FUNDAMENTALS OF
BUSINESS MATHEMATICS

$$\text{Inventory turnover (cost)} = \frac{\text{Cost of goods sold}}{\text{Average inventory (at cost)}}$$

$$\text{Average retail inventory} = \frac{\text{Sum of the retail inventory values}}{\text{Number of inventories}}$$

Chapter 5

Gross Wages pp. 124, 125, 126, 132

Gross earnings (wages) = Rate per hour × Number of hours worked

Gross earnings (piecework) = Rate per unit × Number of units produced

Gross earnings (commissions) = Net sales × Commission rate

Bank Statement Reconciliation p. 168

To the Bank Balance
1. Add the total of all unrecorded deposits.
2. Subtract the total of all outstanding checks.

To the Checkbook Balance
1. Subtract the total of
   a. All previously deposited overdrafts.
   b. All miscellaneous charges.
2. Add the total of all interest and miscellaneous credit.

Chapter 6

Property Tax Calculations p. 190

$$\text{Tax rate} = \frac{\text{Total taxes to be raised}}{\text{Total assessments}}$$

Federal Income Tax Calculations p. 194

1. Compute your *total income.*
2. Compute your *adjustments to income.*
3. Subtract from total income (step 1) your adjustments to income (step 2). The result is your *adjusted gross income.*
4. Compute your total itemized deductions. Subtract from the adjusted gross income (step 3) the *larger* of the total itemized deductions or the *standard deduction.*
5. Multiply your total number of exemptions by $2,300 and subtract this from the amount in step 4. This is your *taxable income.*
6. Compute your tax from the appropriate tax table according to your taxable income and *filing status.*

Chapter 7

Time Calculations pp. 211, 212

Exact Interest

$$t = \frac{\text{Term of the loan in days}}{365}$$

Ordinary Interest

$$t = \frac{\text{Term of the loan in days}}{360}$$

Interest Calculations pp. 208, 209, 219, 220

$$I = Prt \qquad A = P(1 + rt)$$

$$P = \frac{I}{rt} \qquad P = \frac{A}{1 + rt}$$

$$r = \frac{I}{Pt}$$

$$t = \frac{I}{Pr}$$

where I = interest, P = principal (the amount of money borrowed or invested), r = annual rate, t = the length of time (in years) the principal is borrowed or invested, A = maturity value.

Chapter 8

Compound Interest Calculations pp. 227, 232, 237

$$i = \frac{\text{Nominal rate}}{\text{Number of periods per year}}$$

where i = rate per period.

$$A = P(1 + i)^n \qquad P = A(1 + i)^{-n} \qquad A = Pe^{rt}$$

where A = compound amount, P = principal, i = rate per period, and n = total number of periods. t = time in years.

Chapter 9

Simple Discount Calculations pp. 244, 248, 249

$$D = Adt \quad A = \frac{D}{dt} \quad d = \frac{D}{At} \quad t = \frac{D}{Ad} \quad P = A(1 - dt)$$

where D = amount of discount, A = maturity value, d = discount percent, t = term of the loan in years, P = proceeds.

Simple Interest vs. Simple Discount p. 256

$$r = \frac{d}{1 - dt} \qquad d = \frac{r}{1 + rt}$$

where r = simple interest rate, d = discount percent.

Chapter 10

Rule of 78 p. 279

$$R = \frac{n(n + 1)}{m(m + 1)} \times \text{Finance charge}$$

where R = amount of rebate, m = total number of months, and n = m minus number of months before prepay.

Sixth Edition

FUNDAMENTALS OF BUSINESS MATHEMATICS

Walter E. Williams
University of South Florida

James H. Reed
University of South Florida

Wm. C. Brown Publishers
Dubuque, Iowa•Melbourne, Australia•Oxford, England

Book Team

Editor *Earl McPeek/Paula-Christy Heighton*
Developmental Editor *Theresa Grutz*
Production Editor *Karen L. Nickolas*
Designer *Kristyn A. Kalnes*
Art Editor *Joseph P. O'Connell*
Photo Editor *Carrie Burger*

Wm. C. Brown Publishers

A Division of Wm. C. Brown Communications, Inc.

Vice President and General Manager *Beverly Kolz*
Vice President, Publisher *Earl McPeek*
Vice President, Director of Sales and Marketing *Virginia S. Moffat*
Marketing Manager *Julie Joyce Keck*
Advertising Manager *Janelle Keeffer*
Director of Production *Colleen A. Yonda*
Publishing Services Manager *Karen J. Slaght*
Permissions/Records Manager *Connie Allendorf*

Wm. C. Brown Communications, Inc.

President and Chief Executive Officer *G. Franklin Lewis*
Corporate Senior Vice President, President of WCB Manufacturing *Roger Meyer*
Corporate Senior Vice President and Chief Financial Officer *Robert Chesterman*

Cover photos: Background, Middle and Right Insets: © Comstock/
Comstock, Inc.; Left Inset: Jack Elnes/Comstock, Inc.

Copyedited by Lisa L. Burchett-Jacobson

To Elizabeth and June

Contents

5

Payrolls and Banking   123

6

Taxes   183

7

Simple Interest   207

8

Compound Interest   225

9

Simple Discount   243

10

Consumer Credit   259

11

Annuities   283

12

Sinking Funds and Amortization   299

13

Securities   313

14

Topics in Accounting   343

15

Insurance   397

16

Statistics and Graphs   431

17

The Metric System   469

Preface

The sixth edition of *Fundamentals of Business Mathematics* retains the format and style that made the previous editions popular. The book continues to provide basic skills in business mathematics and is written for the first-year community college or university student. While the book is intended for students who plan to major in business, the topics in the book remain pertinent to consumers as well as employers. For this reason, the text is also appropriate for a core course in basic mathematics.

The only prerequisite for the text is standard high school mathematics. In fact, the opening chapter provides a review of basic arithmetic for those students who need to solidify their arithmetic foundations before applying these skills to business situations.

Approach

The philosophy of the text continues to be **"learning by doing,"** and the pedagogy follows the successful formula of **explanation-example-exercise.** New material is reinforced immediately by examples and exercise sets relating to business situations. **Word problems** continue to be a key feature of the text and are valuable training for actual business operations. Additional learning aids in each chapter include **learning objectives, a glossary of key terms,** and **review test.**

Another feature retained in the text is **flexibility.** Once the student masters the material in the first two chapters, the instructor may choose any set of topics from the remaining chapters. This enables the book to be used successfully in courses ranging from one term to a full year.

New to This Edition

The following changes in the sixth edition reflect comments from instructors and reviewers from around the nation.

1. To get students more quickly into the business topics, the review of arithmetic is contained in one chapter.

2. A revised and updated chapter on depreciation covers the latest MACRS depreciation method and expanded coverage of traditional depreciation methods.

3. Updated examples and exercises reflect current wages, interest rates, prices, social security, medicare, federal income tax tables, and stock and bond prices.

4. The section on federal income taxes reflects recent changes in tax legislation.

5. To provide a better ordering of topics, the Topics in Accounting chapter is now chapter 14 and the chapter on Compound Interest (chapter 8) precedes the chapter on Simple Discount (chapter 9).

6. A subsection on real estate loans is new to this edition, as is a new section on mutual funds.

7. Section 15.4 includes updated coverage of group insurance coverage and premiums.

8. Updated coverage of automobile insurance premiums is found in Section 15.6.

9. Calculator solutions are given for selected examples to improve student understanding of the correct calculator keystrokes.

10. Exercises have been revised and updated in most sections.

11. Chapter objectives, glossaries, and chapter review tests have been expanded.

Supplements

In addition to the changes in the text, a number of improvements have been made in the *Instructor's Manual*. Along with complete solutions to all problems in the text, the manual features sections on the purpose of each chapter and includes valuable instructional tips and derivations of important formulas. At the end of each chapter there are six chapter examinations that may be used for in-class testing. These examinations now include multiple-choice tests. Answers to these examinations and to all workbook problems are provided. An additional teaching aid is a set of transparency masters of selected tables and examples in the text.

The *Student's Study Guide* has also been updated and revised. The study guide is designed for those students who need additional practice in solving problems similar to those found in the text.

Our computerized Testing Service provides you with a testing program and the complete *Test Item File* on diskette for use with IBM® PC or Macintosh® computers. The *Computerized Testing Software* requires no programming experience.

The *Test Item File* is a printed version of the *Computerized Testing Software* that allows you to choose test items based on chapter, section, or objective. The objectives are taken directly from *Fundamentals of Business Mathematics,* sixth edition. The items in the *Test Item File* are different from those in the prepared tests in the *Instructor's Manual*. Hence, you will have even more items to choose from for your tests.

Computerized Testing is available free to instructors adopting *Fundamentals of Business Mathematics,* sixth edition.

Business Mathematics Transparencies are available to enhance your instructional time.

Acknowledgments

The continued success of our textbook is due to the comments of the reviewers of this edition and the five earlier editions. We would like to thank the following people for carefully reviewing our sixth edition and providing many invaluable suggestions:

Barbara Sturdevant, State University of New York, College of Technology; Sarah Carpenter, Vincennes University; John Mastriani, El Paso Community College; Carol Crowson DeVille, Louisiana Tech University; Bernadette Antkoviak, Harrisburg Area Community College; Ted Lai, Hudson County Community College; Bobbie Corbett, N. Virginia Community College; James H. Wheeler, Jr., Vance-Granville Community College; Jim Brousard, American Institute of Business; Rhosan Stryker, Delta College.

We would like to thank reviewers of some of our earlier editions:

A. Bruce Wadsworth, Fulton-Montgomery Community College; Maryann Birdsall, Ocean County College; J. David Felt, Northern Virginia Community College; Dorothy Terwilligar, Baker College; Rhosan Stryker, Delta College; Richard Miller, Arizona Western College; Ned W. Schillow, Lehigh County Community College; Ray E. Collings, Tri-County Technical College; and William O. Rider, Westmoreland County Community College.

We would also like to express our appreciation to the editors and staff at Wm. C. Brown Publishers. Their expertise and cooperation are unexcelled. In particular, we wish to thank Earl McPeek, Theresa Grutz, Karen Nickolas, Kristyn Kalnes, and Joseph O'Connell for their superb assistance in the production of this edition. Finally, we wish to thank our wives and children for their encouragement and support.

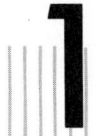

Review of Arithmetic

STUDENT'S SELF EXAMINATION FOR CHAPTER 1

This test will help determine individual strengths and weaknesses in the basic arithmetic skills discussed in chapter 1. The answers are provided in appendix L.

In problems 1–8, perform the indicated operations.

1.   57,973
       +86,718
        44691

2.   3,619
        26,451
          714
       +31,837
        62621

3.   34,514
        −27,638
         6876

4.   7,005
        −6,239
         764

5.   2,746
        × 374
        10984
        19232
        8238
       1027104

6.   9,503
       $\times\ \underline{705}$ **7.** $33,012 \div 63$ **8.** $182,310 \div 354$

In problems 9–16, perform the indicated operations and express your answer as a mixed number or a proper fraction reduced to lowest terms.

9. $\dfrac{1}{3} + \dfrac{1}{12}$

10. $\dfrac{14}{8} - \dfrac{32}{40}$

11. $\dfrac{5}{12} \times \dfrac{18}{35}$

12. $\dfrac{21}{10} \div \dfrac{10}{14}$

13. $2\dfrac{2}{15} + 1\dfrac{1}{5}$

14. $8\dfrac{3}{4} - 4\dfrac{1}{8}$

15. $2\dfrac{1}{3} \times 1\dfrac{1}{4}$

16. $5\dfrac{2}{3} \div 2\dfrac{1}{6}$

Solve.

17.   3,713.42
        144.57
     $+\ \underline{266.98}$

18.   3,713.42
     $-\underline{1,996.87}$

19.   12.43
     $\times\ \underline{0.26}$

20. $123.84 \div 51.6$ **21.** $34.119 \div 2.55$

22. Find the quotient and remainder for $453 \div 7$.

23. Find the quotient and remainder for $2,803 \div 326$.

24. A number added to 2,797 gives 17,423. What is the number?

25. A number divided by 23 is 47. What is the number?

26. When a number is subtracted from 5,617, the result is 1,998. Find the number.

27. A number multiplied by 409 is 15,133. What is the number?

28. When a number is divided by 73, the quotient is 23 and the remainder is 8. Find the number.

29. A video recorder is on sale for $213. If the regular price is $402, how much would be saved by buying the recorder on sale?

30. A local clothing store paid invoices of $23,792, $3,475, and $7,526. What was the total expenditure for the invoices?

31. Last week, a sales representative sold 63 units of product *A* at $14 each, 19 units of product *B* at $223 each, and 37 units of product *C* at $172 each. Find the total sales income for the week.

32. A sporting goods store sold 237 rowing machines for a total profit of $11,613. What profit was made on each machine?

33. A manufacturer filled an order for 57 units of an item at a total cost of $399. Then a second order was filled for 34 units of the same item. What was the cost of the second order?

34. Round 27.492 to **a.** the nearest tenth and **b.** the nearest whole number.

35. Round 4.84675 to **a.** the nearest thousandth and **b.** the nearest hundredth.

36. A contractor purchased 42 acres and subdivided it into $1\frac{1}{2}$ acre lots. How many lots did he have?

37. A job pays $7.80 per hour for a forty-hour week. Overtime hours are paid at $1\frac{1}{2}$ times $7.80. Find the overtime hourly pay.

38. Sara has three apple trees in her backyard. The yield of the first tree was $1\frac{3}{4}$ bushels of apples, the second tree yielded $2\frac{1}{8}$ bushels, and the third tree yielded $1\frac{1}{2}$ bushels. How many total bushels of apples did Sara get from the trees?

39. A salesperson is paid a commission on net sales (total sales less returns). Last week the salesperson had sales of $446.85, $1,268.40, $2,988.69, and $668.75, and returns of $88.25 and $226.50. Find the salesperson's net sales for the week.

40. While modernizing its factory, a company laid off $\frac{1}{6}$ of its 420 workers. Of those laid off, $\frac{1}{7}$ found other jobs. Of the remaining laid-off workers, $\frac{1}{4}$ were retrained for new jobs in the company. How many workers were retrained for new jobs?

Section 1.1 *The Arithmetic of Whole Numbers*

A. Whole Numbers

Numbers in business mathematics are written using the ten digits of the decimal system: 0,1,2,3,4,5,6,7,8,9. Combinations of these digits represent a number because of positional notation as shown in figure 1.1 where each column represents a product of tens.

Figure 1.1
Positional notation

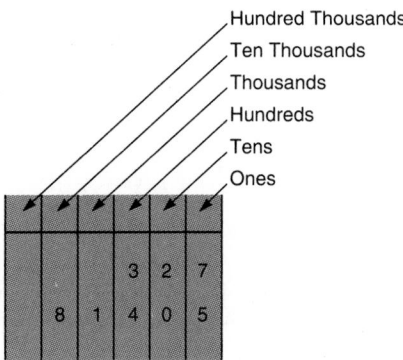

Positional Notation

The number 327 in figure 1.1 means 3 hundreds plus 2 tens plus 7 ones. For clarity, a comma often is inserted after every third positional column, starting from the right. Using this convention, the number 81405 in figure 1.1 is written 81,405. Numbers written using the positional columns in figure 1.1 are called **whole numbers.** The remainder of this section reviews addition, subtraction, multiplication, and division of whole numbers.

B. Adding Whole Numbers

We add two whole numbers by adding the digits in each positional column, beginning with the ones column. The numbers that are to be added are called **addends,** and the result of the addition is called the **sum.** If the sum of the digits in a column results in a two digit number, the first digit of the sum is "carried" to the next column and added with the digits in that column as shown in part (b) of the following example.

E X A M P L E 1   Find: **a.** $52 + $36   **b.** 243 + 162 + 59

Solution: **a.** $52 Addend
  + 36 Addend
  $88 Sum

b.
  ¹¹
  243 Addend
  162 Addend
  + 59 Addend
  464 Sum

One method of checking addition is to reverse the order. That is, if $36 + $52 = $88 and 59 + 162 + 243 = 464, odds are the solution is correct. ∎

C. Subtracting Whole Numbers

To subtract two whole numbers, write the larger (**minuend**) above the smaller (**subtrahend**) so that the positional columns are aligned, then subtract the digits in each column to obtain the **difference**.

EXAMPLE 2   Find: **a.** $58 − $27   **b.** 383 − 61   **c.** 63 − 49

Solution: **a.**
```
$58   Minuend
- 27   Subtrahend
$31   Difference
```
b.
```
  383
-  61
  322
```
c.
```
  5
  ⁶3
- 49
  14
```

Check: **a.**
```
  $31
+  27
  $58
```
b.
```
  322
+  61
  383
```
c.
```
   1
   14
+ 49
   63
```

If a digit of the minuend is smaller than the digit of the subtrahend in any positional column such as in part (c), borrowing is necessary. Borrowing is a rearrangement of the positional notation of the minuend to permit subtraction. In part (c), the rearrangement was as follows:

$$
\begin{array}{rl}
63 = & 5 \text{ tens} + 13 \text{ ones} \\
-49 = - & 4 \text{ tens} + 9 \text{ ones} \\
\hline
14 = & 1 \text{ ten} + 4 \text{ ones}
\end{array}
$$

To check the answer to a subtraction problem, if the difference plus the subtrahend equals the minuend, the answer is correct. ■

D. Multiplying Whole Numbers

In arithmetic, the symbol "×" is usually used to indicate multiplication. In higher mathematics, a dot "·" may be used for multiplication, or if the numbers are in parentheses, the symbol may be omitted entirely. Thus,

$$3 \times 5, \quad 3 \cdot 5, \quad \text{and} \quad (3)(5)$$

all mean the same thing.

To multiply two whole numbers, write the **multiplicand** above the **multiplier** so that the positional columns are aligned, then multiply each digit of the multiplicand by each digit of the multiplier to obtain a **partial product**. The sum of the partial products is the answer or **product**.

E X A M P L E   3   Find: 36×18

Solution:
$$
\begin{array}{r}
36 \\
\times\ 18 \\
\hline
\end{array}
$$

     36   Multiplicand (**or factor**)
$\times$ 18   Multiplier (**or factor**)
     48   Partial product ($8 \times 6 = 48$)
  240   Partial product (8×3 tens $= 24$ tens $= 240$)
    60   Partial product (1 ten $\times 6 = 6$ tens $= 60$)
  300   Partial product (1 ten $\times 3$ tens $= 10 \times 30 = 300$)
  648   Product

With practice, we learn to condense the above solution by employing the carrying device.

     36   Multiplicand
$\times$ 18   Multiplier
  288   Partial product ($8 \times 6 = 48$; write 8, carry 4.
                       $8 \times 3 = 24$; $24 + 4 = 28$; write 28)
  360   Partial product ($10 \times 36 = 360$)
  648   Product

One method of checking multiplication is to reverse the multiplicand and multiplier and find the product.

     18   Multiplicand
$\times$ 36   Multiplier
  108   Partial product
  540   Partial product
  648   Product

E. Dividing Whole Numbers

There are four symbols used to indicate division. Each of the following means the division of 12 by 4.

$$12 \div 4 \qquad \frac{12}{4} \qquad 4\overline{)12} \qquad 12/4$$

Division of two whole numbers is usually performed using long division. Long division of 832 (the **dividend**) by 24 (the **divisor**) is illustrated in the following steps.

Step 1	*Step 2*	*Step 3*	*Step 4*

      3 ($3 \times 24 = 72$)   3   34 ($4 \times 24 = 96$)   34 Quotient
$24\overline{)832}$ $24\overline{)\ 832}$ $24\overline{)832}$ $24\overline{)832}$
  72                    $-\underline{72}\!\downarrow$ $\underline{72}$ $\underline{72}$
                             112   112   112
                                      96      $-\ \underline{96}$
                                                16 Remainder

Steps in long division are repeated until all of the digits in the dividend are used and the subtraction step yields a number less than the divisor. The solution is called the **quotient,** and the number left over is the **remainder.** If the remainder is zero, the divisor is said to divide the dividend evenly. To check an answer to a division problem, multiply the divisor by the quotient and add the remainder; the result should equal the dividend. In the preceding problem, $24 \times 34 = 816$; $816 + 16 = 832$.

E X A M P L E 4   Find and check your result: $7,329 \div 24$

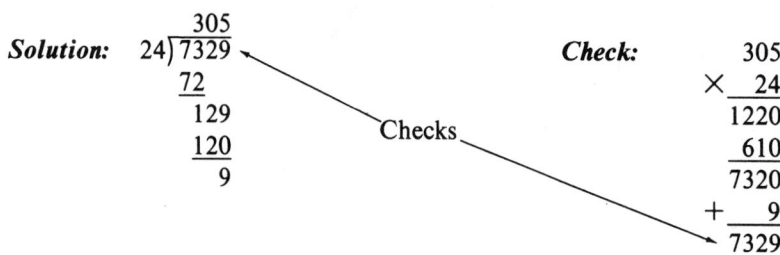

$$\begin{array}{r} 305 \\ 24\overline{)7329} \\ 72 \\ \hline 129 \\ 120 \\ \hline 9 \end{array}$$

Solution: Checks

Check:
$$\begin{array}{r} 305 \\ \times\ 24 \\ \hline 1220 \\ 610 \\ \hline 7320 \\ +\ \ 9 \\ \hline 7329 \end{array}$$

EXERCISES FOR SECTION 1.1

In problems 1–12, find the indicated sums.

1.	153	2.	472	3.	259	4.	458
	+372		+517		+303		+714

5.	467	6.	541	7.	554	8.	6,742
	952		566		506		376
	+280		+279		+234		+ 33

9.	2,721	10.	7,249	11.	3,247,935	12.	8,575,347
	3,723		2,901		+ 348,606		+1,267,749
	+5,429		2,431				
			+1,499				

In problems 13–24, perform the indicated subtraction and check your result.

13.	347	14.	587	15.	371	16.	345	17.	741	18.	541
	− 21		− 34		− 27		− 94		− 72		− 93

19.	5,454	20.	7,867	21.	1,523	22.	7,249	23.	47,775	24.	535,997
	− 706		− 673		− 727		−2,582		−34,822		− 39,267

In problems 25–36, perform the indicated multiplication and check your result.

25.	347	26.	687	27.	677	28.	509	29.	827	30.	541
	× 12		× 43		× 87		× 84		×200		×101

31.	5,384 × 76	32.	2,347 × 63	33.	3,827 × 747	34.	7,116 × 552	35.	4,775 × 822	36.	55,237 × 4,017

In problems 37–52, find the quotient and remainder and check your result.

37. $906 \div 6$ **38.** $225 \div 8$ **39.** $645 \div 43$ **40.** $2,942 \div 32$ **41.** $2,129 \div 23$

42. $4,458 \div 53$ **43.** $1,103 \div 23$ **44.** $7,897 \div 123$ **45.** $3,967 \div 482$ **46.** $4,188 \div 574$

47. $32,886 \div 24$ **48.** $82,993 \div 39$ **49.** $45,776 \div 314$ **50.** $16,468 \div 428$ **51.** $310,846 \div 214$

52. $403,083 \div 486$

Section 1.2   *Introduction to Fractions*

A. Types of Fractions

A fraction consists of two numbers separated by a fraction bar and is written in one of two forms as shown in figure 1.2.

Figure 1.2
Forms of a fraction

$$\begin{array}{ll} 1 & \text{Numerator} \\ - & \text{Fraction Bar} \\ 6 & \text{Denominator} \end{array}$$

Fraction Bar
↓
Numerator ⟶ 1/6 ⟵ Denominator

There are at least four interpretations for a fraction such as $\frac{1}{6}$.

1. **A part of a whole.** If one pie is cut into six equal slices, then a slice is $\frac{1}{6}$ of the whole pie.

2. **A part of a group.** One-sixth of a six-pack of cola is one bottle.

3. **Division of two numbers.** The number $\frac{1}{6}$ can mean $1 \div 6$. In this sense, the fraction bar is just another symbol for the division sign.

4. **Ratio of two numbers.** If during a baseball game a player gets one hit in six times at bat, then we say the player hit $\frac{1}{6}$ of the time. Here the fraction implies a comparison between the numbers 1 and 6.

There are different kinds of fractions. A **proper fraction** is a fraction with numerator less than the denominator. Examples of proper fractions are $\frac{1}{6}$, $\frac{3}{8}$, and $\frac{5}{7}$.

An **improper fraction** is a fraction with numerator greater than or equal to the denominator. Examples of improper fractions are $\frac{9}{7}$, $\frac{8}{3}$, and $\frac{7}{4}$.

B. Mixed Numbers

The sum of a whole number and a proper fraction is called a **mixed number.** Thus $5\frac{3}{4}$ means $5 + \frac{3}{4}$ and $3\frac{2}{9}$ means $3 + \frac{2}{9}$.

A mixed number may be changed to an improper fraction as follows: multiply the whole number by the denominator and add the numerator to get the numerator of the improper fraction. The denominator stays the same. Thus,

$$2\frac{3}{5} = \frac{13}{5} \qquad \text{where } 13 = (5 \times 2) + 3$$

E X A M P L E 1   Convert to an improper fraction: **a.** $2\frac{3}{4}$ **b.** $6\frac{2}{3}$

Solution: **a.** $2\frac{3}{4} = \frac{4 \times 2 + 3}{4} = \frac{11}{4}$

b. $6\frac{2}{3} = \frac{3 \times 6 + 2}{3} = \frac{20}{3}$ ∎

To convert an improper fraction to a mixed number divide the numerator of the improper fraction by the denominator (see interpretation 3 for a fraction on page 7) using the long division technique of the previous section. The quotient is the whole part of the mixed number, the remainder is the numerator of the fraction, and the divisor is the denominator. The conversion of the fraction $\frac{39}{8}$ is shown below.

$$\frac{39}{8} \quad \rightarrow \quad 8\overline{)39} \begin{array}{c} 4 \\ \underline{32} \\ 7 \end{array} \quad \rightarrow \quad 4\frac{7}{8}$$

E X A M P L E 2   Convert to a mixed number: **a.** $\frac{5}{3}$ **b.** $\frac{11}{4}$

Solution: **a.** $3\overline{)5}\begin{array}{c}1\\\underline{3}\\2\end{array}$ thus, $\frac{5}{3} = 1\frac{2}{3}$ **b.** $4\overline{)11}\begin{array}{c}2\\\underline{8}\\3\end{array}$ thus, $\frac{11}{4} = 2\frac{3}{4}$ ∎

C. Equivalent Fractions

The value of a fraction is unchanged if both numerator and denominator of the fraction are multiplied by the same nonzero number. For example,

$$\frac{2}{3} = \frac{2 \times 5}{3 \times 5} = \frac{10}{15}$$

Now suppose we seek to find the answer to the following:

$$\frac{3}{4} = \frac{?}{20}$$

Since $20 \div 4 = 5$, the denominator has been multiplied by 5. To obtain an equal fraction, the numerator must be multiplied by 5. That is,

$$\frac{3}{4} = \frac{3 \times 5}{4 \times 5} = \frac{15}{20}$$

To check the solution, use the fact that two fractions are said to be **equal fractions** if their cross products are equal. For the fractions $\frac{3}{4}$ and $\frac{15}{20}$, the **cross products** are as follows:

$$\frac{3}{4} \diagdown\!\!\!\!\!\diagup \frac{15}{20}$$

Since $3 \times 20 = 60$ and $4 \times 15 = 60$, the cross products are equal and therefore the fractions are equal.

EXAMPLE 3   Solve and check your answer: **a.** $\dfrac{5}{7} = \dfrac{?}{42}$ **b.** $\dfrac{7}{12} = \dfrac{?}{108}$

Solution: **a.** Since $42 \div 7 = 6$, the denominator has been multiplied by 6. Thus,

$$\frac{5}{7} = \frac{5 \times 6}{7 \times 6} = \frac{30}{42} \qquad \textit{Check: } 5 \times 42 = 210 = 7 \times 30$$

b. Since $108 \div 12 = 9$, the denominator has been multiplied by 9. Thus,

$$\frac{7}{12} = \frac{7 \times 9}{12 \times 9} = \frac{63}{108} \qquad \textit{Check: } 7 \times 108 = 756 = 12 \times 63 \qquad \blacksquare$$

D. Fractions in Lowest Terms

A fraction is in **lowest terms** if the only whole number that divides evenly both numerator and denominator is 1. For example the fraction $\frac{2}{3}$ is in lowest terms, since the only whole number divisor of 2 and 3 is 1. The process of reducing a fraction to lowest terms uses equal fractions and the greatest common divisor.

The largest whole number that divides evenly both the numerator and the denominator of a fraction is called the **greatest common divisor (GCD)**. Frequently, the greatest common divisor can be determined by inspection. For instance, it is easy to see that 2 is the GCD of the fraction $\frac{6}{8}$. If the GCD cannot be found by inspection, it can always be found using prime factorization. A **prime** is a whole number larger than 1 that is evenly divisible only by itself and 1. The first ten primes are 2,3,5,7,11,13,17,19,23, and 29. Every whole number is either a prime or can be expressed as a product of primes. This product is called the **prime factorization** of the number. For example, the prime factorization of $60 = 2 \times 2 \times 3 \times 5$ can be found by repeated division with prime divisors as follows:

$$60 \div \boxed{2} = 30$$
$$30 \div \boxed{2} = 15$$
$$15 \div \boxed{3} = 5$$
$$5 \div \boxed{5} = 1 \text{ (Stop when 1 is reached.)}$$

To find the GCD of a fraction, find the prime factorization of the numerator and denominator, then form columns so that only identical primes are in each column. *The GCD is the product of primes that have a pairing.* This process is demonstrated in the next example.

E X A M P L E 4   Find the greatest common divisor of   **a.** 96 and 180   **b.** 75 and 210

Solution: **a.** The prime factorizations are $96 = 2 \times 2 \times 2 \times 2 \times 2 \times 3$ and $180 = 2 \times 2 \times 3 \times 3 \times 5$. Forming columns,

2	2	2	2	2	3		
2	2				3	3	5

the GCD is the product of the paired primes, or $2 \times 2 \times 3 = 12$.

b. The prime factorizations are $75 = 3 \times 5 \times 5$ and $210 = 2 \times 3 \times 5 \times 7$. Forming columns,

	3	5	5		
2	3	5		7	

the GCD is the product of the paired primes, or $3 \times 5 = 15$. ■

Once the GCD is found using the method shown in example 4, the fraction in lowest terms may be found using equal fractions. The next example demonstrates the method.

EXAMPLE 5   Reduce to lowest terms: **a.** $\dfrac{36}{54}$ **b.** $\dfrac{70}{168}$ **c.** $\dfrac{20}{60}$

Solution: **a.** $36 = \begin{array}{|c|c|c|c|c|} 2 & 2 & 3 & 3 & \\ \hline & 2 & 3 & 3 & 3 \end{array}$
$54 =$

The GCD is $2 \times 3 \times 3 = 18$. Since $36 \div 18 = 2$ and $54 \div 18 = 3$,

$\dfrac{36}{54} = \dfrac{2 \times 18}{3 \times 18} = \dfrac{2}{3}$. Thus, the fraction in lowest terms is $\dfrac{2}{3}$.

b. $70 = \begin{array}{|c|c|c|c|c|c|} 2 & & & & 5 & 7 \\ \hline 2 & 2 & 2 & 3 & & 7 \end{array}$
$168 =$

The GCD is $2 \times 7 = 14$. $\dfrac{70}{168} = \dfrac{5 \times 14}{12 \times 14} = \dfrac{5}{12}$.

c. The GCD is 20 by inspection. $\dfrac{20}{60} = \dfrac{1 \times 20}{3 \times 20} = \dfrac{1}{3}$. ∎

EXERCISES FOR SECTION 1.2

In problems 1–10, express the given mixed number as an improper fraction.

1. $4\dfrac{2}{5}$ **2.** $5\dfrac{1}{4}$ **3.** $4\dfrac{4}{5}$ **4.** $7\dfrac{3}{11}$ **5.** $9\dfrac{2}{7}$ **6.** $3\dfrac{2}{3}$

7. $2\dfrac{1}{8}$ **8.** $5\dfrac{5}{6}$ **9.** $3\dfrac{5}{9}$ **10.** $2\dfrac{3}{10}$

In problems 11–20, express the given improper fraction as a mixed number.

11. $\dfrac{14}{9}$ **12.** $\dfrac{11}{4}$ **13.** $\dfrac{15}{6}$ **14.** $\dfrac{21}{4}$ **15.** $\dfrac{24}{15}$ **16.** $\dfrac{62}{7}$

17. $\dfrac{5}{3}$ **18.** $\dfrac{22}{5}$ **19.** $\dfrac{11}{9}$ **20.** $\dfrac{16}{3}$

In problems 21–30, use cross multiplication to determine if the two given fractions are equal.

21. $\dfrac{5}{7}$ and $\dfrac{25}{35}$ **22.** $\dfrac{3}{4}$ and $\dfrac{15}{20}$ **23.** $\dfrac{7}{8}$ and $\dfrac{14}{15}$ **24.** $\dfrac{5}{6}$ and $\dfrac{39}{42}$ **25.** $\dfrac{17}{21}$ and $\dfrac{68}{84}$

26. $\dfrac{27}{28}$ and $\dfrac{81}{94}$ **27.** $\dfrac{32}{33}$ and $\dfrac{192}{198}$ **28.** $\dfrac{75}{625}$ and $\dfrac{3}{25}$ **29.** $\dfrac{33}{120}$ and $\dfrac{11}{40}$ **30.** $\dfrac{13}{41}$ and $\dfrac{65}{205}$

In problems 31–40, find the greatest common divisor of the given numbers.

31. 30 and 36   **32.** 90 and 105   **33.** 42 and 735   **34.** 154 and 770   **35.** 78 and 546

36. 182 and 195   **37.** 42 and 150   **38.** 121 and 385   **39.** 105 and 147   **40.** 165 and 210

In problems 41–52, reduce the given fraction to lowest terms.

41. $\dfrac{7}{14}$ **42.** $\dfrac{15}{30}$ **43.** $\dfrac{24}{36}$ **44.** $\dfrac{8}{12}$ **45.** $\dfrac{21}{28}$ **46.** $\dfrac{95}{100}$

47. $\dfrac{118}{124}$ **48.** $\dfrac{54}{180}$ **49.** $\dfrac{63}{90}$ **50.** $\dfrac{24}{120}$ **51.** $\dfrac{88}{396}$ **52.** $\dfrac{33}{120}$

Express the answers in problems 53–64 as fractions reduced to lowest terms.

53. A restaurant's receipts for one day totaled $1,620. Of this amount, $180 was for liquor. Find the fraction of the total receipts that was due to liquor sales.

54. Sunshine Hardware received a shipment of 64 chain saws and sold 20 of them in one week. Find the fraction of the shipment that was sold during the week.

55. A contractor maintains a fleet of 175 trucks, of which 35 are not in service at a given time. Find the fraction of the total fleet that is in service at a given time.

56. A warehouse contains 32,000 square feet of floor space. Of this space, 24,000 is used for storage and the remainder for offices and shipping. **a.** What fraction is used for storage? **b.** What fraction is used for offices and shipping?

57. W. Mercer bought 625 shares of stock in a land development company. A year later Mercer sold 250 shares of stock. Find the fraction of stock that was sold.

58. Kirby Electronics recently bought a television set for $212 and sold it for $364. What fraction of the selling price was profit?

59. Sally Smith and Dr. Denton entered into a joint business venture and earned a profit of $48,000. Because Sally initially put more money into the venture, they agreed she would receive $30,000 and Dr. Denton would receive $18,000. Find the fraction of the total profit that each received.

60. Arlene Lackey inherited $390,000 and used $210,000 to pay off her creditors. What fraction of the original inheritance did she have left after paying off the debts?

61. According to the personnel officer, 20 employees of the company are single or divorced with no children, 18 are divorced with children, 12 are married with no children, and 32 are married with children.
a. What fraction of the employees has no children?
b. What fraction of the employees is married?

62. A shoe store carries 12 different styles of boys' shoes, 22 different styles of girls' shoes, 16 different styles of men's shoes, and 34 different styles of women's shoes. What fraction of the total shoe styles is for females?

63. Of 110 cars sold by an automobile dealer last month, the number ordered with air conditioning was as follows:

	Two-Door	Four-Door	Sports Coupe
Air Conditioning	28	26	24
No Air Conditioning	12	4	16

a. What fraction of the total cars was ordered with air conditioning?
b. What fraction of the sports coupes was ordered with no air conditioning?
c. What fraction of the total cars sold was two-door or four-door?

64. A check of shopping records at a supermarket revealed the following data.

Number of Shoppers	Total of Purchases
20	Less than $10
120	$10 but less than $40
85	$40 or more

a. What fraction of the shoppers spent less than $40?

b. What fraction of the shoppers spent $10 or more?

Section 1.3 *The Arithmetic of Fractions*

A. Addition of Fractions

To add fractions, two cases must be considered: (1) fractions with the same (common) denominator and (2) fractions with unlike denominators.

The sum of two fractions with a common denominator is a fraction with the same denominator and whose numerator is the sum of the numerators of the given fractions.

EXAMPLE 1   Find: **a.** $\dfrac{2}{7} + \dfrac{3}{7}$ **b.** $\dfrac{4}{11} + \dfrac{7}{11}$

Solution: **a.** $\dfrac{2}{7} + \dfrac{3}{7} = \dfrac{2+3}{7} = \dfrac{5}{7}$ **b.** $\dfrac{4}{11} + \dfrac{7}{11} = \dfrac{4+7}{11} = \dfrac{11}{11} = 1$ ∎

To add fractions with unlike denominators, first convert the given fractions to fractions with a common denominator. One common denominator is the product of the denominators of the given fractions. However, in many cases, the least common denominator is a better choice. The **least common denominator (LCD)** is the smallest nonzero whole number that is divisible by the denominators of the given fractions. In many problems, the least common denominator can be found by inspection. If this is not possible, find the prime factorization of each denominator, then form columns so that only identical primes are in each column. The LCD is the product of representative primes from each column. This process is demonstrated in the next example.

E X A M P L E 2   Find the least common denominator of   **a.** 30 and 36   **b.** 35 and 50

Solution: **a.** The prime factorizations are $36 = 2 \times 2 \times 3 \times 3$ and $30 = 2 \times 3 \times 5$. Forming columns and selecting a representative from each column,

$$\begin{array}{|c|c|c|c|c|} 2 & 2 & 3 & 3 & \\ \hline 2 & & 3 & & 5 \end{array}$$

the LCD is $2 \times 2 \times 3 \times 3 \times 5 = 180$.

b. The prime factorizations are $35 = 5 \times 7$ and $50 = 2 \times 5 \times 5$. Forming columns and selecting a representative from each column,

$$\begin{array}{|c|c|c|c|} 2 & 5 & & 7 \\ \hline 2 & 5 & 5 & \end{array}$$

the LCD is $2 \times 5 \times 5 \times 7 = 350$.   ■

Adding fractions with unlike denominators can now be described using the following steps:

1. find the LCD of the given fractions
2. convert each of the given fractions to a fraction with denominator equal to the LCD (see example 3 of section 1.2)
3. add the new fractions using the technique of example 1

E X A M P L E 3   Add: **a.** $\dfrac{3}{4} + \dfrac{1}{6}$ **b.** $\dfrac{1}{4} + \dfrac{3}{5} + \dfrac{1}{8}$

Solution: **a.** The LCD of 4 and 6 is 12. Thus,

$$\frac{3}{4} + \frac{1}{6} = \frac{9}{12} + \frac{2}{12} = \frac{9 + 2}{12} = \frac{11}{12}$$

b. The LCD of 4, 5, and 8 is 40. Thus,

$$\frac{1}{4} + \frac{3}{5} + \frac{1}{8} = \frac{10}{40} + \frac{24}{40} + \frac{5}{40} = \frac{10 + 24 + 5}{40} = \frac{39}{40}$$ ■

B. Subtraction of Fractions

To subtract fractions, find the LCD if the denominators are unequal. Then, *the difference of two fractions with a common denominator is a fraction with the same denominator and whose numerator is the difference of the numerators of the given fractions.*

EXAMPLE 4   Find: **a.** $\dfrac{9}{20} - \dfrac{3}{20}$ **b.** $\dfrac{3}{5} - \dfrac{1}{4}$

Solution: **a.** $\dfrac{9}{20} - \dfrac{3}{20} = \dfrac{9-3}{20} = \dfrac{6}{20}$

$\dfrac{6}{20} = \dfrac{3 \times 2}{10 \times 2} = \dfrac{3}{10}$

b. The LCD of 4 and 5 is 20. Thus,

$\dfrac{3}{5} - \dfrac{1}{4} = \dfrac{12}{20} - \dfrac{5}{20} = \dfrac{7}{20}$ ∎

C. Multiplication of Fractions

To multiply fractions, multiply their numerators and multiply their denominators.
Follow this rule whether the fractions are proper or improper.

EXAMPLE 5   Find: **a.** $\dfrac{4}{3} \times \dfrac{5}{9}$ **b.** $\dfrac{1}{2} \times \dfrac{3}{4} \times \dfrac{7}{5}$

Solution: **a.** $\dfrac{4}{3} \times \dfrac{5}{9} = \dfrac{4 \times 5}{3 \times 9} = \dfrac{20}{27}$

b. $\dfrac{1}{2} \times \dfrac{3}{4} \times \dfrac{7}{5} = \dfrac{1 \times 3 \times 7}{2 \times 4 \times 5} = \dfrac{21}{40}$ ∎

A modification of the technique for reducing fractions, called **cancellation,**
provides a shortcut for multiplying two or more fractions. To illustrate,

$$\frac{9}{20} \times \frac{8}{27} = \frac{\overset{1}{\cancel{9}}}{\underset{5}{\cancel{20}}} \times \frac{\overset{2}{\cancel{8}}}{\underset{3}{\cancel{27}}} = \frac{1}{5} \times \frac{2}{3} = \frac{2}{15}$$

The canceled numbers represent dividing 20 and 8 by 4, and dividing 27 and 9 by 9.

D. Division of Fractions

The **reciprocal of a fraction** is a fraction found by interchanging the numerator and
the denominator. Thus, the reciprocal of $\frac{3}{4}$ is $\frac{4}{3}$ and the reciprocal of $\frac{1}{6}$ is $\frac{6}{1} = 6$.
*To divide a number by a nonzero fraction, multiply the number by the
reciprocal of the fraction.*

EXAMPLE 6   Find: **a.** $\dfrac{3}{10} \div \dfrac{1}{7}$ **b.** $12 \div \dfrac{1}{3}$ **c.** $\dfrac{35}{62} \div \dfrac{15}{8}$ **d.** $\dfrac{5}{7} \div 9$

Solution: **a.** $\dfrac{3}{10} \div \dfrac{1}{7} = \dfrac{3}{10} \times \dfrac{7}{1} = \dfrac{21}{10} = 2\dfrac{1}{10}$

b. $12 \div \dfrac{1}{3} = \dfrac{12}{1} \times \dfrac{3}{1} = \dfrac{36}{1} = 36$

c. $\dfrac{35}{62} \div \dfrac{15}{8} = \dfrac{\overset{7}{\cancel{35}}}{\underset{31}{\cancel{62}}} \times \dfrac{\overset{4}{\cancel{8}}}{\underset{3}{\cancel{15}}} = \dfrac{28}{93}$

d. $\dfrac{5}{7} \div 9 = \dfrac{5}{7} \times \dfrac{1}{9} = \dfrac{5}{63}$ ■

E. Arithmetic of Mixed Numbers

To add, subtract, multiply, or divide mixed numbers, first convert them to improper fractions and then add, subtract, multiply, or divide as shown in the examples of this section.

EXAMPLE 7   Find: **a.** $3\dfrac{5}{8} + 1\dfrac{7}{12}$ **b.** $9\dfrac{5}{9} - 7\dfrac{3}{4}$ **c.** $2\dfrac{1}{6} \times 3\dfrac{2}{5}$ **d.** $4\dfrac{2}{3} \div 1\dfrac{7}{8}$

Solution: **a.** $3\dfrac{5}{8} + 1\dfrac{7}{12} = \dfrac{29}{8} + \dfrac{19}{12} = \dfrac{87}{24} + \dfrac{38}{24} = \dfrac{125}{24} = 5\dfrac{5}{24}$

b. $9\dfrac{5}{9} - 7\dfrac{3}{4} = \dfrac{86}{9} - \dfrac{31}{4} = \dfrac{344}{36} - \dfrac{279}{36} = \dfrac{65}{36} = 1\dfrac{29}{36}$

c. $2\dfrac{1}{6} \times 3\dfrac{2}{5} = \dfrac{13}{6} \times \dfrac{17}{5} = \dfrac{221}{30} = 7\dfrac{11}{30}$

d. $4\dfrac{2}{3} \div 1\dfrac{7}{8} = \dfrac{14}{3} \div \dfrac{15}{8} = \dfrac{14}{3} \times \dfrac{8}{15} = \dfrac{112}{45} = 2\dfrac{22}{45}$ ■

EXERCISES FOR SECTION 1.3

In problems 1–14, add the fractions and express the answer as a fraction in lowest terms.

1. $\dfrac{1}{12} + \dfrac{5}{12}$ **2.** $\dfrac{2}{9} + \dfrac{4}{9}$ **3.** $\dfrac{3}{16} + \dfrac{9}{16}$ **4.** $\dfrac{6}{25} + \dfrac{4}{25}$ **5.** $\dfrac{1}{2} + \dfrac{1}{5}$

6. $\dfrac{2}{5} + \dfrac{1}{6}$ **7.** $\dfrac{2}{7} + \dfrac{1}{8}$ **8.** $\dfrac{2}{5} + \dfrac{3}{7}$ **9.** $\dfrac{5}{12} + \dfrac{1}{9}$ **10.** $\dfrac{3}{8} + \dfrac{9}{16}$

11. $\dfrac{1}{6} + \dfrac{7}{24}$ **12.** $\dfrac{9}{23} + \dfrac{8}{69}$ **13.** $\dfrac{1}{3} + \dfrac{1}{4} + \dfrac{3}{8}$ **14.** $\dfrac{3}{8} + \dfrac{7}{36} + \dfrac{5}{12}$

In problems 15–26, subtract the fractions and express the answer as a fraction in lowest terms.

15. $\dfrac{5}{6} - \dfrac{1}{6}$ **16.** $\dfrac{7}{8} - \dfrac{3}{8}$ **17.** $\dfrac{9}{20} - \dfrac{3}{20}$ **18.** $\dfrac{13}{18} - \dfrac{5}{18}$ **19.** $\dfrac{3}{10} - \dfrac{1}{7}$

20. $\dfrac{7}{5} - \dfrac{7}{8}$ **21.** $\dfrac{3}{5} - \dfrac{5}{14}$ **22.** $\dfrac{17}{19} - \dfrac{2}{3}$ **23.** $\dfrac{10}{21} - \dfrac{13}{42}$ **24.** $\dfrac{11}{28} - \dfrac{5}{14}$

25. $\left(\dfrac{5}{6} - \dfrac{2}{9}\right) - \dfrac{5}{18}$ **26.** $\left(\dfrac{43}{39} - \dfrac{2}{13}\right) - \dfrac{5}{52}$

In problems 27–36, use cancellation when possible and multiply the fractions. Express the answer as either a mixed number or as a proper fraction reduced to lowest terms.

27. $\dfrac{1}{4} \times \dfrac{1}{3}$ **28.** $\dfrac{7}{9} \times \dfrac{45}{21}$ **29.** $\dfrac{65}{48} \times \dfrac{12}{13}$ **30.** $\dfrac{24}{35} \times \dfrac{7}{12}$

31. $\dfrac{27}{35} \times \dfrac{70}{81}$ **32.** $\dfrac{9}{28} \times \dfrac{14}{3}$ **33.** $\dfrac{4}{9} \times \dfrac{3}{7} \times \dfrac{1}{3}$ **34.** $\dfrac{1}{2} \times \dfrac{2}{3} \times \dfrac{4}{5}$

35. $\dfrac{2}{3} \times \dfrac{4}{5} \times \dfrac{1}{4} \times \dfrac{1}{2}$ **36.** $\dfrac{6}{5} \times \dfrac{3}{2} \times \dfrac{1}{3} \times \dfrac{4}{3}$

In problems 37–46, divide the fractions and express the answer as either a mixed number or as a proper fraction reduced to lowest terms.

37. $\dfrac{3}{7} \div \dfrac{6}{5}$ **38.** $\dfrac{5}{7} \div \dfrac{3}{8}$ **39.** $\dfrac{5}{32} \div \dfrac{1}{16}$ **40.** $\dfrac{3}{2} \div \dfrac{39}{8}$ **41.** $\dfrac{5}{17} \div \dfrac{5}{28}$

42. $\dfrac{7}{12} \div \dfrac{7}{24}$ **43.** $\dfrac{73}{13} \div 9$ **44.** $5 \div \dfrac{1}{3}$ **45.** $\dfrac{143}{69} \div \dfrac{11}{23}$ **46.** $\dfrac{121}{50} \div \dfrac{11}{5}$

In problems 47–62, perform the indicated operation and express the answer as either a mixed number or as a proper fraction reduced to lowest terms.

47. $3\dfrac{5}{6} + 1\dfrac{2}{3}$ **48.** $7\dfrac{3}{7} + 4\dfrac{5}{21}$ **49.** $11\dfrac{3}{5} + 9\dfrac{2}{3}$ **50.** $9\dfrac{7}{8} + 3\dfrac{5}{6}$

51. $3\dfrac{2}{6} - 1\dfrac{1}{4}$ **52.** $4\dfrac{3}{5} - 4\dfrac{1}{10}$ **53.** $17\dfrac{2}{5} - 4\dfrac{1}{3}$ **54.** $8\dfrac{2}{11} - 3\dfrac{5}{22}$

55. $7\dfrac{2}{5} \times 11\dfrac{5}{9}$ **56.** $6\dfrac{2}{3} \times 4\dfrac{7}{8}$ **57.** $7\dfrac{4}{7} \times 9\dfrac{4}{9}$ **58.** $3\dfrac{5}{7} \times 6\dfrac{2}{3}$

59. $5\dfrac{7}{8} \div 3\dfrac{1}{4}$ **60.** $11\dfrac{1}{3} \div 12\dfrac{3}{4}$ **61.** $4\dfrac{2}{3} \div 8\dfrac{2}{3}$ **62.** $3\dfrac{5}{9} \div 2\dfrac{2}{5}$

63. John Barnes purchased a $\frac{3}{8}$ acre lot next to his lot of $\frac{2}{5}$ acres. How much land did John own following the purchase?

64. Lawrence county acquired $\frac{1}{9}$ acre of land from Caryl Cowles and $\frac{2}{7}$ acre of land from Pete McDonald to build entrance ramps for a new road. How much was the total land purchase by the county?

65. Morrison's Music store received a shipment of compact discs and sold $\frac{1}{5}$ of the shipment in one week and $\frac{4}{9}$ of the shipment in the second week. What fraction of the shipment was sold in the two-week period?

66. A company found that $\frac{3}{7}$ of its total production cost for the year was for wages and $\frac{4}{9}$ was for supplies. Find the fraction of total production for wages and supplies.

67. Last year Eastern Storage leased $\frac{2}{5}$ of a building for storage. This year they reduced this amount by $\frac{4}{15}$. How much of the building do they now use for storage?

68. A produce dealer received a shipment of 224 crates of grapes, which are to be repacked in boxes for retail sale. If each box holds $\frac{2}{5}$ of a crate, how many boxes of grapes can be packed?

69. Apco Land Company purchased $\frac{4}{5}$ of an acre of land and divided it equally into four lots. How large was each lot?

70. A contractor estimates that $\frac{7}{8}$ of her fleet of trucks is in service at any time. She also estimates that she needs $\frac{1}{16}$ of her fleet of trucks for each job she undertakes. How many jobs can the contractor undertake at any given time?

71. Weber Enterprises presented a petition to the zoning commission to subdivide a $14\frac{2}{3}$ acre tract into 20 parcels of equal size. If the petition was approved, how many acres did each parcel contain?

72. A citrus grower produced $112\frac{3}{4}$ tons of fruit from one grove and $97\frac{2}{3}$ tons of fruit from another. **a.** How much fruit was produced from the two groves? **b.** If $\frac{7}{8}$ of the fruit was sold to a packing house and the remainder was sold at roadside stands, how many tons of fruit was sold at roadside stands?

73. The J & J Lumber Company received an order for 324 feet of pressure-treated two-by-fours and 48 feet of pressure-treated two-by-sixes. If the two-by-fours cost $18\frac{1}{4}$¢ per foot and the two-by-sixes cost $49\frac{1}{2}$¢ per foot, what was the cost of the order?

74. Delta Rock and Gravel Company purchased $3\frac{1}{2}$ truckloads of decorative rock and gravel and sold $\frac{2}{5}$ of it the day it was delivered. The next day, $\frac{3}{8}$ of the original shipment was sold. Find the number of truckloads sold during the two days.

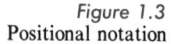 **Section 1.4** *Decimal Fractions and Rounding*

A. Decimal Fractions

A decimal fraction is a fraction in which the denominator is 10 or a product of 10s. In most business applications, decimal fractions are written using an extension of positional notation. In the following display, the decimal point separates columns that are products of 10 from columns that are products of $\frac{1}{10}$.

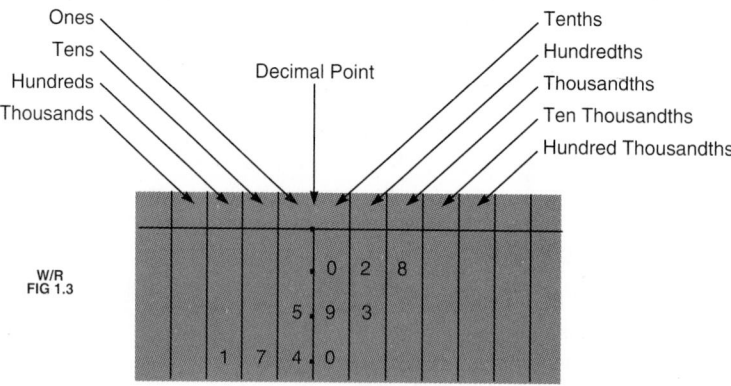

Figure 1.3
Positional notation

Positional Notation

There is an immediate relationship between decimal fractions and fractions:

$$0.1 = \frac{1}{10}$$

$$0.01 = \frac{1}{100}$$

$$0.001 = \frac{1}{1000}$$

$$0.0001 = \frac{1}{10000}$$

etc.

When reading decimal fractions, read the number to the right of the decimal point then the name of the last positional column. Thus, the first number in figure 1.3 (a pure decimal fraction) is read "twenty-eight thousandths." The second number (a mixed decimal fraction) is "five and ninety-three hundredths." The third number is a whole number which could have been written without the decimal point. From figure 1.3, the following are equalities:

$$.028 = \frac{28}{1000} = \frac{7}{250}$$

$$5.93 = 5\frac{93}{100} = \frac{593}{100}$$

$$174.0 = 174$$

B. Addition and Subtraction of Decimal Fractions

To add or subtract decimal fractions, first align the numbers in positional columns. The decimal point is a natural alignment guide. For an addition problem, add the digits in each positional column, using the carrying process if necessary. For a subtraction problem, subtract the digits in each column, using the borrowing process if necessary.

EXAMPLE 1   Find: **a.** 157.496 + 29.0902 + 16.83   **b.** $65.34 − $43.65

Solution: **a.**   157.496
           29.0902
    + 16.83
      203.4162

    b. $65.34
    −43.65
    $21.69

C. Multiplication of Decimal Fractions

To multiply two decimal fractions, if the multiplier is a product of tens, the answer is found by moving the decimal point in the multiplicand to the right one place for each zero in the multiplier. For example,

2.8473 × 10 = 28.473 (One zero; move decimal point right one place.)
2.8473 × 100 = 284.73 (Two zeros; move decimal point right two places.)
2.8473 × 1,000 = 2847.3 (Three zeros; move decimal point right three places.)

If the multiplier is a decimal fraction, the numbers are written and multiplied as if they were whole numbers; then the decimal point is inserted in the answer. *The product will contain digits to the right of the decimal point equal to the sum of the numbers of digits to the right of the decimal points in the factors.*

EXAMPLE 2   Find: 6.354 × 2.7

Solution:

$$
\begin{array}{r}
6.354 \\
\times \quad 2.7 \\
\hline
44478 \\
12\ 708 \\
\hline
17.1558
\end{array}
$$

    6.354   Multiplicand or factor
×   2.7   Multiplier or factor

17.1558   Product

There are 3 + 1 = 4 digits to the right of the decimal places in the factors; thus, the decimal point is located in the product so that there are 4 digits to its right.   ■

EXAMPLE 3   Find: 0.03 × 0.6

Solution:

  0.03   2 digits to right of decimal point
× 0.6   +1 digit to right of decimal point
0.018   3 digits to right of decimal point

A zero was inserted after the decimal point in the product to obtain the correct answer. Since

$$0.03 \times 0.6 = \frac{3}{100} \times \frac{6}{10} = \frac{18}{1,000}$$

this procedure is justified.   ■

D. Division of Decimal Fractions

There are three cases to consider in the division of decimal fractions.

1. **The divisor is a product of tens.** If the divisor is a product of tens, the solution is found by moving the decimal point in the dividend to the *left* for each zero in the divisor. For example:
   26.47 ÷ 10 = 2.647 (One zero; move decimal point one place.)
   26.47 ÷ 100 = 0.2647 (Two zeros; move decimal point two places.)
   26.47 ÷ 1,000 = 0.02647 (Three zeros; move decimal point three places.)
2. **The divisor is a nonzero whole number.** If the divisor is a nonzero whole number, the decimal point in the quotient is located directly above its position in the dividend. Thus, to divide 704.96 by 32,

$$\begin{array}{r} 22.03 \\ 32\overline{)704.96} \\ \underline{64} \\ 64 \\ \underline{64} \\ 96 \\ \underline{96} \\ 0 \end{array}$$

3. **The divisor is a decimal fraction.** If the divisor is a decimal fraction, multiply both the dividend and the divisor by a product of tens that will make the divisor a whole number. Then divide as in case 2 above.

E X A M P L E 4   Find and check your answer.   **a.** $40.096 \div 1.79$ **b.** $3.9567 \div 1.635$

Solution: **a.** Multiplying both numbers by 100, $40.096 \div 1.79 = 4{,}009.6 \div 179$. Hence,

$$\begin{array}{r} 22.4 \\ 179\overline{)4009.6} \\ \underline{358} \\ 429 \\ \underline{358} \\ 716 \\ \underline{716} \\ 0 \end{array}$$

Check:
$$\begin{array}{r} 1.79 \\ \times\ \ 22.4 \\ \hline 716 \\ 358 \\ \underline{358} \\ 40.096 \end{array}$$

b. Multiplying both numbers by 1000, $3.9567 \div 1.635 = 3{,}956.7 \div 1{,}635$. Hence,

$$\begin{array}{r} 2.42 \\ 1635\overline{)3956.70} \\ \underline{3270} \\ 6867 \\ \underline{6540} \\ 3270 \\ \underline{3270} \\ 0 \end{array}$$

Check:
$$\begin{array}{r} 1.635 \\ \times\ \ 2.42 \\ \hline 3270 \\ 6540 \\ \underline{3270} \\ 3.95670 \end{array}$$

E. Rounding

Some calculations yield answers that are not practical. For example, suppose an employee earns $9.37 per hour and works 38.75 hours per week. Then the amount of money earned for the week is

$$\$9.37 \times 38.75 = \$363.0875$$

But this result is not practical because it is an amount of money that cannot be paid in standard coinage.

In problems such as these, the answer is frequently "rounded" to obtain a practical result. To round a number, first locate the digit to the right of the decimal place to which the number is to be rounded. This is the test digit. The number is then rounded according to table 1.1.

Table 1.1 Rounding Rules	Test Digit is Located to the Right of the Decimal Point	Test Digit is Located to the Left of the Decimal Point
Test Digit is Four or Smaller	Delete the test digit and all digits to its right.	Change to zero the test digit and all digits to the decimal point; delete all digits to the right of the decimal point.
Test Digit is Five or Larger	Delete the test digit and all digits to its right. Add one to the digit preceding the test digit.	Change to zero the test digit and all digits to the decimal point; delete all digits to the right of the decimal point. Add one to the digit preceding the test digit.

Using table 1.1 to round $363.08 7 5 to the nearest hundredth, the test digit is the boxed digit 7, which is larger than 5 and located to the right of the decimal point. Thus, $363.0875 rounds to $363.09, and this is the amount that the employee should be paid for the week's work.

EXAMPLE 5   Round to hundredths: **a.** 35.1426   **b.** 35.1476

Solution: The boxed digit is the test digit.
a. 35.14⃞2⃞6 rounds to 35.14
b. 35.14⃞7⃞6 rounds to 35.15   ∎

EXAMPLE 6   Round 1.72546 to the **a.** thousandths place, **b.** hundredths place, **c.** tenths place, and **d.** ones place.

Solution: The boxed digit is the test digit.
a. 1.725⃞4⃞6 rounds to 1.725
b. 1.72⃞5⃞46 rounds to 1.73
c. 1.7⃞2⃞546 rounds to 1.7
d. 1.⃞7⃞2546 rounds to 2   ∎

EXAMPLE 7   Round 8,671.56 to **a.** hundreds **b.** thousands.

Solution: The boxed digit is the test digit.
a. 8,6⃞7⃞1.56 rounds to 8,700
b. 8,⃞6⃞71.56 rounds to 9,000   ∎

For the remainder of the text, answers to exercise problems should be rounded to two decimal places (hundredths) unless otherwise indicated.

(handwritten: 365 days = 1 yr)
(handwritten: 52 wks 1 yr)

EXERCISES FOR SECTION 1.4

In problems 1–32, perform the indicated operation. Do not round answers.

1.   36.5
    $+41.4$

2.   51.8
    $+44.3$

3.   320.7
    $+\ 64.8$

4.   32.9
    $+12.5$

5.   32.94
    $+23.62$

6.   53.62
    $+13.39$

7.   178.449
    161.69
    $+468.041$

8.   509.42
    106.465
    $+818.026$

9.   653.186
    -285.366

10.   981.165
    -314.836

11.   885.4
    $-\ 36.82$

12.   638.77
    $-\ 30.587$

13.   582.7
    $-\ 41.963$

14.   530.9
    $-\ 36.615$

15.   503.94
    $-\ 61.1$

16.   83.84
    $-\ 2.5$

17.   95.007
    -18.0061

18.   59.349
    $-\ 6.8348$

19.   5.126
    $\times\ 5.03$

20.   41.07
    $\times\ 9.24$

21.   68.51
    $\times\ 3.64$

22.   80.02
    $\times 35.07$

23.   80.10
    $\times 50.06$

24.   5.6745
    $\times\ 2.817$

25.   8.5432
    $\times\ 3.008$

26.   3.904
    $\times\ 7.25$

27. $28.182 \div 1.22$

28. $13.271 \div 5.77$

29. $19.8915 \div 4.45$

30. $112.217 \div 7.82$

31. $449.6996 \div 5.32$

32. $13.271 \div 5.77$

Money answers resulting from computations in mathematics of finance are rounded to values that can be paid in standard coinage. In problems 33–40, round the money values.

33. The company John works for changed their pay period from weekly to biweekly. The payroll department recalculated John's biweekly salary to be $1,147.3252. How much was John actually paid?

(handwritten: 47/33)

34. Mary is paid a commission on the total sales she makes. Last week she calculated that her commission amounted to $721.5471. How much did Mary actually receive?

35. Yvonne calculated what her pension would be upon retirement and came up with a figure of $38,262.4583 per year. How much will Yvonne actually receive?

36. A retail firm calculated the selling price of an item should be $37.752 per unit. What was the actual selling price per unit?

37. A government report asked for the average workman's compensation claim for the previous month. Gannon Corporation calculated the average to be $216.8493. What figure was reported to the government?

38. A city council decided to spend 12.3% of the city's receipts from parking on a new city park. The calculated figure was $56,723.72514. How much did the city spend on the new park?

39. To join the union, a worker agreed to a payroll deduction of $\frac{1}{2}$% of his weekly wages. This amounted to $4.2363 per week. How much was actually deducted each week?

40. In calculating the depreciation on an automobile for income tax purposes, a real estate salesperson computed the figure to be $1,801.247. What amount was reported on the tax return?

*In problems 41–50, round the given numbers to **a.** ones, **b.** tenths, and **c.** hundredths.*

41. 34.603   **42.** 35.452   **43.** 328.594   **44.** 659.983

45. 5,320.896   **46.** 6,318.978   **47.** 107,388.872   **48.** 345,699.863

49. 12,341.788   **50.** 86,765.968

*In problems 51–60, round the given numbers to **a.** thousands, **b.** hundreds, and **c.** hundredths.*

51. 3,761.565   **52.** 2,618.938   **53.** 5,863.998   **54.** 8,183.261   **55.** 18,831.082

56. 28,606.981   **57.** 138,489.065   **58.** 259,902.792   **59.** 250,902.702   **60.** 199,996.797

61. A citrus grower operates five groves. During the past year, the income from the crops of each of the groves was as follows: grove A, $11,293.14; grove B, $22,492.36; grove C, $9,403.26; grove D, $17,413.19; grove E, $14,297.93. How much income did the grower receive from the five groves?

62. The monthly storage charge at a warehouse depends on the amount of goods stored. The storage fees for the past six months were $219.72, $413.39, $327.72, $523.78, $319.47, and $209.42. Find the amount paid for storage during the six months.

63. A dentist purchased new office equipment for $1,000 down and twelve payments of $972.31 each for a total cost of $12,667.72. If the cash price of the equipment was $10,727.35, what was the difference in the cash price and the amount actually paid?

64. The W. L. Mercer Company purchased 183.43 acres of land at $1,525.00 per acre for a total cost of $279,730.75. The company then sold 172.85 acres for a total price of $288,572.81. **a.** How many acres of land did the company have left? **b.** How much cash profit did the company make from the sale?

65. A small manufacturing business had total sales of $76,728.72 for one year. The operating expenses for the same year are as follows: rent, $8,723.42; labor, $21,742.41; machinery, $12,242.79; supplies, $13,742.57; and incidentals, $5,429.73. Compute the profit for the year.

66. An apartment complex has 178 units. Of these, 78 are single bedroom units that rent for $460 per month. The remaining apartments are two-bedroom units that rent for $875 per month. Assuming all units are rented, what is the total rental income of the complex per month?

67. A citrus grower has 2,743.47 acres of groves. The grower estimates the income from this year's crop will be $476 per acre. Find the total income the grower will get from the crop.

68. A storage warehouse agreed to store 7,263 barrels of salt for 7¢ per barrel per month. Find the total monthly storage fee.

69. The owner of a restaurant decided to have 572 square yards of carpeting installed. The carpet cost $15.00 per square yard, the padding cost $1.19 per square yard, and the cost of installation was $0.99 per square yard. What was the total bill paid by the owner?

70. The inventory of men's suits in a department store was as follows: 27 suits that sell for $420.50 per suit, 32 suits that sell for $357.95 per suit, and 63 suits that sell for $222.50 per suit. What was the total value of the suits?

71. A discount chain purchased 273 refrigerators for $453 each. The suggested retail price was $970 each, but the chain sold all the refrigerators when they were put on sale for $669.95 each. **a.** What was the chain's profit from the sale? **b.** How much more profit would the chain have made if the refrigerators could have been sold at the suggested retail price?

72. A firm manufactures steel cable that it sells for 92.5¢ per foot. A construction company bought some of the cable for a total price of $573.50. How many feet of cable were purchased?

73. An estate of $737,821.20 was to be divided equally among five heirs. A sixth heir was then found who also was entitled to an equal share. How much less did each of the original five heirs receive?

74. A produce dealer paid a farmer $2,113.75 for 2,742 crates of lettuce and $4,526.04 for 1,372 boxes of tomatoes. The farmer's profit on the lettuce was $825.01 and on the tomatoes was $1,987.84. **a.** How much did it cost the farmer to grow a crate of lettuce? **b.** How much did it cost to grow a box of tomatoes?

Section 1.5 *Calculator Basics (Optional)*

A. General Purpose Calculators

Many of the calculations required in business mathematics can be performed on a hand-held calculator. Calculators used in business now come in many types, from simple general purpose models that cost less than $10 to more expensive multi-function programmable models. In this text, calculator solutions will be performed on a general purpose model using "algebraic logic." Calculations in this logic are performed in the order in which they are entered. This model contains the following keys.

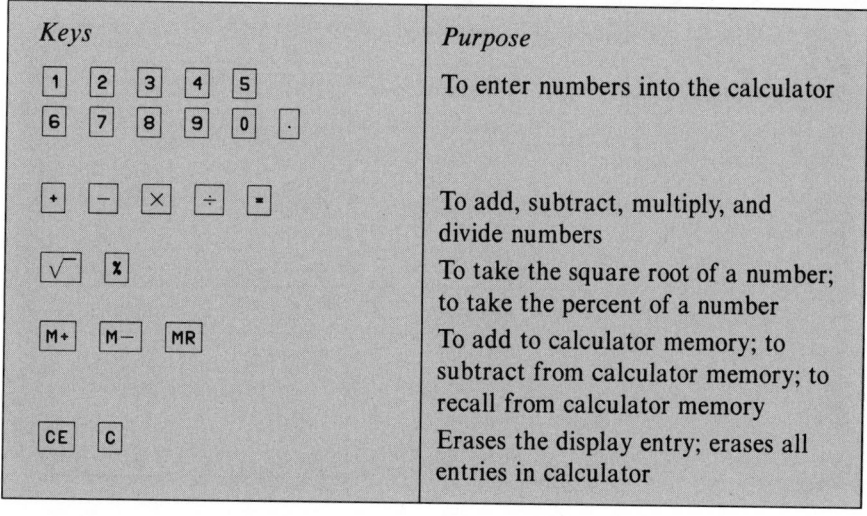

Keys	*Purpose*
1 2 3 4 5 6 7 8 9 0 .	To enter numbers into the calculator
+ − × ÷ =	To add, subtract, multiply, and divide numbers
√ %	To take the square root of a number; to take the percent of a number
M+ M− MR	To add to calculator memory; to subtract from calculator memory; to recall from calculator memory
CE C	Erases the display entry; erases all entries in calculator

B. Calculator Arithmetic

In the following review of basic calculator arithmetic, the column entitled "Entry" indicates the number or key to be entered on the keyboard. The column entitled "Display" indicates the result of the keyboard entry. The first step in any calculation is to press the C key. This puts 0 into the display and into memory. The following examples all assume this first step.

EXAMPLE 1   Find: **a.** 24 + 26   **b.** 461 − 195   **c.** 3,554 × 227   **d.** 11,830 ÷ 455

Solution: **a.**

Entry	Display
24	24
+	24
26	26
=	50

b.

Entry	Display
461	461
−	461
195	195
=	266

c.

Entry	Display
3554	3554
×	3554
227	227
=	806758

d.

Entry	Display
11830	11830
÷	11830
455	455
=	26

Most calculators have a "floating" decimal point that automatically locates the decimal point. To enter decimals, the decimal point key is used.

EXAMPLE 2   Find: **a.** 1.265 + 3.721   **b.** 166 − 33.749   **c.** 1.48 × 9.43   **d.** 27.893 ÷ 14

Solution: **a.**

Entry	Display
1.265	1.265
+	1.265
3.721	3.721
=	4.986

b.

Entry	Display
166	166
−	166
33.749	33.749
=	132.251

c.

Entry	Display
1.48	1.48
×	1.48
9.43	9.43
=	13.9564

d.

Entry	Display
27.893	27.893
÷	27.893
14	14
=	1.9923571

As will be seen in chapter 2, percent (%) means "hundredths." The use of the percent key is shown in parts (a) and (b) of the next example.

A shorthand notation for 5 × 5 is 5^2 (read "5 squared"). Thus, $5^2 = 25$. In turn, the square root of 25 (in symbols $\sqrt{25}$) is 5 because $25 = 5 \times 5$. In like manner, $\sqrt{49} = 7$ because $7 \times 7 = 49$. The use of squared numbers and square roots are found in certain statistical applications (see chapter 16). The square root key on a calculator is demonstrated in parts (c) and (d) of the next example.

EXAMPLE 3   Find: **a.** $200 \times 11\%$ **b.** $1.063 \div 44\%$ **c.** $\sqrt{1521}$ **d.** $\sqrt{7.1289}$

Solution: **a.**

Entry	Display
200	200
$\times$	200
11	11
%	22

b.

Entry	Display
1.063	1.063
$\div$	1.063
44	44
%	2.415909

c.

Entry	Display
1521	1521
$\sqrt{}$	39

d.

Entry	Display
7.1289	7.1289
$\sqrt{}$	2.67

Memory keys can be a considerable convenience when performing arithmetic on a hand-held calculator. Basic use of the M+, M−, and MR keys is as follows (the memory column indicates the number stored in the computer memory):

Entry	Display	Memory	Explanation
120	120	0	
M+	120	120	Puts 120 into memory
30	30	120	
M−	30	90	Subtracts 30 from memory
MR	90	90	Displays number in memory

C. Chain Calculations

Successive calculations (chain calculations) are performed according to the following rules.

1. Do all calculations inside parentheses first.
2. Simplify any expressions with squares and find any square roots.
3. Multiply and divide from left to right.
4. Add and subtract from left to right.

The problems in example 4 illustrate chain calculations in conjunction with the memory keys.

EXAMPLE 4 Find: **a.** $24 + 26 \div 10$ **b.** $75.6 \div (26 + 10)$

c. $620 - (478 \times 40\%)$ **d.** $\dfrac{2 \times 44.3}{195 \times 13 \div 4}$

Solution: **a.** The division is performed before the addition.

Entry	Display	Memory	Explanation
26	26	0	26
÷	26	0	26 ÷
10	10	0	26 ÷ 10
M+	2.6	2.6	2.6 in memory
24	24	2.6	24
+	24	2.6	24 +
MR	2.6	2.6	24 + 2.6
=	26.6	2.6	Answer to 24 + 2.6

b. The addition is performed before the division.

Entry	Display	Memory	Explanation
26	26	0	26
+	26	0	26 +
10	10	0	26 + 10
M+	36	36	36 in memory
75.6	75.6	36	75.6
÷	75.6	36	75.6 ÷
MR	36	36	75.6 ÷ 36
=	2.1	36	Answer to 75.6 ÷ 36

c. The calculation in the parentheses is performed first.

Entry	Display	Memory	Explanation
478	478	0	478
×	478	0	478 ×
40	40	0	478 × 40
%	191.2	0	478 × 40%
M+	191.2	191.2	191.2 in memory
620	620	191.2	620
−	620	191.2	620 −
MR	191.2	191.2	620 − 191.2
=	428.8	191.2	428.8

d. The denominator is calculated first. In the denominator, the multiplication is performed first.

Entry	Display	Memory	Explanation
195	195	0	195
×	195	0	195 ×
13	13	0	195 × 13
÷	2535	0	195 × 13 ÷
4	4	0	195 × 13 ÷ 4
M+	633.75	633.75	633.75 in memory
2	2	633.75	2
×	2	633.75	2 ×
44.3	44.3	633.75	2 × 44.3
÷	88.6	633.75	88.6 (Answer to 2 × 44.3)
MR	633.75	633.75	88.6 ÷ 633.75
=	0.1398027	633.75	Answer to 88.6 ÷ 633.75

Keystrokes using the percent key in chain calculations may vary, even among calculators with algebraic logic. The solution to example 5 below is solved using two possible key sequences. If these fail, use the memory key as demonstrated in the third sequence.

E X A M P L E   5   Find: 684 − (684 × 30%)

Solution: I

Entry	Display
684	684
−	684
30	30
%	478.80

II

Entry	Display
684	684
×	684
30	30
%	205.20
−	478.80

III

Entry	Display	Memory
684	684	0
M+	684	684
×	684	684
.30	.30	684
M−	205.20	478.80
MR	478.80	478.80

D. Fractions and Decimal Fractions

In calculations involving fractions, should the fraction or its decimal representation be used? Before discussing calculator calculations with fractions, recall that every fraction has a decimal representation found by dividing the numerator by the denominator. This decimal representation will be either terminating or infinitely repeating. For example, the following fractions have terminating decimal representations.

$$\frac{1}{2} = 0.5$$

$$\frac{5}{4} = 1.25$$

$$\frac{375}{1000} = 0.375$$

On the other hand, some fractions that have infinitely repeating decimal representations are

$$\frac{1}{3} = 0.3333\ldots \qquad \text{(the 3s repeat indefinitely)}$$

$$\frac{4}{9} = 0.4444\ldots \qquad \text{(the 4s repeat indefinitely)}$$

$$\frac{1}{6} = 0.1666\ldots \qquad \text{(the 6s repeat indefinitely)}$$

$$\frac{5}{11} = 0.454545\ldots \qquad \text{(the pair of digits 45 repeats indefinitely)}$$

On a typical hand-held calculator, the display will show a decimal number up to seven decimal places. Hence, a fraction with an infinitely repeating decimal representation can be approximated at best only to the seventh decimal place. Approximating an infinite decimal introduces a certain amount of error into the calculation. The poorer the approximation, the greater the error. To see this, consider the following calculations of the fraction $\frac{4}{9} = 0.444\ldots$ that were performed on a calculator with a display of seven decimal places.

Product	Answer	Error
$710{,}550 \times \dfrac{4}{9}$	315,800	0
$710{,}550 \times 0.4444444$	315,799.96	0.04
$710{,}550 \times 0.444444$	315,799.68	0.32
$710{,}550 \times 0.44444$	315,796.84	3.16
$710{,}550 \times 0.4444$	315,768.42	31.58
$710{,}550 \times 0.444$	315,484.20	315.8
$710{,}550 \times 0.44$	312,642	3,158
$710{,}550 \times 0.4$	284,220	31,580

In this text, multiplication and division involving fractions with infinitely repeating decimal fractions will be performed using the fraction instead of a decimal approximation. The final answer will be rounded to the desired accuracy. If the fraction has a terminating decimal representation, the decimal representation ordinarily will be used.

EXAMPLE 6   Find: **a.** $710 \times \dfrac{4}{9}$ **b.** $134.20 \times \dfrac{3}{4}$ **c.** $726 \div \dfrac{7}{11}$ **d.** $\dfrac{120}{588 \times \dfrac{5}{18}}$

Solution: **a.** $\dfrac{4}{9}$ has an infinite repeating decimal representation. Hence,

Entry	Display
710	710
×	710
4	4
÷	2840
9	9
=	315.55555

b. $\dfrac{3}{4}$ has a terminating decimal representation equal to 0.75. Hence,

Entry	Display
134.20	134.20
×	134.20
0.75	0.75
=	100.65

c. $726 \div \dfrac{7}{11} = 726 \times \dfrac{11}{7}$. Since $\dfrac{11}{7}$ has an infinitely repeating decimal representation,

Entry	Display
726	726
×	726
11	11
÷	7986
7	7
=	1140.8571

d. Since $\dfrac{5}{18}$ has an infinitely repeating decimal representation,

Entry	Display	Memory
588	588	0
×	588	0
5	5	0
÷	2940	0
18	18	0
M+	163.33333	163.33333
120	120	163.33333
÷	120	163.33333
MR	163.33333	163.33333
=	0.7346938	163.33333

EXERCISES FOR SECTION 1.5

1. $(1,373 + 1,099) - 755$

2. $(16,472 - 11,384) \times 107$

3. $(547 \times 213) - 97,461$

4. $3,472 + (2,520 \div 56)$

5. $(517 \times 213) - 97,461$

6. $17,849 + (324 \times 277)$

7. $23 \times (1,943 \div 29)$

8. $67,892 \times (10,021 - 9,924)$

9. $(247.87 + 113.97) - 14.29$

10. $(165.92 - 54.71) \times 2.39$

11.
```
      143.82
       73.81
      496.14
      501.27
    +  23.79
Total
     -114.72
```

12.
```
    1,572.14
      276.18
       14.92
      978.50
   +1,421.83
Total
 ×    14.00
```

13.
```
      878.22
    5,476.18
    7,985.14
    2,430.02
   +7,218.98
Total
 ×    43.00
```

14.
```
       11.75
      102.09
       14.17
      123.91
    +  98.27
Total
     - 27.83
```

15. $1,872.73 + (5.7 \div 1.25)$

16. $117.83 + (269.85 \div 15.42)$

17. $(1,375.34 \times 279.5) - 216,421.78$

18. $(273.92 + 318.22) \div (49.25 - 28.40)$

19. $(473.25 \times 37.4) - (603.10 \div 40.75)$

20. $(2.133 \div 39.5) + [(47.7 \div 3) + 6.71]$

21. $(5,428.172 - 18.09) \div [(2.81 \times 7.1) - 1.002]$

22. $(328.017 \times 5.11) - (17.21208 \div 2.32)$

23. $(2,148.83 + 4,879.14) - (8,972.04 \times 20\%)$

24. $(10,781.14 - 1,419.27) + (4,275.80 \times 40\%)$

25.
```
1,400 × 14% =
2,750 × 17% =
1,220 × 13% = _____
    Total =
```

26.
```
1,872 × 21% =
3,248 × 19% =
5,710 ×  4% = _____
    Total =
```

27.
```
1,643.10 × 20% =
1,878.40 × 15% =
2,232.50 ×  8% = _____
    Total =
```

28. 6,472.83 × 21% =
   2,391.17 × 12% =
   3,472.08 × 31% =
     984.28 × 17% = _____
          Total =
   Less 24% of total = _____
              =

29. $(2,314.85 - 426.21) \times \dfrac{2}{9}$

30. $(40,625.17 + 431.82) \times \dfrac{7}{11}$

31. $17,249.15 - \left(321.06 \times \dfrac{5}{6}\right)$

32. $8,472.15 \div \left(752.91 \times \dfrac{1}{3}\right)$

33. $\dfrac{1,462.90}{1 + \left(0.09 \times \dfrac{3}{4}\right)}$

34. $\dfrac{2,702.12}{1 + \left(0.07 \times \dfrac{2}{5}\right)}$

35. $\dfrac{1,428.90}{1 + \left(0.1284 \times \dfrac{1}{6}\right)}$

Glossary

Addend   Any of the numbers that are to be added.

Cancellation   Dividing one of the numerators and one of the denominators in the product of fractions by the same nonzero number.

Cross products   Given fractions $\frac{a}{b}$ and $\frac{c}{d}$, the cross products are $a \times d$ and $b \times c$.

Decimal point   A dot used to separate positional columns that are products of 10 from positional columns that are products of $\frac{1}{10}$.

Denominator   That part of a fraction that is below the line signifying division.

Difference   The result of subtracting one number from another.

Digit   Any of the numbers 0,1,2,3,4,5,6,7,8,9. All numbers may be written using these ten digits.

Dividend   In a division problem, the number that is divided by another.

Divisor   In a division problem, the number by which another number is divided.

Equal fractions   Fractions whose cross products are equal.

Factor   Any of the numbers that are to be multiplied in a multiplication problem.

Fraction   A numerical representation of the quotient of two numbers where the indicated division is represented by a horizontal or slanting line.

Greatest common divisor (GCD)   The largest number that evenly divides two or more given numbers.

Improper fraction   A fraction in which the numerator is a number that is greater than or equal to the denominator.

Least common denominator (LCD)   For two or more fractions, the smallest nonzero whole number that is evenly divisible by the denominators of the given fractions.

Lowest terms   A phrase applied to a fraction for which the largest common divisor of the numerator and the denominator is 1.

Minuend   In a subtraction problem, the number from which another number is subtracted.

Mixed number   The sum of a whole number and a proper fraction, written as one number.

Multiplicand   In a multiplication problem, the number that is multiplied by another; the first or top number in the problem.

Multiplier   In a multiplication problem, the number by which another number is multiplied; the second or bottom number in the problem.

Numerator   That part of a fraction that is above the line signifying division.

Operation   Any of the processes of addition, subtraction, multiplication, or division.

Partial product   In a multiplication problem, the result of multiplying the multiplicand by one of the digits in the multiplier.

Prime   A whole number larger than 1 that is evenly divisible only by itself and 1.

Prime factorization   The expression of a whole number larger than 1 as a product of primes.

Product   The result of multiplying two or more numbers (the sum of the partial products).

Proper fraction   A fraction in which the numerator is a number that is smaller than the denominator.

Quotient   The result of dividing one number by another.

Reciprocal   A fraction formed from a given fraction by interchanging the numerator and the denominator.

Reducing a fraction   Dividing the numerator and the denominator of a fraction by the same number.

Remainder   In a division problem, the number remaining at the bottom after the last step of the division process. The sum of the remainder with the product of the divisor times the quotient is equal to the dividend.

Subtrahend   In a subtraction problem, the number that is subtracted from another.

Sum   The result of adding two or more numbers.

Whole number   Any of the numbers 0,1,2,3,4,5,6,7,8,9,10,11 . . .

Review Test

In problems 1–10, perform the indicated operations.

1.   78,548
     + 4,427

2.   62,203
     − 9,648

3.   7,241
     15,896
     8,248
     79,972
     +61,241

4.   9,427
     × 257

5.   115,225
     − 7,336

6.   83,576
     × 427

7. 13,172 ÷ 37

8. 34,398 ÷ 49

9. 40,372 ÷ 71

10. 47,242 ÷ 591

In problems 11–22, perform the indicated operations and write the answer as either a mixed number or as a proper fraction reduced to lowest terms.

11. $\dfrac{2}{5} \times \dfrac{25}{7}$

12. $\dfrac{12}{13} \times \dfrac{7}{24}$

13. $\dfrac{5}{4} - \dfrac{4}{9}$

14. $\dfrac{7}{8} - \dfrac{9}{24}$

15. $\dfrac{2}{3} + \dfrac{1}{12}$

16. $\dfrac{7}{30} + \dfrac{7}{12}$

17. $1\dfrac{3}{7} - \dfrac{15}{35}$

18. $\dfrac{7}{11} \div \dfrac{21}{55}$

19. $\dfrac{3}{7} \div \dfrac{3}{21}$

20. $2\dfrac{8}{9} - \dfrac{5}{6}$

21. $\dfrac{2}{3} \div 4\dfrac{2}{3}$

22. $1\dfrac{1}{24} + \dfrac{5}{16}$

Solve.

23. An assembly-line worker assembled 137 units on Monday, 144 units on Tuesday, and 134 units on Wednesday. How many units were assembled during the three days?

24. A pet supply store purchased 48 cases of dog food for $528. What was the cost per case?

25. For their home, the Smiths purchased new carpeting on sale for $1,847. The regular price for the carpeting was $2,031. How much did the Smiths save by purchasing the carpet on sale?

26. Julie Adams sells real estate. During the month of May, she received commissions of $542, $273, $312, $341, and $428. What was her total commission for the month?

27. Bill Jacobs wrote checks for $112, $49, and $232. The balance in his account before writing the checks was $847. Find the balance in his account after writing the three checks.

28. Atlas Industries manufactures aluminum storage sheds. For the month of March, the total sales of the company amounted to $107,271 for 137 sheds. All of the storage sheds have the same selling price. Find the selling price of each shed.

29. An apartment complex contains 12 one-bedroom apartments and 8 two-bedroom apartments. The one-bedroom apartments rent for $346 per month, and the two-bedroom apartments rent for $432 per month. At full occupancy, what is the total rental income per month from the complex?

30. Fill in the missing entries on the following chart, which shows the daily sales of each salesperson at the Tri-County Furniture Outlet:

	Mon.	Tues.	Wed.	Thurs.	Fri.	Total
J. Beeson	$ 4,271	$8,279	$2,413	$3,892	$ 4,721	—
M. Pruitt	10,114	3,420	4,611	743	3,995	—
P. Baker	2,421	6,744	5,546	2,109	1,815	—
S. Rae	943	5,219	4,428	3,456	11,423	—
Q. Ramirez	6,711	3,978	2,119	5,827	7,319	—
Total	—	—	—	—	—	—

In problems 31–34, perform the indicated operations and round the answer to the nearest hundredth.

31. $24.838 + 16.557$ **32.** $122.936 - 57.78$ **33.** 9.54×3.7 **34.** $1271.808 \div 62.1$

Solve.

35. Waldo's Supermarket received a shipment of 32 cases of cornmeal, 4 of which were later discovered to be infested with insects. What fraction of the shipment was undamaged?

36. A sporting goods store reported monthly sales for the six months of January through June as follows: January, $6,482.35; February, $8,749.87; March, $11,493.73; April, $13,473.71; May, $14,973.71; and June, $12,372.42. Find the total sales for the six-month period.

37. A building contains 4,075 square feet of floor space, of which $\frac{3}{5}$ is used for equipment storage. Of the remaining space, $\frac{1}{3}$ is used for offices. How many square feet are used for offices?

38. One lathe in the M & M Machine Shop can produce $9\frac{3}{5}$ units of a certain item per hour. How many lathes will be required to produce $67\frac{1}{5}$ units per hour?

Formulas, Ratios, and Percent

 **Section 2.1** *Formulas*

A. Introduction

Many of the concepts in business mathematics can be expressed in concise form by means of formulas. For example, in this chapter, the very important formula

$$\text{Percentage} = \text{Base} \times \text{Rate}$$

is developed. This formula is but one of many formulas used in this text, and a proper understanding of formulas and their equivalent forms is crucial. The next section describes how formulas are written and how they can be altered using arithmetic properties.

B. Formulas

As indicated in part A, the formula Percentage = Base × Rate is a key business formula. This formula and its variations are found in chapters throughout this text. This formula is usually abbreviated as

$$P = B \cdot R$$

In a formula the words (letters) stand for numbers. In most formulas, the numbers for all but one of the words (letters) are known, and the solution to the problem requires calculating the value of the remaining word (letter). This process is called **evaluating** the formula and is demonstrated in the next examples.

EXAMPLE 1   Evaluate the formula $P = B \cdot R$ if

    a. $B = 16$ and $R = 12$ **b.** $B = 480$ and $R = \dfrac{3}{4}$

Solution: **a.** $P = B \cdot R$ **b.** $P = B \cdot R$
$$P = 16 \cdot 12$$
$$P = 192$$
$$P = 480 \cdot \frac{3}{4}$$
$$P = 360$$

EXAMPLE 2   Evaluate the formula $I = Prt$ if

    a. $P = 14, r = 6, t = 8$ **b.** $P = 25, r = 14, t = \dfrac{1}{2}$

Solution: **a.** $I = Prt$ **b.** $I = Prt$
$$I = 14 \cdot 6 \cdot 8$$
$$I = 672$$
$$I = 25 \cdot 14 \cdot \frac{1}{2}$$
$$I = 175$$

Sometimes the evaluation of a formula requires a rearrangement of the formula to an equivalent formula. An equivalent formula is created if one or more of the following properties is applied to a formula.

Property 1 The same number (or letter) is added to both sides.
Property 2 The same number (or letter) is subtracted from both sides.
Property 3 Both sides of the equation are multiplied by the same number (or letter).
Property 4 Both sides of the equation are divided by the same nonzero number (or letter).

To **solve** a formula is to rearrange the formula so that a different letter is on the left side of the equals sign. The next examples demonstrate solving formulas.

EXAMPLE 3   Solve for M in the formula $C + M = S$.

Solution: $C - C + M = S - C$ (Property 2)
$M = S - C$ ($C - C = 0$; $0 + M = M$)   ∎

EXAMPLE 4   **a.** Solve the formula $I = Prt$ for t.
b. Find t if $I = 540$, $r = 0.045$, and $P = 6,000$.

Solution: **a.** $I = Prt$

$Prt = I$

$\dfrac{Prt}{Pr} = \dfrac{I}{Pr}$ (Property 4)

$t = \dfrac{I}{Pr}$ (Cancellation property)

b. $t = \dfrac{I}{Pr}$

$t = \dfrac{540}{6,000 \times 0.045}$

$t = 2$ ∎

C. Ratios

As discussed in section 1.2, a ratio is one interpretation for a fraction. Ratios are used to compare numbers. Thus, the fraction $\frac{4}{3}$ is also a comparison of 4 to 3 and in business may be written in one of three ways:

$$\frac{4}{3} \qquad 4 \text{ to } 3 \qquad 4{:}3$$

The last way is used frequently in business transactions. If more than two numbers are being compared, say 3 and 4 and 5, the ratio is written either as 3 to 4 to 5 or 3:4:5. The next examples illustrate some business uses of ratios.

EXAMPLE 5   The Alexander Company had 140 hourly employees and 28 salaried employees. Find the ratio of hourly employees to salaried employees.

Solution: Hourly employees to salaried employees $= \dfrac{\text{Hourly}}{\text{Salaried}}$

$= \dfrac{140}{28}$

$= \dfrac{5}{1}$

Thus, the ratio of hourly workers to salaried workers is 5 to 1 or 5:1 or $\dfrac{5}{1}$.   ∎

When setting up a ratio, the numerator and denominator of the ratio must be in the same units of measurement as demonstrated in the next example.

EXAMPLE 6   After one year on the job, Pierre had earned 16 hours of sick leave and ten days of vacation. Find the ratio of sick leave to vacation if a working day is 8 hours.

Solution: The sick leave is in hours but the vacation is in days. Converting the hours to days, 16 hours = 2 working days. Thus,

$$\text{Ratio of sick leave to vacation} = \frac{\text{Sick leave}}{\text{Vacation}}$$

$$= \frac{2}{10}$$

$$= \frac{1}{5}$$

Thus, the ratio of Pierre's sick leave to vacation is 1:5.   ■

EXAMPLE 7   Zuckerman's Clothing had the following monthly sales in its three departments: Men's—$4,000; Women's—$7,000; Children's—$5,000. Find the ratio of the sales of each department to total sales.

Solution: Total sales = $4,000 + $7,000 + $5,000 = $16,000

a. Ratio of Men's sales to Total Sales $= \dfrac{\text{Men's sales}}{\text{Total sales}}$

$$= \frac{\$4,000}{\$16,000}$$

$$= \frac{1}{4}$$

$$= 1:4$$

b. Ratio of Women's sales to Total Sales $= \dfrac{\text{Women's sales}}{\text{Total sales}}$

$$= \frac{\$7,000}{\$16,000}$$

$$= \frac{7}{16}$$

$$= 7:16$$

c. Ratio of Children's sales to Total Sales $= \dfrac{\text{Children's sales}}{\text{Total sales}}$

$$= \frac{\$5,000}{\$16,000}$$

$$= \frac{5}{16}$$

$$= 5:16$$ ■

D. Proportion

The equality of two ratios is called a **proportion.** Thus, $\frac{2}{5} = \frac{10}{25}$ is a proportion and may be written 2:5 = 10:25 (read 2 is to 5 as 10 is to 25). The numbers 2 and 25 are called the *extremes* of this proportion and the numbers 5 and 10 are called the *means*. Thus, from the equality of fractions (see section 1.2) the product of the means equals the product of the extremes. The next example demonstrates the use of proportions.

E X A M P L E 8   Find k in the proportion $\dfrac{k}{33} = \dfrac{2}{3}$.

Solution: If the unknown number is in the numerator of one of the fractions, it may be found using equivalent fractions (see example 3 of section 1.2). An alternate method is to equate the product of the means and the product of the extremes, then solve and evaluate the resulting formula. This method is demonstrated here.

$$3k = 2 \times 33 \qquad \text{(Product of the means equals the product of the extremes)}$$
$$3k = 66$$
$$\frac{3k}{3} = \frac{66}{3} \qquad \text{(Property 4)}$$
$$k = 22 \qquad \text{(Cancellation property of fractions)}$$

Check: $22 \times 3 = 66 = 2 \times 33$ ∎

E X A M P L E 9   Last year, a homeowner paid \$1,200 in taxes on property assessed at \$90,000. This year the property was assessed at \$105,000. Assuming the ratio of assessed value to taxes will be the same for this year as last, how much will the homeowner pay in taxes this year?

Solution: The problem can be formulated as the following proportion:

$$\frac{\text{This year assessment}}{\text{This year taxes}} = \frac{\text{Last year assessment}}{\text{Last year taxes}}$$

or

$$\frac{105{,}000}{T} \diagdown\!\!\!\!\diagup \frac{90{,}000}{1{,}200}$$
$$90{,}000T = 126{,}000{,}000 \qquad \text{(Product of means = product of extremes)}$$
$$\frac{90{,}000T}{90{,}000} = \frac{126{,}000{,}000}{90{,}000} \qquad \text{(Property 4)}$$
$$T = \$1{,}400$$

Check: $\$105{,}000 \times \$1{,}200 = \$90{,}000 \times \$1{,}400$. Thus, the taxes for this year are \$1,400. ∎

In setting up the proportion of a verbal problem such as example 9, one technique is to make the numerator and denominator of each fraction consist of the same units (time, money, measurements, etc.). Note in example 9, the numerator and denominator of the left fraction consisted of "this year," while the numerator and denominator of the right fraction consisted of "last year." Also, in setting up a proportion, keep in mind that you are setting up fractions that are equal.

EXERCISES FOR SECTION 2.1

1. a. Solve the formula $P = B \cdot R$ for B.
   b. Find B if $P = 1,200$ and $R = 0.06$.

2. a. Solve the formula $A = \frac{1}{2} bh$ for b.
   b. Find b if $A = 20$ and $h = 15$.

3. a. Solve the formula $I = Prt$ for r.
   b. Find r if $I = \$270$, $P = \$2,000$, and $t = 2$.

4. a. Solve the formula $I = Prt$ for P.
   b. Find P if $I = \$108$, $r = 0.12$, and $t = 1.5$.

5. a. Solve the formula $D = Adt$ for d.
   b. Find d if $D = \$570$, $A = \$4,750$, and $t = 1$.

6. a. Solve the formula $D = Adt$ for A.
   b. Find A if $D = \$382.50$, $d = 0.085$, and $t = 3$.

7. a. Solve the formula Acid-test ratio $= \dfrac{\text{Cash} + \text{Receivables}}{\text{Current liabilities}}$ for Current liabilities.
   b. Find Current liabilities if Cash $= \$10,800$, Receivables $= \$82,200$, and Acid-test ratio $= 1.2$.

8. a. Solve the formula Acid-test ratio $= \dfrac{\text{Cash} + \text{Receivables}}{\text{Current liabilities}}$ for Cash.
   b. Find Cash if Current liabilities $= \$40,000$, Receivables $= \$50,000$, and Acid-test ratio $= 1.8$.

9. a. Solve the formula $A = P(1 + rt)$ for P.
   b. Find P if $A = \$1,210$, $r = 0.05$, and $t = 1/6$.

10. a. Solve the formula $A = P(1 + rt)$ for P.
   b. Find P if $A = \$3,087.50$, $r = 0.07$, and $t = 5/12$.

In problems 11–28, reduce the ratio and express in each of the three forms.

11. 12 to 32

12. 18 to 30

13. 18 to 48

14. 15 to 45

15. 24 to 16

16. 45 to 27

17. 45 to 250

18. 72 to 240

19. 65 to 450

20. 200 to 250

21. 250 to 75

22. 350 to 72

23. 216 to 440

24. 145 to 150

25. $920 to $216

26. $550 to $125

27. $1,440 to $3,880

28. $3,820 to $7,480

In problems 29–36, set up a ratio and reduce to lowest terms.

29. 8 inches to 1 foot

30. 2 inches to 1 yard

31. 40¢ to $1

32. 2 dimes to 2 quarters

33. 10 meters to 1 kilometer (1000 meters)

34. 20 ounces to 1 pound

35. 3 hours to 1 day

36. 20 minutes to 1 hour

In problems 37–44, find the missing number in each proportion.

37. $\dfrac{1}{5} = \dfrac{k}{20}$

38. $\dfrac{3}{8} = \dfrac{k}{24}$

39. $\dfrac{1}{k} = \dfrac{7}{42}$

40. $\dfrac{4}{k} = \dfrac{12}{75}$

41. $\dfrac{k}{15} = \dfrac{12}{90}$ **42.** $\dfrac{k}{5} = \dfrac{14}{35}$ **43.** $\dfrac{1}{16} = \dfrac{5}{k}$ **44.** $\dfrac{2}{15} = \dfrac{12}{k}$

45. The formula $G = np$ is used to compute the gross sales G from the sale of n units of a product at a selling price of p dollars per unit. **a.** Solve this formula for n. **b.** If a product sold for $12 per unit and the gross sales were $7,704, how many units were sold?

46. The formula $N = G - C$ is used to compute the net profit N, where G is gross profit and C is production cost. **a.** Solve this formula for C. **b.** Find the production cost if the gross profit is $280,520 and the net profit is $42,520.

47. The checking accounts at the West End bank are subject to a monthly charge of C dollars, where C is given by the formula $C = \$3 + 0.01n$ and n is the number of checks written during the month. Find the charge C for a month in which **a.** 30 checks are written, **b.** 35 checks are written, and **c.** 40 checks are written.

48. The amount of Sam Smooth's weekly paycheck is given by the formula $A = \$425 + \frac{s}{10}$, where s is the total of his sales during the week (in dollars). Find the amount of Sam's paycheck for a week in which his sales were **a.** $900, **b.** $1,150, and **c.** $1,440.

49. A company estimates that its production cost C to produce k units of its product is given by the formula $C = \$5k + \$1,000$. Find C when the number of units produced is **a.** 1,500, **b.** 2,400.

50. The Sporty Shirt Company finds that the amount S of its weekly gross sales is given by the formula $S = \$1,500 + \$100n$, where n is the number of 30-second television commercials per week. Find the weekly gross sales when the number of television commercials per week was **a.** 8, **b.** 15, and **c.** 20.

51. The cost C in dollars of an order of k pounds of premium grade fertilizer from the Gro-Green Fertilizer Company is given by the formula $C = \$0.8k + \$1.00$. Find the cost of an order of **a.** 60 pounds, **b.** 100 pounds, and **c.** 120 pounds.

52. Magnum Corporation determined that the retail price p for its product is given by the formula $p = \$18 - \$\frac{n}{250}$, where n is the number of units produced by the company. Determine the price when the number of units produced is **a.** 250, **b.** 750, and **c.** 1,000.

53. The Drill-Rite Company determined that the demand for their deluxe electric drill is given by the formula $d = 5,000 - \frac{200}{3}p$, where p is the selling price per drill to dealers and d is the number of drills that can be sold. How many drills can be sold if the price p (in dollars) is **a.** 33, **b.** 45, and **c.** 60?

54. Use the formula $G = np$, where $G =$ gross sales, $n =$ number of units sold, and $p =$ price per unit to determine which of the prices in problem 53 yields the maximum gross sales.

55. Budget Beans estimates that the demand d for their small-size can of baked beans is given by the formula $d = 78,000 - 1,250p$, where p is the selling price per can and d is the number of cans that can be sold. Find the number of cans that can be sold if the price p (in cents) is **a.** 32, **b.** 40, and **c.** 44.

56. The Freeland Company found that its cost to manufacture its product is given by the formula $C = \$1.5k + \$250$, where k is the number of units manufactured. Find the cost to manufacture 800 units.

57. Gonzalez & Jimenez spent $4,800 on advertising and had sales of $72,000. What was the ratio of advertising expenses to sales?

58. Out of 360 cases of flu reported in the city, 140 were suffering from a strain of Asian flu. What was the ratio of Asian flu cases to the total number of cases?

59. The city of Wickenden recorded 48 arrests for traffic violations, of which 20 were for DUI (driving under the influence). What was the ratio of DUI arrests to non-DUI driving arrests?

60. A company had a total of 64 computers, of which 12 were laptop computers. Find the ratio of laptop computers to non-laptop computers.

61. Stan Pantling and Will Holmes are business partners. Last year, Stan worked an average of 51 hours per week and Will worked an average of 17 hours per week. The total profit from the business was $81,450, of which Stan received $54,300, and Will received the rest. Find: **a.** the ratio of Stan's average hours per week to Will's average hours per week, and **b.** the ratio of Stan's share of the profit to Will's share of the profit.

62. A hospital employs 161 nurses and 23 physicians. The average salary for a nurse is $36,000 per year and the average salary for a physician is $124,000 per year. Find: **a.** the ratio of nurses to physicians, and **b.** the ratio of the average salary for a nurse to the average salary for a physician.

63. The Algonquin Company is owned and operated by native Indians who manufacture authentic Indian crafts. The company employs 72 people, of which 54 work in the manufacturing area, 12 work in sales, and the remainder work in the office. **a.** What is the ratio of salespersons to manufacturing workers? **b.** What is the ratio of office workers to the total work force?

64. A company employs 120 union employees and 15 management personnel. The annual payroll is $2,250,000 for the union employees and $750,000 for management personnel. Find: **a.** the ratio of union employees to management personnel, and **b.** the ratio of the union payroll to that of management.

65. At the Techmeyer Corporation the ratio of salaried employees to employees paid by the hour is 2:15. Currently, there are 975 hourly employees. How many salaried employees are there?

66. The Willet Company can produce 24 outside light fixtures in 5 hours. The company has received an order for 840 fixtures. How many hours will be required to fill the order?

67. At a sporting goods store, brand R athletic shoes outsells brand N athletic shoes by a ratio of 9:5. Last month the store sold 120 pairs of brand N. How many pairs of brand R were sold?

68. Schulenberg, Inc. advertised on television and radio at a ratio of 5:2. Last year, the company spent $24,000 on radio advertising. How much was spent on television advertising?

69. The law firm of Espinosa, Hernandez, and Rivera used 12 sacks of fertilizer to cover 7,500 square feet of grass surrounding its law offices. The addition of new parking has reduced the grassy area to 6,250 square feet. How many sacks of fertilizer will be needed for the next lawn feeding?

70. Randall Manufacturing obtains 700 BTUs from 25 pounds of a certain grade of coal. If the firm uses 2 tons of coal per day, how many BTUs do they use each day?

71. Ettleman Construction can buy 48 feet of insulating material for $3.36. How much will it cost the company to buy 70 yards?

72. Historically, Chuck's Chips sells thin potato chips and rippled potato chips in a 7:4 ratio. Advance orders have been received for 2,800 cases of thin potato chips. How many cases of rippled potato chips should the company stock?

73. Julia's Concessions operates three stands at the stadium. Last year for the homecoming game, 9,000 hot dogs were sold to 30,000 alumni and students. This year, the attendance is expected to be 42,000. How many hot dogs should Julia's be prepared to sell?

74. In the hospitals of Central City the ratio of nursing positions to nurses employed is 9:8. Currently, there are 480 nurses employed. **a.** How many nursing positions are there? **b.** How many nursing positions are unfilled?

75. Kanabay Mining found uranium ore that contains 0.008 grams of pure uranium per kilogram of ore. How many metric tons (1,000 kilograms) of ore must be processed to obtain 1 gram of pure uranium?

Section 2.2   *The Meaning of Percent*

Business owner Carol meets her banker John for lunch to discuss a business loan of $100,000, a loan that will increase the debt-equity ratio of her business to a projected 24 *percent*. She has brought last year's financial figures with her and proudly points to a gross profit margin of 46 *percent* and an increase in sales of 80 *percent*. Most increases in expenses were on the work force. Each employee had received a 5 *percent* increase in wages, except for the sales personnel who work on a commission rate of 8 *percent*, but who also received bonuses averaging 2 *percent*. The largest increase in expenses occurred in group health insurance premiums which had jumped 21 *percent*. John indicated the loan was promising and agreed to pay the luncheon check. In his expense diary he noted the cost of the lunch which included a 6 *percent* state sales tax plus a tip of 15 *percent*.

The preceding scenario indicates in part the importance of percent in business. In fact, no other concept dominates business calculations more than percent. The word percent stems from the Latin *per centum,* meaning "by the hundred." Over time, the phrase was shortened to *per cent,* and now appears as the single word *percent.*

Because our number system is the decimal system and because our monetary system is decimal based, it is natural to subdivide units into hundredths. In business, these hundredths are called percent.

The symbol for percent is %. Thus 5% means 5 hundredths, and 75% means 75 hundredths. From chapter 1, we conclude that $5\% = \frac{5}{100} = 0.05$ and $75\% = \frac{75}{100} = 0.75$.

The preceding discussion demonstrates simple methods for converting percents to fractions or decimal numbers and vice versa.

To convert a percent to a decimal number:

1. drop the percent symbol
2. convert any fraction to a decimal number
3. move the decimal point two places to the left (inserting zeros as needed)

E X A M P L E 1   Convert the following to decimal numbers.

a. 2%   **b.** 47%   **c.** 6.5%   **d.** $12\frac{3}{4}\%$ **e.** $\frac{1}{2}\%$ **f.** 130%

Solution: Step 1   Step 2   Step 3

		Step 1	Step 2	Step 3
a.		2		0.02
b.		47		0.47
c.		6.5		0.065
d.		$12\frac{3}{4}$	12.75	0.1275
e.		$\frac{1}{2}$	0.5	0.005
f.		130		1.30

To convert a decimal number to a percent:

1. move the decimal point two places to the right (inserting zeros as needed)
2. affix the % symbol

EXAMPLE 2   Convert to percents:

a. 0.03   **b.** 0.1   **c.** 0.045   **d.** 0.8525   **e.** 0.00075   **f.** 1.25

Solution: **a.** $0.03 = 3\%$ **b.** $0.1 = 10\%$

c. $0.045 = 4.5\% \text{ (or } 4\frac{1}{2}\%)$ **d.** $0.8525 = 85.25\% \text{ (or } 85\frac{1}{4}\%)$

e. $0.00075 = 0.075\% \text{ (or } \frac{3}{40}\%)$ **f.** $1.25 = 125\%$ ■

To convert a percent to a fraction:
Convert any decimal to a fraction, drop the % sign, and write as a fraction with denominator 100. Reduce the fraction to lowest terms.

EXAMPLE 3   Convert to fractions:

a. 20%   **b.** 45%   **c.** $\frac{3}{4}\%$ **d.** 0.5%   **e.** $\frac{9}{4}\%$ **f.** 110%

Solution: **a.** $20\% = \dfrac{20}{100} = \dfrac{1}{5}$ **b.** $45\% = \dfrac{45}{100} = \dfrac{9}{20}$ **c.** $\dfrac{3}{4}\% = \dfrac{\frac{3}{4}}{100} = \dfrac{3}{400}$

d. $0.5\% = \dfrac{1}{2}\% = \dfrac{\frac{1}{2}}{100} = \dfrac{1}{200}$ **e.** $\dfrac{9}{4}\% = \dfrac{\frac{9}{4}}{100} = \dfrac{9}{400}$ **f.** $110\% = \dfrac{110}{100} = \dfrac{11}{10}$ ■

To convert a fraction to a percent:

1. divide the numerator of the fraction by the denominator until the quotient contains two places to the right of the decimal point
2. affix the percent sign to the digits of the quotient and the fraction whose numerator is the remainder and whose denominator is the divisor

E X A M P L E 4   Find the percent equal to $\frac{1}{8}$.

Solution: $8\overline{)\begin{array}{l}0.12\\1.00\end{array}}$

$\underline{8}$

20

$\underline{16}$

4 Thus, $\frac{1}{8} = 12\frac{4}{8}\% = 12\frac{1}{2}\%$ ■

E X A M P L E 5   Find the percent equal to $\frac{3}{20}$.

Solution: $20\overline{)\begin{array}{l}0.15\\3.00\end{array}}$

$\underline{2\;0}$

$1\;00$

$\underline{1\;00}$

0 $\frac{3}{20} = 15\%$ ■

E X A M P L E 6   Find the percent equal to $\frac{1}{3}$.

Solution: $3\overline{)\begin{array}{l}0.33\\1.00\end{array}}$

$\underline{9}$

10

$\underline{9}$

1 $\frac{1}{3} = 33\frac{1}{3}\%$ ■

E X A M P L E 7   Find the percent equal to $\frac{7}{5}$.

Solution: $5\overline{)\begin{array}{l}1.40\\7.00\end{array}}$ $\frac{7}{5} = 1.40 = 140\%$

$\underline{5}$

$2\;0$

$\underline{2\;0}$

0

$\underline{0}$ ■

Certain percents occur frequently in business because they are equivalent to simple fractions, which facilitates computations. For example, $33\frac{1}{3}\% = \frac{1}{3}$, $50\% = \frac{1}{2}$, and so on. Table 2.1 shows some of the more common percents and their equivalent fractions.

Table 2.1	Common Percents and Equivalent Fractions

$\frac{1}{2} = 50\%$ $\quad \frac{1}{3} = 33\frac{1}{3}\%$ $\quad \frac{1}{4} = 25\%$ $\quad \frac{1}{5} = 20\%$ $\quad \frac{1}{6} = 16\frac{2}{3}\%$ $\quad \frac{1}{8} = 12\frac{1}{2}\%$ $\quad \frac{1}{12} = 8\frac{1}{3}\%$

$\frac{2}{3} = 66\frac{2}{3}\%$ $\quad \frac{3}{4} = 75\%$ $\quad \frac{2}{5} = 40\%$ $\quad \frac{5}{6} = 83\frac{1}{3}\%$ $\quad \frac{3}{8} = 37\frac{1}{2}\%$ $\quad \frac{5}{12} = 41\frac{2}{3}\%$

$\frac{3}{5} = 60\%$ $\quad \frac{5}{8} = 62\frac{1}{2}\%$ $\quad \frac{7}{12} = 58\frac{1}{3}\%$

$\frac{4}{5} = 80\%$ $\quad \frac{7}{8} = 87\frac{1}{2}\%$ $\quad \frac{11}{12} = 91\frac{2}{3}\%$

Note: An aliquot part of 100 is any number that divides 100 evenly. Each of the percents in line 1 of the table represents an aliquot part of 100.

EXERCISES FOR SECTION 2.2

In problems 1–18, convert the given percents to decimal numbers.

1. 3% $\frac{3}{100} = .03$ **2.** 8% **3.** 67% **4.** 83.5%

5. 83.7% **6.** 79.3% .793 **7.** 8.92% **8.** 6.28%

9. 83.51% **10.** 52.28% .5228 **11.** $13\frac{1}{4}\%$ **12.** $5\frac{1}{2}\%$

13. $\frac{1}{5}\%$ **14.** $\frac{3}{4}\%$ .75 **15.** 212% **16.** 153%

17. 183.4% **18.** 258.4% 2.584

In problems 19–36, convert the given decimal numbers to percents.

19. 0.02 **20.** 0.03 **21.** 0.64 **22.** 0.65 ×100 **23.** 0.8 ×100 **24.** 0.5

25. 0.064 **26.** 0.017 **27.** 0.6045 **28.** 0.5319 **29.** 0.0043 **30.** 0.0036

31. 5.43 **32.** 4.06 **33.** 8.357 **34.** 9.013 **35.** 8.1374 **36.** 7.4641

In problems 37–60, convert the given percents to fractions reduced to lowest terms.

37. 11% **38.** 29% **39.** 46% **40.** 92% Cancel 100 **41.** 0.2% **42.** 0.8%

43. 0.49% **44.** 0.75% **45.** 0.55% **46.** 0.78% **47.** $\frac{7}{8}\%$ **48.** $\frac{5}{6}\%$

49. $\frac{3}{5}\%$ **50.** $\frac{5}{12}\%$ **51.** $\frac{7}{4}\%$ **52.** $\frac{8}{5}\%$ **53.** 104% **54.** 250%

55. 126% **56.** 141% **57.** 87.4% **58.** 61.6% **59.** 145.5% **60.** 136.2%

In problems 61–76, convert the given fractions to percents.

61. $\dfrac{1}{4}$ $+100$
  $1/4 * 100$
  62. $\dfrac{2}{5}$
  63. $\dfrac{3}{4}$
  64. $\dfrac{4}{5}$
  65. $\dfrac{9}{20}$
  66. $\dfrac{7}{20}$

67. $\dfrac{7}{8}$
  68. $\dfrac{5}{8}$
  69. $\dfrac{15}{16}$
  70. $\dfrac{24}{25}$
  71. $\dfrac{9}{11}$
  72. $\dfrac{4}{9}$

73. $\dfrac{7}{15}$
  74. $\dfrac{8}{5}$
  75. $\dfrac{9}{4}$
  76. $\dfrac{15}{8}$

Section 2.3 *Base and Percentage*

Percent is related to two other quantities: base and percentage. The sentence "$95 is 25% of $380" illustrates the relationship. The **base** is a quantity one calculates a percent "of"; in the preceding sentence, the base is $380. The **percentage** is a portion of the base; in the preceding sentence, $95 is 25% (a one-fourth portion) of $380. The relationship between percent, base, and percentage is summarized by the formula

(2–1) $P = B \cdot R$

where P = percentage (portion)
   B = base
   R = rate (percent).

Because the words *percent* and *percentage* are similar, they are frequently used incorrectly. Many times *percent* is used in conversation by someone who is actually discussing *percentage,* or vice versa. Formula 2–1 clarifies the distinction between the two words: percentage is a quantity found by multiplying the base quantity by the percent.

When the base and percent are known, formula 2–1 is used to find the percentage. When the percent and percentage are known, a formula for finding the base is derived by dividing both sides of formula 2–1 by R to obtain

(2–2) $B = \dfrac{P}{R}$

When the percentage and base are the given quantities, a formula for finding the percent is derived by dividing both sides of formula 2–1 by B to obtain

(2–3) $R = \dfrac{P}{B}$

A simple way to remember these formulas uses the triangle below: To find a particular formula, cover one of the letters with a finger. For example, if the top letter is covered, the remaining letters show *RB* which stands for $R \cdot B$ (which is the same as $B \cdot R$), or formula 2–1. However, covering the letter *R* leaves *P* over *B* which stands for $\dfrac{P}{B}$, which is formula 2–3.

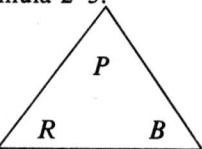

Many problems that involve percent, percentage, or base can be solved using formulas 2–1, 2–2, and 2–3. Choosing the correct formula for a given problem involves correctly identifying the known and unknown quantities. The rate is easily identified by the word percent, or by the percent sign (%). To distinguish between percentage and base, keep in mind that the base is the quantity that we find the percent "of." Thus, the base is usually the quantity or phrase following the word "of." Other terms that refer to the base are the "whole amount," the "original number," or the "total quantity." The next examples demonstrate the use of formulas 2–1, 2–2, and 2–3. Included in representative examples are the calculator calculations.

EXAMPLE 1   What amount is 8% of $3,000?

Solution: The quantity is $3,000, hence this is the base. Thus, $P = ?$, $B = \$3,000$, $R = 8\% = 0.08$. Using formula 2–1,

$P = B \cdot R$
   $= \$3,000 \times 0.08$
   $= \$240$

Eight percent of $3,000 is $240.

Entry	Display
3000	3000
×	3000
8	8
%	240

EXAMPLE 2   Twenty-five percent of what number is 45?

Solution: Following "of" is "what number," hence the base is the unknown. Thus, $P = 45$, $B = ?$, $R = 25\% = 0.25$. Using formula 2–2,

$B = \dfrac{P}{R}$

   $= \dfrac{45}{0.25}$

   $= 180$

Entry	Display
45	45
÷	45
25	25
%	180

EXAMPLE 3   This year's profit of $20,000 is 80% of last year's profit. What was last year's profit?

Solution: The word "of" is used twice in this problem, "of $20,000" and "80% of last year's profit." Since last year's profit is the quantity we are finding a percent of, it is the base. Thus, $P = 20,000$, $B = ?$, $R = 80\% = 0.80$. Using formula 2–2,

$$B = \frac{P}{R}$$

$$= \frac{\$20,000}{0.80} \qquad = \frac{20,000}{80\%}$$

$$= \$25,000$$

■

EXAMPLE 4   A salesperson received a $5.12 commission on a sale of $64.00. What commission percent was paid?

Solution: Following "of" is $64.00, hence this is the base. Thus, $P = \$5.12$, $B = \$64.00$, $R = ?$ Using formula 2–3,

$$R = \frac{P}{B} \qquad \frac{P}{B} = R$$

$$= \frac{\$5.12}{\$64}$$

$$= 0.08$$

$$= 8\%$$

$P =$ Portion / %age amt

$B.$ Principal Amt

$R =$ rate

■

A common application of formulas 2–1, 2–2, and 2–3 is the sales tax imposed by governments on retail sales. In problems involving sales tax, $P =$ amount of the sales tax, $B =$ purchase price, and $R =$ tax rate. The next examples illustrate this application. (Sales tax will be discussed in greater detail in chapter 6.)

EXAMPLE 5   The selling price of an item is $58.95. If the sales tax rate is 6%, find the amount of the sales tax.

Solution: $P = ?$, $B = \$58.95$, $R = 6\% = 0.06$. Using formula 2–1,

$$P = B \cdot R$$

$$= \$58.95 \times 0.06$$

$$= \$3.537$$

$$= \$3.54 \text{ (rounded)}$$

Selling $P = B.$

Tax rate $= R$

Sales tax $= P$

■

E X A M P L E 6   The sales tax on an item was $7.75. If the sales tax rate is 6.25%, what was the selling price of the item?

Solution: $P = \$7.75$, $B = ?$, $R = 6.25\% = 0.0625$. Using formula 2–2,

$$B = \frac{P}{R}$$

$$= \frac{\$7.75}{0.0625}$$

$$= \$124.00$$

E X A M P L E 7   The sales tax on an item that sold for $140.66 was $7.03. To the nearest percent, find the sales tax rate.

Solution: $P = \$7.03$, $B = \$140.66$, $R = ?$ Using formula 2–3,

$$R = \frac{P}{B}$$

$$= \frac{\$7.03}{\$140.66}$$

$$= 0.0499786$$

$$= 5\%$$

EXERCISES FOR SECTION 2.3

1. 5% of 400 is what amount?

2. 9% of 500 is what amount?

3. 18% of 50 is what amount?

4. 16% of 210 is what amount?

5. 57 is 15% of what amount?

6. 182 is 13% of what amount?

7. 4.14 is 1.8% of what amount?

8. 62.15 is 11.3% of what amount?

9. What percent of 420 is 147?

10. What percent of 810 is 162?

11. What percent of 860 is 129?

12. What percent of 945 is 189?

13. 39% of 85 is what amount?

14. 45% of 52 is what amount?

15. 43.4% of 1,450 is what amount?

16. 21.2% of 522 is what amount?

17. 36% of 430 is what amount?

18. 8.9% of 2,620 is what amount?

19. 14.75% of 800 is what amount?

20. 34.9% of 677 is what amount?

21. 60.57 is 18% of what amount?

22. 28.864 is 16% of what amount?

23. 129.339 is 21% of what amount?

24. 385.762 is 37% of what amount?

25. What percent of 77.6 is 3.104?

26. What percent of 38.4 is 2.304?

27. What percent of 123.1 is 9.848?

28. What percent of 477.3 is 42.957?

29. 22.65% of 500 is what amount?

30. 9.225% of 120 is what amount?

31. $\frac{1}{4}$% of 210 is what amount? $\frac{1}{4}\% \times 210$

32. $\frac{2}{5}$% of 925 is what amount?

33. 35.19 is 15.3% of what amount? $35.19 / 15.3\%$

34. 107.214 is 16.7% of what amount?

35. 185.136 is 24.36% of what amount?

36. 275.184 is 47.04% of what amount?

$R =$ 37. What percent of 123.45 is 14.814? $\left(\frac{14.814}{123.45}\right) \times 100$

$R =$ 38. What percent of 616.92 is 431.844?

39. What percent of 1,607.38 is 40.1845?

40. What percent of 1,805.90 is 1,795.0646?

41. Mary sold $885 of women's clothing. At a commission rate of 12%, how much commission will she receive? $885 \times 12\%$

42. A sweater sold for $68.80. If the sales tax rate was 4%, find the amount of the sales tax. $68.80 \times 4\%$

43. Out of 2,250 items manufactured by a machine, 1.2% were defective. Find the number of defective items. $2250 \times 1.2\%$

44. Find the amount of the sales tax on an item priced at $138.02 if the sales tax rate is 5%. $138.02 \times 5\%$

45. Find the sales tax rate on an item that sells for $14.50 if the sales tax was $0.87.

46. The sales tax on an item priced at $140.80 was $7.04. Find the sales tax rate.

47. A worker earning $32,500 received a bonus of $1,300. What percent of the worker's salary was the bonus?

48. A corporation paid income taxes of $54,096 on gross profits of $225,400. Find the income tax rate.

49. Larry Saunders paid a sales tax of $4.03 on a pen and pencil set. If the sales tax rate was 6.25% of the purchase price, what was the purchase price?

50. A stock paid a dividend of 6% of the original investment. If the dividend was $58.50, find the original investment.

51. Chung Chao received a real estate commission of $7,470 which was 6% of the selling price. What was the selling price?

52. A professional quarterback received a bonus of $5,000 for completing 68.18% of the passes he threw in a game. If he completed 30 passes, how many did he attempt?

53. A VCR had a selling price of $249.50. If the sales tax was 5.75% of the selling price, what was the amount of the sales tax?

54. Bruce sold a dining room set for $972. If his sales commission was 18% of the purchase price, how much did Bruce receive?

55. For a magazine advertisement, Hank's Hardware paid $1,522.50. Last year, the same advertisement was 92% of this amount. Find the amount of last year's advertisement.

56. Maria Cubelo purchased a new microwave oven for $249.95. She made a down payment of 15% of the purchase price. Find the amount of the down payment.

57. Louise Hess had a taxable income of $31,620 for last year and paid $6,653 in federal income taxes. What was the federal income tax rate?

58. Of the $210,000 in sales Palm Travel had last year, $181,650 were charged to credit cards. What percent of the sales were credit card purchases?

59. Of 580 employees at McCormick Equipment Company, 435 were union employees. What percent of the company's work force were union employees?

60. The Eltek Corporation reported profits of $26,730 in April on sales of $356,400. What percent of the company's April sales are its profits?

61. Juan Perez received a stock dividend of $450, which was 9% of his original investment. Find his original investment.

62. Mark Stern received a weekly commission check of $194. If the commission rate is 8%, find the amount of his weekly sales.

63. United Heating reported a profit of $26,487 last month, which was 5.4% of sales. Find the amount of last month's sales.

64. During a recent sale at Anderson Electrical Supply, the profit on electric lamps was 45% of the sale price. If the profit on each lamp was $43.20, find the sale price of each lamp.

65. In July, Tire Treads, Inc. reported profits of $26,730 on sales of $356,400. What percent of the company's July sales were its profits?

66. The property of T & H Industries was assessed at $216,000 and the property tax bill was $5,184. Find the property tax rate.

67. Norma Stablik invested $7,400 in a mutual fund and later sold the shares for a profit of $917.60. What percent of her original investment was her profit?

68. The manager of the men's department decided to close out a line of sport coats, so he reduced the price from $280 to $224. What percent of the original price is the reduced price?

69. Hi-Volt Battery Company laid off 5% of their work force because of poor sales. If the company originally employed 3,200 workers, how many workers were laid off?

70. The sales force of a company made 450 calls last month. Eighteen percent of the calls resulted in sales. How many sales were made?

71. Miller Marine Company pays 3% of its monthly net sales to an employee profit sharing plan. Last month, the net sales were $39,742. Find the amount paid to the profit sharing plan.

72. Northwest Motors accepted 160 used cars as trade-ins during February. Of these, 25% were wholesaled to a used car dealer, and 5% were sold as junk. The remaining cars were reconditioned and sold through the company's used car division. **a.** How many cars were reconditioned? **b.** How many cars were junked?

73. A project at Lotus Industries reportedly had an estimated cost of $12,500 which was 80% of the actual cost. What was the actual cost?

74. Nancy Schubert had $157.56 deducted from her monthly paycheck for health insurance, which was 6.5% of her gross pay. Find her gross pay.

75. At the Peachtree Publishing Company, 12.5% of the job applicants could not pass the company employment test. If 18 job applicants failed the employment test, find the number of job applicants.

76. Coal production at the Nichols Coal Company decreased by 2.5% from last week's production. If the decrease was 210.6 tons, find the production for last week.

77. Barb Snyder purchased a new stereo system priced at $734.50. If the sales tax was $22.04, to the nearest percent what percent of the price was the sales tax?

78. Jan Foster paid $13,765.78 in federal income taxes based on an adjusted gross income of $47,468.20. To the nearest percent, what percent of her adjusted gross income did she pay in taxes?

79. Nisha's Produce purchased 640 crates of lettuce, but expects to lose 56 crates due to spoilage. Find the percent of the purchase that will be lost to spoilage.

80. Frances Thomas purchased the Children's Apparel Shop. At the end of the first year, she had $21,200 invested in the shop. If the net income from the shop was $9,200 for the year, to the nearest percent what percent of the investment did she receive as income?

Section 2.4 *Variations of the Percentage Formula*

Prices, costs, and quantities are continually increasing or decreasing in business. For example, a shortage of raw materials can cause the cost of an item to increase. This, in turn, can cause the profit on the item to decrease. The measure of such increase or decrease is in percent. Two types of increases or decreases are calculated: (1) the base is increased (decreased) by a specified amount; (2) the base is increased (decreased) by a specified percent. There are formulas for each type.

If the base is increased (decreased) by a specified *amount,* the percent change is given by

$$(2\text{--}4) \quad R = \frac{\text{Increase (or decrease) in base}}{\text{Base}}$$

The base in formula 2–4 is the original quantity before the increase or decrease is realized.

EXAMPLE 1 The number of electric customers in a southern state increased from 40 million in 1980 to 65.6 million in 1990. Find the percent increase in the number of electric customers during this decade.

Solution: The new base of 65.6 million is an increase from the original base of 40 million.

$$R = \frac{\text{Increase in base}}{\text{Base}}$$
$$= \frac{65.6 - 40}{40}$$
$$= \frac{25.6}{40}$$
$$= 0.64$$
$$= 64\%$$

Entry	Display
65.6	65.6
−	65.6
40	40
÷	25.6
40	40
=	0.64

EXAMPLE 2 The sale price of a swivel rocker was $300 compared to a regular price of $560. By what percent was the price of the rocker reduced?

Solution: The new base of $300 is a decrease from the original base of $560. Using formula 2–4,

$$R = \frac{\text{Decrease in base}}{\text{Base}}$$
$$= \frac{\$560 - \$300}{\$560}$$
$$= \frac{\$260}{\$560}$$
$$= 0.4643$$
$$= 46.43\%$$

Entry	Display
560	560
−	560
300	300
÷	260
560	560
=	0.4642857

EXAMPLE 3 The revenues of Good Shepherd Hospital decreased from $1.3 million last year to $988,000 this year. Calculate the percent decrease in revenue.

Solution: The new base of $988,000 is a decrease from the original base of $1.3 million. Using formula 2–4,

$$R = \frac{\text{Decrease in base}}{\text{Base}}$$
$$= \frac{\$1,300,000 - \$988,000}{\$1,300,000}$$
$$= \frac{\$312,000}{\$1,300,000}$$
$$= 0.24$$
$$= 24\%$$

If the base B is increased (decreased) by a specified *percent* to a new base NB, the amount of the new base is given by

> **(2–5)** $NB = B \pm B \cdot R$

The symbol $\pm$ means "plus or minus." Only one of the signs is used in a given problem. The plus sign is used if the base is increased; the minus sign is used if the base is decreased.

EXAMPLE 4 The Asian Automobile Co. announced a price increase of 3% for next year's model compared to a price of $10,200 for this year's model. What will be the price of next year's model?

Solution: $NB = ?$, $B = \$10,200$, $R = 3\% = 0.03$. Since base has increased, using formula 2–5,

$$NB = B + B \cdot R$$
$$= \$10,200 + 10,200 \times 0.03$$
$$= \$10,200 + 306$$
$$= \$10,506$$

Entry	Display	Memory
10200	10200	0
M+	10200	10200
×	10200	10200
3	3	10200
%	306	10200
M+	306	10506
MR	10506	10506

E X A M P L E 5   Lee Brothers Inc. reported a 6% decline in profits this year. If last year's profits were $128,400, calculate the profits of this year.

Solution: $NB = ?$, $B = \$128,400$, $R = 6\% = 0.06$. Since base has decreased, using formula 2–5,

$$NB = B - B \cdot R$$
$$= \$128,400 - \$128,400 \times 0.06$$
$$= \$128,400 - \$7,704$$
$$= \$120,696$$

EXERCISES FOR SECTION 2.4

In problems 1–12, compute the percent increase or decrease of the given base.

	From	**To**
1.	$60	$90
2.	$370	$444
3.	25 lbs	32.5 lbs
4.	80 kilograms	108 kilograms
5.	400 employees	560 employees
6.	25 cases	60 cases
7.	$472	$401.20
8.	$3,840	$3,264
9.	140 liters	123.2 liters
10.	22 tons	14.08 tons
11.	1,068 gallons	854.4 gallons
12.	290 pairs	174 pairs

In problems 13–24, compute the new base when the original base is increased or decreased by the stated percent.

13. 180 pounds, increased by 60%

14. 64 kilograms, increased by 20%

15. 120 employees, increased by 25%

16. 3,200 students, increased by 12%

17. $4,612.24, increased by 14.2%

18. $16,208, increased by 7.6%

19. 108 shares of stock, decreased by 25%

20. 480 dozen, decreased by 15%

21. 192 square meters, decreased by 38%

22. 120 pairs, decreased by 60%

23. $12,647.16, decreased by 11.6%

24. $6,421.42, decreased by 12.7%

25. Grant Industries granted all hourly employees a wage increase from $11.00 per hour to $11.66 per hour. Find the percent increase in the hourly wage.

26. As a result of a new labor contract, labor costs at a manufacturing plant increased from $48,000 to $60,000. Find the percent increase in labor costs.

27. An insurance company purchased 110,000 shares of a stock. The company began with 500,000 shares of the stock. What was the percent increase in the number of shares owned?

28. J & J Sporting Goods saw their sales increase from $160,000 to $184,000 in one quarter. Find the percent increase in sales in the quarter.

29. Marlin, Inc. increased their quarterly dividend from $0.16 per share to $0.18 per share. Find the percent increase in the quarterly dividend.

30. The value of the inventory in the home furnishings section of a department store increased from $124,000 to $139,500 during the first quarter of the year. Find the percent increase during the first quarter of the year.

31. Dolphin Marine recently reduced the price of an outboard motor from $1,060 to $848. Find the percent decrease in the price.

32. A poor sales performance in the third quarter caused the Brooker Company to reduce its work force from 520 employees to 442 employees. Find the percent decrease in the work force.

33. Major Motors, Inc. reported a decrease in monthly production from 46,000 units to 40,940 units. Find the percent decrease in monthly production.

34. The weekly operating expenses at Wilma's Antiques were reduced from $450 to $414. Find the percent reduction in the weekly operating expenses.

35. A law requiring shrimpers to install a turtle extruder (a device to permit turtles to escape a shrimp net and thus prevent their drowning), resulted in a decrease in the amount of shrimp netted from 6,400 pounds to 6,055 pounds. What was the percent decline in the catch?

36. Computer records indicate that a display should contain 36 bottles of shampoo. Because of theft, only 32 bottles were actually counted. Find the percent decrease in inventory due to theft.

37. This month the city of Fairfield reported a 6% increase in the number of bus riders. If there were 1,250 riders last month, how many riders were there this month?

38. The Daily Independent announced a 5% increase in circulation over last year's figure of 246,000. How many papers were sold this year?

39. Dunbar's Department Store advertised a gas grill at 20% off the regular price of $212. What was the sale price?

40. A truckload of apples arrived at the Super Sweet Cannery. If 15% of the 1,250 pounds of apples in the truckload were spoiled, how many pounds of apples were usable?

41. Jean's house is listed by a realty for $98,000. If the Realtors commission is 8% of the selling price, what will Jean actually receive when her house is sold?

42. A motorcycle is priced at $5,250, which is 18% more than the wholesale price. Find the wholesale price.

43. Atlas Appliances advertised that it would match any competitive advertisement less 10%. A competitor advertised a television set for $462. At what price will Atlas agree to sell the set?

44. Peerless Products installed new equipment that reduced the production cost per unit by 8%. If the old production cost is $120, what is the new production cost?

45. In the decade 1980–90, federal revenues increased some 211%. If 1980 revenues were $517 billion, to the nearest billion find the 1990 revenues.

46. Wanda Phillips recently purchased a gas grill for $182.64, including the sales tax. If the sales tax rate was 6%, find the price of the grill, excluding the sales tax.

47. Susan Prentice purchased a new stereo sound system for a total price of $724.42, including the sales tax. If the sales tax rate was 5.5%, what was the price of the stereo system, excluding the sales tax?

Glossary

Base   A quantity one calculates a percent "of"; the number that is multiplied by a percent.

Evaluating a formula   Calculating the value of a word (letter) when all other words (letters) are replaced by numbers.

Formula   An equation containing more than one variable (letter).

Percent   Means "by the hundred" or "hundredths"; the quotient of the percentage and the base, expressed as hundredths; also called the rate.

Percentage   The product of the base and the percent; a portion of the base.

Proportion   The equality of two ratios.

Rate   See percent.

Ratio   A fraction where the numerator and denominator relate similar things.

Variable   A letter or symbol used to represent or act as a placeholder for numbers.

Review Test

1. Solve the formula $I = Prt$ for t in terms of P, r, and I. Find the value of t if $P = \$15,000$, $r = 0.08$, and $I = \$6,000$.

2. **a.** Solve the formula $A = P(1 + rt)$ for P.
   b. Find P if $A = \$3,245$, $r = 0.06$, and $t = 3$.

3. An entering freshman class had 480 males and 435 females. Express in lowest terms the ratio of female freshmen to total freshmen.

4. Solve $\frac{14}{70} = \frac{a}{60}$ for a.

5. A catering service used 4.5 pounds of butter to prepare a meal for 60 people. How many pounds of butter would be required to prepare the same meal for 40 people?

6. Convert to decimal numbers: **a.** 43%, **b.** $19\frac{1}{2}\%$.

7. Convert to percents: **a.** 0.73, **b.** 0.024.

8. Find: **a.** 18% of 400, **b.** 12% of 780.

9. Express as percents: **a.** $\frac{3}{5}$, **b.** 2.75.

10. Express 65% as a fraction reduced to lowest terms.

11. Express 20 as **a.** a percent, **b.** a decimal.

12. Twelve percent of what amount is 42?

13. What percent of 72.9 is 29.16?

14. What is the percent increase of 78 to 107.64?

15. What is the percent decrease of 125 to 50?

16. Express the percent increase from 55 to 88 as a fraction reduced to lowest terms.

17. If 430 is increased by 30% to a new base, what is the new base?

18. If 75 is decreased by 20% to a new base, what is the new base?

19. A worker paid 27% of her adjusted gross income of \$36,000 in federal income taxes. How much did she pay in taxes?

20. An automobile insurance claim amounted to 44% of the value of the car, which was \$3,800. How much was the claim?

21. Sales at a retail store increased from \$3,200 to \$4,320 in one month. What was the percent increase in sales?

22. A merchant had to raise the price on an item selling for \$68 by 8%. What was the new selling price?

23. During a day's trading, the price of a share of stock decreased from \$46.00 to \$40.25. What was the percent decrease?

24. A corporation reduced its quarterly dividend from \$5.40 per share to \$3.80 per share. To the nearest percent, what percent was the dividend reduced?

25. An employee was given a wage increase of 7.5%. If she was earning \$12.40 per hour before her raise, what is her new hourly rate?

Commercial Discounts

Section 3.1 *Trade Discounts*

A. Introduction

The retail store is the final step of the marketing process that begins with raw materials and ends with a product for sale to the public. Retail stores may be large or small, may be independently owned or part of a nationwide chain, but they have one thing in common: Their managers buy merchandise and then resell it to the public. Over 18 million people are employed in some aspect of retailing, and annual retail trade exceeds $1.5 billion. This chapter covers some basic mathematics of retailing.

A number of special terms are used in retail mathematics:

List price or **suggested retail price** The catalog price or the price on a price list or price tag.

Discount A percentage reduction from the list price.

Net price The list price minus any discounts.

Billing price The net price plus any freight or transportation charges.

Cost price The billing price plus any other charges (for example, storage charges).

Selling price The amount of money the seller receives in exchange for a product.

B. Invoices and Trade Discounts

A **trade discount** is a percentage reduction offered to the retailer by a manufacturer or wholesaler. Often, the manufacturer's list price is approximately the retailer's selling price. Therefore, if the retailer is to cover his or her overhead and earn a net profit, the merchandise must be bought at a discount.

The document that records the sale of merchandise to a retailer is the invoice. A sample invoice is shown in figure 3.1. Note that the trade discount of 50% reduces the list price of $436 by $218. Thus, the net price is $436 − $218 = $218.

The amount of a trade discount is an application of the basic percentage equation $P = B \cdot R$ where P = amount of trade discount, B = list price, and R = trade discount percent.

EXAMPLE 1   Appleton Appliances buys refrigerators from a wholesale appliance dealer. The list price of one model is $978 with a trade discount of 40%. Find **a.** the amount of the trade discount, and **b.** the net price.

Solution: **a.** $P = ?, B = \$978, R = 40\% = 0.40$ **b.** $978.00   List price
$P = B \cdot R$ − 391.20   Trade discount
$\quad = \$978 \times 0.40$ $586.80   Net price
$\quad = \$391.20$

EXAMPLE 2   A wholesale hardware company lists a water heater at $246 with a trade discount of 30%. Find the net price.

Solution: $246.00   List price
− 73.80   Trade discount ($246 × 0.30)
$172.20   Net price

Trade discounts may be in fractional percents such as $16\frac{2}{3}\%$, $33\frac{1}{3}\%$, and so on. In such instances, it may be simpler and more accurate to multiply the list price by the fractional equivalent of the discount percent. Recall from table 2.1 on page 48 that $16\frac{2}{3}\% = \frac{1}{6}$ and $33\frac{1}{3}\% = \frac{1}{3}$.

Figure 3.1
Invoice with trade
discount

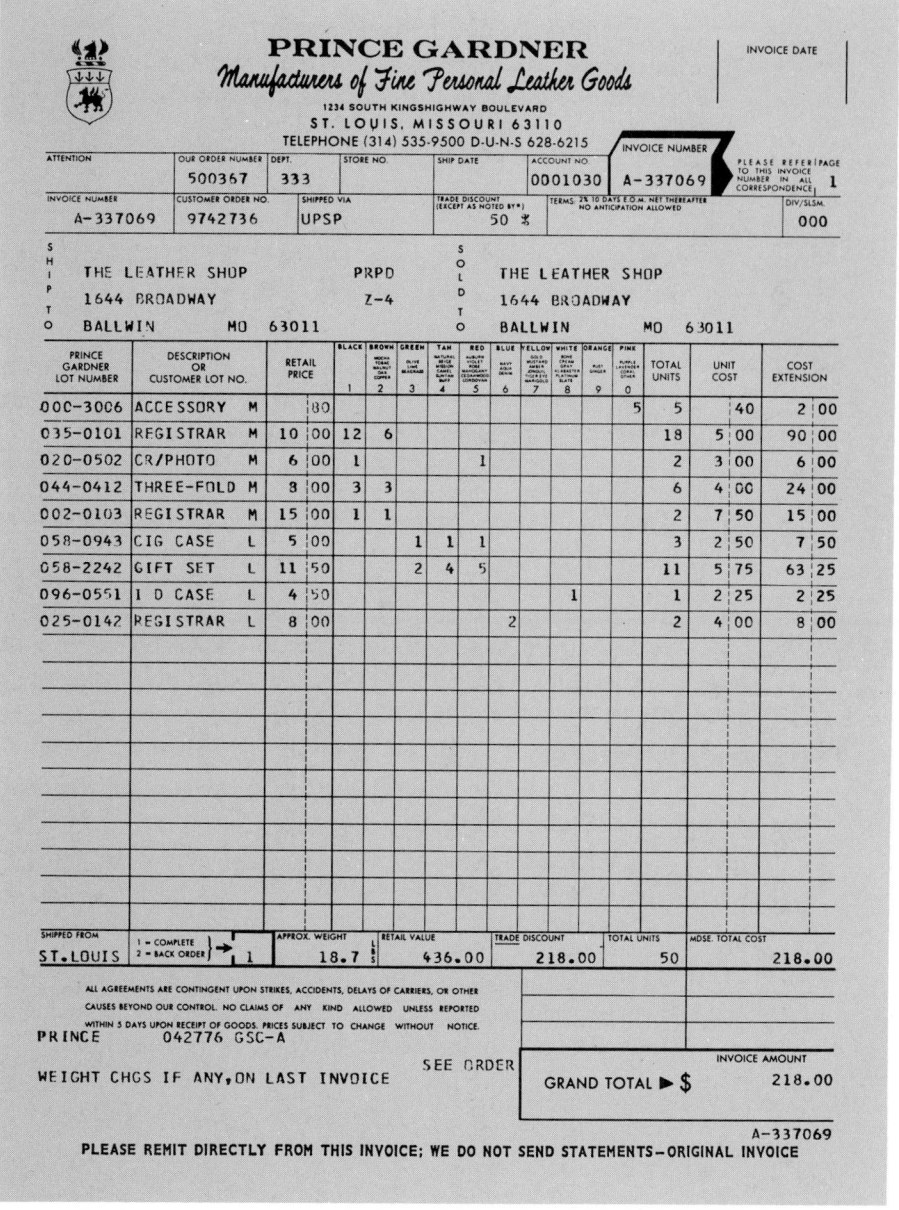

EXAMPLE 3   A bicycle has a list price of $144. The trade discount is $33\frac{1}{3}$%. Find the net price.

Solution:

$144.00   List price
$-\underline{48.00}$ Trade discount ($144 \times \frac{1}{3}$)
$\$96.00$ Net price

C. Complement of the Discount

In example 2, a trade discount of 30% means that the net price is 70% (100% − 30%) of the list price. Multiplying the list price by 0.70 yields

$$
\begin{array}{r}
\$246.00 \\
\times \underline{\quad 0.70} \\
\$172.20
\end{array}
$$

Relative to the 30% discount, 70% is called the **complement of the discount** or the **net price percent.** A discount and its complement are related by the formula

(3–1)   100% − *D* = *C*

where *D* = Trade discount percent
C = Complement of the discount (net price percent)

Thus, *an alternate method of calculating the net price* is to multiply the list price by the net price percent.

EXAMPLE 4   A dining-room suite with a list price of $1,268.00 carries a trade discount of 70%. The freight charges are $94.60. Find the net price using the complement of the discount and then find the billing price.

Solution:

$$
\begin{array}{rl}
\$1{,}268.00 & \text{List price} \\
\times \underline{\quad 0.30} & \text{Net price percent (complement of the discount)} \\
\$\ \ 380.40 & \text{Net price} \\
+ \underline{\quad 94.60} & \text{Freight charges} \\
\$\ \ 475.00 & \text{Billing price}
\end{array}
$$

The complement of the discount for a trade discount of a fractional percent is found by subtracting the fractional equivalent of the discount percent from 1. For example, for a trade discount of $12\frac{1}{2}\% = \frac{1}{8}$, using formula 3–1,

$$
100\% - 12\frac{1}{2}\% = 87\frac{1}{2}\%
$$

$$
1 - \frac{1}{8} = \frac{7}{8}
$$

EXAMPLE 5   A load of fertilizer with a list price of $880 carries a trade discount of $12\frac{1}{2}\%$. Find the net price using the complement of the discount.

Solution: $\$880 \times \dfrac{7}{8} = \$770$

EXERCISES FOR SECTION 3.1

In problems 1–6, find the net price using the discount percent.

	List Price	Discount Percent
1.	$200.00	15% $200 - (200 \times 15?)$
2.	$150.00	20%
3.	$575.00	10%
4.	$445.75	30%

5. $232.40 $5\frac{1}{2}\%$

6. $410.39 $8\frac{1}{3}\%$

In problems 7–12, find the net price using the complement of the discount (net price percent).

7.	$317.00	12% $317 \times .88$
8.	$624.00	17%
9.	$516.25	15%
10.	$284.88	31%

11. $667.70 $7\frac{1}{2}\%$

12. $407.08 $16\frac{2}{3}\%$

Solve:

13. A baby crib has a list price of $269.00 and a trade discount of 60%. Find the net price. $269 \times .40$

14. What is the net price of an exerciser with a list price of $200 and a trade discount of 42%?

15. An automobile club sells a set of luggage for $199. If the set was purchased for list price less 45%, what did the automobile club pay for the set?

16. A collection of women's jeans was purchased by Thompson's Department Store for $48.00 per pair less 28%. What did Thompson's pay per pair of jeans?

48
- 28% 48

17. An eleven piece set of glass cookware was billed to the Kuntry Kitchen Store at $35.50 less a trade discount of 34%. What was the net price of the cookware set?

18. Carl's Camera Shoppe buys a 300mm zoom lens from a wholesaler for a list price of $349.95 less 20%. How much does Carl pay for a 300mm zoom lens?

19. A central air conditioner with a list price of $2,400 was offered with a trade discount of 16%. If the freight charges were $77.40, find the billing price.

2400
$\times$ .84
2112
+ 77.40
2189.4

20. Copper fittings offered by the Kansas City Specialty Company carried a list price of $24.99 less 15%. What was the billing price if freight charges were $5.03?   + freight chgs

21. Stecklers Men's Shop purchased one dozen plain knit shirts with a list price of $20 each and one dozen striped knit shirts with a list price of $25 per shirt. Each type of shirt carried a trade discount of 26%. Find the total net price paid by Stecklers. $\frac{20}{25}$ $45 \times 12 \times 74$

22. Charlene's Intimate Wear bought two dozen sport bras with a list price of $10.50 each and one dozen runner's bras with a list price of $11.00 each. Each bra carried a trade discount of 11%. Find the total net price paid by Charlene's.   10.50   11. 21.50×12 189

23. Overman Office Stores purchased two facsimile machines with a list price of $530 each and 50 rolls of fax paper at $4.00 per roll. The trade discount was 60% on the facsimile machines and 10% per roll on the fax paper. Find the total net price paid by Overman.   530 \times 2 1060 \times 40   504   20 \times 9   = 424   180   604

24. Merrills Appliances purchased 24 hand mixers and 8 counter-top mixers from a wholesale appliance store. The suggested retail prices were $26.95 and $179.95 respectively. The trade discounts were 40% on the hand mixers and 62% on the counter-top mixers. Find the total net price paid by Merrills. $24 \times 26.95 \times .60$ $8 \times 179.95 \times .38$

$\lfloor(162 \times 24) - 16\% \rfloor \lceil 4(184 \times 12) - 20\% \rceil$ $1 - (2380 \div 34.00$

25. A hardware store purchased twenty four cases of latex paint for $162.00 a case less 16% and twelve cases of enamel paint for $184.00 a case less 20%. Find the total net price paid by the hardware store.

26. A floor tile company purchased twelve cases of 8 inch tile at $120.00 per case less 26% and sixteen cases of 12 inch tile at $175.00 per case less $33\frac{1}{3}$%. Find the total net price paid by the floor tile company.

27. A bracelet watch had a list price of $75.00 and a net price of $48.75. Find the trade discount percent. (Hint: use formula 2–4.) $1 - (48.75 \div 75)$

28. A china figurine with a list price of $34.00 was purchased for a net price of $23.80. Find the trade discount percent. (Hint: use formula 2–4.)

29. Radiant Heating Company paid a net price of $72.00 for a space heater with a list price of $120.00. What was the trade discount percent? $x = \frac{72}{120} = 40\%$

30. Ingram Insulation Company bought 30 bags of vermiculite for a net price of $16.83 per bag. If the total list price was $540.00, what was the trade discount percent? $1 - \dfrac{(16.83 \times 30)}{540}$

Section 3.2 *Chain Discounts*

A. Chain Discounts or Series Discounts

Changes in market conditions may affect the selling price of an already discounted product. Improved technology, a reduction in the price of raw materials, or wholesale price adjustments are examples of conditions that may necessitate a price change. Rather than changing the entire price list, the seller may add an additional trade discount. For example, a price might be quoted at $100 less 40% less 20%. This means that the list price is first discounted by 40%, then the result is discounted 20% to obtain the net price. Two or more trade discounts on a single item are called **chain discounts** or **series discounts.**

EXAMPLE 1   A load of paneling with a list price of $684 had trade discounts of 30/15 (30% less 15%). What was the net price?

Solution:

$684.00	List price	
− 205.20	First discount ($684 × 0.30)	
$478.80		
− 71.82	Second discount ($478.80 × 0.15)	
$406.98	Net price	

Entry	Display
684	684
×	684
30	30
%	205.20
−	478.80
×	478.80
15	15
%	71.82
−	406.98

EXAMPLE 2   What is the net price of a musical instrument with a list price of $500 and trade discounts of 60/30/10 (60% less 30% less 10%)?

Solution: $500.00   List price
− 300.00   First discount ($500 × 0.60)
$200.00
− 60.00   Second discount ($200 × 0.30)
$140.00
− 14.00   Third discount ($140 × 0.10)
$126.00   Net price

B. Net Price Percent

The separate calculations in example 2 can be shortened by multiplying the list price by a percent called the **net price percent**. This single percent is the *product of the complements of the chain discount percents.* To illustrate, in example 2

Chain Discount Percent	*Complement of Chain Discount Percent*
60% = 0.60	40% = 0.40
30% = 0.30	70% = 0.70
10% = 0.10	90% = 0.90

The net price percent is the product of the complements or
$0.40 \times 0.70 \times 0.90 = 0.252$. Multiplying the list price by the net price percent,

$500.00   List price
× 0.252   Net price percent
$126.00   Net price

Entry	Display
.4	0.4
×	0.4
.7	0.7
×	0.28
.9	0.9
×	0.252
500	500
=	126

The total trade discount is the difference between the list price and the net price or
$500 − $126 = $374.

EXAMPLE 3   A compact disc player with a list price of $396 has trade discounts of $33\frac{1}{3}/16\frac{2}{3}$. Find the net price using the net price percent.

Solution: Since $33\frac{1}{3}\% = \frac{1}{3}$ and $16\frac{2}{3}\% = \frac{1}{6}$, the product of the complements is $\frac{2}{3} \times \frac{5}{6} = \frac{5}{9}$.

$396 \times \dfrac{5}{9} = $220   Net price

C. Single Discount Percent Equivalent to the Chain Discount

The net price percent goes from the list price to the net price and does not give the sum of the chain discounts. A single discount percent equivalent to the chain discounts can be found by subtracting the net price percent from 100% (or from 1 if the net price percent is in decimal form). To illustrate, in example 2, the net price percent in decimal form was 0.252. Thus,

$$1 - 0.252 = 0.748$$

This is the single discount percent because

$500.00	List price
− 374.00	($500 × 0.748)
$126.00	Net price

E X A M P L E   4   Complete the following invoice.

INVOICE

NO. 287402

DATE 8/2

YOUR ORDER NO. 4749

SOLD TO Eagle Construction Company

1816 High Street

Madison, Wisconsin

SHIPPED TO

4618 Chestnut Street

Watertown, Wisconsin

OUR ORDER NO. K4711	SALESMAN J.D.	TERMS Net	F.O.B.	DATE SHIPPED 7/31	SHIPPED VIA Greyhound			
QUANTITY ORDERED	QUANTITY SHIPPED	STOCK NUMBER/DESCRIPTION				PRICE	UNIT	AMOUNT
1	1	106 – 8490 Home Intercom System				199 90	ea.	
2	2	107 – 8490 Room Stations				21 99	ea.	
		Total List						
		Less 40% less 10%						
		Net						
		Prepaid freight						3 88
		Grand Total						

ORIGINAL

Solution: The net price percent is $0.60 \times 0.90 = 0.54$, thus the single discount percent equivalent to the chain discounts is $1 - 0.54 = 0.46$. The invoice is completed as follows:

$199.90
$+ \underline{\quad 43.98}$ (21.99×2)
$243.88   Total of list prices
$- \underline{\quad 112.18}$ Chain discounts (243.88×0.46)
$131.70   Net price
$+ \underline{\quad\quad 3.88}$ Freight charges
$135.58   Grand total (Billing price)

Entry	Display	Memory
199.90	199.90	0
M+	199.90	199.90
21.99	21.99	199.90
×	21.99	199.90
2	2	199.90
M+	43.98	243.88
MR	243.88	243.88
×	243.88	243.88
.46	0.46	243.88
=	112.1848	243.88
112.18	112.18	243.88
M−	112.18	131.70
MR	131.70	131.70
3.88	3.88	131.70
M+	3.88	135.58
MR	135.58	135.58

EXAMPLE 5   Chieftan Camping offers a camping tent with a list price of $290 and a trade discount of 40%. Chieftan learned that a competitor is selling a similar size tent for a net price of $147.90. What additional trade discount must Chieftan use to match the competitor's price?

Solution: $290.00   List price
$- \underline{\quad 116.00}$ Discount (290×0.40)
$174.00   Net price with one trade discount

To match the competitor, the amount of the additional discount is
$174.00 - $147.90 = $26.10.

$P = \$26.10, B = \$174.00, R = \,?$

$$R = \frac{P}{B}$$

$$= \frac{\$26.10}{\$174.00}$$

$$= 0.15 = 15\%$$

Thus, Chieftan can match the competition with a list price of $290 and chain discounts of 40/15.

EXERCISES FOR SECTION 3.2

*In problems 1–24, find: **a.** the net price percent, and **b.** the single discount percent equivalent to the chain discount.*

1. 50% less 20%
2. 40% less 15%
3. 20% less 5%

4. 55% less 20%
5. 25/10
6. 30/5

7. 18/8
8. 16/5
9. 50% less 10% less 10%

10. 35% less 20% less 10%
11. 40% less 20% less 5%
12. 30% less 20% less 5%

13. 20/20/10
14. 30/10/10
15. 30/20/5

16. 40/15/5
17. 10/10/5
18. 20/15/10

19. $33\frac{1}{3}$% less $33\frac{1}{3}$%
20. $8\frac{1}{3}$% less $8\frac{1}{3}$%
21. $66\frac{2}{3}$% less $8\frac{1}{3}$%

22. $33\frac{1}{3}$% less $16\frac{2}{3}$%
23. $16\frac{2}{3}$% less $16\frac{2}{3}$% less $8\frac{1}{3}$%
24. $33\frac{1}{3}$% less $8\frac{1}{3}$% less $3\frac{1}{3}$%

*In problems 25–36, find: **a.** the amount of each discount, and **b.** the net price.*

25. $27.00 less 40/10
26. $12.50 less 30/15
27. $90.00 less 10/15

28. $46.90 less 35/15
29. $33.00 less 25/10
30. $118.20 less 10/15

31. $480.00 less 10/15/5
32. $204.00 less 20/15/5
33. $235.00 less 10/5/5

34. $540.80 less 30/5/5
35. $1,064.00 less 20/5/15
36. $1,230.50 less 25/20/5

Solve:

37. A digital watch with a list price of $120 had trade discounts of 20% less 15%. Find the net price.

38. A coffee table had a list price of $360 less 60% less 10%. What was the net price?

39. A scientific calculator that listed for $179 carried trade discounts of 12/5. Find the net price.

40. A dehumidifier that had a list price of $96 had trade discounts of 40/5. Find the net price.

41. A set of golf clubs with a list price of $420.00 had trade discounts of 30/15. What was the net price?

42. A gallon of fibered aluminum roof coating with a list price of $24.99 carried trade discounts of 10/5. Find the net price.

43. A trampoline with a list price of $499.99 had trade discounts of 35/10. What was the net price?

44. A 40-foot aluminum extension ladder with a list price of $549.99 had trade discounts of 60/15. What was the net price?

45. Carson Industries sold a computer stand for $99.99 with trade discounts of 30/20. What was the billing price if transportation charges were $14.30?

46. U-Finish Furniture Company offered retail stores trade discounts of 40/20 on an unfinished five-drawer chest. If the suggested retail price was $119.99, how much was the billing price if freight charges were $11.44?

47. Carol Andrews bought a cheval mirror for her curio shop that sold for $139.95 less 20% less 5% less 5%. How much did Carol pay for the mirror?

48. A combination storage cabinet and wardrobe had trade discounts of 20/20/10. If the list price was $149.99, what was the net price?

49. A wholesale hardware store offered an air compressor for $399.99 less 50/10/5/. Find the net price.

50. A bathroom shower curtain with a suggested retail price of $45 had trade discounts of 20/20/5. What was the net price?

51. Pete Polansky is a buyer for a discount chain. Recently, he bought polyester-cotton sheet sets for $29.99 less 10% less 5% less 5% per set. What did Pete pay per set?

52. A-1 Automotive Supply purchased a 215 piece tool set from a wholesale dealer for $219.00 less 30% less 5% less 5%. How much did A-1 pay for the set?

53. A sporting goods store can buy a table tennis table for $280 with trade discounts of 15/10/5. How much will the sporting goods store pay for the table?

54. A camcorder carried a list price of $999.99. If the manufacturer offered trade discounts of 40/10/10, for how much could the camcorder be purchased?

55. An electric range top with a list price of $449.99 carried trade discounts of 30/5. A recent price list added an additional trade discount of 5%. Find the net price.

56. A typewriter with a list price of $399.99 carried trade discounts of 10/10/8. What was the net price?

57. The list price of a lawn mower is $329.80 at two dealers, but at dealer 1 the trade discounts are 10/10/5, while at dealer 2 the trade discounts are 15/5/5. Which dealer offers the lowest net price?

58. A garage door opener carries a list price of $169.95. However, dealer *A* offers trade discounts of 20/10/5 while dealer *B* offers trade discounts of 15/15/5. Which dealer offers the lowest net price?

59. A polished brass faucet is offered by two wholesale suppliers. The first supplier shows a list price of $90.75 with trade discounts of 20/15, while the second supplier shows a list price of $98.50 with trade discounts of 25/15. Which supplier has the lowest net price?

60. Five dozen pajamas can be purchased from company *A* for $1,200 less 20% less 20%. The same order from company *B* costs $1,350 less 30% less 20%. Which company has the lower net price?

Section 3.3   *Quantity Discounts*

A quantity discount is a reduction in price because of the amount purchased and may be offered in addition to any trade discounts. Quantity discounts may be based on:

1. the number of units purchased
2. the dollar value of the entire order
3. the size of the package purchased

Quantity discounts are an application of the basic percentage formula $P = B \cdot R$ where P = amount of quantity discount, B = list price, and R = discount percent.

EXAMPLE 1   The list prices of a manufacturer are subject to the following discounts.

Units	Discounts from List Price
1–24	40%
25–49	43%
50 or more	46%

If an item had a list price of $25, what is the net price on an order of 30 units?

Solution: $750.00 List price ($25 × 30)

− 322.50 Quantity discount ($750 × 0.43)

$427.50 Net price

The solution could also be found using the complement of the discount.

$750.00 List price ($25 × 30)

× 0.57 Complement of the discount (100% − 43%)

$427.50 Net price ∎

EXAMPLE 2 An invoice of the Olympic Sports Company contains the following at the bottom of the page.

Quantity	Discount Allowed
$100 to $499.99	3%
$500 to $899.99	5%
$900 and over	7%

Find the billing price for an order totaling $750.88 if transportation charges are $9.65.

Solution: $750.88 List price

− 37.54 Quantity discount ($750.88 × 0.05)

$713.34 Net price

+ 9.65 Transportation charges

$722.99 Billing price ∎

EXAMPLE 3 A brand of toothpaste with a list price of $8 per dozen tubes had a trade discount of $33\frac{1}{3}$%. An additional discount of 2% was offered for orders by the case (a case contained 12 dozen tubes). What was the net price on an order of two cases?

Solution: $192.00 List price ($8 × 24)

− 64.00 Trade discount ($192 × $\frac{1}{3}$)

$128.00

− 2.56 Quantity discount ($128 × 0.02)

$125.44 Net price ∎

Quantity discounts are offered to induce customers to purchase in larger quantities and are possible because of certain economies realized by the seller. On large orders, there may be a reduction in the salesperson's expenses or in packaging, accounting, or transportation costs. In fact, federal regulations require this. Quantity discounts are subject to the Robinson-Patman Act of 1936, which prohibits lower prices for large orders unless such prices reflect a reduction in the cost of doing business or are needed to meet the prices of a competitor. The purpose of the Robinson-Patman Act is to preserve competition and prevent the creation of monopolies.

EXERCISES FOR SECTION 3.3

Solve:

1. The list prices of a manufacturer are subject to the following discounts.

Units	Discounts from List Price
1–49	10%
50–99	20% 24√70√.8
100 or more	35%

If each unit has a list price of $24, what is the net price on an order of 70 units?

2. The following discounts apply to merchandise purchased at Bishop's Electric Supply Company.

Quantity	Discount Allowed
1–49	5%
50–99	10%
100 or more	16%

Find the net price on an order of 6 dozen units if the list price was $37.30 a dozen.

3. Merchandise purchased at Stratton's Wholesale Hardware is subject to the following discounts.

Total Purchase	Discount Allowed
$100–$299	3%
$300–$599	5%
$600 and over	9%

Find the net price on an order totaling $733.58.

4. Barbara Applegate owns a wholesale lighting company. She offers the following discounts to her retail customers.

Total Purchase	Discount Allowed
$50–$99	2%
$100–$399	4%
$400 and over	8%

What was the net price on an order that totaled $456.87?

5. A wholesale distributor of appliances offered the following discounts on built-in dishwashers.

Quantity	Discount Allowed
1–10	20% .66
11–20	$33\frac{1}{3}$% + 216.30
21 or more	60%

If each dishwasher had a list price of $499.99, what was the billing price on an order of 12 dishwashers if freight charges were $216.30? (499.99 ×12) − (⅓) + 216.30

6. Mayfield Manufacturing offered the following discounts on women's classic oxford shoes that sell for $42.99 a pair.

Quantity (Pairs)	Discount Allowed
1–49	4%
50–199	10%
200 or more	30%

Find the billing price for an order of 80 pairs if transportation charges were $52.79.

7. Griffith Sporting Goods offered the following discounts.

Total Purchase	Discount Allowed
$400–$599.99	$8\frac{1}{3}$% + 97.25
$600–$999.99	12%
$1,000–$1,399.99	16%
$1,400 and over	20%

Find the billing price for an order of $566.40 if transportation charges were $97.25.

8. Jinyong Chen offers the following discounts on purchases from his cloth manufacturing plant.

Total Purchase	Discount Allowed
$200–$699.99	6%
$700–$1,199.99	10½%
$1,200–$1,999.99	14%
$2,000 and over	22% − + 229.78

Find the billing price for an order of $3,650 if transportation charges were $229.78.

9. Purvis Wholesale Pet Supply carries an electronic flea collar with a list price of $39.99. Purvis offers a trade discount of 20% and an additional discount of 10% for orders of 25 or more. Find the net price of an order of 25 collars.

39.99
− 20%
− 10%

10. The Horrigan Company sells a gas shock absorber for $21.99 with a trade discount of 12%. An additional discount of 5% is offered for orders of 50 or more. Find the net price on an order of 70 shock absorbers.

Section 3.4 *Cash Discounts: Ordinary Dating*

A. Credit Terms

The majority of sales to retailers by manufacturers or wholesalers are credit sales; that is, retailers are given a period of time after the sale before payment must be made. Credit sales permit retailers to carry a larger assortment of merchandise. More merchandise can mean more sales, an advantage to both retailers and suppliers.

Credit terms are shown on the invoice, usually in an abbreviated notation. The most common credit period is 30 days and will appear on an invoice as "net 30 days" or "n/30." Similarly, the notations "n/60" and "n/90" mean the credit period is 60 days and 90 days respectively. If credit is not extended to the buyer, the invoice will contain the notation "C.O.D.," which stands for cash on delivery.

An invoice marked "n/30" means the buyer has 30 days after the date of the invoice to make payment. If the invoice amount is not paid within 30 days, it is overdue and may be subject to fees or interest charges.

B. Cash Discounts

While credit sales may be a competitive necessity, the delay in payment can be costly to the seller. With prompt payment, the seller could invest the money, buy more merchandise, or pay bills. One way to encourage buyers to pay promptly is to offer an additional discount called a cash discount. A **cash discount** is a percentage reduction in price for payment within a specified period of time. Cash discounts usually range from 1% to 3% and are indicated on the invoice along with the credit period, as follows:

The cash discount
percent (2%) $\rightarrow$ 2/10, n/30 $\leftarrow$ The number of days after the
invoice date before the bill
becomes overdue

$\uparrow$

The number of days after the
invoice date the cash discount
may be applied

If the preceding notation were on an invoice dated May 1, then the following dates would apply.

May 2–11   2% cash discount applicable

May 12–31   Net price applicable

June 1   Bill is overdue

Cash discounts are calculated in the same way as trade discounts and quantity discounts except cash discounts are taken after all other discounts have been applied. Cash discounts are not applicable to freight charges or to merchandise that has been returned.

EXAMPLE 1   The price on an invoice dated November 1 is $195.50, with terms of 2/10, n/30. How much should be remitted if the bill is paid on **a.** November 10 or **b.** November 30?

Solution: **a.** November 10 falls within the cash discount period of 10 days following November 1. Hence,

$195.50 List price
$-\underline{\quad 3.91}$ Cash discount ($195.50 $\times$ 0.02)
$191.59 Amount to be remitted

b. November 30 is in the period of the eleventh through the thirtieth day following the invoice date. Thus, the amount to be remitted is the list price of $195.50. ■

E X A M P L E   2   If the following invoice is paid on May 10, how much should be paid?

				STORE NO.	CUSTOMER DEPT.	CUSTOMER ORDER NO.	
SHIP TO	Britton Office Supply 2824 Dennison Boulevard Detroit, Michigan			12		11378	
				INVOICE DATE	TERMS (NO ANTICIPATION ALLOWED)		
				4/20	2/30, n/60		
SOLD TO	Britton Office Supply 2824 Dennison Boulevard Detroit, Michigan			ROUTING INSTRUCTIONS			
				NO. OF CNTS.	WGT.	OUR REFERENCE NO.	INVOICE NO.
				1	236	21823	67021

	DESCRIPTION						
STORE USE	STYLE OR LOT	DESCRIPTION			PCS	PRICE	EXTENDED AMOUNT
	113-M	Desk, Executive			1	478.90	478.90

SALESMAN	PAGE NO.	TOTAL NUMBER OF UNIT ➡		SHIPMENT COMPLETE PARTIAL	SUB TOTAL MDSE. AMOUNT	478.90
				Less 70% Less 10%		−349.60
					net	129.30
					FRT. CHARGES	12.68
					GRAND TOTAL	141.98

Solution: May 10 is well within the cash discount period. Hence, both the trade discounts and the cash discount are to be taken.

$478.90   List price
− 349.60   Total trade discounts
$129.30
−   2.59   Cash discounts ($129.30 × 0.02)
$126.71
+   12.68   Freight charges
$139.39   Amount to be paid

More than one cash discount may be offered on a given sale. The notation 3/15, 1/30, n/60 on an invoice dated June 10 means:

June 11–June 25	3% cash discount applicable
June 26–July 10	1% cash discount applicable
July 11–August 9	Billing price due
August 10	Bill is overdue

EXAMPLE 3   An invoice for floor coverings had a billing price of $659.82, but $116.87 of floor coverings had been returned. The invoice was dated July 16 and included freight charges of $42.16 and terms of 5/15, 4/45, n/60. What amount should be remitted if the bill was paid on August 30?

Solution: Freight charges and returned merchandise are not subject to cash discounts.

	$659.82	Billing price
−	116.87	Returned merchandise
−	42.16	Freight charges
	$500.79	
−	20.03	Cash discount ($500.79 × 0.04)
	$480.76	
+	42.16	Freight charges
	$522.92	

EXERCISES FOR SECTION 3.4

page 495

In problems 1–16, find the amount to be remitted.

	Invoice Amount	Invoice Date	Terms	Payment Date	Freight Charges
1.	$235.13	August 11	2/10, n/30	August 20	
2.	$135.65	May 15	2/10, n/30	May 22	
3.	$353.75	December 19	1/10, n/30	December 29	
4.	$984.98	April 8	3/10, n/30	April 16	
5.	$761.83	March 17	2/10, n/60	April 15	$12.48
6.	$576.07	February 10	1/10, n/60	March 9	$76.20
7.	$1,054.91	April 24	3/10, n/90	May 4	$96.10
8.	$2,931.92	October 28	1/10, n/30	November 7	$132.40
9.	$1,059.59	January 19	2/15, n/60	February 3	$206.35
10.	$1,754.37	June 25	3/15, n/60	July 10	$184.16
11.	$2,953.60	September 21	3/10, 1/30, n/60	October 1	$341.32
12.	$1,976.38	June 24	2/10, 1/30, n/60	July 12	$299.06
13.	$2,616.55	February 6	4/10, 2/30, n/45	February 25	$123.54

761.83+12.48

	Invoice Amount	Invoice Date	Terms		Payment Date	Freight Charges
14.	$1,015.25	June 21	3/10, 2/30, n/45		July 2	$66.72
15.	$3,127.71	January 18	3/10, 2/15, 1/30, n/60		February 26	$652.13
16.	$1,234.21	March 2	3/15, 2/30, 1/45, n/60		April 18	$97.36

Solve:

17. A mantle clock with Westminster chimes was priced at $129.95. Find the amount paid if the terms were 2/10, n/30, the invoice was dated March 29, and the invoice was paid on April 8.

18. The list price of a pen and pencil set was $45.00. If the invoice was dated November 16 and paid on November 26, find the amount paid if the terms were 2/10, n/30.

19. Edward Jewelry Company purchased a diamond/sapphire pendant priced at $275.00. The invoice was dated February 26 and contained a trade discount of 70% and terms 3/15, n/45. If payment was made on March 12, how much was remitted?

20. Giles Gun Company sold a 30/30 caliber rifle priced at $249.95. The invoice was dated May 16 and contained a trade discount of 48% and terms 3/10, n/60. Find the amount of the payment made on May 25.

21. Sports Memorabilia, Inc. sold a Stan Musial sports plaque for $89.95 less 25% and terms 3/10, n/30. The invoice was dated March 26 and paid on April 9. Find the amount paid.

22. A 450 × 60 refracting telescope had a list price of $169.95 with trade discounts 60/10 and terms 2/10, n/60. If the invoice was dated April 19 and paid on June 2, find the amount paid.

23. Thompson Ceiling Fans bought six 52″ ceiling fans with a list price of $44.99 per fan. The invoice indicated a trade discount of 18% and terms 2/10, n/30. If Thompson took advantage of both discounts, how much was remitted?

24. A company that specialized in equipment for the elderly sold six aluminum canes with a list price of $24.00 per cane. The invoice indicated a trade discount of 12% and terms 2/10, n/30. If both discounts were taken, find the amount paid.

25. Schooner Fishing Supplies purchased ten tackle boxes with a list price of $47.95 each, trade discounts of 40/15, freight charges of $16.90, and terms 3/15, n/30. The invoice was dated October 6 and paid on October 20. How much was paid?

26. Montgomery Electronics purchased 20 videotape rewinders with a list price of $22.95 each, trade discounts of 15/15/5, and terms 2/10, n/60. The invoice was dated December 5 and paid on February 2. How much was paid?

27. The Wickenden Corporation supplied its security force with 40 transceivers. The list price per transceiver was $54.95, and Wickenden received a quantity discount of 20%. The invoice was dated May 16 and had terms 3/10, 2/30, n/60. Freight charges were $16.60. How much did the transceivers cost if the bill was paid on **a.** May 26, **b.** June 15?

28. For purchasing 50 Carrot Patch dolls at $54.95 each, Teckman Toys received a 21% quantity discount. The invoice was dated July 20 with terms 4/10, 3/30, 2/60, n/90. If freight charges were $26.10, how much did Teckman remit if the bill was paid on **a.** July 29, **b.** August 20, **c.** September 25?

29. The Schmermund Company sold 5 infant car seats with a list price of $66.99 and 8 toddler car seats with a list price of $64.99. Both types carried trade discounts of 15/5/5. Transportation charges were $39.91, and terms were 3/10, 2/30, n/45. One of the toddler car seats was returned because it was damaged during delivery. The invoice was dated August 12 and paid on September 5. Find the amount paid.

30. Jenkins Jeans purchased 48 pairs of boys stonewashed jeans at $32.00 a pair less 15% and 36 boys knit shirts at $22 each less 10%. Transportation charges were $11.16 and on orders of $200 or more an additional 3% discount was allowed. Terms were 3/10, 1/30, n/45. Six pairs of jeans were returned because they were the wrong size. If the invoice was dated July 22 and paid on August 6, find the amount paid.

31. Complete the following invoice and determine the amount to be remitted if the invoice is paid on June 15.

INVOICE

NO <u>2874</u>

DATE <u>6/12</u>

YOUR ORDER NO. <u>11338</u>

SOLD TO <u>Le Bathtique</u> SHIPPED TO <u>Same</u>

<u>714 4th Street</u>

<u>New Orleans, LA</u>

OUR ORDER NO.	SALESMAN	TERMS	FOR	DATE SHIPPED	SHIPPED VIA			
7010	L.R.	4/15,n/30	Dest.	6/12	Overland			
QUANTITY ORDERED	QUANTITY SHIPPED	STOCK NUMBER/DESCRIPTION			PRICE		UNIT	AMOUNT
24	24	FH 1399 Bath Towels			15	50	ea.	
24	24	FH 3027 Hand Towels			9	00	ea.	
24	24	FH 3215 Washcloths			6	00	ea.	
		Less 20% less 5%						
		Net						

32. Complete the following invoice and determine the amount to be remitted if the invoice is paid on July 25.

INVOICE

NO <u>7406</u>

DATE <u>7/18</u>

YOUR ORDER NO. <u>23047</u>

SOLD TO <u>Atlas Plumbing</u> SHIPPED TO <u>Atlas Plumbing</u>

<u>12016 Airport Road</u> <u>12016 Airport Road</u>

<u>St. Louis, MO</u> <u>St. Louis, MO</u>

OUR ORDER NO.	SALESMAN	TERMS	F.O.B.	DATE SHIPPED	SHIPPED VIA			
1104	Art	5/10,n/30		7/17	Stimson Freight			
QUANTITY ORDERED	QUANTITY SHIPPED	STOCK NUMBER/DESCRIPTION			PRICE		UNIT	AMOUNT
8	6	B-0858 Faucet-Dual Handle			52	50	ea.	
8	8	B-0841 Faucet-Single Handle			62	50	ea.	
		Less 40% less 20%						
		Freight Charges						6	38
		Total						

Section 3.5   *Cash Discounts: Other Dating Systems*

A. End of Month Dating

There are other forms of dating used with cash discounts. One of these, **End of Month Dating (E.O.M.)**, also called **proximo dating (Prox.)**, means the cash discount period begins the first day of the month following the date of the invoice. For example, an invoice dated October 12 with terms 2/10, n/30, E.O.M. or 2/10, n/30, Prox. means

October 12	Invoice date
November 1–10	Cash discount period
November 11–30	Billing price due
December 1	Bill is overdue

An exception to the meaning of these terms occurs when the invoice date is after the twenty-fifth day of a month. Then the cash discount period begins the first day of the *second* month following the invoice date. Thus, for an invoice dated October 29 with terms 2/10, n/30, E.O.M.,

October 29	Invoice date
December 1–10	Cash discount period
December 11–30	Billing price due
December 31	Bill is overdue

EXAMPLE 1   The Alberta Company received an invoice for $296.40 dated October 8 with terms 2/10, n/30, E.O.M. The invoice was paid on November 8. Find the amount paid.

Solution: November 8 is within the cash discount period of November 1–10. Thus,

$296.40
− $\underline{\quad 5.93}$ Cash discount ($296.40 × 0.02)
$290.47   Amount to be remitted   ∎

E.O.M. terms are commonly stated without a net credit period, such as 2/10, E.O.M. When this notation is used, it is understood the buyer has 20 days following the discount period to pay the full amount of the invoice.

E.O.M. dating is a convenience to retailers who make frequent purchases from the same supplier in that it permits a single payment for all purchases made during the month.

B. Receipt of Goods Dating

In **receipt of goods dating**, abbreviated **R.O.G.**, the cash discount period begins when the buyer receives the merchandise. Suppose, for example, that an invoice dated April 16 was marked 3/10, n/30, R.O.G. If the buyer received the merchandise on May 12, then

April 16	Invoice date
May 13–22	Cash discount period
May 23–June 11	Billing price due (20 days)
June 12	Bill is overdue

These terms could have also been written 3/10, R.O.G. As with E.O.M. dating, if the net credit period is not indicated, it is understood that the billing price becomes due 20 days after the last day of the discount period.

EXAMPLE 2   Lopez Transmission Service placed an order for parts that were delivered on April 15. An invoice for $1,522.75 had terms 3/10, R.O.G. Find the last day of the cash discount period and the amount paid on that date.

Solution: Ten days from April 15 is April 25.

$1,522.75
$-$ ___45.68___   Cash discount ($1,522.75 $\times$ 0.03)
$1,477.07   Amount remitted

R.O.G. dating is used when shipping time is long, and permits a seller located a considerable distance from a retailer to compete with local vendors offering ordinary dating. It also allows for inspection of the merchandise before the cash discount period begins.

C. Extra Dating

In **extra dating,** the seller allows an added number of days before the cash discount period begins. Thus, an invoice dated July 7 with terms 2/10, 30X, net 60 means

July 7	Invoice date
July 8–August 16	Cash discount period (10 days + 30 extra days)
August 17–September 5	Billing price due
September 6	Bill is overdue

EXAMPLE 3   The Feldhaus Company received an invoice dated March 12 for $598.57 with terms 3/10, 60X, n/30. Find the last day of the cash discount period and the amount paid on that date.

Solution: From appendix B,

X overrides the n
X takes precedent

Date		*Day*
March 12	→	71
		+ ___70___
May 21	←	141

60 + 10 (3/10, 60X

$598.57
$-$ ___17.96___   Cash discount ($598.57 $\times$ 0.03)
$580.61   Amount remitted

Extra dating is used frequently to sell seasonal items in advance of the peak market demand. For example, air conditioners may be sold in the winter in anticipation of summer sales. The extra time may allow the buyer to take the cash discount after the summer sales begin, a particular advantage for a buyer with limited finances. For the seller, the extra time may help stabilize production and eliminate storage costs.

D. Installment Dating

A recent innovation in terms of payment is **installment dating.** In this form of dating, the invoice is paid in two installments over a 60 day period. A cash discount is offered if a specified percent of the total amount is paid within 30 days. A second cash discount is offered if the remaining balance is paid within 60 days. The next example illustrates this form of dating.

E X A M P L E 4   An invoice dated April 20 for $368.44 contains the following information. A 2% discount is offered if 80% of the billing price is paid within 30 days, and another 2% discount is offered if the remaining 20% of the billing price is paid within 60 days. To take advantage of the two discounts, find the amount to be remitted on May 10 and June 5.

Solution: May 10 payment

$294.75   ($368.44 × 0.80)
−   7.37   Cash discount ($368.44 × 0.02)
$287.38   Amount to be remitted

June 5 payment

$73.69   ($368.44 − $294.75)
−   1.47   Cash discount ($73.69 × 0.02)
$72.22   Amount to be remitted

Most buyers choose to pay for merchandise at the end of the discount period, since this allows them the maximum time to use their money. To encourage payment before the last day of the discount period, some vendors offer a form of dating called **anticipation dating.** If an invoice is paid prior to the expiration of the cash discount period, the buyer can deduct an amount determined by the current bank interest rate for the number of days of early payment. Compared to other cash discounts, the amount of this discount is small, but for retail organizations who make a large number of purchases during a year, the savings can be significant. Calculations used in anticipation dating are covered in chapter 9, which also includes examples of anticipation dating.

EXERCISES FOR SECTION 3.5

In problems 1–12, fill in the blanks. Assume the invoice is paid on the last day of the cash discount period and a nonleap year.

	Invoice Date	Terms	Date Rec'd	Date Paid	Invoice Amount	Amount Paid
1.	Apr. 4	2/10, n/30 E.O.M.		—	$512.82	—
2.	Nov. 30	3/10, n/30 E.O.M.		—	$327.43	—
3.	Dec. 6	2/15, n/30 R.O.G.	Feb. 3	—	$842.66	—
4.	May 23	4/10, n/45 R.O.G.	July 5	—	$1,151.38	—
5.	Aug. 24	2/10, 30X, n/60		—	$1,310.55	—
6.	Feb. 4	3/15, 60X, n/30		—	$831.51	—
7.	Feb 16	3/10, E.O.M.		Mar. 10	$1,363.95	—
8.	Feb 28	2/15, E.O.M.		Sept. 15	$262.65	—
9.	Sept. 9	3/10, R.O.G.	Oct. 22	—	$882.05	—
10.	Jan. 13	2/10, R.O.G.	Mar. 5	—	$2,588.15	—
11.	—	4/10, 60X, n/30		June 10	$3,942.22	—
12.	—	3/10, 90X, n/45		Oct. 30	$792.14	—

Solve:

13. An invoice for $286.57 was dated November 21 with terms 2/10, n/30, E.O.M. Find the amount paid if the invoice was paid on **a.** December 9, **b.** December 11.

14. An invoice for $373.60 was dated April 22 with terms 3/10, n/30, E.O.M. How much should be remitted if the bill was paid on **a.** May 9? **b.** May 17?

15. Cray, Inc. received an invoice dated October 27 for $136.95 with terms 3/10, E.O.M. Find the last day of the cash discount and the amount paid on that date.

16. An invoice was dated April 29 with terms 3/10, E.O.M. If the invoice amount was $447.12, find the last day of the cash discount and the amount paid on that date.

17. Flannery's Welding received an invoice dated July 27 with a list price of $966.70 and terms 5/10, Prox. How much was remitted if the bill was paid on **a.** September 8? **b.** September 19?

18. King's Bar-B-Q received an invoice for $857.60 with terms 4/10, Prox., and dated May 16. Find the last day of the cash discount and the amount paid on that date.

19. An invoice dated October 17 was marked 4/10, R.O.G., and the merchandise was received on November 21. If the list price was $572.50, how much was remitted if the bill was paid on **a.** November 30? **b.** December 10?

20. Find the amount that was remitted on an invoice for $473.60 dated January 10 and marked 5/10, R.O.G. if the merchandise was received on February 14 and the invoice was paid on February 20.

21. Cospi and Associates received an invoice dated March 28 for $756.19 at terms 2/10, R.O.G. If the merchandise was received on May 5 and paid on May 12, how much was remitted?

22. The Carpet Connection received an invoice for $2,100.88 dated July 25 with terms 3/15, R.O.G. The merchandise was received on August 21. Find the last day of the cash discount and the amount paid on that date.

23. St. Luke Hospital ordered spare parts for its X-ray machine. The invoice was dated July 14 for $986.57 with terms 2/10, R.O.G. The parts were delivered on September 4. Find the last day of the cash discount and the amount paid on that date.

24. KenCo received an invoice for $665.49 with terms 4/10, R.O.G. The invoice was dated December 4, the merchandise was delivered on January 2, and the bill was paid on February 1. How much was paid?

25. Find the amount to be remitted on August 10 for an invoice dated July 2 with list price of $1,882.72 and terms 3/10, 30X, n/60.

26. An invoice for chemicals was marked 3/15, 20X, n/60. The invoice was dated March 6 and the list price was $844.50. How much was remitted if the bill was paid on April 18?

27. Paul's Plastics received an invoice for $593.63 dated October 10 with terms 3/10, 60X, n/30. If the invoice was paid on December 16, find the amount remitted.

28. TK Products received an invoice dated January 5 for $447.06 with terms 2/10, 30X, n/30. If the bill was paid on February 12, how much was remitted?

29. An invoice for $746.29 was dated February 15 with terms 2/10, 60X, n/30. Assuming a nonleap year, find the last day of the cash discount and the amount paid on that date.

30. Spartan Tire Company received an invoice for some snow tires dated July 15 for $948.00. If the terms were 3/10, 60X, n/30, find the last day of the cash discount and the amount paid on that date.

31. Find the amount remitted on December 12 for an invoice for $679.20 dated November 15 if the merchandise was delivered on November 22 and terms of the invoice were **a.** 4/10, 2/60, n/90; **b.** 2/10, Prox.; **c.** 3/10, R.O.G.; **d.** 3/10, 30X, net 60.

32. An invoice for $824.75 was dated May 6, and the merchandise was delivered on May 23. Find the amount remitted on June 2 if the terms of the invoice were **a.** 3/10, n/30; **b.** 2/10, E.O.M.; **c.** 5/10, R.O.G.; **d.** 4/10, 20X, net 60.

33. Find the amount remitted on February 14 and March 9 for an invoice dated January 19 with a billing price of $658.26 that offers the following installment terms. A 5% discount was offered if 60% of the invoice was paid within 30 days, and another 3% discount was offered if the remaining 40% of the invoice was paid within 60 days.

34. An invoice for $8,842.20 was dated July 7 and offered the following installment dating. A 3% discount was offered if 70% of the invoice was paid within 30 days, and another 2% discount was offered if the remaining 30% of the invoice was paid within 60 days. To take advantage of the two discounts, find the amount to be remitted on August 2 and September 3.

35. Pilar's Florist received an invoice for $2,176 that gave the following terms. A 6% discount was offered if 75% of the invoice was paid within 30 days, and another 2% discount was offered if the remaining 25% of the invoice was paid within 60 days. If the invoice was dated February 26 and paid on March 5 and April 7, find the amount remitted.

36. J & S Electric Company received an invoice for some transformers for $598.50 dated November 10. A 4% discount was offered if 60% of the invoice was paid within 30 days, and another 2% discount was offered if the remaining 40% of the invoice was paid within 60 days. If the invoice was paid on December 10 and January 9, find the amount remitted.

37. Complete the following invoice and determine the amount to be remitted if the invoice is paid on June 10.

INVOICE

NO 287

DATE   5/7

YOUR
ORDER NO.   7003

SOLD TO   Crafts N'Things

106 71st Street

Indianapolis, IN

SHIPPED TO   Crafts N'Things

106 71st Street

Indianapolis, IN

OUR ORDER NO.	SALESMAN	TERMS	F.O.B.	DATE SHIPPED	SHIPPED VIA		
A 205	John	3/10 EOM		5/7	P. Post		

QUANTITY ORDERED	QUANTITY SHIPPED	STOCK NUMBER/DESCRIPTION	PRICE		UNIT	AMOUNT	
2 dz	2 dz	5-Piece Scissor Set	480	00	dz		
		Discount 20/5/5					
		Prepaid freight				7	29
		Total					

ORIGINAL

38. Complete the following invoice and determine the amount to be remitted if the invoice is paid on March 10.

INVOICE

NO   **7410**

DATE 1/6

YOUR
ORDER NO. 7123

SOLD TO   Wallpaper Unlimited

3813 Elm Street

Spartanburg, SC

SHIPPED TO Wallpaper Unlimited

3813 Elm Street

Spartanburg, SC

OUR ORDER NO.	SALESMAN	TERMS	F.O.B.	DATE SHIPPED	SHIPPED VIA		
141B	Bill	3/10,60X		1/4	Rodeway		

QUANTITY ORDERED	QUANTITY SHIPPED	STOCK NUMBER/DESCRIPTION	PRICE		UNIT	AMOUNT	
10	10	Vinyl-coated wallpaper - pattern 03	12	00	Roll		
10	10	Vinyl-coated wallpaper - pattern 04	12	00	Roll		
10	10	Vinyl-coated wallpaper - pattern 07	16	00	Roll		
10	10	Vinyl-coated wallpaper - pattern 10	16	00	Roll		
		Less 35% less 5%					
		Prepaid freight				12	82
		Total					

ORIGINAL

Glossary

Anticipation dating   Terms of sale allowing the buyer to deduct an amount determined by the current bank interest rate for the number of days remaining in the cash discount period.

Billing price   The net price plus freight or transportation charges.

Cash discount   A percentage reduction in price for payment within a specified time.

Cash on delivery (C.O.D.)   When payment is required upon receipt of goods.

Chain discounts   Two or more discounts on a single item of merchandise.

Complement of the discount   Also called net price percent. The difference between 100% and a discount expressed in percent.

Cost price   The billing price plus any additional charges.

Discount   A percentage reduction from the list price.

End of month (E.O.M.) dating   Also called proximo (Prox.) dating. Terms of sale providing a cash discount period beginning the first day of the month following the month of the invoice date.

Extra dating   An extension of the ordinary dating period for a specified number of days.

Installment dating   Terms of sale providing for a cash discount if a specified percent of the total invoice amount is paid within 30 days, and a second cash discount if the remaining balance is paid within 60 days.

List price   The catalog price of an item or the price on a price list or price tag.

Net price   The list price of an item less any discounts.

Net price percent   See *Complement of the discount.*

Ordinary dating   Terms of sale that provide a cash discount period beginning with the date of the invoice.

Proximo dating   See *End of month (E.O.M.) dating.*

Quantity discount   A reduction in price because of the quantity of merchandise purchased.

Receipt of goods (R.O.G.) dating   Terms of sale providing a cash discount period beginning on the day the merchandise is received.

Selling price   The amount of money the seller receives in exchange for a product.

Trade discount   A percentage reduction from the list price offered to the retailer by a manufacturer or wholesaler.

Review Test

1. The _____ is the catalog price or the price on a price list or price tag.

2. Describe the difference between net price and billing price.

3. The complement of a 45% trade discount is _____ %.

4. A lawn fertilizer spreader carries a list price of $25 with a trade discount of 40%. Find the net price.

5. A halogen desk lamp with a list price of $19.90 carried a trade discount of 45%. If freight charges were $4.19, find the billing price.

6. What is the net price of an electric clock with a list price of $48.40 less 25% less 10%?

7. A portable electronic keyboard carried a list price of $179.95 less 40% less 15%. If freight charges are $10.60, find the billing price.

8. An item of merchandise had a list price of $129.91 with trade discounts of 40/20/5. Find the net price percent.

9. An area rug had a list price of $166.50 less 45% less 10%. Find the net price using the single discount percent equivalent to the chain discount.

10. Jensen's sells a diamond studded woman's watch with a list price of $1,195 less a trade discount of 60%. A competitor is selling the same watch for a net price of $444.54. What additional trade discount must Jensen's offer to match the competition?

11. A Bar-B doll had a list price of $14.95. A 6% discount was offered for orders of 10–19, and a 12% discount was offered for orders over 20. If freight charges were $22.17, find the billing price on an order for 25 dolls.

12. An invoice dated May 17 carries a billing price of $614.30 including freight charges of $16.30. What amount should be remitted on June 1 if the terms are 5/10, 4/15, n/30?

13. An invoice dated September 11 is dated 2/10, 30X, net 60. What is the last day of the cash discount?

14. An invoice dated May 16 for $701.53 was marked 2/10, n/30, R.O.G. If the merchandise was received on May 18, find **a.** the last day of the discount period, and **b.** the amount remitted on the last day of the discount period.

15. An invoice dated September 27 for $304.10 contained terms 3/10, n/30, E.O.M. Find **a.** the last day of the discount period, and **b.** the amount remitted on the last day of the discount period.

16. An invoice dated May 19 for $448.63 offered a 2% discount if 80% of the billing price was paid within 30 days, and another 3% discount if the remaining 20% of the billing price was paid within 60 days. Find **a.** the last days of the discount periods, and **b.** the amount remitted on the last days of the discount periods.

4

Pricing and Inventory Control

 Section 4.1   *Markon Based on Cost Price*

A. Introduction

To be successful, retailers must sell merchandise at a price higher than the cost price. This difference, called markon, must be sufficient to cover overhead and provide a net profit. Judicious pricing is one of the keys to any thriving retail operation. If the price is too high, sales will dwindle or be lost to a competitor. If the price is too low, the money generated from the sales may not be sufficient to pay operating expenses and earn a reasonable net profit. For these reasons, pricing is as much an art as it is a science and requires experience coupled with sound judgment.

In addition to the terms defined in chapter 3 are the following special terms used in this chapter:

Markon The difference between the selling price and the cost price. Markon is also known as gross profit or margin.

Overhead The expense of operation, including rent, taxes, salaries, utilities, insurance, and so on.

Net profit Markon minus overhead.

B. The Basic Markon Formula

The selling price of an item is equal to the cost price plus the markon. This fundamental concept can be expressed by the formula

(4–1) $S = C + M$

where

$$S = \text{selling price}$$
$$C = \text{cost price}$$
$$M = \text{markon}$$

C. Markon Based on Cost Price

Small retail businesses frequently express markon as a percentage of the cost price. One method of calculating markon as a percentage of the cost price uses formula 4–1. In this formula, the markon is found using the basic percentage equation where $P = \text{markon}$, $B = \text{cost price}$, and $R = \text{markon percent}$. This is illustrated in the next example.

E X A M P L E 1   Find the selling price of an item if the cost price is $80 and the markon is 40% of the cost price.

Solution: First, the markon is calculated.

$$P = B \cdot R$$
$$= \$80 \times 0.40$$
$$= \$32$$

Using formula 4–1,

$$S = C + M$$
$$= \$80 + \$32$$
$$= \$112$$

A more direct method of calculating markon as a percentage of the cost price uses the formula

P = B × R

(4-2) $S = C \times (100\% + $ Markon % of Cost price)

EXAMPLE 2 What is the selling price of an article if the cost price is $42 and the markon is 30% of the cost price?

Solution: Using formula 4–2,

P = B +   R

$S = C \times (100\% +$ Markon % of Cost price)
$= \$42 \times (100\% + 30\%)$
$= \$42 \times (130\%)$
$= \$42 \times 1.3$
$= \$54.60$

EXAMPLE 3 The invoice for a group of furniture pieces indicated a list price of $528.60, a trade discount of 40%, and transportation charges of $29.25. The retailer determined a markon of 60% of the cost price, rounded to the nearest dollar. What should be the selling price of the furniture pieces?

Solution:

$528.60	List price	
− 211.44	Trade discount ($528.60 × 0.40)	
+ 29.25	Transportation charges	
$346.41	Cost price	

100
100
200

Using formula 4–2,

$S = C \times (100\% +$ Markon % of Cost price)
$= \$346.41 \times (100\% + 60\%)$
$= \$346.41 \times (160\%)$
$= \$346.41 \times 1.6$
$= \$554.256$
$= \$554.00$

Formula 4–2 may also be used to solve for the cost price or markon percent as shown in the next examples.

H.W. 4. 1, 2, 3

E X A M P L E 4   A lamp that sells for $50 cost the retailer $20. What is the markon percent based on cost price?

Solution: $S = C \times (100\% + \text{Markon \% of Cost price})$

$\$50 = \$20 \times (100\% + \text{Markon \% of Cost price})$

$\dfrac{\$50}{\$20} = (100\% + \text{Markon \% of Cost price})$

$2.5 = 1.0 + \text{Markon \% of Cost price}$

$1.5 = \text{Markon \% of Cost price}$

$150\% = \text{Markon \% of Cost price}$

■

E X A M P L E 5   A patio set sells for $220, which includes a markon of 58% of the cost price. Find the cost price.

Solution: $S = C \times (100\% + \text{Markon \% of Cost price})$

$\$220 = \text{Cost price} \times (100\% + 58\%)$

$\$220 = \text{Cost price} \times (158\%)$

$\$220 = \text{Cost price} \times 1.58$

$\dfrac{\$220}{1.58} = \text{Cost price}$

$\$139.24 = \text{Cost price}$

$B \quad \dfrac{P}{R}$

$P = B \times R$

$\dfrac{P}{R}$

$\dfrac{S}{mo}$
139.24

■

✓ EXERCISES FOR SECTION 4.1

In problems 1–12, fill in the blanks if the markon percents are on cost price.

	Cost Price	Markon Percent	Selling Price
1.	$25.00	20%	— ×1.20
2.	$39.00	30%	—
3.	$154.00	42%	—
4.	$182.00	8%	—
5.	$156.91	—	$238.50 $\frac{S}{C}$
6.	$194.53	—	$311.25
7.	$197.65	—	$336.00
8.	$373.52	—	$504.25
9.	—	$33\frac{1}{3}\%$	$185.95 ÷1.33
10.	—	46%	$328.30
11.	—	$66\frac{2}{3}\%$	$405.75
12.	—	38%	$684.90

Solve: C+1.86

13. A pool table with a cost price of $674 had a markon of 86% of the cost price. What was the selling price?

14. A pair of golf shoes had a markon of 40% of the cost price of $28.50. Find the selling price.   ×1.40

15. The cost price of a certain lighting fixture was $79. What was the selling price if the markon was 40% of the cost price?

16. Find the selling price of an article of clothing if the cost price was $47 and the markon was **a.** 60% of the cost price and **b.** 62% of the cost price.

17. If the cost price of a digital clock radio was $22.50, find the selling price if the markon was **a.** 25% of the cost price and **b.** 32% of the cost price.

18. What was the selling price of a set of drapes with a cost price of $80 and a markon of **a.** 68% and **b.** 72% of the cost price?

19. The cost price of an adjustable exercise bench was $129. What was the selling price if the markon was **a.** 45% of the cost price or **b.** 60% of the cost price?

20. The list price for a washing machine was $424.50. If the trade discount was 40% and freight charges were $34.70, find the cost price. If the markon was 55% of the cost price, what was the selling price of the washer?

21. An invoice for a color television set shows a list price of $724.24, a trade discount of 35%, and freight charges of $11.40. The retailer decides on a markon of 40% of the cost price. What should be the selling price for the television set?

22. Franklin Clothiers bought thirty men's ties for a total of $198.00. If the markon percent of the cost price was 50%, find the selling price of each tie.

23. The Bride-To-Be Shop bought a bridal gown for $120 and sold it for $200. To the nearest percent, find the markon percent of the cost price.

24. The selling price of an article is $72.00, which includes a markon of $14.40. To the nearest percent, find the markon percent of the cost price.

25. Tri-State Automotive sold a stainless steel hood-latch for $14.99, compared to the cost price of $10.20. To the nearest percent, find the markon percent of the cost price.

26. A box of stationery that sold for $5.97 cost the retailer $4.30. To the nearest percent, what is the markon percent of the cost price?

27. A baby wind-up swing cost $20.00 and sold for $38.99. To the nearest percent, find the markon percent of the cost price.

28. A retailer buys blank cassette tapes at $42.00 a dozen and sells them for $4.48 each. Per cassette, what is the amount of the markon and the markon percent of the cost price?

29. A sewing machine with a selling price of $324.60 had a markon of 85% of the cost price. What was the cost price?

30. A mattress that sold for $140 had a markon of 60% of the cost price. What was the cost price?

31. A 5-hp tiller sold for $339.99, which included a 54% markon of the cost price. Find the cost price.

32. A department store sold a steel bed frame for $41, which included a markon of 70% of the cost price. What was the cost price?

33. The Deerfield Men's Shop sold 25 pairs of slacks for $750, which included a markon of 26% of the cost price. What was the cost price per pair of slacks?

34. Gina's Glass sold 8 sets of water goblets for a total of $191.92. Each set had a markon of 18% of the cost price. What was the cost price per set?

Section 4.2   *Markon Based on Selling Price*

A. Markon Formula Based on Selling Price

Most large retail establishments calculate markon on the selling price. There are several reasons for this: sales data are more available than cost data; trade statistics are expressed using a sales base; and a number of internal operations, such as sales commissions, taxes, and advertising, are based on sales.

The formula for calculating the selling price when the markon is based on the selling price is:

$$(4\text{--}3) \quad S = \frac{C}{100\% - \text{Markon \% of Selling price}}$$

E X A M P L E 1   A hardware item that costs \$4.60 had a markon of $33\frac{1}{3}\%$ of the selling price. Find the selling price.

Solution: With a markon of $33\frac{1}{3}\%$, calculations are simplified using the fraction $\frac{1}{3}$. Using formula 4–3,

$$S = \frac{C}{100\% - \text{Markon \% of Selling price}}$$

$$= \frac{\$4.60}{100\% - 33\frac{1}{3}\%}$$

$$= \frac{\$4.60}{1 - \frac{1}{3}}$$

$$= \frac{\$4.60}{\frac{2}{3}}$$

$$= \$4.60 \times \frac{3}{2}$$

$$= \$6.90$$

■

Formula 4–3 may also be used to solve for the cost price or markon percent, as demonstrated in the next examples.

E X A M P L E 2   An item that sells for \$61.50 carried a markon of 16% of the selling price. What was the cost price?

Solution: Using formula 4–3,

$$S = \frac{C}{100\% - \text{Markon \% of Selling price}}$$

$$\$61.50 = \frac{C}{100\% - 16\%}$$

$$\$61.50 = \frac{C}{84\%}$$

$$\$61.50 = \frac{C}{0.84}$$

$$\$61.50 \times 0.84 = C$$

$$\$51.66 = C$$

■

EXAMPLE 3   After examination of a brand of tennis rackets, a sporting goods retailer estimated that she could sell the rackets for $70 each. If she had to maintain a markon of 40% of the retail price, what was the top price the retailer could afford to pay and still sell the rackets for $70 each?

Solution: Using formula 4–3,

$$S = \frac{C}{100\% - \text{Markon \% of Selling price}}$$

$$\$70 = \frac{C}{100\% - 40\%}$$

$$\$70 = \frac{C}{60\%}$$

$$\$70 = \frac{C}{0.60}$$

$$\$70 \times 0.60 = C$$

$$\$42 = C$$

B. Conversion of the Markon Base

If an item cost $10 and sells for $15, the markon of $5 is 50% of the cost price and $33\frac{1}{3}\%$ of the selling price. The markon based on selling price appears to be smaller, another reason that this base is used to determine markon. Under certain conditions, it is desirable to convert from one markon base to the other. The formulas used for this conversion are

(4–4)   Markon % of Cost price = $\dfrac{\text{Markon \% of Selling price}}{100\% - \text{Markon \% of Selling price}}$

(4–5)   Markon % of Selling price = $\dfrac{\text{Markon \% of Cost price}}{100\% + \text{Markon \% of Cost price}}$

E·X A M P L E 4   The markon on an item is 40% of the selling price. What is the markon percent of the cost price?

Solution: Using formula 4–4,

$$\text{Markon \% of Cost price} = \frac{\text{Markon \% of Selling price}}{100\% - \text{Markon \% of Selling price}}$$

$$= \frac{40\%}{100\% - 40\%}$$

$$= \frac{0.40}{1 - 0.40}$$

$$= \frac{0.40}{0.60}$$

$$= 0.666 \ldots$$

$$= 66\frac{2}{3}\%$$

■

E X A M P L E 5   The markon on an item is 20% of the cost price. What is the markon percent of the selling price?

Solution: Using formula 4–5,

$$\text{Markon \% of Selling price} = \frac{\text{Markon \% of Cost price}}{100\% + \text{Markon \% of Cost price}}$$

$$= \frac{20\%}{100\% + 20\%}$$

$$= \frac{0.20}{1 + 0.20}$$

$$= \frac{0.20}{1.20}$$

$$= 0.1666 \ldots$$

$$= 16\frac{2}{3}\%$$

■

EXERCISES FOR SECTION 4.2

In problem 1–12 find the missing price. Assume that markon is a percent of the selling price.

Cost Price	Markon Percent	Selling Price		Cost Price	Markon Percent	Selling Price
1. $27.00	10%	—		4. $26.70	40%	—
2. $17.00	15%	—		5. $116.50	$33\frac{1}{3}\%$	—
3. $42.45	25%	—				

Cost Price	Markon Percent	Selling Price
6. $331.75	$16\frac{2}{3}\%$	—
7. —	34%	$19.50
8. —	31%	$37.00
9. —	15%	$49.95
10. —	21%	$99.99
11. —	$22\frac{1}{2}\%$	$122.40
12. —	$18\frac{1}{4}\%$	$124.95

Solve:

13. An infant walker is to have a markon of 38% of the selling price. If the cost price is $42, find the selling price.

14. An article of clothing with a cost price of $47.50 is to have a markon of 51% of the selling price. Find the selling price.

15. Bob's Building Supplies paid $4.80 for a five gallon can of joint compound. If the markon was 40% of the selling price, what was the selling price?

16. The manager of Atlas Building Supplies decided on a markon of 32% of the selling price for a workbench. If the cost price of the workbench was $120.70, what was the selling price?

17. A miniature grandfather clock cost the Granville Company $84.00. If the markon was 40% of the selling price, what was the selling price?

18. The cost price for a piece of electronic equipment was $82.32. What was the selling price if the markon is 45% of the selling price?

19. A brass bed frame with a selling price of $300 had a markon of 40% of the selling price. Find the cost price.

20. A mattress that sold for $140 carried a markon of 60% of the selling price. What was the cost price?

21. Kool-Air sold a portable air conditioner for $250 which included a markon of 38% of the selling price. What was the cost price?

22. A multi-panel folding door that sold for $49.00 had a markon of 22% of the selling price. Find the cost price.

23. A retailer sold a line of glassware with a markon of 47% of the selling price of $16.00 per set. If transportation and handling charges averaged $1.80 per set, what was the net price the retailer paid for a set of the glassware?

24. A 10′ × 8′ storage shed that sold for $218 had a markon of 26% of the selling price. If transportation charges were $26.00, what price did the retailer pay for the shed?

25. The owner of a shoe store examined a new style of shoes that she believed she could sell at $52 a pair. Her standard markon was 42% of the selling price. At what cost price could she afford to buy the shoes?

26. A buyer for a department store found a line of junior dresses that should sell for $40 per dress. The store maintains a markon of 39% of the selling price in that department. At what cost price per dress did the buyer plan to buy the dresses?

27. A buyer can buy stuffed toy animals at $40.00 a dozen. He estimates that the toy animals could be sold for $4.95 each. If the markon on stuffed animals is 38% of the selling price, what trade discount (to the nearest percent) must the buyer seek to buy one dozen of the stuffed animals?

28. A store purchased 50 table lamps for $1,800. Fifteen of the lamps were sold for $60 each and 25 of the lamps were sold for $40 each. At what price must each of the remaining lamps be sold to have an overall markon of 20% of the selling price?

29. Bikini Beachwear purchased 80 bathing suits for $2,341.50. They sold 15 at $45 each and 30 at $40 each. At what price must each of the remaining suits be sold to have an overall markon of 30% of the selling price?

In problems 30–34, round all markon percents to the nearest percent.

30. A retailer decided on a markon of 62% of the cost price for one model of a microwave oven. What was the markon percent of the selling price?

31. Find the markon percent of the cost price if the markon percent of the selling price was **a.** 40% and **b.** 45%.

32. What was the markon percent of the selling price if the markon percent of the cost price was **a.** 70% and **b.** 90%?

33. A trash compactor had a markon of 58% of the selling price. **a.** What was the markon percent of the cost price? **b.** Using **a,** if the cost price was $142.50, what was the selling price?

34. **a.** Find the markon percent of the selling price for a lawn mower that had a markon of 84% of the cost price. **b.** Using **a,** if the selling price was $382.40, what was the cost price?

Section 4.3 *Markdown and Extent of Markdown*

A. Markdown

The dynamics of retailing require a continuous adjustment in pricing. Economic conditions and competition cause prices to fluctuate both upward and downward. Price adjustments include discounts to employees, markup (an additional markon), and the most significant of all, markdowns.

A **markdown** is a reduction in the selling price of an item. While some markdowns are planned, most occur for other reasons. Among these are buying at the wrong time, overbuying, poor stock rotation, pricing mistakes, and the need to clear out merchandise that is obsolete, shopworn, unpopular, or part of broken assortments.

Markdowns are ordinarily expressed as a percentage of the original selling price and are calculated as a straight application of the basic percentage formula $P = B \cdot R$ with P = amount of markdown, B = selling price, and R = markdown percent.

EXAMPLE 1   The price of a book was marked down from $7.95 to $4.95. To the nearest percent, what was the markdown percent?

Solution: The amount of the markdown was $P = \$7.95 - \$4.95 = \$3.00$, $B = \$7.95$, and $R = ?$

$$R = \frac{P}{B}$$
$$= \frac{\$3.00}{\$7.95}$$
$$= 0.377$$
$$= 38\%$$

EXAMPLE 2   A department store advertised women's blouses on sale at 20% off the regular price. If the blouses originally sold at $35, what was the new selling price?

Solution: The new selling price is the original selling price less the markdown.

$35.00   Original selling price
− 7.00   Markdown ($35 × 0.20)
$28.00   New selling price

A markdown of 20% means that the selling price is 100% − 20% = 80% of the original selling price. Thus, an alternate solution is

$35.00   Original selling price
× 0.80   Complement of the markdown percent
$28.00   New selling price

EXAMPLE 3   A large scratch was discovered on a dining-room table on display in a furniture store. The selling price of the table included a markon of 60% of the selling price. The retailer decided to mark down the table 30% of the selling price because of the scratch. If the cost price of the table was $178, find **a.** the original selling price and **b.** the new selling price.

Solution: **a.** $S = \dfrac{C}{100\% - \text{Markon \% of Selling price}}$

$= \dfrac{\$178}{100\% - 60\%}$

$= \$445.00$ Original selling price

b. $445.00   Original selling price
× 0.70   Complement of the markdown percent
$311.50   New selling price

B. Extent of Markdown

The question of how much to mark down an item is as difficult to answer as the question of how much markon an item should have. The general rule is that the markdown must be large enough to appeal to a prospective buyer. A dress reduced from $60.00 to $58.50 is not likely to attract attention, but a markdown to $46.00 may result in a quick sale. An old adage in retailing is, "The first markdown is the least expensive," meaning that efforts to clear out merchandise should be in one step rather than a series of successive markdowns.

While the markdown should be large enough to sell the merchandise, there are practical restraints on the size of the markdown. These can be made clear from an examination of the price structure. From formula 4–1, the selling price equals the cost price plus markon. As previously mentioned, markon includes overhead plus net profit. Thus,

(4–1) $S = C + M$

and

> **(4–6)** $M = O + P$

where O = overhead and P = net profit. Substituting,

> **(4–7)** $S = C + O + P$

This formula is illustrated in figure 4.1.

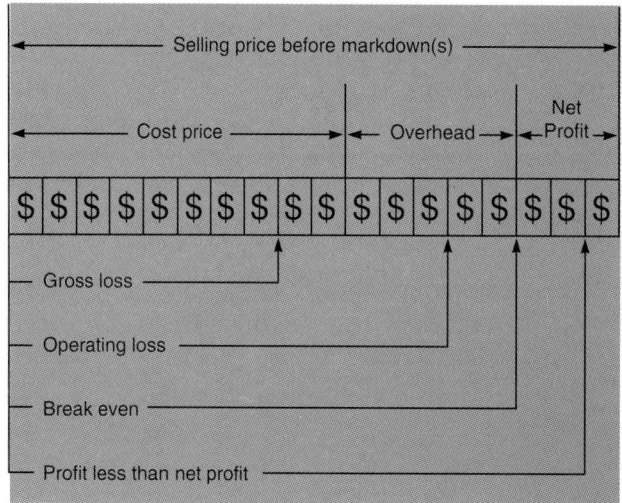

Figure 4.1
Profit and loss Regions

If possible, the markdown should be confined to the net profit region where the retailer still makes a profit, even though smaller than the desired net profit (see figure 4.1). A markdown equal to the total net profit results in a selling price called the **break-even point.** At the break-even point the selling price covers the cost price plus overhead. Thus, there is no profit, but neither is there a loss. If the markdown causes the selling price to fall below the break-even point, then the retailer suffers an **operating loss.** If the markdown causes the selling price to fall below the cost price, then the retailer suffers a **gross loss.** By comparing the selling price after markdown(s) with the break-even point and the cost price, the extent of markdown can be determined.

EXAMPLE 4   The original selling price on an item of toddler's wear at the R. J. Taylor Department Store was $6.95. Included in this price is a markon of $2.78. Estimated overhead on the item is $2.08. During an end-of-season sale, the item was marked down to $5.00. Determine whether the sale resulted in a profit or a loss.

Solution: $6.95   Original selling price
            − 2.78   Markon
            $4.17   Cost price
            + 2.08   Overhead
            $6.25   Break-even point

Since the final selling price is smaller than the break-even point, the store had an operating loss of $6.25 − $5.00 = $1.25.   ■

EXAMPLE 5   A stereo receiver on display was marked down 25% of the selling price of $369.99. Soon afterwards, it was discovered that a switch was broken and the receiver was marked down another 20%. The cost price was $231.84, and overhead was estimated at 40% of the cost price. Determine whether the sale resulted in a profit or a loss.

Solution: $231.84   Cost price $369.99   Original selling price
            + 92.74   Overhead ($231.84 × 0.40)   − 92.50   1st markdown
            $324.58   Break-even point   ($369.99 × 0.25)
                                              $277.49   Markdown selling price
                                              − 55.50   2nd markdown
                                                        ($277.49 × 0.20)
                                              $221.99   Final selling price

The final selling price is less than the cost price, so the retailer had a gross loss.   ■

EXAMPLE 6   A department store bought ten men's suits at a cost price of $228 per suit. Five of the suits were sold at the selling price of $320 per suit, three of the suits sold after they were marked down to $270, and the remaining two suits sold after they were marked down again to $225. If the overhead is 18% of the cost price, determine if the store made a profit or loss.

Solution: $2,280.00   Total cost ($228.00 × 10) $1,600.00   ($320.00 × 5)
            + 410.40   Overhead ($2,280.00 × 0.18)   + 810.00   ($270.00 × 3)
            $2,690.40   Break-even point   + 450.00   ($225.00 × 2)
                                                   $2,860.00   Total sales
                                                  −$2,690.40   Break-even point
                                                     $169.60   Net profit

While the store made a profit, it is less than the net profit of $3,200 − $2,690.40 = $509.60 the store would have made had the suits sold at the original selling price.   ■

EXERCISES FOR SECTION 4.3

1. A pair of women's shoes with an original selling price of $60 is on sale for $45. Find the markdown percent. $(\frac{45}{60}) - 1 = 25\%$

2. The price of an air-conditioning unit was marked down from $599.99 to $479.99. Find the markdown percent. $\frac{479.99}{599} - 1$

3. A woman's blouse that had lipstick on the collar was marked down from $38 to $25. To the nearest percent, find the markdown percent. $(\frac{25}{38}) - 1$

4. Find the markdown percent on a bumper pool table marked down from $329.99 to $279.99.

5. A riding lawn mower was advertised at 30% off the selling price. If the original selling price was $2,899, find the sale price. $\div 7$

6. A clothing store advertised men's suits on sale at 25% off the regular price. If the suits originally sold for $298, find the sale price.

7. A padded toilet seat was marked down 20% from the selling price of $19.88. Find the new selling price. $\times .8$

8. Find the new selling price of a boy's hooded fleece jacket if the original selling price of $14 was marked down 40%.

9. A computer game was marked down 60% from its original selling price of $99.95. What was the new selling price? $\times .4$

10. A child's stroller was marked down 25% from the original selling price of $159.95. Find the new selling price.

11. A man's leather jacket was marked down 20% from its original selling price of $159.99. When the jacket still did not sell, it was marked down 15% from the new selling price. What was **a.** the selling price after the first markdown and **b.** the final selling price? $\times .85$ $\times .80$

12. An air purifier with an original selling price of $250 was marked down 24%. When the purifier still did not sell, it was marked down 15% from the new selling price and sold. What was **a.** the selling price after the first markdown and **b.** the final selling price?

13. A personal organizer with an original selling price of $549.95 was marked down 12%. However, to meet the price of a competitive brand, it was necessary to mark down the organizer 6% from the new selling price. What was **a.** the selling price after the first markdown and **b.** the final selling price? $\times .88$ $\times .84$

14. To make room for spring fashions, a woman's wool suit was marked down 18% from its original selling price of $204. When the suit did not sell, it was marked down 12% from the new selling price. What was **a.** the selling price after the first markdown and **b.** the final selling price?

15. A department store had seven adjustable piano lamps in stock. Two lamps sold when the selling price of $45 was marked down 20%. When the remaining lamps were marked down 15% from the new selling price, three lamps were sold. The remaining lamps did not sell until a third markdown of 10% of the second new selling price. How much money was received from the sale of the seven lamps?

16. Four cutlery sets sold when the selling price of $90 was marked down 22%. When the cutlery sets were marked down 12% of the new selling price, five more sets sold. The three remaining sets sold when a markdown of 10% of the second new selling price was made. How much money was received from the sale of the cutlery sets?

17. A dent in the side of a washing machine dictated a markdown in the price of the machine by 30%. The cost price of the machine was $321.96, and the markon was 40% of the selling price. Find **a.** the original selling price and **b.** the new selling price. $\div 60$ $\times .7$ 536.60 375

18. A living-room easy chair was found to have a small tear in the fabric. The cost price of the chair was $140, and the markon was 160% of the cost price. The retailer decided to mark down the selling price of the chair by 25%. Find **a.** the original selling price and **b.** the new selling price. 273

19. A graphite backboard had an initial selling price of $129.98, which included a markon of $48.50. The estimated overhead of the item was $8.50. If the backboard was marked down and sold at $99.98, did the sale result in a profit or loss?

$NS = P$
$old \$ = B$

$CI = 89 \times 4.48$

$Sf \quad 99 - 6$

$SP = MU + 850 - 99.98$

$COP = 89.98 \quad Gam \, 8/0$

20. A pair of 14k gold filigree earrings with a selling price of $69.95 was marked down to $49.97. Overhead on the earrings was estimated to be $14.00 and the markon was $40.00. Did the sale result in a profit or loss?

21. A set of pole-top draperies was advertised at $49.99. *11.99* The cost price of the draperies was $38.00 and the overhead was estimated to be 20% of the cost price. If the markon was $11.99, determine if a sale resulted in a profit or loss.

22. A trolling motor was marked down from $299.95 to $269.97. If the cost price was $191.25, markon was $108.70, and overhead was 30% of the cost price, did a sale result in a profit or loss?

23. A 66-piece silverplated flatware service was originally priced at $299.99. The cost price was $150.00 and overhead was estimated to be 20% of the cost price. Find the smallest selling price for which the service could be sold and not incur an operating loss. — $180.00

24. A rolled-edged desk had a selling price of $229.95. The cost price was $90.95 and overhead was estimated to be 40% of the cost price. Find the sale price of the desk if it was sold at the break-even price.

127.33

25. A home improvement store purchased 12 bath light bars for $216. Five were sold at the initial selling price of $29.99, five were sold at a marked down price of $19.99, one was damaged and sold at $9.99, and one was missing from inventory and unaccounted for. If overhead was 26% of the cost price, determine if the store made a profit or loss on the light bars.

Loss $12.27

26. A department store purchased 400 boxes of Christmas cards at a cost of $3.20 per box. Of the 400 boxes, 250 were sold at the selling price of $6.95, 90 were sold after they were marked down to $3.95, and the remaining 60 were sold after Christmas at $1.50 per box. If the overhead was estimated to be 30% of the cost price, determine if the store made a profit or loss on the Christmas cards.

27. After 60 days on display, a salon hair dryer was marked down from $56.95 to $41.97. Shortly afterwards, the off-on switch was found to be damaged and the dryer was sold at a clearance price of $29.99. If overhead was 25% of the cost price and markon was 40% of the selling price, determine if the sale resulted in a profit or loss.

(56.95×.6
34.17×.25
8.54
42.71 —
29.99
12.72
loss

28. A satin dress with floral lace had an initial selling price of $190, but after 45 days was marked down to $140. When a tear was discovered in the lace, the dress was sold at a clearance price of $69.99. If the markon was 60% of the selling price and overhead was 15% of the cost price, did the sale result in a profit or a loss?

Section 4.4 *Maintaining Markon*

A. Markon of Perishables

In previous sections, the markon was per item, because it was assumed that each item in stock was saleable. For some products, however, this is not the case. Vendors of perishable items such as fruit, produce, dairy and bakery products, and flowers recognize that because of spoilage some items cannot be sold at the regular price, or perhaps not at all. As a consequence, the selling price of the saleable items must be adjusted to maintain the desired markon percent. This is accomplished by calculating the markon on the entire stock, then dividing the result by the number of saleable items. The technique is illustrated in the next example.

178.78   *81.48*

SP
129.98   38

EXAMPLE 1   A grocer purchased 500 lbs. of ripe peaches at $0.20 per pound. The grocer anticipated that 20% of the peaches would spoil and have to be discarded. What was the selling price per pound if the markon was 40% of the cost price?

Solution: The formula is

$$\text{Price per pound} = \frac{\text{Total desired selling price}}{\text{Pounds of saleable peaches}}$$

The total cost of the peaches was $0.20 × 500 = $100.00. Using formula 4–2, the total desired selling price was

$S = C × (100\% + \text{Markon \% of Cost price})$
    $= \$100(140\%)$
    $= \$100(1.40)$
    $= \$140$

A spoilage rate of 20% means 100% − 20% = 80% of the peaches will be saleable. Using the basic percentage equation with $P = ?$, $B = 500$, and $R = 0.80$,

$P = B · R$
    $= 500 × 0.80$
    $= 400 \text{ pounds of saleable peaches}$

$$\text{The price per pound} = \frac{\$140}{400}$$
    $= \$0.35 \text{ per pound}$

Had all the peaches been saleable in the previous example, a markon of 40% of the cost price would have meant a selling price of $0.20 × 1.40 = $0.28 per pound and the grocer would have received $0.28 × 500 = $140 for the peaches. With only 400 pounds of saleable peaches, it takes a selling price of $0.35 per pound for the grocer to receive $0.35 × 400 = $140.

EXAMPLE 2   The Open Hearth Bakery baked 30 coffee cakes at a total cost of $49.78. The bakery expected 10% of the cakes to become stale and to be donated to charity. If the bakery wanted to maintain a markon of 60% of the cost price, what was the selling price of each coffee cake?

Solution: The formula is

$$\text{Price per cake} = \frac{\text{Total desired selling price}}{\text{Number of saleable cakes}}$$

Using formula 4–2, the total desired selling price is

$S = C × (100\% + \text{Markon \% of Cost price})$
    $= \$49.78(160\%)$
    $= \$49.78(1.60)$
    $= \$79.65$

A spoilage rate of 10% means 100% − 10% = 90% of the cakes will be saleable. Using the basic percentage equation with $P =$?, $B = 30$, and $R = 0.90$,

$P = B \cdot R$
  $= 30 \times 0.90$
  $= 27$ saleable cakes

The price per cake $= \dfrac{\$79.65}{27}$
  $= \$2.95$ ■

B. Markon of Irregulars

Manufacturers may produce some items that cannot be sold at the regular selling price because of defects or blemishes in manufacture. If the defects or blemishes are minor, these irregular items may be sold to retailers at a reduced price. To maintain the desired markon percent, the selling price of the regular merchandise without defects must be adjusted, as illustrated in the next example.

EXAMPLE 3   The Keystone Clothing Company manufactured a brand of women's blouses at a cost of $12 per blouse. The company found that 7% of the blouses contained defects and were sold as irregulars at $16 each. Find the selling price per blouse on the manufacture of 2,200 blouses if the markon was 45% of the selling price.

Solution: The formula is

$$\text{Price per item} = \frac{\text{Selling price of entire stock} - \text{Income from sale of irregulars}}{\text{Number of regular items}}$$

The total cost of the blouses is $12 × 2,200 = $26,400.
Using formula 4–3,

$S = \dfrac{C}{100\% - \text{Markon \% of Selling price}}$
  $= \dfrac{\$26,400}{100\% - 45\%}$
  $= \dfrac{\$26,400}{55\%}$
  $= \dfrac{\$26,400}{0.55}$
  $= \$48,000$ Selling price of entire stock

The number of irregulars is found by an application of the basic percentage formula with $P =$?, $B = 2,200$, and $R = 0.07$:

$P = B \cdot R$
  $= 2,200 \times 0.07$
  $= 154$ irregular blouses

The income from the sale of the irregulars is $16 \times 154 = \$2,464$. With 154 irregular blouses there are $2,200 - 154 = 2,046$ regular blouses. Hence,

$$\text{Price per blouse} = \frac{\$48,000 - \$2,464}{2,046}$$
$$= \frac{\$45,536}{2,046}$$
$$= \$22.26$$

Thus, a selling price of $22.26 for the regular blouses and $16 for the irregular blouses will provide the manufacturer with the desired markon.   ■

C. Markon for Planned Markdowns

Some retailers set a price on an item with planned markdowns in mind. The purpose is to attract bargain hunters who like to shop for items on sale. The initial selling price is calculated so that even with one or more markdowns, the retailer will maintain a desired markon percent. This is illustrated in the next examples.

EXAMPLE 4   Ace Appliances wants to maintain a markon of 40% of the final selling price for a home freezer that cost $300. What should be the initial selling price if Ace plans to offer the freezer at "20% off"?

Solution: First, the final selling price after markdown is calculated using formula 4–3.

$$S = \frac{C}{100\% - \text{Markon \% of Selling price}}$$
$$= \frac{\$300}{100\% - 40\%}$$
$$= \frac{\$300}{60\%}$$
$$= \frac{\$300}{0.60}$$
$$= \$500$$

The initial selling price is calculated using formula 2–2 with $P = \$500$, $B = ?$, and $R = $ *complement of the markdown percent* $= 80\%$

$$B = \frac{P}{R}$$
$$= \frac{\$500}{0.80}$$
$$= \$625$$

To verify that this is the correct initial selling price,

$625.00   Initial selling price
− 125.00   Markdown ($625 × 0.20)
$500.00   Selling price after markdown

EXAMPLE 5   The price on a mattress at Trader Dan's Discount store indicated a markdown of 25% of the selling price, and on this sale day, the buyer was instructed to deduct another 10% from the markdown price. What initial selling price was placed on the mattress if Trader Dan wanted to maintain a markon of 150% of the cost price of $114.75?

Solution: First, the final selling price is calculated using formula 4–2.

$S = C × (100\% + \text{Markon \% of Cost price})$
$= \$114.75 × (100\% + 150\%)$
$= \$114.75 × (250\%)$
$= \$114.75 × (2.50)$
$= \$286.88$

The initial selling price is calculated using formula 2–2 with $P = \$286.88$, $B = ?$, and $R = $ *product of the complements of the markdown percents*
$= 0.75 × 0.90 = 0.675$

$$B = \frac{P}{R}$$
$$= \frac{\$286.88}{0.675}$$
$$= \$425$$

EXERCISES FOR SECTION 4.4

1. A grocer bought 500 pounds of tomatoes but 100 pounds spoiled before they could be sold. If the grocer wanted to maintain a markon of 68% of the cost price of $0.43 per pound, what should be the selling price per pound of the remaining tomatoes?

2. Val's Florist Shoppe purchased 100 dozen long stem roses at $10 per dozen. Val found that 30% of the roses had to be discarded because of spoilage. What was the selling price per dozen if Val maintained a markon of 60% of the cost price?

3. A produce dealer purchased 400 pounds of apples at $0.40 per pound. The dealer wanted to maintain a markon of 50% of the cost price. If the dealer expects 15% of the apples to spoil and be discarded, what was the selling price per pound?

4. A grocer anticipated that 25% of an order of 300 pounds of grapes would spoil. If the grapes cost $0.35 per pound, and if markon was to be maintained at 50% of the selling price, what was the selling price per pound of the grapes?

5. A manufacturer made a production run of 2,000 golf balls at a total cost of $1,800. The manufacturer expects 4% of the golf balls will have defects and will be sold for $0.70 each. To maintain an overall markon of 25% of the selling price, what price should the manufacturer place on a golf ball without defect?

6. The Tifton Company manufactured 2,000 men's shirts at a cost of $8.00 per shirt. The company found that 10% of the shirts were defective and were sold at $12 per shirt. Find the selling price per shirt if Tifton maintained an overall markon of 60% of the selling price.

7. A manufacturer maintained a markon of 30% of the cost price. Find the selling price per unit if 3,000 units were manufactured at a cost of $14 each, and the company sold 20% of the items as irregulars for $10 each.

8. A company manufactured 1,500 items of its product at a cost of $5.00 per item. If the maintained markon is 40% of the selling price, and if the company sold 15% of the items as irregulars at $6.00 each, find the selling price per item.

9. An electric three-hole punch cost the owner of an office supplies store $52.94. What initial selling price should be placed on the punch if the owner plans a markdown of 40% of that price and still maintains a markon of 70% of the cost price?

10. A phone mart advertised a telephone answering machine for 35% off the "list price." The machine cost $69.31, and despite the markdown, the phone mart maintained a markon of $33\frac{1}{3}$% of the selling price. Find the list price.

11. Big Al's Furniture Store purchased a bunk bed with storage chest that cost $202.30. To the nearest dollar, what initial selling price should Big Al place on the bunk bed so that it can be marked down 30%, then that price marked down 15% and still maintain an overall markon of 30% of the selling price?

12. Cal's Camp Goods purchased a 16′ × 10′ nylon tent for $122.21. If Cal wants to maintain a markon of 80% of the cost price and still mark down the initial selling price by 30% and that price by 10%, to the nearest dollar what should be the initial selling price?

Section 4.5 *Inventory Valuation*

A. Inventory Control

One key to successful business management is proper inventory control. **Inventory control** means the determination of how much merchandise should be on hand, how much is on hand, and the value of what is on hand. To determine how much, two methods are commonly used: (1) perpetual inventory and (2) periodic inventory.

Perpetual inventory is a system whereby a constant record is maintained of all inventory transactions. For small stores, a perpetual inventory card such as that shown in figure 4.2 may be sufficient. The card indicates a description of the item, the quantity received, the quantity issued, and the remaining balance.

Large firms with a computer can record inventory transactions almost instantaneously. Each item is assigned a product code which is entered into the cash register and the sale is recorded and inventory adjusted by the computer program. Those with optical scanning equipment can record inventory transactions by reading the uniform product code. A uniform product code (UPC) on a product package or container appears as a series of black and white stripes with numbers below them such as that shown in figure 4.3.

Each item is assigned its own UPC. When passed over an optical scanner the number is read and transmitted to a computer that records the sale and adjusts the inventory. The computer indicates the selling price to the cash register, compiles a detailed receipt for the customer, and may be programmed to order replacement merchandise.

Figure 4.2
Perpetual inventory card

ARTICLE						SIZE UNIT	MAX. MIN.		LOCATION		STOCK NO.	

RECEIVED			ISSUED			BALANCE	RECEIVED			ISSUED			BALANCE
DATE	ORDER	QUAN.	DATE	ORDER	QUAN.		DATE	ORDER	QUAN.	DATE	ORDER	QUAN.	

TOPS form 490   LITHO IN U.S.A.

Figure 4.3
A uniform product code

0   30020   01350   2

Even with electronic inventory control, most businesses will take a **periodic inventory** at least once a year, a physical count of all merchandise on hand. The purpose of this inventory is to reconcile the book inventory with the physical count. Discrepancies between the two figures may be due to improper coding, failure to record inventory transactions, computer malfunction, or theft.

Small stores may record merchandise count using a physical inventory sheet such as that shown in figure 4.4. The key items on the inventory sheet include the quantity on hand, a description of the item, and the unit price. Larger stores may use electronic recording equipment to record this information.

B. Inventory Valuation Methods

Once an inventory has been completed, its value must be determined. Four methods of inventory valuation are (1) specific identification, (2) average cost, (3) first in, first out (FIFO), and (4) last in, first out (LIFO).

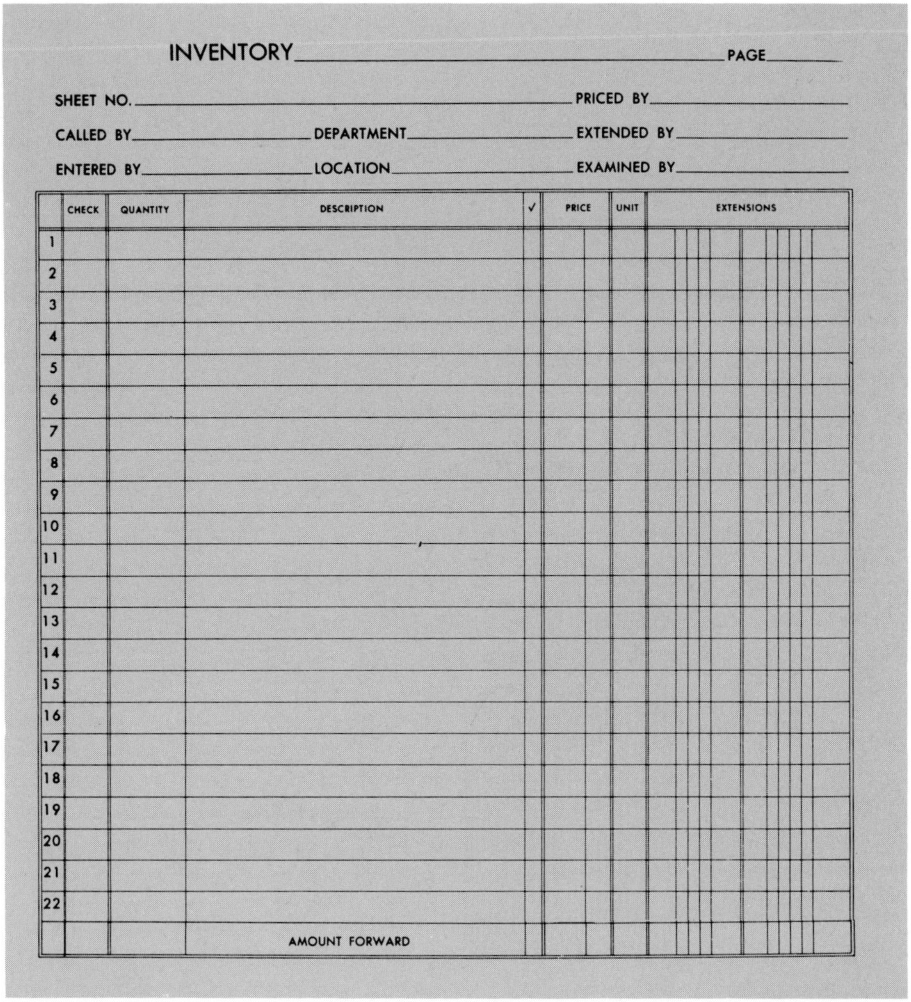

Figure 4.4
Physical inventory sheet

	CHECK	QUANTITY	DESCRIPTION	✓	PRICE	UNIT	EXTENSIONS
1							
2							
3							
4							
5							
6							
7							
8							
9							
10							
11							
12							
13							
14							
15							
16							
17							
18							
19							
20							
21							
22							
			AMOUNT FORWARD				

INVENTORY_____ PAGE_____

SHEET NO._____ PRICED BY_____

CALLED BY_____ DEPARTMENT_____ EXTENDED BY_____

ENTERED BY_____ LOCATION_____ EXAMINED BY_____

When the **specific identification** method is used, each item in stock is specifically identified, counted, and listed. This method works well when the number of units is small and each item is cost coded so its exact cost is known. In the inventory illustrated in figure 4.5, the value of the inventory is the sum of the extensions, or $535.

In the **average cost** inventory method, the average cost of an item is the sum of the total costs divided by the total items available for sale. The value of the inventory is the product of the average cost and the number of items counted.

Figure 4.5
Inventory of television
picture tubes

	CHECK	QUANTITY		DESCRIPTION	✓	PRICE	UNIT	EXTENSIONS
1		1	A 4301	TV Picture Tube		$120 00	ea.	12 0 00
2		2	K 2064	TV Picture Tube		$160 00	ea.	32 0 00
3		1	T 1062	TV Picture Tube		$ 95 00	ea.	95 00
4								
5								

EXAMPLE 1   Use the average cost method to determine the December 30 inventory value from the following inventory card.

ARTICLE:

Single switch outlet box

SIZE: **MAX:** 90   **LOCATION:**

UNIT: Each   **MIN:** 30   Bin 28-D

DATE	ORDER	QUAN.	UNIT COST	ORDER	QUAN.	CURRENT BALANCE
		RECEIVED		ISSUED		
12-31	Beg. Inv.	40	$ 0.22			40
3-5				12073	12	28
3-20	1-4072	30	$0.24			58
4-9				13071	30	28
6-6	1-6073	60	$0.26			88
7-20				14043	24	64
8-12				15116	44	20
9-1	1-8840	30	$0.28			50
12-30	End. Inv.					50

FIFO 40 + 22 + 10 24

Excluded

LIFO

30 + 28 a
20 + 26 a

Solution:

$0.22 × 40 = $ 8.80 $40.00 ÷ 160 = $0.25   Average cost of one item
$0.24 × 30 = $ 7.20 $0.25 × 50 = $12.50   Inventory value
$0.26 × 60 = $15.60
$0.28 × 30 = $ 8.40
         160    $40.00

The average cost method assumes that when prices have varied over a period, the average cost should be charged against sales revenue.

Most business people attempt to sell merchandise that they bought first before they sell their newer items. This is sound management practice in that it keeps stock fresh and merchandise new. The **first in, first out (FIFO)** inventory valuation method is based on the concept that the merchandise on hand is the newest and that the older merchandise has been sold.

E X A M P L E 2   Given the inventory card from example 1, find the December 30 inventory using the FIFO method.

Solution: Assuming that the 50 boxes in inventory are the latest purchased, then the 50 units include all of the September 1 purchase and 20 units of the June 6 purchase. Thus,

$0.28 × 30 = $ 8.40   September purchase
$0.26 × 20 = $ 5.20   June purchase
           $13.60   Inventory value   ■

FIFO is an advantage to a business when prices are decreasing but a disadvantage when prices are increasing. When prices are increasing, replacement costs tend to absorb profits that appear to exist but that in reality have been used to purchase higher-priced merchandise.

The **last in, first out (LIFO)** inventory valuation method assumes that the merchandise on hand is the oldest and that the merchandise sold was the latest purchased.

E X A M P L E 3   Given the inventory card from example 1, find the December 30 inventory using the LIFO method.

Solution: Assuming that the 50 boxes in inventory are the first purchased, then the 50 units include all of the December 31 beginning inventory and 10 units from the March 20 purchase. Thus,

$0.22 × 40 = $ 8.80   December 31 beginning inventory
$0.24 × 10 = $ 2.40   March purchase
           $11.20   Inventory value   ■

In contrast to the FIFO inventory valuation method, LIFO is an advantage to a business if costs are increasing and a disadvantage to a business if costs are decreasing. When costs are increasing, the LIFO method produces a lower inventory value and a lower profit, and therefore lower income taxes.

C. Inventory Valuation Estimation

Because it is time consuming and expensive, a periodic inventory may be conducted only once or twice a year. But businesses often need to monitor their financial status more frequently than this. Thus, methods have been developed to approximate inventory values. Two popular methods for estimating inventory values are (1) the gross profit method and (2) the retail method.

The **gross profit method** of estimating inventory is as follows:

> Beginning inventory (at cost)
> + Purchases (at cost)
>
> Merchandise available for sale (at cost)
> − Cost of goods sold
>
> Ending inventory (at cost)

Except for cost of goods sold, the preceding entries are available from current records. Cost of goods sold can be calculated from formula 4–3 found on page 94 solved for *C*.

EXAMPLE 4   The December 31 inventory value of a company was $148,000. Through March 31, the company recorded purchases of $125,000 and net sales of $200,000. Estimate the value of the inventory on March 31 if the company used a markon percent of 35% of the selling price.

Solution: First, the cost of goods sold is calculated. Using formula 4–3 with $S = $200,000 and markon percent $= 35\%$

$$S = \frac{C}{100\% - \text{Markon \% of Selling price}}$$

$S(100\% - \text{Markon \% of Selling price}) = C$ (Mult. both sides by denominator)

$C = S(100\% - \text{Markon \% of Selling price})$
  $= \$200,000 (100\% - 35\%)$
  $= \$200,000 (65\%)$
  $= \$200,000 (0.65)$
  $= \$130,000$

$148,000	Beginning inventory (December 31)
+ 125,000	Purchases
$273,000	Merchandise available for sale
− 130,000	Cost of goods sold
$143,000	Ending inventory (March 31)

■

grose profit margin

The second method for estimating inventory value is called the **retail method** because it requires a company to maintain records of all purchases at both cost and retail prices. The retail method utilizes the same format as the gross profit method except that all entries are at retail prices. This means that net sales must be used instead of cost of goods sold. That is,

> Beginning inventory (at retail)
> + Purchases (at retail)
>
> Merchandise available for sale (at retail)
> − Net sales
>
> Ending inventory (at retail)

The ending inventory value at retail is then converted to an estimated value at cost by multiplying it by the ratio of the merchandise available for sale (at cost) to the merchandise available for sale (at retail). The retail method assumes that this ratio is equal to that of the ending inventory (at cost) divided by the ending inventory (at retail).

EXAMPLE 5   The December 31 inventory of the Stocton Corporation was valued at $6,000 (cost), $10,000 (retail). During the next three months, the company made purchases totaling $30,000 (cost), $50,000 (retail) and had net sales of $48,000. Estimate the value of the inventory at cost as of March 31.

Solution:

	Cost	*Retail*
Previous inventory	$ 6,000	$10,000
+ Purchases	+ 30,000	+ 50,000
Merchandise available for sale	$36,000	$60,000
− Net sales		− 48,000
March 31 inventory (at retail)		$12,000

$\dfrac{\$36,000}{\$60,000} = 0.60$ Ratio of the merchandise available for sale at cost to the merchandise available for sale at retail

$\$12,000 \times 0.60 = \$7,200$ Estimated value of March 31 inventory (at cost)   ■

Estimation of the inventory value by the retail method is a paper figure. When physical inventories are conducted, these paper figures must be adjusted to reflect actual conditions. The primary advantage of the retail method is that gross profits can be determined more quickly than by any other method. The chief disadvantage of the retail method is the extensive bookkeeping required to maintain records at both cost and retail prices.

D. Inventory Turnover

Another important part of inventory control is inventory turnover. **Inventory turnover** (also known as *stock turnover* or *stockturn*) is the number of times during a given period that the average inventory on hand is sold and replaced. Inventory turnover varies according to the type of business. For example, inventory turnover for food markets is about once a month; for hardware stores, it is about twice a year.

The first step in calculating inventory turnover is finding the average inventory. The **average inventory** is the sum of the values of the inventories during the period divided by the number of inventories.

EXAMPLE 6   A company recorded the following inventories, each valued at retail: January 1, $26,300; July 1, $18,500; December 31, $25,700. Determine the average retail inventory.

Solution: Average retail inventory $= \dfrac{\text{Sum of the retail inventory values}}{\text{Number of inventories}}$

$$= \frac{\$26,300 + \$18,500 + \$25,700}{3}$$

$$= \$23,500 \qquad ∎$$

The inventory turnover may be computed on the basis of cost or retail, depending on the inventory control method used by the business. The formulas are

(4–8)	Inventory turnover (retail) $=$	$\dfrac{\text{Net sales}}{\text{Average inventory (at retail)}}$
(4–9)	Inventory turnover (cost) $=$	$\dfrac{\text{Cost of goods sold}}{\text{Average inventory (at cost)}}$

EXAMPLE 7   The Kotton Kandy Company had annual sales of $146,000. To the nearest tenth, find the inventory turnover if the average inventory (at retail) for the year was $10,500.

Solution: Using formula 4–8,

$$\text{Inventory turnover} = \frac{\$146,000}{\$10,500} \rightarrow \text{average}$$
$$= 13.9$$

Thus, the company sold and replaced its average inventory on hand 13.9 times during the year.   ∎

EXAMPLE 8   For a six-month period, the cost of goods sold at an appliance store was $245,000. Find the inventory turnover if the average inventory (at cost) was $98,000.

Solution: Using formula 4–9,

$$\text{Inventory turnover} = \frac{\$245,000}{\$98,000}$$
$$= 2.5$$

In general, an increase in inventory turnover means stocks are fresher, less capital is tied up in inventory, and storage space is reduced. However, if the turnover becomes too great, sales may be lost because of reduced customer selection, quantity discounts may be lost because of smaller quantities ordered, and operating expenses may increase because of additional paperwork. Clearly, proper inventory control is a central task of management.

EXERCISES FOR SECTION 4.5

1. Apex Hardware Store's inventory of galvanized fencing is shown on the following inventory sheet.

	CHECK	QUANTITY	DESCRIPTION	PRICE		UNIT	EXTENSIONS
1		15	100-foot rolls	$ 59	00	Each	
2		12	50-foot rolls	$ 31	00	Each	
3		9	25-foot rolls	$ 17	00	Each	
4							
5							

Fill in the blanks on the sheet and use the specific identification method to find the value of the inventory.

2. The inventory of tropical-fish aquariums at Sea World Shop is shown on the following inventory sheet.

	CHECK	QUANTITY	DESCRIPTION	PRICE		UNIT	EXTENSIONS
1		8	10-gallon	$ 9	85	Each	
2		13	20-gallon	$ 17	59	Each	
3		3	30-gallon	$ 24	39	Each	
4		7	50-gallon	$ 41	79	Each	
5		2	60-gallon	$ 63	29	Each	

Fill in the blanks on the sheet and use the specific identification method to find the value of the inventory.

In problems 3–5, use the information shown on the following perpetual inventory card.

ARTICLE:						
Model 114-S pocket calculator						

SIZE:		MAX: 80		LOCATION:		
UNIT: Each		MIN: 10		Shelf C-3		

	RECEIVED				ISSUED		CURRENT
DATE	ORDER	QUAN.	UNIT COST	ORDER	QUAN.	BALANCE
12-31-88	Beg. Inv.	15	$ 8.40			15
1-5-89	A-2071	40	$ 9.20			55
2-11-89				B-411	15	40
4-28-89				B-517	22	18
6-2-89	A 5713	60	$9.60			78
9-17-89				B-771	30	48
10-20-89				B-901	38	10
11-6-89	A-7621	45	$10.00			55
12-30-89	End. Inv.					55

3. Use the average cost method to find the December 30 inventory value of the pocket calculators.

4. What is the December 30 inventory value of the pocket calculators using the FIFO method?

5. Use the LIFO method to find the December 30 inventory value of the pocket calculators.

In problems 6–8, use the information shown on the following perpetual inventory card.

ARTICLE: AM-FM radio-tape player 214D						
SIZE: UNIT: Each		MAX: 60 MIN : 15		LOCATION: Shelf 210		

RECEIVED				ISSUED		CURRENT
DATE	**ORDER**	**QUAN.**	**UNIT COST**	**ORDER**	**QUAN.**	**BALANCE**
12-31-88	Beg. Inv.	23	$41.50			23
2-10-89				25107	18	5
2-16-89	4-111	40	$43.00			45
3-8-89				27810	15	30
5-7-89				31642	20	10
6-1-89	4-714	42	$45.25			52
7-4-89				33872	15	37
10-11-89				37412	20	17
11-15-89				41062	15	2
11-20-89	4-992	45	$49.20			47
12-30-89	End. Inv.					47

6. What is the December 30 inventory value of the radio-tape players using the average cost method?

7. Use the FIFO method to find the December 30 inventory value of the radio-tape players.

8. Use the LIFO method to find the December 30 inventory value of the radio-tape players.

In problems 9–11, use the information shown on the following perpetual inventory card.

ARTICLE: Video cassette tape TR120						
SIZE: 6-hour **MAX:** 150				**LOCATION:** Shelf 142		
UNIT: Each **MIN:** 40						

RECEIVED				ISSUED		CURRENT
DATE	ORDER	QUAN.	UNIT COST	ORDER	QUAN.	BALANCE
12-31-88	Beg. Inv.	55	$ 9.24			55
1-27-89				B-513	20	35
2-15-89	A-273	100	$ 9.78			135
3-20-89				B-601	50	85
4-5-89				B-692	30	55
6-2-89				B-748	50	5
6-15-89	A-814	150	$10.40			155
7-23-89				B-920	30	125
8-14-89				B-1102	40	85
10-10-89				B-1310	20	65
11-18-89				B-1408	50	15
11-30-89	A-1022	125	$11.20			140
12-30-89	End. Inv.					140

9. What is the December 30 inventory value of the videotapes using the average cost method?

10. Use the FIFO method to find the December 30 inventory value of the videotapes.

11. Use the LIFO method to find the December 30 inventory value of the videotapes.

STOP WORRY + FOLLOW THE
PRINCIPLE + EXAMPLE

12. Use the gross profit method to estimate the value of the ending inventory at cost for a company if the beginning inventory at cost was $175,000, purchases at cost total $123,000, net sales total $186,000, and the company used a markon of 48% of the retail price.

13. For the first quarter of the last year, the beginning inventory of the Symms Company was $423,000. During the quarter, the company had purchases of $372,000, and net sales of $594,000. If the company used a markon of 32% of the retail price, estimate the value of the inventory at the end of the quarter using the gross profit method.

14. Butler Industries recorded a beginning inventory at cost of $515,000. During the next quarter, the company had purchases of $231,715, $302,930, and $391,030. The company used a markon of 52% of the retail price. Use the gross profit method to estimate the value of the ending inventory at the end of the quarter if net sales were $785,435.

15. The March 31 inventory value of Heintzelman, Inc. was $87,160. Through June 30, the company made purchases of $43,200, $29,885, and $56,710. Use the gross profit method to estimate the value of the inventory on June 30 if the company used a markon of 37% of the retail price, and net sales for the three month period were $153,140.

16. The net sales of the Lephart Corporation for the first six months were $803,100. The beginning inventory at cost was $415,790 and the company had purchases of $209,550, $265,300, and $99,770. If the company used a markon of 46% of the retail price, use the gross profit method to estimate the value of the inventory at the end of the six month period.

17. Use the retail inventory method to estimate the current inventory value at cost from the following records of Cardoso & Sons.

	Cost	Retail
Previous inventory	$22,933	$48,700
Purchases	+ 35,300	+ 50,000
Merchandise available for sale	$58,233	$98,700
Less Net sales		− 46,500
Current inventory (at retail)		$52,200

Stop worry your head its simple
cost ÷ Retail × Curi Inventory to find
current I v at cost

18. From the following records of the Bransilver Company, estimate the current inventory value at cost using the retail inventory method.

	Cost	Retail
Previous inventory	$140,604	$248,700
Purchases	+ 85,300	+ 154,700
Merchandise available for sale	$225,904	$403,400
Less Net sales	C/R × C,J	− 146,500
Current inventory (at retail)		$256,900

19. The June 30 inventory of Castella & Giotto was valued at $32,530 (cost), $60,300 (retail). During the next three months, the company had purchases totaling $60,200 (cost), $108,300 (retail), and had net sales of $117,200. Use the retail inventory method to estimate the value of the inventory at cost on September 30.

20. Estimate the value of the inventory at cost on June 30 for the Les' Garage using the retail inventory method and the following data: March 31 inventory was valued at $37,500 (cost), $70,000 (retail); purchases between March 31 and June 30 totaled $87,450 (cost), $175,000 (retail); the garage had net sales of $93,800 during the three month period.

21. Palmer Paper Company took three inventories (at retail) last year. The amounts were $65,889, $73,580, and $66,940. Find the average inventory (at retail) for the year.

22. Pan-Am Supply Company recorded four inventories (at cost) last year in the amounts of $25,840, $23,100, $39,090, and $28,510. What was the average inventory (at cost) for the year?

23. Marine Service, Inc. took three inventories (at retail) last year in the amounts of $933,600, $1,410,000, and $828,600. If the corporation had net annual sales of $5,815,700, find the inventory turnover for the year.

24. The net sales at Pro Line Golf Products last year was $483,500. The company recorded the following inventories (at retail): $99,120, $104,400, $69,710, and $105,350. Find the inventory turnover for the year.

= 92730 - 168600

CI = 51400

25. Sunbelt Framing and Glass took inventory (at cost) four times during the year. The amounts were $19,310, $33,490, $26,700, and $32,000. The cost of goods sold during this period was $490,890. Find the inventory turnover for the year.

26. The cost of goods sold by a company during the past year was $939,175. The company took inventory (at cost) three times during the year, recording amounts of $272,139, $291,920, and $251,530. What was the inventory turnover for the year?

Glossary

Average cost   For a unit of merchandise, the sum of the total costs divided by the total units available for sale during the period; used in the average cost inventory valuation method.

Average inventory   The sum of the inventories during a period divided by the number of inventories.

Break-even point   When the selling price of an item equals the cost price plus operating expenses.

First in, first out (FIFO)   An inventory valuation method that assumes that the merchandise on hand is the newest and that the oldest merchandise has been sold.

Gross loss   When the markdown on an item exceeds the markon.

Gross profit method   A procedure for estimating the value of an inventory using the formula

Ending inventory (at cost) = Beginning inventory (at cost) + Purchases (at cost) − Cost of goods sold

Inventory control   The determination of how much merchandise is on hand, how much should be on hand, and the value of what is on hand.

Inventory turnover   The number of times during a given period that the average inventory on hand is sold and replaced.

Last in, first out (LIFO)   An inventory valuation method that assumes that the merchandise on hand is the oldest and that the newest merchandise has been sold.

Markdown   A reduction in the selling price of an item.

Markon   The difference between the selling price and the cost price.

Net profit   Markon less overhead.

Operating loss   When the markdown exceeds the net profit but is less than the net profit plus operating expenses.

Overhead   The expense of operation, including rent, taxes, salaries, utilities, and so on. Also called operating expenses.

Periodic inventory   The physical count of all merchandise on hand.

Perpetual inventory   A system whereby a constant record is maintained of all inventory transactions.

Retail method   A procedure for estimating the value of an inventory using the formula

Ending inventory (at retail) = Beginning inventory (at retail) + Purchases (at retail) − Net sales

Specific identification   An inventory valuation method wherein each item in stock is specifically identified, counted, and listed.

Review Test

1. The expense of operation, such as rent, taxes, and salaries, is called _____ .

2. A reduction in the selling price of an item is called _____ .

3. What is the selling price of an article if the cost price is $63 and the markon is 46% of the cost price?

4. A wallpaper pasting machine that cost $67.60 had a markon of 60% of the selling price. Find the selling price.

5. A combination speakerphone and answering machine had a markon of 48% of the selling price of $99.90. Find the cost price.

6. The markon of an item is 30% of the cost price. What is the markon percent of the selling price? (Round to the nearest percent.)

7. The markon on an item was 36% of the selling price. What was the markon percent of the cost price?

8. The price of a dress is marked down from $78.95 to $56.00. What is the markdown percent? (Round to the nearest percent.)

9. A Chippendale style curio with a selling price of $229 was advertised at $129. The cost price is $78, and overhead is estimated at 45% of the cost price. Determine whether a sale results in a profit or a loss.

10. A grocer purchased 450 pounds of apples at $0.38 per pound. The grocer anticipated that 8% of the apples would spoil and have to be discarded. If the grocer maintained a markon of 25% of the selling price, what was the selling price per pound of the non-spoiled apples?

11. A company manufactured children's rain coats at a cost of $6.70 per coat. On a production run of 2,000 coats, 4% were defective and sold for $7.25 each. To the nearest dollar, find the selling price per coat if the company maintained a markon of 35% of the selling price.

12. An inventory card indicated the following purchases and unit costs: 120 at $1.16; 110 at $1.21; 90 at $1.30; 150 at $1.18. If there are 35 currently on hand, find the value of the inventory using the average cost method.

13. A merchant's beginning inventory was 10 bottles of antacid valued at $2.00 per bottle. Purchases were 24, 12, and 24 bottles at cost prices of $2.12, $2.15, and $2.05, respectively. If the ending inventory was 30 bottles, find the value of the ending inventory using (a) the LIFO method and (b) the FIFO method.

14. A company recorded the following data: previous inventory: $30,100 (cost), $36,120 (retail); purchases: $45,832 (cost), $56,480 (retail); net sales at retail: $50,100. Estimate the value of the inventory using the retail method.

15. During one year, a company had the following inventories, each valued at retail: $18,200, $24,650, $19,240, and $21,060. Find the inventory turnover (rounded to the nearest tenth) if net sales for the year were $88,452.

Payrolls and Banking

Section 5.1   *Gross Earnings: Salary and Wages*

A. Introduction

The company payroll is a record of employee earnings. Preparation of the payroll is one of the most important office functions of any company. Accuracy is essential; nothing is more damaging to employee morale than being paid an incorrect amount. The payroll begins with the calculation of **gross earnings,** the total earnings of an employee within a pay period. Subtracted from this total are **deductions,** amounts withheld from the employee's pay. The employee receives the difference, called **net earnings.** Figure 5.1 shows the process of preparing a payroll. This section covers two forms of gross earnings, salaries and wages. A third form, commissions, is covered in the next section.

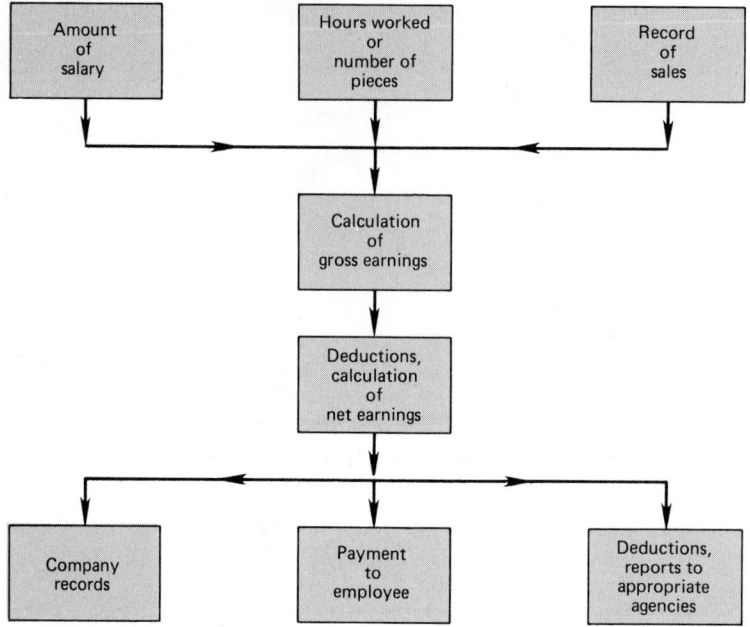

Figure 5.1
Actions of the payroll
department

B. Salaries

The word **salary** describes the earnings of executives, supervisors, office personnel, and others who are paid according to a specified period of employment. A salary is independent of both production and working time. A salary is paid at specified intervals called **pay periods.** Pay periods may be monthly, semimonthly, biweekly, or weekly. To find the gross earnings per pay period, divide the annual earnings by the number of pay periods per year.

$$\textbf{(5–1)} \quad \text{Gross earnings per pay period (salary)} = \frac{\text{Annual earnings}}{\text{No. of pay periods per year}}$$

EXAMPLE 1 The president of Triton Manufacturing Company earned a salary of $312,000 per year. Calculate the gross earnings if the president was paid **a.** monthly, **b.** semimonthly, **c.** biweekly, and **d.** weekly.

Solution: **a.** There are *12* pay periods if the pay period is *monthly*. Thus,

$$\text{Gross earnings} = \frac{\$312,000}{12} = \$26,000 \text{ per month}$$

b. There are *24* pay periods if the pay period is *semimonthly*.

$$\text{Gross earnings} = \frac{\$312,000}{24} = \$13,000 \text{ twice each month}$$

c. There are *26* pay periods if the pay period is *biweekly.*

$$\text{Gross earnings} = \frac{\$312,000}{26} = \$12,000 \text{ every two weeks}$$

d. There are *52* pay periods if the pay period is *weekly.*

$$\text{Gross earnings} = \frac{\$312,000}{52} = \$6,000 \text{ per week}$$

C. Wages

The majority of workers in this country are paid according to actual time at work. Their earnings are called **wages** and are calculated on a per hour basis. Gross earnings for hourly workers are found by multiplying the hourly rate by the number of hours worked per pay period as shown in formula 5–2.

(5–2)	Gross earnings (wages) = Rate per hour × Number of hours worked

EXAMPLE 2   An electrician wiring apartments in a new complex worked the following hours in a two week period.

	Sun.	Mon.	Tues.	Wed.	Thurs.	Fri.	Sat.
Week 1	0	8	6	4	8	8	4
Week 2	0	8	8	8	8	8	0

At an hourly rate of $11.56, calculate the electrician's gross earnings for the biweekly pay period.

Solution: The electrician worked 38 hours in week 1 and 40 hours in week 2 for a total of 78 hours.

$$\text{Gross earnings} = \$11.56 \times 78$$
$$= \$901.68$$

D. Piecework

In addition to the hourly rate, the term wages also refers to compensation based on production. The oldest form of production wages is called **piecework** or **piece-rate.** Workers under this payment plan earn according to the number of units produced.

(5–3)	Gross earnings (piecework) = Rate per unit × Number of units produced

The piecework plan of the next example is known as **straight piece-rate.**

EXAMPLE 3 Jeanine sews elastic bands in underwear, receiving $0.78 for each item of underwear. Calculate her gross earnings on a day when she completed 92 items.

Solution: Using formula 5–3,

$$\text{Gross earnings} = \$0.78 \times 92$$
$$= \$71.76$$

For workers engaged in production, it has long been known that extra effort is obtained only if some incentive exists. **Differential piecework** is a plan that offers an additional production incentive by providing a higher piece rate for greater production.

EXAMPLE 4 Patterson Manufacturing Co. pays its pieceworkers as follows:

Items produced	*Rate per item*
1–100	$0.80
101–140	0.95
141+	1.10

During one shift John produced 92 items, Harold produced 121 items, and Marsha produced 145 items. Find their gross earnings for the shift.

Solution:

John
$0.80 \times 92 = \$73.60$

Harold
$0.95 \times 121 = \$114.95$

Marsha
$1.10 \times 145 = \$159.50$

As shown in examples 3 and 4, straight piece-rate and differential piecework rewards the fast, efficient worker who can exceed the average production. To ensure quality is not sacrificed for speed, such plans may include a penalty for producing substandard items. Called **chargebacks** or **dockings,** these charges are usually less than standard rate, since a small amount of production error is normal.

EXAMPLE 5 Kevin solders connections on a circuit board. He is paid $1.95 for each board that passes inspection, with a chargeback of $0.60 for each board that fails inspection. His production for one week was as follows:

	Sun.	Mon.	Tues.	Wed.	Thurs.	Fri.	Sat.
Passed	0	38	44	45	48	42	0
Failed	0	5	3	2	2	3	0

Find his gross earnings for the week.

Solution: Kevin produced a total of 232 boards for the week, of which 15 failed inspection.

$$\$1.95 \times 217 = \$423.15$$
$$0.60 \times 15 = \quad -9.00$$
$$\text{Gross earnings} = \$414.15$$

■

Incentive piecework plans reward the fast, efficient worker who can exceed the average production, but it penalizes the slower below-average worker. Today there is considerable pressure (particularly by unions) to guarantee a minimum wage to the pieceworker, regardless of production. This minimum wage is set near a "standard," a production amount set by work measurement methods.

E X A M P L E 6   A lathe operator is paid $1.05 for each part machined and has a guaranteed weekly wage of $580.00. His production for the week was as follows:

	Sun.	Mon.	Tues.	Wed.	Thurs.	Fri.	Sat.
Week	0	100	107	106	110	102	0

Calculate his gross earnings for the week.

Solution: The worker machined a total of 525 parts during the week. Using formula 5–3,

$$\text{Gross earnings} = \$1.05 \times 525$$
$$= \$551.25$$

Since this is less than the guaranteed wage, his weekly gross earnings are $580.00 ■

Another wage plan based on production is the standard hour plan. In this plan, a worker is paid an hourly rate based on a "standard" number of units produced per hour and a piece-rate. For instance, suppose the lathe operator in example 6 normally machines 13 parts per hour. At a piece-rate of $1.05 per part, this comes to an hourly wage of $1.05 × 13 = $13.65. The "standard" production level per hour is the basis for a guaranteed minimum wage; production exceeding the standard is rewarded in the form of an "incentive bonus."

E X A M P L E 7   A worker in a company manufacturing electrical devices normally can assemble 340 units per week (40 hours). At an hourly rate of $9.50, find the gross earnings of a worker who assembled 374 units in a week.

Solution: A production of 374 units is an efficiency of $\frac{374}{340} = 110\%$. Accordingly, the worker received the regular wage plus a 10% incentive bonus.

$$\text{Regular pay} = \$9.50 \times 40 \quad = \$380.00$$
$$\text{Incentive bonus} = \$380.00 \times 0.10 = \quad \$38.00$$
$$\text{Gross earnings} \quad\quad = \$418.00$$

■

EXERCISES FOR SECTION 5.1

Round all answers to the nearest cent.

1. Bruce Dyer earns an annual salary of $32,000 at Boynton Industries, where the pay period is biweekly. Find his gross earnings per pay period.

2. The Alliance Company pays draftspeople a beginning salary of $27,400 per year. If the pay period at Alliance is biweekly, find the gross earnings per pay period of a beginning draftsperson.

3. Find the gross earnings per pay period of the president of Liberbaum & Co. if her salary is $92,000 per year and the pay period is weekly.

4. Lewers Sanitary Service pays its comptroller a salary of $66,000 per year. If the pay period is weekly, find the comptroller's gross earnings per pay period.

5. Find the gross earnings per pay period of an employee whose annual salary is $24,668 if the pay period is monthly.

6. Kelly Malone is a payroll clerk at the Hampton Corporation, where she earns $19,400 per year. If the company's pay period is monthly, find her salary per pay period.

7. Steve Kinnan receives an annual salary of $18,820 as a bookkeeper for the Peterson Construction Company. Find his gross earnings per pay period if the pay period is semimonthly.

8. Oneila Sanchez is the senior vice-president of Sanchez Legal Services. Her annual salary is $48,600, and the pay period is semimonthly. Find her gross earnings per pay period.

9. Christine Moore is an office manager at Merlin & Jones where she earns a salary of $2,088 per month. Find her gross earnings per pay period if the pay period is weekly. (Hint: first compute the annual salary.)

10. John Elliot earns $1,840 per month at Wellington Motors, where the pay period is biweekly. Compute his gross earnings per pay period. (Hint: first compute the annual salary.)

11. The weekly earnings of Rene Elias are currently $856. When the company converts to a semimonthly pay period, what will be her gross earnings per pay period?

12. Arthur Brennan's current gross earnings are $430 per week. Next year, his company will switch to a monthly pay period. What will be his gross earnings per pay period after the switch?

13. Mark Gard earns $14.56 per hour as a mechanic. Compute his gross earnings for a week in which he worked 36 hours.

14. Last week, Mimi Siegel worked 32 hours, and the previous week she worked 30 hours. At a wage rate of $9.86 per hour, find her gross earnings for the two-week period.

15. Ed Osler, a fork-lift operator, worked the following hours during the past two weeks.

	Sun.	Mon.	Tues.	Wed.	Thurs.	Fri.	Sat.
Week 1	0	8	6	5	7.5	7	0
Week 2	0	8	7.5	4	8	8	0

Find his gross earnings for the two-week period if he earned $8.91 per hour.

16. Charles Hobbs earned $12.05 per hour working for a local radiator repair shop. Calculate his gross earnings for a two-week period during which he worked the following hours.

	Sun.	Mon.	Tues.	Wed.	Thurs.	Fri.	Sat.
Week 1	0	7.5	5	8	4.5	7	0
Week 2	0	6.5	4	7	8	2.5	0

17. Julian Jimenez was laid off his regular job as a pipefitter. Last week he worked part-time for 20 hours at $7.00 per hour. His wife Anita earns $12.50 per hour for a 40 hour week as a customer service representative. Find their combined gross earnings for the past week.

18. Tammy Ho works 15 hours per week after school at Lee's Drugstore where she earns $5.50 per hour. Last week she also made $5.00 per hour for babysitting for four hours. Find her gross earnings for the past week.

19. Single parent Jean Jones works at two jobs to support herself and her children. By day she works at a factory where she earns $11.90 per hour for a 35 hour workweek. In the evening she works at a bakery where she earns $9.50 per hour for 24 hours per week. Find her gross earnings for a week.

20. Del Harris finished his apprenticeship at Hickok's Steel Fabrication Company and received an increase in pay to $10.75 per hour for a 40 hour workweek, compared to last week when he was paid $7.25 per hour. If the pay period is biweekly, find his gross earnings for the past two weeks.

21. Christine Hobson packages arts and crafts at Hobbies Unlimited. She is paid on a straight piecework basis of $0.52 per package assembled. Find her gross earnings on a day that she assembled 84 packages.

22. Benito Roman is paid on a straight piecework basis of $1.08 per piece. What were his gross earnings on a day that his production was 46 pieces?

23. Roy Veal assembled 39 units on Monday and 48 units on Tuesday. If he is paid $4.50 for each unit assembled, find his gross earnings for the two days.

24. Because of plant cutbacks in production, Robin Chapman worked only two days last week. She produced 460 and 472 items, and was paid $0.73 per item produced. What were her gross earnings for the week?

25. Faulkner Products pays its pieceworkers according to the following scale.

Items produced	Rate per item
1–50	$3.40
51+	$3.80

During week 1, an employee produced 46 items. The second week the employee produced 55 items. If the pay period is biweekly, find the gross earnings of the employee for the pay period.

26. Mitchell Manufacturing pays its pieceworkers according to the following scale.

Items produced	Rate per item
1–120	$0.69
121–135	0.78
136+	0.85

On the last shift Shelly produced 114 items, Grant produced 122 items, and Heather produced 136 items. Find each employee's gross earnings for the shift.

27. Carmen works at a plant that pays its pieceworkers according to the following scale.

Units assembled	Rate per unit
1–225	$0.92
226–250	1.10
251+	1.19

During week 1 Carmen assembled 247 units. In week 2, she assembled 269 units. If the pay period is biweekly, find her gross earnings for the pay period.

28. Gwen is paid a piece-rate according to the following scale.

Pieces	Rate per unit
1–200	$0.24
201–230	0.32
231+	0.40

Her production was 212 pieces on Monday and 238 on Tuesday. On Wednesday, after producing 78 pieces she became ill at work and left. She was sick the remainder of the workweek. Find her weekly gross wages.

29. At GlenCo Fittings, Luis grinds and polishes fittings. He is paid $0.40 a fitting with a chargeback of $0.28 for each fitting that fails inspection. His production for the week was as follows:

	Sun.	Mon.	Tues.	Wed.	Thurs.	Fri.	Sat.
Production	0	96	106	104	118	98	0
Rejects	0	12	5	6	9	8	0

Find Luis' gross earnings for the week.

30. J. L. Barney earns a piece-rate of $0.81 per piece with a chargeback of $0.44 for each substandard piece. Last week he produced 370 pieces, of which 11 were substandard. Find his gross earnings for the week.

31. An employee is paid a piece-rate of $0.62 per piece with a chargeback of $0.39 for each piece rejected. Find the gross earnings on a day that the employee produced 96 pieces including 4 rejects.

32. Risa assembled 44 units today, but 3 failed inspection. She is paid a piece-rate of $1.88 per assembly with a chargeback of $1.02 for each assembly that fails inspection. Find her gross earnings for the day.

33. The Chandon Company employs Louise Reeves to operate a machine that produces components for electric motors. Louise is paid $1.08 per unit produced with a guaranteed weekly wage of $485.00. Find her gross earnings for a week during which her production was as follows:

	Sun.	Mon.	Tues.	Wed.	Thurs.	Fri.	Sat.
Production	0	88	89	94	90	85	0

34. Dandy Draperies pays sewing machine operator Ruby Nesbit $1.12 per unit produced with a guaranteed weekly wage of $285.00. Find her gross earnings for a week during which her production was as follows:

	Sun.	Mon.	Tues.	Wed.	Thurs.	Fri.	Sat.
Production	0	50	52	47	51	48	0

35. Wilma Hogue is a packer for Wellington Industries. She is paid $0.30 per item packed, with a guaranteed weekly wage of $420.00. Find her gross earnings for a week during which her production was as follows:

	Sun.	Mon.	Tues.	Wed.	Thurs.	Fri.	Sat.
Production	0	257	265	261	259	255	0

36. At the Merritt Company, Theresa Dinsmore is an assembler, receiving $1.46 per unit assembled with a guaranteed weekly wage of $435.00. Find her gross earnings for a week during which her daily assembly was as follows:

	Sun.	Mon.	Tues.	Wed.	Thurs.	Fri.	Sat.
Assembled	0	62	59	57	63	59	0

37. In problem 33, suppose the Chandon Company decided to convert to the standard hour plan and set Louise Reeves' standard level of production at 460 units per week (40 hours). Using her piece-rate of $1.08 per unit produced, find her hourly wage. (Hint: first find her hourly wage, using her piece-rate of $1.08 per unit.)

38. In problem 34, calculate Ruby Nesbit's hourly wage (using her piece-rate of $1.12 per unit produced) if the company converted to the standard hour plan and set Ruby's weekly (40 hours) production level at 245 units per week. (Hint: first find her piece-rate, using the piece-rate of $1.12 per unit.)

39. In problem 35, if Wellington Industries converted to the standard hour plan and set Wilma Hogue's weekly (40 hours) production level at 1,400 units, find her gross earnings for a week during which she produced 1,390 units. (Hint: first find her hourly wage, using her piece-rate of $0.30 per unit.)

40. In problem 36, the Merritt Company converted to the standard hour plan and set Theresa Dinsmore's weekly (40 hours) production level at 320 units. What were her gross earnings for a week during which she produced 352 units? (Hint: first find her hourly wage, using her piece-rate of $1.46 per unit.)

41. Clyde Shaw is an assembler in a manufacturing company that uses the standard hour plan. Clyde is paid $9.60 per hour, and his standard production level is 200 units per 40 hour workweek. Find his gross earnings for a week during which he produced 215 units.

42. Sally Greer is paid according to the standard hour plan. Her production level is 280 units per 40 hour workweek and her hourly wage is $10.30. What were her gross earnings for a week during which she produced 294 units?

Section 5.2 *Gross Earnings: Commissions*

Commissions are earnings of sales personnel. Three common commission plans are straight commission, graduated commission, and salary and commission.

A. Straight Commission

Salespeople on straight commission are paid according to their **net sales** (total sales less returns and cancellations). This may be a set amount, but more often is a percentage of the dollar amount of their net sales. Gross earnings are calculated using the basic percentage formula $P = B \cdot R$ where the commission (percentage) equals the net sales (base) times the commission rate (percent):

(5–4)   Gross earnings (commission) = Net sales × Commission rate

---

EXAMPLE 1   Charles Schulz submitted orders for $16,450 worth of machinery during the first week of September. During the same week, the company received a cancellation of an order from one of Schulz's customers for $1,220. At a straight commission rate of 8%, calculate Shulz's gross earnings for the week.

Solution: The net sales were $16,450 − $1,220 = $15,230. Using formula 5–4,

Gross earnings = $15,230 × 0.08
                     = $1,218.40   ∎

The chief advantage of the straight commission plan is its simplicity. However, because sales tend to vary from month to month, the income of the salesperson will also fluctuate. Also, new or inexperienced salespersons may not sell enough to earn a reasonable income. To offset these disadvantages, a company may offer a straight commission plan with a drawing account. A drawing account is essentially an advance on future commissions; it is repaid from future commissions, as illustrated in the next example.

EXAMPLE 2   During her first four months of employment with the Glover Company, sales representative Sarah Cook had sales of $10,800, $12,800, $14,500, and $9,800. Carol received a straight commission of $12\frac{1}{2}\%$ of net sales with a draw of $1,500 per month. Calculate Carol's gross earnings for the four-month period.

Solution:

Sales	Earned Commissions	Draw Advance	Draw Deficit Brought Fwd.	Gross Earnings	Draw Deficit Carried Fwd.
$10,800	$1,350.00	$150.00	—	$1,500.00	$150.00
12,800	1,600.00	—	$150.00	1,500.00	50.00
14,500	1,812.50	—	50.00	1,762.50	—
9,800	1,225.00	275.00	—	1,500.00	275.00

As a result of her drawing account, Carol would receive $1,500, $1,500, $1,762.50, and $1,500 respectively, as gross earnings for the four months.   ■

B. Graduated Commissions

As an additional incentive, commissions may be on a graduated scale, meaning that the commission percent increases as sales volume increases. Companies can offer a graduated commission plan because travel, meals, and other sales expenses paid by the company remain relatively constant regardless of the sales volume.

E X A M P L E 3   The Shelby Corporation pays its sales personnel monthly according to the following graduated scale.

6% of the first $7,500 in net sales
$7\frac{1}{4}$% of the next $7,500 in net sales
8% of all net sales over $15,000

Last month, Travis Clark had net sales of $24,750. Calculate his gross earnings.

Solution: Sales

$ 7,500 × 0.06	=	$450.00
$ 7,500 × 0.0725	=	543.75
$ 9,750 × 0.08	=	780.00
$24,750		$1,773.75

■

C. Salary and Commission

Sales personnel under a salary and commission plan receive a salary plus a percentage of net sales. Since the sales representative receives a guaranteed salary, the commission percent is usually less than a straight commission percent.

SALES PROFESSIONALS

Sabal Products, Inc. is looking for sales professionals to promote its products in this area. Responsibilities include: prospecting, cold calling, and installation. The ideal candidate should be able to work independently, have 1–2 years strong sales experience, and possess good oral and written communication skills. BA/BS degree preferred. This is a commission only position with additional incentives based on achievement! We provide business-related expenses and health benefits are available. To apply, call 504–638–9514 or fax 504–638–4486. We are an equal opportunity employer.

Sabal Products

EXAMPLE 4   During a week that Harry Carson sold $12,750 worth of supplies, the company had returns of $1,400 from one of his customers. Harry received a salary of $325 plus a commission of 3% of his net sales. Calculate his gross earnings for the week.

Solution:

Gross sales	= $12,750.00	Commission	= $340.50 ($11,350 × 0.03)
Returns	= 1,400.00	Salary	= 325.00
Net sales	= $11,350.00	Gross earnings	= $665.50

Retail stores commonly offer a salary and commission plan wherein a commission is paid only when sales exceed a specified quota.

EXAMPLE 5   Nancy Sherman is a salesclerk in the women's wear section of a department store. She is paid a weekly salary of $228 for a 35 hour workweek, plus a commission of 4% of net sales in excess of $1,800 per week. Calculate her gross earnings in a week that she had sales of $2,960.

Solution: Nancy will be paid a commission on $2,960 − $1,800 = $1,160 of sales.

Salary	$228.00
Commission	+ 46.40 ($1,160 × 0.04)
Gross earnings	$274.40

Department heads or sales managers often are paid a commission that is a percentage of the net sales of the people they supervise. This type of commission is called an **override**.

EXAMPLE 6   In addition to her weekly salary of $450, Joan Littlefield receives a commission of 5% of her personal net sales in excess of $1,500, plus an override of $\frac{1}{2}$% of the net sales of four employees she supervises. Last week her personal sales were $1,970 and the net sales of the four employees was $9,455. Find her gross earnings for the week.

Solution:

Salary	$450.00
Commission	23.50 ($470 × 0.05)
Override	+ 47.28 ($9,455 × 0.005)
Gross earnings	$520.78

D. Commission Agents

Some individuals or agencies known as **commission agents**, **brokers**, or **factors** act as intermediaries in the sale or purchase of merchandise. For example, agricultural products are often grown on farms that are far away from their city markets. In

Figure 5.2
An account sales

\multicolumn{5}{c}{*Account Sales*}
\multicolumn{5}{c}{**Adams & Adams**}
Tel: (617) 556-4100		*1296 State Street*	*Reg. No. 140678*	
Fax: (617) 556-2507		*Boston, Mass., 02190*		
		Account of Thorton Farms	*Date* Mar 10	
		Plant City, Florida		

Feb	24	230 flats strawberries @ $5.10	$1,173.00	
	27	310 flats strawberries @ $4.95	1,534.50	
Mar	1	305 flats strawberries @ $4.60	1,403.00	
		Gross proceeds		$4,110.50
		Charges		
		Commission, 7%	$287.74	
		Freight	101.88	
		Refrigerated Storage	48.00	
				437.62
		Net Proceeds		$3,672.88

such an instance a farmer (the consignor) may ship his product to a commission agent (the consignee) on consignment. The commission agent then sells the shipment at the best possible price, called the **gross proceeds.** From this is deducted a straight commission along with any expenses such as freight, storage, etc. The remainder, called the **net proceeds,** is paid to the farmer. Accompanying the net proceeds is an **account sales,** a printed record of the transaction such as that illustrated in figure 5.2.

Commission agents may also be buyers for their clients. Such agents typically specialize in items not readily available through wholesale distributors. Following delivery of the desired items which were purchased at the best possible price, the agent sends the buyer an **account purchase** which details the items purchased and their price plus the agent's straight commission (of the purchase price) and any expenses. An account purchase is shown in figure 5.3.

Figure 5.3
An account purchase

Account Purchase

Horton and Mann

1100 Sixth Ave., San Diego, Calif., 92115

Quality Imports
12361 Dover Street
St. Louis, Missouri

Oct	12	200 Wooden bowls @ $4.10		$820.00
	14	125 Hand painted mugs @ $1.80		225.00
	16	50 22cm Figurines @ $3.00		150.00
	16	75 10cm Figurines @ $1.65		123.75
				$1,318.75
		Charges:		
		Commission, 6%		$79.13
		Freight and import duties		99.20
		Insurance		26.20
				204.53
		Gross cost		$1,523.28

EXERCISES FOR SECTION 5.2

1. Mark Conrad is paid a straight commission of 11% on his net sales. During April, his net sales totaled $21,350. Find his gross earnings for the month.

2. Last month, Eleanor Jordan sold $41,720 worth of merchandise. At a straight commission rate of 9%, how much were her gross earnings for the month?

3. During the month of February, Bob Reynolds submitted orders for $27,481 worth of fittings. Two of the orders totaling $2,350 were subsequently canceled. Calculate his gross earnings for the month if he is paid a straight commission of 7% on net sales.

4. Lila Maddox is paid a straight commission of 6% on net sales. In May, her sales were $31,240, with returns and cancellations totaling $3,942. What was her commission for the month?

5. Last month, Ron Dillon sold $31,415 worth of furniture, with returns and cancellations totaling $1,323. If he is paid a straight commission of 9% on net sales, find his gross earnings for the month.

6. Tony Gonzalo sells plumbing fixtures on a straight commission of 8% of net sales. Find his gross earnings for a month in which he submitted orders totaling $31,616 and cancellations amounted to $4,115.

7. Janelle Horner is paid a straight commission of $7\frac{1}{2}$% of her net sales. During the past week, she had sales of $1,077 on Monday, $915 on Tuesday, $637 on Wednesday, $920 on Thursday, and $615 on Friday. Returned merchandise totaled $401 for the week. What were her gross earnings for the week?

8. Vince Rocco sold $1,372 on Monday, $1,340 on Tuesday, $942 on Wednesday, $1,008 on Thursday, and $531 on Friday. If returned merchandise totaled $656 for the week, find his gross earnings for the week at a straight commission rate of 11%.

9. Stockbroker Willard Myers received a commission of $184.80 on the purchase of some stock for a customer. The sale price of the stock was $9,240. If he is paid a straight commission on the stock, what was his commission rate?

10. Real estate salesperson Linda Nanz received a commission of $5,490 on the sale of a home. If her commission rate is 6% of the selling price, find the selling price of the home.

11. Glenn Olander recently accepted a sales position with Hoffman Industries, where he receives a straight commission of 9% of net sales with a draw of $1,575 per month. Complete the following record of his monthly gross earnings for his first three months with the company.

Month	Net Sales	Earned Commission	Draw Advance	Draw Deficit Brought Fwd.	Gross Earnings	Draw Deficit Carried Fwd.
Jan.	$15,200	$1,368.00	$207.00	—	$1,575.00	$207.00
Feb.	11,850			$207.00		
Mar.	20,540					

12. Fashion Flair, a wholesale clothing firm, pays its sales personnel 7% of net sales with a draw of $1,020 per month. Complete the following record of the monthly gross earnings for sales representative Patricia Wolfe.

Month	Net Sales	Earned Commission	Draw Advance	Draw Deficit Brought Fwd.	Gross Earnings	Draw Deficit Carried Fwd.
Sept.	$ 9,560			$71.50		
Oct.	13,225					
Nov.	15,140					

13. Oldsmar Industries pays salesperson Mary Read a straight commission of 14% with a monthly draw of $1,750. Complete the following record of her gross earnings for a three-month period.

Month	Net Sales	Earned Commission	Draw Advance	Draw Deficit Brought Fwd.	Gross Earnings	Draw Deficit Carried Fwd.
April	$12,842			$70.00		
May	11,540					
June	18,760					

14. Claude Redman is paid a straight commission of 12% with a draw of $1,700 per month. Complete the following record of his gross earnings for a three-month period.

Month	Net Sales	Earned Commission	Draw Advance	Draw Deficit Brought Fwd.	Gross Earnings	Draw Deficit Carried Fwd.
Aug.	$14,225			$44.00		
Sept.	14,850					
Oct.	$14,975					

15. Dora Rose is paid a graduated commission of 9% of the first $10,000 in net sales and 11.5% of net sales over $10,000. Last month she had net sales of $14,920. Find her gross earnings for the month.

16. The Valin Corporation pays its sales personnel a graduated commission of 15% of the first $3,000 in net sales and 18% of net sales over $3,000. Compute the gross earnings for a salesperson who had sales of $6,250 during a month.

17. Epler & Futch pays its sales personnel a graduated commission of 6% of the first $8,000 in net sales, 8% of the next $4,000 in net sales, and 9.5% of all net sales over $12,000. In a month that Bill Walker had net sales of $14,500, what were his gross earnings?

18. Grace James is paid a weekly graduated commission of 8% of the first $2,000 in net sales, 9.25% of the next $1,500 in net sales, and 10.5% of all net sales over $3,500. Find her gross earnings for a week that her net sales were $3,622.

19. During the month of August, salesperson Terry Frank submitted orders totaling $25,483. Terry is paid a monthly graduated commission of 10% of the first $10,000 in net sales, 11.25% of the next $8,000 in net sales, and 12% of all net sales over $18,000. Compute Terry's gross earnings for the month if $4,120 of his orders were canceled.

20. Pam Hendry submitted orders totaling $17,563 in February, with $2,657 in cancellations. Pam is paid a monthly graduated commission of 8.5% of the first $9,000 in net sales, 10% of the next $4,000 in net sales, and 12% of all net sales over $13,000. What were her gross earnings for the month?

21. Jean Nicole is employed as a salesclerk in the sporting goods section of a large store. She is paid a salary of $335 a week plus a commission of 3.25% of her weekly net sales. Find her gross earnings for a week that her sales were $1,242 with returns of $165.

22. Jay Incorporated pays Phillip Lund $360 per week plus a commission of 2.75% of net sales. Last week Phillip sold $2,720 of supplies, with returns of $323. What were his gross earnings for the week?

23. Fernando Rivera is paid a monthly salary of $1,075 plus a commission of 5% of net sales in excess of $5,500. Last month he sold $11,424 worth of goods, with cancellations of $2,720. How much were his gross earnings for the month?

24. Cheryl Minich is employed at Milroy Optical Company where she is paid a weekly salary of $232 plus a commission of 5.25% of net sales in excess of $1,200. Find her gross earnings for a week that her sales were $1,572 with returns of $117.

25. Tom Weber is the manager of the men's wear section in a department store. He is paid a salary of $330 per week plus a commission of 5% of net sales over $1,800 and an override of 0.75% of the net sales of the clerks working under him. His sales last week totaled $3,300 with returns of $143. The people working under him had sales of $17,240 with returns of $619. What were his gross earnings for the week?

26. Michele Turner manages the Hillside branch of Bentlys, a women's clothing chain. She receives a salary of $330 per week plus a commission of 5.5% of net sales over $1,500 and an override of 0.5% of the net sales of the clerks working under her. Find her gross earnings for a week that she sold $3,125 in merchandise with returns of $217 and her employees sold $12,240 in merchandise with returns of $757.

27. The following payroll records give the net sales, commission rates, quota, returns, and salary for each of five salespersons employed at Sam's Style Shoppe. Find the gross earnings of each salesperson for the week.

Sam's Style Shoppe							Week ending April 6
Name	Sales	Returns	Net Sales	Quota	Commission	Salary	Gross Earnings
Mazurek, S.	$2,452	$47	2405	$ 800	6.5% -104.32	$245	349.33
Reese, S.	3,187	63	—	—	4.0	255	—
Taylor, J.	2,740	18	—	1,200	7.0	250	—
Velasco, R.	3,416	27	—	—	5.5	240	—
Williams, P.	3,141	36	—	1,000	5.75	260	—

28. Frieda's Card & Gift Shop employs five salespersons. Complete the following payroll for the week ending June 7.

Frieda's Card & Gift Shop							Week ending June 7
Name	Sales	Returns	Net Sales	Quota	Commission	Salary	Gross Earnings
Darke, L.	$1,720	$102	—	$500	8%	$250	—
Hargraves, E.	1,542	182	—	600	8.5	255	—
Taylor, J.	1,912	94	—	—	4.5	240	—
Velasco, R.	2,004	114	—	—	5.25	235	—
Williams, P.	1,643	83	—	700	9	260	—

29. Complete the following account sales.

942.01

Account Sales

Benson Brothers
Denver, Colorado

FOR THE ACCOUNT OF: Lexington Farms
Sonoma Valley, Calif.

1486.43

15700.25

Apr	4	2,000 crates oranges @ $2.96	5920	
	12	1,400 crates oranges @ $3.01	4214	
	16	1,825 crates oranges @ $3.05	5566.25	
		Gross proceeds	15700.25	
		Charges:		
		Freight	$577.80 +	
		Commission, 6%	942.02	
		Net proceeds		

907.47

976.68

30. Find the amount remitted to the seller for the following entries from an account sales: March 16—400 containers of roses at $12.96 per container; March 20—325 containers of gardenias at $8.80 per container; commission, 8%; freight and insurance, $261.30.

31. Complete the following account purchase.

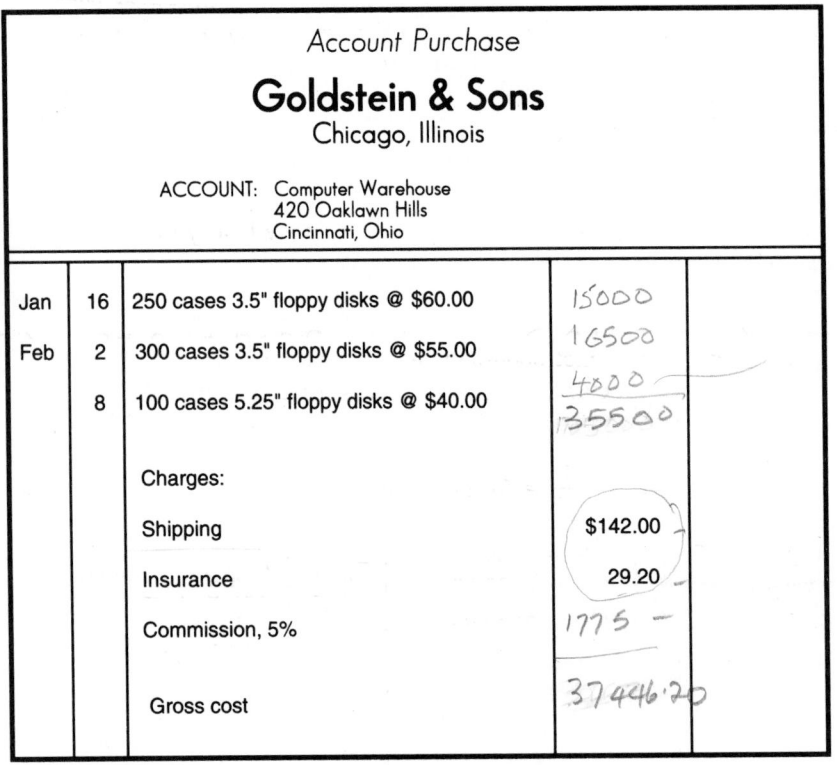

		Account Purchase		
		Goldstein & Sons		
		Chicago, Illinois		
		ACCOUNT: Computer Warehouse 420 Oaklawn Hills Cincinnati, Ohio		
Jan	16	250 cases 3.5" floppy disks @ $60.00	15000	
Feb	2	300 cases 3.5" floppy disks @ $55.00	16500	
	8	100 cases 5.25" floppy disks @ $40.00	4000 35500	
		Charges:		
		Shipping	$142.00	
		Insurance	29.20	
		Commission, 5%	1775	
		Gross cost	37446·20	

32. Find the amount remitted to the agent for the following entries from an account purchase: 400 kg black tea at $8.00 per kg; 100 kg green tea at $6.00 per kg; 300 kg oolong tea at $6.90 per kg; freight charges, $117.90; commission, 7%.

Cost
− Expenses (freight / comm)
Net

Section 5.3 *Overtime*

For workers in the United States covered by the Fair Labor Standards Act, hours on the job must be separated into two categories: regular and overtime. First passed by Congress in 1938, this act (also known as the Federal Wage and Hour Law) establishes minimum wages, overtime pay, and other labor standards for every employee engaged in interstate or foreign commerce or in the production of goods for such commerce. Under the latest amendment of the act, regular hours consist of a workweek of 40 hours. Hours worked in excess of 40 during a workweek constitute **overtime** hours. The act specifies the rate of pay for overtime to be $1\frac{1}{2}$ times the rate for regular hours. While the act is aimed primarily at wage earners, its overtime provisions also apply to certain categories of salaried and commissioned employees, as will be seen in this section.

A. Wages

Overtime for employees paid an hourly wage is $1\frac{1}{2}$ times the hourly rate for hours in excess of a 40 hour workweek.

E X A M P L E   1   A switchboard operator for a metropolitan telephone company earns $8.40 an hour for a 40 hour workweek. Calculate her gross earnings for a week that she worked 48 hours.

Solution: The overtime rate is \$8.40 $\times 1\frac{1}{2} =$ \$12.60. Thus,

Regular wages $= \$8.40 \times 40 = \$336.00$
Overtime wages $= \$12.60 \times 8 = \underline{100.80}$
Gross earnings $= \$436.80$

Entry	Display	Memory
8.4	8.4	0
×	8.4	0
40	40	0
M+	336	336
12.6	12.6	336
×	12.6	336
8	8	336
M+	100.8	436.8
MR	436.8	436.8

Many payroll employees compute the overtime wages by multiplying the number of overtime hours by $1\frac{1}{2}$ instead of the rate. The result is the same. For example 1,

Regular wages $= \$8.40 \times 40 = \$336.00$

Overtime wages $= \$8.40 \times 12 = \underline{100.80}\left(12 = 8 \times 1\frac{1}{2}\right)$

Gross earnings $ = \$436.80$

First used in cost accounting and becoming increasingly popular, the overtime-premium method is still another equivalent way of computing overtime. In this method, the regular rate is multiplied by the total number of hours worked. Overtime is found by multiplying half the regular rate by the number of overtime hours. In example 1,

Regular wages = \$8.40 × 48 = \$403.20
Overtime   = \$4.20 × 8 =   33.60
Gross earnings   = \$436.80

Since employees are paid a higher rate for overtime, it is important that the employer keep accurate records of the hours worked. Most employers accomplish this by time sheets or by a time card such as that shown in the next example. A more sophisticated device utilizes a plastic card that is inserted into a timing device directly linked to a computer. The computer records and stores the time worked and during the payroll-run calculates the regular and overtime hours.

E X A M P L E 2   George Welch earns \$6.20 an hour for a 40 hour workweek. Calculate his gross earnings for the week using the information on the following time card.

WEEKLY TIME CARD   FROM 3/7 TO 3/13
(DATE)   (DATE)

(Notice-This card must be turned in to the proper authority before payment can be made)

EMPLOYEE'S NAME _George C. Welch_   S.S. ACCT. No. _321-54-9876_
ADDRESS _110 Oak Street_
POSITION _____   DEPT. _Production_   BADGE No. _10479_
NAME OF EMPLOYER _____

	A. M.		P. M.		Overtime		Total Hours	
	IN	OUT	IN	OUT	IN	OUT	REGULAR	OVERTIME
MONDAY	8:00	12.01	12:30	4:30			8	
TUESDAY	8:02	12.00	12:30	4:30	6:00	9:30	8	3½
WEDNESDAY	8:01	12.01	12:30	4:32	4:32	8:00	8	3½
THURSDAY	8:01	12:00	12:31	4:31			8	
FRIDAY	8:00	12:05	12:35	4:30			8	
SATURDAY								
SUNDAY								
I, the undersigned, certify that this is a true and accurate record of my working time for the period above mentioned.					WEEKLY TOTAL		40	7

SIGNATURE _George C. Welch_

Form W.T.C. Redi-Record Payroll Systems Inc. Oceanside, N.Y.

Solution: The overtime rate is $6.20 \times 1\frac{1}{2} = \$9.30$

Regular wages = \$6.20 × 40 = \$248.00
Overtime wages = 9.30 × 7   =   65.10
Gross earnings   = \$313.10

While the wage and hour law defines overtime as work in excess of 40 hours per workweek, some wage agreements recognize other forms of overtime as well. "Time-and-a-half" ($1\frac{1}{2}$ times the regular rate) may be paid for hours in excess of 8 hours per day, and "double-time" (two times the regular rate) is often paid for work on Sundays or holidays. Hours for which an employee receives time-and-a-half or double-time are still counted as part of the 40 hour workweek when computing overtime.

EXAMPLE 3   The time card of an employee indicated the following hours worked during the week of Sunday, June 30, through Saturday, July 6.

	6/30	7/1	7/2	7/3	7/4	7/5	7/6
Week	8	0	$8\frac{1}{2}$	8	$4\frac{1}{2}$	8	8

The regular hourly rate for the employee is $9.40, and he receives time-and-a-half for work in excess of 8 hours a day or 40 hours a week, plus double-time for Sundays or holidays. Find his gross earnings for the week.

Solution: The hours worked are distributed as regular (R), overtime or time-and-a-half (OT), and double-time (DT).

	6/30	7/1	7/2	7/3	7/4	7/5	7/6	Total	Rate	Total Wages
R			8	8		8	3	27	$9.40	$253.80
OT		$\frac{1}{2}$					5	$5\frac{1}{2}$	14.10	77.55
DT	8				$4\frac{1}{2}$			$12\frac{1}{2}$	18.80	235.00
									Gross earnings	$566.35

Note that the $4\frac{1}{2}$ double-time hours on 7/4 are because of a holiday, and that only 3 hours of the 8 hours worked on 7/6 are regular hours since the employee had already worked 37 hours of the 40 hour workweek during the preceding six days. ■

Employees on piecework also receive overtime pay for work in excess of a 40 hour workweek. To calculate overtime pay, the total wages earned by piecework first must be converted to an hourly rate; the overtime rate is $1\frac{1}{2}$ times the hourly equivalent.

E X A M P L E 4   An employee on piecework earns $0.87 per piece. What were his gross earnings for a week during which he worked 50 hours and he produced 400 pieces?

Solution: The total amount earned by piecework for the week was $0.87 \times 400 = \$348.00$. Accordingly, the regular hourly rate was $\frac{\$348.00}{50} = \$6.96$, and the overtime hourly rate was $\$6.96 \times 1\frac{1}{2} = \$10.44$.

Regular wages $= \$6.96 \times 40 = \$278.40$
Overtime wages $= \$10.44 \times 10 = \underline{104.40}$
Gross earnings $= \$382.80$ ■

E X A M P L E 5   Donna Appleton is paid a piece-rate of $0.32 with a guaranteed weekly wage of $280.00. She produced 860 pieces during a week that she worked 44 hours. Calculate her gross earnings for the week.

Solution: The guaranteed weekly wage is $\frac{\$280.00}{40} = \$7.00$ per hour. The total amount earned by piecework is $\$0.32 \times 860 = 275.20$, which converts to $\frac{\$275.20}{44} = \$6.25$ per hour. Since this is less than the guaranteed wage, she is paid the guaranteed wage. The overtime rate is $\$7.00 \times 1\frac{1}{2} = \$10.50$.

Regular wages $= \$7.00 \times 40 = \$280.00$
Overtime wages $= \$10.50 \times 4 = \underline{42.00}$
Gross earnings $= \$322.00$ ■

B. Salaries

If a salary is paid to an employee for a specified number of hours to be worked per week, then the employee is covered by the Fair Labor Standards Act and must be paid the overtime rate for the hours worked in excess of the specified workweek. Before the overtime rate can be calculated, an hourly rate of pay is found by dividing the weekly salary (or biweekly or semimonthly salary converted to a weekly salary) by the specified weekly hours.

E X A M P L E 6   Vivian Moore is employed as a secretary with a salary of $448.00 per 40 hour workweek. Calculate her gross earnings for a week during which she worked 46 hours.

Solution: A salary of $448.00 for a 40 hour workweek amounts to a regular hourly rate of $\frac{\$448.00}{40} = \$11.20$ per hour. The overtime hourly rate is $\$11.20 \times 1\frac{1}{2} = \$16.80$. Thus,

Regular pay $= \$11.20 \times 40 = \$448.00$
Overtime pay $= \$16.80 \times 6 = \underline{100.80}$
Gross earnings $= \$548.80$ ■

EXAMPLE 7   The Spring Pure Water Company pays one of its office workers a salary of $1,716 per month. The salary is for a workweek of 40 hours, but during a recent two-week period, the following hours were worked.

	Sun.	Mon.	Tues.	Wed.	Thurs.	Fri.	Sat.
Week 1	0	10	7	10	8	8	4
Week 2	0	7	9	8	9	7	4

Calculate the gross earnings of the office worker if the pay period is biweekly.

Solution: The monthly salary is converted to an hourly rate in two steps:

	Weekly salary	$= \$1,716 \times \frac{12}{52} =$	$396.00
	Hourly rate	$= \$396 \div 40 =$	$9.90
	Overtime rate	$= \$9.90 \times 1\frac{1}{2} =$	$14.85
Week 1	Regular pay	$= \$9.90 \times 40 =$	$396.00
	Overtime pay	$= \$14.85 \times 7 =$	103.95
	Subtotal		$499.95
Week 2	Regular pay	$= \$9.90 \times 40 =$	$396.00
	Overtime pay	$= \$14.85 \times 4 =$	59.40
	Subtotal		455.40
	Gross earnings		$955.35 ∎

C. Commissions

"Outside" sales personnel (that is, sales representatives who spend most of their time away from their employer's place of business) are not covered by the Fair Labor Standards Act. However, "inside" sales personnel are covered by the act, and their commission (and any salary) must be converted to an hourly rate to determine an overtime rate, as demonstrated in the next example.

EXAMPLE 8   A salesclerk for Gilbert's Department Store is paid $260 per week for a 40 hour workweek and 3% of her sales in excess of $1,200. Calculate her gross earnings for a week that she worked 44 hours and recorded sales of $1,844.

Solution: Regular hourly rate (salary) $= \frac{\$260}{40} = \$6.50$
Overtime hourly rate (salary) $= \$6.50 \times 1\frac{1}{2} = \$9.75$
Commission $= \$644 \times 0.03 = \$19.32$
Regular hourly rate (commission) $= \frac{\$19.32}{44} = \$0.44$
Overtime hourly rate (commission) $= \$0.44 \times 1\frac{1}{2} = \$0.66$

Regular pay	$= \$6.50 \times 40 =$	$260.00
Overtime pay	$= \$9.75 \times 4 =$	39.00
Subtotal		$299.00
Regular commission	$= \$0.44 \times 40 =$	$17.60
Overtime commission	$= \$0.66 \times 4 =$	2.64
Subtotal		20.24
Gross earnings		$319.24 ∎

EXERCISES FOR SECTION 5.3

1. If Randy Brown is paid $8.80 for a 40 hour workweek, what was his gross earnings for a week during which he worked 45 hours?

2. Find Jewel Davis' gross earnings for a week during which she worked 43 hours, if she receives $10.40 per hour for a specified 40 hour workweek.

3. Douglas Johnson earns $12.60 per hour for a 40 hour workweek. Calculate his gross earnings for a week when his time report was as follows:

	Sun.	Mon.	Tues.	Wed.	Thurs.	Fri.	Sat.
Week	0	8	12	8	10	10	0

4. Diane Gaskins filed the following time report for the week of April 15 through April 21. If she is paid $8.20 per hour for a 40 hour workweek, complete her gross earnings for the week.

	4/15	4/16	4/17	4/18	4/19	4/20	4/21
Week	0	8	8	9	14	11	0

5. Hutton Contractors pays its employees time-and-a-half for work in excess of 8 hours a day or 40 hours a week plus double-time for Sundays and holidays. Richard Ivey, a carpenter at Hutton, is paid $15.80 per hour. Compute his gross earnings for the week of Sunday, December 30, through Saturday, January 5, during which he worked the following hours.

	12/30	12/31	1/1	1/2	1/3	1/4	1/5
Hours	4	4	6	$7\frac{1}{2}$	9	$8\frac{1}{2}$	4

6. Cindy Jantzen is employed at Classic Quilting, where she receives $4.40 per hour with time-and-a-half for work in excess of 8 hours a day or 40 hours a week plus double-time for Sundays and holidays. Find her gross earnings for the week of Sunday, September 6, through Saturday, September 12 (September 7 was Labor Day), during which she worked the following hours.

	9/6	9/7	9/8	9/9	9/10	9/11	9/12
Hours	3	6	$7\frac{1}{2}$	5	$9\frac{1}{2}$	4	0

7. Gene Walters is an assembler at Fairline Industries, where he is paid a straight piecework of $0.48 per part assembled. Last week he worked 48 hours and assembled 558 units. Calculate his gross earnings for the week.

8. An employee at the Brookwood Company is paid a straight piecework of $0.75 per piece. Find the gross earnings for a week during which the employee worked 45 hours and produced 408 pieces.

(handwritten notes at top: 24 = 902 440 = 360×.86 = 310.33 47 86 62.56 (24-360)×1.5+7 39 2 86)

9. Louise Quick is paid a piece-rate of $0.86 per piece with a guaranteed weekly wage of $312.00. What was her gross earnings for a week during which she worked 47 hours and produced 424 pieces?

10. The Halleck Company pays its employees in the shipping department $0.94 per unit packed for shipment, with a guaranteed weekly wage of $320.00. Compute the gross earnings for a week during which the employee worked 47 hours and packed 420 pieces.

11. Norma Beard is paid a piece-rate of $0.80 per piece with a guaranteed weekly wage of $224.00. What are her gross earnings for a week during which she worked 42 hours and produced 296 pieces?

12. Juan Lopez works for the Winters Company where he is paid a piece-rate of $0.58 per piece with a guaranteed weekly wage of $184.00. What are his gross earnings for a week during which he worked 45 hours and produced 344 pieces?

13. Joe Bazer is paid a salary of $334.40 per 40 hour workweek. Using the three methods of computing overtime described in this section, calculate his gross earnings for a week during which he worked 44 hours.

14. Jan Whitlock is a salaried employee at the Comtech Company, where she earns $326.80 per 40 hour workweek. Using the three methods of computing overtime described in this section, find her gross earnings for a week during which she worked 46 hours.

15. Frank Larkin is an office manager at the Bissett Paint Company. He is paid a monthly salary of $4,160 for a 40 hour workweek. The pay period at the company is biweekly, and during the last pay period Frank worked the following hours.

	Sun.	Mon.	Tues.	Wed.	Thurs.	Fri.	Sat.
Week 1	0	8	6	7	6	8	6
Week 2	0	7	8	8	8	7	5

(handwritten: ×12÷26; 41(4×1.5; 43); 4160÷80×17×1.544 = overtime)

Compute Frank's gross earnings for this pay period.

16. The Amazon Marine Equipment Company pays one of its office workers a monthly salary of $1,560 for a 40 hour workweek. If the pay period at Amazon is biweekly, find the worker's gross earnings for the following two-week period.

	Sun.	Mon.	Tues.	Wed.	Thurs.	Fri.	Sat.
Week 1	0	7	8	6	7	8	6
Week 2	0	8	8	8	8	6	6

17. Robinson's Metal Works pays Joan Schyler an annual salary of $16,432. The workweek at Robinson's is 40 hours, and the pay period is biweekly. Find Joan's gross earnings for a pay period during which she worked the following hours.

	Sun.	Mon.	Tues.	Wed.	Thurs.	Fri.	Sat.
Week 1	0	8	8	6	8	7	7
Week 2	0	8	8	7	7	6	6

18. Hallamore Industries pays one of its branch office managers an annual salary of $37,856 for a 40 hour workweek. The pay period at Hallamore is biweekly, and during the last pay period the manager worked the following hours.

	Sun.	Mon.	Tues.	Wed.	Thurs.	Fri.	Sat.
Week 1	0	8	8	7	7	7	8
Week 2	0	8	7	7	8	8	7

Compute the manager's gross earnings for this pay period.

19. Vernon Kyle works in the sporting goods section of a department store. He is paid a salary of $340 for a 40 hour workweek, plus a commission of 4% of sales in excess of $1,500. Find his gross earnings for a week during which he worked 50 hours and sold $1,725 worth of merchandise.

20. Isabel Keene sells leisure wear at the Fun-N-Frolic Shoppe. She receives a salary of $328 for a 40 hour workweek, plus a commission of 2.5% of sales in excess of $600. Calculate her gross earnings for a week during which she worked 45 hours and recorded sales of $1,176.

21. The sales personnel at Apple's Appliance Store are paid $284 per 40 hour workweek, plus a commission of 2.5% of sales in excess of $2,000. What were the gross earnings of a sales representative for a week during which the representative worked 43 hours and sold $2,688 worth of merchandise?

22. Ed Alexander worked 42 hours last week at the Futura Furniture Store. He is paid a salary of $180 for a 40 hour workweek, plus a commission of 3% of sales in excess of $1,800. If he recorded sales for the week totaling $2,668, what were his gross earnings?

Section 5.4 *Net Earnings*

Following the computation of gross earnings, the next step in preparation of the payroll is the calculation of net earnings. As previously stated, net earnings are gross earnings less deductions. Deductions are amounts that the employer withholds from the employee's earnings. The payroll department subtracts deductions from gross earnings and pays the employee the difference, or net earnings. A record is maintained of all deductions, and periodically, these sums are sent to the appropriate agency.

Deductions may be voluntary or required by law. We examine the latter category first.

A. Federal Income Tax

The federal government has authorized employers to withhold a percentage of the employee's gross earnings each payday as advance payment of the employee's federal income tax.

The percentage subtracted from gross earnings depends on three factors: (1) gross earnings, (2) marital status, and (3) the number of withholding allowances. A **withholding allowance** reduces the amount of tax withheld from an employee's earnings. The government grants one withholding allowance for each person supported by the employee and additional allowances on the basis of certain special circumstances. At the time of employment, each employee is required to complete an Employee's Withholding Allowance Certificate (Form W-4) on which the employee declares the number of allowances he or she wishes to claim (see figure 5.4). A person with a spouse and two children may claim four allowances, one for

1992 Form W-4

Department of the Treasury
Internal Revenue Service

Purpose. Complete Form W-4 so that your employer can withhold the correct amount of Federal income tax from your pay.

Exemption From Withholding. Read line 7 of the certificate below to see if you can claim exempt status. *If exempt, complete line 7; but do not complete lines 5 and 6.* No Federal income tax will be withheld from your pay. Your exemption is good for one year only. It expires February 15, 1993.

Basic Instructions. Employees who are not exempt should complete the Personal Allowances Worksheet. Additional worksheets are provided on page 2 for employees to adjust their withholding allowances based on itemized deductions, adjustments to income, or two-earner/two-job situations. Complete all worksheets that apply to your situation. The worksheets will help you figure the number of withholding allowances you are entitled to claim. However, you may claim fewer allowances than this.

Head of Household. Generally, you may claim head of household filing status on your tax return only if you are unmarried and pay more than 50% of the costs of keeping up a home for yourself and your dependent(s) or other qualifying individuals.

Nonwage Income. If you have a large amount of nonwage income, such as interest or dividends, you should consider making estimated tax payments using Form 1040-ES. Otherwise, you may find that you owe additional tax at the end of the year.

Two-Earner/Two-Jobs. If you have a working spouse or more than one job, figure the total number of allowances you are entitled to claim on all jobs using worksheets from only one Form W-4. This total should be divided among all jobs. Your withholding will usually be most accurate when all allowances are claimed on the W-4 filed for the highest paying job and zero allowances are claimed for the others.

Advance Earned Income Credit. If you are eligible for this credit, you can receive it added to your paycheck throughout the year. For details, get Form W-5 from your employer.

Check Your Withholding. After your W-4 takes effect, you can use **Pub. 919,** Is My Withholding Correct for 1992?, to see how the dollar amount you are having withheld compares to your estimated total annual tax. Call 1-800-829-3676 to order this publication. Check your local telephone directory for the IRS assistance number if you need further help.

Personal Allowances Worksheet

For 1992, the value of your personal exemption(s) is reduced if your income is over $105,250 ($157,900 if married filing jointly, $131,550 if head of household, or $78,950 if married filing separately). Get Pub. 919 for details.

A   Enter "1" for **yourself** if no one else can claim you as a dependent . . . . **A** _1_

B   Enter "1" if:
- You are single and have only one job; or
- You are married, have only one job, and your spouse does not work; or
- Your wages from a second job or your spouse's wages (or the total of both) are $1,000 or less.

B ____

C   Enter "1" for your **spouse.** But, you may choose to enter -0- if you are married and have either a working spouse or more than one job (this may help you avoid having too little tax withheld) . . . . **C** ____

D   Enter number of **dependents** (other than your spouse or yourself) whom you will claim on your tax return . . . . **D** ____

E   Enter "1" if you will file as **head of household** on your tax return (see conditions under "Head of Household," above) . **E** ____

F   Enter "1" if you have at least $1,500 of **child or dependent care expenses** for which you plan to claim a credit . **F** ____

G   Add lines A through F and enter total here. **Note:** *This amount may be different from the number of exemptions you claim on your return* ▶ **G** ____

For accuracy, do all worksheets that apply.
- If you plan to **itemize or claim adjustments to income** and want to reduce your withholding, see the Deductions and Adjustments Worksheet on page 2.
- If you are **single** and have **more than one job** and your combined earnings from all jobs exceed $29,000 **OR** if you are **married** and have a **working spouse or more than one job,** and the combined earnings from all jobs exceed $50,000, see the Two-Earner/Two-Job Worksheet on page 2 if you want to avoid having too little tax withheld.
- If **neither** of the above situations applies, **stop here** and enter the number from line G on line 5 of Form W-4 below.

- - - - - - - - - **Cut here and give the certificate to your employer. Keep the top portion for your records.** - - - - - - - - -

Form **W-4** Department of the Treasury Internal Revenue Service	**Employee's Withholding Allowance Certificate** ▶ **For Privacy Act and Paperwork Reduction Act Notice, see reverse.**	OMB No. 1545-0010 19**92**

1 Type or print your first name and middle initial   _Jane J._   Last name _Doe_ | **2** Your social security number _123-45-6798_

Home address (number and street or rural route)   _2824 Spring Street_

3 ☐ Single ☒ Married ☐ Married, but withhold at higher Single rate.
Note: *If married, but legally separated, or spouse is a nonresident alien, check the Single box.*

City or town, state, and ZIP code   _Anytown, USA   00000_

4 If your last name differs from that on your social security card, check here and call 1-800-772-1213 for more information . ▶ ☐

5 Total number of allowances you are claiming (from line G above or from the Worksheets on back if they apply)   **5** _2_

6 Additional amount, if any, you want deducted from each paycheck   **6** $ ____

7 I claim exemption from withholding and I certify that I meet **ALL** of the following conditions for exemption:
- Last year I had a right to a refund of **ALL** Federal income tax withheld because I had **NO** tax liability; **AND**
- This year I expect a refund of **ALL** Federal income tax withheld because I expect to have **NO** tax liability; **AND**
- This year if my income exceeds $600 and includes nonwage income, another person cannot claim me as a dependent.

If you meet all of the above conditions, enter the year effective and "EXEMPT" here . . ▶ **7** 19

8 Are you a full-time student? **(Note:** *Full-time students are not automatically exempt.)* . . . . **8** ☐ Yes ☒ No

Under penalties of perjury, I certify that I am entitled to the number of withholding allowances claimed on this certificate or entitled to claim exempt status.

Employee's signature ▶ _Jane J. Doe_   Date ▶ _March 16_   , 19

9 Employer's name and address (Employer: Complete 9 and 11 only if sending to the IRS)   _The Conglomerate Corporation Industrial Park Anytown, USA 00000_ | **10** Office code (optional) | **11** Employer identification number _241-2883_

Cat. No. 10220Q

Figure 5.4   Employee's withholding allowance certificate (Form W-4)

the employee and one for each of the other family members. If both spouses work, then the couple may split the allowances as they see fit.

A detailed discussion of withholding allowances and eligible dependents is beyond the scope of this text, but it should be noted that an employee may claim fewer allowances than the number to which he or she is entitled. Since the amount of tax withheld is only an approximation, the employee may owe additional taxes on April 15, the deadline for filing income tax returns. By claiming fewer allowances, a greater amount is withheld, thus reducing the likelihood of owing additional tax upon filing the return. The government refunds any amount in excess of the taxes the employee owes.

To assist the payroll clerk in computing the amount of income tax to be withheld, the Internal Revenue Service has prepared tables. The table most frequently used is the Wage Bracket Table. This table categorizes employees by the three factors previously mentioned: marital status, gross earnings, and number of withholding allowances. Portions of this table are shown in tables 5.1 and 5.2 (pp. 151–153).

To illustrate the use of these tables, consider a married employee claiming four withholding allowances who is paid biweekly a salary of $1,325. To determine the tax to be withheld, we locate the table entitled Married Persons—Biweekly Payroll (table 5.2) and find the employee's wage bracket in the left column headed "And the wages are." A biweekly salary of $1,325 falls in the wage bracket "at least $1,320 but less than $1,340." We then proceed to the right along this line until we reach the column for four allowances. The amount to be withheld is $112.00.

EXAMPLE 1	Derek Tracy is single and claims one withholding allowance (S–1). His job at the Carson Publishing Company pays $12.22 per hour for a 40 hour workweek. How much income tax was withheld each pay period?
Solution:	The tax to be withheld is found in table 5.1, Single Persons—Weekly Payroll

Gross earnings = $12.22 × 40 = $488.80

The gross earnings lie in the wage bracket of "at least $480 but less than $490." The tax for one allowance is $59.00. ∎

EXAMPLE 2	Perry Watson sells chemical products on a straight commission of 30%. During the last biweekly pay period, his sales were $1,748 for the first week and $2,232 for the second week. Perry's wife works in an office, and they have one child. How much tax should be deducted from Perry's gross earnings if he claims two allowances on his W-4 form?

Table 5.1

SINGLE Persons—**WEEKLY** Payroll Period

(For Wages Paid After February 1992)

And the wages are—		And the number of withholding allowances claimed is—										
At least	But less than	0	1	2	3	4	5	6	7	8	9	10
		The amount of income tax to be withheld shall be—										
$0	$50	$0	$0	$0	$0	$0	$0	$0	$0	$0	$0	$0
50	55	1	0	0	0	0	0	0	0	0	0	0
55	60	2	0	0	0	0	0	0	0	0	0	0
60	65	2	0	0	0	0	0	0	0	0	0	0
65	70	3	0	0	0	0	0	0	0	0	0	0
70	75	4	0	0	0	0	0	0	0	0	0	0
75	80	5	0	0	0	0	0	0	0	0	0	0
80	85	5	0	0	0	0	0	0	0	0	0	0
85	90	6	0	0	0	0	0	0	0	0	0	0
90	95	7	0	0	0	0	0	0	0	0	0	0
95	100	8	1	0	0	0	0	0	0	0	0	0
100	105	8	2	0	0	0	0	0	0	0	0	0
105	110	9	2	0	0	0	0	0	0	0	0	0
110	115	10	3	0	0	0	0	0	0	0	0	0
115	120	11	4	0	0	0	0	0	0	0	0	0
120	125	11	5	0	0	0	0	0	0	0	0	0
125	130	12	5	0	0	0	0	0	0	0	0	0
130	135	13	6	0	0	0	0	0	0	0	0	0
135	140	14	7	0	0	0	0	0	0	0	0	0
140	145	14	8	1	0	0	0	0	0	0	0	0
145	150	15	8	2	0	0	0	0	0	0	0	0
150	155	16	9	3	0	0	0	0	0	0	0	0
155	160	17	10	3	0	0	0	0	0	0	0	0
160	165	17	11	4	0	0	0	0	0	0	0	0
165	170	18	11	5	0	0	0	0	0	0	0	0
170	175	19	12	6	0	0	0	0	0	0	0	0
175	180	20	13	6	0	0	0	0	0	0	0	0
180	185	20	14	7	0	0	0	0	0	0	0	0
185	190	21	14	8	1	0	0	0	0	0	0	0
190	195	22	15	9	2	0	0	0	0	0	0	0
195	200	23	16	9	3	0	0	0	0	0	0	0
200	210	24	17	10	4	0	0	0	0	0	0	0
210	220	25	19	12	5	0	0	0	0	0	0	0
220	230	27	20	13	7	0	0	0	0	0	0	0
230	240	28	22	15	8	2	0	0	0	0	0	0
240	250	30	23	16	10	3	0	0	0	0	0	0
250	260	31	25	18	11	5	0	0	0	0	0	0
260	270	33	26	19	13	6	0	0	0	0	0	0
270	280	34	28	21	14	8	1	0	0	0	0	0
280	290	36	29	22	16	9	3	0	0	0	0	0
290	300	37	31	24	17	11	4	0	0	0	0	0
300	310	39	32	25	19	12	6	0	0	0	0	0
310	320	40	34	27	20	14	7	2	0	0	0	0
320	330	42	35	28	22	15	9	3	0	0	0	0
330	340	43	37	30	23	17	10	3	0	0	0	0
340	350	45	38	31	25	18	12	5	0	0	0	0
350	360	46	40	33	26	20	13	6	0	0	0	0
360	370	48	41	34	28	21	15	8	1	0	0	0
370	380	49	43	36	29	23	16	9	3	0	0	0
380	390	51	44	37	31	24	18	11	4	0	0	0
390	400	52	46	39	32	26	19	12	6	0	0	0
400	410	54	47	40	34	27	21	14	7	1	0	0
410	420	55	49	42	35	29	22	15	9	2	0	0
420	430	57	50	43	37	30	24	17	10	4	0	0
430	440	58	52	45	38	32	25	18	12	5	0	0
440	450	61	53	46	40	33	27	20	13	7	0	0
450	460	63	55	48	41	35	28	21	15	8	1	0
460	470	66	56	49	43	36	30	23	16	10	3	0
470	480	69	58	51	44	38	31	24	18	11	4	0
480	490	72	59	52	46	39	33	26	19	13	6	0
490	500	75	62	54	47	41	34	27	21	14	7	1
500	510	77	65	55	49	42	36	29	22	16	9	2
510	520	80	68	57	50	44	37	30	24	17	10	4
520	530	83	71	58	52	45	39	32	25	19	12	5
530	540	86	73	61	53	47	40	33	27	20	13	7
540	550	89	76	64	55	48	42	35	28	22	15	8
550	560	91	79	67	56	50	43	36	30	23	16	10
560	570	94	82	69	58	51	45	38	31	25	18	11
570	580	97	85	72	60	53	46	39	33	26	19	13
580	590	100	87	75	63	54	48	41	34	28	21	14

Page 28

Table 5.2

MARRIED Persons—**BIWEEKLY** Payroll Period
(For Wages Paid After February 1992)

And the wages are—		And the number of withholding allowances claimed is—										
At least	But less than	0	1	2	3	4	5	6	7	8	9	10
		The amount of income tax to be withheld shall be—										
$0	$235	$0	$0	$0	$0	$0	$0	$0	$0	$0	$0	$0
235	240	1	0	0	0	0	0	0	0	0	0	0
240	245	2	0	0	0	0	0	0	0	0	0	0
245	250	3	0	0	0	0	0	0	0	0	0	0
250	260	4	0	0	0	0	0	0	0	0	0	0
260	270	5	0	0	0	0	0	0	0	0	0	0
270	280	7	0	0	0	0	0	0	0	0	0	0
280	290	8	0	0	0	0	0	0	0	0	0	0
290	300	10	0	0	0	0	0	0	0	0	0	0
300	310	11	0	0	0	0	0	0	0	0	0	0
310	320	13	0	0	0	0	0	0	0	0	0	0
320	330	14	1	0	0	0	0	0	0	0	0	0
330	340	16	2	0	0	0	0	0	0	0	0	0
340	350	17	4	0	0	0	0	0	0	0	0	0
350	360	19	5	0	0	0	0	0	0	0	0	0
360	370	20	7	0	0	0	0	0	0	0	0	0
370	380	22	8	0	0	0	0	0	0	0	0	0
380	390	23	10	0	0	0	0	0	0	0	0	0
390	400	25	11	0	0	0	0	0	0	0	0	0
400	410	26	13	0	0	0	0	0	0	0	0	0
410	420	28	14	1	0	0	0	0	0	0	0	0
420	430	29	16	3	0	0	0	0	0	0	0	0
430	440	31	17	4	0	0	0	0	0	0	0	0
440	450	32	19	6	0	0	0	0	0	0	0	0
450	460	34	20	7	0	0	0	0	0	0	0	0
460	470	35	22	9	0	0	0	0	0	0	0	0
470	480	37	23	10	0	0	0	0	0	0	0	0
480	490	38	25	12	0	0	0	0	0	0	0	0
490	500	40	26	13	0	0	0	0	0	0	0	0
500	520	42	29	15	2	0	0	0	0	0	0	0
520	540	45	32	18	5	0	0	0	0	0	0	0
540	560	48	35	21	8	0	0	0	0	0	0	0
560	580	51	38	24	11	0	0	0	0	0	0	0
580	600	54	41	27	14	1	0	0	0	0	0	0
600	620	57	44	30	17	4	0	0	0	0	0	0
620	640	60	47	33	20	7	0	0	0	0	0	0
640	660	63	50	36	23	10	0	0	0	0	0	0
660	680	66	53	39	26	13	0	0	0	0	0	0
680	700	69	56	42	29	16	3	0	0	0	0	0
700	720	72	59	45	32	19	6	0	0	0	0	0
720	740	75	62	48	35	22	9	0	0	0	0	0
740	760	78	65	51	38	25	12	0	0	0	0	0
760	780	81	68	54	41	28	15	1	0	0	0	0
780	800	84	71	57	44	31	18	4	0	0	0	0
800	820	87	74	60	47	34	21	7	0	0	0	0
820	840	90	77	63	50	37	24	10	0	0	0	0
840	860	93	80	66	53	40	27	13	0	0	0	0
860	880	96	83	69	56	43	30	16	3	0	0	0
880	900	99	86	72	59	46	33	19	6	0	0	0
900	920	102	89	75	62	49	36	22	9	0	0	0
920	940	105	92	78	65	52	39	25	12	0	0	0
940	960	108	95	81	68	55	42	28	15	2	0	0
960	980	111	98	84	71	58	45	31	18	5	0	0
980	1,000	114	101	87	74	61	48	34	21	8	0	0
1,000	1,020	117	104	90	77	64	51	37	24	11	0	0
1,020	1,040	120	107	93	80	67	54	40	27	14	0	0
1,040	1,060	123	110	96	83	70	57	43	30	17	3	0
1,060	1,080	126	113	99	86	73	60	46	33	20	6	0
1,080	1,100	129	116	102	89	76	63	49	36	23	9	0
1,100	1,120	132	119	105	92	79	66	52	39	26	12	0
1,120	1,140	135	122	108	95	82	69	55	42	29	15	2
1,140	1,160	138	125	111	98	85	72	58	45	32	18	5
1,160	1,180	141	128	114	101	88	75	61	48	35	21	8
1,180	1,200	144	131	117	104	91	78	64	51	38	24	11
1,200	1,220	147	134	120	107	94	81	67	54	41	27	14
1,220	1,240	150	137	123	110	97	84	70	57	44	30	17
1,240	1,260	153	140	126	113	100	87	73	60	47	33	20
1,260	1,280	156	143	129	116	103	90	76	63	50	36	23
1,280	1,300	159	146	132	119	106	93	79	66	53	39	26

Page 34

Table 5.2 Continued

MARRIED Persons—BIWEEKLY Payroll Period
(For Wages Paid After February 1992)

And the wages are—		And the number of withholding allowances claimed is—										
At least	But less than	0	1	2	3	4	5	6	7	8	9	10
		The amount of income tax to be withheld shall be—										
$1,300	$1,320	$162	$149	$135	$122	$109	$96	$82	$69	$56	$42	$29
1,320	1,340	165	152	138	125	112	99	85	72	59	45	32
1,340	1,360	168	155	141	128	115	102	88	75	62	48	35
1,360	1,380	171	158	144	131	118	105	91	78	65	51	38
1,380	1,400	174	161	147	134	121	108	94	81	68	54	41
1,400	1,420	177	164	150	137	124	111	97	84	71	57	44
1,420	1,440	180	167	153	140	127	114	100	87	74	60	47
1,440	1,460	183	170	156	143	130	117	103	90	77	63	50
1,460	1,480	186	173	159	146	133	120	106	93	80	66	53
1,480	1,500	189	176	162	149	136	123	109	96	83	69	56
1,500	1,520	192	179	165	152	139	126	112	99	86	72	59
1,520	1,540	196	182	168	155	142	129	115	102	89	75	62
1,540	1,560	202	185	171	158	145	132	118	105	92	78	65
1,560	1,580	207	188	174	161	148	135	121	108	95	81	68
1,580	1,600	213	191	177	164	151	138	124	111	98	84	71
1,600	1,620	219	194	180	167	154	141	127	114	101	87	74
1,620	1,640	224	200	183	170	157	144	130	117	104	90	77
1,640	1,660	230	205	186	173	160	147	133	120	107	93	80
1,660	1,680	235	211	189	176	163	150	136	123	110	96	83
1,680	1,700	241	216	192	179	166	153	139	126	113	99	86
1,700	1,720	247	222	197	182	169	156	142	129	116	102	89
1,720	1,740	252	228	203	185	172	159	145	132	119	105	92
1,740	1,760	258	233	208	188	175	162	148	135	122	108	95
1,760	1,780	263	239	214	191	178	165	151	138	125	111	98
1,780	1,800	269	244	220	195	181	168	154	141	128	114	101
1,800	1,820	275	250	225	200	184	171	157	144	131	117	104
1,820	1,840	280	256	231	206	187	174	160	147	134	120	107
1,840	1,860	286	261	236	212	190	177	163	150	137	123	110
1,860	1,880	291	267	242	217	193	180	166	153	140	126	113
1,880	1,900	297	272	248	223	198	183	169	156	143	129	116
1,900	1,920	303	278	253	228	204	186	172	159	146	132	119
1,920	1,940	308	284	259	234	209	189	175	162	149	135	122
1,940	1,960	314	289	264	240	215	192	178	165	152	138	125
1,960	1,980	319	295	270	245	220	196	181	168	155	141	128
1,980	2,000	325	300	276	251	226	201	184	171	158	144	131
2,000	2,020	331	306	281	256	232	207	187	174	161	147	134
2,020	2,040	336	312	287	262	237	212	190	177	164	150	137
2,040	2,060	342	317	292	268	243	218	193	180	167	153	140
2,060	2,080	347	323	298	273	248	224	199	183	170	156	143
2,080	2,100	353	328	304	279	254	229	204	186	173	159	146
2,100	2,120	359	334	309	284	260	235	210	189	176	162	149
2,120	2,140	364	340	315	290	265	240	216	192	179	165	152
2,140	2,160	370	345	320	296	271	246	221	197	182	168	155
2,160	2,180	375	351	326	301	276	252	227	202	185	171	158
2,180	2,200	381	356	332	307	282	257	232	208	188	174	161
2,200	2,220	387	362	337	312	288	263	238	213	191	177	164
2,220	2,240	392	368	343	318	293	268	244	219	194	180	167
2,240	2,260	398	373	348	324	299	274	249	225	200	183	170
2,260	2,280	403	379	354	329	304	280	255	230	205	186	173
2,280	2,300	409	384	360	335	310	285	260	236	211	189	176
2,300	2,320	415	390	365	340	316	291	266	241	217	192	179
2,320	2,340	420	396	371	346	321	296	272	247	222	197	182
2,340	2,360	426	401	376	352	327	302	277	253	228	203	185
2,360	2,380	431	407	382	357	332	308	283	258	233	209	188
2,380	2,400	437	412	388	363	338	313	288	264	239	214	191
2,400	2,420	443	418	393	368	344	319	294	269	245	220	195
2,420	2,440	448	424	399	374	349	324	300	275	250	225	201
2,440	2,460	454	429	404	380	355	330	305	281	256	231	206
2,460	2,480	459	435	410	385	360	336	311	286	261	237	212
2,480	2,500	465	440	416	391	366	341	316	292	267	242	217
2,500	2,520	471	446	421	396	372	347	322	297	273	248	223
2,520	2,540	476	452	427	402	377	352	328	303	278	253	229
2,540	2,560	482	457	432	408	383	358	333	309	284	259	234
2,560	2,580	487	463	438	413	388	364	339	314	289	265	240
2,580	2,600	493	468	444	419	394	369	344	320	295	270	245

$2,600 and over   Use Table 2(b) for a **MARRIED person** on page 26. Also see the instructions on page 24.

Page 35

Solution: Perry's total sales for the pay period are $3,980.

Commissions = $3,980 × 0.30 = $1,194

In the table entitled Married Persons—Biweekly Payroll Period (table 5.2), Perry's tax bracket is "at least $1,180 but less than $1,200." His tax for two allowances is $117.00.   ◼

B. Social Security

The economic depression of the 1930s spawned a number of emergency measures and legislation. Perhaps the most significant of these was the **Federal Insurance Contributions Act** of 1937. Better known as the Social Security Act, it established a fund to provide monthly benefits to retired or disabled workers and to pay burial and survivors' benefits to the surviving family of a deceased worker. A recent amendment to the act provides health insurance benefits under the Medicare Program.

More a compulsory insurance program than a tax, the act requires employers to withhold a percentage of the employee's gross earnings as contributions. These contributions are matched by the employer until the total annual contribution reaches a maximum established by the act. Both the contribution percent and the maximum to be withheld are amended by Congress periodically to liberalize benefits. This is necessary because of the rise in the cost of living and inflation. The contributions of the employee are matched by the employer, and periodically, these sums are deposited with a bank authorized to accept these taxes. Tax tables are furnished by the Internal Revenue Service, or the tax may be computed by multiplying the employee's gross earnings by the appropriate percent. The percent is different for Social Security and for Medicare. In this text the 1992 rates shown in table 5.3 are used.*

Table 5.3	Social Security and Medicare Tax Rates		
	Tax Rate	**Maximum Annual Pay Taxed**	**Maximum Tax per Worker**
Social Security	6.2%	$55,000	$3,410.00
Medicare	1.45%	$130,200	$1,887.90

EXAMPLE 3   Juan Hernandez earns $11.75 for a forty hour workweek. How much was deducted for SSM taxes the second week of February?

Solution: The maximum tax per worker cannot be met in the second week of February, so the combined rate of 7.65% can be used to calculate the deductions.

$11.75 × 40 × 0.0765 = $35.96   ◼

In this chapter, the abbreviation "SSM" will be used for "Social Security and Medicare."

EXAMPLE 4 Wade Taylor is a salesperson whose commission is 18% of net sales with a draw of \$400 per week. Last week, his sales were \$2,100. Assuming the maximum tax per worker has not been reached for either Social Security or Medicare, how much should be deducted?

Solution: The earned commission for the week is $\$2{,}100 \times 0.18 = \$378$; hence, Wade's gross earnings for the week will be the draw of \$400. The SSM taxes on this amount are $\$400 \times 0.0765 = \$30.60$. ■

EXAMPLE 5 Last year the comptroller of the Barrett Corporation was paid a salary of \$84,000. How much was deducted for SSM taxes for the monthly pay period of August?

Solution: An annual salary of \$84,000 amounts to gross earnings of $\$84{,}000 \div 12 = \$7{,}000$ per month. The comptroller's tax per month was:

Social Security
$\$7{,}000 \times 0.062 = \$434.00$ per month. After 7 months, a total of
$\$434.00 \times 7 = \$3{,}038$ will have been deducted. Since the maximum deduction per worker is \$3,410, the deduction for August was $\$3{,}410 - \$3{,}038 = \$372.00$.

Medicare
$\$7{,}000 \times 0.0145 = \$101.50$ per month.
Total SSM deduction for August
$\$372.00 + \$101.50 = \$473.50$ ■

C. Other Deductions

Deductions for Social Security, Medicare, and federal income tax are the main required payroll deductions. Some states may have compulsory deductions for state income tax or disability insurance. Additionally, there may be voluntary deductions made by the employer as a service to the employee. Group insurance premiums, union dues, United States Savings Bonds, credit union loan payments, or contributions to charitable organizations are examples of such deductions. Figure 5.5 shows a sample paycheck stub with deductions listed.

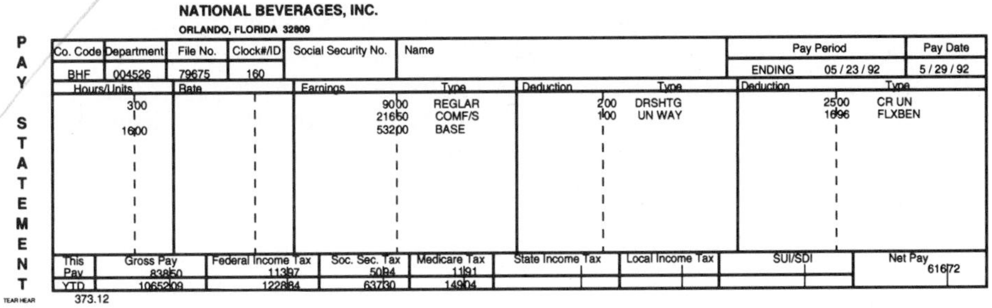
NATIONAL BEVERAGES, INC.
ORLANDO, FLORIDA 32809

PAY STATEMENT

Co. Code	Department	File No.	Clock#/ID	Social Security No.	Name	Pay Period	Pay Date
BHF	004526	79675	160			ENDING 05 / 23 / 92	5 / 29 / 92

Hours/Units	Rate	Earnings	Type	Deduction	Type	Deduction	Type
3 00		90 00	REGLAR	2 00	DRSHTG	25 00	CR UN
		216 50	COMF/S	1 00	UN WAY	16 96	FLXBEN
16 00		532 00	BASE				

	Gross Pay	Federal Income Tax	Soc. Sec. Tax	Medicare Tax	State Income Tax	Local Income Tax	SUI/SDI	Net Pay
This Pay	838 50	113 97	50 94	11 91				616 72
YTD	10652 09	1228 84	637 30	149 04				

TEAR HEAR 373.12

Figure 5.5
Sample paycheck stub

EXAMPLE 6 Harrison Keely is a die-maker who is single and earns $13.15 per hour for a 40 hour workweek. In addition to deduction for federal income tax (S–1) and Social Security, and Medicare, union dues of $9.25 per month are also withheld from his pay. Find Keely's net earnings for a 40 hour workweek if the company pay period is weekly and the maximum FICA deductions have not been met.

Solution:

Gross earnings $= \$13.15 \times 40$		$= \$526.00$
Income tax	$= \$71.00$	
SSM $\$526 \times 0.0765$	$= 40.24$	
Union dues $\$9.25 \times \frac{12}{52}$	$= 2.13$	
Total deductions		$\$113.37$
Net earnings		$\$412.63$

EXAMPLE 7 Charles Patton is paid weekly and earns $8.40 per hour for a 40 hour workweek. He has joined the payroll savings plan and purchases a bond a month for $25.00. He participates in the company group insurance plan, which costs him $65.10 a month. He is classified S–3. Calculate his net earnings for a week in March during which he worked 42 hours.

Solution: The overtime rate is $\$8.40 \times 1\frac{1}{2} = \$12.60$ per hour.

Regular wages	$= \$8.40 \times 40$	$= \$336.00$
Overtime wages	$= \$12.60 \times 2$	$= 25.20$
Gross earnings		$\$361.20$
Federal income tax		$= \$28.00$
SSM	$= \$361.20 \times 0.0765$	$= 27.63$
Savings bond	$= \$25.00 \times \frac{12}{52}$	$= 5.77$
Group insurance	$= \$65.10 \times \frac{12}{52}$	$= 15.02$
Total deductions		$\$ 76.42$
Net earnings		$\$284.78$

EXAMPLE 8 Virginia Krisloff sells cosmetics. She receives a salary of $350.00 per week, plus 5% of all weekly sales in excess of $3,000.00. During the last biweekly pay period, her weekly sales were $3,800.00 and $4,600.00. Virginia is married and claims three allowances for income tax purposes. In addition to Social Security and Medicare, she contributes $22.20 per month to the company retirement plan. To insure her family under the group insurance plans costs $87.00 per month, and Virginia has agreed to a deduction of $2.00 per month as a pledge to the United Fund. Assuming she has not reached the maximum SSM deductions, what were her net earnings for the last pay period?

Solution:

Salary	$= \$350 \times 2$	$= \$700.00$
Commissions	$= \$2,400 \times 0.05$	$= \underline{120.00}$
Gross earnings		$\$820.00$
Income tax (M–3)		$= \$50.00$
SSM	$= \$820 \times 0.0765$	$= 62.73$
Retirement	$= \$22.20 \times \frac{12}{26}$	$= 10.25$
Group Insurance	$= \$87 \times \frac{12}{26}$	$= 40.15$
United Fund	$= 2 \times \frac{12}{26}$	$= \underline{0.92}$
Total deductions		$\underline{\$164.05}$
Net earnings		$\$655.95$

EXERCISES FOR SECTION 5.4

1. Tony Di Salvo is single and claims one withholding allowance. His weekly salary is $314. How much income tax is withheld from his gross earnings?

2. Find the income tax withheld from the biweekly gross earnings of an employee who is married, claims two allowances, and is paid a monthly salary of $2,920.

3. Joanne McMannis is an office manager at the Carleton Company, where she receives a salary of $48,450 per year. She is married with two children, and she claims all four allowances. If the pay period at Carleton is biweekly, how much income tax is withheld from her biweekly gross earnings?

4. Ray Baker earns $6.80 an hour for a 40 hour workweek at the Calvert Manufacturing Company. He is single, claims one allowance, and is paid weekly. Find the amount of income tax withheld for a week during which he worked 47 hours.

5. Accutex Scientific Equipment operates on a biweekly pay period. Richard Thaxton, an employee at Accutex, is married with four children and claims three allowances. He is paid $14.20 for a 40 hour workweek. How much income tax was withheld from his gross earnings for a pay period during which he worked 43 hours the first week and 47 hours the second week?

6. Glenn Darnell sells office furniture on a straight commission of 20% of net sales. He is married with one child and claims three allowances. How much income tax was withheld from his last biweekly gross earnings if he sold $2,340 worth of merchandise the first week and $2,984 the second week?

7. Beverly Morrow is employed by Cory Products Company where she is paid weekly a straight commission of 14% of her net sales. She is single and claims one allowance. Find the amount of income tax withheld from her gross earnings for a week during which she sold $3,142.60 worth of merchandise, with returns of $211.40.

8. Cecil Beamon is paid a biweekly graduated commission of 9% of the first $3,500.00 in net sales and 11.5% of net sales in excess of $3,500.00. He is married with two children and claims four allowances. How much income tax was withheld from his gross earnings for a pay period during which he sold $9,842.40 worth of merchandise, with cancellations and returns of $622.50?

9. The Doyle Company pays its sales personnel a weekly graduated commission of 7% of the first $4,500.00 in net sales and 9% of net sales in excess of $4,500.00. Find the income tax withheld from the gross earnings of a single salesperson claiming two allowances for a week during which sales totaled $5,240.00 with returns of $291.72.

10. Judy Roberts receives a salary of $330.00 per week, plus a commission of 6.25% of net sales. Judy is single and claims one allowance. How much income tax was withheld from her gross earnings for a week during which she had sales of $2,140.50, with returns of $110.80?

11. Nelson's Computer Supplies pays its salespeople $380 a week, plus 9.25% of weekly net sales. If the pay period is biweekly, find the income tax withheld from the gross earnings of a married salesperson claiming three allowances who reported the following sales.

	Total Sales	Returns
Week 1	$1,142.41	$203.72
Week 2	1,003.39	114.78

In the following problems, use the Social Security and Medicare contribution rates of table 5.3 on page 154 when calculating Social Security and Medicare deductions.

12. Ted Lee is paid $579.42 per week. How much is deducted from his gross earnings for SSM taxes each biweekly pay period? How much will Ted have contributed in SSM taxes in a year?

13. Julia Tibbetts is a department manager for the Drexel Company and is paid an annual salary of $50,000. How much is deducted each biweekly pay period from her gross earnings for SSM taxes? For how many pay periods of the year will she contribute to SSM?

14. David Bland, a salesperson, receives a commission of 16% of net sales with a guaranteed draw of $310.00 per week. How much SSM taxes was deducted from his gross earnings for a week during which his net sales totaled $1,242.50?

15. Nancy Miller sells cookware on a biweekly commission basis of 14.5% of net sales with a guaranteed biweekly draw of $575. During the last two-week period, she reported the following sales.

	Total Sales	Returns and Cancellations
Week 1	$2,352.63	$ 72.41
Week 2	$2,411.71	$153.69

How much was deducted for SSM taxes this pay period?

16. Morehouse Metal Works employs Charles McDonald as a machinist. He receives $12.20 per hour for a 40 hour workweek. In addition to deductions for federal income tax (his classification is S–2), Social Security and Medicare, he also has deducted from his weekly gross earnings **a.** union dues of $5.90 per month and **b.** a group insurance payment of $32.14 per month. Find his net earnings for a week during which he worked 42 hours.

17. John Ritch is paid biweekly at Timsco Industries. He is paid $9.90 per hour for a 40 hour workweek. His group insurance payment is $77.42 per month, his union dues are $10.11 per month, and he has $50.00 per pay period deducted from his earnings and deposited with the company credit union. His classification is M–3. Compute his net earnings for the last two-week period, during which he worked 47 hours the first week and 44 hours the second week.

18. Madison's Department Store employs Cheryl Watts as a salesclerk. She is paid biweekly a salary of $360.00 per week, plus a commission of 4.75% of weekly sales in excess of $1,200.00. This pay period she also received a $200 bonus. She is classified M–2. In addition to SSM, she contributes $13.75 per month to the company retirement plan. She also has $82.14 per month for insurance, $5.00 per month for the United Fund, and $8.72 per month for union dues deducted from her earnings. Calculate her net earnings for a pay period during which she sold $1,432.71 worth of merchandise the first week and $1,563.42 the second week.

19. Terry Gilbreath is paid weekly a salary of $325.00, plus a commission of 7.5% of net sales in excess of $1,400.00. He is classified S–3, and in addition to SSM, he contributes $22.72 per month to the company retirement plan. He also has deductions to cover **a.** his union dues of $8.43 per month, **b.** his group insurance payment of $67.15 per month, **c.** his credit union payment of $50.00 per month, and **d.** his United Fund contribution of $10.00 per month. Find his net earnings for a week during which he sold $1,873.17 worth of merchandise, with returns and cancellations totaling $94.12.

20. Ben Darlington earns $34,720.00 per year as a supervisor at the Busbee Corporation. He is classified M–1, and in addition to SSM, he contributes $49.31 per month to the company retirement plan. He also has deductions for **a.** $14.42 per month union dues, **b.** $81.17 per month group insurance, and **c.** $18.75 per month for savings bonds. If the pay period at Busbee is biweekly, find his net earnings for the first pay period in February.

21. The vice president of Holstrum Enterprises is paid $110,500 per year. She is classified M–2. She has deductions from her biweekly earnings to cover **a.** $994.57 in federal income tax withholding; **b.** $387.21 per month for the company retirement plan, in addition to SSM; **c.** $56.25 per month for savings bonds; **d.** $200.00 per month for savings in the credit union; and **e.** $96.82 per month for group insurance. If the pay period at Holstrum is biweekly, what are her net earnings for the first pay period in March? What are her net earnings for the last pay period in November?

Section 5.5   *Employer Contributions, Records, and Reports*

Except for income tax, most payroll deductions are payments for employee benefits. Ordinarily, the employee pays only a portion of the total cost of these benefits; the remainder is paid by the employer. Some employer contributions are required by law, while others are voluntary in the form of fringe benefits to the employee.

A. Social Security

The employer is required to match the Social Security and Medicare contributions of the employee.

EXAMPLE 1   An employee had gross earnings of $536.42 for a weekly pay period in April. Find the total amount to be deposited for Social Security and Medicare.

Solution:
Employee SSM deductions	$= \$536.42 \times 0.0765 = \$41.04$
Employer SSM contributions	$= \underline{41.04}$
Total SSM taxes	$= \$82.08$

B. Federal Unemployment Tax

Employees who lose their jobs or who are temporarily laid off may receive limited compensation through a provision of the Social Security Act. A fund called the

Unemployment Trust Fund has been established from taxes on industry. From this fund, payments are made to unemployed workers either for a limited time period or until reemployment, whichever comes first.

The **federal unemployment tax** is currently 6.2% of the first $7,000 of the employee's gross earnings and is paid entirely by the employer. However, most states also have unemployment tax laws, and an employer can credit state unemployment taxes against the federal tax up to a maximum of 5.4% of the first $7,000. In other words, if the state tax exceeds 5.4% of the first $7,000, the employer pays the state tax plus a federal tax of 0.8%. If the state tax is less than 5.4% of the first $7,000, then the combined federal and state tax paid by the employer is 6.2% of the first $7,000. Each state sets its own tax rate. In many states, the lower the company's unemployment rate, the lower the tax.

E X A M P L E 2 The K & C Company is located in a state that has a standard unemployment tax of 6.3% of the first $7,000 of gross earnings of each employee. However, as a result of favorable employment experience, the current tax rate for the K & C Company is 5.7%. If the company employed 36 people last year and all 36 employees earned in excess of $7,000, calculate the total unemployment taxes paid by the employer.

Solution: The state tax is $7,000 × 0.057 = $399 per person. Since the state tax is more than 5.4% of $7,000 per person, the employer must pay the state tax plus a federal tax of 0.8% of $7,000 = $56 per person.

State tax	= $399 × 36 =	$14,364
Federal tax	= $ 56 × 36 =	2,016
Total unemployment tax	=	$16,380

C. Group Life and Health Insurance

A common employee fringe benefit is **group insurance.** Under a master policy issued to the company, employees may be insured for life insurance, hospitalization, surgery, and other medical expenses. In addition, most policies extend the health benefits to the employee's family, if the employee wishes to contract for this option. Group insurance is usually available without medical examination and is less expensive than individual insurance for two reasons. First, the policy is sold to a group, thus reducing paperwork and administrative expenses, and second, it is customary for the employer to pay a portion of the cost. The employer's share of the insurance premium varies from company to company. Some employers pay the entire premium; others pay a percentage, say 50%. A common arrangement is for the employer to pay the employee's premium while the employee, in turn, pays the cost of insuring his or her family. Group insurance is discussed again in chapter 15.

EXAMPLE 3   The Bradford Dry Goods Company has a group insurance plan whereby each employee is covered under a group health plan. In addition, each employee is insured for $5,000 term life insurance except the officers of the company, who are insured for $12,000. The premiums are as follows:

Life insurance $0.68 per $1,000.00 per month
Medical
    Employee only $35.42 per month
    Dependents only $86.15 per month

The company has agreed to pay for the cost of the employee benefits; the employee must pay for any dependents. If the company has 42 employees and 4 officers, and if 24 of the 28 married employees elect to insure their families, what is **a.** the total monthly premium and **b.** the cost to the employer?

Solution: The life insurance costs $0.68 \times 5 = $3.40 per month for $5,000 insurance and $0.68 \times 12 = $8.16 for $12,000 of coverage.

Life insurance premiums		
Officers ($8.16 \times 4)	$ 32.64	
Other employees ($3.40 \times 42)	142.80	
Subtotal		$175.44
Medical premium		
Employee ($35.42 \times 46)	$1,629.32	
Dependents ($86.15 \times 24)	2,067.60	
Subtotal		$3,696.92
Total monthly premium		$3,872.36
Cost to the employer ($1,629.32 + $175.44)		$1,804.76

D. Records and Reports

Employers are required by the Fair Labor Standards Act to keep accurate employee records that include the following information:

Identifying information Employee's full name, address, Social Security number, birth date, sex, and occupation

Hours (wage earners) Time and day of week when the workweek begins, hours worked each day, total hours worked each workweek

Earnings Basis on which earnings are paid, regular hourly rate, total regular earnings, total overtime earnings, all additions to or deductions from the employee's earnings for each pay period

Figure 5.6
Earnings Record

QTR	EARN-INGS	DEDUCTIONS					NET PAID
		FICA	WITH-HLDG	LO-CAL	INS	UNION DUES	
1st	8433.40	645.13	1369.00		279.50	57.00	6082.77
2nd							
3rd							
4th							
Tot							

NAME _____   EXEMPTIONS _1_
ADDRESS _____ TEL. _____
S.S. NO. _____ CLOCK NO. ___ SEX ___ SINGLE ✓MARRIED ___
DATE BORN ____ DATE EMPLOYED ___ HRS. PER DAY ___ PER WK. ___
POSITION ___ DATE TERMINATED ____ REMARKS _____
RATE: DATE ____ $ _14.90_ PER _hr._ DATE _____ $ _____ PER ____

FIRST QUARTER – 19_____

PAY PERIOD	REGULAR TIME		OVER TIME		TOTAL EARNINGS	NON-TAXABLE SICK PAY ETC.	AMT TAXABLE	DEDUCTIONS							NET EARNINGS	
	TIME	RATE	HRS	RATE				FICA	WITH-HOLDING	LO-CAL	INS	UNION DUES			AMOUNT	DATE PAID
JAN. 4-8	40	14.90	8	22.35	774.80			59.27	114.00		21.50	19.00			554.03	1-8
11-15	40		8		774.80			59.27	114.00		21.50				553.03	1-15
18-22	40		8		774.80			59.27	114.00		21.50				553.03	1-22
25-29	40				596.00			45.59	90.00		21.50				438.91	1-29
FEB. 1-5	40				596.00			45.59	90.00		21.50	19.00			419.91	2-5
8-12	32				476.80			36.48	58.00		21.50				360.82	2-12
15-19	32				476.80			36.48	58.00		21.50				360.82	2-19
22-26	40		4	29.80	715.20			54.71	124.00		21.50				514.99	2-26
MAR. 1-5	40		8		774.80			59.27	114.00		21.50	19.00			534.03	3-5
8-12	40		4		685.40			52.43	115.00		21.50				496.47	3-12
15-19	40				596.00			45.59	90.00		21.50				438.91	3-19
22-26	40				596.00			45.59	90.00		21.50				438.91	3-26
29-2	40				596.00			45.59	90.00		21.50				438.91	4-2
TOTAL QTR.	504		40		8433.40			645.13	1369.00		279.50	57.00			6082.77	

Earnings Record

One method of recording this information is an employee earnings record. A sample earnings record is shown in figure 5.6. Often, this form has quarterly totals because quarterly reports are required by federal and state governments. The calendar quarters of a year are January 1 to March 31, April 1 to June 30, July 1 to September 30, and October 1 to December 31.

The Employer's Quarterly Tax Return (Form 941) is an example of a quarterly report required by the federal government. (See figure 5.7.) Deductions for Social Security, Medicare and federal income tax are reported on this form. Also, the employer must remit to the United States Treasury Department (through a Federal Reserve Bank or any commercial bank authorized to receive federal taxes) the SSM taxes levied on him or her as an employer, the SSM taxes withheld from employees' wages, and the federal income tax deducted from employees' wages. The frequency of these deposits depends on the amount of taxes withheld. The rules for deposits are given in the instructions for Form 941.

Figure 5.7
Employer's quarterly
Federal Tax Return
(Form 941)

Form **941**
(Rev. January 1991)
Department of the Treasury
Internal Revenue Service

4141

Employer's Quarterly Federal Tax Return

▶ See Circular E for more information concerning employment tax returns.

Please type or print.

OMB No. 1545-0029
Expires: 5-31-93

Your name, address, employer identification number, and calendar quarter of return. (If not correct, please change.)

Name (as distinguished from trade name)
John Norton

Date quarter ended
March

Trade name, if any
Norton Hydraulics

Employer identification number
68-1592041

Address and ZIP code
P.O. Box 1784, Riverside, Illinois, 60546

T	
FF	
FD	
FP	
I	
T	

If address is different from prior return, check here ▶ ☐

1 1 1 1 1 1 1 1 1 1 1   2   3 3 3 3 3 3   4 4 4

5 5 5   6   7   8 8 8 8 8 8   9 9   10 10 10 10 10 10 10 10 10 10

If you do not have to file returns in the future, check here . . . ☐   Date final wages paid . . .

If you are a seasonal employer, see **Seasonal employers** on page 2 and check here . ▶ ☐

1a Number of employees (except household) employed in the pay period that includes March 12th	**1a**	8	
b If you are a subsidiary corporation AND your parent corporation files a consolidated Form 1120, enter parent corporation employer identification number (EIN) ▶ **1b** ☐ –			
2 Total wages and tips subject to withholding, plus other compensation	**2**	$64,216	00
3 Total income tax withheld from wages, tips, pensions, annuities, sick pay, gambling, etc. . .	**3**	11,558	00
4 Adjustment of withheld income tax for preceding quarters of calendar year (see instructions) .	**4**		
5 Adjusted total of income tax withheld (line 3 as adjusted by line 4—see instructions) .	**5**	11,558	00
6a Taxable social security wages **(Complete line 7)** $ 64,216 00 × 12.4% (.124) =	**6a**	7,962	78
b Taxable social security tips $ × 12.4% (.124) =	**6b**		
7 Taxable Medicare wages and tips . . . . . $ 64,216 00 × 2.9% (.029) =	**7**	1,862	26
8 Total social security and Medicare taxes (add lines 6a, 6b, and 7)	**8**	9,825	04
9 Adjustment of social security and Medicare taxes (see instructions for required explanation) .	**9**		
10 Adjusted total of social security and Medicare taxes (line 8 as adjusted by line 9—see instructions)	**10**	9,825	04
11 Backup withholding (see instructions)	**11**		
12 Adjustment of backup withholding tax for preceding quarters of calendar year	**12**		
13 Adjusted total of backup withholding (line 11 as adjusted by line 12)	**13**		
14 **Total taxes** (add lines 5, 10, and 13)	**14**	21,383	04
15 Advance earned income credit (EIC) payments made to employees, if any	**15**		
16 Net taxes (subtract line 15 from line 14). **This should equal line IV below** (plus line IV of Schedule A (Form 941) if you have treated backup withholding as a separate liability) . . .	**16**	21,383	04
17 **Total deposits for quarter,** including overpayment applied from a prior quarter, from your records.	**17**	21,383	04
18 **Balance due** (subtract line 17 from line 16). This should be less than $500. Pay to IRS . . .	**18**	0	00
19 **Overpayment,** if line 17 is more than line 16, enter here ▶ $ _____ and check if to be:			

☐ Applied to next return   **OR**   ☐ Refunded.

Record of Federal Tax Liability (You must complete if line 16 is $500 or more and Schedule B is not attached.) See instructions before checking these boxes.
Check only if you made deposits using the 95% rule ☐   Check only if you are a first time 3-banking-day depositor. . . . ▶ ☐

Show tax liability here, **not deposits.** IRS gets deposit data from FTD coupons.

Date wages paid		First month of quarter		Second month of quarter		Third month of quarter
1st through 3rd	A	$3,549.70	I	$3,510.17	Q	$3,590.27
4th through 7th	B		J		R	
8th through 11th	C		K		S	
12th through 15th	D		L		T	
16th through 19th	E	3,578.46	M	3,589.28	U	3,565.16
20th through 22nd	F		N		V	
23rd through 25th	G		O		W	
26th through the last	H		P		X	
Total liability for month	I	$7,128.16	II	$7,099.45	III	$7,155.43
IV Total for quarter (add lines **I, II,** and **III**). This should equal line 16 above . . . . . . ▶						$21,383.04

Do **NOT** Show Federal Tax Deposits Here

Sign Here

Under penalties of perjury, I declare that I have examined this return, including accompanying schedules and statements, and to the best of my knowledge and belief, it is true, correct, and complete.

Signature ▶ *John Norton*

Print Your Name and Title John Norton, Pres.

Date April 15

For Paperwork Reduction Act Notice, see page 2.

EXERCISES FOR SECTION 5.5

Use table 5.3 when calculating Social Security and Medicare deductions.

1. Thelma Baxter earns a weekly salary of $586.42. How much total SSM taxes per week (employee deduction plus employer contribution) will be deposited for? What total amount will be deposited for in one year?

2. An employee has gross earnings of $29,450 per year. How much total SSM taxes per biweekly pay period (employee deduction plus employer contribution) is deposited for? What total amount is deposited for in one year?

3. Everett Hawkins earns $72,800 per year as the vice president of Alco, Inc. Find the total SSM taxes per week (employee deduction plus employer contribution) to be deposited for during February. How much total tax will be deposited for the year?

4. Carol Paige is a branch manager at Pittman Industries. She is paid $58,500 per year, and the pay period is biweekly. Find the total SSM taxes per pay period (employee deduction plus employer contribution) deposited for during March. How much total tax will be deposited for the year?

5. Sterling Imports is located in a state that has a standard unemployment tax of 5.2% of the first $7,000 of gross earnings of each employee. Because of favorable employment experience, the state tax rate for Sterling is 4.2%. The company employs 43 people, and all of the employees earn more than $7,000 per year. Find the total unemployment taxes paid by the company.

6. Superior Plastics pays a state unemployment tax of 5.9% of the first $7,000 of gross earnings of each employee. The company employs 57 people, and all 57 employees earn in excess of $7,000 per year. How much total unemployment tax does Superior pay?

7. Find the total federal unemployment tax paid by a company that has 23 employees, each earning more than $7,000 per year, if the state unemployment tax is 4.4% of the first $7,000 earned by each employee.

8. The Drewfield Company employs 18 people, and each employee earns more than $7,000 per year. Last year, the company paid a total of $5,670 in federal unemployment tax. How much total state unemployment tax was paid?

9. The Simpson Machinery Company provides group insurance plans for its employees. Each employee is insured for $10,000 of term life insurance at a cost of $0.72 per $1,000 per month, and each officer of the company is insured for an additional $10,000 at the same rate. Also, each employee is covered under a health insurance plan that costs $21.54 per month for the employee only, plus $67.20 per month for dependents. The company has 37 employees, 3 of whom are officers, and 24 employees elect to insure dependents. If the company pays only for the cost of employee benefits, find **a.** the total monthly insurance premium and **b.** the monthly cost to the employer.

10. A company has group insurance plans for its employees for life insurance, medical insurance, and disability insurance. Each officer of the company receives $15,000 of life insurance, and all other employees receive a $10,000 policy. Every employee is provided disability insurance, and each employee is covered under a medical plan that costs $38.15 per month for the employee only, plus $65.60 per month for dependents. The cost of the life insurance is $0.92 per $1,000 per month, and the monthly disability premium is $12.82 per month. If there are 78 employees, 7 of whom are officers, and 56 employees elect to cover dependents on the medical plan, find the monthly cost to the employer if the employer pays for **a.** all life insurance, 50% of all disability insurance, and all medical insurance for each employee, excluding dependent coverage; and **b.** all disability insurance, all life insurance, all medical insurance for each employee, and 50% of the cost of dependent medical coverage.

Bank Statement Reconciliation

A. Checking Accounts

Most businesses and individuals prefer to pay their obligations by check. There are two reasons for this: (1) checks are safer than cash, and (2) checks provide written legal receipts of transactions.

A **checking account** is a service provided by a bank whereby funds of a business, institution, or an individual are placed in a bank for safekeeping and for future use. The owner of a checking account is called the **depositor.** A **check** is a written order directing the bank to pay a specified amount of money to a specified party, called the **payee.** A typical check is shown in figure 5.8.

Figure 5.8
Sample check

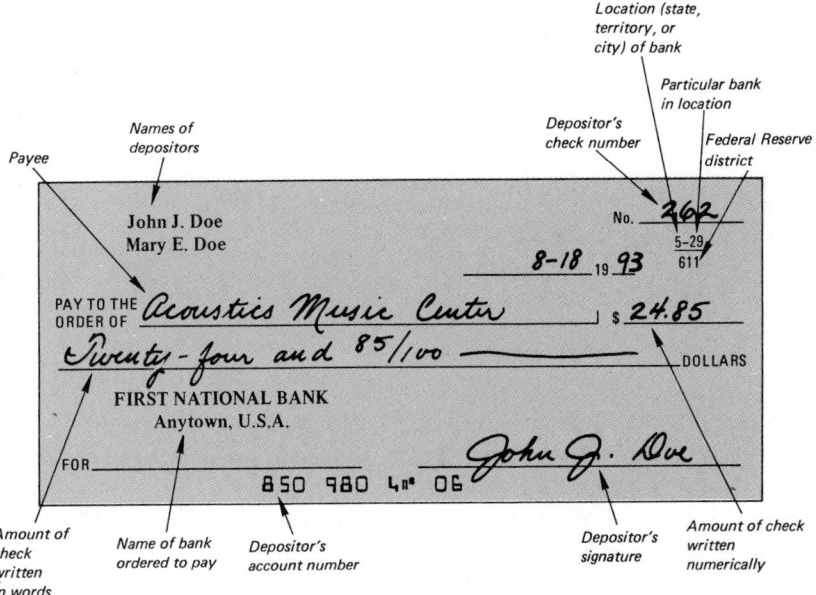

The act of placing funds in a checking account is called a **deposit.** Deposits are accompanied by a deposit slip, which classifies the deposit funds according to coin, currency, or checks. Checks are usually listed on the deposit slip according to bank number, an identification number located in the upper right corner of the check. An example of a completed deposit slip is shown in figure 5.9.

Before the payee can cash or deposit a check, it should be endorsed. An **endorsement** provides written instructions for the disposition of the funds. An endorsement can direct the bank to (1) pay the amount of the check to the payee (a blank endorsement), (2) deposit the amount of the check in the payee's checking account (restrictive endorsement), or (3) pay the amount of the check to a third party (special endorsement). These kinds of endorsements are illustrated in figure 5.10. The blank endorsement should not be executed until the payee is ready to cash

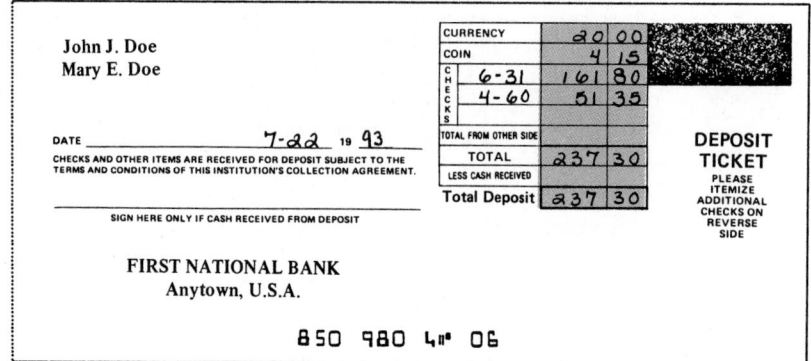

Figure 5.9
Completed deposit slip

(a)

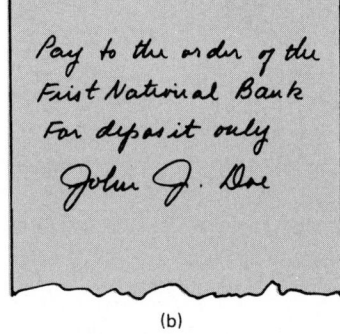

(b)

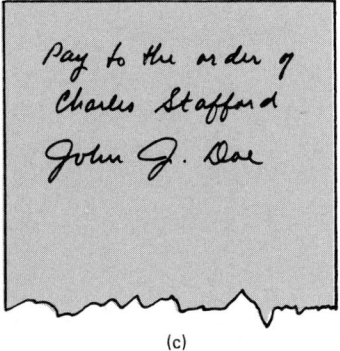

(c)

Figure 5.10
The three types of endorsements

the check because a check with a blank endorsement that is lost or stolen can be cashed by another person, who simply endorses the check below the payee's signature.

Both the depositor and the bank keep a record of all transactions (checks written, deposits made, etc.) within the account. The record maintained by the depositor is on a **check stub or check register.** (See figure 5.11.) Beginning with the current amount of money in the checking account, called the **balance,** deposits are added to the balance, and written checks are subtracted from the balance.

Figure 5.11
Check register

PLEASE BE SURE TO DEDUCT ANY PER CHECK CHARGES OR SERVICE CHARGES THAT MAY APPLY TO YOUR ACCOUNT

CHECK NUMBER	DATE	CHECKS ISSUED TO OR DESCRIPTION OF DEPOSIT	(–) AMOUNT OF CHECK	√ T	(–) CHECK FEE (if any)	(+) AMOUNT OF DEPOSIT	BALANCE
							1216 47
415	5/30	To/For City Electric Co.	185 16				$ 1031 31
	6/1	To/For Deposit				973 80	$ 2005 11
416	6/10	To/For Brooks Wholesale Plumbing	216 75				$ 1788 36
417	6/10	To/For Stinson's Sheet Metal Co.	101 40				$ 1686 96
		To/For					$
		To/For					$

EXAMPLE 1   As of February 19, the Reffitt Company had a balance of $4,692.17 in its bank checking account. On February 20, a deposit of $316.40 was made, and a check was written in the amount of $172.95. What was the balance in the company checking account as of February 20?

Solution:
$4,692.17	Balance on February 19
+ 316.40	Deposit on February 20 *credit*
5,008.57	Total
− 172.95	Check written on February 20 *debit*
$4,835.62	Balance as of February 20

The record of checks and deposits maintained by the bank is the **bank statement.** Periodically (usually monthly), a copy of the bank statement is sent to the depositor. The bank statement indicates the balance at the beginning of the period; provides an account of deposits, checks, fees, and miscellaneous credits recorded by the bank for the period; and gives the balance in the account at the end of the period. A typical bank statement is shown in figure 5.12.

The balance on the bank statement (the bank balance) at the end of a period seldom agrees with the balance shown on the check stub or check register (the checkbook balance). This may be due to an arithmetic error by either party, but more often it is the result of one or more of the following:

1. **Outstanding checks** Checks written on the account and subtracted on the check stub or check register that have not yet been received by the bank and hence are not listed on the bank statement.   *or cleared*

2. **Unrecorded deposits** Deposits that are added to the balance on the check register that have not yet been recorded on the bank statement.

3. **Overdrafts** Checks written on a checking account when there are insufficient funds in the account to pay the payee. If a depositor receives a check from a third party and submits it to the bank for deposit in his or her account, and if the bank is unable to collect the funds, then the amount is deducted from the depositor's account, and the check is returned to the depositor.

4. **Miscellaneous charges or credits** Credits or fees on the bank statement that are not recorded on the check register. Many banking institutions now pay interest on funds in a checking account, and this interest appears as a credit on the statement. Fees on the statement could include charges for providing the checking account service (service charges), charges for the printing of new checks, transactions at an automated teller machine (ATM), charges for overdrafts, or corrections of previously undetected bank errors.

B. Reconciliation

When the bank balance and the checkbook balance are not in agreement, the depositor should attempt to **reconcile** the account. This is accomplished as follows:

Figure 5.12
Typical bank statement

	ACCOUNT NUMBER
	1-01138
	7-20-93
	STATEMENT DATE

Johnson Drug Store
101 Main Street
Anytown, U.S.A.

BALANCE LAST STATEMENT	CHECKS		DEPOSITS		SERVICE CHARGE	BALANCE THIS STATEMENT
	NO	TOTAL AMOUNT	NO	TOTAL AMOUNT		
942.81	13	2,044.85	4	2,226.70	2.75	1,121.91

DATE	CHECKS AND DEBIT CHARGES				DEPOSITS & CREDITS	BALANCE
	CHECK NO.	AMOUNT	CHECK NO.	AMOUNT		
6-23	111	14.65	109	38.40	623.17	1,512.93
6-25	112	101.60				1,411.33
7-1		28.75 RT			402.70	1,785.28
7-8	115	33.50				1,751.78
7-9	108	472.70			602.20	1,881.28
7-12	114	114.78	110	192.80		1,573.70
7-12	102	321.40	116	50.00		1,202.30
7-15	117	66.80	119	73.40		1,062.10
7-16		2.75 SC	121	536.07	598.63	1,121.91

CODES			
CM-CREDIT MEMO DC-DEPOSIT CORRECTION	DM-DEBIT MEMO EC-ERROR CORRECTION	RT-RETURN CHECK SC-SERVICE CHARGE	RC-RETURN CHECK CHARGE

SHOULD FURTHER INFORMATION BE HELPFUL PLEASE REFER TO YOUR ACCOUNT NO. WHEN MAKING INQUIRIES.
PLEASE EXAMINE AT ONCE. IF NO ERROR IS REPORTED IN TEN DAYS THE ACCOUNT WILL BE CONSIDERED CORRECT.

To the Bank Balance

1. Add the total of all unrecorded deposits.
2. Subtract the total of all outstanding checks.

To the Checkbook Balance

1. Subtract the total of
   a. All previously deposited overdrafts.
   b. All miscellaneous charges.
2. Add the total of all interest and miscellaneous credits.

Figure 5.13
Format for bank
statement reconciliation

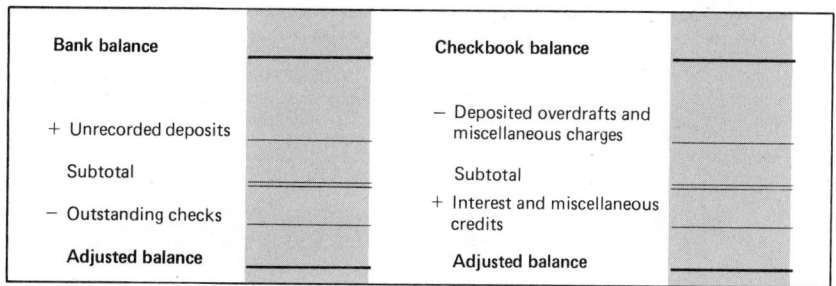

The result of this arithmetic is an adjusted bank balance and an adjusted checkbook balance. These two balances will be identical, provided that all transactions were recorded correctly and that there were no mathematical errors. The adjusted balance represents the true balance in the checking account, and the check register should be corrected to reflect the adjusted balance. A format for bank statement reconciliation is shown in figure 5.13.

E X A M P L E 2 The bank statement of Dunn's Flower & Gift Shop indicated a balance of $794.15. The shop's checkbook balance was $945.60. For the preceding period, there was an unrecorded deposit of $424.18, service charges of $3.80, and outstanding checks of $100.64, $39.95, $12.48, and $123.46. Reconcile the checking account.

Solution: The total of the outstanding checks is $276.53. Using the format of figure 5.13,

Bank balance	$ 794.15	Checkbook balance	$945.60
Unrecorded deposit	+ 424.18	Service charge	− 3.80
Subtotal	1,218.33	Subtotal	941.80
Outstanding checks	− 276.53	Interest and misc. credits	+ 0.00
Adjusted balance	$941.80	Adjusted balance	$941.80

If the adjusted balances fail to agree following a reconciliation attempt, there has been an error. This may be an error on the part of the bank, but more likely it is a mistake by the depositor. The most common errors include adding or subtracting incorrectly, copying numbers incorrectly, or failing to record a check or deposit. Checks, check stubs, and deposit slips should be examined for these errors, and a new reconciliation statement prepared. If, after repeated attempts, the account cannot be reconciled, the depositor should seek assistance from the bank. ■

E X A M P L E   3   Reconcile the following checking account. Items on the register marked with a check (✓) indicate items that appeared on the previous month's bank statement. (The code SC on the bank statement means **"service charge"**; the code RT means **"returned check,"** that is, a previously deposited overdraft; and the code INT means **"interest credited."**)

Bank Statement

Checks and Debits				Deposits	Date	Balance
Check No.	Amount	Check No.	Amount			
					9–30	924.16
613	64.46				10–2	859.70
616	124.30				10–11	735.40
615	58.70		74.36		10–14	602.34
			RT			
617	515.00			3.02 INT	10–15	90.36
				189.60	10–16	279.96
618	16.60		2.60 SC		10–24	260.76

Check Register

Date	Check No.	Check Issued to	Amount	✓	Deposits	Balance
						1,095.16
9–24	612	J.R. Discon	43.20	✓		1,051.96
9–26	613	Armis Co.	64.46			987.50
9–27	614	Security Alarms	127.80	✓		859.70
10–8	615	Jackson Supply	58.70			801.00
10–10	616	Farmington Co.	124.30			676.70
10–11	617	Payroll	515.00		189.60	351.30
10–20	618	Terrell's Off. Supply	16.60			334.70
10–25	619	Lawson Lumber Co.	122.40			212.30

Solution:

Bank balance	$260.76	Checkbook balance	$212.30
Outstanding check	− 122.40	Returned check	− 74.36
		Service charge	− 2.60
		Interest	+ 3.02
Adjusted balance	$138.36	Adjusted balance	$138.36

■

EXAMPLE 4   Mary Jo Reynolds was unable to reconcile her checking account. Her checkbook stubs, bank statement, and reconciliation attempt follow. What went wrong?

Mary's Check Stubs

672.12
29.07
———
643.05
92.16
———
0.89

145	IF TAX DEDUCTIBLE CHECK HERE ☐	
	$ 29.07	
	3-7 19 93	
To	Allied Dept. Store.	
For	Bedspread	
	DOLLARS	**CENTS**
BAL FWD	672	12
DEPOSIT		
DEPOSIT		
TOTAL	672	12
THIS ITEM	29	07
SUB-TOTAL		
OTHER DEDUCT. (IF ANY)		
BAL FWD	643	05

146	IF TAX DEDUCTIBLE CHECK HERE ☐	
	$ 92.16	
	3-10 19 93	
To	Safeway	
For	Groceries	
	DOLLARS	**CENTS**
BAL FWD	643	05
DEPOSIT		
DEPOSIT		
TOTAL	643	05
THIS ITEM	92	16
SUB-TOTAL		
OTHER DEDUCT. (IF ANY)		
BAL FWD	551	89

550.89

147	IF TAX DEDUCTIBLE CHECK HERE ☐	
	$ 375.00	
	3-10 19 93	
To	Shady Villas Inc.	
For	Rent	
	DOLLARS	**CENTS**
BAL FWD	551	89
DEPOSIT		
DEPOSIT		
TOTAL	551	89
THIS ITEM	375	00
SUB-TOTAL		
OTHER DEDUCT. (IF ANY)		
BAL FWD	176	89

175.89 ✓

148	IF TAX DEDUCTIBLE CHECK HERE ☐	
	$ 78.44	
	3-15 19 93	
To	Tallowondy Electric	
For	Feb. Electric Bill	
	DOLLARS	**CENTS**
BAL FWD	176	89
DEPOSIT	1086	42
DEPOSIT		
TOTAL	1273	31
THIS ITEM	78	44
SUB-TOTAL		
OTHER DEDUCT. (IF ANY)		
BAL FWD	1194	87

1262.31
1883.87.

Bank Statement (as of 3–16–93)

Checks and Debits		Deposits	Date	Balance
Check No.	**Amount**			
				672.12
145	29.07		3–11	643.05
147	375.00		3–12	268.05
146	92.16	1,086.42	3–16	1,262.31
	2.60 SC		3–16	1,259.71

Mary's Reconciliation Statement

Bank balance	$1,239.71	Checkbook balance	$1,194.87
Outstanding check	− 78.44	Service charge	− 2.60
Adjusted balance	$1,161.27	Adjusted balance	$1,192.27

Solution: Mary Jo made three errors: a subtracting error on check stub 146, an adding error on check stub 148, and a copying error when writing the bank balance on her reconciliation statement. Once these errors are corrected, the adjusted bank balance and the adjusted checkbook balance is $1,181.27.   ■

EXERCISES FOR SECTION 5.6

In problems 1–10, use the given information to find the balance in the account as of the indicated date.

1. April 6: Balance = $1,325.14
   April 10: Check written for $211.15
   April 12: Check written for $947.20
   Balance as of April 12 = ?

2. September 8: Balance = $4,712.42
   September 9: Check written for $1,621.29
   September 14: Check written for $2,142.41
   Balance as of September 14 = ?

3. January 28: Balance = $4,331.78
   January 30: Deposit of $1,620.71
   February 3: Check written for $2,247.60
   Balance as of February 3 = ?

4. October 14: Balance = $947.21
   October 15: Deposit of $347.98
   October 17: Check written for $211.19
   Balance as of October 17 = ?

5. May 8: Balance = $2,113.78
   May 9: Check written for $217.15
   May 11: Deposit of $412.42
   May 15: Check written for $709.39
   Balance as of May 15 = ?

6. November 21: Balance = $2,124.08
   November 25: Check written for $1,342.71
   November 26: Deposit of $727.77
   November 27: Check written for $942.31
   Balance as of November 27 = ?

7. June 28: Balance = $3,271.11
   June 29: Deposit of $426.07
   June 30: Checks written for $7.11 and $45.80
   July 2: Check written for $1,247.12
   Balance as of July 2 = ?

8. August 2: Balance = $1,724.13
   August 6: Checks written for $143.12 and $913.72
   August 10: Check written for $547.08
   August 11: Deposit of $322.27
   Balance as of August 11 = ?

9. October 17: Balance = $1,914.37
   October 18: Deposit of $398.14
   October 19: Checks written for $177.43 and $313.79
   October 23: Deposit of $211.14
   October 25: Check written for $97.14
   Balance as of October 25 = ?

10. February 16: Balance = $1,247.63
    February 18: Deposit of $619.17
    February 21: Check written for $523.14
    February 26: Checks written for $113.14 and
            $422.73
    March 1: Deposit of $241.47
    Balance as of March 1 = ?

11. Fill in the missing entries on the following check stubs, proceeding in numerical order and carrying each balance to the next stub.

No. 82 $32.00
May 3, 1993
To: J. Best
For: Insurance

Bal. Brt. Forward	947.10
Amt. Dep. Total	182.00
Amt. This Check	32.00
Bal. Car. Forward	1097.1

No. 83 $157.21
May 7, 1993
To: Fla. Power
For: Elec. Bill

Bal. Brt. Forward	1097.1
Amt. Dep. Total	0.00
Amt. This Check	157.21
Bal. Car. Forward	939.89

No. 84 $ 87.13
May 12, 1993
To: S.F.U.W.
For: Auto Repair

Bal. Brt. Forward	939.89
Amt. Dep. Total	431.82
Amt. This Check	87.13
Bal. Car. Forward	1284.58

No. 85 $221.37
May 13, 1993
To: B. Gadsden
For: Pump Service

Bal. Brt. Forward	1284.58
Amt. Dep. Total	0.00
Amt. This Check	221.37
Bal. Car. Forward	1063.21

No. 86 $200.00
May 13, 1993
To: Mastercharge
For: Payment

Bal. Brt. Forward	1063.21
Amt. Dep. Total	379.14
Amt. This Check	200.00
Bal. Car. Forward	1242.35

No. 87 $333.14
May 14, 1993
To: Amer. Finance
For: Loan Payment

Bal. Brt. Forward	1242.35
Amt. Dep. Total	0.00
Amt. This Check	333.14
Bal. Car. Forward	909.21

12. Fill in the blanks on the following check register.

Check Register						
Check No.	Date	Check Issued to or Description of Deposit	Amount of Check	✓	Amount of Deposit	Balance
						782.15
354	5–13	Colony Shops	47.12	—		_____
355	5–17	Dr. Cone	29.00	—		_____
	5–23	Deposit			582.14 +	_____
356	5–24	Daily Enterprise	12.50	—		_____
357	5–26	Vol. Fire Dept.	12.20	—		_____
358	5–26	Hecht Company	82.14	—		_____
359	5–28	Sterling Savings & Loan	254.13	—		_____
360	6–1	Mutual Life Ins.	74.32	—		_____
	6–7	Deposit			241.72 +	_____
361	6–9	W.P. Black	187.50	—		_____

13. A checking account has a bank statement balance of $514.13, a checkbook balance of $386.09, outstanding checks of $12.14 and $120.15, and a service charge of $4.25. Use the format of figure 5.13 to reconcile the account.

14. The bank statement of El Dorado Auto Upholstery indicated a balance of $2,350.15, and the checkbook balance was $1,576.52. For the preceding period, there was an unrecorded deposit of $732.14, a service charge of $4.20, and outstanding checks of $302.64, $417.81, $306.02, and $483.50. Use the format of figure 5.13 to reconcile the account.

15. The latest bank statement received by Drummond Enterprises indicated a balance in the company's checking account of $3,114.27. The company's checkbook balance was $3,197.81. There were unrecorded deposits of $2,113.17 and $1,011.10, and outstanding checks of $742.14, $311.10, $108.82, $473.14, and $1,415.03. There was a charge of $9.50 on the account for printing new checks. Use the format of figure 5.13 to reconcile the account.

16. Using the format of figure 5.13, reconcile the following account: The bank statement balance was $4,321.19, and the checkbook balance was $5,249.61. There were unrecorded deposits of $1,517.12, $509.13, and $714.98. Outstanding checks were in the amounts of $444.45, $123.19, $1,509.23, $4.42, and $52.49. There was a charge of $8.50 on the account for printing new checks, and a check for $312.47 that was deposited was returned because of insufficient funds (an overdraft).

17. Use the format of figure 5.13 to reconcile the following account of the Dolby Company: The bank statement balance was $2,251.19, and the checkbook balance was $2,986.12. The unrecorded deposits were in the amounts of $237.15, $975.83, $1,214.58, $547.19, and $642.81. There were outstanding checks of $171.46, $858.88, $619.92, $741.08, $1,106.41, $213.41, $109.29, and $19.17. There was a service charge of $5.15, and a charge for new checks of $9.27. Also, two checks in the amounts of $321.14 and $621.43 that had been deposited were returned because of insufficient funds.

18. The bank statement and check register for the account of Lory's Boutique follow. The items on the register marked with a check (✓) indicate items that appeared on the previous month's bank statement. Fill in the missing entries on the check register, find the outstanding checks and unrecorded deposits, and reconcile the account. (The code SC on the bank statement means "service charge," the code RT means "returned check," and the code INT means "interest credited.")

Check Register

Check No.	Date	Check Issued to or Description of Deposit	Amount of Check	✓	Amount of Deposit	Balance
						1,241.46
121	6–24	Pacific Light	112.46	✓		1,129.00
122	6–26	Sizemore's Office Supply	41.14			1,087.86
123	6–27	Apex Fuel Company	82.24			1,005.62
124	6–27	Reese Wholesale	214.82	✓		790.80
	6–29	Deposit			527.31 ✓	1,318.11
125	7–2	Global Imports	92.37			1,225.74
	7–4	Adjustment for Service Charge	2.75	✓		1,222.99
126	7–9	Gerrell Fashions	153.91			1069.08
	7–10	Deposit			417.84 ✓	1486.92
127	7–16	Financial Trust	321.47			1165.45
128	7–23	Ray-Mar Designs	472.14			693.31
129	7–27	J.T. Whittington	29.36			663.95
	7–30	Deposit			687.81 ✓	1351.76

Bank Statement

Check No.	Amount	Check No.	Amount	Deposits	Date	Balance
					6–30	911.43 1318.11
123	82.24		317.81 RT		7–2	511.38
				527.31 ✓	7–3	1,038.69
125	92.37				7–9	946.32
126	153.91			417.84 ✓	7–14	1,364.16
127	321.47	122	41.14	2.86 INT	7–21	1,004.41
128	472.14		1.50 SC		7–31	530.77

19. Fill in the missing entries on the following check register and bank statement. The items marked with a check (✓) on the register appeared on the previous month's statement. Find the <u>outstanding checks</u> and <u>unrecorded deposits</u> and reconcile the account. (The codes INT, SC, RT, and DM on the bank statement mean, respectively, "interest credited," "service charge," "returned check," and "debit memo.")

Check Register

Check No.	Date	Check Issued to or Description of Deposit	Amount of Check	✓	Amount of Deposit	Balance
						2,475.91
387	10–23	Cities Supply Co.	215.82	✓		2,260.09
388	10–23	Martin Plumbing	83.14			2,176.95
	10–26	Deposit		✓	485.30	2,662.25
389	10–26	Consolidated Elec.	138.41	✓		2,523.84
390	10–30	Haynes Transport	47.18			2,476.66
391	11–2	Justin Construction	914.82			1,561.84
	11–4	Adjustment for SC	2.65	✓		1,559.19
	11–6	Deposit			842.13	_____
392	11–9	Delta Engineering	1,417.10			_____
	11–15	Deposit			817.10	_____
393	11–16	Holiga Glass Co.	123.72			_____
394	11–20	Midwest Finance	782.37			_____
395	11–21	E. J. Reed	23.10			_____
396	11–27	Central Heating	214.02			_____
	11–28	Deposit			392.68	_____
397	11–29	Avco Tile	514.27			_____

Bank Statement

Checks and Debits				Deposits	Date	Balance
Check No.	Amount	Check No.	Amount			
					10–31	2,604.33
391	914.82				11–6	1689,51
				842.13	11–10	2531·64
388	83.14		121.13 RT	11.02 INT	11–14	2580,65
				817.10	11–18	3397.75
	224.15 RT				11–19	3621·90
392	1,417.10				11–20	220 4.8
395	23.10		7.50 DM		11–23	2174.2
394	782.37				11–24	1391, 83
	3.42 SC	393	123.72		11–30	1388·41

20. The bank statement and check register for the account of Warner's Hardware follow. Fill in the missing entries, find the outstanding checks and unrecorded deposits, and reconcile the account. Items marked with a check (✓) on the register appeared on the previous month's statement. (The codes SC, RT, DM, CM, and INT on the bank statement mean, respectively, "service charge," "returned check," "debit memo," "credit memo," and "interest credited.")

Check Register

Check No.	Date	Check Issued to or Description of Deposit	Amount of Check	✓	Amount of Deposit	Balance
						1,892.01
211	4–21	Lake City Supply	182.77	✓		1,709.24
212	4–23	A. R. Robbins	86.13			1,623.11
	4–26	Deposit		✓	1,478.04	3,101.15
213	4–26	Johnson Sheet Metal	287.12			2,814.03
214	4–27	Superior Rubber Products	513.21	✓		2,300.82
215	5–1	Wood Products Inc.	918.42	✓		1,382.40
	5–8	Adjustment for SC	2.25	✓		1,380.15
	5–10	Deposit			914.22	
216	5–14	Statewide Electric	192.14			
217	5–17	Foster Tools	478.13			
218	5–18	Amer. Whlsl. Supply	742.91			
219	5–18	W. E. Williams	47.18			
	5–19	Deposit			849.47	
220	5–21	United Savings & Loan	271.17			
221	5–23	Greenwell Fertilizer Co.	381.41			
222	5–25	Perma-Plastics Inc.	172.10			
	5–26	Deposit			1,724.29	
223	5–27	T. R. Bascomb	14.81			
224	5–27	Central Realty	92.36			
225	5–29	Standard Sales Inc.	147.90			
	5–30	Deposit			1,141.13	

Bank Statement

Checks and Debits

Check No.	Amount	Check No.	Amount	Deposits	Date	Balance
					4–30	2,671.82
213	287.12	215 ✓	918.42		5–4	
	392.10 RT			9.64 INT	5–8	
			83.10 RT	914.22	5–14	
216	192.14				5–17	
				849.47	5–22	
220	271.17	218	742.91		5–23	
219	47.18		15.20 DM		5–25	
224	92.36			10.00 CM	5–28	
221	381.41			1,724.29	5–29	
	2.75 SC				5–31	

Glossary

Account purchase   An itemized statement of merchandise purchased by a commission agent.

Account sales   An itemized statement of merchandise sold by a commission agent.

Balance   The current amount of money in a checking account.

Bank statement   A record of the transactions in a checking account (checks written, deposits made, fees charged, etc.) maintained by the bank.

Chargeback (or docking)   A reduction in gross earnings for the production of substandard items.

Check   A written order directing a bank to pay a specified amount of money from a checking account to a specified party.

Checking account   A service provided by a bank whereby funds of a business, institution, or individual are placed in the bank for safekeeping and future use.

Check register or check stub   A record maintained by the owner of a checking account of the checks and deposits in the account.

Commission   Earnings of sales personnel based on the amount of items sold; usually a percentage of net sales.

Commission Agent (or broker or factor)   An individual or agency that buys or sells merchandise for another party.

Deduction   Money withheld from an employee's earnings as requested by the employee or required by law.

Deposit   The act of placing funds in a checking account.

Depositor   The owner of a checking account.

Differential piecework   An incentive wage plan that provides two different piece-rates, one for all units produced up to a specified standard and a second (higher) piece-rate for all units if the worker's production exceeds the standard.

Drawing account   A fund from which salespeople may receive advances against future commissions.

Endorsement   An inscription on the back of a check by the payee providing instructions for the disposition of the check.

Fair Labor Standards Act   A federal law (also known as the Federal Wage and Hour Law) enacted in 1938 that establishes minimum wages, overtime pay, and other labor standards for all employees covered by the act.

Federal income tax   A federal tax based on an employee's earnings, marital status, and number of withholding allowances.

Federal unemployment tax   A federal tax used to support a fund to provide compensation to workers who are unable to find employment. The tax is paid entirely by the employer.

Federal Insurance Contributions Act (Social Security) An act that established a fund to provide monthly benefits to retired or disabled workers and to the surviving families of deceased workers.

Graduated commission   Commissions that are based on a graduating scale; that is, the commission rate increases as sales volume increases.

Gross earnings   The total earnings of an employee within a specified pay period, before any deductions are made.

Gross proceeds   The value of merchandise sold by a commission agent before deducting the commission and expenses of the agent.

Group insurance   Insurance issued to a company that provides benefits for the employees.

Incentive wage plan   Any method of computing wages for workers engaged in production that rewards extra or sustained effort (for example, piecework or standard hour plans).

Interest credited   Interest paid on funds in a checking account and shown as a credit on a bank statement.

Net earnings   The actual earnings paid to a worker after all deductions are made.

Net proceeds   The amount paid to the seller by a commission agent equal to the gross proceeds minus commission and expenses.

Net sales   Total sales less returns and cancellations.

Outstanding check   A check written on a checking account but not yet received by the bank and hence not entered on the bank statement.

Overdraft   A check written on a checking account when there are insufficient funds in the account to pay the payee.

Override   A commission paid to supervisory personnel based on the net sales of the people they supervise.

Overtime   Hours worked in excess of a specified workweek (usually 40 hours, but sometimes less). The Fair Labor Standards Act specifies the rate of pay for overtime hours to be $1\frac{1}{2}$ times the rate for regular hours.

Pay period   The interval between earnings payments to an employee.

Payee   The party named to receive the funds from a check.

Piecework or piece-rate   Wage compensation based on the number of units produced by workers engaged in production.

Reconciliation   Adjustments to the bank statement and the check register of a checking account to determine that both records of the account are in agreement.

Returned check   A check returned to the party that deposited it because there are insufficient funds in the account on which the check was written.

Salary   Gross earnings that are paid according to a specified period of employment. A salary is independent of both production and actual working time.

Service charge   A fee charged by a bank for providing a checking account service.

Standard hour plan   An incentive wage plan based on a standard production level of a specified number of units per hour.

Straight piece-rate   A production wage plan where gross earnings equals the product of the rate per unit and the number of units produced.

Unrecorded deposit   A deposit that has been added to the balance of a checking account on the check register but has not yet been listed on the bank statement.

Wages   Gross earnings of workers that are paid according to actual time at work; usually calculated on a per hour basis as the rate per hour times the number of hours worked.

Withholding allowance   Allowance granted by the federal government that reduces the amount of income tax withheld from gross earnings.

Review Test

1. Jennifer Collins earns a salary of $2,240 per month. Compute her gross earnings per pay period if the pay period is biweekly.

2. Bob Richert sells lighting fixtures on a straight commission of 12% of net sales. During April, his sales were $21,417, with returns and cancellations totaling $1,742. Find his gross earnings for the month.

3. For each part machined, an operator is paid $0.97, with a guaranteed weekly wage of $502. Last week the operator's production was: Monday, 98; Tuesday, 114; Wednesday, 109; Thursday, 107; Friday, 101. Find the operator's gross earnings for the week.

4. In August, Pete Clark submitted orders totaling $23,420. Pete is paid a monthly graduated commission of 4% of the first $10,000 of net sales, 6% of the next $10,000, and 8.5% of net sales in excess of $20,000. Find his gross earnings for the month if returns and cancellations totaled $1,740.

5. Pam Stephens is employed as an assembler by a company that uses the standard hour plan. Pam is paid $4.60 per hour, and her standard production level is 140 units per 40 hour workweek. Find her gross earnings for a week during which she produces 161 units.

6. In addition to her weekly salary of $422 per week, Juanita receives a commission of 6% of her net sales plus an override of 1/2% of the net sales of the five employees she supervises. Last week her personal net sales were $2,137 and those of her employees were $11,269. Find Juanita's gross earnings for the week.

7. An account purchase listed the following items (unit prices in parentheses): 50 Parrot design bird feeders ($9.48), 125 Recycled paper stationery sets ($4.12), 500 boxes holiday wraps and labels ($9.78). If the agent's commission was 5 3/4% and transportation charges were $59.70, find the gross cost.

8. Richard Stringline earns $2,028 per month. His salary is based on a 40 hour workweek, but during the last two weeks he worked the following hours.

	Sun.	Mon.	Tues.	Wed.	Thurs.	Fri.	Sat.
Week 1	0	8	9	8	8	7	3
Week 2	0	8	8	10	8	7	4

Calculate Richard's gross earnings for this two-week period.

9. Marilyn earns $12.40 per hour for a forty hour workweek. For the past four weeks she worked 40, 45, 50, and 40 hours. Calculate her gross earnings for the past four weeks.

10. Lee Long is single and claims one withholding allowance. He is paid a straight commission of 12% of net sales. Using tables 5.1–5.2, find his net earnings for a week in February when his net sales were $3,700 if the only deductions were for federal income and Social Security and Medicare taxes.

11. Brenda Sales is paid biweekly and earns $15.60 per hour for a 40 hour workweek. In addition to deductions for federal income tax (M–2) and Social Security and Medicare, union dues of $18.60 per month and group insurance premiums of $28.10 per week are also withheld from her pay. Use tables 5.1–5.2 to find Brenda's net earnings for a two-week period (assume Social Security and Medicare maximums have not been reached).

12. The McPherson Company pays a state unemployment tax of 6.1% of the first $7,000 of gross earnings of each employee. The company employs 34 people, and all 34 employees earn in excess of $7,000 per year. How much total (state and federal) unemployment tax does the company pay?

13. A checking account has a bank statement balance of $451.53, a checkbook balance of $330.74, outstanding checks totaling $242.81, unrecorded deposits of $116.22, and a service charge of $5.80. Reconcile the account.

14. Reconcile the following checking account: Bank balance, $1,417.40; checkbook balance, $917.32; returned check, $413.28; unrecorded deposits, $218.41 and $709.52; service charge, $5.40; outstanding checks, $311.81, $904.72, $622.14, and $8.02.

15. The Brooker Corporation pays Susan Wecksler a straight commission of 9% of net sales with a monthly draw of $1,800. Complete the following record of her monthly gross earnings.

Month	Net Sales	Earned Commissions	Draw Advance	Draw Deficit Brought Fwd.	Gross Earnings	Draw Deficit Carried Fwd.
Jan.	$19,422	1747.98	52.02 +	$600.00	1800	652.02 –
Feb.	21,112	1900.08		–652.02 –	1800	551.94
Mar.	18,748	1687.32	112.68	551.94	1800	664.62

50 + 9.48   474
125 + 4.12   515
500 + 9.78   4890

5879 6 5¾   338.04
+338 04   +59.70
+ 59.70   497.70
6276.74

① 1747.98 – 1800 = 52.02
② 52.02 + 600 = 652.02
③ 1900.08 – 652.02 – 1800 = 551.94
④ 1687.32 – 551.94 – 1800 = 664.62
⑤ 664.62 – 551.94 = 112.68
6 — Sale was over 1800

chapter

6

Taxes

Section 6.1 *Sales and Excise Taxes*

A. Introduction
Revenue for federal, state, and local governments is obtained from three sources: taxation, borrowing, and service fees. Of these, taxation is the most important source of income. Taxes absorb over 30% of total income in the United States, which means that the average American works over four months out of every twelve to support federal, state, and local governments.

For these tax dollars, Americans receive a variety of services and benefits. Among these are education, health care, national defense, police and fire protection, public housing, streets and highways, recreation facilities, and park lands. While dislike of taxes is universal, most people would agree with Chief Justice Oliver Wendell Holmes, Jr. who said that "Taxes are the price we pay for civilization."

B. Sales Taxes
Sales tax is a primary source of revenue for state governments. Table 6.1 lists states that currently have a sales tax. Some states also permit municipalities to impose a

sales tax, but these local sales rates usually are less than the state percent. Retail merchants are responsible for collecting sales taxes and forwarding them to the appropriate governmental agency.

Table 6.1	State Sales Tax						
0.00%	**3.00%**	**4.00%**	**4.225%**	**4.25%**	**4.50%**	**5.00%**	
Alaska	Colorado	Alabama	Missouri	Kansas	Oklahoma	Arizona
Delaware	Wyoming	Arkansas			Virginia	Idaho
Montana		Connecticut				Indiana
New Hampshire		Georgia				Iowa
Oregon		Hawaii				Maine
		Louisiana				Maryland
		Michigan				Massachusetts
		New York				Nebraska
		South Dakota				New Mexico
						North Carolina
						North Dakota
						Ohio
						South Carolina
						Vermont
						Wisconsin

5.50%	**5.75%**	**6.00%**	**6.25%**	**6.50%**	**7.00%**
Tennessee	Nevada	California	Illinois	Minnesota	New Jersey
		D.C.	Texas	Washington	Rhode Island
		Florida	Utah		
		Kentucky			
		Mississippi			
		Pennsylvania			
		West Virginia			

The sales tax is a percentage of retail sales. Calculation of the sales tax is an application of the basic percentage formula

$$P = B \cdot R$$

where

P = amount of the sales tax
B = purchase price
R = tax rate

In retail stores with electronic cash registers, the tax is automatically calculated and added to the total selling price. Stores without electronic cash registers utilize a tax table that enables salesclerks to read the appropriate tax.

EXAMPLE 1   A ceiling fan sells for $130. If the sales tax is 4%, find: **a.** the amount of the sales tax and **b.** the total price paid by the buyer.

Solution: **a.** $P = ?, B = \$130, R = 4\% = 0.04$

$$P = B \cdot R$$
$$= \$130 \times 0.04$$
$$= \$5.20$$

b. The total price paid is the purchase price plus the sales tax.

$$\begin{array}{r} \$130.00 \\ + \quad 5.20 \\ \hline \$135.20 \end{array}$$

In some states, sales of less than one dollar are taxed according to tax brackets arbitrarily established by state or local tax authorities. Table 6.2 illustrates sample tax brackets for a sales tax of 4%, 5%, and 6%. Thus, with a 4% sales tax, an item that sells for $0.30 would be taxed $0.02; had the percentage formula been used, the tax would have been $0.01.

Table 6.2		Sales Tax Intervals			
Sales Amt	**4%**	**Sales Amt**	**5%**	**Sales Amt**	**6%**
$0.01–$0.09	$0.00	$0.00–$0.10	$0.00	$0.00–$0.10	$0.00
0.10– 0.25	0.01	0.11– 0.25	0.01	0.11– 0.22	0.01
0.26– 0.50	0.02	0.26– 0.45	0.02	0.23– 0.39	0.02
0.51– 0.75	0.03	0.46– 0.65	0.03	0.40– 0.56	0.03
0.76– 0.99	0.04	0.66– 0.85	0.04	0.57– 0.73	0.04
		0.86– 0.99	0.05	0.74– 0.90	0.05
				0.91– 1.08	0.06

For sales involving dollars and cents, one method of computing the sales tax is to use the basic percentage equation to calculate the tax on the dollars and the tax brackets to find the tax on the cents.

EXAMPLE 2   Using table 6.2 and the basic percentage formula, find the sales tax on a battery powered radio priced at $19.29 if the tax rate is 4%.

Solution: $\$19.29 = \$19.00 + \$0.29$

$$\begin{array}{ll} \$ 0.76 & (\$19.00 \times 0.04) \\ + \quad 0.02 & \text{Table 6.2} \\ \hline \$ 0.78 & \text{Total sales tax} \end{array}$$

In certain instances, the sales tax is not applicable. For example, sales taxes on interstate sales are prohibited by the United States Constitution, and local sales taxes normally are limited to the local taxing districts. Thus, an item sold in a state with a sales tax but outside the limits of a city with a municipal sales tax would be subject only to the state sales tax.

There may also be exemptions or exclusions from the sales tax. An exemption means that a specific item is not subject to the tax. Groceries and prescription drugs are common exemptions. Thus, a steak purchased at a supermarket would not be taxed, but a steak ordered at a restaurant would be taxed. An exclusion means that purchases by a particular organization are not taxed. Religious groups, charitable organizations, and nonprofit hospitals typically receive such exclusions.

EXAMPLE 3 A state sales tax is 5% of retail sales, excluding food items. Use the basic percentage equation to find the amount of the sales tax on the following items purchased at a supermarket.

Meat	$24.48
Vegetables	4.35
Shampoo	3.98
Laundry soap	4.70
Milk	2.96
Razor blades	1.79

Solution: The prices for the nonfood items (shampoo, soap, and razor blades) total $10.47.

$$P = B \cdot R$$
$$= \$10.47 \times 0.05$$
$$= \$0.52$$

If the total paid by the buyer and the sales tax rate are known, it is possible to find the purchase price using formula 2–5

$$NB = B \pm B \cdot R$$

where
$$NB = \text{total paid by the buyer}$$
$$B = \text{purchase price}$$
$$R = \text{sales tax rate}$$

EXAMPLE 4 In going over the daily sales, a store manager came upon a sales slip for $23.10 that indicated only the total paid by the buyer. If the sales tax rate is 5%, find: **a.** the purchase price and **b.** the amount of the tax.

Solution: **a.** Using formula 2–5 with $NB = \$23.10$, $R = 5\% = 0.05$, $B = ?$

$$NB = B \pm B \cdot R$$
$$\$23.10 = B + 0.05B$$
$$\$23.10 = 1.05B$$
$$\frac{\$23.10}{1.05} = B \quad \text{(Dividing both sides by 1.05)}$$
$$\$22.00 = B$$

b. $23.10   Total paid by buyer
  −   22.00   Purchase price
  $ 1.10   Amount of sales tax

C. Excise Taxes

Excise taxes are taxes on nonessential items and luxury items. Excise taxes are imposed by governments at the federal, state, or local level and may be a percentage of the manufacturer's selling price or a fixed amount per quantity sold. Table 6.3 shows the federal excise tax on selected items. Excise taxes that are a percentage of the manufacturer's selling price are calculated using the basic percentage formula.

Table 6.3   Federal Excise Taxes

Item	Tax	Item	Tax
Air Transportation (per fare)		Heavy trucks (sale price)	12%
Domestic	10%	Luxury items (by sale price)	
International	$6	*Autos (over $30,000)*	10%
Coal (per ton or s.p.)		*Boats (over $100,000)*	10%
Underground (lesser amt)	$1.10 or 4.4%	*Aircraft (over $250,000)*	10%
Surface mined (lesser amt)	$0.55 or 4.4%	*Furs/Jewels (over $10,000)*	10%
Fuels (per gallon)		Ozone Depleting Chemicals (per pound)	
Commercial aviation	14.1¢	*CFC-11*	$1.67
Diesel	20.1¢	*Halon-1211*	5.01
Gasohol	8.7¢	*Carbon tetrachloride*	1.84
Gasoline	14.1¢	Sporting Equipment (by sale price)	
Gas guzzler (models by mpg)		*Bows and Arrows*	11%
21.5–22.5 MPG	$1,000	*Sport fishing equip.*	10%
16.5–17.5	3,000	*Electric outboard motors*	3%
12.5–13.5	6,400	Telephone Service (per bill)	3%

EXAMPLE 5   A fishing rod on sale for $26 is subject to a sales tax of 4% and an excise tax of 10%. Find the total amount paid by the buyer.

Solution: $P = ?, B = \$26, R = 4\% = 0.04$ (sales tax), $R = 10\% = 0.10$ (excise tax)

   $26.00   Sale price
+   1.04   Sales tax ($26 × 0.04)
+   2.60   Excise tax ($26 × 0.10)
  $29.64   Total paid by the buyer

EXERCISES FOR SECTION 6.1

In problems 1–10, find **a.** *the amount of the sales tax using the basic percentage formula and* **b.** *the total price paid by the buyer.*

Price	Sales Tax Rate	Price	Sales Tax Rate
1. $ 60.00	4%	6. $ 414.85	5%
2. $ 82.00	4%	7. $ 533.88	$6\frac{1}{2}\%$
3. $115.00	5%	8. $ 716.44	$4\frac{1}{2}\%$
4. $240.00	5%	9. $1,237.95	5%
5. $123.68	6%	10. $2,662.75	6%

In problems 11–20, find the total sales tax by using the basic percentage formula on the dollars and table 6.2 to find the tax on the cents.

Price	Sales Tax Rate	Price	Sales Tax Rate
11. $ 35.74	6%	16. $ 534.90	4%
12. $ 44.16	6%	17. $ 468.65	5%
13. $123.56	5%	18. $ 921.38	5%
14. $286.48	5%	19. $2,973.45	6%
15. $351.16	4%	20. $1,034.40	6%

In problems 21–26, find the total paid by the buyer if the sales tax is calculated using the basic percentage formula.

Price	Sales Tax Rate	Excise Tax Rate
21. $ 65.00	3%	10%
22. $ 48.00	4%	8%
23. $ 173.50	5%	11%
24. $ 637.15	5%	5%
25. $1,945.76	4%	10%
26. $6,449.60	6%	11%

Solve.

27. The purchase price of some overhead lighting fixtures is $584.92. If the sales tax is 5%, find: **a.** the amount of the tax using only the basic percentage formula, and **b.** the amount of the tax using the basic percentage formula for the dollars and the tax brackets in table 6.2 for the cents.

28. A piece of china is priced at $37.79. If the sales tax is 6%, find: **a.** the amount of the tax using only the basic percentage formula, and **b.** the amount of the tax using the basic percentage formula for the dollars and the tax brackets in table 6.2 for the cents.

In problems 29–35, use the basic percentage formula to find the sales and excise taxes. Assume that food items are tax-exempt.

29. Find the total sales tax paid on the following items purchased in a state with a 6% sales tax.

Canned goods	$13.92
Produce	6.14
Paper goods	8.44
Toiletries	5.23
Meat	27.17

30. In a state with a sales tax rate of 5%, find the total sales tax paid on the following items.

Frozen food	$11.28
Bakery items	6.24
Toothpaste	2.79
Dog food	7.89
School supplies	4.71
Household cleaner	6.43

31. Cal Morgan purchased a new word processor for a total of $472.45, including 5% sales tax. Find the purchase price (excluding tax) and the amount of the sales tax.

32. Mona Peters paid a total of $621.78, including tax, for a new television set. If the sales tax rate is $4\frac{1}{2}\%$, find the purchase price (excluding tax) and the amount of the sales tax.

33. An airline ticket for $275.00 is subject to a sales tax of 6% and an excise tax of 10%. Find the total amount paid by the buyer.

34. Find the total amount paid for a man's gold ring priced at $1,249.50 if the sales tax is 4% and the excise tax is 10%.

35. A camera is subject to a sales tax of 6% and a local excise tax of 9%. Judy Phillips purchased the camera for a total price of $500.83, including taxes. Find the purchase price of the camera, excluding taxes.

Section 6.2 *Property Taxes*

The primary source of revenue of county governments, municipalities, and school districts is the property tax. One reason for this is that the property tax can be most readily administered at the local level. Another reason is that property owners benefit more from community services and, therefore, pay more to support these services.

The word **property** in property tax can mean real property (land and the building improvements on it) as well as personal property (automobiles, furniture, jewelry, and so on). Property tax consists of two factors: assessed valuation and the tax rate.

The **assessed value** of real property is a percentage of its fair market value as determined by the tax assessor, a local official. Suppose, for example, that real property in Central City is assessed at 80% of its fair market value. Then an office building with a fair market value of $220,000 would have an assessed value of $220,000 × 0.80 = $176,000.

After the assessed value of all property has been determined and the total taxes required to provide the needed services are determined, the property tax rate is found by dividing the total taxes to be raised by the total of the assessments. For example, if the annual budget of the Franklin County School District is $1,760,000 and the total assessed value of the property in the school district is $62,857,142, then the tax rate is

$$\text{Tax rate} = \frac{\text{Total taxes to be raised}}{\text{Total assessments}} = \frac{\$1,760,000}{\$62,857,142} = 0.028$$

This tax rate can be expressed in several different ways.

1. Percent of assessed value. 0.028 is 2.8%.
2. Per $100 of assessed value or $2.80.
3. Per $1,000 of assessed value or $28.
4. In **mills** ($\frac{1}{1000}$ of a dollar) or 28 mills.

The number of decimal places in the tax rate varies among taxing authorities. Rounding practices also vary. One method is to round the final digit up, regardless of the value of the next digit; mills are rounded up to the next mill. Thus, while normal rounding of 0.02423 as a percent to two decimal places would be 2.42%, for tax purposes, it is commonly rounded to 2.43%. Rounded to the next whole mill, this tax rate would be 25 mills.

Calculation of the property tax is an application of the basic percentage formula

where
$$P = B \cdot R$$
$$P = \text{Property tax}$$
$$B = \text{Assessed value}$$
$$R = \text{Tax rate}$$

E X A M P L E 1   Find the property tax on property with an assessed value of $234,000 if the tax rate is 2.12%.

Solution: $P = ?, B = \$234,000, R = 2.12\% = 0.0212$

$P = B \cdot R$
$\quad = \$234,000 \times 0.0212$
$\quad = \$4,960.80$

E X A M P L E 2   An office building has an assessed value of $380,000 in a city where property is taxed at a rate of $1.63 per $100 of assessed value. Find the property tax.

Solution: $P = ?, B = \$380,000, R = \dfrac{1.63}{100} = 0.0163$

$P = B \cdot R$
$\quad = \$380,000 \times 0.0163$
$\quad = \$6,194$

EXAMPLE 3   Property in Johnson County is assessed at 78% of its fair market value. If the tax rate is 34 mills, what is the property tax on property with a fair market value of $144,500?

Solution: The assessed value of the property is $144,500 \times 0.78 = \$112,710$.

$$P = ?, B = \$112,710, R = 34 \text{ mills} = \frac{34}{1,000} = 0.034$$

$$P = B \cdot R$$
$$= \$112,710 \times 0.034$$
$$= \$3,832.14 \qquad \blacksquare$$

If the property tax rates are known, the assessed value can be found using the formula

$$B = \frac{P}{R}$$

EXAMPLE 4   The property tax on a building is $1,602.54. If the tax rate is 1.74%, find the assessed value.

Solution: $P = \$1,602.54, B = ?, R = 1.74\% = 0.0174$

$$B = \frac{P}{R}$$
$$= \frac{\$1,602.54}{0.0174}$$
$$= \$92,100 \qquad \blacksquare$$

If the property tax and assessed value are known, the tax rate can be found using the formula

$$R = \frac{P}{B}$$

EXAMPLE 5   Property taxes on property with an assessed value of $416,000 are $8,569.60. Find the tax rate expressed in dollars per $1,000 of assessed value.

Solution: $P = \$8,569.60, B = \$416,000, R = ?$

$$R = \frac{P}{B}$$
$$= \frac{\$8,569.60}{\$416,000}$$
$$= 0.0206$$
$$0.0206 \times \$1,000 = \$20.60 \qquad \blacksquare$$

EXERCISES FOR SECTION 6.2

In problems 1–16, find the property tax.

	Assessed Value	Tax Rate			Assessed Value	Tax Rate
1.	$ 75,000	3.14%		9.	$ 75,420	$15.70 per $1,000
2.	$ 92,650	2.91%		10.	$ 156,250	$16.30 per $1,000
3.	$ 250,475	1.82%		11.	$ 524,375	$27.00 per $1,000
4.	$1,144,000	2.27%		12.	$1,722,800	$19.75 per $1,000
5.	$ 40,600	$1.65 per $100		13.	$ 18,480	14 mills
6.	$ 164,850	$1.73 per $100		14.	$ 166,775	16.5 mills
7.	$ 728,600	$2.60 per $100		15.	$1,264,600	18 mills
8.	$2,246,300	$3.20 per $100		16.	$2,416,000	26 mills

Solve.

17. Find the assessed value of a piece of property if the tax rate is 1.60% and the property tax is $2,126.

18. What is the assessed value of an office building if the property tax on the building is $12,870 and the tax rate is 1.98%?

19. Anderson County property is assessed at 90% of its fair market value. If the property tax rate is $24 per $1,000 of assessed value, what is the property tax on property assessed at $874,000?

20. Property in Canyon County is assessed at 67% of its fair market value. Find the fair market value of a piece of property if the tax rate is 1.46% and the property tax is $720.93.

21. Property in the city of Glenville is assessed at 72% of its fair market value. What is the tax on a building with a fair market value of $450,000 if the tax rate is **a.** $24.40 per $1,000 of assessed value, **b.** 30 mills?

22. If property in the county of Oakley is assessed at 85% of its fair market value, find the property tax on some acreage with a fair market value of $820,000 when the tax rate is **a.** $2.52 per $100 of assessed value, **b.** 28 mills.

23. Joe and Jeri Jackson received their property tax bill which included taxes from the county, city, and the local school district. The county tax rate was $2.74 per $100 of assessed value, the city tax rate was $1.63 per $100 of assessed value, and the local school district was 10 mills. If Joe and Jeri's house was assessed at $96,000, what was the total of their tax bill?

24. Patricia Aitello owns a house assessed at $110,000. Her property tax bill included the following tax rates: 27 mills from the city, 16.1 mills from the county, and 4.52 mills from the flood control district. Find the total that Patricia paid in property taxes.

25. Dorothy Holloway lives in a city where property is assessed at 76% of its fair market value. The fair market value of her house is $88,500, and in addition to a city tax rate of $3.60 per $100 of assessed value, there is a charge of 1.5 mills by the district air pollution control, and voters had approved a tax of $0.75 per $100 of assessed value for improvements to the high school. What was Dorothy's total tax bill?

26. Pedro Sanchez lives in a city where property is assessed at 80% of its fair market value. The fair market value of his house is $72,650, and the city tax rate is 38 mills. In addition, the sanitary district imposes a tax of 1.55 mills, and the soil conservation district adds a tax of $1.45 per $1,000 of assessed value. Find Pedro's total tax bill.

27. Faircraft Industries is planning to open a branch in either the city of Marion or McArthur. Property in Marion is assessed at 82% of its fair market value and has a tax rate of 2.68%. In McArthur, property is assessed at 70% of its fair market value with a tax rate of 32 mills. Faircraft estimates that its new branch will have a fair market value of $1,260,000. Where should Faircraft locate its branch to have the lowest property tax bill?

28. Compton, Inc. has the option of locating a new plant with a fair market value of $14,750,000 in Aberdeen County or across the state line in the county of Mayfield. In Aberdeen County, property is assessed at 60% of its fair market value and has a tax rate of $3.90 per $100 of assessed value. In the county of Mayfield, property is assessed at 78% of its fair market value and the tax rate is $28.40 per $1,000 of assessed value. Where should Compton, Inc. locate its new plant to have the lowest property tax bill?

29. The new assessment on the property of the Rathcamp Company was $4,200,000. Last year, the property was assessed at $3,700,000. This year the city tax rate was also raised from 3.15% to 3.50%. Rathcamp claims the assessment was too high and has threatened to close their plant and move to another location if their property taxes are more than $21,700 from last year. If the company does close their plant many people will lose their jobs and the economic loss to the city would be $22,000,000 annually. City officials have ordered a reassessment of the Rathcamp Company property. If the city gives in to the company's demands, what should be the new assessment of the Rathcamp Company property?

30. Phyllis Powell had the assessed value on her house increase from $68,000 to $74,500. Property in her city is taxed at a rate of 22 mills. Phyllis felt the new assessment was too high and appealed. She won and her property tax was reduced to $1,573. What was the new assessment on her house?

Section 6.3 *Federal Income Tax*

A. Basic Steps

In 1913, ratification of the Sixteenth Amendment to the United States Constitution gave Congress the "power to lay and collect taxes on incomes, from whatever source derived." Since that time, the individual income tax has become the mainstay of the federal tax system, as shown in figure 6.1.

Figure 6.1
The budget dollar (fiscal year 1991 estimate)
Source: Office of Management and Budget

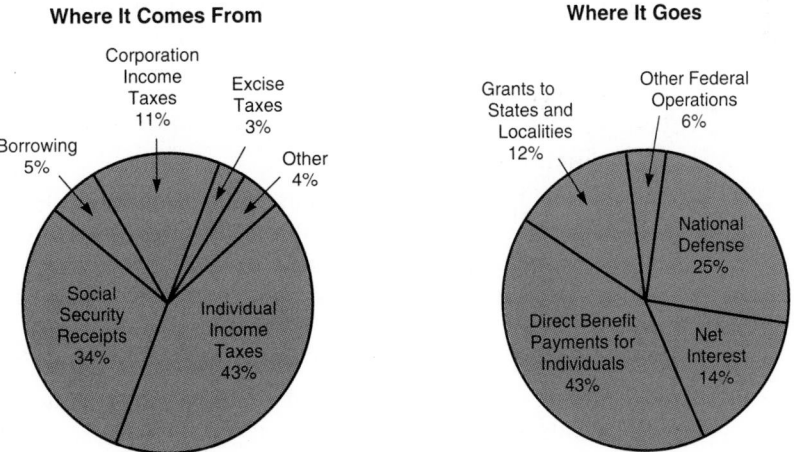

The Budget Dollar (Fiscal 1991 Estimate)

All citizens of the United States are required to file an income tax return if their income exceeds an amount determined by age and marital status. A tax return is filed on government form 1040 (or 1040A or 1040EZ) for income earned the previous calendar year and must be submitted before midnight on April 15th. The Internal Revenue Service (IRS) is the government agency responsible for collecting federal taxes.

The following are basic steps in computing personal income tax.

1. Compute your *total income.*
2. Compute your *adjustments to income.*
3. Subtract from total income (step 1) your adjustments to income (step 2). The result is your *adjusted gross income.*
4. Compute your total itemized deductions. Subtract from the adjusted gross income (step 3) the *larger* of the total itemized deductions or the *standard deduction.* In 1992, the standard deduction amounts were*

Single	$3,600
Married filing jointly	6,000
Married filing separately	3,000
Head of household	5,250
Qualifying widow(er)	6,000

*Taxpayers who are 65 and older and/or blind receive different deductions.

5. Multiply your total number of exemptions by $2,300 and subtract this from the amount in step 4. This is your *taxable income.*
6. Compute your tax from the appropriate tax table according to your taxable income and *filing status.*

B. Total Income

For most people, total income means the income from employment, from interest on savings or bonds, or from stock dividends. For income from employment, employers must furnish each employee with an IRS form W-2 Wage and Tax Statement that indicates the amount earned by the employee the previous calendar year (see figure 6.2). Annual income from interest or dividends is reported to the recipient on IRS form 1099 or a similar statement.

C. Adjustments to Income

Adjustments to income are amounts that are subtracted from the total income. Examples are deductions for reimbursed employee business expenses, penalties for early withdrawal of savings, alimony payments, contributions to a Keogh retirement plan, or contributions to an individual retirement account.

D. Adjusted Gross Income

The adjusted gross income is found by subtracting from total income the total adjustments to income.

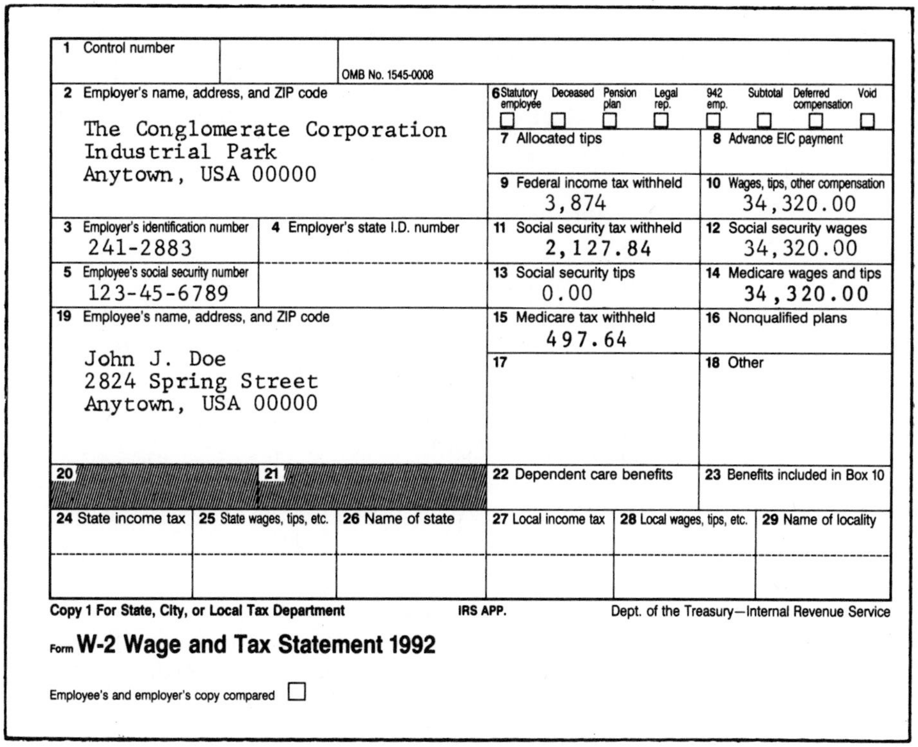

Figure 6.2
Wage and tax statement
(Form W-2)

1 Control number								
		OMB No. 1545-0008						

2 Employer's name, address, and ZIP code

The Conglomerate Corporation
Industrial Park
Anytown, USA 00000

6 Statutory employee	Deceased	Pension plan	Legal rep.	942 emp.	Subtotal	Deferred compensation	Void

7 Allocated tips	**8 Advance EIC payment**
9 Federal income tax withheld 3,874	**10 Wages, tips, other compensation** 34,320.00

3 Employer's identification number 241-2883
4 Employer's state I.D. number

11 Social security tax withheld 2,127.84	**12 Social security wages** 34,320.00

5 Employee's social security number 123-45-6789

13 Social security tips 0.00	**14 Medicare wages and tips** 34,320.00

19 Employee's name, address, and ZIP code

John J. Doe
2824 Spring Street
Anytown, USA 00000

15 Medicare tax withheld 497.64	**16 Nonqualified plans**
17	**18 Other**

20	**21**	**22 Dependent care benefits**	**23 Benefits included in Box 10**

24 State income tax	**25** State wages, tips, etc.	**26** Name of state	**27** Local income tax	**28** Local wages, tips, etc.	**29** Name of locality

Copy 1 For State, City, or Local Tax Department   IRS APP.   Dept. of the Treasury—Internal Revenue Service

Form **W-2 Wage and Tax Statement 1992**

Employee's and employer's copy compared ☐

E X A M P L E 1   Julie Stone earned $64,000 last year as a computer programmer. During that time she contributed $2,500 to a Keogh. In addition to her salary, Julie earned $1,375 in stock dividends. Find Julie's adjusted gross income.

Solution:

$64,000   Employment income
+ 1,375   Stock dividends
$65,375   Total income
− 2,500   Adjustments to income
$62,875   Adjusted gross income

E. Deductions

Deductions are expenses that reduce the taxable income. Examples of such expenses are

Medical and dental expenses in excess of a percent of the adjusted gross income as determined by the IRS

Home mortgage interest

State and local income taxes

Real estate taxes

Contributions to charitable organizations

The government has calculated an average amount an individual or family is expected to incur in deductible expenses during a year, called the **standard deduction.** The taxpayer has the option of subtracting from the adjusted gross income either the standard deduction or the total of all **itemized deductions,** whichever is greater.

F. Exemptions

In general, an exemption is the taxpayer or a relative who depends on the taxpayer for financial support. For example, a married taxpayer with two small children could claim four exemptions: the taxpayer, the taxpayer's spouse, and the two children. Exemptions are used to reduce the adjusted gross income. The 1992 deduction was $2,300 per exemption.

G. Taxable Income

The **taxable income** is the adjusted gross income minus the total for exemptions and minus either **a.** the total of itemized deductions, or **b.** the standard deduction, whichever is greater.

EXAMPLE 2   Joe Mullins had an adjusted gross income of $51,500 last year. His total itemized deductions were $6,955, compared with a standard deduction of $6,000. Find his taxable income if he had four exemptions.

Solution: The total itemized deductions exceeds the standard deductions. Thus,

$51,500   Adjusted gross income
− 9,200   Exemptions ($2,300 × 4)
− 6,955   Total of itemized deductions
$35,345   Taxable income   ■

EXAMPLE 3   Rita Wilson earned an adjusted gross income of $37,000 last year. Her deductible expenses (in excess of IRS exclusions) were as follows: medical and dental expenses, $290; interest charges, $830; real estate taxes, $1,200; contributions to charitable organizations, $440. Find her taxable income if she claims one exemption and the standard deduction is $3,600.

Solution: Itemizing Rita's deductions,

$ 290   Medical and dental expenses
830   Interest charges
1,200   Real estate taxes
440   Contributions to charitable organizations
$2,760   Total of deductions

Since her itemized deductions do not exceed the standard deduction, Rita should not itemize her deductions on her tax return. Thus,

$37,000   Adjusted gross income
− 2,300   Exemption
− 3,600   Standard deduction
$31,100   Taxable income   ∎

H. Tax

The amount of the tax is found in tax tables (used if the taxable income is less than $100,000) or a tax rate schedule (used if the taxable income is $100,000 or more). In the examples and problems of this text, tax tables for 1992 are used. A portion of the tables is shown on the next three pages as table 6.4. The amount of the tax is the intersection of the taxable income row with the filing status column.

EXAMPLE 4   A married taxpayer filing a joint return had a taxable income of $23,630. Find the amount of the tax.

Solution: From table 6.4, the intersection of the row 23,600–23,650 and the column "Married filing jointly" is $3,544.   ∎

EXAMPLE 5   A single taxpayer had a taxable income of $48,230. Find the amount of the tax.

Solution: From table 6.4, the intersection of the row 48,200–48,250 and the column "Single" is $10,715.   ∎

EXAMPLE 6   Joanna Sparks had an adjusted gross income of $51,750 and itemized deductions of $3,936. She is single but claims her mother as an exemption. Find the amount of her tax if she files as head of household.

Solution: $51,750   Adjusted gross income
− 5,250   Standard deductions
− 4,600   Exemptions ($2,300 × 2)
$41,900   Taxable income

From table 6.4, the intersection of the row 41,900–41,950 and the column "Head of a household" is $8,002.   ∎

Table 6.4

1992 Tax Table—Continued

If line 37 (taxable income) is—		Single	Married filing jointly *	Married filing separately	Head of a household
At least	But less than			**Your tax is—**	
14,000					
14,000	14,050	2,104	2,104	2,104	2,104
14,050	14,100	2,111	2,111	2,111	2,111
14,100	14,150	2,119	2,119	2,119	2,119
14,150	14,200	2,126	2,126	2,126	2,126
14,200	14,250	2,134	2,134	2,134	2,134
14,250	14,300	2,141	2,141	2,141	2,141
14,300	14,350	2,149	2,149	2,149	2,149
14,350	14,400	2,156	2,156	2,156	2,156
14,400	14,450	2,164	2,164	2,164	2,164
14,450	14,500	2,171	2,171	2,171	2,171
14,500	14,550	2,179	2,179	2,179	2,179
14,550	14,600	2,186	2,186	2,186	2,186
14,600	14,650	2,194	2,194	2,194	2,194
14,650	14,700	2,201	2,201	2,201	2,201
14,700	14,750	2,209	2,209	2,209	2,209
14,750	14,800	2,216	2,216	2,216	2,216
14,800	14,850	2,224	2,224	2,224	2,224
14,850	14,900	2,231	2,231	2,231	2,231
14,900	14,950	2,239	2,239	2,239	2,239
14,950	15,000	2,246	2,246	2,246	2,246
15,000					
15,000	15,050	2,254	2,254	2,254	2,254
15,050	15,100	2,261	2,261	2,261	2,261
15,100	15,150	2,269	2,269	2,269	2,269
15,150	15,200	2,276	2,276	2,276	2,276
15,200	15,250	2,284	2,284	2,284	2,284
15,250	15,300	2,291	2,291	2,291	2,291
15,300	15,350	2,299	2,299	2,299	2,299
15,350	15,400	2,306	2,306	2,306	2,306
15,400	15,450	2,314	2,314	2,314	2,314
15,450	15,500	2,321	2,321	2,321	2,321
15,500	15,550	2,329	2,329	2,329	2,329
15,550	15,600	2,336	2,336	2,336	2,336
15,600	15,650	2,344	2,344	2,344	2,344
15,650	15,700	2,351	2,351	2,351	2,351
15,700	15,750	2,359	2,359	2,359	2,359
15,750	15,800	2,366	2,366	2,366	2,366
15,800	15,850	2,374	2,374	2,374	2,374
15,850	15,900	2,381	2,381	2,381	2,381
15,900	15,950	2,389	2,389	2,389	2,389
15,950	16,000	2,396	2,396	2,396	2,396
16,000					
16,000	16,050	2,404	2,404	2,404	2,404
16,050	16,100	2,411	2,411	2,411	2,411
16,100	16,150	2,419	2,419	2,419	2,419
16,150	16,200	2,426	2,426	2,426	2,426
16,200	16,250	2,434	2,434	2,434	2,434
16,250	16,300	2,441	2,441	2,441	2,441
16,300	16,350	2,449	2,449	2,449	2,449
16,350	16,400	2,456	2,456	2,456	2,456
16,400	16,450	2,464	2,464	2,464	2,464
16,450	16,500	2,471	2,471	2,471	2,471
16,500	16,550	2,479	2,479	2,479	2,479
16,550	16,600	2,486	2,486	2,486	2,486
16,600	16,650	2,494	2,494	2,494	2,494
16,650	16,700	2,501	2,501	2,501	2,501
16,700	16,750	2,509	2,509	2,509	2,509
16,750	16,800	2,516	2,516	2,516	2,516
16,800	16,850	2,524	2,524	2,524	2,524
16,850	16,900	2,531	2,531	2,531	2,531
16,900	16,950	2,539	2,539	2,539	2,539
16,950	17,000	2,546	2,546	2,546	2,546

If line 37 (taxable income) is—		Single	Married filing jointly *	Married filing separately	Head of a household
At least	But less than			**Your tax is—**	
17,000					
17,000	17,050	2,554	2,554	2,554	2,554
17,050	17,100	2,561	2,561	2,561	2,561
17,100	17,150	2,569	2,569	2,569	2,569
17,150	17,200	2,576	2,576	2,576	2,576
17,200	17,250	2,584	2,584	2,584	2,584
17,250	17,300	2,591	2,591	2,591	2,591
17,300	17,350	2,599	2,599	2,599	2,599
17,350	17,400	2,606	2,606	2,606	2,606
17,400	17,450	2,614	2,614	2,614	2,614
17,450	17,500	2,621	2,621	2,621	2,621
17,500	17,550	2,629	2,629	2,629	2,629
17,550	17,600	2,636	2,636	2,636	2,636
17,600	17,650	2,644	2,644	2,644	2,644
17,650	17,700	2,651	2,651	2,651	2,651
17,700	17,750	2,659	2,659	2,659	2,659
17,750	17,800	2,666	2,666	2,666	2,666
17,800	17,850	2,674	2,674	2,674	2,674
17,850	17,900	2,681	2,681	2,681	2,681
17,900	17,950	2,689	2,689	2,692	2,689
17,950	18,000	2,696	2,696	2,706	2,696
18,000					
18,000	18,050	2,704	2,704	2,720	2,704
18,050	18,100	2,711	2,711	2,734	2,711
18,100	18,150	2,719	2,719	2,748	2,719
18,150	18,200	2,726	2,726	2,762	2,726
18,200	18,250	2,734	2,734	2,776	2,734
18,250	18,300	2,741	2,741	2,790	2,741
18,300	18,350	2,749	2,749	2,804	2,749
18,350	18,400	2,756	2,756	2,818	2,756
18,400	18,450	2,764	2,764	2,832	2,764
18,450	18,500	2,771	2,771	2,846	2,771
18,500	18,550	2,779	2,779	2,860	2,779
18,550	18,600	2,786	2,786	2,874	2,786
18,600	18,650	2,794	2,794	2,888	2,794
18,650	18,700	2,801	2,801	2,902	2,801
18,700	18,750	2,809	2,809	2,916	2,809
18,750	18,800	2,816	2,816	2,930	2,816
18,800	18,850	2,824	2,824	2,944	2,824
18,850	18,900	2,831	2,831	2,958	2,831
18,900	18,950	2,839	2,839	2,972	2,839
18,950	19,000	2,846	2,846	2,986	2,846
19,000					
19,000	19,050	2,854	2,854	3,000	2,854
19,050	19,100	2,861	2,861	3,014	2,861
19,100	19,150	2,869	2,869	3,028	2,869
19,150	19,200	2,876	2,876	3,042	2,876
19,200	19,250	2,884	2,884	3,056	2,884
19,250	19,300	2,891	2,891	3,070	2,891
19,300	19,350	2,899	2,899	3,084	2,899
19,350	19,400	2,906	2,906	3,098	2,906
19,400	19,450	2,914	2,914	3,112	2,914
19,450	19,500	2,921	2,921	3,126	2,921
19,500	19,550	2,929	2,929	3,140	2,929
19,550	19,600	2,936	2,936	3,154	2,936
19,600	19,650	2,944	2,944	3,168	2,944
19,650	19,700	2,951	2,951	3,182	2,951
19,700	19,750	2,959	2,959	3,196	2,959
19,750	19,800	2,966	2,966	3,210	2,966
19,800	19,850	2,974	2,974	3,224	2,974
19,850	19,900	2,981	2,981	3,238	2,981
19,900	19,950	2,989	2,989	3,252	2,989
19,950	20,000	2,996	2,996	3,266	2,996

If line 37 (taxable income) is—		Single	Married filing jointly *	Married filing separately	Head of a household
At least	But less than			**Your tax is—**	
20,000					
20,000	20,050	3,004	3,004	3,280	3,004
20,050	20,100	3,011	3,011	3,294	3,011
20,100	20,150	3,019	3,019	3,308	3,019
20,150	20,200	3,026	3,026	3,322	3,026
20,200	20,250	3,034	3,034	3,336	3,034
20,250	20,300	3,041	3,041	3,350	3,041
20,300	20,350	3,049	3,049	3,364	3,049
20,350	20,400	3,056	3,056	3,378	3,056
20,400	20,450	3,064	3,064	3,392	3,064
20,450	20,500	3,071	3,071	3,406	3,071
20,500	20,550	3,079	3,079	3,420	3,079
20,550	20,600	3,086	3,086	3,434	3,086
20,600	20,650	3,094	3,094	3,448	3,094
20,650	20,700	3,101	3,101	3,462	3,101
20,700	20,750	3,109	3,109	3,476	3,109
20,750	20,800	3,116	3,116	3,490	3,116
20,800	20,850	3,124	3,124	3,504	3,124
20,850	20,900	3,131	3,131	3,518	3,131
20,900	20,950	3,139	3,139	3,532	3,139
20,950	21,000	3,146	3,146	3,546	3,146
21,000					
21,000	21,050	3,154	3,154	3,560	3,154
21,050	21,100	3,161	3,161	3,574	3,161
21,100	21,150	3,169	3,169	3,588	3,169
21,150	21,200	3,176	3,176	3,602	3,176
21,200	21,250	3,184	3,184	3,616	3,184
21,250	21,300	3,191	3,191	3,630	3,191
21,300	21,350	3,199	3,199	3,644	3,199
21,350	21,400	3,206	3,206	3,658	3,206
21,400	21,450	3,214	3,214	3,672	3,214
21,450	21,500	3,225	3,221	3,686	3,221
21,500	21,550	3,239	3,229	3,700	3,229
21,550	21,600	3,253	3,236	3,714	3,236
21,600	21,650	3,267	3,244	3,728	3,244
21,650	21,700	3,281	3,251	3,742	3,251
21,700	21,750	3,295	3,259	3,756	3,259
21,750	21,800	3,309	3,266	3,770	3,266
21,800	21,850	3,323	3,274	3,784	3,274
21,850	21,900	3,337	3,281	3,798	3,281
21,900	21,950	3,351	3,289	3,812	3,289
21,950	22,000	3,365	3,296	3,826	3,296
22,000					
22,000	22,050	3,379	3,304	3,840	3,304
22,050	22,100	3,393	3,311	3,854	3,311
22,100	22,150	3,407	3,319	3,868	3,319
22,150	22,200	3,421	3,326	3,882	3,326
22,200	22,250	3,435	3,334	3,896	3,334
22,250	22,300	3,449	3,341	3,910	3,341
22,300	22,350	3,463	3,349	3,924	3,349
22,350	22,400	3,477	3,356	3,938	3,356
22,400	22,450	3,491	3,364	3,952	3,364
22,450	22,500	3,505	3,371	3,966	3,371
22,500	22,550	3,519	3,379	3,980	3,379
22,550	22,600	3,533	3,386	3,994	3,386
22,600	22,650	3,547	3,394	4,008	3,394
22,650	22,700	3,561	3,401	4,022	3,401
22,700	22,750	3,575	3,409	4,036	3,409
22,750	22,800	3,589	3,416	4,050	3,416
22,800	22,850	3,603	3,424	4,064	3,424
22,850	22,900	3,617	3,431	4,078	3,431
22,900	22,950	3,631	3,439	4,092	3,439
22,950	23,000	3,645	3,446	4,106	3,446

* This column must also be used by a qualifying widow(er).

Continued on next page

Table 6.4 Continued

1992 Tax Table—Continued

23,000

At least	But less than	Single	Married filing jointly *	Married filing separately *	Head of a household
23,000	23,050	3,659	3,454	4,120	3,454
23,050	23,100	3,673	3,461	4,134	3,461
23,100	23,150	3,687	3,469	4,148	3,469
23,150	23,200	3,701	3,476	4,162	3,476
23,200	23,250	3,715	3,484	4,176	3,484
23,250	23,300	3,729	3,491	4,190	3,491
23,300	23,350	3,743	3,499	4,204	3,499
23,350	23,400	3,757	3,506	4,218	3,506
23,400	23,450	3,771	3,514	4,232	3,514
23,450	23,500	3,785	3,521	4,246	3,521
23,500	23,550	3,799	3,529	4,260	3,529
23,550	23,600	3,813	3,536	4,274	3,536
23,600	23,650	3,827	3,544	4,288	3,544
23,650	23,700	3,841	3,551	4,302	3,551
23,700	23,750	3,855	3,559	4,316	3,559
23,750	23,800	3,869	3,566	4,330	3,566
23,800	23,850	3,883	3,574	4,344	3,574
23,850	23,900	3,897	3,581	4,358	3,581
23,900	23,950	3,911	3,589	4,372	3,589
23,950	24,000	3,925	3,596	4,386	3,596

24,000

At least	But less than	Single	Married filing jointly *	Married filing separately *	Head of a household
24,000	24,050	3,939	3,604	4,400	3,604
24,050	24,100	3,953	3,611	4,414	3,611
24,100	24,150	3,967	3,619	4,428	3,619
24,150	24,200	3,981	3,626	4,442	3,626
24,200	24,250	3,995	3,634	4,456	3,634
24,250	24,300	4,009	3,641	4,470	3,641
24,300	24,350	4,023	3,649	4,484	3,649
24,350	24,400	4,037	3,656	4,498	3,656
24,400	24,450	4,051	3,664	4,512	3,664
24,450	24,500	4,065	3,671	4,526	3,671
24,500	24,550	4,079	3,679	4,540	3,679
24,550	24,600	4,093	3,686	4,554	3,686
24,600	24,650	4,107	3,694	4,568	3,694
24,650	24,700	4,121	3,701	4,582	3,701
24,700	24,750	4,135	3,709	4,596	3,709
24,750	24,800	4,149	3,716	4,610	3,716
24,800	24,850	4,163	3,724	4,624	3,724
24,850	24,900	4,177	3,731	4,638	3,731
24,900	24,950	4,191	3,739	4,652	3,739
24,950	25,000	4,205	3,746	4,666	3,746

25,000

At least	But less than	Single	Married filing jointly *	Married filing separately *	Head of a household
25,000	25,050	4,219	3,754	4,680	3,754
25,050	25,100	4,233	3,761	4,694	3,761
25,100	25,150	4,247	3,769	4,708	3,769
25,150	25,200	4,261	3,776	4,722	3,776
25,200	25,250	4,275	3,784	4,736	3,784
25,250	25,300	4,289	3,791	4,750	3,791
25,300	25,350	4,303	3,799	4,764	3,799
25,350	25,400	4,317	3,806	4,778	3,806
25,400	25,450	4,331	3,814	4,792	3,814
25,450	25,500	4,345	3,821	4,806	3,821
25,500	25,550	4,359	3,829	4,820	3,829
25,550	25,600	4,373	3,836	4,834	3,836
25,600	25,650	4,387	3,844	4,848	3,844
25,650	25,700	4,401	3,851	4,862	3,851
25,700	25,750	4,415	3,859	4,876	3,859
25,750	25,800	4,429	3,866	4,890	3,866
25,800	25,850	4,443	3,874	4,904	3,874
25,850	25,900	4,457	3,881	4,918	3,881
25,900	25,950	4,471	3,889	4,932	3,889
25,950	26,000	4,485	3,896	4,946	3,896

26,000

At least	But less than	Single	Married filing jointly *	Married filing separately *	Head of a household
26,000	26,050	4,499	3,904	4,960	3,904
26,050	26,100	4,513	3,911	4,974	3,911
26,100	26,150	4,527	3,919	4,988	3,919
26,150	26,200	4,541	3,926	5,002	3,926
26,200	26,250	4,555	3,934	5,016	3,934
26,250	26,300	4,569	3,941	5,030	3,941
26,300	26,350	4,583	3,949	5,044	3,949
26,350	26,400	4,597	3,956	5,058	3,956
26,400	26,450	4,611	3,964	5,072	3,964
26,450	26,500	4,625	3,971	5,086	3,971
26,500	26,550	4,639	3,979	5,100	3,979
26,550	26,600	4,653	3,986	5,114	3,986
26,600	26,650	4,667	3,994	5,128	3,994
26,650	26,700	4,681	4,001	5,142	4,001
26,700	26,750	4,695	4,009	5,156	4,009
26,750	26,800	4,709	4,016	5,170	4,016
26,800	26,850	4,723	4,024	5,184	4,024
26,850	26,900	4,737	4,031	5,198	4,031
26,900	26,950	4,751	4,039	5,212	4,039
26,950	27,000	4,765	4,046	5,226	4,046

27,000

At least	But less than	Single	Married filing jointly *	Married filing separately *	Head of a household
27,000	27,050	4,779	4,054	5,240	4,054
27,050	27,100	4,793	4,061	5,254	4,061
27,100	27,150	4,807	4,069	5,268	4,069
27,150	27,200	4,821	4,076	5,282	4,076
27,200	27,250	4,835	4,084	5,296	4,084
27,250	27,300	4,849	4,091	5,310	4,091
27,300	27,350	4,863	4,099	5,324	4,099
27,350	27,400	4,877	4,106	5,338	4,106
27,400	27,450	4,891	4,114	5,352	4,114
27,450	27,500	4,905	4,121	5,366	4,121
27,500	27,550	4,919	4,129	5,380	4,129
27,550	27,600	4,933	4,136	5,394	4,136
27,600	27,650	4,947	4,144	5,408	4,144
27,650	27,700	4,961	4,151	5,422	4,151
27,700	27,750	4,975	4,159	5,436	4,159
27,750	27,800	4,989	4,166	5,450	4,166
27,800	27,850	5,003	4,174	5,464	4,174
27,850	27,900	5,017	4,181	5,478	4,181
27,900	27,950	5,031	4,189	5,492	4,189
27,950	28,000	5,045	4,196	5,506	4,196

28,000

At least	But less than	Single	Married filing jointly *	Married filing separately *	Head of a household
28,000	28,050	5,059	4,204	5,520	4,204
28,050	28,100	5,073	4,211	5,534	4,211
28,100	28,150	5,087	4,219	5,548	4,219
28,150	28,200	5,101	4,226	5,562	4,226
28,200	28,250	5,115	4,234	5,576	4,234
28,250	28,300	5,129	4,241	5,590	4,241
28,300	28,350	5,143	4,249	5,604	4,249
28,350	28,400	5,157	4,256	5,618	4,256
28,400	28,450	5,171	4,264	5,632	4,264
28,450	28,500	5,185	4,271	5,646	4,271
28,500	28,550	5,199	4,279	5,660	4,279
28,550	28,600	5,213	4,286	5,674	4,286
28,600	28,650	5,227	4,294	5,688	4,294
28,650	28,700	5,241	4,301	5,702	4,301
28,700	28,750	5,255	4,309	5,716	4,309
28,750	28,800	5,269	4,316	5,730	4,320
28,800	28,850	5,283	4,324	5,744	4,334
28,850	28,900	5,297	4,331	5,758	4,348
28,900	28,950	5,311	4,339	5,772	4,362
28,950	29,000	5,325	4,346	5,786	4,376

29,000

At least	But less than	Single	Married filing jointly *	Married filing separately *	Head of a household
29,000	29,050	5,339	4,354	5,800	4,390
29,050	29,100	5,353	4,361	5,814	4,404
29,100	29,150	5,367	4,369	5,828	4,418
29,150	29,200	5,381	4,376	5,842	4,432
29,200	29,250	5,395	4,384	5,856	4,446
29,250	29,300	5,409	4,391	5,870	4,460
29,300	29,350	5,423	4,399	5,884	4,474
29,350	29,400	5,437	4,406	5,898	4,488
29,400	29,450	5,451	4,414	5,912	4,502
29,450	29,500	5,465	4,421	5,926	4,516
29,500	29,550	5,479	4,429	5,940	4,530
29,550	29,600	5,493	4,436	5,954	4,544
29,600	29,650	5,507	4,444	5,968	4,558
29,650	29,700	5,521	4,451	5,982	4,572
29,700	29,750	5,535	4,459	5,996	4,586
29,750	29,800	5,549	4,466	6,010	4,600
29,800	29,850	5,563	4,474	6,024	4,614
29,850	29,900	5,577	4,481	6,038	4,628
29,900	29,950	5,591	4,489	6,052	4,642
29,950	30,000	5,605	4,496	6,066	4,656

30,000

At least	But less than	Single	Married filing jointly *	Married filing separately *	Head of a household
30,000	30,050	5,619	4,504	6,080	4,670
30,050	30,100	5,633	4,511	6,094	4,684
30,100	30,150	5,647	4,519	6,108	4,698
30,150	30,200	5,661	4,526	6,122	4,712
30,200	30,250	5,675	4,534	6,136	4,726
30,250	30,300	5,689	4,541	6,150	4,740
30,300	30,350	5,703	4,549	6,164	4,754
30,350	30,400	5,717	4,556	6,178	4,768
30,400	30,450	5,731	4,564	6,192	4,782
30,450	30,500	5,745	4,571	6,206	4,796
30,500	30,550	5,759	4,579	6,220	4,810
30,550	30,600	5,773	4,586	6,234	4,824
30,600	30,650	5,787	4,594	6,248	4,838
30,650	30,700	5,801	4,601	6,262	4,852
30,700	30,750	5,815	4,609	6,276	4,866
30,750	30,800	5,829	4,616	6,290	4,880
30,800	30,850	5,843	4,624	6,304	4,894
30,850	30,900	5,857	4,631	6,318	4,908
30,900	30,950	5,871	4,639	6,332	4,922
30,950	31,000	5,885	4,646	6,346	4,936

31,000

At least	But less than	Single	Married filing jointly *	Married filing separately *	Head of a household
31,000	31,050	5,899	4,654	6,360	4,950
31,050	31,100	5,913	4,661	6,374	4,964
31,100	31,150	5,927	4,669	6,388	4,978
31,150	31,200	5,941	4,676	6,402	4,992
31,200	31,250	5,955	4,684	6,416	5,006
31,250	31,300	5,969	4,691	6,430	5,020
31,300	31,350	5,983	4,699	6,444	5,034
31,350	31,400	5,997	4,706	6,458	5,048
31,400	31,450	6,011	4,714	6,472	5,062
31,450	31,500	6,025	4,721	6,486	5,076
31,500	31,550	6,039	4,729	6,500	5,090
31,550	31,600	6,053	4,736	6,514	5,104
31,600	31,650	6,067	4,744	6,528	5,118
31,650	31,700	6,081	4,751	6,542	5,132
31,700	31,750	6,095	4,759	6,556	5,146
31,750	31,800	6,109	4,766	6,570	5,160
31,800	31,850	6,123	4,774	6,584	5,174
31,850	31,900	6,137	4,781	6,598	5,188
31,900	31,950	6,151	4,789	6,612	5,202
31,950	32,000	6,165	4,796	6,626	5,216

* This column must also be used by a qualifying widow(er).

Continued on next page

Table 6.4 Continued

1992 Tax Table—Continued

If line 37 (taxable income) is—		And you are—			
At least	But less than	Single	Married filing jointly *	Married filing separately	Head of a household
		Your tax is—			

41,000

At least	But less than	Single	MFJ	MFS	HoH
41,000	41,050	8,699	6,833	9,160	7,750
41,050	41,100	8,713	6,847	9,174	7,764
41,100	41,150	8,727	6,861	9,188	7,778
41,150	41,200	8,741	6,875	9,202	7,792
41,200	41,250	8,755	6,889	9,216	7,806
41,250	41,300	8,769	6,903	9,230	7,820
41,300	41,350	8,783	6,917	9,244	7,834
41,350	41,400	8,797	6,931	9,258	7,848
41,400	41,450	8,811	6,945	9,272	7,862
41,450	41,500	8,825	6,959	9,286	7,876
41,500	41,550	8,839	6,973	9,300	7,890
41,550	41,600	8,853	6,987	9,314	7,904
41,600	41,650	8,867	7,001	9,328	7,918
41,650	41,700	8,881	7,015	9,342	7,932
41,700	41,750	8,895	7,029	9,356	7,946
41,750	41,800	8,909	7,043	9,370	7,960
41,800	41,850	8,923	7,057	9,384	7,974
41,850	41,900	8,937	7,071	9,398	7,988
41,900	41,950	8,951	7,085	9,412	8,002
41,950	42,000	8,965	7,099	9,426	8,016

42,000

At least	But less than	Single	MFJ	MFS	HoH
42,000	42,050	8,979	7,113	9,440	8,030
42,050	42,100	8,993	7,127	9,454	8,044
42,100	42,150	9,007	7,141	9,468	8,058
42,150	42,200	9,021	7,155	9,482	8,072
42,200	42,250	9,035	7,169	9,496	8,086
42,250	42,300	9,049	7,183	9,510	8,100
42,300	42,350	9,063	7,197	9,524	8,114
42,350	42,400	9,077	7,211	9,538	8,128
42,400	42,450	9,091	7,225	9,552	8,142
42,450	42,500	9,105	7,239	9,566	8,156
42,500	42,550	9,119	7,253	9,580	8,170
42,550	42,600	9,133	7,267	9,594	8,184
42,600	42,650	9,147	7,281	9,608	8,198
42,650	42,700	9,161	7,295	9,622	8,212
42,700	42,750	9,175	7,309	9,636	8,226
42,750	42,800	9,189	7,323	9,650	8,240
42,800	42,850	9,203	7,337	9,664	8,254
42,850	42,900	9,217	7,351	9,678	8,268
42,900	42,950	9,231	7,365	9,692	8,282
42,950	43,000	9,245	7,379	9,706	8,296

43,000

At least	But less than	Single	MFJ	MFS	HoH
43,000	43,050	9,259	7,393	9,720	8,310
43,050	43,100	9,273	7,407	9,734	8,324
43,100	43,150	9,287	7,421	9,748	8,338
43,150	43,200	9,301	7,435	9,762	8,352
43,200	43,250	9,315	7,449	9,776	8,366
43,250	43,300	9,329	7,463	9,791	8,380
43,300	43,350	9,343	7,477	9,806	8,394
43,350	43,400	9,357	7,491	9,822	8,408
43,400	43,450	9,371	7,505	9,837	8,422
43,450	43,500	9,385	7,519	9,853	8,436
43,500	43,550	9,399	7,533	9,868	8,450
43,550	43,600	9,413	7,547	9,884	8,464
43,600	43,650	9,427	7,561	9,899	8,478
43,650	43,700	9,441	7,575	9,915	8,492
43,700	43,750	9,455	7,589	9,930	8,506
43,750	43,800	9,469	7,603	9,946	8,520
43,800	43,850	9,483	7,617	9,961	8,534
43,850	43,900	9,497	7,631	9,977	8,548
43,900	43,950	9,511	7,645	9,992	8,562
43,950	44,000	9,525	7,659	10,008	8,576

44,000

At least	But less than	Single	MFJ	MFS	HoH
44,000	44,050	9,539	7,673	10,023	8,590
44,050	44,100	9,553	7,687	10,039	8,604
44,100	44,150	9,567	7,701	10,054	8,618
44,150	44,200	9,581	7,715	10,070	8,632
44,200	44,250	9,595	7,729	10,085	8,646
44,250	44,300	9,609	7,743	10,101	8,660
44,300	44,350	9,623	7,757	10,116	8,674
44,350	44,400	9,637	7,771	10,132	8,688
44,400	44,450	9,651	7,785	10,147	8,702
44,450	44,500	9,665	7,799	10,163	8,716
44,500	44,550	9,679	7,813	10,178	8,730
44,550	44,600	9,693	7,827	10,194	8,744
44,600	44,650	9,707	7,841	10,209	8,758
44,650	44,700	9,721	7,855	10,225	8,772
44,700	44,750	9,735	7,869	10,240	8,786
44,750	44,800	9,749	7,883	10,256	8,800
44,800	44,850	9,763	7,897	10,271	8,814
44,850	44,900	9,777	7,911	10,287	8,828
44,900	44,950	9,791	7,925	10,302	8,842
44,950	45,000	9,805	7,939	10,318	8,856

45,000

At least	But less than	Single	MFJ	MFS	HoH
45,000	45,050	9,819	7,953	10,333	8,870
45,050	45,100	9,833	7,967	10,349	8,884
45,100	45,150	9,847	7,981	10,364	8,898
45,150	45,200	9,861	7,995	10,380	8,912
45,200	45,250	9,875	8,009	10,395	8,926
45,250	45,300	9,889	8,023	10,411	8,940
45,300	45,350	9,903	8,037	10,426	8,954
45,350	45,400	9,917	8,051	10,442	8,968
45,400	45,450	9,931	8,065	10,457	8,982
45,450	45,500	9,945	8,079	10,473	8,996
45,500	45,550	9,959	8,093	10,488	9,010
45,550	45,600	9,973	8,107	10,504	9,024
45,600	45,650	9,987	8,121	10,519	9,038
45,650	45,700	10,001	8,135	10,535	9,052
45,700	45,750	10,015	8,149	10,550	9,066
45,750	45,800	10,029	8,163	10,566	9,080
45,800	45,850	10,043	8,177	10,581	9,094
45,850	45,900	10,057	8,191	10,597	9,108
45,900	45,950	10,071	8,205	10,612	9,122
45,950	46,000	10,085	8,219	10,628	9,136

46,000

At least	But less than	Single	MFJ	MFS	HoH
46,000	46,050	10,099	8,233	10,643	9,150
46,050	46,100	10,113	8,247	10,659	9,164
46,100	46,150	10,127	8,261	10,674	9,178
46,150	46,200	10,141	8,275	10,690	9,192
46,200	46,250	10,155	8,289	10,705	9,206
46,250	46,300	10,169	8,303	10,721	9,220
46,300	46,350	10,183	8,317	10,736	9,234
46,350	46,400	10,197	8,331	10,752	9,248
46,400	46,450	10,211	8,345	10,767	9,262
46,450	46,500	10,225	8,359	10,783	9,276
46,500	46,550	10,239	8,373	10,798	9,290
46,550	46,600	10,253	8,387	10,814	9,304
46,600	46,650	10,267	8,401	10,829	9,318
46,650	46,700	10,281	8,415	10,845	9,332
46,700	46,750	10,295	8,429	10,860	9,346
46,750	46,800	10,309	8,443	10,876	9,360
46,800	46,850	10,323	8,457	10,891	9,374
46,850	46,900	10,337	8,471	10,907	9,388
46,900	46,950	10,351	8,485	10,922	9,402
46,950	47,000	10,365	8,499	10,938	9,416

47,000

At least	But less than	Single	MFJ	MFS	HoH
47,000	47,050	10,379	8,513	10,953	9,430
47,050	47,100	10,393	8,527	10,969	9,444
47,100	47,150	10,407	8,541	10,984	9,458
47,150	47,200	10,421	8,555	11,000	9,472
47,200	47,250	10,435	8,569	11,015	9,486
47,250	47,300	10,449	8,583	11,031	9,500
47,300	47,350	10,463	8,597	11,046	9,514
47,350	47,400	10,477	8,611	11,062	9,528
47,400	47,450	10,491	8,625	11,077	9,542
47,450	47,500	10,505	8,639	11,093	9,556
47,500	47,550	10,519	8,653	11,108	9,570
47,550	47,600	10,533	8,667	11,124	9,584
47,600	47,650	10,547	8,681	11,139	9,598
47,650	47,700	10,561	8,695	11,155	9,612
47,700	47,750	10,575	8,709	11,170	9,626
47,750	47,800	10,589	8,723	11,186	9,640
47,800	47,850	10,603	8,737	11,201	9,654
47,850	47,900	10,617	8,751	11,217	9,668
47,900	47,950	10,631	8,765	11,232	9,682
47,950	48,000	10,645	8,779	11,248	9,696

48,000

At least	But less than	Single	MFJ	MFS	HoH
48,000	48,050	10,659	8,793	11,263	9,710
48,050	48,100	10,673	8,807	11,279	9,724
48,100	48,150	10,687	8,821	11,294	9,738
48,150	48,200	10,701	8,835	11,310	9,752
48,200	48,250	10,715	8,849	11,325	9,766
48,250	48,300	10,729	8,863	11,341	9,780
48,300	48,350	10,743	8,877	11,356	9,794
48,350	48,400	10,757	8,891	11,372	9,808
48,400	48,450	10,771	8,905	11,387	9,822
48,450	48,500	10,785	8,919	11,403	9,836
48,500	48,550	10,799	8,933	11,418	9,850
48,550	48,600	10,813	8,947	11,434	9,864
48,600	48,650	10,827	8,961	11,449	9,878
48,650	48,700	10,841	8,975	11,465	9,892
48,700	48,750	10,855	8,989	11,480	9,906
48,750	48,800	10,869	9,003	11,496	9,920
48,800	48,850	10,883	9,017	11,511	9,934
48,850	48,900	10,897	9,031	11,527	9,948
48,900	48,950	10,911	9,045	11,542	9,962
48,950	49,000	10,925	9,059	11,558	9,976

49,000

At least	But less than	Single	MFJ	MFS	HoH
49,000	49,050	10,939	9,073	11,573	9,990
49,050	49,100	10,953	9,087	11,589	10,004
49,100	49,150	10,967	9,101	11,604	10,018
49,150	49,200	10,981	9,115	11,620	10,032
49,200	49,250	10,995	9,129	11,635	10,046
49,250	49,300	11,009	9,143	11,651	10,060
49,300	49,350	11,023	9,157	11,666	10,074
49,350	49,400	11,037	9,171	11,682	10,088
49,400	49,450	11,051	9,185	11,697	10,102
49,450	49,500	11,065	9,199	11,713	10,116
49,500	49,550	11,079	9,213	11,728	10,130
49,550	49,600	11,093	9,227	11,744	10,144
49,600	49,650	11,107	9,241	11,759	10,158
49,650	49,700	11,121	9,255	11,775	10,172
49,700	49,750	11,135	9,269	11,790	10,186
49,750	49,800	11,149	9,283	11,806	10,200
49,800	49,850	11,163	9,297	11,821	10,214
49,850	49,900	11,177	9,311	11,837	10,228
49,900	49,950	11,191	9,325	11,852	10,242
49,950	50,000	11,205	9,339	11,868	10,256

* This column must also be used by a qualifying widow(er).

Continued on next page

EXAMPLE 7 Juan Garcia and his wife have a combined income of $62,506 and interest income of $500. They receive an adjustment to income of $1,450. Their deductible expenses (in excess of IRS exclusions) include doctor and dentist bills of $1,688, $1,922 in state income taxes, $1,690 in real estate taxes, home mortgage interest, $1,040, charitable contributions of $1,056, and $163 in miscellaneous deductions. The Garcias are filing a joint return claiming five exemptions. Find the amount of the tax if the standard deduction is $6,000.

Solution:

$62,506	Employment income
+ 500	Interest income
− 1,450	Adjustment to income
$61,556	Adjusted gross income

$1,688	Medical and dental expenses
1,922	State income taxes
1,690	Real estate taxes
1,040	Home mortgage interest
1,056	Contributions
163	Finance charges
$7,559	Total itemized deductions

$61,556	Adjusted gross income
−$ 7,559	Total itemized deductions
− 11,500	Exemptions ($2,300 × 5)
$42,497	Taxable income

From table 6.4, the intersection of the row 42,450–42,500 and the column "Married filing jointly" is $7,239. ∎

EXAMPLE 8 Charles Kirk had a taxable income of $16,290 last year. Charles is single and claimed one exemption. He is paid weekly, and $34 was withheld from his pay. Determine if at the end of the year Charles paid additional taxes or received a refund.

Solution: From table 6.4, Charles' tax was $2,441. The total withheld from his pay was $34 × 52 = $1,768. Thus, Charles paid an additional amount of $2,441 − $1,768 = $673. ∎

EXAMPLE 9 Last year, John Higgins earned $42,400. He also received $2,016 in interest on savings and made payments of $3,120 to a Keogh pension plan. John is paid every two weeks and has $190 withheld each payday. In preparing his federal income tax return, John itemized deductions, and the total was $5,420. John is married with one child and filed a joint return. Determine if John paid additional taxes or received a refund.

	$42,400	Employment income
+	2,016	Interest
	$44,416	Total income
−	3,120	Adjustments to income
	$41,296	Adjusted gross income
−	6,000	Standard Deduction
−	6,900	Exemptions
	$28,396	Taxable income

	$ 4,940	Withheld ($190 × 26)
−	4,256	Tax (table 6.4)
	$ 684	Refunded to John

Solution:

EXERCISES FOR SECTION 6.3

In problems 1–6, use the information given to find the adjusted gross income.

1. Earned income, $24,752; interest income, $257; adjustments to income, $782.

2. Earned income, $33,284; interest income, $792; dividend income, $147; payments to a Keogh plan, $1,141; other adjustments to income, $857.

3. Earned income, $47,214; interest income, $1,214; dividend income, $392; payments to a Keogh plan, $482; other adjustments to income, $700.

4. Earned income, $28,427; interest income, $108; dividend income, $210; payments to an IRA, $160 per month; other adjustments to income, $319.

5. Earned income, $51,908; interest income, $1,942; dividend income, $4,249; payments to a Keogh plan, $410 per month; other adjustments to income, $2,317.

6. Earned income, $24,425; interest income, $685; payments to an IRA, $200 per month; alimony, $220 per month.

In problems 7–12, determine whether the taxpayer should itemize deductions or use the standard deduction. (All deduction items are in excess of any IRS exclusion.)

7. Medical and dental expenses, $1,308; state income tax, $672; charitable contributions, $1,243; miscellaneous deductions, $340. Single.

8. Medical and dental expenses, $440; real estate taxes, $1,600; state income tax, $1,500; home mortgage interest, $1,250; charitable contributions, $900. Head of household.

9. Real estate taxes, $2,465; state income tax, $1,900; home mortgage interest, $760; charitable contributions, $1,214. Married filing jointly.

10. Medical and dental expenses, $228; state income tax, $1,520; charitable contributions, $940. Married filing separately.

11. Medical and dental expenses, $139; real estate taxes, $1,466; home mortgage interest, $2,666; charitable contributions, $975; miscellaneous deductions, $200. Head of household.

12. Medical and dental expenses, $116; real estate taxes, $822; state income tax, $1,720; home mortgage interest, $1,072; charitable contributions, $1,335; miscellaneous deductions, $700. Married filing jointly.

In problems 13–28, find the tax using the given information. Assume that the reduction for exemptions is $2,300 per exemption and that all deductions are in excess of any IRS exclusions.

13. Married taxpayer; filing separately; taxable income, $29,200.

14. Married taxpayer; joint return; taxable income, $41,480.

15. Single taxpayer; one exemption; adjusted gross income, $21,014; total itemized deductions, $2,842.

16. Head of household; two exemptions; adjusted gross income, $27,573; total itemized deductions, $3,214.

17. Adjusted gross income, $36,214; total itemized deductions, $5,287; head of household; two exemptions.

18. Adjusted gross income, $41,702; total itemized deductions, $6,142; married filing jointly; four exemptions.

19. Adjusted gross income, $22,578; medical expenses, $312; mortgage interest, $1,935; real estate taxes, $841; charitable contributions, $428. Single; one exemption.

20. Adjusted gross income, $35,551; mortgage interest, $3,326; real estate taxes, $1,918; charitable contributions, $622; miscellaneous, $326. Married filing jointly; three exemptions.

21. Adjusted gross income, $53,700. Deductible expenses: medical, dental, and drug expenses, $470; mortgage interest, $2,700; miscellaneous, $440; real estate taxes, $1,850; charitable contributions, $280. Married filing jointly, two exemptions.

22. Adjusted gross income, $53,500. Deductible expenses: medical, dental, and drug expenses, $125; mortgage interest, $1,400; real estate taxes, $1,670; state income tax, $1,250; charitable contributions, $1,500. Head of household; two exemptions.

23. Earned income, $40,201; interest income, $821; adjustments to income, $1,750; medical expenses, $578; mortgage interest, $1,826; real estate taxes, $1,226; charitable contributions, $1,394; miscellaneous, $418. Married filing jointly; four exemptions.

24. Earned income, $31,802; interest income, $278; adjustments to income, $1,492. Deductions: mortgage interest, $1,737; real estate taxes, $1,892; charitable contributions, $1,246; miscellaneous, $495. Married filing jointly; three exemptions.

25. Income from employment, $57,800; interest income, $920; dividend income, $800. Deductions: medical, dental, and drug expenses, $415; mortgage interest, $2,620; real estate taxes, $1,860; charitable contributions, $1,420. Married filing jointly; five exemptions.

26. Income from employment, $68,600; adjustments to income, $1,300; dividend income, $1,500. Deductions: medical, dental, and drug expenses, $1,370; mortgage interest, $4,900; state income tax, $1,200; real estate taxes, $1,100; charitable contributions, $4,000; miscellaneous, $320. Married filing jointly; three exemptions.

27. Bob and Jean Farrell have a combined income from their jobs of $92,000. They also have dividend income of $1,800 and payments to a Keogh plan of $18,400. Their deductions include medical, dental, and drug expenses of $235, state income taxes of $2,700, mortgage interest of $5,240, real estate taxes of $4,600, charitable contributions of $4,500 and miscellaneous, $210. If the Farrells file a joint return claiming four exemptions, how much federal income tax will they owe?

28. Last year, Pat and Jim Roberts had a combined income from employment of $63,100. They also had interest income of $600 and dividend income of $800. Their deductible expenses for the year were: medical, dental, and drug expenses, $895; mortgage interest, $5,800; real estate taxes, $2,100; state income tax, $1,150; miscellaneous, $840; charitable contributions, $1,200. The Roberts filed a joint return claiming five exemptions. Find the amount of federal income tax they owe.

Glossary

Adjusted gross income   Total income less adjustments to income.

Adjustments to income   Expenses that may be subtracted from total income to obtain adjusted gross income; includes such expenses as deductions for reimbursed employee business expenses, penalties for early withdrawal of savings, alimony payments, contributions to a Keogh pension plan, or for taxpayers not covered by a company pension plan, contributions to an individual retirement account.

Assessed value   A percentage of the estimated market value of property.

Deduction   An expense that reduces the amount of taxable income.

Excise tax   A tax imposed by federal, state, or local governments on specific nonessential or luxury items.

Exemption   An allowance used to reduce the adjusted gross income. In general, an exemption is the taxpayer or any relative of the taxpayer who is dependent on the taxpayer for financial support.

Itemized deductions   A listing of each allowable deduction and the amount. Used only if the total exceeds the standard deduction.

Mill   1/1,000 of a dollar.

Property   For tax purposes, this term can mean real property (land and the building improvements on the land) or personal property (automobiles, furniture, jewelry, and so on).

Property tax rate   The quotient obtained by dividing the total taxes to be raised by the total assessments.

Sales tax   A tax on retail sales imposed by state or local governments.

Standard deduction   The average amount an individual or family is expected to incur in deductible expenses during a year.

Taxable income   The adjusted gross income minus the total for exemptions and minus either **a.** the total of itemized deductions, or **b.** the standard deduction, whichever is greater.

Total income   For most people, the income from employment, from interest on savings or bonds, and from stock dividends.

Review Test

1. A tax imposed on a nonessential or luxury item is called a(n) _____ tax.

2. A percentage of the estimated market value of property is called the _____ of the property.

3. A _____ is 1/1,000 of a dollar.

4. The difference between total income and adjustments to income is called the _____ .

5. The average amount of deductible expenses an individual or family is expected to incur during a year is called the _____ .

In problems 6–10, use only the basic percentage formula to compute sales and excise taxes.

6. The selling price of a baby car seat is $69.99. Find the amount of the sales tax if the tax rate is 6%.

7. Find the total cost of a coffeemaker if the selling price is $46.95 and the sales tax rate is 4%.

8. A theater owner decides that the total price of a ticket for a movie (selling price plus sales tax) should be $5.50. What is the selling price if the sales tax rate is 5%?

9. A fishing rod that sells for $72.95 is subject to a 4% sales tax and a 10% excise tax. What is the total cost to the buyer?

10. A state sales tax was $5\frac{1}{2}$% on all items except groceries and prescription drugs. Mildred made the following purchases at Jody's Discount Drugs: Deodorant, $2.35; magazine, $2.95; aspirin, $1.40; four 2-liter bottles of cola at $1.19 per bottle; mouthwash, $3.10; corn chips, $2.15. She also paid $15.80 for a prescription that had been filled. Find the total amount Mildred paid the cashier.

11. Find the property tax on a warehouse. The property is assessed at 80% of its market value of $1,434,000 and the tax rate is 28 mills.

12. Property taxes for a house with a fair market value of $139,700 were $4,302.76. If assessments were 88% of the fair market value, find the property tax percent.

13. A businessperson paid $5,355 in property taxes. The tax rate was $4.25 per $100 of assessed value and the property was assessed at 70% of its fair market value. Find the fair market value.

14. Harold Haines's salary was $32,800 last year. During the same year, he had adjustments to income of $2,870, and he made $50 per month in interest from a savings account. What was his adjusted gross income for the year?

15. The Petersons had combined salaries of $89,400, 15% of which was contributed to a Keogh plan. They also received $2,025 in stock dividends, of which 20% was in tax free investments not subject to federal income taxes. The Petersons have two children and filed a joint federal income tax return using the standard deduction. Find their taxable income for the year.

16. Edith Miller earned a salary of $28,500 last year. In addition, she received $1,400 in dividends, and she had medical and dental expenses of $822 in excess of the IRS exclusion. Other expenses for the year included mortgage interest charges of $1,040, real estate taxes of $1,677, and charitable contributions of $1,516. Calculate her taxable income if she claims two exemptions and files a return as head of household.

Simple Interest

 **Section 7.1** *Simple Interest*

A. Introduction

Money paid for the use of money is called **interest.** Much of the American economy depends on keeping in circulation money that people have but temporarily do not need. The charge for rent of this money is called interest.

Nearly every adult receives or pays interest. We receive interest from our savings accounts or from bonds because we, in effect, are loaning our money for others to use. But we pay interest in the mortgage payments for our home, in our automobile payments, and often in the payment of credit card accounts. In these instances we have borrowed money, and our payments include interest charges.

Businesses and governmental bodies also pay interest when they borrow money to finance special projects. They obtain funds by borrowing from banks or insurance companies, or by the issuance of bonds. In each case, interest is paid to the party supplying the money.

In this chapter, we begin a study of the kinds of interest and the methods of calculating interest.

B. The Simple Interest Formula

Simple interest is an annual percentage of the amount of money borrowed or invested. The formula for simple interest is a modification of the basic percentage formula. The formula is

(7-1) $I = Prt$

where I = simple interest,
        P = **principal** (the amount of money borrowed or invested)
        r = annual rate
        t = the length of time the principal is borrowed or invested.

The principal is expressed in dollars, the rate is expressed in percent, and the time is expressed in years.

Because simple interest is used primarily for short term loans, a time fraction must be used when the term of the loan is in months. The time fraction is given by

(7-2) $\dfrac{\text{Term of the loan in months}}{12}$

EXAMPLE 1   Find the time fraction for a loan with a term of: **a.** three months, **b.** four months, **c.** six months, and **d.** nine months.

Solution: Using formula 7–2,

a. $\dfrac{3}{12} = \dfrac{1}{4} = 0.25$

b. $\dfrac{4}{12} = \dfrac{1}{3}$

c. $\dfrac{6}{12} = \dfrac{1}{2} = 0.5$

d. $\dfrac{9}{12} = \dfrac{3}{4} = 0.75$ ■

EXAMPLE 2   A person borrowed $500 for four months at a simple interest rate of 9%. How much interest did the person pay?

Solution: $I = ?, P = \$500, r = 9\% = 0.09, t = \dfrac{4}{12} = \dfrac{1}{3}$

Using formula 7–1,

$I = Prt$

$= \$500 \times 0.09 \times \dfrac{1}{3}$

$= \$15$ ■

E X A M P L E   3   Find the interest paid on a $4,400 loan for six months at $6\frac{1}{4}$% simple interest.

Solution: $I = ?, P = \$4,400, r = 6\frac{1}{4}\% = 0.0625, t = \dfrac{6}{12} = 0.5$

Using formula 7–1,

$I = Prt$
$= \$4,400 \times 0.0625 \times 0.5$
$= \$137.50$

C. Variations of the Simple Interest Formula

In formula 7–1, the interest I is the unknown. However, it may be necessary to solve for one of the other quantities. From

$$I = Prt$$

we can derive

(7–3) $P = \dfrac{I}{rt}$ (Dividing both sides of formula 7–1 by rt)

(7–4) $r = \dfrac{I}{Pt}$ (Dividing both sides of formula 7–1 by Pt)

(7–5) $t = \dfrac{I}{Pr}$ (Dividing both sides of formula 7–1 by Pr)

E X A M P L E   4   At a simple interest rate of 8%, what principal would earn $288 interest in nine months?

Solution: Using formula 7–3 with $I = \$288, P = ?, r = 8\% = 0.08, t = \dfrac{9}{12} = 0.75$

$P = \dfrac{I}{rt}$

$= \dfrac{\$288}{0.08 \times 0.75}$

$= \$4,800$

Entry	Display	Memory
0.08	0.08	0
×	0.08	0
0.75	0.75	0
M+	0.06	0
288	288	0.06
÷	288	0.06
MR	0.06	0.06
=	4800	0.06

EXAMPLE 5   Find the simple interest rate necessary for $4,800 to earn $162 interest in six months.

Solution: Using formula 7–4 with $I = 162, $P = $4,800$, $r = ?$, $t = \dfrac{6}{12} = 0.5$

$$r = \frac{I}{Pt}$$
$$= \frac{\$162}{\$4,800 \times 0.5}$$
$$= 0.0675$$
$$= 6.75\%$$

■

EXAMPLE 6   How long will it take for $5,400 to earn $405 in interest if the simple interest rate is 5%?

Solution: Using formula 7–5 with $I = 405, $P = $5,400$, $r = 5\% = 0.05$, $t = ?$

$$t = \frac{I}{Pr}$$
$$= \frac{\$405}{\$5,400 \times 0.05}$$
$$= 1.5 \text{ years}$$

■

EXERCISES FOR SECTION 7.1

In problems 1–16, use the simple interest formula to solve for the missing letter.

	I	P	r	t		I	P	r	t
1.	—	$500	7%	2 years	9.	—	$3,800	$6\frac{1}{4}\%$	8 months
2.	—	$2,000	5%	1 year	10.	$382.50	—	9%	15 months
3.	$150	—	10%	6 months	11.	$67.20	$630	—	16 months
4.	$210	—	7%	9 months	12.	$1,443.75	$22,000	$8\frac{3}{4}\%$	—
5.	$720	$12,000	—	8 months	13.	$780.80	—	6.1%	2 years
6.	($4,250)	$1,500	—	4 months	14.	$155.63	$4,025	—	$\frac{2}{3}$ year
7.	$204	$600	$8\frac{1}{2}\%$	—	15.	—	$15,000	9.42%	1.5 years
8.	$37.40	$1,360	$5\frac{1}{2}\%$	—	16.	$3,075	$125,500	7.35%	—

Solve.

17. Bob Parker borrowed $3,000 for four months at a simple interest rate of 12%. How much interest will Bob pay for the loan?

$$3000 \times \frac{4}{12} \times \frac{12}{100} = 120$$

18. Find the interest paid for a loan of $1,800 for 10 months at 9% simple interest.

$$1800 \times \frac{10}{12} \times \frac{9}{100} = 45$$

19. What is the interest on a $1,500 loan for six months at $8\frac{3}{4}\%$ simple interest?

20. Myra Williams borrowed $2,400 for 18 months at a simple interest rate of $7\frac{1}{2}\%$. How much interest will she pay for the loan?

21. Sue Cunningham owns a $5,000 bond that pays $10\frac{1}{4}\%$ simple interest. How much does she receive quarterly from the bond?

22. Bill Foster invested $10,000 in a <u>six</u> month savings certificate offered by his credit union. If the interest rate on the certificate was 11.65%, how much interest did Bill earn?

23. At a simple interest rate of 9%, how much money would have to be invested to earn $315 in seven months?

24. Mel Phillips paid $675 interest on a $5,000 loan at 9% simple interest. What was the length of the loan?

25. Brenda Jones invested $15,000 in U.S. Treasury bills. At the end of three months, she received $368.75 in interest. What was the simple interest rate?

26. To earn $85 in eight months, how much money would have to be invested at $8\frac{1}{2}\%$ simple interest?

27. Find the simple interest rate necessary for $2,500 to earn $443.75 in 18 months.

28. How long will it take $1,300 invested at $9\frac{1}{2}\%$ to earn $61.75 in simple interest?

29. Wilma Smith arranged for a loan of $7,500 for $1\frac{1}{2}$ years at $8\frac{3}{4}\%$ simple interest. How much interest will she pay?

30. Brett Walker needs to borrow $4,000 to pay for remodeling his store. If the rate of simple interest Brett must pay is 7%, and if he is not willing to pay more than $210 in interest, for how long can he borrow the money?

31. Ned Peters needs to borrow $3,900 for 16 months. If he cannot pay more than $360 in interest, and if the least simple interest rate at which he can borrow the money is $6\frac{3}{4}\%$, can he obtain the loan?

32. The new owner of a small business wishes to borrow some money for operating capital. At a simple interest rate of $10\frac{1}{2}\%$, how much can she borrow for three months and not pay more than $100 in interest?

33. June Richardson has arranged to loan $2,700 to a friend for four months. To receive at least $100 in simple interest, what is the smallest interest rate that she can charge?

Section 7.2 *Exact Time and Ordinary Time*

Time is measured in years in the simple interest formula; hence, in the previous section a **time fraction** was used when the term of the loan was in months. When time is measured in days, there are two time fractions, one based on an astronomical calendar and one based on a financial calendar. The astronomical calendar, called **exact time,** is based on the revolution of the earth about the sun. One revolution takes $365\frac{1}{4}$ days; hence a calendar year consists of 365 days, with a leap year of 366 days every fourth year.* The year is divided into months of 28, (29), 30, or 31 days, irregularly spaced. Thus, for exact time, the time fraction is

$$(7\text{-}6) \quad \frac{\text{Term of the loan in days}}{365}$$

*Leap years account for the $\frac{1}{4}$ day accumulation each year, with the extra day added to the month of February (February 29). Leap years occur on years divisible by 4 or for century years divisible by 400. 1992, 1996, 2000, 2004, and so on are leap years, but 1900 was not.

365 for Deposit + Interest. — Exact
360 for Loans - Ordinary

The financial calendar, called **ordinary time** or **banker's year,** eliminates the irregularities of the astronomical calendar by defining a year to be 12 months of thirty days per month. As a result, a year in ordinary time consists of $12 \times 30 = 360$ days. Thus, the time fraction for ordinary time is

(7–7) $$\frac{\text{Term of the loan in days}}{360}$$

Ordinary time is a calendar of convenience since 360 is divisible by 30, 60, 90, 120, and 180, numbers that are frequently used for the term of a loan.

In most interest transactions, *if the term of the loan is expressed in days, exact time is used. Also, an interest bearing document begins to earn interest on the day following its execution and continues to earn interest until the day it is paid. Thus, in counting the days between two dates, the last day is counted, but the first day is not.*

Calculations of exact time may be simplified by the use of appendix B—The Number of Each Day of the Year—found at the end of the book. The examples that follow illustrate the use of appendix B in finding exact time. Unless specified, the years are nonleap years and the dates are in the same year.

E X A M P L E 1   Using exact time, find the number of days from May 14 to September 20.

Solution:
Date		*Day*
September 20	=	263
May 14	=	−134
		129

There are 129 days from May 14 to September 20.   ■

E X A M P L E 2   Using exact time, find the number of days from January 4, 1992 to April 30, 1992.

Solution: The year 1992 was a leap year; thus,

Date		*Day*
April 30, 1992	=	121 (120 + 1 day for leap year)
January 4, 1992	=	− 4
		117

■

E X A M P L E 3   Find the number of days from November 14, 1993 to January 10, 1994.

Solution: Because this period includes two different years, the interval must be separated into 1993 time and 1994 time. Then the solutions are added to find the total time.

Date		Day
December 31, 1993	=	365
November 14, 1993	=	$-\underline{318}$
		47
January 10, 1994	=	$+\underline{\ \ 10}$
		57

■

E X A M P L E   4   A loan is executed on June 10 for a term of six months. Find the due date of the loan. *360*

Solution: Since the term of the loan is stated in months, six months from June 10 is December 10. This is true using either exact time or ordinary time. ■

One exception to the reasoning of example 4 occurs when the term of a loan ends on a day that does not exist. For instance, a one month loan executed on March 31 would be due on April 30, since there is no April 31.

E X A M P L E   5   A loan is executed on June 10 for 180 days. Find the due date of the loan using exact time.

Solution: The term of the loan is in days; hence from appendix B,

Date		Day
June 10	→	161
		$+\underline{180}$
December 7	←	341

■

EXERCISES FOR SECTION 7.2

In problems 1–10, use appendix B and exact time to find the number of days from the first date to the second. Unless specified, the dates are in the same year.

1. April 22 to September 23

2. July 26 to November 16

3. May 5 to July 4

4. June 23 to October 1

5. March 9 to June 26

6. January 20 to October 23

7. May 7 to January 14 of the following year

8. July 3 to March 4 of the following year

9. October 25 to August 2 of the following year

10. September 5 to April 14 of the following year

In problems 11–20, use exact time to find the due date of a loan executed on the given date for the given term.

11. April 5, two months

12. August 4, seven months

13. September 28, 90 days

14. April 17, 120 days

15. March 21, 60 days

16. February 6, 90 days

17. March 6, 90 days

18. February 18, 120 days

19. December 23, 120 days

20. January 27, 60 days

Section 7.3 *Exact Interest and Ordinary Interest*

In the previous section, it was shown that there are two time fractions when the term of a loan is in days. These time fractions are

(7–8)	$\dfrac{\text{Term of the loan in days}}{365}$
(7–9)	$\dfrac{\text{Term of the loan in days}}{360}$

Interest calculations using time fraction 7–8 are called **exact interest.** Exact interest is used by the federal government and by Federal Reserve banks in their transactions with member banks. Interest calculations using time fraction 7–9 are called **ordinary interest, banker's interest,** or **banker's rule.** Ordinary interest was once favored by commercial institutions because it generates more interest than exact interest. However, recent federal regulations requiring that lending institutions disclose true interest rates to borrowers has resulted in a decline in ordinary interest loans.

EXAMPLE 1   Find the exact interest on $3,000 at $9\frac{3}{4}$% from August 12 to December 5.

Solution: From appendix B, the number of days from August 12 to December 5 is 115 days. Thus, with $I = ?$, $P = \$3,000$, $r = 9\frac{3}{4}\% = 0.0975$, and $t = \frac{115}{365}$,

$$I = Prt$$
$$= \$3,000 \times 0.0975 \times \frac{115}{365}$$
$$= \$92.16$$

Entry	Display
3000	3000
$\times$	3000
0.0975	0.0975
$\times$	292.50
115	115
$\div$	33637.5
365	365
$=$	92.157534

EXAMPLE 2   Find the ordinary interest on $900 at $6\frac{1}{2}\%$ for 30 days.

Solution: $I = ?, P = \$900, r = 6\frac{1}{2}\% = 0.065,$ and $t = \dfrac{30}{360} = \dfrac{1}{12}$

$= \$900 \times 0.065 \times \dfrac{1}{12}$

$= \$4.88$ ∎

EXAMPLE 3   A loan for $1,500 is executed on January 10 at a simple interest rate of 8% and is due on February 20. Calculate the interest using **a.** exact interest and **b.** ordinary interest.

Solution: From appendix B, the exact time from January 10 to February 20 is 41 days. Thus, with $P = \$1,500$ and $r = 8\% = 0.08,$

a. $I = Prt$

$= \$1,500 \times 0.08 \times \dfrac{41}{365}$

$= \$13.48$

b. $I = Prt$

$= \$1,500 \times 0.08 \times \dfrac{41}{360}$

$= \$13.67$

In this case, ordinary interest earned $0.19 more than exact interest.   ∎

EXAMPLE 4   A loan of $1,200 for 70 days earned exact interest in the amount of $16.11. What was the interest rate?

Solution: $P = \$1,200, I = \$16.11, r = ?, t = \dfrac{70}{365}$

$r = \dfrac{I}{Pt}$

$= \dfrac{\$16.11}{\$1,200 \times \dfrac{70}{365}}$

$= 0.07 = 7\%$

Entry	Display	Memory
1200	1200	0
×	1200	0
70	70	0
÷	84000	0
365	365	0
M+	230.13698	230.13698
16.11	16.11	230.13698
÷	16.11	230.13698
MR	230.13698	230.13698
=	0.0700017	230.13698

∎

EXAMPLE 5 How many days would it take to earn \$247.50 ordinary interest on \$20,000 invested at $8\frac{1}{4}\%$?

Solution: $I = \$247.50$, $P = \$20,000$, $r = 8\frac{1}{4}\% = 0.0825$, $t = ?$

$$t = \frac{I}{Pr}$$

$$= \frac{\$247.50}{\$20,000 \times 0.0825}$$

$$= 0.15 \text{ years}$$

$$= 0.15 \times 360 \quad \text{(Multiplying by 360 to convert to days)}$$

$$= 54 \text{ days} \qquad \blacksquare$$

As shown in section 3–4, it is a common practice for vendors to offer buyers a cash discount for prompt payment. It is usually profitable for a buyer to take advantage of a cash discount, even if it is necessary to borrow money to do so. The next examples demonstrate why.

EXAMPLE 6 An invoice for \$600 contains terms 2/10, n/30. At what exact interest rate could the buyer afford to borrow to take advantage of the cash discount?

Solution: The first step is to calculate the cash discount and the amount to be borrowed:

$$
\begin{array}{rl}
\$600 & \text{Net amount} \\
-\underline{\quad 12} & \text{Cash discount (\$600} \times 0.02) \\
\$588 & \text{Amount to be borrowed}
\end{array}
$$

If the buyer is to save money, the interest on the loan must be less than \$12. Since the net amount is due 20 days after the last day of the cash discount, the term of the loan is $\frac{20}{365}$. Thus, using formula 7–4 with $I = \$12$, $P = \$588$, $r = ?$, and $t = \frac{20}{365}$,

$$r = \frac{I}{Pt}$$

$$= \frac{\$12}{\$588 \times \dfrac{20}{365}}$$

$$= 0.3724$$

$$= 37.24\%$$

The buyer could borrow \$588 for 20 days at any interest rate less than 37.24% and save money on the transaction. $\qquad \blacksquare$

EXAMPLE 7   An invoice for $480 contains terms 3/10, n/60. At an exact interest rate of $10\frac{1}{2}\%$, calculate **a.** how much would have to be borrowed to take advantage of the cash discount and **b.** how much would be saved on the transaction.

Solution: **a.** $480.00   Net amount
          −   14.40   Cash discount ($480 × 0.03)
             $465.60   Amount to be borrowed

b. $I = ?, P = \$465.60, r = 10\frac{1}{2}\% = 0.105,$ and $t = \dfrac{50}{365}$

$I = Prt$

$= \$465.60 \times 0.105 \times \dfrac{50}{365}$

$= \$6.70$

The interest on the loan is $6.70. Hence, the amount saved is

$14.40 − $6.70 = $7.70.

EXERCISES FOR SECTION 7.3

In problems 1–16, find the exact interest for the given loans. (Always assume nonleap years.)

1. $8,600 at 9% for 90 days
2. $5,400 at 11% for 180 days
3. $4,300 at $8\frac{1}{4}\%$ for 60 days
4. $3,600 at $9\frac{1}{2}\%$ for 90 days
5. $6,500 at $8\frac{3}{4}\%$ for 45 days
6. $9,100 at $6\frac{3}{4}\%$ for 65 days
7. $5,000 at $7\frac{1}{2}\%$ from June 4 to September 2
8. $5,300 at $10\frac{1}{4}\%$ from January 5 to October 4

9. $4,650 at $9\frac{3}{4}\%$ from February 27 to July 7
10. $8,100 at $10\frac{1}{2}\%$ from September 15 to March 4
11. $8,925 at $8\frac{3}{4}\%$ from October 1 to August 9
12. $6,675 at $8\frac{1}{2}\%$ from September 12 to January 14
13. $6,550 at 9.24% from August 18 to January 25
14. $9,120 at 7.68% from December 5 to March 29
15. $13,810 at 8.44% from March 15 to May 19
16. $12,125 at 6.96% from April 10 to August 22

In problems 17–22, find the ordinary interest for the given loan.

17. $2,900 at 6% for 120 days
18. $8,250 at $7\frac{1}{2}\%$ for 90 days
19. $4,100 at $8\frac{1}{2}\%$ from January 5 to April 23

20. $5,500 at 10% from March 21 to May 11
21. $9,260 at $9\frac{1}{4}\%$ from May 12 to October 9
22. $10,125 at $6\frac{1}{2}\%$ from August 14 to November 3

*In problems 23–39, find: **a.** the exact interest and **b.** the ordinary interest for the given loans.*

23. $8,500 at 10% for 90 days
24. $4,500 at 6% for 180 days
25. $6,200 at $8\frac{1}{4}\%$ for 60 days

26. $3,700 at $9\frac{1}{2}\%$ for 180 days
27. $4,600 at $8\frac{3}{4}\%$ for 45 days
28. $8,200 at $6\frac{3}{4}\%$ for 65 days

29. $3,000 at $11\frac{1}{2}$% from May 15 to August 13

30. $7,200 at $10\frac{1}{4}$% from July 8 to September 6

31. $2,500 at $9\frac{3}{4}$% from February 4 to August 3

32. $8,200 at $10\frac{1}{2}$% from January 18 to August 6

33. $8,800 at $8\frac{3}{4}$% from September 26 to February 3

34. $6,700 at $8\frac{1}{2}$% from November 12 to July 10

35. $6,450 at $9\frac{1}{2}$% from October 23 to February 15

36. $9,230 at $10\frac{3}{4}$% from August 18 to January 20

37. $13,720 at $9\frac{1}{4}$% from December 5 to February 18

38. $15,570 at $7\frac{1}{2}$% from March 12 to May 15

39. $22,800 at $6\frac{3}{4}$% from September 4 to October 19

In problems 40–49, find the interest rate for the given loans.

40. $3,000 earns $180 ordinary interest in 180 days.

41. $9,600 earns $144 ordinary interest in 60 days.

42. $4,500 earns $99.86 exact interest in 90 days.

43. $5,700 earns $149.92 exact interest in 120 days.

44. $2,800 earns $121.33 ordinary interest from March 15 to November 10.

45. $3,800 earns $140.39 ordinary interest from May 6 to September 23.

46. $6,400 earns $153.42 exact interest from November 11 to February 19.

47. $7,200 earns $258.90 exact interest from December 4 to July 2.

48. $5,200 earns $136.50 ordinary interest from October 28 to February 5.

49. $3,100 earns $151.34 ordinary interest from September 18 to March 27.

In problems 50–55, find the number of days necessary to earn the given amount of interest on the given loan.

50. $600 ordinary interest on $20,000 at 12%

51. $37.50 ordinary interest on $2,500 at 9%

52. $136.50 ordinary interest on $4,200 at $9\frac{3}{4}$%

53. $706.85 exact interest on $8,600 at 10%

54. $270.74 exact interest on $7,200 at 7.25%

55. $330.82 exact interest on $9,200 at $8\frac{3}{4}$%

In problems 56–63, an investment of P dollars yields the given amount of interest. Find P. (Round to the nearest dollar.)

56. $160 ordinary interest in 180 days at 8%

57. $80 ordinary interest in 60 days at 9%

58. $94.93 exact interest in 90 days at 11%

59. $98.63 exact interest in 120 days at 12%

60. $79.75 ordinary interest at $7\frac{1}{2}$% from May 6 to August 4

61. $142.92 ordinary interest at $8\frac{1}{4}$% from September 5 to January 23

62. $573.25 exact interest at $9\frac{1}{4}$% from July 22 to April 8

63. $483.29 exact interest at $10\frac{1}{2}$% from August 10 to June 6

In problems 64–69, for the given invoice amount and cash discount terms, find the ordinary interest rate at which a buyer could afford to borrow to take advantage of the cash discount.

64. $100; 1/10, n/30

65. $450; 2/15, n/30

66. $680; 3/10, n/30

67. $144.60; 2/15, n/60

68. $375.45; 4/15, n/60

69. $920.33; 5/10, n/30

In problems 70–74, for the given invoice amount, cash discount terms, and ordinary interest rate, find: **a.** *the amount to be borrowed and* **b.** *how much would be saved on the transaction.*

70. $200; 2/10, n/30; 9%

71. $500; 3/10, n/30; 12%

72. $1,370; 4/15, n/60; $8\frac{1}{2}$%

73. $782.50; 2/15, n/60; 11%

74. $947.65; 5/15, n/90; $10\frac{3}{4}$%

Section 7.4   *Maturity Value and Present Value*

A. Maturity Value

When a loan is repaid, the borrower pays the principal plus interest. This sum is called the **amount** or **maturity value.** In symbols,

(7–10) $A = P + I$

In example 1 of section 7.3, the maturity value is

$$A = P + I$$
$$= \$3,000 + \$92.16$$
$$= \$3,092.16$$

Thus, at the end of 115 days, the borrower paid $3,092.16.

The maturity value can be expressed by a different formula. Since

$$A = P + I$$

and

$$I = Prt$$

it follows that

$$A = P + Prt \quad \text{(Substitution)}$$

Factoring P yields

(7–11) $A = P(1 + rt)$

If the principal, rate, and time are given, then maturity value may be found directly from formula 7–11.

EXAMPLE 1   Find the maturity value of $1,280 invested at a simple interest rate of 9% for three months.

Solution: $A = ?, P = \$1,280, r = 9\% = 0.09, t = \frac{3}{12} = 0.25$. Using formula 7–11,

$$A = P(1 + rt)$$
$$= \$1,280[1 + (0.09 \times 0.25)]$$
$$= \$1,280[1 + 0.0225]$$
$$= \$1,280[1.0225]$$
$$= \$1,308.80$$

The result may be checked using formulas 7–1 and 7–10:

$$I = Prt$$
$$= \$1,280 \times 0.09 \times 0.25$$
$$= \$28.80$$
$$A = P + I$$
$$= \$1,280 + \$28.80 = \$1,308.80$$

B. Present Value at Simple Interest

If formula 7–11 is solved for P, the result is

$$A = P(1 + rt)$$
$$P(1 + rt) = A$$

(7–12) $P = \dfrac{A}{1 + rt}$

When formula 7–12 is used, P is referred to as **present value.** Formulas 7–11 and 7–12 solve opposite kinds of problems. Formula 7–11 answers the question, "What amount A results from the investment of principal P at rate r for time t?" On the other hand, formula 7–12 answers the question, "What principal P invested at rate r for time t will result in amount A?"

E X A M P L E   2   What investment at 12% simple interest would have a maturity value of \$500 in 18 months?

Solution: $A = \$500, P = ?, r = 12\% = 0.12, t = \dfrac{18}{12} = 1.5$

$$P = \dfrac{A}{1 + rt}$$
$$= \dfrac{\$500}{1 + (0.12 \times 1.5)}$$
$$= \dfrac{\$500}{1 + 0.18}$$
$$= \dfrac{\$500}{1.18}$$
$$= \$423.73$$

EXAMPLE 3   Find the present value of $2,000 at 12% for eight months.

Solution: $A = \$2,000$, $P = ?$, $r = 12\% = 0.12$, $t = \dfrac{8}{12} = \dfrac{2}{3}$. Using formula 7–12,

$$P = \frac{A}{1 + rt}$$

$$= \frac{\$2,000}{1 + (0.12 \times 2/3)}$$

$$= \frac{\$2,000}{1 + 0.08}$$

$$= \frac{\$2,000}{1.08}$$

$$= \$1,851.85$$

■

EXAMPLE 4   In one year, John Sparks plans to modernize his shop by buying new equipment. He estimates that it will require $6,000 for the new machines. To have the money to purchase the equipment, he wishes to make an investment that will yield $6,000 one year from now. At $8\frac{1}{2}\%$ simple interest, how much must he invest now to have a total of $6,000 in one year?

Solution: $A = \$6,000$, $P = ?$, $r = 8\frac{1}{2}\% = 0.085$, $t = 1$

$$P = \frac{A}{1 + rt}$$

$$= \frac{\$6,000}{1 + (0.085 \times 1)}$$

$$= \frac{\$6,000}{1.085}$$

$$= \$5,529.95$$

■

Lending institutions change their interest rates in response to changing economic conditions, but also in response to competition. The average interest rate is referred to as the cost of money or the **rate money is worth.** Present value can be used to compare investments with the rate money is worth.

EXAMPLE 5   Bob Simons deals in antique cars. At a recent show he was offered $40,000 cash for a vintage auto or $42,800 in nine months. If money is worth 9%, which is the better offer?

Solution: The better offer is the larger of $40,000 or the present value of $42,800.

$$A = \$42,800, P = ?, r = 9\% = 0.09, t = \frac{9}{12} = 0.75$$

$$P = \frac{A}{1 + rt}$$

$$= \frac{\$42,800}{1 + (0.09 \times 0.75)}$$

$$= \frac{\$42,800}{1.0675}$$

$$= \$40,093.68$$

The cash in nine months offer is better by $40,093.68 − $40,000 = $93.68.   ■

EXERCISES FOR SECTION 7.4

In problems 1–10, use the formula A = P(1 + rt) to compute the maturity value A for the given values of P, r, and t.

1. $P = \$2,000, r = 6\%, t = 1$ year $200(1 + 6 \times 1)$

2. $P = \$3,000, r = 10\%, t = 1$ year

3. $P = \$4,000, r = 12\%, t = 2$ months

4. $P = \$3,600, r = 9\frac{1}{2}\%, t = 4$ months

5. $P = \$2,400, r = 7\frac{1}{4}\%, t = 15$ months

6. $P = \$1,600, r = 11\frac{3}{4}\%, t = 6$ months

7. $P = \$3,250, r = 8\frac{1}{4}\%, t = 9$ months

8. $P = \$1,750, r = 9\frac{1}{4}\%, t = 8$ months

9. $P = \$2,250, r = 8\frac{3}{4}\%, t = 4$ months

10. $P = \$4,410, r = 6\frac{3}{4}\%, t = 10$ months

In problems 11–20, use the formula P = $\frac{A}{1+rt}$ to find the present value P for the given values of A, r, and t.

11. $A = \$1,221, r = 7\%, t = 3$ months $\frac{1221}{1 + (7\% + \frac{3}{12})}$

12. $A = \$2,426, r = 6\frac{1}{2}\%, t = 2$ months $\frac{2}{12}$

13. $A = \$1,022.50, r = 9\%, t = 3$ months $\frac{3}{12}$

14. $A = \$1,563.75, r = 8\frac{1}{2}\%, t = 6$ months

15. $A = \$2,046.26, r = 9\frac{1}{4}\%, t = 3$ months

16. $A = \$2,922.50, r = 8\frac{3}{4}\%, t = 6$ months

17. $A = \$3,802.50, r = 7\frac{1}{2}\%, t = 9$ months

18. $A = \$4,141.67, r = 8\frac{1}{2}\%, t = 5$ months

19. $A = \$3,000, r = 9\frac{3}{4}\%, t = 4$ months

20. $A = \$2,832.81, r = 6\frac{1}{4}\%, t = 4$ months

Solve. $2000(1 + 7\% \times \frac{3}{12})$

21. John Richards borrowed $2,500 from Leslie Small at 7% interest for three months. How much will John repay Leslie at the end of three months?

22. Dick Welch loaned his neighbor $2,000 for six months at $8\frac{1}{4}\%$ interest. What amount of money will the neighbor repay Dick at the end of six months? $\frac{6}{12}$

23. Find the maturity value for a loan of $3,500 for 14 months at 7.5% interest.

24. If $2,800 is borrowed for five years at 8.5% interest, what is the maturity value of the loan?

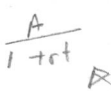

$$\frac{A}{1 + rt} \quad R$$

25. Joan Parker is planning to spend $3,000 one year from now for a European tour. How much should she invest now at $8\frac{3}{4}\%$ interest to have the money for her trip?

26. Find the present value of $1,500 at $10\frac{1}{4}\%$ interest for nine months.

27. What is the present value of $2,400 at $8\frac{1}{2}\%$ interest for three months?

28. Roger Simmons borrowed $2,800 for 18 months at $6\frac{3}{4}\%$ interest to pay for new equipment for his auto repair shop. What amount will he repay for the loan?

29. Mary Schmidt was offered $20,000 for a piece of property or $21,000 in eight months. If money can be invested at the interest rate of $10\frac{1}{2}\%$, which is the better offer?

30. Arthur Samuels owns some old silver coins. A buyer offered to pay him $1,800 cash or $2,000 in 10 months. If money can be invested at the simple interest rate of 7.5%, which is the better offer?

31. For her antique clock, Sandi King was offered $1,600 cash or $1,000 now and $625 in six months. If money can be invested at the interest rate of 6.25%, which is the better offer?

32. Paul Baker estimates that in eighteen months he will need $4,500 to replace some aging equipment in his grocery store. He has $4,000 in an investment that will yield the equivalent of 7% simple interest. Will he be able to purchase the equipment?

33. Max Phillips plans to remodel his store in 15 months. He estimates that the remodeling will cost $13,800, and he has $12,000 to invest. Find the least interest rate at which he can invest his money so as to meet his remodeling expenses.

34. At an interest rate of $6\frac{1}{2}\%$, how long will it take for an investment of $4,800 to have a maturity value of $5,736?

35. June Porter has an opportunity to invest $2,400 at 7.8% interest. How long will it take for the maturity value of the investment to reach $2,681?

36. At what rate of interest will $3,200 have a maturity value of $3,386 in nine months?

Glossary

Amount   See *maturity value*.

Banker's interest   See *ordinary interest*.

Banker's rule   See *ordinary interest*.

Banker's year   See *ordinary time*.

Exact interest   Interest calculations using the time fraction $\dfrac{\text{Exact time in days}}{365}$.

Exact time   The calendar based on the revolution of the earth around the sun. The year consists of 365 days, with a leap year of 366 days every fourth year. The months have 28, (29), 30, or 31 days, irregularly spaced.

Interest   Money paid for the use of money.

Maturity value   Also called *amount*. The total amount due (principal plus interest) when a loan is repaid.

Ordinary interest   Also called *banker's interest* or *banker's rule*. Interest calculations using the time fraction $\dfrac{\text{Exact time in days}}{360}$.

Ordinary time   Also called *banker's year*. A financial calendar consisting of 12 months of 30 days per month. A year in ordinary time thus consists of 360 days.

Present value   The amount of money (principal) that must be borrowed or invested at a given interest rate for a given length of time to result in a specified maturity value.

Principal   The amount of money borrowed or invested.

Simple interest   An annual percentage of the amount of money borrowed or invested.

Time fraction   A fraction used to express the length of a loan when the loan is specified to be for a number of days or months.

Review Test

1. Hal Morris borrowed $1,600 for six months at 7% simple interest. How much did Hal pay in interest?

2. Find the simple interest earned on a $2,000 loan for four months at $10\frac{1}{2}\%$.

3. Jenny paid $140.25 interest on a nine-month loan at a simple interest rate of $8\frac{1}{2}\%$. Find the principal.

4. At a simple interest rate of $11\frac{1}{4}\%$, what principal would earn $90 interest in three months?

5. Gary needs to earn $3,100 simple interest in sixteen months from an investment of $30,000. What minimum interest rate must Gary find for his investment?

6. Find the simple interest rate necessary for $6,500 to earn $487.50 interest in eight months.

7. How many months would it take to earn $180.60 simple interest on a principal of $1,720 invested at a rate of 9%?

8. Mary Cunningham invested $2,800 at $10\frac{3}{4}\%$ simple interest. How many months will it take for her investment to earn $75.25 in interest?

9. Bill Pell borrowed $2,000 for 45 days at $9\frac{1}{2}\%$ ordinary interest. How much interest did he pay for the loan?

10. How many days would it take $1,825 to earn $90.75 exact interest at 11%?

11. Mary and Kerry each borrowed $1,450 for 90 days at 8% simple interest. However, Mary's loan was at exact interest while Kerry's loan was at ordinary interest. Find the amount of interest each paid.

12. Monica borrowed $720 for 90 days at $8\frac{1}{4}\%$ exact interest. At what ordinary interest rate would she have paid the same amount of interest? Round your answer to two decimal places.

13. An invoice for $800 contains terms 3/10, n/30. At what interest rate (ordinary interest) could the buyer afford to borrow to take advantage of the cash discount?

14. Find the maturity value of a $750 loan at 12% exact interest for 80 days.

15. What investment at $6\frac{3}{4}\%$ exact interest for 120 days would result in a maturity value of $574.65?

16. Six months from now, Julia Bennett plans to remodel her real estate office. She estimates that the remodeling will cost $6,000. How much money must she invest now at $12\frac{1}{2}\%$ simple interest to have $6,000 in six months?

17. For his stamp collection, Fred was offered $1,200 now or $400 now and $825 in three months. If money can be invested at $7\frac{1}{2}\%$ simple interest, which offer should Fred accept?

18. Mel Bridges was offered $1,500 cash for his woodworking tools. Another prospective buyer then offered him $1,000 now and $525 in six months. If money can be invested at the interest rate of 7%, which is the better offer?

8

Compound Interest

 Section 8.1 *Compound Interest Formula*

A. Introduction

Compound interest differs from simple interest in that simple interest is computed on a principal that never changes, while compound interest is computed on the principal plus previously earned interest. For this reason, compound interest is frequently described as "interest on interest."

To illustrate the difference between simple interest and compound interest, consider $100 invested for three years at 9% simple interest and at 9% interest compounded annually. Both calculations use the simple interest formula $I = Prt$ where the rate $\times$ time $= 0.09 \times 1 = 0.09$.

	Simple Interest*		*Compound Interest*	
Year 1	$100.00	Principal	$100.00	Principal
	× 0.09	Rate × Time	× 0.09	Rate × Time
	$ 9.00	Interest	$ 9.00	Interest
Year 2	$100.00	Principal	$109.00	Principal ($100 + $9)
	× 0.09	Rate × Time	× 0.09	Rate × Time
	$ 9.00	Interest	$ 9.81	Interest
Year 3	$100.00	Principal	$118.81	Principal ($109.90 + $9.81)
	× 0.09	Rate × Time	× 0.09	Rate × Time
	$ 9.00	Interest	$ 10.69	Interest

The simple interest is $9.00 + $9.00 + $9.00 = $27.00, while the compound interest is $9.00 + $9.81 + $10.69 = $29.50 for the same period, because interest is computed on interest for the last two years. Thus,

$$A = P + I \qquad\qquad A = P + I$$
$$= \$100 + \$27 \qquad\quad = \$100 + \$29.50$$
$$= \$127 \qquad\qquad\quad = \$129.50$$

In the preceding illustration, compound interest generated more interest than the corresponding rate of simple interest, and generally this is the case. Despite this, compound interest is paid to investors by banks, savings and loan institutions, and the U.S. government bond program. One reason for this is that compound interest encourages the investor to keep the interest on deposit; the savings institution thus has funds on hand that it would otherwise have to pay out in interest.

Notice that both simple interest and compound interest use the formula $A = P + I$. However, in compound interest A is called the **compound amount** (also future value), P is the **original principal,** and I is called **compound interest.** Also, in compound interest the quoted interest rate is the **nominal rate** (rate per annum), and the length of the investment is the **term.** The intervals when interest is added to the principal are called **conversion periods,** or just **periods.** In the previous illustration, the compound amount is $129.50, the original principal is $100, the compound interest is $29.50, the nominal rate is 9%, the term is three years, and the conversion period is one year.

The most frequently used conversion periods are monthly, quarterly, semiannually, and annually. The greater the number of conversion periods, the greater the compound interest for a given investment.

B. The Compound Interest Formula
One method of computing compound interest is to use the simple interest formula as in the previous illustration. However, for most calculations, this would be cumbersome. A more efficient way is to use the following formula.

---

*The simple interest calculation using $I = Prt$ is $100 × 0.09 × 3 = $27. However, for this illustration, the interest is calculated annually. The result is the same.

$$(8-1) \quad A = P(1 + i)^n$$

where

$A =$ Compound amount
$P =$ Original principal
$i =$ Rate per period $= \dfrac{\text{Nominal rate}}{\text{No. of conversion periods in one year}}$
$n =$ Total number of conversion periods
$(1 + i)^n =$ Product of n $(1 + i)$s

In the previous illustration,

$$P = \$100$$
$$i = \frac{0.09}{1} = 0.09$$
$n = 1$ period per year $\times$ 3 years $= 3$ conversion periods
$(1 + i)^n = (1.09)^3$ where $(1.09)^3$ is the product of three (1.09)s
or $1.09 \times 1.09 \times 1.09$

thus

$$
\begin{aligned}
A &= \$100 \times (1.09)^3 \\
&= \$100 \times 1.295029 \qquad (1.09 \times 1.09 \times 1.09 = 1.295029) \\
&= \$125.5029 \\
&= \$125.50 \text{ (Rounded)}
\end{aligned}
$$

C. Compound Interest Tables

When n is large, the calculation of $(1 + i)^n$ becomes difficult, even with the help of a calculator (unless it is equipped with a y^x key*). While $(1.09)^3 = 1.03 \times 1.03 \times 1.03$ is not difficult to calculate, $(1.09)^{30}$ is another matter. To simplify these calculations, appendix C provides the value of $(1 + i)^n$ for various combinations of i and n. For instance, to find the value of $(1.09)^3$, locate in appendix C the page labeled 9% and column C labeled "Compound Amount." Row 3 of this column is 1.29502900.

EXAMPLE 1   Find the compound amount on \$4,000 at 11% compounded quarterly for five years.

Solution: $P = \$4,000,\ i = \dfrac{11\%}{4} = 2\dfrac{3}{4}\% = 0.0275,$

$n = 4$ periods per year $\times$ 5 years $= 20$ periods
$$
\begin{aligned}
A &= P(1 + i)^n \\
&= \$4,000(1.0275)^{20} \\
&= \$4,000(1.72042843) \qquad \text{(Appendix C)} \\
&= \$6,881.71372 \\
&= \$6,881.71
\end{aligned}
$$

\■

Calculators equipped with a y^x key may be used to calculate $(1 + i)^n$. For example, to find $(1.09)^3$, enter "1.09," "y^x," "3," "=."

EXAMPLE 2   Find the compound amount and the compound interest for an investment of $2,000 for three years that pays 10% compounded semiannually.

Solution: $P = \$2,000, i = \dfrac{10\%}{2} = 5\% = 0.05, n = 2 \times 3 = 6$

$A = P(1 + i)^n$
$ = \$2,000(1 + 0.05)^6$
$ = \$2,000(1.05)^6$
$ = \$2,000(1.34009564)$ (Appendix C)
$ = \$2,680.19128$
$ = \$2,680.19$

$I = A - P$
$ = \$2,680.19 - \$2,000$
$ = \$680.19$

Appendix C can also be used to find values of i or n.

EXAMPLE 3   How long will it take for $2,000 to accumulate to $2,612.10 if the $2,000 is compounded quarterly at 9%?

Solution: $A = \$2,612.10, P = \$2,000, i = \dfrac{9\%}{4} = 2\dfrac{1}{4}\% = 0.0225, n = \, ?$

$A = P(1 + i)^n$

$\dfrac{A}{P} = (1 + i)^n$ (Dividing both sides by P)

$\dfrac{\$2,612.10}{\$2,000.00} = (1.0225)^n$

$1.30605 = (1.0225)^n$

In appendix C on the $2\frac{1}{4}\%$ page, 1.30604999 is the entry for $n = 12$; thus, the term is 12 quarters or three years.

EXAMPLE 4   What interest rate compounded semiannually would be required for $4,400 to accumulate to $14,111.40 in 10 years?

Solution: $A = \$14,111.40, P = \$4,400, i = \, ?, n = 2 \times 10 = 20$
$A = P(1 + i)^n$

$\dfrac{A}{P} = (1 + i)^n$ (Dividing both sides by P)

$\dfrac{\$14,111.40}{\$4,400} = (1 + i)^{20}$

$3.2071363 = (1 + i)^{20}$

A horizontal scan of the $n = 20$ line of appendix C shows that the entry very close to 3.2071363 is on the page labeled $i = 6\%$. Since interest is compounded semiannually, the nominal rate is 6% $\times$ 2 = 12%.

EXAMPLE 5   John Talbot invested \$900 in a savings account that paid $6\frac{1}{2}\%$ compounded semiannually. After $3\frac{1}{2}$ years, he withdrew \$1,000 from the account and invested it in a certificate of deposit paying 11% compounded quarterly, leaving the remainder in the savings account. How much was his total compound amount two years after purchasing the certificate of deposit?

Solution: *First $3\frac{1}{2}$ years*

Using calculator

$1.0325; y^{xc}; 900, =$

$$P = \$900, \; i = \frac{6\frac{1}{2}\%}{2} = 3\frac{1}{4}\% = 0.0325, \; n = 2 \times 3\frac{1}{2} = 7$$

$$A = P(1 + i)^n$$
$$= \$900(1.0325)^7$$
$$= \$900(1.2509225) \quad \text{(Appendix C)}$$
$$= \$1,125.83$$

Next 2 years (Certificate of Deposit)

$$P = \$1,000, \; i = \frac{11\%}{4} = 2\frac{3}{4}\% = 0.0275, \; n = 4 \times 2 = 8$$

$$A = P(1 + i)^n$$
$$= \$1,000(1.0275)^8$$
$$= \$1,000(1.24238055) \quad \text{(Appendix C)}$$
$$= \$1,242.38$$

Next 2 years (Savings Account)

$$P = \$125.83, \; i = 3\frac{1}{4}\% = 0.0325, \; n = 2 \times 2 = 4$$

$$A = P(1 + i)^n$$
$$= \$125.83(1.0325)^4$$
$$= \$125.83(1.13647593) \quad \text{(Appendix C)}$$
$$= \$143.00$$

Total compound amount = \$1,242.38 + \$143.00 = \$1,385.38

The last half of the twentieth century has been an inflationary period for much of the world, an era of continually increasing prices. Many people are unaware that an inflation rate of 6% per year means that on the average prices are increasing at a rate of 6% compounded annually and that such an increase can impact prices dramatically. The next example demonstrates the effects of continued inflation.

EXAMPLE 6   Suppose an automobile costs $10,000. What will the same automobile cost in five years if the inflation rate is **a.** 5%, **b.** 8%, **c.** 10%?

Solution: **a.** $A = ?, P = \$10,000, i = 5\% = 0.05, n = 1 \times 5 = 5$

$A = P(1 + i)^n$
$= \$10,000(1.05)^5$
$= \$10,000(1.27628156)$ (Appendix C)
$= \$12,762.82$

b. $A = ?, P = \$10,000, i = 8\% = 0.08, n = 1 \times 5 = 5$

$A = P(1 + i)^n$
$= \$10,000(1.08)^5$
$= \$10,000(1.46932808)$ (Appendix C)
$= \$14,693.28$

c. $A = ?, P = \$10,000, i = 10\% = 0.10, n = 1 \times 5 = 5$

$A = P(1 + i)^n$
$= \$10,000(1.10)^5$
$= \$10,000(1.61051)$ (Appendix C)
$= \$16,105.10$

The decade of the 90s began with an inflation rate of about 4% per year, except for energy and medical care, which were about 10% and 15% per year, respectively. Table 8.1 indicates the cost of some familiar items should this rate continue for the next twenty years. (All items except the last two are rounded to the nearest dollar.)

Table 8.1   Effects of Inflation

Item	Today	In Ten Years	In Twenty Years
House	$100,000	$148,024	$219,112
Doctor Visit	$40	$162	$655
Dinner at Restaurant	$15	$22	$33
In-Hospital Stay	$2,500	$10,114	$40,916
Athletic Shoes	$60	$89	$131
Motel Room	$75	$111	$164
Movie Ticket	$4.50	$6.66	$9.86
Gallon of Gasoline	$1.25	$3.24	$8.41

EXERCISES FOR SECTION 8.1

In problems 1–8, use the formula $A = P(1 + i)^n$ *and appendix C to find the compound amount for the given original principal at the given compound interest rate for the indicated term.*

1. $2,000 for 2 years at 7% compounded annually

2. $800 for 3 years at 8% compounded annually

3. $700 for 2 years at 10% compounded semiannually

4. $600 for 2 years at 9% compounded semiannually

5. $1,200 for 1 year at 9% compounded quarterly

6. $800 for 1 year at 10% compounded quarterly

Pg 10→

$7\% = 0.07$

$0.07 + 1 = 1.07; \ 1.07, \times 4, 2, =, X, 2000$

7. $900 for 2 years at 8% compounded semiannually

8. $200 for 4 years at $11\frac{1}{2}$% compounded semiannually

In problems 9–16, use the formula $A = P(1 + i)^n$ *and appendix C to find the compound interest on the given original principal at the given compound interest rate for the indicated term.*

9. $2,000 for 2 years at 8% compounded annually

10. $4,000 for 3 years at 12% compounded annually

11. $900 for 3 months at 6% compounded monthly 13.57

12. $300 for 5 months at 12% compounded monthly

13. $1,500 for 2 years at 11% compounded semiannually

14. $2,100 for 4 years at 8% compounded semiannually

15. $1,100 for 12 years at 9% compounded quarterly

16. $500 for 10 years at 10% compounded quarterly

In problems 17–22, use appendix C to find how long it would take for the given original principal to accumulate to the given amount at the given compound interest rate.

17. $2,000 to $2,928.10 at 10% compounded annually

18. $3,000 to $18,522.73 at 11% compounded semiannually

19. $650 to $1,045.48 at 8% compounded quarterly

20. $700 to $800.77 at 9% compounded monthly

21. $1,300 to $1,436.36 at 6% compounded monthly

22. $1,150 to $1,612.93 at 7% compounded annually

In problems 23–28, use appendix C to find the compound interest rate that would make the given original principal accumulate to the given amount in the given length of time.

23. $500 to $670.05 in 3 years, interest compounded semiannually

24. $3,500 to $4,094.50 in 2 years, interest compounded semiannually

25. $1,400 to $1,776.58 in 4 years, interest compounded quarterly

26. $2,600 to $3,247.93 in $2\frac{1}{2}$ years, interest compounded quarterly

27. $1,600 to $1,648.60 in 6 months, interest compounded monthly

28. $900 to $994.16 in 10 months, interest compounded monthly

Solve.

$$A = 5000\left(1 + \frac{.08}{4}\right)^{3t}$$

29. Lynn Bishop placed $5,000 in a money market account that pays 8% interest compounded quarterly. How much will be in the account after one year?

30. On the day his son was born, Pedro Dominguez planned for his son's education by placing $8,000 in an account paying 9% compounded semiannually. Pedro closed the account 18 years later and used the compound amount to send his son to college. How much was the compound amount?

$$2000\left(1 + \frac{.09}{12}\right)^{10}$$

31. In preparation for a tax payment, Janice Jones placed $2,000 in an account paying 9% compounded monthly. After 10 months she closed the account. How much did she receive?

32. A professional baseball player's contract called for $50,000 to be placed in an account paying 11% compounded quarterly, with the player to receive the

$$2000\left(\left(\frac{9\%}{12} + 1\right)\right)^{10}$$

compound amount when he retired. If he retired seven years later, how much did he receive from the account?

33. Following a job transfer, Kerry Grant sold his condominium for $162,000. While looking for a new home, he put his money into an account that paid 10% compounded quarterly. Eighteen months later he withdrew the compound amount. How much did he withdraw?

34. Carol and Carolyn each have $4,000 in a savings account. Carol's money is in a bank that pays 8% compounded annually. Carolyn's money is invested in a credit union paying $8\frac{1}{2}$% compounded annually. After two years, how much more will Carolyn have than Carol?

35. Find the length of time for $5,000 to double if it is invested in an account that pays 12% compounded quarterly.

36. If the rate of inflation is 4% per year, how much will a house cost in five years if it costs $90,000 today?

37. During the 1980s some Latin American countries had inflation rates of 150% per year. At this inflation rate, calculate the price of a loaf of bread in two years if it cost $0.90 today.

38. Your current wages are $400 per week. During the next 3 years, the inflation rate is expected to be 5.9%. How much should your wages be at the end of this period if you are to have the same standard of living?

39. John Foster has $4,000 to invest for 3 years. He can either invest it at 10% simple interest or $9\frac{1}{2}\%$ compounded annually. Which interest rate should he choose?

40. Mary Watkins placed $450 in a savings account paying 9% interest compounded quarterly. After four years, she withdrew $500 from the account and bought a certificate of deposit that paid 12% compounded semiannually, leaving the remainder in the savings account. How much was her total compound amount one year after purchasing the certificate of deposit?

41. Art Landon opened a savings account with $1,200. The account paid 8% compounded semiannually. After $3\frac{1}{2}$ years he withdrew $1,000 from the account and bought a certificate of deposit that paid 10% compounded quarterly, leaving the remainder in the savings account. How much was his total compound amount $1\frac{1}{2}$ years after purchasing the certificate of deposit?

Section 8.2   *Present Value*

In chapter 7 on simple interest, present value was defined as the current value of a future sum of money. This definition also applies to present value at compound interest. The procedure for finding present value is also the same; the formula for A is solved for P.

$$A = P(1 + i)^n$$
$$P(1 + i)^n = A$$
$$\frac{P(1 + i)^n}{(1 + i)^n} = \frac{A}{(1 + i)^n} \qquad \text{(Dividing both sides by } (1 + i)^n)$$
$$P = \frac{A}{(1 + i)^n} = A \times \frac{1}{(1 + i)^n}$$

Another way of writing $\dfrac{1}{(1 + i)^n}$ is $(1 + i)^{-n}$. Thus,

---

(8–2) $P = A(1 + i)^{-n}$

Present value at compound interest can be calculated by using appendix D, which lists the values of $(1 + i)^{-n}$. Similar to finding an entry in the compound interest table, an entry in appendix D is found by locating the appendix page for the rate of interest i and the nth row of column D "Present Value." This entry is the value of $(1 + i)^{-n}$.

EXAMPLE 1   Find the principal that must be deposited at 9% compounded annually to have a compound amount of $10,000 in eight years.

Solution: $P = ?$, $A = \$10,000$, $i = 9\% = 0.09$, $n = 8$

$(109 \ Y^x \ 8 \ +- \ =) 10,000$

$P = A(1 + i)^{-n}$

$\quad = \$10,000(1.09)^{-8}$

$\quad = \$10,000(0.50186628)$ (Appendix D)

$\quad = \$5,018.66$

■

EXAMPLE 2   Find the principal that must be deposited at 8% compounded quarterly to have a compound amount of $15,000 in five years.

Solution: $P = ?$, $A = \$15,000$, $i = \dfrac{8\%}{4} = 0.02$, $n = 4 \times 5 = 20$

$102 \ V^x \ 20 -$

$P = A(1 + i)^{-n}$

$\quad = \$15,000(1.02)^{-20}$

$(1.02 \ 4x \ 20 \ -- \ =) 15000$

$\quad = \$15,000(0.67297133)$ (Appendix D)

$\quad = \$10,094.57$

Check: If a principal of $10,094.57 was invested at 8% compounded quarterly for five years, then by formula 8–1

$A = P(1 + i)^n$

$\quad = \$10,094.57(1.02)^{20}$

$\quad = \$10,094.57(1.4859474)$

$\quad = \$14,999.99$

$\quad = \$15,000$

■

EXAMPLE 3   The parents of newborn Terry Morton wanted to establish a savings account that would provide $24,000 for college expenses at age 18. Their banker calculated the amount to be placed in an account that paid 12% compounded semiannually. How much was put in the savings account?

Solution: $P = ?$, $A = \$24,000$, $i = \dfrac{12\%}{2} = 0.06$, $n = 2 \times 18 = 36$

$P = A(1 + i)^{-n}$

$\quad = \$24,000(1.06)^{-36}$

$(106 \ y^x \ 36 - \ =) 24000$

$\quad = \$24,000(0.12274077)$ (Appendix D)

$\quad = \$2,945.78$

■

The present value of expected future income from an investment is often used to compare alternate investment proposals.

$Principal = A(1+i)^{-n}$

E X A M P L E   4   Paul Hawkins is considering two different investment programs. Each program requires the same initial investment, and the projected income of the two programs for each of the first three years is as follows:

Year	Program A	Program B
1	$2,000	$1,000
2	1,500	1,200
3	1,000	2,300

If money is worth 9% compounded annually, which is the better investment?

Solution: Since present value is the current value of a future sum of money, the better investment will be the one for which the sum of the present values of the future incomes is largest. The present values of the projected yearly incomes from the two programs are:

Program A

Year	Income	Present Value	
1	$2,000	$2,000(1.09)^{-1}$	$= \$1,834.86$
2	1,500	$1,500(1.09)^{-2}$	$=\ \ 1,262.52$
3	1,000	$1,000(1.09)^{-3}$	$=\ \ \ \ 772.18$
		Sum	$= \$3,869.56$

Program B

Year	Income	Present Value	
1	$1,000	$1,000(1.09)^{-1}$	$=\ \$\ \ 917.43$
2	1,200	$1,200(1.09)^{-2}$	$=\ \ 1,010.02$
3	2,300	$2,300(1.09)^{-3}$	$=\ \ 1,776.02$
		Sum	$= \$3,703.47$

Since the sum of the present value of the yearly incomes from program A exceeds that of program B, program A is the better investment.   ■

EXERCISES FOR SECTION 8.2

In problems 1–10, use appendix D to find the principal that must be invested at the given interest rate to have the given amount after the given period of time.

1. $4,000 in two years at 12% compounded semiannually

2. $5,000 in five years at 10% compounded semiannually

3. $3,000 in three years at 7% compounded annually

4. $1,600 in one year at 8% compounded quarterly

5. $1,500 in ten years at 12% compounded quarterly

6. $20,000 in twenty years at 12% compounded monthly

7. $5,000 in four years at 9% compounded monthly

8. $4,000 in ten years at 6% compounded semiannually

9. $1,400 in six years at 11% compounded quarterly

10. $10,000 in twenty years at 8% compounded quarterly

Solve.

11. Ten years ago, Jack Philips opened a savings account that paid 6% interest compounded quarterly. He made no deposits or withdrawals after his initial deposit. Today, there is $3,083.83 in the account. How much did he place in the account initially?

12. John Foster, who is 40 years old, wishes to place enough money in a savings account that pays 10% interest compounded quarterly so that he will have $20,000 in the account at age 65 to use for retirement. How much should he put in the account?

13. Pam Shuster just inherited $15,000. She wishes to put enough of her inheritance into a savings account so that five years from now she will still have $15,000. If the account pays 9% compounded semiannually, how much should she put in the account? $= P(1 + \frac{.09}{2})^{2 \times 5}$

14. Joyce Ruth is planning to tour Europe two years from now, and she estimates that she will need $3,000 for the trip. How much should she place in a savings account now to have enough money for her trip if the account pays 12% compounded quarterly?

15. John Perry is considering two different investment programs, each requiring the same initial investment. The projected net incomes for each of the first three years are: program A—$2,500, $2,500, $1,500; program B—$3,000, $2,500, $1,000. If money is worth 10% compounded annually, which is the better investment?

16. The Jensens are considering two investment programs, each requiring the same initial investment. Program A is expected to return a net income of $1,000, $4,000, $2,500, and $500 for each of the first four years. Program B is expected to return $3,000, $1,500, $2,000, and $1,500. At an interest rate of $9\frac{1}{2}$% compounded annually, which is the better investment?

17. A company is considering the proposals of two advertising firms. Each proposal requires an investment of $65,000. The first proposal is expected to result in a semiannual increase in net income of $10,000, $15,000, and $20,000 for the first 18 months. The second proposal is expected to return $10,000, $12,000, and $23,000 over the same period. At an interest rate of 10% compounded semiannually, which proposal should the company accept?

Section 8.3 *Daily and Continuous Compounding*

A. Daily Compounding

Traditionally, savings institutions offered interest at periods that were annual, semiannual, or quarterly. However, in recent years, competition for the savings dollar has resulted in savings plans with shorter conversion periods. The first to be studied is interest compounded daily.

Interest compounded daily has two advantages. First, the investor earns higher interest, for it has already been demonstrated that the shorter the conversion period, the greater the generated interest. Second, since interest is calculated according to the number of days invested, there is no penalty for early withdrawal as there often is on accounts with conversion periods of a quarter or longer.

Daily interest is calculated using formula 8–1, $A = P(1 + i)^n$, the same as for any other interest calculation. However, since the conversion period is one day, $i = \frac{r}{365}$, where r is the nominal rate. For ease of calculation, appendix I is a table of values of $(1 + \frac{r}{365})^n$. The headings at the top of the table are values of r; the values of n are given in the left-hand column. An appropriate entry in the table is multiplied by the principal P to obtain the compound amount A.

EXAMPLE 1

Find the compound amount of $1,500 invested on July 14 and withdrawn on September 9 if interest is compounded daily at a rate of 10%.

Solution: From appendix B there are 57 days from July 14 to September 9. Thus, $A = ?$, $P = \$1,500$, $r = 10\% = 0.10$, $n = 57$

how many yrs   , 16 156

$$A = P\left(1 + \frac{r}{365}\right)^n$$

$$= \$1,500\left(1 + \frac{0.10}{365}\right)^{57}$$

$$= \$1,500(1.01573684) \qquad \text{(Appendix I)}$$

$$= \$1,523.61$$

EXAMPLE 2

Consuela Vargas invested $2,000 on January 22 in a credit union that paid interest at a rate of 9% compounded daily. If the credit union credits the interest to her account quarterly, what was her balance at the end of the quarter?*

Solution: From appendix B, there are 68 days from January 22 to March 31 (the end of the quarter). Thus,

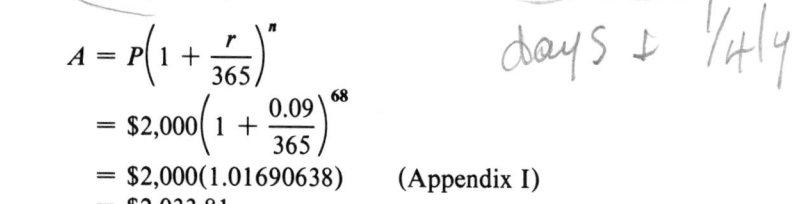

$$A = P\left(1 + \frac{r}{365}\right)^n$$

days ÷ 1/4/4

$$= \$2,000\left(1 + \frac{0.09}{365}\right)^{68}$$

$$= \$2,000(1.01690638) \qquad \text{(Appendix I)}$$

$$= \$2,033.81$$

The balance as of March 31 is $2,033.81. The interest earned to this date is $2,033.81 − \$2,000 = \$33.81$.

Note

EXAMPLE 3

Continental Federal pays investors interest at a rate of $8\frac{1}{2}\%$ compounded daily. Jim Click opened an account with a $500 deposit on April 1 and made an additional deposit of $700 on May 15. **a.** What was the compound amount at the end of the quarter? **b.** If Jim receives an interest check quarterly, how much did he receive at the end of the quarter?

---

*Ending dates of the four quarters in a year are March 31, June 30, September 30, and December 31.

Solution: **a.** There are 90 days from April 1 to June 30 (the end of the quarter), and 46 days from May 15 to June 30.

April Deposit

$$A_1 = P\left(1 + \frac{r}{365}\right)^n$$

$$= \$500\left(1 + \frac{.085}{365}\right)^{90}$$

$$= \$500(1.02117759)$$

$$= \$510.588795$$

$$= \$510.59$$

May Deposit

$$A_2 = P\left(1 + \frac{r}{365}\right)^n$$

$$= \$700\left(1 + \frac{.085}{365}\right)^{46}$$

$$= \$700(1.01076865)$$

$$= \$707.538055$$

$$= \$707.54$$

The compound amount A is the sum $A_1 + A_2$. Thus,

$$A = A_1 + A_2$$

$$= \$510.59 + \$707.54$$

$$= \$1,218.13$$

b. Interest is calculated using

$$I = A - P$$

$$= \$1,218.13 - \$1,200.00 \qquad (\$1,200 = \$500 + \$700)$$

$$= \$18.13$$

B. Continuous Compounding

The most recent innovation in savings plans is the ultimate in compounding: interest compounded continuously. The formula for this form of compounding is

(8–3) $A = Pe^{rt}$

where A = Compound amount
P = Original principal
r = Nominal rate
t = Time in years
e = A mathematical constant approximately equal to 2.7183

A table of values for e^{rt} is found in appendix J.*

E X A M P L E   4   Find the compound amount of \$1,200 compounded continuously at 10% for six months.

Solution: $A = ?,\ P = \$1,200,\ r = 10\% = 0.10,\ t = \dfrac{6}{12} = 0.5$

$$A = Pe^{rt}$$

$$= \$1,200e^{(0.10)(0.5)}$$

$$= \$1,200e^{0.05}$$

$$= \$1,200(1.0513) \qquad \text{(Appendix J)}$$

$$= \$1,216.56$$

Calculators equipped with an e^x key may also be used to find e^{rt}. For example to find $e^{0.05}$, enter ".05," "e^x."

EXAMPLE 5   Marv Hanson invested $7,000 in an account that pays $8\frac{1}{2}\%$ compounded continuously. How much was in the account after four years?

Solution: $A = ?, P = \$7,000, r = 0.085, t = 4$

$A = Pe^{rt}$

$\quad = \$7,000e^{(0.085)(4)}$

$\quad = \$7,000e^{0.34}$

$\quad = \$7,000(1.4049) \quad$ (Appendix J)

$\quad = \$9,834.30$

How does daily and continuous compounding of interest compare with compounding of interest over longer conversion periods? The entries in table 8.2 give the compound interest earned on $1,000 invested at a rate of 12% for a range of conversion periods. Note that the shorter the conversion period, the greater the amount of compound interest earned.

Table 8.2	Compound Interest on $1,000 Invested at 12%			
Conversion Period	**One Year**	**Five Years**	**Ten Years**	**Twenty Years**
Annually	$120.00	$762.34	$2,105.84	$8,646.29
Semiannually	123.60	790.85	2,207.14	9,285.72
Quarterly	125.51	806.11	2,262.04	9,640.89
Monthly	126.83	816.70	2,300.39	9,892.55
Daily	127.47	821.94	2,319.46	10,018.83
Continuously	127.50	822.12	2,320.12	10,023.18

EXERCISES FOR SECTION 8.3

In problems 1–10, use appendix I to find the compound amount of the given principal invested at the given compound interest rate when interest is compounded daily.

1. $600 from August 15 to December 7 at 8%

2. $1,000 from March 14 to September 7 at $9\frac{1}{2}\%$

3. $950 from April 14 to June 27 at 7.25%

4. $1,600 from October 2 to November 11 at $8\frac{1}{2}\%$

5. $2,500 from May 30 to August 23 at 10%

6. $900 from June 5 to September 29 at 11.75%

7. $2,450 from January 3 to September 13 at 11% (assume nonleap year)

8. $1,575 from July 29 to October 4 at 6.25%

9. $1,825 from September 8 to January 27 at 9%

10. $682 from November 18 to January 15 at 11%

In problems 11–16, assume that interest is compounded daily and credited quarterly. Find the amount at the end of the quarter when the given principal is placed in an account that pays the given rate of compound interest.

11. $500 deposited July 20 at 10%

12. $1,500 deposited October 12 at 12%

13. $2,800 deposited November 19 at $8\frac{1}{2}$%

14. $2,200 deposited June 6 at $9\frac{1}{2}$%

15. $600 deposited January 20 at 11% (nonleap year)

16. $1,470 deposited January 15 at $6\frac{1}{2}$% (nonleap year)

17. Pete Thomas opened an account at a savings and loan association that pays 8% interest compounded daily. If Pete opened his account on August 1 with $600 and made an additional deposit on September 1 of $400, what was the balance in his account at the end of the quarter?

18. Carolyn James opened a savings account at Fiduciary Federal with $500 on October 1. On November 1, she made an additional deposit of $400. If Fiduciary Federal pays 9% interest compounded daily what was the balance in her account at the end of the quarter?

In problems 19–26, use appendix J to find the compound amount of the given principal invested at the given compound interest rate when interest is compounded continuously.

19. $1,400 at 7% for two years

20. $1,840 at 11% for three years

21. $950 at 12% for six months

22. $1,800 at 9% for four months

23. $1,950 at 10% for eighteen months

24. $2,830 at $6\frac{1}{2}$% for four years

25. $1,440 at $11\frac{1}{2}$% for four years

26. $3,740 at 7% for ten years

27. Jeanne Phillips wishes to invest $5,000 for two years. She can invest the money at $9\frac{1}{2}$% compounded continuously or 10% compounded semiannually. Which is the better investment?

||||||| **Section 8.4** *Nominal Rate versus Effective Rate*

The rate quoted in a compound interest transaction is an annual rate, or nominal rate. When the conversion period is less than one year, the action of interest generating interest results in a rate greater than the nominal rate. For example, if $100 is invested for one year at 9% compounded quarterly, then

$$
\begin{aligned}
A &= P(1 + i)^n \\
&= \$100(1.0225)^4 \\
&= \$100(1.09308332) \quad \text{(Appendix C)} \\
&= \$109.31
\end{aligned}
$$

The interest earned in one year is $9.31, which is 9.31% of $100.00. This is equivalent to $100.00 invested at 9.31% simple interest, since

$$
\begin{aligned}
I &= Prt \\
&= \$100 \times 0.0931 \times 1 \\
&= \$9.31
\end{aligned}
$$

Compared with the nominal rate of 9%, 9.31% is called the **effective rate** of interest or the **true interest rate,** since it indicates the real earning power of the funds invested.

The effective rate can be read directly from appendix C. For example, consider a principal P invested at 8% compounded semiannually. This means that the rate per period is 4% and that the table entry from appendix C for $n = 2$ is 1.0816.

The table entry of 1.0816 is the compound amount per $1.00 of principal; that is, $1.00 invested at 8% compounded semiannually amounts to $1.0816 in one year. Thus, $1.00 earns $0.0816 simple interest in one year. This is equivalent to a simple interest rate of 8.16%, since by the simple interest formula $I = Prt,$ the interest I on $1.00 at 8.16% for one year is $I = \$1 \times 0.0816 \times 1 = \$0.0816$. Thus, the effective rate of interest is 0.0816 or 8.16%.

EXAMPLE 1   A sum of money is invested at an interest rate of 9% compounded monthly. Find the effective rate of interest.

Solution: $i = \dfrac{9\%}{12} = 0.75\% = 0.0075, n = 12$

From appendix C, $(1.0075)^{12} = 1.0938069$

The effective rate is 0.0938069. To the nearest hundredth of a percent, this is 9.38%.

■

Given the effective rate of interest, the nominal rate can be found.

EXAMPLE 2   A credit union announces the issuance of savings certificates paying an effective rate of 12.68%. If interest is compounded monthly, what is the nominal rate r?

Solution: An effective rate of 12.68% means that for $n = 12$,

$(1 + i)^{12} = 1.1268$

From appendix C, $(1.01)^{12} = 1.12682503$; thus,

$i = \dfrac{r}{12} = 0.01$

$r = 12 \times 0.01$ (Multiplying both sides by 12)

$r = 0.12$

$r = 12\%$

■

EXERCISES FOR SECTION 8.4

In problems 1–10, find the effective interest rates (to the nearest hundredth of a percent) for the given rates of compound interest.

1. 11% compounded quarterly

2. 10% compounded semiannually

3. 9% compounded quarterly

4. 12% compounded quarterly $\left[\left(1\frac{2\%}{4}\right)+1\right]^{4}$

5. 8% compounded quarterly

6. 12% compounded semiannually

7. 9% compounded semiannually

8. 7% compounded semiannually

9. 6% compounded monthly

10. 10% compounded quarterly

In problems 11–15, find the nominal interest rates for the given effective rates of interest.

11. 11.30%, interest compounded semiannually

12. 8.16%, interest compounded semiannually

13. 7.19%, interest compounded quarterly

14. 10.38%, interest compounded quarterly

15. 6.17%, interest compounded monthly

16. A savings and loan association issues $1,000 savings certificates with an effective rate of 11.46%. If interest is compounded quarterly, what is the nominal rate?

Glossary

Compound amount   Also called *future value*. The total amount accumulated (principal plus interest) from a loan or investment at compound interest.

Compound interest   Interest that is periodically computed and added to the previous principal, yielding a new principal for the next interest computation.

Conversion periods   The intervals of time when interest is computed and added to the principal.

Effective rate   The simple interest rate that generates the same amount of interest in one year as a given compound interest rate.

Nominal rate   The rate per annum; the quoted compound interest rate.

Original principal   The original amount of money borrowed or invested at compound interest.

Present value   The amount of money (original principal) that must be borrowed or invested at a given interest rate for a given length of time to result in a specified compound amount.

Rate per period   The nominal rate divided by the number of conversion periods per year.

Term   The length of an investment or loan.

True interest rate   See *effective rate*.

Review Test

1. Find the rate per period for
   a. 10% compounded quarterly
   b. 9% compounded monthly
   c. 6% compounded semiannually
   d. 9% compounded quarterly

2. Using appendix C, find the compound amount for $900 invested for one year in an account that pays 12% interest compounded semiannually.

3. Using appendix C, find the compound amount and the compound interest for $2,600 invested for three years at 11% compounded quarterly.

4. Using Appendix C, what interest rate compounded quarterly would be required for $12,200 to accumulate to $14,511.22 in $2\frac{1}{2}$ years?

5. A South American country recently had an inflation rate of 20% per year. If that happened in this country, what would be the price of a gallon of milk in two years if it presently costs $2.70? (*Hint:* Use the simple interest formula.)

6. Gloria Winters will need $25,000 in 18 months for new display cases. Use appendix D to determine how much she should deposit now in an account that pays 12% compounded quarterly to have the money for the cases.

7. How long will it take for $1,000 to accumulate to $1,500 if money is worth 11% compounded quarterly? Use appendix C.

8. On May 14, Henry Stone deposited $800 in an account that pays 9% interest compounded daily. What is the compound amount of the account on June 24? Use appendices B and I.

9. What amount invested at 7% compounded continuously would accumulate to $5,676.40 in five years?

10. Cynthia Lewis places $1,500 in an account that pays 8% interest compounded quarterly. Use appendix C to find the effective rate of interest.

11. Which investment for three years yields the largest compound amount: (a) $5,000 at 6% compounded quarterly, (b) $5,125 at 5% compounded continuously, or (c) $4,950 at $6\frac{1}{2}$% compounded annually?

12. Harold Cruz is considering two different investment programs. Each program requires the same initial investment, and the projected income of the two programs for each of the first three years is as follows:

Year	Program A	Program B
1	$1,000	$1,200
2	1,400	1,300
3	1,600	1,500

If money is worth 11% compounded semiannually, which is the better investment? Use appendix D.

Simple Discount

 **Section 9.1** *The Simple Discount Formula*

A. Introduction

In chapter 7, we discussed simple interest. Another kind of interest is called **simple discount.** For example, suppose John Webster asks a bank to loan him $1,000 for one year. The bank agrees to the loan, but presents Webster with $880 and indicates that the $120 difference is a 12% interest charge ($1,000 \times 0.12 = $120). Webster accepts the $880, and in one year, he will owe the bank $1,000.

The primary difference between this loan and a simple interest loan is that interest is computed on the maturity value instead of on the principal. This difference between simple interest and simple discount is worth repeating. *Simple interest is a percentage of the principal; simple discount is a percentage of the maturity value.*

B. The Simple Discount Formula

Simple discount is another application of the basic percentage equation. The formula is

> **(9–1)** $D = Adt$

where

$$D = \text{Amount of discount}$$
$$A = \text{Maturity value}$$
$$d = \text{Discount percent}$$
$$t = \text{Term of the loan in years}$$

In the John Webster loan, the calculations were

$D = ?, A = \$1,000, D = 12\% = 0.12, t = 1$
$D = Adt$
$\quad = \$1,000 \times 0.12 \times 1$
$\quad = \$120$

The amount paid to the borrower in a simple discount loan is called the **proceeds** of the loan, rather than the principal. The proceeds of a simple discount transaction are equal to the maturity value minus the discount. That is,

> **(9–2)** $P = A - D$

where

$$P = \text{Proceeds}$$
$$A = \text{Maturity value}$$
$$D = \text{Amount of discount}$$

In the Webster transaction,

$P = A - D$
$\quad = \$1,000 - \$120$
$\quad = \$880$

The proceeds may also be thought of as the **present value** of the loan at simple discount.

EXAMPLE 1   The Farmers State Bank offered to discount a loan of $800 at 7% for six months. Find: **a.** the discount and **b.** the proceeds of the loan.

Solution: **a.** $D = ?, A = \$800, d = 7\% = 0.07, t = \dfrac{1}{2} = 0.5$

$D = Adt$
$\quad = \$800 \times 0.07 \times 0.5$
$\quad = \$28$

$D = Adt \quad (Adt)$

b. $P = ?, A = \$800, D = \$28$
   $P = A - D$
   $ = \$800 - \$28$
   $ = \$772$ ■

EXAMPLE 2   For a $680 loan discounted at $11\frac{1}{4}\%$ for two months, find: **a.** the discount and **b.** the present value.

Solution: **a.** $D = ?, A = \$680, d = 11\frac{1}{4}\% = 0.1125, t = \frac{1}{6}$

$D = Adt$

$= \$680 \times 0.1125 \times \frac{1}{6}$

$= \$12.75$

b. $P = ?, A = \$680, D = \$12.75$
   $P = A - D$
   $ = \$680 - \$12.75$
   $ = \$667.25$ ■

For a given transaction, 12% simple discount is not equivalent to 12% simple interest. To see this, let us return to the John Webster loan and calculate the simple interest rate. $I = \$120, P = \$880, r = ?$, and $t = 1$; hence,

$$r = \frac{I}{Pt}$$
$$ = \frac{\$120}{\$880 \times 1}$$
$$ = 0.13636$$
$$ = 13.64\% \text{ (Rounded)}$$

Thus, a 12% simple discount rate on this loan is equivalent to a simple interest rate of 13.64%. In other words, for a given simple discount percent, it takes a higher simple interest percent to produce the same amount of interest.

Because simple discount earns more interest than the same simple interest percent, simple discount was once popular with banks for short-term loans. But in 1969, Congress enacted legislation requiring lending institutions to disclose the interest charges in terms of a simple interest percent (see section 10.4). As a result, many financial institutions use simple discount only for certain transactions with other banks and in some instances that involve the sale of interest-bearing notes to the public. For example, the Treasury Department uses the terms of simple discount to quote the rates at which short-term Treasury securities (commonly known as T-bills) are sold to the public. Also, simple discount is still used in transactions where the federal disclosure act does not apply, such as personal loans between individuals.

E X A M P L E   3   Linda Parsons purchased a $10,000 three-month Treasury bill discounted at 7.75%. Find: **a.** the discount and **b.** the present value.

Solution: **a.** $D = ?$, $A = \$10,000$, $d = 7.75\% = 0.0775$, $t = \dfrac{1}{4} = 0.25$

$$D = Adt$$
$$= \$10,000 \times 0.0775 \times 0.25$$
$$= \$193.75$$

b. $P = ?$, $A = \$10,000$, $D = \$193.75$
$$P = A - D$$
$$= \$10,000 - \$193.75$$
$$= \$9,806.25$$

For short-term simple discount loans, ordinary interest is usually used if the term of the loan is in days.

E X A M P L E   4   Find the discount on a $1,200 loan at $7\frac{1}{2}\%$ for 45 days.

Solution: $D = ?$, $A = \$1,200$, $d = 7\dfrac{1}{2}\% = 0.075$, $t = \dfrac{45}{360} = \dfrac{1}{8} = 0.125$

$$D = Adt$$
$$= \$1,200 \times 0.075 \times 0.125$$
$$= \$11.25$$

E X A M P L E   5   A loan of $575 is executed on November 28 and is due on January 15. What is **a.** the discount and **b.** the proceeds if the loan is discounted at 9%?

Solution: From appendix B, there are 48 days from November 28 to January 15. Thus, with $A = \$575$, $d = 9\% = 0.09$, and $t = \frac{48}{360} = \frac{2}{15}$,

a. $D = Adt$
$$= \$575 \times 0.09 \times \frac{2}{15}$$
$$= \$6.90$$

b. $P = A - D$
$$= \$575.00 - \$6.90$$
$$= \$568.10$$

As discussed in chapter 3, some vendors offer anticipation dating to encourage payment of an invoice before the last day of the discount period. If an invoice is paid prior to the expiration of the cash discount period, the buyer can deduct an amount equal to the current bank discount rate for the number of days of early payment. This is demonstrated in the next example.

EXAMPLE 6　An invoice for $2,500 dated June 1 contains terms 2/10, n/30, anticipation. If the current discount rate is 8% and the invoice is paid on June 5, find the amount to be remitted.

Solution:　　$2,500　List price
− ____50　Cash discount ($2,500 × 0.02)
　$2,450

The number of days of early payment is the number of days from June 5 through June 11, or 6 days. Thus,

$$D = ?, A = \$2,450, d = 8\% = 0.08, t = \frac{6}{360} = \frac{1}{60}$$

$$D = Adt$$

$$= \$2,450 \times 0.08 \times \frac{1}{60}$$

$$= \$3.27$$

Thus, the amount to be remitted is $2,450.00 − $3.27 = $2,446.73.　■

EXERCISES FOR SECTION 9.1

In problems, 1–15, find the discount and the proceeds of the given loan.

1. $5,000 discounted at 10% for three years

2. $3,000 discounted at 9% for two years

3. $2,720 discounted at 7½% for one year

4. $1,420 discounted at 6¼% for nine months

5. $2,250 discounted at 11¾% for six months

6. $450 discounted at 8½% for three months

7. $2,875 discounted at 10¾% for ten months

8. $1,150 discounted at 9½% for eight months

9. $4,275 discounted at 11½% for eighteen months

10. $1,800 discounted at 9¼% for six months

11. $1,900 discounted at 6% for 30 days

12. $1,400 discounted at 7¾% for 60 days

13. $1,350 discounted at 6¾% for 50 days

14. $760 discounted at 8½% for 200 days

15. $1,350 discounted at 9¼% for 170 days

16. A $1,200 loan is executed on April 10 and is due July 15. If the loan is discounted at 10%, find the discount and the proceeds.

17. John Blocker negotiated a loan at the bank for $7,500 for two years, discounted at 6½%. Find the discount and the proceeds of the loan.

18. The Midwest Bank offered to lend Janice Baxter $3,200 discounted at 11¾% for 40 days. Find the discount and the proceeds of the loan.

19. To obtain additional operating capital for his new business, Bob Perkins borrowed $12,000 from his bank, discounted at 7¼% for 245 days. Find the discount and the proceeds of the loan.

20. Ray Pittman purchased a $5,000 three-month Treasury bill discounted at 7.42%. Find: **a.** the discount and **b.** the present value.

21. Find: **a.** the discount and **b.** the present value for a $10,000 six-month Treasury bill discounted at 6.89%.

22. An invoice for $428.60 dated January 18 contains terms 3/10, n/30, with anticipation. If the current discount rate is 9% and the invoice is paid on January 21, find the amount to be remitted.

23. The terms of an invoice dated October 15 were 2/15, n/30, with anticipation. If the list price was $522.48, the invoice was paid on October 18, and the current discount rate is 8.25%, find the amount to be remitted.

Section 9.2 *Other Discount Formulas*

As with simple interest, the formula for simple discount can be solved for any of the other variables.

(9–3)	$A = \dfrac{D}{dt}$	(Dividing both sides of formula 9–1 by *dt*)
(9–4)	$d = \dfrac{D}{At}$	(Dividing both sides of formula 9–1 by *At*)
(9–5)	$t = \dfrac{D}{Ad}$	(Dividing both sides of formula 9–1 by *Ad*)

You should learn to solve formula 9–1 for the appropriate letter rather than attempt to memorize formulas 9–3, 9–4, and 9–5.

E X A M P L E   1   If a bank discounts a loan at 10% for four months, what is the maturity value if the discount is $40?

Solution: $D = \$40, A = ?, d = 10\% = \dfrac{1}{10}, t = \dfrac{4}{12} = \dfrac{1}{3}$

$$A = \frac{D}{dt}$$

$$= \frac{\$40}{\dfrac{1}{10} \times \dfrac{1}{3}}$$

$$= \frac{\$40}{\dfrac{1}{30}}$$

$$= \$1,200$$

EXAMPLE 2   Gilbert Evans received $375 from Paul Decker and promised to pay him $400 in nine months. What was the simple discount rate?

Solution: $D = \$400 - \$375 = \$25, A = \$400, d = ?, t = \dfrac{9}{12} = 0.75$

$$d = \frac{D}{At}$$

$$= \frac{\$25}{\$400 \times 0.75}$$

$$= \frac{\$25}{\$300}$$

$$= 0.0833$$

$$= 8.33\%$$

EXAMPLE 3   J. D. Godwin received $192.50 from Clyde McKeever and agreed to repay him $200.00. If the note Godwin signed was discounted at a simple discount rate of 9%, what was the term of the loan?

Solution: $D = \$200.00 - \$192.50 = \$7.50, A = \$200.00, d = 9\% = 0.09, t = ?$

$$t = \frac{D}{Ad}$$

$$= \frac{\$7.50}{\$200.00 \times 0.09}$$

$$= \frac{\$7.50}{\$18.00} = \frac{7.5}{18} = \frac{15}{36} = \frac{5}{12}$$

$$= 5 \text{ months}$$

The proceeds also can be expressed by a different formula. Since

$$P = A - D$$

and

$$D = Adt$$

it follows that $P = A - Adt$ (Substitution)

(9–6) $P = A(1 - dt)$

EXAMPLE 4 Find the proceeds of a $670 loan discounted at 12% for five months.

Solution: $P = ?, A = \$670, d = 12\% = 0.12, t = \dfrac{5}{12}$

$$P = A(1 - dt)$$
$$= \$670 \left(1 - \left(0.12 \times \dfrac{5}{12} \right) \right)$$
$$= \$670(1 - 0.05)$$
$$= \$670(0.95)$$
$$= \$636.50$$

EXAMPLE 5 The proceeds of a loan are $1,560. What is the maturity value of the loan if the discount rate is $11\frac{1}{4}\%$ and the term of the loan is 80 days?

Solution: $P = \$1,560, A = ?, d = 11\dfrac{1}{4}\% = 0.1125,$

$t = \dfrac{80}{360} = \dfrac{2}{9}$

$P = A(1 - dt)$

$A = \dfrac{P}{1 - dt}$ (Dividing both sides by $1 - dt$)

$= \dfrac{\$1,560}{1 - (0.1125 \times 2/9)}$

$= \dfrac{\$1,560}{0.975}$

$= \$1,600$

Entry	Display	Memory
0.1125	0.1125	0
×	0.1125	0
2	2	0
÷	0.225	0
9	9	0
M−	0.025	−0.025
1	1	−0.025
M+	1	0.975
1560	1560	0.975
÷	1560	0.975
MR	0.975	0.975
=	1600	0.975

EXERCISES FOR SECTION 9.2

In problems 1–12, solve the formula D = Adt *for the appropriate variable and compute the value of the indicated quantity.*

1. $A = \$1,800, d = 10\%, D = \$540$. Find t.

2. $d = 12\%, t = 3$ years, $D = \$216$. Find A.

3. $A = \$1,450, t = 2$ years, $D = \$246.50$. Find d.

4. $A = \$3,750, d = 9\frac{1}{2}\%, t = 4$ years. Find D.

5. $A = \$600, t = 6$ months, $D = \$33$. Find d.

6. $A = \$1,300, d = 11\%, D = \$35.75$. Find t.

7. $d = 10\frac{1}{2}\%, t = 4$ months, $D = \$94.50$. Find A.

8. $A = \$2,400, t = 7$ months, $D = \$157.50$. Find d.

9. $A = \$1,440, d = 6\frac{1}{2}\%, t = 40$ days. Find D.

10. $A = \$2,800, t = 72$ days, $D = \$57.40$. Find d.

11. $d = 11\frac{3}{4}\%, t = 180$ days, $D = \$129.25$. Find A.

12. $A = \$900, t = 64$ days, $D = \$15.60$. Find d.

Solve.

13. Bill Harris borrowed $4,500 for six months, discounted at 11%. Find the proceeds of the loan.

14. What is the discount on a loan of $1,200 discounted at 12% if the loan is executed on May 24 and is due on November 2?

15. Clementine Williams executed a loan on October 12 for $1,100 discounted at $8\frac{1}{2}$%. If the loan is due February 16, what are the proceeds?

16. Karen Peters can borrow money from her bank discounted at 10% for two years. If she needs proceeds of $2,600, how much should she borrow?

17. John Butcher needs $6,000 to cover operating expenses for his new store. How much should he borrow if the loan is to be discounted at 12% for six months?

18. The First City Bank approved a loan of $2,000 for two years. If the proceeds are $1,580, what was the discount rate?

19. If the proceeds of a $1,200 loan for six months were $1,149, what was the discount rate?

20. Jennifer Smith needs $7,350 to remodel her store. What is the least amount (maturity value) that she can borrow if the loan is discounted at 6% for 120 days?

21. John Baxter signed a promissory note agreeing to pay the bank $950.00 in 45 days. If the bank charged $10.20 for the loan, what was the discount rate?

22. Paula Forsythe received $1,257.75 from P. J. Thomas and agreed to repay him $1,300.00. If the note Paula signed was discounted at $6\frac{1}{2}$%, what was the term of the loan?

Section 9.3 *Discounting Interest-bearing Notes*

An individual who borrows money is usually required to sign a written agreement that states the conditions of the loan—the term, the rate of interest or discount, and the principal or maturity value of the loan. An example of such an agreement is the **promissory note** shown in figure 9.1. Promissory notes can be written at simple interest, simple discount, or no interest at all. In any event, a note is a promise to pay the maturity value of the loan on the date specified.

A promissory note is both a legal and a negotiable instrument. That is, in addition to a promise to pay, a note may be sold to a third party. In this sense, a promissory note is similar to a personal check; it may be endorsed to a third party for cash, in payment for goods or services, or in retirement of a debt.

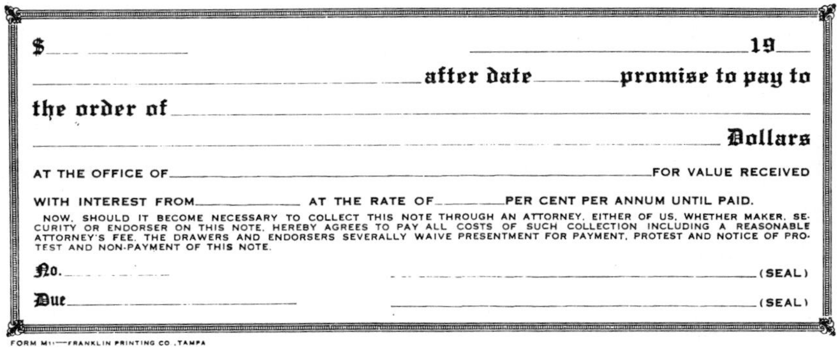
$ ______ ______ 19__

______ after date ______ promise to pay to

the order of ______

______ Dollars

AT THE OFFICE OF ______ FOR VALUE RECEIVED

WITH INTEREST FROM ______ AT THE RATE OF ______ PER CENT PER ANNUM UNTIL PAID.

NOW, SHOULD IT BECOME NECESSARY TO COLLECT THIS NOTE THROUGH AN ATTORNEY, EITHER OF US, WHETHER MAKER, SECURITY OR ENDORSER ON THIS NOTE, HEREBY AGREES TO PAY ALL COSTS OF SUCH COLLECTION INCLUDING A REASONABLE ATTORNEY'S FEE. THE DRAWERS AND ENDORSERS SEVERALLY WAIVE PRESENTMENT FOR PAYMENT, PROTEST AND NOTICE OF PROTEST AND NON-PAYMENT OF THIS NOTE.

No. ______ ______ (SEAL)

Due ______ ______ (SEAL)

FORM M1—FRANKLIN PRINTING CO., TAMPA

Figure 9.1
Promissory note

Banks are the principal purchasers of promissory notes and do so at a discount. For instance, a businessperson may own a number of promissory notes that must be sold to meet unusual expenses. By discounting the notes at a bank, the businessperson obtains the needed cash, and the bank earns a profit equal to the discount percentage.

When the payee of an interest-bearing note sells the note to a bank, he or she receives the proceeds of the newly discounted note.

EXAMPLE 1 On March 1, Hal Miller loaned a friend $1,500 at a simple interest rate of $8\frac{1}{2}\%$ with a due date of June 29. On April 10, Hal sold the note to a bank that discounted the note at 10%. How much did Hal receive from the bank?

Solution: From appendix B, there are 120 days from March 1 to June 29 and 80 days from April 10 to June 29. Before the proceeds of the discounted note can be found, we must calculate the maturity value of the simple interest loan using formula 7–11.

$$A = ?, P = \$1,500, r = 8\frac{1}{2}\% = 0.085, t = \frac{120}{360} = \frac{1}{3}$$

$$A = P(1 + rt)$$

$$= \$1,500 \left(1 + \left(0.085 \times \frac{1}{3}\right)\right)$$

$$= \$1,542.50$$

The proceeds are now calculated using formula 9–6.

$$P = ?, A = \$1,542.50, d = 10\% = 0.1, t = \frac{80}{360} = \frac{2}{9}$$

$$P = A(1 - dt)$$

$$= \$1,542.50 \left(1 - \left(0.1 \times \frac{2}{9}\right)\right)$$

$$= \$1,508.22$$

The transactions between the two parties can be summarized as follows:

	Hal	*Bank*
Received	$1,508.22	$1,542.50
Expended	− 1,500.00	− 1,508.22
Earned	$ 8.22	$ 34.28

Hal receives $1,508.22 and realizes $8.22 on the loan, despite having to sell the note prior to the maturity date. The bank realizes $34.28 on the transaction. ■

EXAMPLE 2   Thirty days before the due date of a $1,200, ninety-day loan discounted at 11%, Granite City Bank rediscounted (sold) the note to Franklin Federal Bank at a rate of 9%. How much did Granite City Bank receive from Franklin Federal Bank? How much did Granite City Bank make on the transaction?

Solution: First, the proceeds of the original loan are calculated.

$$P = ?, A = \$1,200, d = 11\% = 0.11, t = \frac{90}{360} = 0.25$$

$$\begin{aligned} P &= A(1 - dt) \\ &= \$1,200\,(1 - (0.11 \times 0.25)) \\ &= \$1,200(0.9725) \\ &= \$1,167 \end{aligned}$$

Next, the proceeds of the rediscounted note are calculated.

$$P = ?, A = \$1,200, d = 9\% = 0.09, t = \frac{30}{360} = \frac{1}{12}$$

$$\begin{aligned} P &= A(1 - dt) \\ &= \$1,200 \left(1 - \left(0.09 \times \frac{1}{12}\right)\right) \\ &= \$1,200(0.9925) \\ &= \$1,191 \end{aligned}$$

The transactions between the two banks can be summarized as follows:

	Granite City Bank	*Franklin Federal Bank*
Received	$1,191	$1,200
Expended	− 1,167	− 1,191
Earned	$ 24	$ 9

Granite City Bank received $1,191 from Franklin Federal Bank and earned $1,191 − $1,167 = $24 on the transaction.   ■

As illustrated in example 2, it is a common practice for financial institutions to charge each other a discount rate lower than that charged to individual borrowers and businesses.

In section 7.3, it was shown that merchants could usually save money by taking advantage of a cash discount in the payment of a bill, even if it meant borrowing at simple interest to do so. An analogous situation occurs when a merchant borrows money at simple discount to take advantage of a cash discount. While an invoice is not an interest-bearing document, it acts as such in that a higher price is paid if the purchaser fails to take advantage of the cash discount. As in the case of borrowing at simple interest, borrowing at simple discount is prudent only if the discount on the loan is less than the cash discount. The maximum possible savings occur when the bill is paid on the last day that the cash discount is offered.

EXAMPLE 3   The terms of a bill for $1,200 are 2/30, n/60. If the discount rate at a bank is 8%, **a.** how much must be borrowed (proceeds) and **b.** how much will be saved by taking advantage of the cash discount?

Solution: **a.** The cash discount is $1,200 $\times$ 0.02 = $24; hence,

$1,200   n/60

$-$ $\underline{24}$ Cash discount

$1,176   Amount to be borrowed (proceeds)

b. The net amount is due 30 days after the last day of the cash discount. Thus, we must calculate the maturity value necessary to generate proceeds of $1,176 in 30 days.

$$A = ?, P = \$1,176, d = 8\% = 0.08, t = \frac{30}{360} = \frac{1}{12}$$

Solving formula 9–6 for A,

$$A = \frac{P}{1 - dt}$$
$$= \frac{\$1,176}{1 - (0.08 \times 1/12)}$$
$$= \$1,183.89$$

The discount is $1,183.89 $-$ $1,176.00 = $7.89. Thus, the amount saved by borrowing is $24.00 $-$ $7.89 = $16.11.   ■

EXAMPLE 4   A merchant receives a consignment of goods for $840 with terms 1/10, n/30. At what discount rate could he afford to borrow money to take advantage of the cash discount?

Solution: The cash discount is $840 $\times$ 0.01 = $8.40; hence,

$840.00   n/30

$-$ $\underline{8.40}$ Cash discount

$831.60   Amount to be borrowed

The net amount is due 20 days after the last day of the cash discount. In borrowing from the bank, the discount percentage must not exceed $8.40 (the cash discount), or the merchant will lose money. Thus, using formula 9–4, with $D = \$8.40$, $A = \$840.00$, $d = ?$, and $t = \frac{20}{360} = \frac{1}{18}$

$$d = \frac{D}{At}$$
$$= \frac{\$8.40}{\$840.00 \times 1/18}$$
$$= 0.18$$
$$= 18\%$$

The merchant could afford to borrow money at a discount rate up to 18% and still break even on the transaction.   ■

EXERCISES FOR SECTION 9.3

1. Paul Prentice loaned Bill Butler $3,000 for 90 days at a simple interest rate of 8%. Then, 60 days later, Paul sold the note to a bank that discounted it at 9%. How much did Paul receive from the bank? How much did Paul make on the loan?

2. A $1,400 note bearing 9% simple interest with a term of six months is sold to a bank two months before the due date. If the bank discounts the note at 11%, how much did the payee receive for the note? How much did the payee make on the loan?

3. Two months before the due date, Gateway Bank purchased a one year, $8,000 note bearing $8\frac{1}{2}\%$ simple interest. If the bank discounted the note at $10\frac{1}{2}\%$, how much did the bank make on the transaction? How much did the original owner of the note make?

4. On April 10, Mary Phillips loaned her sister $2,400 at a simple interest rate of $6\frac{1}{4}\%$. The due date of the note was July 19, but on June 29, Mary sold the note to the bank, which discounted it at $8\frac{3}{4}\%$. How much did Mary receive for the note? How much did she make on the loan? How much did the bank make on the transaction?

5. Jim Butler loaned his brother-in-law $2,800 on March 2 at a simple interest rate of $7\frac{3}{4}\%$. The due date of the note was September 18, but because of an illness in his family, Jim was forced to sell the note to the bank on April 1, and the bank discounted it at $9\frac{1}{4}\%$. How much did Jim receive for the note? How much did he lose on the loan? How much did the bank make?

6. Forty-five days before the due date of an $1,800, 180 day loan discounted at 12%, Pacific Bank sold the note to Western Bank at a discount rate of 10%. How much did Pacific Bank receive from Western Bank? How much did Pacific Bank make on the transaction?

7. On June 7, Union Bank loaned $3,700 discounted at $11\frac{1}{4}\%$. The due date of the note was November 4, but on September 5, Union Bank sold the note to Central Bank at a discount of $9\frac{3}{4}\%$. How much did Union Bank receive for the note? How much did Union Bank make on the transaction?

8. The terms of a bill for $900 are 3/30, n/90. If the discount rate at a bank is 12%, how much must be borrowed (proceeds) to take advantage of the cash discount? How much is saved by taking advantage of the discount?

9. Packard Products receives a consignment of goods for $1,600 with terms of 2/10, n/30. The discount rate at the bank is $8\frac{1}{4}\%$. How much should Packard borrow (proceeds) to take advantage of the cash discount? How much will Packard save by borrowing the money?

10. If the terms of a $1,400 bill are 2/20, n/60, find the maximum discount rate at which money could be borrowed to take advantage of the cash discount.

11. Howell Services receives a bill for $2,100 with terms of 2/30, n/120. If the current discount rate for borrowing money is 9%, should the company borrow money to take advantage of the cash discount? Why?

12. Should a company borrow money at a discount rate of 10% to take advantage of the cash discount of an $1,800 bill with terms of 1/10, n/40? Why?

Section 9.4 | *Simple Interest versus Simple Discount*

In section 9.1, it was shown that for a given discount rate, it takes a higher simple interest rate to generate the same amount of interest. In this section, the precise relationship between simple interest and simple discount is given by deriving formulas to convert from one rate to the other. If the formulas

$$A = P(I + rt) \text{ and } P = A(1 - dt)$$

are solved for the common variable P, then

$$P = \frac{A}{1 + rt} \text{ and } P = A(1 - dt)$$

Since P is equal to each of these quantities,

(9–7) $\dfrac{A}{1 + rt} = A(1 - dt)$

or

(9–8) $\dfrac{1}{1 + rt} = 1 - dt$ (Dividing both sides of 9–7 by A)

Solving 9–8 for r,

(9–9) $r = \dfrac{d}{1 - dt}$

Solving 9–8 for d,

(9–10) $d = \dfrac{r}{1 + rt}$

Formulas 9–9 and 9–10 give the relationship between simple interest and simple discount. Given one rate, we can solve for the other by using the appropriate formula. Note that only time affects the relationship between the two rates; the maturity value has no effect.

E X A M P L E   1   What simple interest rate corresponds **a.** to a 12% discount rate on a loan for one year and **b.** to a $10\frac{1}{2}$% discount rate on a loan for 90 days?

Solution: **a.** $d = 12\% = 0.12, t = 1$

$r = \dfrac{d}{1 - dt}$

$= \dfrac{0.12}{1 - (0.12 \times 1)}$

$= 0.1364$ (Rounded)

$= 13.64\%$

(Compare with the calculations for the John Webster loan in section 9.1.)

b. $d = 10\frac{1}{2}\% = 0.105$, $t = \dfrac{90}{360} = 0.25$

$$r = \frac{d}{1 - dt}$$

$$= \frac{0.105}{1 - (0.105 \times 0.25)}$$

$$= 0.1078 \quad \text{(Rounded)}$$

$$= 10.78\%$$

EXAMPLE 2 Find the discount rate corresponding to a simple interest rate of **a.** 9% and **b.** $12\frac{1}{4}\%$ if the term of the loan is six months.

Solution: **a.** $r = 9\% = 0.09$, $t = \dfrac{1}{2} = 0.5$

$$d = \frac{r}{1 + rt}$$

$$= \frac{0.09}{1 + (0.09 \times 0.5)}$$

$$= 0.0861 \quad \text{(Rounded)}$$

$$= 8.61\%$$

b. $d = 12\frac{1}{4}\% = 0.1225$, $t = \dfrac{1}{2} = 0.5$

$$d = \frac{r}{1 + rt}$$

$$= \frac{0.1225}{1 + (0.1225 \times 0.5)}$$

$$= 0.1154 \quad \text{(Rounded)}$$

$$= 11.54\%$$

EXERCISES FOR SECTION 9.4

In problems 1–8, find the simple interest rate that corresponds to the given discount rate for the given time.

1. 8%, two years

2. 10%, six months

3. $11\frac{1}{4}\%$, 18 months

4. $11\frac{1}{2}\%$, one year

5. $9\frac{3}{4}\%$, 90 days

6. $8\frac{3}{4}\%$, 40 days

7. $12\frac{1}{4}\%$, 100 days

8. $11\frac{1}{4}\%$, 72 days

In problems 9–17, find the discount rate that corresponds to the given simple interest rate for the given time.

9. 8%, two years

10. 12%, 18 months

11. $9\frac{1}{4}\%$, one year

12. $8\frac{3}{4}\%$, four years

13. $6\frac{1}{4}\%$, three months

14. $7\frac{3}{4}\%$, 40 days

15. $9\frac{3}{4}\%$, 180 days

16. $10\frac{3}{4}\%$, 20 days

17. $11\frac{1}{2}\%$, 60 days

Solve.

18. Mary Miller needs to borrow some money for 90 days to cover her expenses in opening a new clothing shop. She can obtain the money by borrowing it from a bank at $6\frac{3}{4}\%$ simple interest, or she can borrow it from a friend at $6\frac{1}{2}\%$ discount. Where should she borrow the money?

19. John Parsons is opening a restaurant and wants to borrow some money to buy equipment. He plans to borrow the money for two years. He can get the money from the bank at $9\frac{1}{4}\%$ discount, or he can borrow from a friend at $11\frac{1}{4}\%$ simple interest. Where should he get the money?

20. Jack Bentley can borrow money for two years from the bank at $8\frac{3}{4}\%$ discount, or he can borrow money elsewhere at 10% simple interest. Should he borrow from the bank or obtain the money elsewhere?

21. C. J. Peterson wants to borrow money for four years so that she can remodel her gift shop. Should she obtain the money from the bank at $7\frac{1}{2}\%$ discount or borrow from other sources at 10% simple interest?

Glossary

Present value Also called proceeds. The value in current dollars of a future sum found by the formulas $P = A - D$ or $P = A(1 - dt)$, where P is the present value, A is the maturity value, D is the amount of the discount, d is the discount percent, and t is the term of the loan or investment in years.

Proceeds See *present value*.

Promissory note A written promise to pay a sum of money at a specified future date.

Simple discount Interest computed on the maturity value of a loan according to the formula $D = Adt$, where D is the amount of simple discount, A is the maturity value, d is the discount percent, and t is the term of the loan in years.

Review Test

1. The Lodesville State Bank offered to discount a loan of $2,700 at 10% for three months. Find: **a.** the discount and **b.** the present value.

2. Find the discount and the proceeds on a $1,600 loan at 6.5% for 45 days.

3. If a bank discounts a loan at 12% for four months, what is the maturity value if the discount is $150?

4. Morton Nickel received $764 from Pat Osten and promised to pay Pat $800 in 180 days. What was the simple discount rate?

5. Find the proceeds of a $950 loan at 8% discount for five months.

6. Find the proceeds of a $1,750 loan at 7% discount for 90 days.

7. What simple interest rate corresponds to a 10% discount rate on a loan for 90 days?

8. What discount rate corresponds to an $11\frac{1}{4}\%$ simple interest rate on a loan for 40 days?

9. The terms of a bill for $900 are 3/10, n/30. If the discount rate is 9%, **a.** how much must be borrowed, and **b.** how much will be saved by taking advantage of the cash discount?

10. An $840 note for 90 days bearing 9% simple interest is sold to a bank 60 days before the due date. If the bank discounts the note at $10\frac{1}{2}\%$, how much does the seller receive from the bank?

10

Consumer Credit

Section 10.1 *Distribution of Partial Payments*

A. Introduction

Credit has become an American Institution. "Buy now—pay later" is an accepted way of life for the consumer, and Americans buy houses, automobiles, appliances, home furnishings, and clothing on credit. In fact, nearly anything may be obtained on credit. The extent to which Americans buy on credit is demonstrated in figure 10.1.

Credit permits the purchase of items that consumers might not otherwise be able to afford. By dividing the total cost of an item into a series of partial payments over time, consumers are able to purchase items that they could not buy if cash were required.

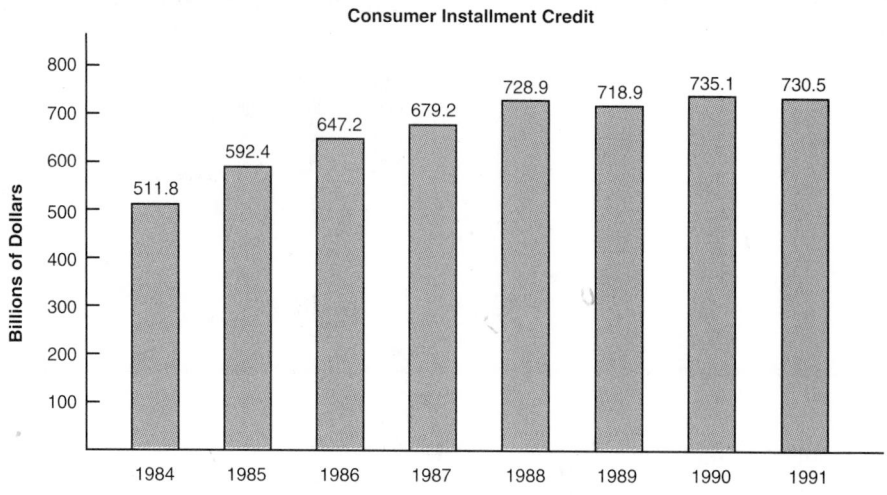

Figure 10.1
Consumer installment credit

Consumer Installment Credit

Consumer Installment Credit Amounts Outstanding

The ease of buying without the need to carry cash is a second reason for the increase in credit sales. However, consumers often pay dearly for this convenience, as will be seen in this chapter. Nonetheless, credit purchases by consumers, business, and government are expected to increase, leading to predictions of a future "credit economy" and a "cashless-checkless" society.

The consumer credit covered in this chapter includes charge accounts, credit cards, and installment contracts.

B. The United States Rule

There is a key difference in paying off a simple interest loan and paying off a loan by a series of partial payments. In a simple interest loan, the borrower has the use of the principal for the entire term of the loan. But when a loan is paid off by a series of partial payments, each payment normally includes part of the principal and an interest charge. The United States Supreme Court has established certain principles on how a partial payment is to be allocated. These principles have become known as the United States Rule and are applied for *each* partial payment in the following steps:

1. *Calculate the interest on the remaining principal from the first day of the loan (or last partial payment) to the day of the current partial payment.*
2. *Subtract the amount in step 1 from the amount of the current partial payment.*
3. *Subtract the amount in step 2 from the remaining principal.*

If the partial payments do not pay off the loan, the amount to be paid on the due date is the remaining principal plus interest on the remaining principal.

The above steps assume each partial payment will be larger than the calculated interest. If a partial payment is smaller than the calculated interest, it is just held by the lender; interest continues to accumulate until the held payment plus subsequent partial payments equals or exceeds the interest due. In calculating interest, banker's rule, $\frac{\text{No. of days}}{360}$, is used.

EXAMPLE 1   On a $3,000 loan at 10% interest, payments of $300, $50, and $200 were made at three-month intervals. What was the amount due if the loan was paid off in one year?

Solution:

Principal		$3,000.00
Payment 1	$300.00	
Less interest ($3,000 $\times$ 0.10 $\times$ $\frac{1}{4}$)	75.00	
Applied to principal		225.00
New principal		$2,775.00
Payment 2	$ 50.00	
Less interest ($2,775 $\times$ 0.10 $\times$ $\frac{1}{4}$)	69.38	
Applied to principal		0.00
New principal		$2,775.00
Payment 3 ($200 + $50)*	$250.00	
Less interest ($2,775 $\times$ 0.10 $\times$ $\frac{1}{2}$)	138.75	
Applied to principal		111.25
New principal		$2,663.75
Plus interest ($2,663.75 $\times$ 0.10 $\times$ $\frac{1}{4}$)		66.59
Amount due		$2,730.34

The total interest paid in the previous example was $75.00 + $138.75 + $66.59 = $280.34. Simple interest for one year would have been $3,000 $\times$ 0.10 $\times$ 1 = $300. Thus, a savings of $300 − $280.34 = $19.66 was realized by making partial payments.

EXERCISES FOR SECTION 10.1

In problems 1–10, find the amount due at the end of one year on the given loan when the indicated partial payments are made at three-month intervals.

Loan Amount	Interest Rate	Payments			
1. $1,000	12%	$200, $200, $400	6. $3,000	7%	$400, $75, $500
2. $2,000	8%	$400, $350, $650	7. $1,500	$10\frac{1}{2}$%	$100, $350, $600
3. $5,000	7%	$1,000, $2,000, $400	8. $2,500	$6\frac{1}{2}$%	$450, $100, $600
4. $6,000	9%	$2,000, $1,500, $2,000	9. $5,200	$7\frac{3}{4}$%	$100, $700, $1,600
5. $8,000	6%	$4,000, $200, $2,100	10. $2,700	$8\frac{1}{4}$%	$80, $50, $200

*Because the previous payment was not as large as the interest charge, the previous payment is added to this payment. Interest is calculated for six months on the next payment.

Solve.

11. Joan Reynolds borrowed $6,000 at 10% interest and made payments at two-month intervals of $1,000, $500, $75, $1,200, and $30. How much was due on the loan at the end of the first year?

12. Bob Johnson borrowed $4,000 for two years at 12% interest so that he could remodel his clothing shop. If he made partial payments at three-month intervals of $500, $150, $60, $300, $1,000, $40, and $1,000, how much did he owe at the end of two years?

Section 10.2 *Open-end Credit*

A. The Finance Charge

The potential uses of credit are many; so are the abuses. Lured by clever advertisements and catch phrases such as "no money down" and "easy terms," some consumers purchase items solely on the amount of the monthly payments, not realizing that the total purchase price may include exorbitant fees and high interest rates. Often, those who can least afford such charges are susceptible to such sales approaches, and in some cases they have incurred enormous debts from repeated and unwise credit purchases.

The Truth-in-Lending Act was passed by Congress to make consumers aware of the true cost of credit and to enable them to make comparisons of credit terms. Regulation Z is a Federal Reserve System Document that carries out the provisions of this act and applies to banks, savings and loans, credit card issuers, automobile dealers, residential mortgage brokers, and all other individuals or groups that offer or arrange for consumer credit.

Two important concepts contained in Regulation Z are the finance charge and the annual percentage rate. The finance charge is covered in this section; the annual percentage rate is covered in section 10.4.

In credit purchases covered by Regulation Z, the total price paid by the customer often includes fees other than interest charges. Examples of such fees are credit investigation fees, credit life insurance, or carrying charges. Carrying charges (also called time payment differential) refer to the additional bookkeeping expenses incurred by the seller in a transaction. Regulation Z lumps all such fees, along with interest charges, under the term **finance charge.**

B. Open-end Credit

Most consumers are acquainted with open-end credit, for this is the credit associated with major credit cards and with the revolving charge accounts of most department stores and retail businesses. In most open-end credit accounts, a monthly finance charge is included if the entire balance is not paid by the **payment due date,** usually 25 days after the billing date. The finance charge is a percentage of (1) the unpaid balance or (2) the average daily balance.

In the unpaid balance method, the finance charge is computed on the unpaid balance as of the end of the previous month. The amount of the finance charge varies according to the institution offering the credit and the state in which the

Many consumer's rely on
several credit cards

account is located, but typically ranges from 1% to 2% of the unpaid balance. In recording payments and finance charges on open-end accounts, the United States Rule is used.

EXAMPLE 1

The balance on a credit card account with a finance charge of 1.75% per month on the unpaid balance is $76.40. If monthly payments of $22.00, $12.00, $10.00, and $15.00 are made, find: **a.** the remaining balance due and **b.** the total paid in finance charges during this period.

Solution:

Month	Previous Balance	Payments	Finance Charge	Credited to Balance	New Balance
1	$76.40	$22.00	$1.34 ($76.40 × 0.0175)	$20.66	$55.74
2	55.74	12.00	0.98 ($55.74 × 0.0175)	11.02	44.72
3	44.72	10.00	0.78 ($44.72 × 0.0175)	9.22	35.50
4	35.50	15.00	0.62 ($35.50 × 0.0175) $3.72	14.38	21.12

The remaining balance is $21.12 and a total finance charge of $3.72 was paid during the period. ∎

EXAMPLE 2 The outstanding balance on a revolving charge account that carries a finance charge of 1.5% per month on the unpaid balance is $36.20. The following purchases, returns, and payments were made on the account.

Month	Purchases	Returns	Payments
1	$ 7.48		$15.00
2	67.60	$45.00	10.00
3			20.00

What was the remaining balance following the third payment?

Solution:

Month	Previous Balance	Current Purchases	Returns	Payments	Finance Charge	Credited to Balance	New Balance
1	$36.20	$ 7.48		$15.00	$0.54	$14.46	$29.22
2	29.22	67.60	45.00	10.00	0.44	9.56	42.26
3	42.26			20.00	0.63	19.37	22.89

The finance charge as a percentage of the unpaid balance has all but been replaced by the finance charge as a percentage of the average daily balance because the latter method generates more interest. The **average daily balance** is the sum of the daily balances during the billing cycle divided by the number of days in the cycle. Each **daily balance** is the previous balance plus purchases and cash advances,* less any payments or credits, and excluding any unpaid finance charges made during the billing period.

Like the unpaid balance method, the amount of the finance charge under the average daily balance method varies according to the institution offering the credit and the state in which the account is located, but typically ranges from 1% to 2% of the average daily balance. The finance charge percent may change during the year. Many companies offering open-end credit now link changes in the finance charge percent to changes in some federal index, for example the average interest rate of Treasury bills. The finance charge percent and the amount of the finance charge appear on the monthly statement following the month in which the finance charge was generated.

EXAMPLE 3 Joanne Miller has a revolving charge account at a department store. Her monthly statement contained the following information.

Bank-sponsored credit cards often provide limited cash loans as a part of their service.

Previous balance		$45.93	June 23 = 20.93
6–20 Payment	$25.00CR	
6–25 Women's wear	26.80	Charge
6–28 Auto department	24.74	
7–2 Craft department	12.00	20.93 + 63.57 = 84.47
7–10 Billing date		

Find: **a.** the payment due date and **b.** the daily balance for Joanne's account on June 23 and July 5.

Solution: **a.** The payment due date is 25 days from July 10, or August 4.
b. The daily balance on June 23 is $45.93 − $25.00 = $20.93
The daily balance on July 5 is $20.93 + $26.80 + $24.74 + $12.00 = $84.47. ■

E X A M P L E 4   A monthly statement for a credit card account with billing date the 20th of each month contained the following information.

Previous balance		$112.40
10–27 Credit	$46.80CR	
10–31 Charge	22.00	
11–5 Payment	20.00CR	
11–10 Cash Advance	50.00	
11–20 Billing date		

Find: the average daily balance for the November 20 billing date.

Solution: Since the previous billing date was October 20, the daily balances are as follows:

Daily Balance

10–20	Seven days	$112.40	
10–27	Four days	65.60	($112.40 − $46.80 = $65.60)
10–31	Five days	87.60	($65.60 + $22.00 = $87.60)
11–5	Five days	67.60	($87.60 − $20.00 = $67.60)
11–10	Ten days	117.60	($67.60 + $50.00 = $117.60)
11–20			

$$\begin{array}{rcl}
\$112.40 \times 7 &=& \$\ \ 786.80 \\
65.60 \times 4 &=& 262.40 \\
87.60 \times 5 &=& 438.00 \\
67.60 \times 5 &=& 338.00 \\
117.60 \times 10 &=& \underline{1,176.00} \\
31 && \$3,001.20
\end{array}$$

$3,001.20 ÷ 31 = $96.81   Average daily balance   ■

EXAMPLE 5   Rosemary Morley's latest monthly statement from Bank-A-Card (billing date the 18th of each month) contained the following information.

Previous balance		$355.00
8–5	Payment	$155.00CR
8–8	Marshall's Department Store	42.18
8–10	Fancy French Restaurant	18.60
8–12	Cash Advance—Sunshine National Bank	100.00
8–18	Billing date	

If the finance charge is 1.5% of the average daily balance, find: **a.** the average daily balance and **b.** the finance charge.

Solution: **a.** There are 18 days from the previous billing date of July 18 to the payment date, 3 days to the department store charge, 2 days to the restaurant charge, 2 days to the cash advance, and 6 days to the August 18th billing date. Hence,

$$\$355.00 \times 18 = \$\ 6,390.00$$
$$\$200.00 \times \ \ 3 = \ \ \ \ 600.00 \quad (\$355 - \$155 = \$200)$$
$$\$242.18 \times \ \ 2 = \ \ \ \ 484.36 \quad (\$200 + \$42.18 = \$242.18)$$
$$\$260.78 \times \ \ 2 = \ \ \ \ 521.56 \quad (\$242.18 + \$18.60 = \$260.78)$$
$$\underline{\$360.78 \times \ \ 6 = \ \ \underline{2,164.68}} \quad (\$260.78 + \$100.00 = \$360.78)$$
$$\ \ \ \ \ \ \ \ \ \ \ \ \ \ \ \ \ 31 \ \ \ \ \ \$10,160.60$$

$$\$10,160.60 \div 31 = \$327.76 \quad \text{Average daily balance}$$
b. $\$327.76 \times 0.015 = \$4.92 \quad \text{Finance charge}$ ■

Consumers who incur a finance charge by failing to pay off their new balance in full by the payment due date pay dearly for this credit. For example, a finance charge of 1.5% per month is equivalent to an annual percentage rate of $1.5 \times 12 = 18\%$, and a finance charge of 2% per month is equivalent to an annual percentage rate of $2 \times 12 = 24\%$. However, because the monthly finance charge seems relatively small, many consumers seem content to pay such exorbitant interest charges.

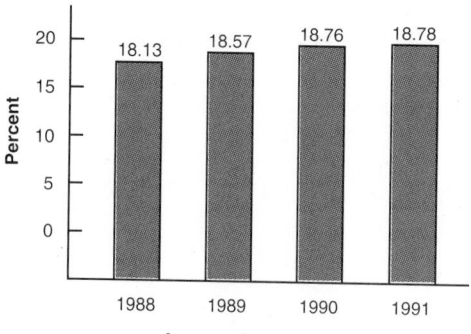

Average Credit Card Rates

EXERCISES FOR SECTION 10.2

*In problems 1–6, find: **a.** the remaining balance due and **b.** the total paid in finance charges if the finance charge is computed on the unpaid balance at the end of the previous month.*

1. Unpaid balance of $424.20; 1.7% per month finance charge; monthly payments of $30.00, $50.00, and $60.00.

2. Unpaid balance of $294.16; 1.5% per month finance charge; monthly payments of $20.00, $15.00, and $25.00.

3. Unpaid balance of $342.26; 1.75% per month finance charge; monthly payments of $20.00, $45.00, and $70.00.

4. Unpaid balance of $628.14; 1.5% per month finance charge; monthly payments of $35.00, $65.00, and $45.00.

5. Unpaid balance of $1,034.22; 1.667% per month finance charge; monthly payments of $120.00, $115.00, $70.00, $80.00, and $125.00.

6. Unpaid balance of $1,210.21; 1.6% per month finance charge; monthly payments of $220.00, $100.00, $125.00, $80.00, and $110.00.

In problems 7–12, find the remaining balance of each account if the finance charge is computed on the unpaid balance at the end of the previous month.

7. Previous balance of $404.01; 1.8% per month finance charge

Month	Purchases	Returns	Payments
1	$11.56		$15.00
2	23.41		10.00
3	17.85	$21.50	20.00

8. Previous balance of $228.11; 1.55% per month finance charge

Month	Purchases	Returns	Payments
1	$41.23	$12.00	$25.00
2	12.41		20.00
3	68.72		20.00

9. Previous balance of $188.27; 1.75% per month finance charge

Month	Purchases	Returns	Payments
1	$12.71	$12.71	$25.00
2	87.62		20.00
3	41.41		50.00

10. Previous balance of $622.25; 1.75% per month finance charge

Month	Purchases	Returns	Payments
1	$14.85	$14.85	$25.00
2	38.26		20.00
3	86.72		40.00

11. Previous balance of $522.26; 1.552% per month finance charge

Month	Purchases	Returns	Payments
1	$82.71	$14.85	$25.00
2	53.92		50.00
3	48.07		60.00
4	11.15	22.15	75.00

12. Previous balance of $622.25; 1.705% per month finance charge

Month	Purchases	Returns	Payments
1	$69.52		$120.00
2	73.94		150.00
3	20.37		160.00
4	52.63		175.00

In problems 13–18, information from the monthly statement of a credit card is given. For each account the payment due date is 25 days from the billing date. Find: **a.** the payment due date and **b.** the daily balance on the specified dates. (Use appendix B to find the due dates.)

13. Previous balance $266.40
    4–15 Payment   50.00CR
    4–20 Charge   80.12
    4–21 Charge   54.22
    5–6   Billing date
    (1) April 18, (2) April 25

14. Previous balance $412.23
    5–21 Charge   48.90
    5–25 Charge   63.95
    5–31 Credit   96.21CR
    6–3   Payment   100.00CR
    6–10 Charge   37.61
    6–19 Billing date
    (1) May 23, (2) June 2,
    (3) June 11

15. Previous balance $382.75
    12–30 Credit   23.60CR
    1–4   Charge   58.61
    1–9   Credit   66.33CR
    1–15 Payment   150.00CR
    1–28 Billing date
    (1) January 3, (2) January 20

16. Previous balance $366.36
    10–5   Cash advance   50.00
    10–12 Charge   90.13
    10–16 Charge   96.21
    10–19 Cash advance   75.00
    10–30 Billing date
    (1) October 18, (2) October 24

17. Previous balance $452.29
    4–4   Cash advance   80.00
    4–10 Credit   88.14CR
    4–15 Charge   33.21
    4–24 Payment   120.00CR
    5–1   Billing date
    (1) April 12, (2) April 25

18. Previous balance $106.94
    8–15 Payment   50.00CR
    8–18 Charge   90.13
    8–21 Charge   96.21
    8–31 Cash advance   75.00
    9–12 Billing date
    (1) August 16, (2) August 29

In problems 19–24, find the average daily balance as of the given billing date. For each problem, the billing dates fall on the same day of the month.

19. Previous balance $126.90
    1–20 Charge   83.00
    1–31 Payment   90.00CR
    2–15 Billing date

20. Previous balance $45.26
    3–21 Credit   39.00CR
    4–1   Charge   27.81
    4–4   Payment   25.00CR
    4–12 Billing date

21. Previous balance $482.60
    7–20 Payment   200.00CR
    7–25 Charge   62.30
    8–2   Cash advance   40.00
    8–12 Charge   56.60
    8–15 Billing date

22. Previous balance $649.06
    8–12 Charge   66.20
    8–16 Credit   37.63CR
    8–19 Credit   58.00CR
    9–1   Payment   300.00CR
    9–9   Billing date

23. Previous balance $92.20
    5–10 Payment   50.00CR
    5–12 Charge   57.00
    5–18 Charge   30.32
    5–20 Cash advance   75.00
    5–25 Credit   57.00CR
    6–1   Billing date

24. Previous balance $487.33
    4–26 Charge   14.67
    4–30 Charge   18.30
    5–9   Payment   200.00CR
    5–13 Charge   45.00
    5–15 Charge   52.00
    5–25 Billing date

For each of the credit card accounts in problems 25–30, calculate the finance charge on the average daily balance at the given percent. For each problem, the billing dates fall on the same day of the month.

25. Previous balance $240.14
    4–20 Charge   50.72
    4–28 Charge   24.72
    5–10 Payment   140.00CR
    Billing date: May 15
    Finance Charge: 1.55% of the
    average daily balance

26. Previous balance $360.24
    3–26 Charge   24.16
    4–2   Payment   175.00CR
    4–15 Payment   20.00CR
    Billing date: April 20
    Finance Charge: 1.7% of the
    average daily balance

27. Previous balance $416.18
    8–20 Payment   200.00CR
    8–25 Cash advance   50.00
    9–4   Charge   16.72
    9–8   Charge   72.42
    Billing date: September 10
    Finance Charge: 1.8% of the
    average daily balance

28. Previous balance $182.78
    6–12 Cash advance   100.00
    6–20 Payment   40.00CR
    6–28 Charge   17.42
    6–30 Payment   50.00CR
    Billing date: July 1
    Finance Charge: 1.5% of the
    average daily balance

29. Previous balance $316.40
    4–20 Payment   150.00CR
    4–22 Credit   27.16CR
    4–28 Cash advance   50.00
    5–4 Payment   100.00CR
    Billing date: May 10
    Finance Charge: 1.625% of the
    average daily balance

30. Previous balance $512.16
    7–22 Charge   100.00
    7–28 Charge   40.00
    7–29 Credit   17.42CR
    8–7 Payment   50.00CR
    8–12 Cash advance   75.00
    8–16 Charge   41.16
    Billing date: August 20
    Finance Charge: 1.75% of the
    average daily balance

In problems 31–34, find the balance of the account as of the last given billing date.

31. Previous balance $74.35
    4–9 Payment   50.00CR
    4–10 Charge   16.20
    4–20 Charge   104.35
    4–25 Charge   34.50
    5–1 Billing date
    5–10 Charge   22.79
    5–12 Credit   16.20CR
    5–26 Charge   20.40
    6–1 Billing date
    Finance Charge: 1.5% of the
    average daily balance

32. Previous balance $82.31
    6–5 Charge   12.16
    6–15 Payment   25.00CR
    6–17 Charge   33.38
    6–20 Charge   41.00
    7–1 Billing date
    7–8 Charge   7.83
    7–10 Charge   16.40
    7–12 Charge   76.70
    7–14 Credit   41.00CR
    8–1 Billing date
    Finance Charge: 1.6% of the
    average daily balance

33. Previous balance $63.94
    9–12 Credit   14.30CR
    9–16 Charge   44.80
    9–25 Cash advance   75.00
    9–25 Charge   34.50
    10–10 Billing date
    10–13 Charge   4.70
    10–20 Charge   16.35
    10–30 Charge   21.25
    11–5 Payment   100.00CR
    11–10 Billing date
    Finance Charge: 1.55% of the
    average daily balance

34. Previous balance $180.00
    3–18 Charge   27.62
    3–20 Credit   33.28CR
    3–30 Cash advance   100.00
    4–3 Payment   200.00CR
    4–15 Billing date
    4–18 Cash advance   50.00
    4–23 Charge   72.16
    4–30 Charge   61.14
    5–4 Payment   75.00CR
    5–11 Charge   22.17
    5–15 Billing date
    Finance Charge: 1.6% of the
    average daily balance

Section 10.3 *Installment Plans*

A second type of consumer credit is credit in return for a series of equal payments at equal intervals over a fixed period of time. This credit, called the **installment plan,** is used in the purchase of "big ticket" items, such as automobiles, furniture, and major appliances. The major features of the installment plan are the down payment, the amount financed, and the amount and schedule of payments.

An accepted principle of the installment plan is that the buyer pay a part of the cash price in the form of a **down payment** or **trade-in.** This creates a sense of ownership for the buyer and provides a safety margin for the vendor. The amount of down payment varies according to the item purchased; for furniture and appliances, 10% of the cash price is a common figure.*

The cash price minus the down payment or trade-in is the **amount financed.**** The sum of the cash price, the finance charge, and any other charges is called the **deferred payment price.**

The **schedule of payments** is determined by dividing the deferred payment price minus the total down payment into a series of equal partial payments. There are two factors to consider. First, the amount of the payment should be relative to the buyer's income and credit status and should correlate with the buyer's pay period. Second, the unpaid balance should be no greater than the resale value of the merchandise.

EXAMPLE 1   To purchase a new car, Terry Bacon agreed to pay $2,500 down and a finance charge of 9% per year of the amount financed. If the cash price was $19,880, and if Terry paid off the debt in 48 monthly payments, what was **a.** the amount of the finance charge, **b.** the deferred payment price, and **c.** the monthly payment?

Solution: **a.** ($19,880 − $2,500) × 0.09 × 4 = $6,256.80   Amount of finance charge

b. $19,880.00   Cash price
+   6,256.80   Finance charge
$26,136.80   Deferred payment price

c. $26,136.80   Deferred payment price
−   2,500.00   Down payment
$23,636.80
$23,636.80 ÷ 48 = $492.43

Since the division does not result in an even number of cents, the monthly payment would likely be $492.43 for 47 months and $492.59 for the final month.

$23,144.21 ($492.43 × 47)
+   492.59
$23,636.80

---

*The credit rating of the customer may also influence the amount of the down payment.

**The amount financed is also called the unpaid balance of the cash price. Actually, the amount financed may include other items, but these are not discussed in this text.

E X A M P L E   2   Sarah Compton purchased a refrigerator with a cash price of $629.99 from a department store. Sarah paid $63 down and $38.75 per month for 18 months. Find **a.** the amount financed, **b.** the deferred payment price, and **c.** the finance charge.

Solution: **a.** $629.99   Cash price
                  −   63.00   Down payment
                      $566.99   Amount financed

         b. $697.50   ($38.75 × 18)
                  +   63.00   Down payment
                      $760.50   Deferred payment price

         c. $760.50   Deferred payment price
                  −   629.99   Cash price
                      $130.51   Finance charge

Businesses offering installment plans must provide their customers with a description of the financing. This description must be in printed form (usually a sales contract) and clearly state the terms of the plan, including the items covered in the previous examples, the annual rate, the charge for default or delinquency, and the penalty for prepayment of principal. A sample of the disclosure information required by Regulation Z is shown in figure 10.2.

EXERCISES FOR SECTION 10.3

In problems 1–10, the cash price of an item is given along with the percent of the amount financed that is the finance charge. For the given down payment and number of monthly payments, find: a. the amount of the finance charge, b. the deferred payment price, and c. the monthly payment.

1. Cash price of $882.14, finance charge of 10% per year of amount financed, down payment of $100.00, 18 monthly payments

2. Cash price of $661.23, finance charge of 12% per year of amount financed, down payment of $50.00, 12 monthly payments

3. Cash price of $1,052.18, finance charge of 11% per year of amount financed, down payment of $150.00, 12 monthly payments

4. Cash price of $1,623.34, finance charge of 8% per year of amount financed, down payment of $162.33, 18 monthly payments

5. Cash price of $1,612.26, finance charge of 9% per year of amount financed, down payment of $225.00, 18 monthly payments

6. Cash price of $2,549.34, finance charge of $9\frac{1}{2}$% per year of amount financed, down payment of $401.72, 24 monthly payments

7. Cash price of $3,271.60, finance charge of $8\frac{1}{2}$% per year of amount financed, down payment of $375.46, 24 monthly payments

8. Cash price of $4,923.36, finance charge of $10\frac{1}{4}$% per year of amount financed, down payment of $492.34, 30 monthly payments

9. Cash price of $4,239.45, finance charge of $7\frac{3}{4}$% per year of amount financed, down payment of $518.27, 36 monthly payments

10. Cash price of $4,332.60, finance charge of $8\frac{3}{4}$% per year of amount financed, down payment of $421.18, 36 monthly payments

Figure 10.2
Disclosure information
required by Regulation Z

Seller's Name: _____   **Contract #**_____

_____

RETAIL INSTALLMENT CONTRACT AND SECURITY AGREEMENT

The undersigned (herein called Purchaser, whether one or more) purchases from _____(seller) and grants to _____ a security interest in, subject to the terms and conditions hereof, the following described property.

QUANTITY	DESCRIPTION	AMOUNT

Description of Trade-in:

Sales Tax	
Total	

Insurance Agreement

The purchase of insurance coverage is voluntary and not required for credit.   (Type of Ins.) insurance coverage is available at a cost of $_____ for the term of credit.

   I desire insurance coverage

Signed_____ Date_____

   I do not desire insurance coverage

Signed_____ Date_____

PURCHASER'S NAME_____
PURCHASER'S ADDRESS_____
CITY_____STATE___ZIP_____

1. CASH PRICE $_____
2. LESS: CASH DOWN PAYMENT $_____
3.   TRADE-IN   _____
4.   TOTAL DOWN PAYMENT _____$_____
5. UNPAID BALANCE OF CASH PRICE $_____
6. OTHER CHARGES:

   _____ $_____
   _____

7. AMOUNT FINANCED $_____
8. FINANCE CHARGE $_____
9. TOTAL OF PAYMENTS $_____
10. DEFERRED PAYMENT PRICE (1+6+8) $_____
11. ANNUAL PERCENTAGE RATE   _____%

Purchaser hereby agrees to pay to_____ _____ at their offices shown above the "TOTAL OF PAYMENTS" shown above in _____ monthly installments of $_____(final payment to be $_____) the first installment being payable _____ 19____, and all subsequent installments on the same day of each consecutive month until paid in full. The finance charge applies from   (Date)

Signed_____

Notice to Buyer: You are entitled to a copy of the contract you sign. You have the right to pay in advance the unpaid balance of this contract and obtain a partial refund of the finance charge based on the "Actuarial Method." [Any other method of computation may be so identified, for example, "Rule of 78's," "Sum of the Digits," etc.]

This form, when properly completed, will show how a creditor may comply with the disclosure requirements of the provisions of paragraphs (b) and (c) of §226.8 of Regulation Z for the type of credit extended in this example. This form is intended solely for purposes of demonstration and it is not the only format which will permit a creditor to comply with disclosure requirements of Regulation Z.

In problems 11–20, the cash price of an item is given along with the down payment, the amount paid per month, and the number of months payments are to be made. Find: **a.** *the amount financed,* **b.** *the deferred payment price, and* **c.** *the finance charge.*

11. Cash price of $511.25, down payment of $75.00, monthly payments of $21.85 for 24 months

12. Cash price of $824.11, down payment of $122.14, monthly payments of $46.02 for 18 months

13. Cash price of $421.18, down payment of $45.26, monthly payments of $32.80 for 12 months

14. Cash price of $729.18, down payment of $72.92, monthly payments of $43.07 for 18 months

15. Cash price of $1,124.18, down payment of $172.18, monthly payments of $50.84 for 24 months

16. Cash price of $1,021.11, down payment of $212.14, monthly payments of $75.17 for 12 months

17. Cash price of $992.95, down payment of $110.72, monthly payments of $55.91 for 18 months

18. Cash price of $1,795.92, down payment of $333.21, monthly payments of $64.60 for 30 months

19. Cash price of $2,892.11, down payment of $363.81, monthly payments of $89.71 for 36 months

20. Cash price of $2,214.87, down payment of $385.75, monthly payments of $66.05 for 36 months

Solve.

21. Judy Anderson purchased a living-room suite for $321.18 down and a finance charge of 8% per year of the amount financed. If the cash price was $2,163.33, and if Judy paid off the furniture in 20 monthly payments, find: **a.** the amount of the finance charge, **b.** the deferred payment price, and **c.** the monthly payment.

22. Tom Phillips purchased a washing machine for $60.00 down and $42.98 per month for 12 months. If the cash price of the machine was $512.42, find: **a.** the amount financed, **b.** the deferred payment price, and **c.** the finance charge.

Section 10.4   *The Annual Percentage Rate*

A key feature of the truth-in-lending legislation is the requirement that the seller disclose not only the amount of the finance charge but also the annual percent. Because interest is normally expressed as a rate per annum, the requirement that finance charges also be expressed as an annual rate provides the consumer with a truer picture of the cost of consumer credit.

As defined by Regulation Z, the **annual percentage rate** is found by multiplying the unit-period rate by the number of unit-periods in a given year. The regulation further states that the computation must be accurate to the nearest quarter of 1% and that payments are applied first to the finance charge and any remainder to the unpaid balance of the amount financed.

In open-end credit, the unit period is normally one month, and the unit period rate is the percent per month charge on the unpaid or average daily balance, Thus, a charge of 1% per month is an annual percentage rate (APR) of 1% $\times$ 12 = 12%, $1\frac{1}{2}$% per month is an APR of $1\frac{1}{2}$% $\times$ 12 = 18%, and $3\frac{1}{2}$% per month is an APR of 42%.

For installment plans, the computation is more involved, and APR tables have been prepared by the government to simplify the computation. A portion of these tables is found in appendix K at the end of the book. To calculate the APR using appendix K,

Step 1 Divide the finance charge by the total amount financed and multiply by $100. (This gives the finance charge per $100 of the amount to be financed.)

Step 2 Find the number of payments in the first column of appendix K. Follow horizontally across this row to the column with the amount nearest the value obtained in step 1. The top of this column shows the annual percentage rate.

The sample page from appendix K shown on page 275 can be used for the next example.

EXAMPLE 1   An installment contract for a color television set contains the following information: cash price of $695.00, total down payment of $150.00, deferred payment price of $799.25. What is the annual percentage rate if the plan calls for 24 monthly payments?

Solution:

$799.25   Deferred payment price
$-$ 695.00   Cash price
$104.25   Finance charge

$695.00   Cash price
$-$ 150.00   Down payment
$545.00   Amount financed

Step 1: $\dfrac{\$104.25}{\$545.00} \times \$100.00 = \$19.13$

Step 2:   In line 24 of appendix K, the nearest value to $19.13 is $19.24. The top of this column shows that the annual percentage rate is 17.5%.   ■

EXAMPLE 2   Thelma Fricks purchased a vacuum cleaner by paying $30.00 down and $25.20 per month for twelve months. If the cash price was $299.99, find the annual percentage rate.

Solution:

$302.40   ($25.20 $\times$ 12)
$+$ 30.00   Down payment
$332.40   Deferred payment price

$332.40   Deferred payment price
$-$ 299.99   Cash price
$ 32.41   Finance charge

$299.99   Cash price
$-$ 30.00   Down payment
$269.99   Amount financed

$$\frac{\$32.41}{\$269.99} \times 100 = 12.00$$

In line 12 of appendix K, the APR is 21.50%.   ■

SAMPLE PAGE FROM TABLE FOR COMPUTING ANNUAL PERCENTAGE RATE FOR LEVEL MONTHLY PAYMENT PLANS

ANNUAL PERCENTAGE RATE

(FINANCE CHARGE PER $100 OF AMOUNT FINANCED)

NUMBER OF PAYMENTS	14.00%	14.25%	14.50%	14.75%	15.00%	15.25%	15.50%	15.75%	16.00%	16.25%	16.50%	16.75%	17.00%	17.25%	17.50%	17.75%
1	1.17	1.19	1.21	1.23	1.25	1.27	1.29	1.31	1.33	1.35	1.37	1.40	1.42	1.44	1.46	1.48
2	1.75	1.78	1.82	1.85	1.88	1.91	1.94	1.97	2.00	2.04	2.07	2.10	2.13	2.16	2.19	2.22
3	2.34	2.38	2.43	2.47	2.51	2.55	2.59	2.64	2.68	2.72	2.76	2.80	2.85	2.89	2.93	2.97
4	2.93	2.99	3.04	3.09	3.14	3.20	3.25	3.30	3.36	3.41	3.46	3.51	3.57	3.62	3.67	3.73
5	3.53	3.59	3.65	3.72	3.78	3.84	3.91	3.97	4.04	4.10	4.16	4.23	4.29	4.35	4.42	4.48
6	4.12	4.20	4.27	4.35	4.42	4.49	4.57	4.64	4.72	4.79	4.87	4.94	5.02	5.09	5.17	5.24
7	4.72	4.81	4.89	4.98	5.06	5.15	5.23	5.32	5.40	5.49	5.58	5.66	5.75	5.83	5.92	6.00
8	5.32	5.42	5.51	5.61	5.71	5.80	5.90	6.00	6.09	6.19	6.29	6.38	6.48	6.58	6.67	6.77
9	5.92	6.03	6.14	6.25	6.35	6.46	6.57	6.68	6.78	6.89	7.00	7.11	7.22	7.32	7.43	7.54
10	6.53	6.65	6.77	6.88	7.00	7.12	7.24	7.36	7.48	7.60	7.72	7.84	7.96	8.08	8.19	8.31
11	7.14	7.27	7.40	7.53	7.66	7.79	7.92	8.05	8.18	8.31	8.44	8.57	8.70	8.83	8.96	9.09
12	7.74	7.89	8.03	8.17	8.31	8.45	8.59	8.74	8.88	9.02	9.16	9.30	9.45	9.59	9.73	9.87
13	8.36	8.51	8.66	8.81	8.97	9.12	9.27	9.43	9.58	9.73	9.89	10.04	10.20	10.35	10.50	10.66
14	8.97	9.13	9.30	9.46	9.63	9.79	9.96	10.12	10.29	10.45	10.62	10.78	10.95	11.11	11.28	11.45
15	9.59	9.76	9.94	10.11	10.29	10.47	10.64	10.82	11.00	11.17	11.35	11.53	11.71	11.88	12.06	12.24
16	10.20	10.39	10.58	10.77	10.95	11.14	11.33	11.52	11.71	11.90	12.09	12.28	12.46	12.65	12.84	13.03
17	10.82	11.02	11.22	11.42	11.62	11.82	12.02	12.22	12.42	12.62	12.83	13.03	13.23	13.43	13.63	13.83
18	11.45	11.66	11.87	12.08	12.29	12.50	12.72	12.93	13.14	13.35	13.57	13.78	13.99	14.21	14.42	14.64
19	12.07	12.30	12.52	12.74	12.97	13.19	13.41	13.64	13.86	14.09	14.31	14.54	14.76	14.99	15.22	15.44
20	12.70	12.93	13.17	13.41	13.64	13.88	14.11	14.35	14.59	14.82	15.06	15.30	15.54	15.77	16.01	16.25
21	13.33	13.58	13.82	14.07	14.32	14.57	14.82	15.06	15.31	15.56	15.81	16.06	16.31	16.56	16.81	17.07
22	13.96	14.22	14.48	14.74	15.00	15.26	15.52	15.78	16.04	16.30	16.57	16.83	17.09	17.36	17.62	17.88
23	14.59	14.87	15.14	15.41	15.68	15.96	16.23	16.50	16.78	17.05	17.32	17.60	17.88	18.15	18.43	18.70
24	15.23	15.51	15.80	16.08	16.37	16.65	16.94	17.22	17.51	17.80	18.09	18.37	18.66	18.95	19.24	19.53
25	15.87	16.17	16.46	16.76	17.06	17.35	17.65	17.95	18.25	18.55	18.85	19.15	19.45	19.75	20.05	20.36
26	16.51	16.82	17.13	17.44	17.75	18.06	18.37	18.68	18.99	19.30	19.62	19.93	20.24	20.56	20.87	21.19
27	17.15	17.47	17.80	18.12	18.44	18.76	19.09	19.41	19.74	20.06	20.39	20.71	21.04	21.37	21.69	22.02
28	17.80	18.13	18.47	18.80	19.14	19.47	19.81	20.15	20.48	20.82	21.16	21.50	21.84	22.18	22.52	22.86
29	18.45	18.79	19.14	19.49	19.83	20.18	20.53	20.88	21.23	21.58	21.94	22.29	22.64	22.99	23.35	23.70
30	19.10	19.45	19.81	20.17	20.54	20.90	21.26	21.62	21.99	22.35	22.72	23.08	23.45	23.81	24.18	24.55
31	19.75	20.12	20.49	20.87	21.24	21.61	21.99	22.37	22.74	23.12	23.50	23.88	24.26	24.64	25.02	25.40
32	20.40	20.79	21.17	21.56	21.95	22.33	22.72	23.11	23.50	23.89	24.28	24.68	25.07	25.46	25.86	26.25
33	21.06	21.46	21.85	22.25	22.65	23.06	23.46	23.86	24.26	24.67	25.07	25.48	25.88	26.29	26.70	27.11
34	21.72	22.13	22.54	22.95	23.37	23.78	24.19	24.61	25.03	25.44	25.86	26.28	26.70	27.12	27.54	27.97
35	22.38	22.80	23.23	23.65	24.08	24.51	24.94	25.36	25.79	26.23	26.66	27.09	27.52	27.96	28.39	28.83
36	23.04	23.48	23.92	24.35	24.80	25.24	25.68	26.12	26.57	27.01	27.46	27.90	28.35	28.80	29.25	29.70
37	23.70	24.16	24.61	25.06	25.51	25.97	26.42	26.88	27.34	27.80	28.26	28.72	29.18	29.64	30.10	30.57
38	24.37	24.84	25.30	25.77	26.24	26.70	27.17	27.64	28.11	28.59	29.06	29.53	30.01	30.49	30.96	31.44
39	25.04	25.52	26.00	26.48	26.96	27.44	27.92	28.41	28.89	29.38	29.87	30.36	30.85	31.34	31.83	32.32
40	25.71	26.20	26.70	27.19	27.69	28.18	28.68	29.18	29.68	30.18	30.68	31.18	31.68	32.19	32.69	33.20
41	26.39	26.89	27.40	27.91	28.41	28.92	29.44	29.95	30.47	30.97	31.49	32.01	32.52	33.04	33.56	34.08
42	27.06	27.58	28.10	28.62	29.15	29.67	30.19	30.72	31.25	31.78	32.31	32.84	33.37	33.90	34.44	34.97
43	27.74	28.27	28.81	29.34	29.88	30.42	30.96	31.50	32.04	32.58	33.13	33.67	34.22	34.76	35.31	35.86
44	28.42	28.97	29.52	30.07	30.62	31.17	31.72	32.28	32.83	33.39	33.95	34.51	35.07	35.63	36.19	36.76
45	29.11	29.67	30.23	30.79	31.36	31.92	32.49	33.06	33.63	34.20	34.77	35.35	35.92	36.50	37.08	37.66
46	29.79	30.36	30.94	31.52	32.10	32.68	33.26	33.84	34.43	35.01	35.60	36.19	36.78	37.37	37.96	38.56
47	30.48	31.07	31.66	32.25	32.84	33.44	34.03	34.63	35.23	35.83	36.43	37.04	37.64	38.25	38.86	39.46
48	31.17	31.77	32.37	32.98	33.59	34.20	34.81	35.42	36.03	36.65	37.27	37.88	38.50	39.13	39.75	40.37
49	31.86	32.48	33.09	33.71	34.34	34.96	35.59	36.21	36.84	37.47	38.10	38.74	39.37	40.01	40.65	41.29
50	32.55	33.18	33.82	34.45	35.09	35.73	36.37	37.01	37.65	38.30	38.94	39.59	40.24	40.89	41.55	42.20
51	33.25	33.89	34.54	35.19	35.84	36.49	37.15	37.81	38.46	39.12	39.79	40.45	41.11	41.78	42.45	43.12
52	33.95	34.61	35.27	35.93	36.60	37.27	37.94	38.61	39.28	39.96	40.63	41.31	41.99	42.67	43.36	44.04
53	34.65	35.32	36.00	36.68	37.36	38.04	38.72	39.41	40.10	40.79	41.48	42.17	42.87	43.57	44.27	44.97
54	35.35	36.04	36.73	37.42	38.12	38.82	39.52	40.22	40.92	41.63	42.33	43.04	43.75	44.47	45.18	45.90
55	36.05	36.76	37.46	38.17	38.88	39.60	40.31	41.03	41.74	42.47	43.19	43.91	44.64	45.37	46.10	46.83
56	36.76	37.48	38.20	38.92	39.65	40.38	41.11	41.84	42.57	43.31	44.05	44.79	45.53	46.27	47.02	47.77
57	37.47	38.20	38.93	39.68	40.42	41.16	41.91	42.65	43.47	44.15	44.91	45.66	46.42	47.18	47.94	48.71
58	38.18	38.93	39.68	40.43	41.19	41.95	42.71	43.47	44.23	45.00	45.77	46.54	47.32	48.09	48.87	49.65
59	38.89	39.66	40.42	41.19	41.96	42.74	43.51	44.29	45.07	45.85	46.64	47.42	48.21	49.01	49.80	50.60
60	39.61	40.39	41.17	41.95	42.74	43.53	44.32	45.11	45.91	46.71	47.51	48.31	49.12	49.92	50.73	51.55

EXAMPLE 3   Gene Roberts purchased a set of four automobile tires by making six monthly payments of $33.56. He received $12.00 credit for his old tires as a trade-in. The cash price was $51.00 per tire. What annual percentage rate did Gene pay as a result of buying on credit?

Solution:

$201.36	($33.56 × 6)
+ 12.00	Trade-in
$213.36	Deferred payment price

$213.36	Deferred payment price
− 204.00	Cash price ($51 × 4)
$ 9.36	Finance charge

$204.00	Cash price
− 12.00	Trade-in
$192.00	Amount financed

$$\frac{\$9.36}{\$192.00} \times \$100.00 = \$4.88$$

In line 6 of appendix K, the nearest value to $4.88 is $4.87; hence, the APR is 16.5%. ■

The annual percentage rate of 16.5% in example 3 means that if interest is computed at 16.5% only on the remaining balance each month, and if the $33.56 payment is applied to the outstanding balance according to the United States Rule, then the six payments will equal the $192.00 amount financed plus the $9.36 finance charge. This is illustrated in the schedule of payments shown in the following table (the final balance of −$.03 is due to rounding and the approximate annual percentage rate of 16.5%):

(1)	(2)	(3)	(4)	(5)	(6)
Month	Previous Balance	Payment	Interest ($Prt = I$)	Credited to Balance (3)–(4)	New Balance (2)–(5)
1	$192.00	$33.56	$192.00 × .165 × $\frac{1}{12}$ = $2.64	$30.92	$161.08
2	161.08	33.56	161.08 × .165 × $\frac{1}{12}$ = 2.21	31.35	129.73
3	129.73	33.56	129.73 × .165 × $\frac{1}{12}$ = 1.78	31.78	97.95
4	97.95	33.56	97.95 × .165 × $\frac{1}{12}$ = 1.35	32.21	65.74
5	65.74	33.56	65.74 × .165 × $\frac{1}{12}$ = 0.90	32.66	33.08
6	33.08	33.56	33.08 × .165 × $\frac{1}{12}$ = 0.45	33.11	−.03
			$9.33	$192.03	

EXERCISES FOR SECTION 10.4

In problems 1–6, find the annual percentage rate for revolving charge accounts with the given monthly interest rate.

1. 1.25%   **2.** 2.25%   **3.** 2.5%   **4.** 1.55%   **5.** 1.8%   **6.** 1.75%

In problems 7–27, use appendix K to find the annual percentage rate for the given installment contract.

7. Cash price of $472, down payment of $75, deferred payment price of $525, 18 monthly payments

8. Cash price of $782.40, down payment of $110.00, deferred payment price of $896.62, 24 monthly payments

9. Cash price of $1,287.40, down payment of $225.00, deferred payment price of $1,575.80, 40 monthly payments

10. Cash price of $1,896.52, down payment of $425.50, deferred payment price of $2,245.80, 36 monthly payments

11. Cash price of $2,692.49, down payment of $510.25, deferred payment price of $2,972.75, 26 monthly payments

12. Cash price of $979.42, down payment of $220.15, deferred payment price of $1,142.60, 30 monthly payments

13. Cash price of $1,475.83, down payment of $283.49, deferred payment price of $1,695.43, 28 monthly payments

14. Cash price of $1,064.89, down payment of $106.49, deferred payment price of $1,289.09, 42 monthly payments

15. Cash price of $4,287.50, down payment of $723.89, deferred payment price of $4,893.80, 22 monthly payments

16. Cash price of $485.42, 24 monthly payments of $21.79 each, down payment of $50

17. Cash price of $859.63, 12 monthly payments of $71.82 each, down payment of $85

18. Cash price of $1,152.16, 15 monthly payments of $77.86 each, down payment of $100

19. Cash price of $987.24, 30 monthly payments of $35.25 each, down payment of $90

20. Cash price of $647.83, 18 monthly payments of $35.96 each, down payment of $65

21. Cash price of $743.85, down payment of $50.00, 18 monthly payments of $42.65 each

22. Cash price of $1,142.86, down payment of $225.00, 12 monthly payments of $83.15 each

23. Cash price of $1,857.64, down payment of $410.00, 24 monthly payments of $71.20 each

24. Cash price of $858.19, down payment of $95.00, 20 monthly payments of $43.66 each

25. Cash price of $1,042.80, down payment of $140.00, 18 monthly payments of $55.11 each

26. Bob Johnson purchased a new outboard motor by paying $75.00 down and $54.03 a month for 18 months. If the cash price was $957.75, find the annual percentage rate Bob is paying.

27. Sylvia Stephens purchased a new sewing machine by paying $50.00 down and $27.66 a month for 24 months. If the cash price was $621.80, find the annual percentage rate Sylvia is paying.

Section 10.5 *The Rule of 78*

Installment contracts are designed to pay off the principal and interest charge (finance charge) by a series of partial payments; thus, each payment is part principal and part interest. Should the full amount of the obligation be paid prior to the maturity date, the borrower may be entitled to a rebate on the unearned interest.

The Truth-in-Lending Act requires the lender to disclose the method of calculating such a rebate when the loan is initiated. In the language of the act, the lender must give "a statement of the amount or method of computation of any charge that may be deducted from the amount of any rebate of such unearned finance charge that will be credited to an obligation or refunded to the customer."[*]

A method commonly used to calculate this rebate is called the **Rule of 78,** or the sum-of-the-balances method. This method assumes that on a 12 month loan, 12 units of principal are outstanding the first month, 11 units are outstanding the second month, 10 units are outstanding the third month, and so on, to the last or twelfth month, when 1 unit of principal is outstanding. Since the sum of the numbers from 1 to 12 is 78, the total finance charge is divided into 78 units (hence, the name Rule of 78).

Division of the finance charge into 78 units has the following effect on the amount of the rebate. Clearly, there is no rebate if the loan is not paid off until the end of the twelfth month or the maturity date, but if the loan is paid off at the end of the eleventh month, the borrower is entitled to a rebate of $\frac{1}{78}$ of the finance charge. If the loan is paid off at the end of the tenth month, the borrower is entitled to a rebate of $\frac{1}{78} + \frac{2}{78} = \frac{1+2}{78} = \frac{3}{78}$ of the finance charge, and if the loan is paid off at the end of the ninth month, the borrower is entitled to a rebate of $\frac{1+2+3}{78}$ of the finance charge. In general, if a 12 month loan is paid in full at the end of the nth month, then the amount of the rebate R is given by the formula

$$\textbf{(10–1)} \quad R = \frac{1 + 2 + \ldots + (12 - n)}{78} \times \text{Finance charge}$$

EXAMPLE 1   Beverly McMillan purchased a set of golf clubs on a 12 month installment contract that included a finance charge of $40. If she decided to pay off the entire contract at the end of the seventh month, how much would her rebate be under the Rule of 78?

Solution: $n = 7$ and $12 - n = 12 - 7 = 5$

Hence, by formula 10–1,

$$R = \frac{1 + 2 + 3 + 4 + 5}{78} \times \$40$$

$$= \frac{15}{78} \times \$40$$

$$= \$7.69$$

*If the correct contract does not provide for any rebate of unearned finance charges upon prepayment in full, this must be disclosed.

Rebate calculations for contracts other than 12 months duration are the same, except that the number of units is different. For a six month loan, there are $1 + 2 + 3 + 4 + 5 + 6 = 21$ units; for an 18 month loan, there are 171 units; for a two year loan, there are 300 units; and so on.

A general formula for the amount of rebate under the sum-of-the-balances method is as follows: if R = amount of rebate, m = total number of months, and $n = m$ minus number of months before prepay, then

(10–2) $R = \dfrac{n(n + 1)}{m(m + 1)} \times$ Finance charge

In example 1, $m = 12$, $n = 12 - 7 = 5$, and the finance charge was $40; thus

$$R = \frac{5(6)}{12(13)} \times \$40$$

$$= \frac{5}{26} \times \$40$$

$$= \$7.69$$

(handwritten: $5(5+1) \quad \dfrac{30}{156} = \dfrac{5}{26} \times 40 = \dfrac{200}{26} = 7.69$)

E X A M P L E   2   To get a new roof put on his house, Danny Swisshelm signed a contract calling for a finance charge of $234.00 and 24 monthly payments of $84.75. At the end of the fifteenth month, Danny decided to pay off the entire debt. Under the sum-of-the-balances method, what rebate did Danny receive?

Solution: $m = 24$, $n = 24 - 15 = 9$

$$R = \frac{9(10)}{24(25)} \times \$234$$

$$= 0.15 \times \$234$$

$$= \$35.10$$

E X A M P L E   3   K. May McCluskey purchased a vacuum cleaner for a finance charge of $18 and six payments of $23 per month. At the end of the fourth month, Mrs. McCluskey decided to pay off the entire amount of the obligation. Find: **a.** the amount of the rebate and **b.** the amount of the final payment.

Solution: **a.** $m = 6$, $n = 6 - 4 = 2$

$$R = \frac{2(3)}{6(7)} \times \$18$$

$$= \frac{1}{7} \times \$18$$

$$= \$2.57$$

b. If the debt is to be paid off at the end of the fourth month, three payments have been made with three remaining. The remaining payments total $3 \times \$23.00 = \$69.00$. With the rebate, the final payment is $\$69.00 - \$2.57 = \$66.43$.

EXERCISES FOR SECTION 10.5

In problems 1–5, use the Rule of 78 to compute the rebate when a 12 month installment contract with the given finance charge is paid off at the end of the given month.

1. Finance charge of $60, paid off at the end of the fifth month

2. Finance charge of $18, paid off at the end of the third month

3. Finance charge of $24, paid off at the end of the tenth month

4. Finance charge of $36, paid off at the end of the fourth month

5. Finance charge of $48, paid off at the end of the eighth month

In problems 6–10, use the sum-of-the-balances method to compute the rebate when an installment contract of the given duration with the given finance charge is paid off at the end of the given month.

6. Two year contract, $180 finance charge, paid off at the end of the twelfth month

7. 18 month contract, $110 finance charge, paid off at the end of the tenth month

8. Six month contract, $24 finance charge, paid off at the end of the third month

9. 14 month contract, $90 finance charge, paid off at the end of the ninth month

10. 20 month contract, $160 finance charge, paid off at the end of the fourteenth month

Solve.

11. Bob Jacobs purchased a color television set on a one year installment contract that included a finance charge of $68. If Bob paid off the contract at the end of the eighth month, what was his rebate?

12. Jennifer Childress signed a one year installment contract to purchase some furniture. If the contract included a finance charge of $74, and if Jennifer paid off the contract at the end of the fifth month, what was her rebate?

13. Craig Ross bought some new equipment for his radiator shop on a 20 month installment contract that included a finance charge of $236. He was then able to pay off the contract at the end of the sixteenth month. How much was his rebate?

14. Diane Dennis signed an 18 month installment contract to buy some new display items for her clothing shop. If the contract included a finance charge of $210, and if Diane paid off the contract at the end of the fourteenth month, what was her rebate?

15. Ralph Thomas bought a fishing boat on an installment plan of $52 a month for one year. At the end of the seventh month, Ralph paid off the contract. If the finance charge was $64, find the amount of the final payment.

16. Marcia Brennan purchased a refrigerator for a finance charge of $36 and sixteen monthly payments of $63 each. At the end of the sixth month, Marcia paid off the contract. What was the amount of the final payment?

||||||||||||||||||||||||||||||||||| Glossary |||||||||||||||||||||||||||||||||||||||||||

Amount financed   The difference between the cash price and the down payment or trade-in.

Annual percentage rate   The cost of credit expressed as an annual percent in accordance with the regulations contained in Regulation Z of the Truth-in-Lending Act.

Average daily balance   The sum of the daily balances during a billing cycle divided by the number of days in the cycle.

Daily balance   The previous balance plus purchases and cash advances, less any payments or credits, and excluding any unpaid finance charges made during the billing period.

Deferred payment price   The sum of the cash price, the finance charge, and any other charges.

Down payment   In an installment contract, a portion of the cash price paid at the time of the sale.

Finance charge   The total of all costs to the buyer for obtaining credit, including interest, credit investigation fees, credit life insurance, and carrying charges.

Installment plan   A payment plan calling for a series of equal payments over a fixed period of time.

Open-end credit   A payment plan in which a finance charge (depending on the balance of the account) is imposed at the end of each billing period and in which the number of payments is not fixed.

Payment due date   The date by which full payment must be made on an open-end account to avoid a finance charge.

Regulation Z   A Federal Reserve System document implementing the provisions of the Truth-in-Lending Act.

Rule of 78   A method used to calculate the amount of the rebate when the full amount owed under an installment contract is paid prior to the maturity date.

Schedule of payments   In an installment plan, a series of equal partial payments found by dividing the deferred payment price minus the total down payment by the total number of payments.

Trade-in   An item of merchandise accepted as the down payment on an installment plan.

Truth-in-Lending Act   A federal disclosure act requiring sellers to inform buyers of the cost of credit.

United States Rule   A method established by a decision of the United States Supreme Court for crediting partial payments toward a debt. The fundamental principle of the rule is that a partial payment is applied first to the interest on the unpaid balance, with any remainder applied to the reduction of the principal.

Review Test

In problems 1–5, indicate whether the statement is true or false.

1. A principle of the United States Rule is that if the partial payment does not exceed the accumulated interest, the partial payment is applied only to the principal for that period.

2. The Truth-in-Lending Act was designed to regulate interest charges.

3. In open-end credit, a finance charge is imposed if the entire balance of the account is not paid by the payment due date.

Solve.

6. Using the United States Rule, find the amount due at the end of one year on a loan of $600 at 10% if the following payments are made at three-month intervals: $90, $50, $75.

$$\frac{12(13}{24(24+1)} \quad \sqrt{180} \quad = \quad \frac{156}{600} \quad -46.8$$

4. The average daily balance is the sum of the daily balances during the billing cycle divided by the number of days in the cycle.

5. The cash price minus the down payment or trade-in is the amount financed.

$$\frac{9(9+1)}{12(12+1} = \quad \frac{90}{156} = 31.2 = 10.38$$

7. Find the new balance after month 2 on the following credit card account if the finance charge is $1\frac{1}{2}\%$ per month of the unpaid balance.

Month	Previous Balance	Purchases	Payments	Finance Charge	Credited to Balance	New Balance
1	$142.00	$0.00	$60.00	—	—	—
2	—	200.00	50.00	—	—	—

8. The monthly charge on the following account is 1.8% of the average daily balance. Compute the finance charge. The billing dates fall on the same day of each month.
   Previous balance $160.70
   6–20, Charge   134.50
   6–26, Charge   64.48
   7–1, Payment   50.00CR
   7–10, Billing date

9. An item of furniture with a cash price of $639.95 is purchased with a payment of $64.00 down, 18 monthly payments, and a finance charge of 11.75% per year of the amount financed. Find: **a.** the amount of the finance charge, **b.** the deferred payment price, and **c.** the monthly payment.

10. **a.** Compute the rebate on an 18 month installment contract with a finance charge of $75.00 if the contract is paid off at the end of the eighth month. **b.** If the contract called for monthly payments of $36.50, find the amount of the final payment.

chapter

11

Annuities

 Section 11.1 *Ordinary Annuities*

A. Introduction

An **annuity** is a series of payments at regular intervals. The payments are normally equal but need not be so. The time interval between payments is called the **period,** and the **term** of an annuity is the time from the beginning of the first period to the end of the last period. Examples of annuities are Social Security payments, mortgage payments on a house, endowments, and installment plan payments.

The type of annuity to be studied in this chapter is the **annuity certain.** The beginning and ending dates of an annuity certain are specified.* There are two basic kinds of annuity certain. If the payment is made at the end of a period, the annuity

*If either the beginning or ending date of an annuity is not specified, then the annuity is called a **contingent annuity.** Proceeds of a life insurance policy that are paid in installments are an example of this kind of annuity, in that the beginning payment is contingent on the death of the insured.

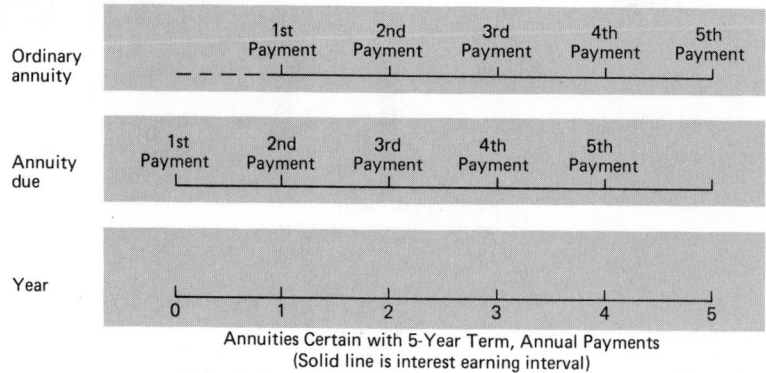

Figure 11.1
Annuities certain with
five-year term,
annual payments

Annuities Certain with 5-Year Term, Annual Payments
(Solid line is interest earning interval)

Pension | montly salary

is called an **ordinary annuity;** if the payment is made at the beginning of a period, the annuity is called an **annuity due.** (See figure 11.1.)

— beginng at month.

B. The Ordinary Annuity Formula

To understand an ordinary annuity and its formulas, suppose that on May 1 of each year for five years, $1 is deposited in a savings account paying 10% interest compounded annually. What is the accumulated amount immediately following the last deposit?

The fifth deposit, having just been made, earns no interest; the fourth deposit earns one year's interest; the third deposit earns two years' interest; and so on. By formula 8–1 for compound interest (using appendix C),

Fifth deposit	$1	= $1.00000000
Fourth deposit	$1 $(1.10)^1$	= 1.10000000
Third deposit	$1 $(1.10)^2$	= 1.21000000
Second deposit	$1 $(1.10)^3$	= 1.33100000
First deposit	$1 $(1.10)^4$	= 1.46410000
Accumulated deposit		= $6.10510000

The accumulated amount for deposits of $1 is $6.10510000. By the same reasoning, it can be shown that had the deposits been $100 per year, the accumulated amount would be $100 \times 6.10510000 = \$610.510000$, and that deposits of $1,000 per year would result in an accumulated amount of $1,000 \times 6.10510000 = \$6,105.10000$.

This special case leads to a generalization. Consider an ordinary annuity with n payments of $1 each ($n$ = a counting number) made once a year, and let the annual compound interest rate be i. Then, if the accumulated amount is denoted by $s_{\overline{n}|i}$

(11–1) $s_{\overline{n}|} = 1 + (1 + i) + (1 + i)^2 + (1 + i)^3 + \ldots + (1 + i)^n$

The right-hand side of this equation can be simplified; the result is

$$\textbf{(11-2)} \quad s_{\overline{n}|i} = \frac{(1 + i)^n - 1}{i}$$

To demonstrate formula 11–2, consider the previous illustration.

$$s_{\overline{5}|0.10} = \frac{(1.10)^5 - 1}{0.10}$$

$$= \frac{1.61051000 - 1}{0.10} \quad \text{(Appendix C)}$$

$$= \frac{.61051000}{0.10}$$

$$= 6.1051000$$

One final step in the generalization remains. Formula 11–2 is the accumulated amount for payments of $1. If the payments are P dollars per year, and if the accumulated amount is denoted by S, then

$$\textbf{(11-3)} \quad S = P \cdot s_{\overline{n}|i}$$

C. Annuity Tables

Annuity computations can be made using a compound interest table such as appendix C. However, the computations are tedious, and for that reason, tables have been prepared for values of $s_{\overline{n}|i}$. Appendix E at the end of the book is such a table. The heading of each page is the value of i; the values of n are in the left-hand column.

EXAMPLE 1   What is the accumulated amount for annual deposits of $1,000 in an account paying 8% compounded annually following the twelfth deposit?

Solution: $S = ?, P = \$1,000, n = 12, i = 0.08$

$S = P \cdot s_{\overline{n}|i}$

$= \$1,000 \cdot s_{\overline{12}|0.08}$

$= \$1,000 \times 18.97712646$ (Appendix E)

$= \$18,977.12646$

$= \$18,977.13$

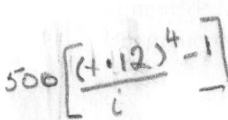

EXERCISES FOR SECTION 11.1

In problems 1–19, use appendix E and the formula $S = P \cdot s_{\overline{n}|i}$ to find the accumulated amount S when P dollars are invested annually n times in an account paying the given interest rate i compounded annually.

1. $P = \$500, n = 4, i = 12\%$ **2.** $P = \$800, n = 6, i = 9\%$ **3.** $P = \$1,200, n = 5, i = 8\%$

4. $P = \$1,200, n = 8, i = 8\frac{1}{2}\%$ **5.** $P = \$600, n = 15, i = 6\%$ **6.** $P = \$1,600, n = 10, i = 10\%$

(look under 9% for 6) 800

$1.12 \; yx^4 - 1 = \div .12 = \times 500$

7. $P = \$750$, $n = 15$, $i = 9\frac{1}{2}\%$ 8. $P = \$400$, $n = 20$, $i = 11\%$ 9. $P = \$900$, $n = 40$, $i = 10\%$

10. $P = \$1,300$, $n = 10$, $i = 7\%$ 11. $P = \$1,850$, $n = 14$, $i = 8\%$ 12. $P = \$1,750$, $n = 22$, $i = 12\%$

13. $P = 1,250$, $n = 25$, $i = 7\%$ 14. $P = \$2,000$, $n = 20$, $i = 8\%$ 15. $P = \$3,600$, $n = 18$, $i = 11\%$

16. $P = \$4,750$, $n = 14$, $i = 9\%$ 17. $P = \$9,500$, $n = 12$, $i = 8\frac{1}{2}\%$ 18. $P = \$6,500$, $n = 25$, $i = 6\frac{1}{2}\%$

19. $P = \$7,000$, $n = 30$, $i = 12\%$ $A = P\left[\dfrac{(1+i)^n - 1}{L}\right] = 1 + i \; yx^n - 1 = \div i = \times P$

Solve.

20. Carl Jennings decides to start a savings plan by placing $1,000 a year in a savings account that pays 10% interest compounded annually. How much will Carl have in his savings account after he makes his twentieth deposit?

21. Myra Miller works in a women's clothing store. She wants to open her own shop, so she decides to put $1,200 a year into a savings account that pays 12% interest compounded annually. How much will she have in her account after she makes her fifth deposit? After she makes her eighth deposit?

22. John Atkins is placing $800 a year in an account that pays 11% interest compounded annually. He intends to use this savings plan to educate his children. How much will John have in the account after he makes his fifteenth deposit?

$1 + \cdot 12 = 4 \times 5 \; \underline{\quad} 1 = \div \; \cdot 12 = \times /1200$

$1 + \cdot 12 = 4x^8 - 1 = \div \; \cdot 12 = \times /1200$

23. Sarah Stephens is putting $1,600 a year into an account that pays $9\frac{1}{2}\%$ interest compounded annually to save money for a new house. How much will she have in the account after she makes her sixth deposit? After she makes her twelfth deposit?

24. Mechanic Jack Ruse places $2,000 a year in an account paying 6% interest compounded annually to save money to purchase his own auto repair shop. How much will Jack have in the account after he makes his seventh deposit? After he makes his tenth deposit?

25. Janet Richards has decided to put $1,500 a year into an account that pays 10% interest compounded annually so that one day she will be able to open her own business. How much will she have in the account after she makes her fourth deposit? After she makes her seventh deposit?

Section 11.2 *Nominal Rate*

The word annuity implies annual payments and a nominal rate, but in practice, the payments and conversion period may be semiannual, quarterly, or monthly.* Analogous to compound interest, formula 11–3 can be used in any annuity calculation as long as the conversion period and the payment period are the same time interval.**

EXAMPLE 1   Payments of $1,000 are made twice a year and are accumulated at 9% compounded semiannually. What is the accumulated amount following the tenth payment?

Solution: $S = ?$, $P = \$1,000$, $n = 10$, $i = \frac{9\%}{2} = 4\frac{1}{2}\% = 0.045$

$S = P \cdot s_{\overline{n}|i}$

$= \$1,000 \cdot s_{\overline{10}|0.045}$

$= \$1,000 \times 12.28820937$ (Appendix E)

$= \$12,288.20937$

$= \$12,288.21$

Nominal rate and conversion period were discussed in section 8.1.
**The conversion period and payment period are not always the same, but such cases are not considered here.*

EXAMPLE 2   To provide for the replacement of machinery, the Krane Company made quarterly deposits of $1,800 in an account that paid 11% interest compounded quarterly. How much was in the fund after the twelfth deposit, and how much interest was earned?

Solution: $S = ?, P = \$1,800, n = 12, i = \frac{11\%}{4} = 2\frac{3}{4}\% = 0.0275$

$$S = P \cdot s_{\overline{n}i}$$
$$= \$1,800 \cdot s_{\overline{12}0.0275}$$
$$= \$1,800 \times 13.99213729 \quad \text{(Appendix E)}$$
$$= \$25,185.85 \; -(1800 \times 12) = Ans$$

The total of the deposits is $12 \times \$1,800 = \$21,600$; thus, the interest earned is $\$25,185.85 - \$21,600.00 = \$3,585.85$. ■

EXAMPLE 3   How many monthly payments of $150 would it take to accumulate $5,000 if the payments were deposited in an account paying 6% compounded monthly?

Solution: $S = \$5,000, P = \$150, n = ?, i = \frac{6\%}{12} = \frac{1}{2}\% = 0.005$

$$S = P \cdot s_{\overline{n}i}$$
$$P \cdot s_{\overline{n}i} = S$$
$$s_{\overline{n}i} = \frac{S}{P} \quad \text{(Dividing both sides by } P)$$
$$s_{\overline{n}i} = \frac{\$5,000}{\$150}$$
$$= 33.33333333$$

Appendix E on the page headed $\frac{1}{2}\%$ shows that the entry nearest to but larger than 33.33333333 is 33.44141666 for $n = 31$. Thus, a minimum of $n = 31$ payments are required. This results in an accumulation of $\$150 \times 33.44141666 = \$5,016.22$. ■

EXERCISES FOR SECTION 11.2

In problems 1–10, find the accumulated amount S at the end of the n equal payments of P dollars each into an account that pays the given nominal interest rate.

1. Semiannual payments of $P = \$200$ each, $n = 10$ payments, 8% interest compounded semiannually

2. Semiannual payments of $P = \$350$ each, $n = 15$ payments, 12% interest compounded semiannually

3. Quarterly payments of $P = \$900$ each, $n = 20$ payments, 7% interest compounded quarterly

4. Quarterly payments of $P = \$750$ each, $n = 24$ payments, 10% interest compounded quarterly

5. Monthly payments of $P = \$50$ each, $n = 50$ payments, 6% interest compounded monthly

6. Quarterly payments of $P = \$80$ each, $n = 25$ payments, 8% interest compounded quarterly

7. Semiannual payments of $P = \$350$ each, $n = 12$ payments, 9% interest compounded semiannually

8. Monthly payments of $P = \$200$ each, $n = 100$ payments, 9% interest compounded monthly

9. Quarterly payments of $P = \$175$ each, $n = 80$ payments, 10% interest compounded quarterly

10. Quarterly payments of $P = \$225$ each, $n = 30$ payments, 11% interest compounded quarterly

$A = P\left[\frac{1-(1+i)^{-n}}{i}\right] = 50\left[\frac{1-(1+\frac{.06}{12})^{-50}}{.005}\right]$

$1 + .005 = Yx^{50} - = - + 1 = \div .005 \times 50 = 2832.26$

Solve.

11. How many quarterly payments of $500 each would it take to accumulate $20,000 if the payments were deposited in an account paying 8% interest compounded quarterly?

12. Find the number of quarterly payments of $250 each that must be paid into an account earning 6% interest compounded quarterly for there to be $8,000 in the account.

13. If monthly deposits of $1,000 were put into an account paying 6% compounded monthly, how long would it take to become a millionaire?

14. How many monthly payments of $9,000 would it take to accumulate $400,000 if the payments were deposited in an account paying 9% compounded monthly? How much would actually accumulate?

15. John Peterson has decided to place $200 each month in a credit union savings account that pays 4% compounded monthly so that he can purchase a new car that costs $10,500. How long will it take for the accumulated amount in the account to reach $10,500? How much interest will be earned by the time the account accumulates to $10,500?

16. To offset future expansion expenses, Martin Industries made semiannual deposits of $1,500 each into an account that paid 8% interest compounded

semiannually. How much was in the account after the fifteenth deposit? How much interest was earned?

17. Taylor's Transit Company is making quarterly payments of $1,750 into an account that pays 6% interest compounded quarterly to accumulate $20,000 for the purchase of new equipment. How long will it take for the account to accumulate to $20,000? How much interest will be earned by that time?

18. To provide for future remodeling expenses, the owner of a restaurant made semiannual payments of $500 into an account that paid 11% interest compounded semiannually. How much was in the account after the tenth deposit? How much interest was earned?

19. The Phillips Produce Company is making monthly payments of $600 into an account that pays 9% interest compounded monthly to provide funds for business expansion. How much will be in the account after the twentieth deposit? How much interest will be earned at that time?

20. To provide funds for new research equipment, Conco Labs made semiannual payments of $2,000 each into an account that paid 12% interest compounded semiannually. How long did it take for the account to accumulate to $30,000? How much interest was earned at that time? How much was in the account after the twentieth deposit?

Section 11.3 *Present Value of an Ordinary Annuity*

The present value of an annuity is that current amount that, if invested at a given rate, will result in a specified series of future payments. To understand the formulas for the present value of an ordinary annuity, consider the special case of how much must be deposited now in a bank paying 9% compounded annually to provide for five annual withdrawals of $1, the first withdrawal to be made in one year. See figure 11.1.

The amount to be deposited is the sum of the present values of the separate withdrawals. That is (using appendix D),

First withdrawal	$1 (1.09)^{-1}$ =	$0.91743119
Second withdrawal	$1 (1.09)^{-2}$ =	0.84167999
Third withdrawal	$1 (1.09)^{-3}$ =	0.77218348
Fourth withdrawal	$1 (1.09)^{-4}$ =	0.70842521
Fifth withdrawal	$1 (1.09)^{-5}$ =	0.64993139
Amount deposited now		= $3.88965126

Thus, a deposit of slightly less than $3.89 in an account paying 9% compounded annually would provide a fund that would permit $1 to be withdrawn annually for five years. To withdraw $100 a year for five years, the deposit would have to be $100 × 3.88965126 = $388.965126, and to withdraw $1,000 a year for five years, a deposit of $1,000 × 3.88965126 = $3,889.65126 would be required.

There is a similarity between the preceding discussion and that for the accumulated amount of an ordinary annuity. This similarity extends to the development of a formula for the present value of an annuity. The formula is

(11–4) $A = P \cdot a_{\overline{n}|i}$

where

A = present value of an ordinary annuity
P = amount of each future payment,
$a_{\overline{n}|i}$ = present value of a deposit of $1 at interest rate per period i for n conversion periods.

The values of $a_{\overline{n}|i}$ can be found in appendix F. The values in this table are multiplied by P to obtain A.

EXAMPLE 1

Carl Jefferson sold his business and retired on his sixtieth birthday. He used a part of the money from the sale to purchase an annuity that would pay him $4,500 a quarter until he began to receive Social Security at age 65. If money is worth 10% compounded quarterly, how much did the annuity cost?

5 yrs $\frac{10}{4}$

Solution: $A = ?, P = \$4,500, n = 20, i = \frac{10\%}{4} = 2\frac{1}{2}\% = 0.025$

$A = P \cdot a_{\overline{n}|i}$
   $= \$4,500 \cdot a_{\overline{20}|0.025}$
   $= \$4,500 \times 15.58916229$ (Appendix F)
   $= \$70,151.23$

Carl received 20 × $4,500 = $90,000 in payments; thus, $90,000 − $70,151.23 = $19,848.77 was earned in interest.   ■

EXAMPLE 2

For her corner lot, Con Oil offered Margaret Prescott $40,000 and semiannual payments of $5,000 for the next five years. If money is worth 12% compounded semiannually, what is the equivalent cash price of the lot?

Solution: $A = ?, P = \$5,000, n = 10, i = \frac{12\%}{2} = 6\% = 0.06$

$A = P \cdot a_{\overline{n}|i}$
   $= \$5,000 \cdot a_{\overline{10}|0.06}$
   $= \$5,000 \times 7.36008705$ (Appendix F)
   $= \$36,800.44$

Thus, the cash price of the lot is $40,000 + $36,800.44 = $76,800.44.   ■

EXAMPLE 3   If $75,000 is used to purchase an annuity that pays $950 a month, and if the interest rate is 9% compounded monthly, approximately how many payments are possible?

Solution: $A = \$75,000, P = \$950, n = ?, i = \frac{9\%}{12} = \frac{3}{4}\% = 0.0075$

$$A = P \cdot a_{\overline{n}|i}$$

$$P \cdot a_{\overline{n}|i} = A$$

$$a_{\overline{n}|i} = \frac{A}{P} \quad \text{(Dividing both sides by } P)$$

$$a_{\overline{n}|0.0075} = \frac{\$75,000}{\$950}$$

$$\checkmark = 78.94736842$$

Appendix F on the page headed $\frac{3}{4}\%$ shows that the value for $a_{\overline{120}|0.0075}$ is 78.94169267. This is the largest entry in the table that is still less than 78.94736842. Thus, $n = 120$ payments are possible. ⌐

EXERCISES FOR SECTION 11.3

In problems 1–10, find the present value of an annuity that will provide the given payments for the given length of time when money is worth the given nominal compound interest rate.

1. $2,000 per year for 10 years, 7% interest compounded annually

2. $3,500 per year for eight years, 11% interest compounded annually

3. $800 per quarter for four years, 7% interest compounded quarterly

4. $1,200 per quarter for two years, 12% interest compounded quarterly

5. $400 semiannually for six years, 8% interest compounded semiannually

6. $750 semiannually for 12 years, 10% interest compounded semiannually

7. $1,500 per month for four years, 9% interest compounded monthly

8. $1,750 per month for $3\frac{1}{2}$ years, 6% interest compounded monthly

9. $3,000 per quarter for six years, 11% interest compounded quarterly

10. $4,750 per quarter for five years, 10% interest compounded quarterly

Solve.

11. If $15,000 is used to purchase an annuity that pays $400 a month, and if the interest rate is 6% compounded monthly, how many full payments will be received from the annuity?

12. How many full payments will be received from an annuity that costs $10,000 if the payments are $750 semiannually and money is worth 7% compounded semiannually?

13. Bob Brewster sold some real estate for $15,000 down and quarterly payments of $500 for 10 years. If money is worth 8% compounded quarterly, what is the equivalent cash price of the real estate?

14. Sue Johnson purchased an annuity that would pay her son $400 per month while he was getting his education. How much did the annuity cost if the payments were to continue for four years and money was worth 6% compounded monthly?

(handwritten) eg 3

(handwritten) eg # 2

(handwritten) $800\left[\dfrac{1-(1+0.175)^{-16}}{.0175}\right]$

(handwritten) $= 1 + .0175 = y^{x^{16}} \div = \div + 1 = \div .0175 = x\ 800 = 11080.4$

15. Jesse Phillips won $20,000 in a sweepstakes and purchased an annuity with the money that would pay him $750 quarterly. If money was worth 10% compounded quarterly at the time he purchased the annuity, how many full payments will he receive?

16. Sarah Steadman sold her retail clothing store for $20,000 in cash and monthly payments of $500 for four years. If money was worth 12% compounded monthly, what was the equivalent cash selling price of the store?

17. Carol Jackson purchased an annuity that would pay her daughter $150 a month for 40 months. How much did the annuity cost if money was worth 9% compounded monthly?

18. Ron Jacobson sold one of the branch stores of his business for $65,000 and used the money to purchase an annuity that would pay him $5,000 semiannually. If money was worth 12% compounded semiannually at the time he purchased the annuity, how many full payments will he receive?

Section 11.4   *Annuities Due*

The second type of annuity certain is the annuity due. In an annuity due, payments are made at the beginning of the period. Insurance premiums and rent payments are common examples of annuities due.

The accumulated amount and the present value of an annuity due have the same meanings as for an ordinary annuity. Thus, formulas for annuities due can be derived from the formulas and tables of the ordinary annuity.

To determine a formula for the accumulated amount of an annuity due, consider figure 11.1 on page 282 and our first illustration of a $1 annual payment for five years. Note that the annuity due has five interest-earning periods, one more than for the ordinary annuity. This is true in general; that is, if an ordinary annuity has n interest-earning periods, then for the same term an annuity due has $n + 1$ interest-earning periods. Also, the formulas for $s_{\overline{n}|i}$ include the last payment of an ordinary annuity that earns no interest (this is the first term in formula 11–1). The annuity due has no such payment; thus it must be deducted from $s_{\overline{n}|i}$.

Combining this information, the accumulated amount of an annuity due is

(11–5) $\overline{S} = P \cdot (s_{\overline{n+1}|i} - 1)$

where

$\overline{S}$ = accumulated amount of annuity due*
P = payment or deposit
n = number of payments or deposits
i = rate per period.

*It is customary to designate the accumulated amount and the present value of an annuity due by boldface letters **S** and **A**. For ease of writing, the notations $\overline{S}$ and $\overline{A}$ are used in this text.

E X A M P L E 1   For 10 years, an annual deposit of $4,000 was made on April 1 in an account paying 7% compounded annually. Find the accumulated amount on April 1 of the eleventh year.

Solution: $\overline{S} = ?, P = \$4,000, n = 10, i = 7\% = 0.07$

$\overline{S} = P \cdot (s_{\overline{n+1}|i} - 1)$

$= \$4,000(s_{\overline{11}|0.07} - 1)$

$= \$4,000(15.78359932 - 1)$ (Appendix E)

$= \$4,000(14.78359932)$

$= \$59,134.40$

E X A M P L E 2   How long will it take to accumulate $25,000 if $1,620 is deposited at the beginning of each month in an account that pays interest at 6% compounded monthly?

Solution:

$\overline{S} = \$25,000, P = \$1,620, n = ?, i = \frac{6\%}{12} = \frac{1}{2}\% = 0.005$

$\overline{S} = P \cdot (s_{\overline{n+1}|i} - 1)$

$P \cdot (s_{\overline{n+1}|i} - 1) = \overline{S}$

$s_{\overline{n+1}|i} - 1 = \dfrac{\overline{S}}{P}$ (Dividing both sides by P)

$s_{\overline{n+1}|i} = \dfrac{\overline{S}}{P} + 1$ (Adding 1 to both sides)

$s_{\overline{n+1}|0.005} = \dfrac{\$25,000}{\$1,620} + 1$

$s_{\overline{n+1}|0.005} = 16.43209877$

Appendix E on the page headed $\frac{1}{2}\%$ shows that the smallest entry greater than 16.43209877 is $s_{\overline{16}|0.005} = 16.61423026$. Since $n + 1 = 16, n = 15$. Thus, 15 months will be required.

E X A M P L E 3   For 20 semiannual deposits of $1,800 invested at 7% compounded semiannually, find the accumulated amount of **a.** an ordinary annuity and **b.** an annuity due.

Solution: **a.** $S = ?, P = \$1,800, n = 20, i = \frac{7\%}{2} = 3.5\% = 0.035$

$S = P \cdot s_{\overline{n}|i}$

$= \$1,800 \cdot s_{\overline{20}|0.035}$

$= \$1,800 \times 28.27968181$ (Appendix E)

$= \$50,903.43$

b. $\overline{S} = ?, P = \$1,800, n = 20, i = \frac{7\%}{2} = 3.5\% = 0.035$

$\overline{S} = P \cdot (s_{\overline{n+1}|i} - 1)$

$= \$1,800(s_{\overline{21}|0.035} - 1)$

$= \$1,800(30.26947068 - 1)$ (Appendix E)

$= \$1,800(29.26947068)$

$= \$52,685.05$

Note that the accumulated amount for the annuity due is greater than that for the ordinary annuity.

EXERCISES FOR SECTION 11.4

$-S = P(s \overline{n+1}|i - 1)$

In problems 1–10, find the accumulated amount of the given annuity due when n payments of P dollars each are deposited in an account that pays the given nominal interest rate.

$= 1600(s \overline{21}|0.0275 - 1)$

1. $1,000 per year for five years, 12% interest compounded annually $1000 \times (n+1)i - 1$
$= 1000 \times 60.12 - 1 = 1000 \times (8.115189 - 1)$

6. $150 per month for one year, 12% interest compounded monthly

$1600(27.9178593)$

2. $1,500 per year for 15 years, 7% interest compounded annually
$15000(16.07 - 1)$

7. $450 per quarter for four years, 6% interest compounded quarterly $= 1600 (26.9178593)$

3. $700 semiannually for five years, 8% interest compounded semiannually

8. $1,600 per quarter for five years, 11% interest compounded quarterly $= 4306852$

4. $400 semiannually for 12 years, 10% interest compounded semiannually

9. $400 per month for four years, 9% interest compounded monthly

5. $200 per month for three years, 6% interest compounded monthly

10. $775 per quarter for five years, 10% interest compounded quarterly

Solve. $350[a$

as in #11

11. A deposit of $350 is made each month for 24 months into an account that pays 4% interest compounded monthly. Find the accumulated amount in the account at the beginning of the twenty-fifth month.

A. D

17. To provide funds for an expected increase in operating expenses at her restaurant, Myra Cole decides to deposit $200 each month into an account that pays 9% interest compounded monthly. How much will she have in the account 24 months from now if she makes the first deposit immediately?

12. For five years, a deposit of $550 is made at the beginning of each quarter into an account that pays 7% interest compounded quarterly. What is the accumulated amount in the account at the beginning of the first quarter of the sixth year?

18. Bob Schwartz decides to begin a savings plan by depositing $125 each quarter into an account that pays 7% interest compounded quarterly. If he makes his first deposit now, how much will be in the account three years from now?

000
700 +1

13. How long will it take to accumulate $10,000 if $700 is deposited at the beginning of each year into an account that pays interest at 10% compounded annually?

19. At the beginning of the year, Donna Deer took $2,000 from her savings and placed it in an Individual Retirement Account (IRA) that pays 9.5% compounded annually. If Donna continues this practice for the next 35 years, how much will she have in her IRA account? # 11

14. If $500 is paid quarterly into an account that pays 12% interest compounded quarterly, how many years will it take to accumulate $15,000 in the account?

15. For 10 quarterly deposits of $600 each invested at 8% compounded quarterly, find the accumulated amount of **a.** an ordinary annuity and **b.** an annuity due.

20. Each month, Jack and Kay put $187.50 in an IRA account that pays 12% compounded monthly. If they continue to make these deposits until Jack retires in 9 years and 11 months, how much will they have in their IRA account?

16. For 20 monthly deposits of $75 each invested at 6% compounded monthly, find the accumulated amount of **a.** an ordinary annuity and **b.** an annuity due.

$(a) \ 600 \cdot \frac{10\frac{2\%}{8}}{4} = 600 \times 10.94972100$
$NB = 6569.83$

$s \overline{n+1}|i = \frac{S}{P} + 1$

$s \overline{n+1}|0.10 = \frac{10,000}{700} + 1 = 15.28571429$

$b \ 600 \times \overline{11}|.02 - 1 = 600 \times (9.78684805 - 1$
$NB = 600 18.7867$

if $n+1 = 10$ $n = 9$ Ans 9 yrs

Section 11.5   *Present Value of an Annuity Due*

To determine a formula for the present value of an annuity due, again consider figure 11.1 on page 284. With an annuity due, the present value of the first payment of $1 is $1 since there is no interest-earning period. As a result, there are only four periods for calculation of present value, one less than the ordinary annuity. This is true in general; if an ordinary annuity has n periods, the annuity due has $n - 1$ periods when calculating present value. The initial payment is then added to this calculation. Combining this information, the present value of an annuity due is

$$(11-6) \quad \overline{A} = P(a_{\overline{n-1}|i} + 1)$$

where

$\overline{A}$ = Present value of an annuity due
P = Amount of each future payment
n = Number of payments
i = Rate per period.

EXAMPLE 1   Find the present value of an annuity due with semiannual payments of $3,000 for a term of 10 years if interest is compounded at 7% semiannually.

Solution: $\overline{A} = ?, P = \$3,000, n = 20, i = \frac{7\%}{2} = 3\frac{1}{2}\% = 0.035$

$\overline{A} = P(a_{\overline{n-1}|i} + 1)$

$\quad = \$3,000(a_{\overline{19}|0.035} + 1)$

$\quad = \$3,000(13.70983742 + 1) \quad$ (Appendix F)

$\quad = \$3,000(14.70983742)$

$\quad = \$44,129.51$

EXAMPLE 2   A company retirement fund pays Bob Simmons $980 at the beginning of each month. If money is worth 9% compounded monthly, what is the present value of the pension for **a.** one year and **b.** four years?

Solution: **a.** $\overline{A} = ?, P = \$980, n = 12, i = \frac{9\%}{12} = \frac{3}{4}\% = 0.0075$

$\overline{A} = P(a_{\overline{n-1}|i} + 1)$

$\quad = \$980(a_{\overline{11}|0.0075} + 1)$

$\quad = \$980(10.52067452 + 1) \quad$ (Appendix F)

$\quad = \$980(11.52067452)$

$\quad = \$11,290.26$

b. $\overline{A} = ?, P = \$980, n = 48, i = \frac{9\%}{12} = \frac{3}{4}\% = 0.0075$

$\overline{A} = P(a_{\overline{n-1}|i} + 1)$

$\quad = \$980(a_{\overline{47}|0.0075} + 1)$

$\quad = \$980(39.48616775 + 1) \quad$ (Appendix F)

$\quad = \$980(40.48616775)$

$\quad = \$39,676.44$

EXAMPLE 3   What is the present value of **a.** an ordinary annuity and **b.** an annuity due if $P = \$750$ per month, the term is 30 months, and interest is compounded at 12% monthly?

Solution: **a.** $A = ?, P = \$750, n = 30, i = \frac{12\%}{12} = 1\% = 0.01$

$$A = P \cdot a_{\overline{n}|i}$$
$$= \$750 \cdot a_{\overline{300}|0.01}$$
$$= \$750 \times 25.80770822 \qquad \text{(Appendix F)}$$
$$= \$19,355.78$$

b. $\overline{A} = ?, P = \$750, n = 30, i = \frac{12\%}{12} = 1\% = 0.01$

$$\overline{A} = P(a_{\overline{n-1}|i} + 1)$$
$$= \$750(a_{\overline{29}|0.01} + 1)$$
$$= \$750(25.06578530 + 1) \qquad \text{(Appendix F)}$$
$$= \$750(26.06578530)$$
$$= \$19,549.34$$

Note that the present value of the annuity due is greater than that of the ordinary annuity.

$P=800 \quad n= 5 \quad i=.12 \qquad 800\left(\overset{4}{a_{\overline{7}|}}\cdot 12 + 1\right) = 800(\$.03734935$

EXERCISES FOR SECTION 11.5

In problems 1–10, find the present value for each annuity due using the information provided.

1. $800 per year for five years, 12% interest compounded annually

2. $1,400 per year for 10 years, $9\frac{1}{2}$% interest compounded annually

3. $700 per quarter for four years, 8% interest compounded quarterly

4. $400 per quarter for five years, 6% interest compounded quarterly

5. $1,200 semiannually for five years, 8% interest compounded semiannually

$P = 4200 \quad n= 20 \quad i=.055 / 5\cdot 5\%$

Solve, **(a)** $4200 \quad a_{\overline{20}|}\cdot055 = 4200(14.95038248)$
$= 50,191\cdot61$

6. $2,000 semiannually for eight years, 7% interest compounded semiannually
$\Rightarrow A=?, etc$
$A = P(a_{\overline{n-1}|}i+1)$

7. $200 per month for 48 months, 6% interest compounded monthly $= 350(a_{\overline{47}|0.01} +1)$

8. $350 per month for 20 months, 12% interest compounded monthly
$= 350(17.226008501)$
$350(18.226008601)$

9. $1,250 per quarter for nine years, 10% interest compounded quarterly $= 6379.10$

10. $3,400 semiannually for eight years, 9% interest compounded semiannually

$6 \quad 980(a_{\overline{20-1}|}\cdot055 +1$
$= 980(a_{\overline{19}|}\cdot055 = 12.60765352$
$= 52952.14$

11. Find the present value of **a.** an ordinary annuity and **b.** an annuity due if $P = \$4,200$ semiannually, the term is 10 years, and interest is compounded at 11% semiannually.

12. What is the present value of **a.** an ordinary annuity and **b.** an annuity due if $P = \$250$ monthly, the term is three years, and interest is compounded at 9% monthly?

13. As payment to satisfy an old debt, John Baker agrees to pay his neighbor $500 quarterly for two years, with the first payment to be made immediately. If money is worth 11% compounded quarterly, what is the equivalent cash value of John's debt to his neighbor?

$P = 500 \quad n = 8 \quad i = \frac{11}{4}$

annuity due
immediately

14. Some teenagers vandalized Lisa Carter's clothing store, and their parents agreed to pay Lisa $50 per month for two years to cover damages, with the first payment to be made immediately. What is the equivalent cash amount of damage done to the store if money is worth 12% compounded monthly?

15. When Ella Richards graduated from college, her father gave her $50 and promised to pay her $50 each month for the next 12 months. If money is worth 9% compounded monthly, what is the equivalent cash value of Ella's gift? (Hint: $n = 13$.)

16. To satisfy a debt to one of its creditors, a company agrees to pay $3,000 semiannually for six years, with the first payment to be made immediately. If money is worth 7% compounded semiannually, what is the amount of the debt?

17. Atlas Plumbing Supply agreed to pay John Simmons $2,500 quarterly for five years as compensation for injuries John received on the job. If the first payment was made immediately and if money was worth 12% compounded quarterly, what was the equivalent cash value of the settlement?

18. Bob Jacobs, a truck driver, lost control of his truck and knocked down a wall of a restaurant while making a delivery. To pay for the damages, Bob paid the owner of the restaurant $100 a month for two years, with the first payment made immediately. If money was worth 6% compounded monthly, what was the equivalent cash value of the damage?

Glossary

Annuity   Any series of payments at regular intervals of time. The payments are usually equal but need not be so.

Annuity certain   An annuity for which the beginning and ending dates are specified.

Annuity due   An annuity for which payments are made at the beginning of each period; for example, apartment rent or insurance premiums.

Contingent annuity   An annuity for which either the beginning or ending date is not specified.

Conversion period   The intervals of time when interest is computed and added to the accumulated amount of an annuity.

Nominal rate   The rate per annum; the quoted compound interest rate of an annuity.

Ordinary annuity   An annuity for which payments are made at the end of each period; for example, salaries or interest payments.

Period of an annuity   The time interval between the payments of an annuity.

Present value of an annuity   The current amount of money that, if invested at a given rate, will result in a specified series of future payments.

Term of an annuity   The time from the beginning of the first period to the end of the last period of an annuity.

Review Test

Use appendices E and F to solve the following problems.

1. What is the accumulated amount of quarterly payments of $400 invested in an ordinary annuity at 11% compounded quarterly following the twelfth payment?

2. James Richards sold some real estate for $25,000 down and semiannual payments of $2,000 for the next 10 years, with the first payment due in six months. If money is worth 9% compounded semiannually, what is the equivalent cash price of the real estate?

3. Which generates the larger accumulated amount: an ordinary annuity of $200 per quarter for two years at 10% compounded quarterly or an annuity due of $65 per month for two years at 12% compounded monthly?

4. How long will it take to accumulate $20,000 if $350 is deposited at the beginning of each month in an account that pays interest at 9% compounded monthly?

5. Find the present value of an annuity due with semiannual payments of $1,500 for a term of six years if money is worth 7% compounded semiannually.

6. Jim Justin purchased 50 shares of stock for his infant daughter and placed the dividends (paid at the end of each quarter) in a savings account paying 9% compounded quarterly. During the first two years, the quarterly dividends were $2.60 per share. Find the amount in the savings account after two years.

7. Sandra Locke used an inheritance of $40,000 to purchase an ordinary annuity that paid $2,500 a quarter. If money was worth 11% compounded quarterly, how many full payments did she receive?

8. Lou Martin is paid on the fifteenth of each month. For 18 months, he placed 15% of his monthly pay of $1,200 in an account paying 9% compounded monthly. How much was in the account on the fifteenth day of the nineteenth month?

9. A business property was purchased for $150,000 down and monthly payments of $10,000 for four years. Find the equivalent cash price if money was worth 9% compounded monthly.

10. Find the difference between the present values of an ordinary annuity and an annuity due if the semiannual payment is $800, the term is 14 years, and money is worth 7% compounded semiannually.

chapter

12

Sinking Funds and Amortization

 *Section 12.1* *Sinking Funds*

A. Introduction
An annuity established to meet a future obligation is called a **sinking fund.** Businesses establish sinking funds to redeem bonds, to replace worn-out equipment, to expand facilities, or to meet a future debt or anticipated expense. In general, sinking funds retire only the principal of a debt.

If both the principal and accrued interest are gradually retired by partial payments, the process is called **amortization.**

This chapter examines the fundamentals of sinking funds and amortization. While the methods developed are applicable to both kinds of annuities certain, discussion is limited to the ordinary annuity.

B. A Formula for Sinking Funds

In a sinking fund, the amount of the obligation, the term, and the current interest rate are known; the unknown is the periodic payment P (called the rent in a sinking fund). This means solving the annuity formula for P. The result is

$$(12\text{–}1) \quad P = S \times \frac{1}{s_{\overline{n}|i}}$$

Appendix G shows the values for $\dfrac{1}{s_{\overline{n}|i}}$.

E X A M P L E 1

The Scorpio Corporation estimates that its plant machinery will be obsolete in another three years. The replacement cost is $240,000, and the current interest rate is 8% compounded quarterly. To be able to purchase the machinery in three years, how much should the company pay into a sinking fund at the end of each quarter?

Solution: $S = \$240,000, P = ?, n = 12, i = \frac{8\%}{4} = 2\% = 0.02$

$$P = S \times \frac{1}{s_{\overline{n}|i}}$$

$$= \$240,000 \times \frac{1}{s_{\overline{12}|0.02}}$$

$$= \$240,000 \times 0.07455960 \qquad \text{(Appendix G)}$$

$$= \$17,894.304$$

$$= \$17,894.30 \qquad\qquad\qquad\qquad\qquad\qquad\qquad ∎$$

E X A M P L E 2

Grey Enterprises plans to remodel its fleet of trucks in three years at an estimated cost of $140,000. The company established a sinking fund in an account that earned interest at 9% compounded semiannually. What was the amount of the payment at the end of each six months?

Solution: $S = \$140,000, P = ?, n = 6, i = \frac{9\%}{2} = 4\frac{1}{2}\% = 0.045$

$$P = S \times \frac{1}{s_{\overline{n}|i}}$$

$$= \$140,000 \times \frac{1}{s_{\overline{6}|0.045}}$$

$$= \$140,000 \times 0.14887839 \qquad \text{(Appendix G)}$$

$$= \$20,842.97 \qquad\qquad\qquad\qquad\qquad\qquad\qquad ∎$$

E X A M P L E 3

The Davidson Corporation borrowed $200,000 by issuing bonds redeemable in 10 years. To be able to redeem the bonds at maturity, the company established a sinking fund into which payments were made at the end of each quarter. If the interest rate was 10% compounded quarterly, **a.** what was the amount of each payment, and **b.** how much total interest was earned?

Solution: **a.** $S = \$200,000, P = ?, n = 40, i = \frac{10\%}{4} = 2\frac{1}{2}\% = 0.025$

$$P = S \times \frac{1}{s_{\overline{n}|i}}$$

$$= \$200,000 \times \frac{1}{s_{\overline{40}|0.025}}$$

$$= \$200,000 \times 0.01483623 \qquad \text{(Appendix G)}$$

$$= \$2,967.25$$

b.
$$
\begin{array}{rl}
\$200,000 & \text{Accumulated amount} \\
-\ \underline{118,690} & \text{Total payments } (\$2,967.25 \times 40) \\
\$\ 81,310 & \text{Earned interest}
\end{array}
$$

■

Frequently, it is convenient to have a schedule showing the operation of the sinking fund.

EXAMPLE 4   To be able to remodel their display rooms 18 months from now, the Regency Company established a sinking fund by making quarterly payments into an account paying 7% compounded quarterly. Prepare a schedule for a remodeling cost of $28,000.

Solution: $S = \$28,000, P = ?, n = 6, i = \frac{7\%}{4} = 1\frac{3}{4}\% = 0.0175$

$$P = S \times \frac{1}{s_{\overline{n}|i}}$$

$$= \$28,000 \times \frac{1}{s_{\overline{6}|0.0175}}$$

$$= \$28,000 \times 0.15952256 \qquad \text{(Appendix G)}$$

$$= \$4,466.63$$

Period	Accumulated Amt. Beginning of Period (1)	Earned Interest (2)	Periodic Payment (3)	Accumulated Amt. End of Period (1) + (2) + (3)
1	0	0	$4,466.63	$ 4,466.63
2	$ 4,466.63	$ 78.17	4,466.63	9,011.43
3	9,011.43	157.70	4,466.63	13,635.76
4	13,635.76	238.63	4,466.63	18,341.02
5	18,341.02	320.97	4,466.63	23,128.62
6	23,128.62	404.75	4,466.63	28,000.00

Since each line in the schedule is a separate interest problem, the interest can be calculated using the simple interest formula. For instance, the earned interest in period 2 is $4,466.63 \times 0.0175 = \$78.17$.

■

See back of book

EXERCISES FOR SECTION 12.1

In problems 1–6, find the amount of the periodic payment P for the given sinking fund.

1. $S = \$70,000$, quarterly payments for five years, 8% interest compounded quarterly

2. $S = \$40,000$, semiannual payments for 10 years, 10% interest compounded semiannually

3. $S = \$90,000$, quarterly payments for six years, 9% interest compounded quarterly

4. $S = \$27,000$, semiannual payments for eight years, 7% interest compounded semiannually

5. $S = \$16,000$, monthly payments for three years, 9% interest compounded monthly

6. $S = \$35,000$, semiannual payments for six years, 11% interest compounded semiannually

In problems 7–12, find the amount of the periodic payment P for the given sinking fund, set up a schedule showing the operation of the fund, and compute the total interest earned by the fund.

7. $S = \$22,000$, quarterly payments for two years, 8% interest compounded quarterly

8. $S = \$31,000$, semiannual payments for three years, 6% interest compounded semiannually

9. $S = \$8,000$, monthly payments for six months, 6% interest compounded monthly

10. $S = \$40,000$, semiannual payments for four years, 8% interest compounded semiannually

11. $S = \$36,000$, quarterly payments for 15 months, 10% interest compounded quarterly

12. $S = \$42,000$, semiannual payments for three years, 8% interest compounded semiannually

In problems 13–16, fill in the missing entries in the sinking fund schedules.

13.

	Beginning of Period	**End of Period**		
Period	Accumulated Amount (1)	Earned Interest (2)	Periodic Payment (3)	Accumulated Amount (1) + (2) + (3)
1	$ 0.00	$ 00.00	$2,073.72	$2,073.72
2	2,073.72	207.37	2073.72	4354.81
3	4354.81	435.48 +	2073.72	6864.06 @ 10%
4				
5				
6				

① $70000\,(207.02) = \$2880.97$

#8

$31,000 \quad 3 \text{ yrs} \quad 2\frac{1}{2} \quad 6\% = 31000 = \dfrac{1}{67.03}) = 0.15459750(31000 = 4792.52$

			4792.52	4792.52
1	4792.52	143.77	4792.52	9728.82
2	4727.72	291.86		14,818.20
3	14802.52	444.40		20,050.52
4	20,050.52	601.40		25,444.14
	25444.14	703.32		30,999.98
		2244.86		

14.

	Beginning of Period	End of Period		
Period	Accumulated Amount (1)	Earned Interest (2)	Periodic Payment (3)	Accumulated Amount (1) + (2) + (3)
1	$ 0.00	$00.00		
2	1,332.62	59.97		
3				
4				
5				
6				
7				
8				

15.

	Beginning of Period	End of Period		
Period	Accumulated Amount (1)	Earned Interest (2)	Periodic Payment (3)	Accumulated Amount (1) + (2) + (3)
1	$ 0.00	$ 00.00		
2	6,694.41	167.36		
3				
4				
5				
6				
7				
8				
9				
10				

16.

	Beginning of Period	End of Period		
Period	Accumulated Amount (1)	Earned Interest (2)	Periodic Payment (3)	Accumulated Amount (1) + (2) + (3)
1	$ 0.00	$00.00		
2	647.61	4.86		
3				
4				
5				
6				
7				
8				
9				
10				
11				
12				

Solve.

17. The Hudson Manufacturing Company plans to replace some of its machinery in two years at an estimated cost of $220,000. The company established a sinking fund in an account that earns interest at 10% compounded quarterly. Find the amount of each quarterly payment.

18. Scott Processors issued bonds totaling $725,000 to raise capital for plant modifications. The bonds were redeemable in six years, and the company established a sinking fund, into which payments were made quarterly, to redeem the bonds. If the interest rate was 11% compounded quarterly, find: **a.** the amount of each payment and **b.** the total interest earned.

19. The owner of an appliance store established a sinking fund so that she could remodel her display room in two years. If the account earned interest at 9% compounded monthly, and if the remodeling cost was $9,000, find the amount of the monthly payments into the account.

20. The Harris Company plans to open a branch office in three years at an estimated cost of $430,000. To provide the funds, the company established a sinking fund in an account that pays 9% interest compounded semiannually. Find the amount of the semiannual payments into the fund. Prepare a schedule showing the operation of the fund.

Section 12.2   *Amortization*

A. Introduction

In example 3 of section 12.1, a sinking fund was established to redeem bonds that had been issued. But investors buy bonds because bonds are interest bearing; that is, not only does the bondholder receive at maturity the original cost of the bond (principal), but also periodic interest payments while the bond is in force. In example 3, a sinking fund was created to pay off the principal; the interest on the bonds would have to be paid from some other source. Had both the principal and accrued interest been retired by the partial payments, the debt would have been *amortized*. Other examples of amortization occurred in section 10.3 on installment plans; although the interest calculation is different, the partial payments paid off the entire debt, both principal and finance charge.

B. The Amortization Formula

Consider a debt A drawing interest at rate i per period. To pay off the entire debt in n periodic payments of amount P, the present value of these future payments must equal A. That is,

$$P \times a_{\overline{n}i} = A$$

Solving this formula for P yields

(12–2) $P = A \times \dfrac{1}{a_{\overline{n}i}}$

Each payment using formula 12–2 is distributed between principal and interest according to the United States Rule. Values for $\dfrac{1}{a_{\overline{n}i}}$ are found in appendix H.

EXAMPLE 1   The Growth Corporation acquired a piece of property for $750,000 by paying $150,000 down and signing a mortgage for 48 quarterly payments (payments to be made at the end of each quarter). What was the amount of each payment if the nominal rate was 9%?

Solution: $A = \$750,000 - \$150,000 = \$600,000$, $P = ?$, $n = 48$, $i = 2\frac{1}{4}\% = 0.0225$

$$P = A \times \frac{1}{a_{\overline{n}|i}}$$

$$= \$600,000 \times \frac{1}{a_{\overline{48}|0.0225}} \quad \text{(Appendix H)}$$

$$\$600,000 \times 0.03428233$$

$$= \$20,569.40$$

■

EXAMPLE 2   A debt of $4,400 bears interest at 8% compounded semiannually. What semiannual payment is required to amortize the debt in $2\frac{1}{2}$ years if the payments are made at the end of each six months?

Solution: $A = \$4,400$, $P = ?$, $n = 5$, $i = 4\% = 0.04$

$$P = A \times \frac{1}{a_{\overline{n}|i}}$$

$$= \$4,400 \times \frac{1}{a_{\overline{5}|0.04}}$$

$$= \$4,400 \times 0.22462711 \quad \text{(Appendix H)}$$

$$= \$988.36$$

■

EXAMPLE 3   Construct a schedule showing the distribution of payments in example 2 of this section.

Solution: A schedule showing the distribution of payments is called an *amortization schedule*. To determine the interest in column 3 of the schedule, recall that compound interest is a series of simple interest calculations, with the simple interest formula applied to the entry in column 1. For instance, the first entry in column three is $\$4,400 \times 0.04 = \$176.00$.

	Beginning of Period	End of Period			
Period	Amount of Debt (1)	Payment (2)	Interest (3)	Applied to Principal (4) = (2) − (3)	Remaining Debt (5) = (1) − (4)
1	$4,400.00	$988.36	$176.00	$812.36	$3,587.64
2	3,587.64	988.36	143.51	844.85	2,742.79
3	2,742.79	988.36	109.71	878.65	1,864.14
4	1,864.14	988.36	74.57	913.79	950.35
5	950.35	988.36	38.01	930.35	0.00

■

C. Real Estate Loans

Perhaps the most common example of amortization is mortgage payments on a real estate loan. Two popular forms of real estate loans are **a.** the fixed rate mortgage and **b.** the adjustable rate mortgage.

a. The Fixed Rate Mortgage

The fixed rate mortgage is the traditional mortgage. In a typical fixed rate mortgage, the borrower borrows a fixed amount of money at a fixed interest rate for a fixed period of time. The loan is repaid in equal payments for the term of the loan. The real estate loan in example 1 is an example of a fixed rate mortgage. For the typical mortgage on a home, the term of the loan is 30 years and the payments are monthly. A portion of each payment is applied to accrued interest, with the remainder applied to the outstanding principal, in accordance with the United States Rule.

EXAMPLE 4   Joan and Jerry Hemlepp signed a mortgage in the amount of $100,000 at an interest rate of 9% compounded monthly and a term of 30 years. Find: **a.** the amount of the monthly payment, and **b.** the total interest paid.

Solution: **a.** $A = \$100,000$, $P = ?$, $n = 360$, $i = \frac{9}{12}\% = 0.0075$

$$P = A \times \frac{1}{a_{\overline{n}i}}$$

$$= \$100,000 \times \frac{1}{a_{\overline{360}0.0075}} \qquad \text{(Appendix H)}$$

$$= \$804.62$$

b. $\$289,663.20$ Total of payments $\$804.62 \times 360$
       $- \ \underline{100,000.00}$ Amount of loan
       $\$189,663.20$ Interest   ■

Note in the previous example that if the mortgage is paid off, the homeowner pays almost 3 times the original amount borrowed. In the first years of a mortgage, most of the payment goes to interest. It is only in the later years that most of the payment goes to principal. This is illustrated in table 12.1 which shows an amortization schedule of the loan in example 4 for the first six months and the last six months.

Table 12.1   Amortization Schedule

Period	Beginning of Period Amount of Debt (1)	End of Period Payment (2)	Interest (3)	Applied to Principal (4) = (2) − (3)	Remaining Debt (5) = (1) − (4)
1	$100,000.00	$804.62	$750.00	$ 54.62	$99,945.38
2	99,945.38	804.62	749.59	55.03	99,890.35
3	99,890.35	804.62	749.18	55.44	99,834.90
4	99,834.90	804.62	748.76	55.86	99,779.04
5	99,779.04	804.62	748.34	56.28	99,722.76
6	99,722.76	804.62	747.92	56.70	99,666.06
355	4,703.48	804.62	35.28	769.34	3,934.14
356	3,934.14	804.62	29.51	775.11	3,159.03
357	3,159.03	804.62	23.69	780.93	2,378.10
358	2,378.10	804.62	17.84	786.78	1,591.32
359	1,591.32	804.62	11.93	792.69	798.63
360	798.63	804.62	5.99	798.63	0.00

The major advantage of the fixed rate mortgage is that the interest rate and the payment amount remain the same for the term of the loan. This gives peace of mind to the borrower. The major disadvantage of the fixed rate mortgage is that the borrower may not be able to afford the loan when interest rates are high.

Table 12.2   Monthly Mortgage Payments (30 year fixed rate loan)

Loan Amt.	Interest Rate 7.5%	8%	8.5%	9%	9.5%	10%	10.5%	11%	11.5%	12%
60,000	419.53	440.26	461.35	482.77	504.51	526.54	548.84	571.39	594.17	617.17
65,000	454.49	476.95	499.79	523.00	546.55	570.42	594.58	619.01	643.69	668.60
70,000	489.45	513.64	538.24	563.24	588.60	614.30	640.32	666.63	693.20	720.03
75,000	524.41	550.32	576.69	603.47	630.64	658.18	686.05	714.24	742.72	771.46
80,000	559.37	587.01	615.13	643.70	672.68	702.06	731.79	761.86	792.23	822.89
85,000	594.33	623.70	653.58	683.93	714.73	745.94	777.53	809.47	841.75	874.32
95,000	664.25	697.08	730.47	764.39	798.81	833.69	869.00	904.71	940.78	977.18
100,000	699.21	733.76	768.91	804.62	840.85	877.57	914.74	952.32	990.29	1028.61

The monthly payments in table 12.2 represent only principal plus interest. In both the fixed rate mortgage and the adjustable rate mortgage described next, it is common for lenders to require $\frac{1}{12}$ of the estimated property taxes and insurance as a part of the monthly payment. This money is placed in an **escrow account** and used by the lender to pay these bills when they come due. Consumer advocates oppose such a practice, since the lender can invest the money in the escrow account and earn interest on it. Some lenders now pay interest on such accounts.

b. Adjustable Rate Mortgage

In an adjustable rate mortgage, the beginning interest rate is almost always lower than the rate of a fixed rate mortgage, but the rate is subject to an adjustment, typically at the end of each year. This adjustment is usually based on some index* such as the interest rates on one-year treasury securities. Thus, if the interest rates on the securities increase, the interest rate on the adjustable rate mortgage goes up; if the interest rate on the securities goes down, the interest rate on the adjustable rate mortgage goes down. As the mortgage rate goes up or down, so do the monthly payments of the homeowner. To protect the homeowner from "payment shock" as a result of an unusual increase in interest rates, most adjustable rate mortgages have a "cap" or maximum amount the interest rate may increase. There may also be a lifetime interest cap, meaning that the interest rate may not exceed a certain percent, regardless of increases in interest rates. To protect the lender, there may also be an interest rate floor, meaning that the mortgage rate may not go lower than a certain percent.

In addition to the increase (decrease) in the index, the new interest rate includes the *margin* percent, a percent that covers the lender's operating expenses and some profit. The next example illustrates the calculation of a new adjustable mortgage rate.

EXAMPLE 5   An adjustable rate mortgage has the following features:

Beginning rate	7%	Lifetime interest rate cap	5%
Current index rate	7.5%	Adjustment period	1 yr
Margin rate	2.5%	Interest rate floor	6%
Annual interest rate cap	2%	Term of loan	30 yrs

Find the interest rate for the second year of the term.

Solution:

Current index rate	7.5%	Present rate	7%
Margin rate	+ 2.5%	Annual cap	+ 2%
Proposed new rate	10.0%	Maximum new rate	9%

Since the proposed new rate exceeds the present rate plus the annual cap, the rate for the second year is 9%.   ∎

Compared to fixed rate mortgages, an adjustable rate mortgage has the advantage of a lower beginning interest rate, usually from 1 to 3 percent. This allows more people to qualify for a loan since the monthly payments are lower.

*See chapter 17 for a discussion of indexes.

Homeowners also benefit from lower interest rates, since their mortgage rates may also decline. The major disadvantage of an adjustable rate mortgage is that monthly payments may go up with increasing interest rates. Even with annual and lifetime caps, continued increases in monthly payments may cause financial hardships for many homeowners.

Home Ownership Rates (By states and district)

State	Rate	State	Rate	State	Rate
Ala.	67.7%	Ky.	64.9%	N.D.	67.1%
Alaska	58.7	La.	66.3	Ohio	69.6
Ariz.	63.9	Maine	73.6	Okla.	71.4
Ark.	66.3	Md.	65.5	Ore.	63.4
Calif.	53.6	Mass.	58.9	Pa.	72.8
Colo.	58.6	Mich.	73.2	R.I.	61.2
Conn.	66.4	Minn.	68.3	S.C.	71.0
Del.	68.7	Miss.	72.2	S.D.	65.8
D.C.	38.7	Mo.	63.7	Tenn.	67.3
Fla.	64.4	Mont.	67.9	Texas	61.0
Ga.	64.7	Neb.	67.2	Utah	70.4
Hawaii	54.7	Nev.	54.3	Vt.	69.7
Idaho	70.2	N.H.	67.0	Va.	70.2
Ill.	70.2	N.J.	63.7	Wash.	64.3
Ind.	68.2	N.M.	65.5	W.Va.	74.8
Iowa	69.6	N.Y.	52.3	Wisc.	69.3
Kan.	68.1	N.C.	69.4	Wyo.	69.6

EXERCISES FOR SECTION 12.2

In problems 1–6, find the periodic payment required to amortize the given debt in the given time.

1. $4,000 debt, bearing interest at 6% compounded annually, annual payments for 10 years

2. $10,000 debt, bearing interest at 8% compounded quarterly, quarterly payments for 12 years

3. $16,000 debt, bearing interest at 10% compounded semiannually, semiannual payments for 20 years

4. $12,500 debt, bearing interest at 12% compounded monthly, monthly payments for $3\frac{1}{2}$ years

5. $7,500 debt, bearing interest at 9% compounded monthly, monthly payments for three years

6. $25,000 debt, bearing interest at 7% compounded semiannually, semiannual payments for 10 years

In problems 7–12, find the periodic payment required to amortize the given debt in the given time and construct a schedule showing the distribution of payments.

7. $5,250 debt, bearing interest at 8% compounded annually, annual payments for four years

8. $7,420 debt, bearing interest at 9% compounded semiannually, semiannual payments for three years

9. $3,200 debt, bearing interest at 11% compounded quarterly, quarterly payments for two years

10. $9,450 debt, bearing interest at 12% compounded monthly, monthly payments for 10 months

11. $8,700 debt, bearing interest at 9% compounded monthly, monthly payments for one year

12. $2,400 debt, bearing interest at 12% compounded semiannually, semiannual payments for six years

In problems 13–16, fill in the missing entries in the amortization schedules.

13.

Period	Beginning of Period Amount of Debt (1)	End of Period Payment (2)	Interest (3)	Applied to Principal (4) = (2) − (3)	Remaining Debt (5) = (1) − (4)
1	$1,500.00		$75.00		
2					
3					
4					

14.

Period	Beginning of Period Amount of Debt (1)	End of Period Payment (2)	Interest (3)	Applied to Principal (4) = (2) − (3)	Remaining Debt (5) = (1) − (4)
1	$5,000.00		$200.00		
2					
3					
4					
5					

15.

Period	Beginning of Period Amount of Debt (1)	End of Period Payment (2)	Interest (3)	Applied to Principal (4) = (2) − (3)	Remaining Debt (5) = (1) − (4)
1	$11,000.00		$357.50		
2					
3					
4					
5					
6					
7					
8					

16.

Period	Beginning of Period	End of Period			
	Amount of Debt (1)	Payment (2)	Interest (3)	Applied to Principal (4) = (2) − (3)	Remaining Debt (5) = (1) − (4)
1	$32,500.00		$2,437.50		
2					
3					
4					
5					
6					
7					
8					
9					
10					

Solve.

17. Johnson Properties acquired some acreage for $340,000 by paying $100,000 down and signing a mortgage for 24 quarterly payments. If the interest rate is 8% compounded quarterly, what is the amount of each quarterly payment?

18. The Centaur Corporation borrowed $200,000 to open a new branch office. If the interest rate is 7% compounded semiannually, and if the debt is to be amortized by semiannual payments for 10 years, find the amount of each payment.

19. The Everwear Carpet Outlet borrowed $175,000 to construct a new warehouse. The company is to amortize the loan in four years by making quarterly payments. If the interest rate is 10% compounded quarterly, find the amount of each payment.

20. For a $50,000 debt, bearing interest at 10% compounded quarterly, **a.** how much total interest is paid if the debt is amortized in eight years? **b.** How much more interest is paid if the debt is amortized in ten years?

21. To buy their new house, George and Susan made a down payment and signed a 30-year mortgage for $78,000. If the interest rate is 9% compounded monthly, find the amount of their monthly mortgage payment.

22. The Haycox Corporation purchased an apartment building for $180,000 down and a 20-year mortgage for $788,400. If the interest rate is 6% compounded monthly, find the amount of the corporation's monthly mortgage payment.

23. Four years after borrowing $60,000, to be amortized at 9% compounded semiannually for 10 years, the Decker Company was forced to refinance the remaining principal at 12% compounded semiannually for 20 years. Find: **a.** the semiannual payment for the original debt, **b.** the semiannual payment for the refinanced debt, and **c.** the total additional interest paid as a result of the refinancing.

In problems 24–28, find the interest rate for the next year of the adjustable rate mortgage if the adjustment period is one year.

	Present Rate	Current Index	Margin	Annual Cap	Floor		Present Rate	Current Index	Margin	Annual Cap	Floor
24.	6.5%	8%	2.5%	2%	6.25%	**27.**	8.25%	7%	2.75%	2%	6.5%
25.	7%	7.8%	2%	2.2%	7%	**28.**	8.75%	8.5%	2%	1.5%	7.5%
26.	9%	8.5%	2.25%	2.25%	6.5%						

Glossary

Adjustable rate mortgage A mortgage where the amount and time are fixed, but the interest rate varies according to a specified index.

Amortization The retirement of the principal and accrued interest of a debt by a series of partial payments.

Escrow account Money over and above the monthly mortgage payment, accumulated in a fund and used to pay property taxes, insurance, etc.

Fixed rate mortgage A mortgage where the interest rate, amount, and time are fixed.

Sinking fund An annuity established to meet a future obligation.

Review Test

1. A sinking fund is to be established to accumulate $110,000 in four years. How much should be invested quarterly if the interest rate is 11% compounded quarterly?

2. The Fraley Company borrowed $450,000 by issuing bonds that were redeemable in 20 years. To be able to redeem the bonds at maturity, the company established a sinking fund into which payments were made at the end of each six months. If the interest rate was 12% compounded semiannually, find: **a.** the amount of each payment and **b.** the total interest earned.

3. A debt of $16,000 bears interest at 9% compounded quarterly. What quarterly payment is required to amortize the debt in five years if payments are made at the end of each quarter?

4. How much interest is paid if a $6,000 debt, bearing interest at 7% compounded annually, is amortized over four years with payments at the end of each year?

5. Construct an amortization schedule showing the distribution of payments for a $4,700 debt, bearing interest at 10% compounded semiannually, with semiannual payments for three years.

6. Maria Valdez plans to replace a piece of equipment in three years. She anticipates that by that time the equipment will cost 15% more than its present price of $14,400. If money is worth 11% compounded semiannually, how much should she invest at the end of each six months to be able to purchase the equipment in three years?

7. Marion Brothers paid $20,000 down and made payments at the end of each month for three years to amortize the cost of a $200,000 computer. The interest rate was 9% compounded monthly. Find: **a.** the amount of each payment, **b.** the interest paid on the loan, and **c.** the total cost of the computer.

8. The McPherson Company purchased some acreage for a down payment of $20,000 and a 10-year mortgage for $227,000. If the interest rate was 6% compounded monthly, find the amount of the company's monthly mortgage payment.

13

Securities

Section 13.1   *Corporate Stock*

A. Introduction

There are times when a corporation may need funds in excess of those in the
company treasury. Plant expansion, acquisition of another company, modernization
of facilities, even the birth of the corporation itself may require capital beyond the
ability of the company to supply. It may be possible to borrow the money from a

Figure 13.1
Sample stock certificate

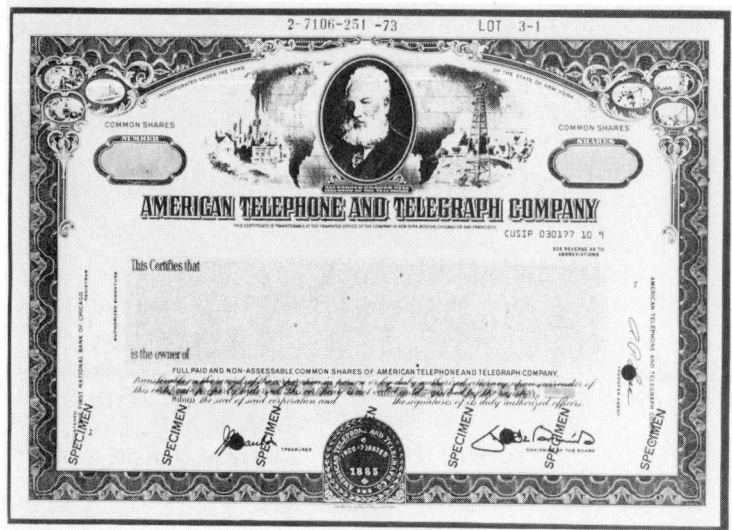

lending institution, but a more advantageous way of raising capital is to sell securities to the public. Two of these securities—corporate stocks and corporate bonds—are the subject of this chapter.

B. Common Stock

When a company issues **common stock,** it offers for sale to the public part ownership in the company. The unit of ownership is the **share.** For example, an individual who owns 1,000 shares of a total of 100,000 shares owns 1% of the corporation. If 100 persons each bought 1,000 shares, then the corporation would be owned by 100 persons. Evidence of stock ownership is the stock certificate, an engraved or lithographed document on which are entered the owner's name, the number of shares, and the date of issue (see figure 13.1).

Although shareholders own the corporation, direction of the corporation is entrusted to the board of directors, elected by the stockholders. In turn, the board of directors hires the executives of the company, such as the president, vice president, and so on, to manage the daily operations of the corporation.

C. Advantages and Disadvantages of Investing in Common Stock

There are several advantages to investing in common stock. Among these are (1) dividends, (2) capital gain, (3) liquidity and minimum management, and (4) inflation protection. Let us examine these in some detail.

Dividends. **Stock dividends** are a percentage of the after-tax profits of a corporation and are usually distributed by the board of directors on a per share basis. For example, a dividend of $0.25 per share to a stockholder who owns 1,000 shares means a payment of $0.25 $\times$ 1,000 = $250.00. Dividends are normally in cash, but may be in additional shares of stock.

The amount of a dividend often exceeds returns from other forms of investment (for example, bonds or savings accounts), but it should be understood that dividends are paid from the corporation's net earnings. A firm that has made no money or that is in financial distress may reduce the amount of the dividend or pay no dividend at all.

EXAMPLE 1   The board of directors of the Craft Corporation voted to distribute 60% of the company's net profits of $600,000 to the corporation's stockholders. If there are 450,000 outstanding shares of common stock, what was the amount of the declared dividend?

Solution: The amount to be distributed is $600,000 × 0.60 = $360,000.

$$\frac{\$360,000}{450,000} = \$0.80 \quad \text{Dividend per share of common stock}$$

■

Capital Gain.
It is possible for the value of common stock to increase, thus allowing an individual to sell the stock for more than its purchase price. This is called **capital gain.**

EXAMPLE 2   John Jacobs purchased 500 shares of common stock at $38.00 per share and later sold them for $42.50 per share. What was his capital gain?

Solution:
```
 $21,250   Selling price ($42.50 × 500)
- 19,000   Purchase price ($38 × 500)
 $ 2,250   Capital gain
```
■

Liquidity and Minimum Management.
Stocks require little attention and may be readily sold for cash. This is not true for all investments, such as real estate.

Inflation Protection.
In general, stock prices increase as prices rise for other commodities, thus protecting the buyer from devaluation of the dollar. Some investments (savings accounts, for example) do not afford this protection.

As with any investment, there are risks. The primary disadvantages of owning common stock is the potential loss of your profits and part of your investment as a result of poor performance by the corporation, or by a decline in the stock market.

D. Preferred Stock

A company may issue another class of stock, called preferred stock. Preferred stock differs from common stock in three important ways.

1. Preferred stock dividends are usually fixed and are paid before any dividends are paid to common stockholders.

2. Should corporation earnings be insufficient to pay the full dividend per share, the difference may be carried over to subsequent dividend payments.
3. In the event of bankruptcy and after all debts are paid, remaining assets are paid first to preferred stockholders then to common stockholders.

E X A M P L E   3   The board of directors for the Orion Corporation voted $362,000 in dividends for the fourth quarter. The company has issued 70,000 shares of preferred stock that pays a quarterly dividend of $0.60 per share, and there are 640,000 shares of common stock outstanding. Determine the dividend per share of common stock.

Solution: The preferred dividends are paid first.

$362,000   Amount to be distributed
−   42,000   Preferred stock dividends ($0.60 × 70,000)
$320,000   For distribution to common stockholders

$$\frac{\$320,000}{640,000} = \$0.50 \quad \text{Per share dividend for common stock}$$ ■

E X A M P L E   4   Koger Business Systems has issued 300,000 shares of common stock and 50,000 shares of preferred stock that pays a quarterly dividend of $0.80 per share. For the past three quarters Koger has paid no dividends, but this quarter the board of directors voted to distribute $235,000 in dividends. Find the dividend per share of stock for the current quarter.

Solution: Dividends for four quarters first must be paid to the preferred stockholders.

$0.80 × 50,000 × 4 = $160,000

This leaves $235,000 − $160,000 = $75,000 to be distributed to the common stockholders.

$$\frac{\$75,000}{300,000} = \$0.25$$

Thus, the preferred stock dividend was $0.80 × 4 = $3.20 per share and the common stock dividend was $0.25 per share.   ■

Preferred stock is often described as a hybrid stock because it has characteristics of both common stock and bonds. The chief advantage of preferred stock is its dividend, but there are disadvantages. The right to buy additional shares is limited, and the dividend is usually fixed, regardless of the prosperity of the corporation. Preferred stock thus occupies an intermediate position between common stock and bonds and must be considered a moderately conservative investment.

EXERCISES FOR SECTION 13.1

1. The board of directors of Quiklube, Inc. approved a dividend of $192,500 at the end of the first quarter. If there were 175,000 shares of common stock outstanding, what was the dividend per share?

2. The Huron Company is distributing 40% of its net profits of $450,000 to its stockholders. There are 200,000 outstanding shares of common stock in the company. What is the dividend per share of common stock?

3. John Porter owns 200 shares of common stock in the Martin Mining Company. The company has decided to distribute 50% of its first quarter profits of $700,000 to its stockholders. If there are 500,000 outstanding shares of common stock, how much will John receive in dividends?

4. Lucille Porter purchased 100 shares of common stock in the Owens Corporation. The company's board of directors voted to distribute 60% of the company's profits of $225,000 to its stockholders, and there are 300,000 outstanding shares of common stock. How much did Lucille receive?

5. There are 240,000 outstanding shares of common stock in the Otis Manufacturing Company. The company's quarterly profits in 1993 were
Quarter I: $208,000
Quarter II: $160,000
Quarter III: $140,000
Quarter IV: $172,000
If the company distributed 60% of its profits to its 1,800 stockholders, what was the quarterly dividend per share of common stock in 1993?

6. Myron Industries recorded the following profits in 1993, with the given percentages distributed among the company's stockholders
Quarter I: $110,000; 60%
Quarter II: $180,000; 70%
Quarter III: $90,000; 40%
Quarter IV: $105,000; 40%
If there are 200,000 outstanding shares of common stock, what was the quarterly dividend per share of common stock in 1993?

7. Joan Richards purchased 150 shares of common stock in Continental Industries at $22.25 per share and a year later sold the stock for $26.75 per share. What was her capital gain?

8. At the beginning of the second quarter, Tim O'Connor bought 300 shares of Data Systems common stock at $14.75 per share. The company's board of directors voted to distribute 40% of the company's second-quarter profits of $350,000 among its stockholders, and there are 400,000 outstanding shares of common stock. Tim sold his stock at the end of the quarter for $17.25 per share. What was his capital gain? How much did he receive in dividends? What was his total profit on the transaction?

9. The board of directors of the Babson Company voted $150,000 in dividends for the third quarter. The company has issued 30,000 shares of preferred stock that pays a quarterly dividend of $0.20 per share, and there are 400,000 shares of common stock outstanding. Determine the dividend per share of common stock.

10. There are 800,000 outstanding shares of common stock in the Lyonkraft Company and 70,000 shares of preferred stock that pay a quarterly dividend of $0.60 per share. For the second quarter, the company will distribute $410,000 in dividends. Determine the dividend per share of common stock.

11. Rhonda Myer has 100 shares of preferred and 400 shares of common stock in the Scott Manufacturing Company. For the first quarter, the company will distribute $257,000.00 in dividends. If the preferred stock pays a quarterly dividend of $0.50 a share, and if there are 580,000 shares of common and 50,000 shares of preferred stock outstanding, how much will Rhonda receive in dividends?

12. The board of directors of Sundberg Industries declared a dividend of 80% of the $71,500 in earnings last quarter. If there were 12,000 shares of preferred stock with an annual dividend of $4.40 per share outstanding and 110,000 shares of common stock outstanding, find the dividend per share for last quarter.

13. Following two quarters during which no dividends were paid, the board of directors of the Gannett Company voted to distribute $41,950 in dividends. If Gannett has issued 10,000 shares of preferred stock with a quarterly dividend of $0.50 per share and 180,000 shares of common stock, find the dividend per share for the current quarter.

14. The board of directors of Nettles, Inc. voted to
distribute $41,950 in dividends for the current
quarter. This follows five consecutive quarters that
the board voted no dividends. If Nettles has 15,000
shares of preferred stock with a quarterly dividend of
$0.35 per share and 95,000 outstanding shares of
common stock, find the dividend per share for the
current quarter.

$$41950$$
$$31500$$
$$\overline{}$$
$$10450$$

$$(0.35 \times 15000 \times 6)$$

$$\frac{10450}{95000} = 0.11\text{¢}$$

Section 13.2   *Transactions in Stocks*

A. Buying and Selling

When a corporation first issues stock, it is usually sold at par value, the amount
printed on a stock certificate. After a share of stock is purchased, the issuing
corporation can no longer control its ownership or price. As a result, stock is bought
and sold like any other commodity.

Figure 13.2
Stock ownership in the
U.S.

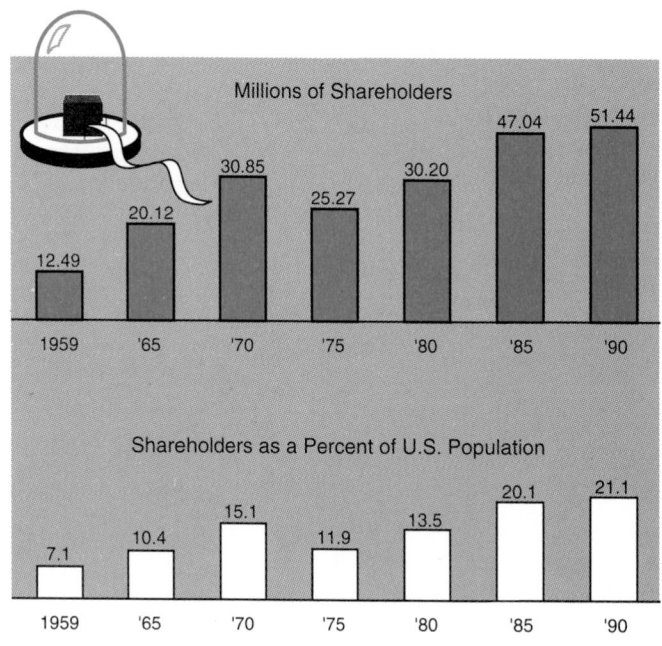

Stock Ownership in the U.S.

For major corporations, the principal market for stocks is a stock exchange. In
the United States, the largest stock exchanges are the New York Stock Exchange
and the American Stock Exchange. At a stock exchange, the price of a share is
determined by the most fundamental of economic concepts—the law of supply and
demand. Shares are sold by a two-way auction: buyers compete with other buyers
for the lowest price, and sellers compete with other sellers for the highest price.

The actual trading (buying and selling) of a stock is carried out by stock exchange members, called brokers. If an investor wants to buy or sell a share of stock, an order is placed with a broker at a local brokerage office. Once the order is placed, the broker bargains for the best possible price, whether the order is a purchase or a sale.

Because the trading of stocks is subject to supply and demand, the price of a share fluctuates daily. The financial sections of many daily newspapers carry an account of the previous day's activity on an exchange. A portion of such an account is shown in figure 13.3. The meaning of the underlined entry in figure 13.3 is as follows:

34	The highest selling price during the past 52 weeks. Stocks are sold in whole dollars and units of eighths of a dollar ($12\frac{1}{2}$¢ or \$0.125). Thus, the high is \$34.00 per share for the past 52 weeks.
$26\frac{1}{4}$	The lowest selling price during the past 52 weeks (\$26.25).
AshOil	Abbreviation for Ashland Oil, the name of the stock.
1.00	The amount of the annual dividend.
3.3	The yield. This is discussed in section 13.3.
12	The price-earnings ratio. This is discussed in section 13.3.
309	The number of reported shares sold for the day, in hundreds.
31	The highest selling price of the day (\$31).
$30\frac{5}{8}$	The lowest selling price of the day (\$30.625).
$30\frac{5}{8}$	The last or closing price of the day (\$30.625).
$-\frac{1}{2}$	The difference between today's closing price and the closing price of the last session in which the stock was traded.

Figure 13.3
Sample newspaper account of stock transactions

52 Week High	52 Week Low	Stock	Div	Yld	PE	Vol 00's	High	Low	Close	Chg
6⅝	4	Armco	...	...	...	1402	5¾	5⅝	5¾	...
41¼	30½	Armc pfA	4.50	11.0	...	21	41¼	41	41	− ¼
36½	23½	ArmWI	1.20	3.3	31	675	36⅝	35⅞	36	− ¼
18½	7⅜	ArowE	1.94	11.2	51	618	17¾	17¼	17¼	− ¼
30	16¾	ArwE pf	1.94	6.8	84	33	28⅝	28¼	28½	+ ⅛
11¼	5¾	Artra	...	...	...	72	5⅞	5⅝	5¾	− ⅛
26½	17⅜	Arvin	0.68	2.7	25	44	25⅝	25½	25⅝	...
55½	44½	Arvin pf	3.75	7.0	52	21	54⅛	53⅝	53⅝	− ¼
2⅜	1	ARX	...	...	...	33	1⅞	1¾	1⅞	...
56	40¾	ASA	2.00	4.7	29	514	43⅜	42⅝	43	+ ⅜
29¼	18¼	Asarco	x0.80	3.0	24	404	26¾	26	26⅝	+ ⅜
38	22½	AsCoal	0.40	1.2	14	129	33⅝	32⅝	33⅛	− ⅝
34	26¼	AshOil	1.00	3.3	12	309	31	30⅝	30⅝	− ½
16⅛	11	AsiaPc	e0.23	1.5	...	250	15½	15¼	15½	− ⅛
16⅝	10¾	AsetInv	2.00	15.5	6	345	12⅞	12⅝	12⅞	+ ⅛
30	18⅛	AsdNG	0.12	0.6	25	24	19⅝	19½	19⅝	− ⅛
16½	10⅝	Athlne	1.00	6.2	14	117	16¼	16	16¼	+ ¼
37⅜	30¼	AtlGas	2.08	6.1	15	306	34⅜	34	34⅜	+ ⅛
44⅝	33¾	AltEnrg	3.00	6.8	12	131	44⅜	44⅛	44⅜	...
22¾	21	AltEnrg wi	...	...	6	34	22⅝	22⅛	22½	...
125¾	98⅛	AtlRich	5.50	5.0	33	1979	110¼	109½	109⅞	− ⅛
8⅜	5½	Atlas	...	...	...	27	6⅛	6	6	...
23	16¾	ATMOS	1.24	5.9	16	64	21	20¾	21	+ ¼
21	9⅛	Atwod	e0.77	6.4	12	2776	12⅛	11¾	12⅛	+ ⅜
10¼	5½	AudVd	...	...	14	101	6¾	6½	6⅝	+ ⅛
14⅛	7⅞	Augat	...	...	...	129	11½	11½	11½	...
10⅝	7⅞	Austr e	0.22	2.6	...	187	8½	8⅜	8½	...
49	29½	AutoDt	s0.40	0.8	27	2266	48	47	47⅞	+ ¾
42	14⅝	Autozn s	...	...	48	266	37⅛	36¼	36⅝	− ½
28	19⅝	AVMCO	s0.40	1.6	22	16	25⅛	24⅞	25⅛	+ ¼
28⅛	20	AveryD	0.80	2.9	26	673	28⅛	27⅞	28	...
30	23¼	Avnet	0.60	2.3	19	221	26	25⅞	26	...
54	37⅛	Avon a	1.40	2.7	25	3313	51⅝	51⅛	51¼	− ⅜
28⅞	16	Aydin e	...	...	8	41	17⅛	16¾	16¾	...

52 Week High	52 Week Low	Stock	Div	Yld	PE	Vol 00's	High	Low	Close	Chg
22½	15	Clarcor	f0.60	3.7	14	60	16½	16⅛	16⅜	...
30½	20½	ClarkE	...	...	...	1142	25⅞	25¼	25⅝	+ ½
27⅛	11	ClaytHs s	...	...	20	407	22½	22	22¼	...
9¾	8¼	ClemGlb	e0.35	3.8	...	249	9⅜	9⅛	9¼	− ⅛
40⅜	29½	ClvClf	1.10	3.2	10	308	34⅞	34⅝	34¾	...
52	36½	Clorox	1.68	3.4	39	1032	50⅞	49⅜	49⅜	− 2⅝
32¾	19⅝	ClubMd	0.30	1.2	12	21	25⅛	24¾	25	...
44	17⅝	CMLs e	0.08	0.2	24	337	43⅞	42⅜	42⅜	− 1⅜
27½	14⅞	CMS Eng	0.48	3.0	...	1440	15¾	15⅝	15¾	+ ¼
5⅛	2	CMSEnh	...	...	...	11	2½	2½	2½	...
104½	75½	CNAFn	...	...	9	94	86	84⅝	84¾	− 1¾
12½	10¼	CNAI	1.16	9.3	11	39	12½	12½	12½	+ ⅛
8⅞	4⅛	Coachm	0.08	1.0	...	29	8¼	8	8⅛	+ ⅛
12¼	3¾	CoastSv	...	...	4	1182	11¼	10⅝	10⅝	− ⅝
36¾	22	Coastal	0.40	1.5	44	3077	27½	27	27⅛	− ⅛
84⅜	53	CocaCl	1.12	1.3	33	7238	84⅝	83	u84½	+ 1⅛
42⅛	41¼	CocaCl wi	...	...	17	651	42⅜	41⅝	u42⅜	+ ⅝
19½	11¾	CocaCE	0.05	0.4	...	1707	12⅞	12⅝	12¾	− ¼
23	13⅜	Coeur e	0.15	1.0	...	445	15¼	14¾	14⅞	+ ⅜
28⅛	23	Colemn n	...	...	29	124	24⅞	24¼	24½	− ⅛
52	35⅝	ColgP s	1.06	2.1	60	4551	51⅛	50	51	...
9⅜	8¼	ColHln	0.68	8.2	11	425	8½	8⅜	8⅜	− ⅛
11½	10⅜	Collln	1.20	10.7	9	174	11¼	11⅛	11¼	+ ⅛
6⅝	5⅜	CollHI	0.78	11.6	8	280	6¾	6½	u6¾	+ ⅛
12¼	11⅜	Collnv	0.86	7.4	13	98	11¾	11⅝	11¾	+ ⅛
8⅞	7½	ColMu	0.63	8.0	6	143	8	7⅞	7⅞	...
21¾	17	Coltec n	...	...	...	448	21⅝	21⅜	21⅝	+ ¼
40⅞	12⅞	vjColGas j	...	...	...	3028	14⅞	14	14⅞	+ ⅝
24 21/32	12½	Comdis	b0.28	1.8	27	907	15½	15⅜	15½	...
60⅝	36	Comeric	s1.88	3.1	12	524	60¼	59¾	59⅞	− ⅜
19⅝	12¾	CmlTek	0.68	3.7	26	97	18¼	18⅛	18¼	...
19¼	10⅛	Comdre	...	...	8	2352	12⅜	12	12⅛	− ⅛
42⅝	29⅝	CmwE	3.00	8.9	89	3730	34	33⅜	33⅞	− ⅛
100	90	CwE pfl	8.38	8.5	...	20	98¼	98	98¼	+ ¾

B. Buying and Selling Costs

The basic unit of stock purchase or sale is the **round lot,** which is 100 shares or a multiple of 100 shares.* Orders for other than round lots are called **odd lots.** For example, the trading price of 300 shares of a stock at a price per share of $15\frac{1}{4}$ is $15.25 \times 300 = \$4,575$.

In addition to the trading price, buyers or sellers must also pay a commission to the broker who executes the order. The amount of the commission depends on the trading price. Commission schedules not only vary from broker to broker but may be negotiable on large stock purchases. For odd lots, $\frac{1}{8}$ point ($12\frac{1}{2}$ cents) is added to the broker's commission. This is called the **odd-lot differential.**

handwritten: Charged as extra when dealt by in lots

Sellers of stock are subject to fees and taxes along with the broker's commission. **The Securities and Exchange Commission (SEC),** a federal agency that regulates stock exchanges, levies a fee of $0.01 per $500 in value (or any fraction of $500). Some state and local governments may also charge a transfer tax when the stock is sold.

The costs of buying or selling stocks are summarized as follows:

Buyer Pays	Seller Receives
Trading price	Trading price
plus	*less*
Basic broker commission	Basic broker commission
plus	*less*
Any odd-lot differential	Any odd-lot differential
	less
	SEC fee
	less
	Any transfer taxes

EXAMPLE 1 Find the total cost of purchasing 100 shares of stock at $40\frac{1}{2}$ if the broker's commission is a flat fee of $50 for each order under $5,000.

Solution:

$4,050.00	Trading price ($40.50 × 100)
+ 50.00	Broker's commission
$4,100.00	Total cost

handwritten: round lot straight

---

*For low-volume stocks, a round lot may consist of only 10 shares.

E X A M P L E   2   What is the total cost of purchasing 40 shares of stock at $35\frac{1}{8}$ if the broker's basic commission is 2.2% of the trading price?

Solution:

$1,405.00 Trading price ($35.125 × 40)
+   30.91 Broker's bas. comm. ($1,405 × 0.022)
+   5.00 Odd-lot differential ($0.125 × 40)
$1,440.91 Total cost

Entry	Display	Memory
1405	1405	0
M+	1405	1405
×	1405	1405
.022	0.022	1405
M+	30.91	1435.91
.125	0.125	1435.91
×	0.125	1435.90
40	40	1435.91
M+	5	1440.91
MR	1440.91	1440.91

E X A M P L E   3   Janis McGuire sold 200 shares of stock at $37\frac{5}{8}$. If the broker's commission was 1.4% of the trading price, what did Janis net from the sale?

Solution:

$7,525.00 Trading price ($37.625 × 200)
−   105.35 Broker's commission ($7,525 × 0.014)   *memory net income so deduct BC + SEC fee*
−   0.16 SEC fee ($7,525 ÷ $500 = 15.05; 16 × $0.01 = $0.16)
$7,419.49 Net to Janis

E X A M P L E   4   How much would a seller net from the sale of 80 shares of stock at $16\frac{7}{8}$ if the transfer taxes were $3.35 and the broker's basic commission was 2% of the trading price?

Solution:

$1,350.00 Trading price ($16.875 × 80)
−   27.00 Broker's commission ($1,350 × 0.02)
−   10.00 Odd-lot differential ($0.125 × 80)
−   3.35 Transfer taxes
−   0.03 SEC fee ($1,350 ÷ $500 = 2.7; 3 × $0.01 = $0.03)
$1,309.62 Net to seller

EXAMPLE 5   Lowell Fraley sold 300 shares of stock at $27\frac{1}{4}$. The same day, he purchased 250 shares of stock at $31\frac{1}{8}$. If the broker's basic commission was 1.4% of the trading price on the sale and 1.5% on the purchase, and if transfer taxes were $12, how much did Lowell receive after the sale and the purchase?

Solution:

	$8,175.00	Trading price ($27.25 × 300)
−	114.45	Broker's commission ($8,175 × 0.014)
−	12.00	Transfer tax
−	0.17	SEC fee ($8,175 ÷ $500 = 16.35; 17 × $0.01 = $0.17)
	$8,048.38	Net to Lowell from sale
	$7,781.25	Trading price ($31.125 × 250)
+	116.72	Broker's basic commission ($7,781.25 × 0.015)
+	6.25	Odd-lot differential ($0.125 × 50)
	$7,904.22	Total cost
	$8,048.38	
−	7,904.22	
	$ 144.16	Received by Lowell after sale and purchase

EXERCISES FOR SECTION 13.2

In problems 1–10, determine the total cost of purchasing the indicated number of shares of stock at the given price per share and with the given basic broker commission.

1. 100 shares at $9.50 per share; $20.40 commission

2. 100 shares at $22.00 per share; $41.25 commission

3. 100 shares at $42\frac{3}{8}$ per share; $57.91 commission

4. 400 shares at $3\frac{3}{4}$ per share; $52.90 commission

5. 900 shares at $57\frac{1}{8}$ per share; 0.8% of the trading price

6. 1,300 shares at $40\frac{3}{8}$ per share; 0.9% of the trading price

7. 80 shares at $19\frac{1}{2}$ per share; 2.2% of the trading price

8. 55 shares at $32\frac{5}{8}$ per share; 1.8% of the trading price

9. 140 shares at $15\frac{7}{8}$ per share (100 round lot, 40 odd lot); 2% of the trading price

10. 225 shares at $60\frac{1}{8}$ per share (200 round lot, 25 odd lot); 1.2% of the trading price

In problems 11–20, find the net amount to the seller given a. the number of shares and the price per share, b. the basic broker commission, and c. transfer taxes.

11. a. 100 shares at $12.00 per share; **b.** $23.60

12. a. 100 shares at $22.50 per share; **b.** $40.00

13. a. 400 shares at $38\frac{1}{2}$ per share; **b.** $141.25; **c.** $11.25

14. a. 1500 shares at $43\frac{3}{4}$ per share; **b.** $461.50; **c.** $21.65

15. a. 600 shares at $14\frac{5}{8}$ per share; **b.** $135.60; **c.** $8.70

16. a. 500 shares at $22\frac{3}{8}$ per share; **b.** $154.94; **c.** $11.44

17. a. 70 shares at $7\frac{7}{8}$ per share; **b.** $10.70

18. a. 65 shares at $14\frac{1}{2}$ per share; **b.** $20.56

19. a. 150 shares at $10\frac{3}{4}$ per share (100 round lot, 50 odd lot); **b.** $39.99

20. a. 325 shares at $26\frac{5}{8}$ per share (300 round lot, 25 odd lot); **b.** $102.80

In problems 21–24, find the net result of the transactions given a. the number of shares and the price per share, b. the basic broker commission, and c. transfer taxes.

21. Sold **a.** 100 shares at $20\frac{3}{8}$ per share; **b.** $38.16
Bought **a.** 200 shares at $12\frac{1}{2}$ per share; **b.** $46.30

22. Sold **a.** 500 shares at $16\frac{3}{4}$ per share; **b.** $95.12
Bought **a.** 300 shares at 22 per share; **b.** $111.40

23. Sold **a.** 175 shares at $32\frac{1}{2}$ per share; **b.** $50.04;
c. $5.34
Bought **a.** 400 shares at $12\frac{3}{8}$ per share; **b.** $68.35

24. Sold **a.** 160 shares at $9\frac{5}{8}$ per share; **b.** $29.50;
c. $2.50
Bought **a.** 80 shares at $13\frac{7}{8}$ per share; **b.** $36.20

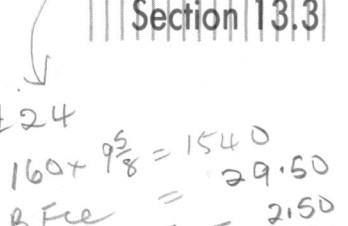

Section 13.3 *Valuation Indices: Stocks*

The fluctuation of stock prices makes it possible to make a lot of money in the stock market and also to lose a lot of money in the stock market.* Consequently, investors are continually searching for a formula that will predict market behavior. While some formulas have been successful when applied over a long period of time, no one has yet found a way to "beat the market." The old axiom is still true: "The market can do anything."

While market behavior may be unpredictable, there are several indicators that investors use to evaluate an individual stock. Among these are (1) earnings per share, (2) the price-earnings ratio, and (3) the yield.

A. Earnings per Share

The earnings per share for common stock is found by dividing earnings available for common stock by the number of outstanding shares.

$$(13\text{-}1) \quad E/S = \frac{\text{Net profit} - \text{Preferred dividends}}{\text{Outstanding shares}}$$

EXAMPLE 1   In the previous year, Gartco Corporation had a net profit of $4,600,000, from which preferred stock dividends were $520,000. If there were 1,800,000 outstanding shares, find the earnings per share.

Solution: $E/S = \dfrac{\$4,600,000 - \$520,000}{1,800,000}$

$= \dfrac{\$4,080,000}{1,800,000}$

$= \$2.266$

$= \$2.27$

*Two examples of this are Bernard Baruch and Daniel Drew. Baruch once made $700,000 on one stock, Amalgamated Copper. On the other hand, "Uncle Daniel," one of the most ruthless men in Wall Street history and who amassed a fortune of some $13 million, lost it all in the end and died with less than $1,000.

Earnings per share may be found in a company's annual report and theoretically represents the earnings of one share of stock. It is not to be confused with dividends, which is actually distributed to stockholders. In examining earnings per share, investors look for an upward trend, for example a company whose E/S have increased in four of the last five years.

B. Price-earnings Ratio

The price-earnings ratio is a number found by dividing the current market price of a share by the earnings per share.

$$(13\text{-}2) \quad P/E = \frac{\text{Current market price}}{\text{Earnings per share}}$$

eg $15

10 per share | mue yea

EXAMPLE 2   Find the price-earnings ratio of a stock selling for $64 with earnings per share of $4.

Solution: $P/E = \dfrac{\$64}{\$4}$

$= 16$

$= \dfrac{16}{1}$

The price-earnings ratio is 16 to 1.   ■

The price-earnings ratio is the most frequently used indicator of the relationship between stock prices and earnings and represents the amount that investors are currently paying for $1 of the company's earnings. Over a period of time, the price-earnings ratio of a given stock tends to fluctuate over a wide range. While analysts hold varying opinions on what is the ideal price-earnings ratio, a P/E of between 6–10 is regarded as conservative. A P/E below 6 signals uncertainty about the company's financial soundness, and a P/E over 10 means the investor is paying a premium for the stock.

C. Yield

Another simple tool for measuring stock valuation is the yield. The yield is that percent (rounded to the nearest tenth) found by dividing the annual dividend by the current market price.

$$(13\text{-}3) \quad \text{Yield} = \frac{\text{Annual dividend}}{\text{Current market price}}$$

11 ⟶ $PE = \dfrac{62.375}{5620,000 - 752000}$ $= \dfrac{62.375}{4143000} = 14.08$

$\overline{11\ 000,000}$

$= 14:1$

EXAMPLE 3   Find the yield of a stock if it is currently selling at $36\frac{1}{4}$ and paying an annual dividend of $1.60.

Solution: $\text{Yield} = \dfrac{\$1.60}{\$36.25}$

$\quad\quad\quad\quad = 0.0441$

$\quad\quad\quad\quad = 4.4\%$

Div on C share = Yield
Pb Stock

Yield is considered a definite indicator of the reasonableness of a stock price. Slow-growth stocks may be expected to yield as much as 5%, while future-growth stocks may average only 2% to 3%.

EXERCISES FOR SECTION 13.3

In problems 1–6, find the earnings per share for the indicated common stock.

1. Net profit of $281,000; preferred dividends of $180,000; 50,000 outstanding shares

2. Net profit of $2,255,000; preferred dividends of $410,000; 900,000 outstanding shares

3. Net profit of $4,415,000; preferred dividends of $1,100,000; 1,500,000 outstanding shares

4. Net profit of $3,592,000; preferred dividends of $820,000; 1,400,000 outstanding shares

5. Net profit of $6,313,000; preferred dividends of $2,150,000; 2,300,000 outstanding shares

6. Net profit of $1,885,000; preferred dividends of $126,600; 1,120,000 outstanding shares

In problems 7–12, find the price-earnings ratio of the given stock. (Round to the nearest whole number.)

7. Selling price of stock, $47.25; earnings per share, $1.80

8. Selling price of stock, $27.50; earnings per share, $1.85

9. Selling price of stock, $73.00; earnings per share, $2.10

10. Selling price of stock, $43\frac{1}{8}$; earnings per share, $2.25

11. Net profit of company, $5,620,000; preferred dividends, $750,000; outstanding shares of common stock, 1,100,000; selling price of stock, $62\frac{3}{8}$

12. Net profit of company, $4,750,000; preferred dividends, $1,150,000; outstanding shares of common stock, 875,000; selling price of stock, $52\frac{7}{8}$

In problems 13–20, find the yield of the given stock. (Round to the nearest tenth of a percent.)

13. Annual dividend per share, $1.80; selling price, $61.25

14. Annual dividend per share, $0.60; selling price, $24.25

15. Annual dividend per share, $1.20; selling price, $31.25

16. Annual dividend per share, $1.55; selling price, $18\frac{1}{8}$

17. Annual dividend per share, $0.88; selling price, $33\frac{3}{4}$

18. Total annual dividends paid, $3,111,000; outstanding shares of common stock, 920,000; selling price, $54\frac{3}{8}$

19. Total annual dividends paid, $2,300,000; outstanding shares of common stock, 1,875,000; selling price, $19\frac{7}{8}$

20. Jane Travis is deciding which of three stocks to purchase. Stock *A* pays dividends of $1.80 and sells for $28\frac{1}{8}$, stock *B* pays dividends of $0.20 and sells for $3\frac{1}{4}$, stock *C* pays dividends of $0.90 and sells for $14\frac{1}{8}$. If Jane is interested in income, which stock should she purchase?

Section 13.4 *Bonds*

A. Corporate Bonds

Bonds are a second way in which corporations can acquire capital. When a company issues bonds, it is borrowing money from investors. Thus, a bond is like a long-term promissory note. Each bond is an agreement to repay the principal (**face value** or **par value**) at a specified time and to pay a set annual rate of interest from the day of issue to the day of redemption. Although the set interest is nominal, it is customary to pay the interest semiannually.

As an investment, corporate bonds differ from corporate stocks in the following ways.

1. Bonds are "debt instruments" in that a bondholder simply lends money to the company, while stocks are "equity instruments" in that a stockholder is a part owner of the company.
2. A bondholder receives only a fixed interest payment while a stockholder shares in the profits of the company in the form of dividends. However, a stockholder's dividends may fluctuate or may not be paid at all, but a bondholder receives interest payments when due. Failure of the company to pay bond interest constitutes insolvency of the company.
3. In the event of insolvency, the claims of bondholders are paid first, then preferred stockholders, then common stockholders.

Obviously, bonds are a more conservative investment than common stock. But, as the risk is smaller, so is the return. Financial risk affects both the price and the profits of corporate securities. The additional investment security of bonds makes them popular with insurance companies, banks, pension funds, and other investors seeking guaranteed incomes. Common stocks are for investors willing to accept financial risk for potential growth and increased profits.

There are several types of corporate bonds, but the most popular is the **mortgage bond,** which pledges the physical property of the corporation as security. This is an example of a secured bond. Unsecured bonds, called **debentures,** are backed only by the general credit of the corporation.

Since the quality of a bond is a measure of its security, it is a practice to rate bonds according to their security features. There are two companies that rate all major corporations in the United States, Moody's Investment Service and Standard and Poor's. Their ratings and approximate quality definitions are shown in table 13.1.

Bond ratings demonstrate the relationship between yield and risk. The lower the rating the higher the interest rate the company is expected to pay, since the risk to the investor is higher. Ratings are not shown in the newspaper listings, but their results are reflected in the yield column. Those bonds with the highest yields, comparatively, are those that have the lowest ratings.

Since 1983 all corporate bonds are **registered bonds,** meaning that they are issued to specifically named owners. Interest on registered bonds is paid by check, and the bonds must be returned to a transfer office for reissue when acquired by new owners.

Table 13.1

Standard & Poor's	Moody's	Quality
AAA	Aaa	Highest
AA+	Aa1	High
AA	Aa2	
AA−	Aa3	
A+	A1	Upper Medium
A	A2	
A−	A3	
BBB+	Baa1	Medium
BBB	Baa2	
BBB−	Baa3	
BB+	Ba1	Speculative
BB	Ba2	
BB−	Ba3	
B+	B1	Very speculative
B	B2	
B−	B3	
CCC	Caa	Poor quality, may be in default
CC	Ca	Highly speculative
C	C	Poorest quality
D	D	In default

B. Transactions in Bonds

Bonds are sold in denominations ranging from $50 to $10,000, but the most popular denomination for corporate bonds is $1,000. Bonds are marketed at a securities exchange or on the over-the-counter market.* Bond transactions at an exchange are reported daily in the financial section of many newspapers. Figure 13.4 shows a sample of such a report.

The meaning of the underlined entry is as follows:

AT&T	Abbreviation for American Telephone and Telegraph.
$7\frac{1}{8}$	The annual interest rate of the bond ($7\frac{1}{8}$%).
03	The maturity date of the bond (2003).
7.5	The bond yield. This is discussed in section 13.5.
291	The volume of sales in thousands of dollars.
$94\frac{7}{8}$	The highest selling price of the day in percent of $1,000 face value; that is, the price is $1,000 × 0.94875 = $948.75.
$94\frac{1}{2}$	The lowest selling price of the day; that is, $945.00.
$94\frac{3}{4}$	The last or closing price of the day; that is, $947.50.
$+\frac{1}{4}$	The change in closing price from the last trading session.

*An over-the-counter market is made up of securities dealers who may or may not be members of an exchange. Stock of companies with insufficient financial qualifications to be listed on an exchange also are traded on over-the-counter markets.

Figure 13.4
Sample newspaper account of bond transactions

Bonds	Cur. Yld.	Sales 1000s	High	Low	Close	Net Chg.
Ancp 13⅞02f	cv	12	105	105	105	− ¼
Andarko 6¼14	cv	76	95	94	95	+ ½
Anheu 8s96	7.9	8	101½	101½	101½	−1½
Anheu 8⅝16	8.6	35	100½	100	100	
ARch 10½95	10.2	55	103¼	103	103	− ¼
ARch 7.7s00	7.7	10	99¾	99¾	99¾	− ⅛
ARch 9¼93	9.0	15	103⅛	103⅛	103⅛	− ⅛
ARch 9½96	9.2	35	102⅞	102	102⅞	− ⅛
ARch 9⅞16	8.9	4	111¼	111¼	111¼	+ ⅛
Arml 13½94	12.9	20	105	105	105	
Arml 9.2s00	10.6	10	87	87	87	−3
ATT 5⅛01	6.2	82	83¼	83	83¼	
ATT 5½97	5.9	40	94	93⅞	94	− ½
ATT 5⅝95	5.7	33	98¾	98	98¾	+ ½
ATT 6s00	6.7	265	89⅞	89½	89½	− ½
ATT 7s01	7.3	340	95⅝	95⅛	95½	− ½
ATT 7⅛s03	7.5	291	94⅞	94½	94¾	+ ¼
ATT 8⅛22		376	96⅝	96¼	96½	
ATT 8⅝26	8.6	331	100⅛	99⅞	99⅞	
ATT 8⅝31	8.6	460	100⅛	99¾	99¾	

Bonds	Cur. Yld.	Sales 1000s	High	Low	Close	Net Chg.
Chiquta 10¼05	10.4	23	100	99	99	+ ⅛
Chiquta 10½04	10.6	108	99¾	99½	99½	
Chiquta 11⅞03	11.3	245	105⅛	104¾	104¾	− ⅛
ChmNY 8½99	8.4	10	100½	100½	100½	+ ½
ChockFull 7s12	cv	26	85¾	84½	85¾	+1½
ChPotVa 8⅝09		15	101¾	101¾	101¾	+ ⅜
ChryF 13¼99	12.2	70	108⅜	108	108⅜	
ChryF 8⅛94	8.3	244	98⅛	98	98⅛	
ChryF 8⅜97	9.0	77	92⅞	92⅝	92⅝	− ⅛
ChryF 9.30s94	4.7	415	99⅜	99⅜	99⅜	
Chrysl 10.40s99	10.6	429	98	97⅝	98	+ ⅛
Chrysl 10.95s17	11.8	242	93¼	93	93⅛	− ⅛
Chrysl 12s15	12.2	1667	99	98⅛	98½	+ ¼
Chrysl 13s97	12.4	230	104⅝	104⅜	104½	− ¼
Chrysl 8s98	8.8	82	91¼	91	91¼	+ ¾
Chrysl 8⅞95	8.9	15	100	100	100	+ ¾
Chrysl 9.60s94	9.6	425	100⅜	100	100¼	
CIGNA 8.20s10	cv	65	103	102¼	103	+1
viCircK 12¾97		10	16	16	16	−1¾
viCircK 13s97f		12	4¼	4¼	4¼	− ⅛

Bonds	Cur. Yld.	Sales 1000s	High	Low	Close	Net Chg.
DanaCp dc5⅞06	cv	97	88½	88	88	− ½
DataGen 8⅜02	10.1	97	83¾	83	83	+1
Datpnt 8⅞06	cv	55	58	56	58	+ ½
DaytPL 8⅛01	8.1	10	100	100	100	−1½
DetEd 7⅜01	7.7	30	95½	95⅜	95½	+1⅛
DetEd 8.15s00	8.1	8	100⅛	100⅛	100⅛	− ⅛
DetEd 8⅛01	8.2	7	99½	99½	99½	− ¾
Disney zr05		592	49½	49	49⅛	− ⅜
DowCh 7⅞07	8.2	15	96½	96½	96½	− ¾
DowCh 8.90s00	8.6	8	103⅞	103½	103⅞	+1⅞
DowCh 8½06	8.4	5	100⅞	100⅞	100⅞	− ½
DukePw 7¾03	7.8	15	99¾	99¾	99¾	+ ⅛
DukePw 8⅛03	8.0	17	101¼	100¾	101¼	+1¼
DukePw 8⅛07	8.0	25	101	101	101	+ ⅜
DukePw 8⅜06	8.2	25	102	102	102	+1¼
duPont 8.45s04	8.3	44	102¼	102	102¼	
duPont 8½06	8.4	203	101¾	101½	101½	− ½
duPont 8½16	8.4	15	100⅞	100¾	100⅞	+ ⅛
duPont dc6s01		22	87⅞	87¼	87⅞	+ ⅝
DuqsnLt 8⅜07	8.4	40	100⅛	100⅛	100⅛	+ ⅛

C. Buying and Selling Costs

As indicated in part A, the market price of a bond is expressed as a percent of its face value, which is customarily \$1,000. A price of 95 means that the current market price is 95% of \$1,000, or \$950. Similarly, a price of 103 means that the current market price is 103% of \$1,000, or \$1,030. The difference between the market price and the face value is known as a **discount** when the market price is less than the face value, and a **premium** when the market price is greater than the face value.

Why should the market price of a bond be other than the face value? There are two reasons: financial risk and interest rates. A decline in confidence in a company such as the lowering of the bond rating means an increase in risk, and only potentially greater rewards will entice investors to accept the risk. Since the interest rate of a bond is fixed, a larger reward is accomplished by lowering the selling price.

Prevailing interest rates also play a major role in the market price of a bond. Again, since the interest rate of a bond is fixed, bonds can be marketed competitively only by adjusting the selling price. To illustrate, if a \$1,000 bond with an interest rate of 6% is sold for \$612.25, then the actual return on the investment is $\frac{\$60.00}{\$612.25} = 0.098 = 9.8\%$. Thus, the bond interest plus the difference between the face value and the selling price is equivalent to investing at a simple interest rate of 9.8%. In general, as prevailing interest rates increase, bond prices decrease; as prevailing interest rates decrease, bond prices increase.

Another factor in the cost of bonds is accrued interest. Because interest is paid only to the owner of a bond, the purchaser pays the seller for all accrued interest since the last interest payment. The interest is calculated using the simple interest formula $I = Prt$, using the financial calendar of a 30 day month and a 360 day year. Most bond interest is paid semiannually.

Both buyer and seller pay a broker's commission, which also adds to the cost of a bond. A typical commission is \$10 per bond or \$25, whichever is greater. Finally, the seller of a bond is subject to an SEC fee of \$0.01 per \$500 quotation or fraction thereof.

The costs of buying and selling bonds can be summarized as follows:

Purchase price = Market price + Accrued interest + Commission
Selling price = Market price + Accrued interest − Commission − SEC fee.

In the examples and problems of this section, the face value of the bonds is $1,000.

9%

EXAMPLE 1   Find the cost of buying five Con Oil 9s02 bonds quoted at $89\frac{1}{2}$ if the date of the sale is March 1 and interest is paid on January 1 and July 1.

Solution: A quote of $89\frac{1}{2}$ means the market price per bond is $1,000 × 0.895 = $895 per bond. January 1 to March 1 is 60 days, thus $t = \frac{60}{360} = \frac{1}{6}$. Using the simple interest formula the accrued interest per bond is $1,000 × 0.09 × $\frac{1}{6}$ = $15. In summary,

$4,475   Market price ($895 × 5)
+   75   Accrued interest ($15 × 5)
+   50   Commission ($10 × 5)
$4,600   Total cost   ■

EXAMPLE 2   Alice Blake bought ten Evco $11\frac{1}{2}$ s96 bonds quoted at $114\frac{1}{4}$. If the date of the sale was October 1 and interest is paid on January 1 and July 1, what did Alice pay for the bonds?

Solution: A quote of $114\frac{1}{4}$ means the market price per bond is $1,000 × 1.1425 = $1,142.50 per bond. July 1 to October 1 is 90 days, thus $t = \frac{90}{360} = \frac{1}{4}$. Using the simple interest formula the accrued interest per bond is $1,000 × 0.115 × $\frac{1}{4}$ = $28.75. In summary,

$11,425.00   Market price ($1,142.50 × 10)
+   287.50   Accrued interest ($28.75 × 10)
+   100.00   Commission ($10 × 10)
$11,812.50   Total cost   ■

EXAMPLE 3   Richard Whitlock sold two BiCon $8\frac{1}{4}$ s98 bonds on November 25. The bonds were quoted at $99\frac{1}{8}$ and paid interest semiannually on March 1 and September 1. How much did Richard net from the sale?

Solution: A quote of $99\frac{1}{8}$ means the market price per bond is $1,000 × 0.99125 = $991.25 per bond. The time from the last interest payment is two months and 24 days or 84 days.* Using the simple interest formula the accrued interest per bond is $1,000 × 0.0825 × $\frac{84}{360}$ = $19.25. In summary,

$1,982.50   Market price ($991.25 × 2)
+   38.50   Accrued interest ($19.25 × 2)
−   25.00   Commission minimum
−   0.04   SEC fee ($1,982.50 ÷ 500 = 3.965; 4 × $0.01 = $0.04)
$1,995.96   Net to Richard   ■

*The settlement date *is the date that the buyer makes payment and acquires title to the bond. Thus, the interest paid is:*

September 1 to November 1 = 2 months = 60 days
November 1 to November 25 = 24 days
Interest period = 84 days

[handwritten top margin: Cost 882.50×2 = 1765 = ⅙ = 90/360 = 0.25/1000×0.09×0.25=20, Int 22.50×2 = 45 = 25/1835, Con comm 183]

EXERCISES FOR SECTION 13.4

[handwritten: Hint 9s 06–2ch ×4 90½ = 90.50, 90.50, 88.25 ×10 / 882.50]

In problems 1–8, find the cost of buying the given bonds. (The face value of the bonds is $1,000.)

1. Ten WyCo 7s99 bonds quoted at $82\frac{1}{2}$; date of sale, April 1; interest paid on January 1 and July 1

2. Two Chry 9s06 bonds quoted at $88\frac{1}{4}$; date of sale, October 1; interest paid on January 1 and July 1

3. Eight Grmn $8\frac{1}{4}$ s02 bonds quoted at $92\frac{1}{8}$; date of sale, July 1; interest paid on April 1 and October 1

4. Fifteen GMe $7\frac{5}{8}$ s14 bonds quoted at $91\frac{1}{2}$; date of sale, July 14; interest paid on January 1 and July 1 *[handwritten: – 13days]*

[handwritten: 1000 × 0.67625 + 13/360 = 275; 915 × 15 = 13725 — cost; 2.75 × 15 = 41.25 Int; 10 × 15 = 150 Comn → #13916.25]

5. Nine SCN $6\frac{7}{8}$ s08 bonds quoted at $88\frac{1}{2}$; date of sale, April 22; interest paid on February 1 and August 1

6. Four Medco $7\frac{5}{8}$ s03 bonds quoted at $94\frac{1}{2}$; date of sale, August 28; interest paid on April 1 and October 1

7. Eight MePw $10\frac{1}{2}$ s11 bonds quoted at 103; date of sale, April 1; interest paid on January 1 and July 1

8. Twelve TMA $11\frac{1}{4}$ s98 bonds quoted at $105\frac{3}{4}$; date of sale, May 18; interest paid on February 1 and August 1

In problems 9–16, find the net proceeds from the sale of the given bonds. (The face value of the bonds is $1,000.)

9. Three SPac $7\frac{1}{2}$ s04 bonds quoted at 98; date of sale, May 1; interest paid on January 1 and July 1

10. Five Arpw $5\frac{1}{4}$ s04 bonds quoted at $71\frac{1}{8}$; date of sale, December 1; interest paid on January 1 and July 1

11. Six SunP $6\frac{7}{8}$ s02 bonds quoted at $82\frac{1}{8}$; date of sale, February 16; interest paid on February 1 and August 1

12. Nine FnCo $9\frac{1}{4}$ s05 bonds quoted at $95\frac{1}{2}$; date of sale, May 27; interest paid on May 1 and November 1

13. Fifteen OCC $8\frac{7}{8}$ s03 bonds quoted at $98\frac{1}{4}$; date of sale, June 18; interest paid on March 1 and September 1

14. Twelve BnkC $7\frac{5}{8}$ s07 bonds quoted at $84\frac{1}{4}$; date of sale, May 19; interest paid on February 1 and August 1

15. Fifteen MaCr $12\frac{1}{4}$ s14 bonds quoted at $108\frac{5}{8}$; date of sale, June 12; interest paid on March 1 and September 1

16. Ten NoGa $11\frac{3}{8}$ s09 bonds quoted at $112\frac{1}{2}$; date of sale, February 12; interest paid on February 1 and August 1

Solve.

17. David Truitt sold four A&O $7\frac{1}{8}$ s06 bonds, each with face value of $1,000, on April 14. The bonds were quoted at $82\frac{3}{4}$ and paid semiannual interest on February 1 and August 1. That same day, he used part of the proceeds to purchase three PaC $8\frac{7}{8}$ s04 bonds, each with face value of $1,000 and quoted at $92\frac{1}{8}$. If the PaC bonds paid interest on January 1 and July 1, how much did David have left of the proceeds from the sale of the A&O bonds?

[handwritten: #12, 955 × 9 = 8595, 26 days, 6.68 × 9 = 60.12, 10.9 × 9 = 90.00, − 0.18, 8564.94]

18. Janis Boyd sold five StO $8\frac{1}{4}$ s07 bonds, each with face value of $1,000, on March 23. The bonds were quoted at $87\frac{1}{8}$ and paid semiannual interest on January 1 and July 1. That same day, she decided to use the proceeds to purchase some MCM $9\frac{1}{8}$ s99 bonds, each with face value of $1,000 and quoted at $98\frac{1}{2}$. If the MCM bonds paid interest on March 1 and September 1, how many MCM bonds was she able to buy? How much did she have left of the proceeds from the sale of the StO bonds?

[handwritten: Feb 1 to May 1 = 90 days – MCM, may 1 – 19 = 18 days/108, 1000 × 07625 × 108/360 = 22.88, 842.5 × 12 = 10110, 22.88 × 12 = 274.56, 10 × 12 = −120.00, SES = .21, 10264.35]

Section 13.5   *Valuation Indices: Bonds*

Aside from the yield stated on the bond itself, which is the **nominal yield** (annual interest rate), there are two other valuation indices commonly used by bond investors: current yield and yield to maturity.

A. Current Yield

The current yield is that percent found by dividing the annual interest by the current market price:

> **(13–4)**   Current yield = $\dfrac{\text{Annual interest}}{\text{Current market price}}$

As indicated in section 13.4, the current yield is the simple interest rate at which one could invest the market price of the bond and earn the same amount of interest as that generated by the bond. The current yield is the yield quoted in the financial section of a newspaper.

EXAMPLE 1   Verify the yield for the DataGen $8\frac{3}{8}$ 02 in figure 13.4. (The face value of the bond is $1,000.)

Solution: Since $8\frac{3}{8}$ = 8.375%, the annual interest is $1,000 × 0.08375 = $83.75. From figure 13.4, the closing price was $1,000 × 0.83 = $830.00. Thus,

$$\text{Current yield} = \frac{\$83.75}{\$830.00}$$
$$= 0.10090$$
$$= 0.101$$
$$= 10.1\%$$

B. Yield to Maturity

The most common measure of bond yields is the yield to maturity, a percent found by dividing the combined annual gain by the average investment. Yields to maturity are normally published in specially prepared bond tables but may be approximated by the following formula:

> **(13–5)**   Yield to maturity = $\dfrac{\text{Annual interest} + \text{Average capital gain}}{500 + 1/2 \text{ Market price}}$

where the average capital gain (or loss) is the difference between the face value and the market price divided by the remaining term of the bond.*

---

*If there is an average capital loss rather than an average capital gain, then the formula is

$$\text{Yield to maturity} = \frac{\text{Annual interest} - \text{Average capital gain}}{500 + 1/2 \text{ Market price}}$$

E X A M P L E 2   Find the yield to maturity on a $1,000 bond quoted at 80 if the interest rate is 7% and the remaining term of the bond is 20 years.

Solution: Annual interest $= \$1,000 \times 0.07 = \$70$

$$\text{Average capital gain} = \frac{\$1,000 - \$800}{20} = \$10$$

$$500 + \frac{1}{2} \text{ market price} = \$500 + \$400 = \$900$$

$$\begin{aligned}\text{Yield to maturity} &= \frac{\$70 + \$10}{\$900} \\ &= 0.0888888 \\ &= 8.9\%\end{aligned}$$

■

EXERCISES FOR SECTION 13.5

In problems 1–8, compute the current yield for the given bonds with face value of $1,000. (Round answers to the nearest tenth of a percent.)

1. GaPw $8\frac{1}{4}$ s92 quoted at 93

2. UCar $7\frac{1}{8}$ s04 quoted at 82

3. ConP $6\frac{1}{4}$ s94 quoted at $71\frac{1}{4}$

4. SMP $7\frac{1}{4}$ s99 quoted at $84\frac{3}{8}$

5. DayCo $8\frac{1}{4}$ s06 quoted at $97\frac{1}{2}$

6. MWCr $6\frac{1}{4}$ s02 quoted at $67\frac{3}{8}$

7. PAA $7\frac{1}{4}$ s95 quoted at $85\frac{1}{4}$

8. Bghs $8\frac{1}{4}$ 01 quoted at $89\frac{1}{8}$

In problems 9–17, find the yield to maturity for the given bonds with face value of $1,000. (Round answers to the nearest tenth of a percent.)

9. TwCF $7\frac{1}{4}$ s quoted at 83; remaining term, 10 years

10. TPL $8\frac{1}{4}$ s quoted at 91; remaining term, 20 years

11. PCC $9\frac{1}{4}$ s quoted at 94; remaining term, 15 years

12. WstnC $6\frac{1}{4}$ s quoted at $71\frac{1}{4}$; remaining term, 8 years

13. LTP $7\frac{1}{4}$ s quoted at $83\frac{1}{8}$; remaining term, 14 years

14. IntH $8\frac{1}{4}$ s quoted at $92\frac{5}{8}$; remaining term, 12 years

15. Frmt $6\frac{1}{4}$ s quoted at $68\frac{7}{8}$; remaining term, 6 years

16. John Boswell is considering purchasing DTT $7\frac{7}{8}$ s bonds, each with face value of $1,000 and quoted at $87\frac{5}{8}$. The remaining term of the bonds is 22 years. Compute the current yield and the yield to maturity.

17. Kathy Forbes is trying to decide whether to buy GPL $6\frac{1}{8}$ s bonds, each with face value of $1,000 and quoted at $71\frac{1}{8}$, or NLL $8\frac{1}{4}$ s bonds, each with face value of $1,000 and quoted at $87\frac{1}{8}$. If the remaining term of the GPL bonds is 12 years and the remaining term of the NLL bonds is eight years, which of the bonds has the greatest yield to maturity?

Section 13.6 *Mutual Funds*

A. Introduction

Brokerage houses and institutional investors such as insurance companies and pension funds employ scores of investment analysts. Armed with giant computers and expertise in economics, accounting, and finance, these professionals examine the many factors that can affect company performance such as product line, production efficiency, marketing personnel, finances, and management capabilities. Today, the individual investor can utilize the same sophisticated research techniques as the institutional investor through mutual funds.

A **mutual fund** is a professionally managed investment company that pools the money of many people and invests it in stocks, bonds, and other securities. This money is entrusted to a fund manager who determines which securities are to be traded and when. Since different investors have different investment objectives, there are different mutual funds, such as growth funds, stock funds, bond funds, money market funds, and income funds. A description of a mutual fund including its history, investment objectives, performance, and management is contained in a prospectus that the fund is required to publish, and is free to anyone who requests it.

B. Advantages and Disadvantages of Mutual Funds

Mutual funds offer several advantages to the investor. Among these are

a. *Reduction of risk.* The assets of a mutual fund are spread over many different securities. There are two risks in owning securities. Either the entire market can drop in value, or an individual security can drop in value. Since the latter is more likely than the former, this risk is minimized through diversity of investment.

b. *Liquidity.* Mutual funds are a very liquid form of investment. You can get your money out of a mutual fund by making a phone call, writing a check, or by having the money wired to your bank.

c. *Professional management.* Mutual fund managers are highly qualified portfolio managers with the same expertise and technology as the other institutional investors mentioned above.

d *Reduction of transaction costs.* Today, as much as 90% of the volume of trades on a securities market comes from life insurance companies, pension funds, and mutual funds. With millions of dollars at their disposal, the money managers of these organizations buy in bulk, and thus can negotiate commissions at a much lower rate than an individual investor.

e. *Convenience.* Investments in a mutual fund can be made by mail, by telephone, or in person. The income earned by the fund can be reinvested in the fund or paid by check. Mutual funds handle all the details of transactions, mail dividend checks promptly, and provide year-end summaries for income tax purposes.

There is one primary disadvantage to investing in mutual funds, particularly the popular no-load funds; they often perform poorly in a "bear" market, a time when the average price of stocks is declining. One reason for this is that mutual fund managers are required by law to state and then follow their investment policies, and it may not be possible to react to a down market without violating these investment promises.

C. Buying and Selling Costs

Mutual funds set a minimum amount required for investment, typically $1,000, but sometimes as little as $250, and in some instances as low as $50 if invested on a regular monthly basis. Like corporate stocks, the unit of purchase in a mutual fund is a share. The purchase price of a share is based on the **net asset value** (**NAV**) of a share and is equal to the current value of the total fund assets minus the fund liabilities and expenses all divided by the total number of outstanding shares. That is,

$$(13\text{–}6) \quad NAV = \frac{\text{Assets} - \text{Liabilities and Expenses}}{\text{No. of shares}}$$

EXAMPLE 1 The Excalibur fund had total assets of $148,500,000, total liabilities and expenses of $1,400,000, and 12,000,000 outstanding shares. Find the NAV.

Solution: Using formula 13–6,

$$NAV = \frac{\$148,500,000 - \$1,400,000}{12,000,000}$$
$$= \$12.258$$
$$= \$12.26$$

The most popular mutual funds come in two forms, load funds and no-load funds. A load is a sales charge or commission paid by the buyer to cover selling costs. Load funds are purchased from a stockbroker, insurance agent, or mutual fund salesperson. Load funds come in two forms.

1. *Front-end load.* These load funds charge a sales fee that is typically from 1% to 8.5% of the amount invested. Funds with a sales fee in the 1%–3% range are typically called *low front-end load* funds.

2. *Back-end load.* Sometimes called a redemption fee, exit fee, or deferred sales charge, this charge can amount from 4% to 6% of the amount withdrawn from the fund. Some back-end load funds impose the full fee if the shares are redeemed within the first year of ownership, reducing by 1% for each additional year owned.

EXAMPLE 2   Johnna invested $20,000 in a load fund with a 8.5% sales fee. Find: **a.** the amount of the fee, **b.** the net investment, and **c.** the percent earned by the salesperson on the net investment.

Solution: **a.** The amount of the fee is calculated using the basic percentage formula with

P = amount of fee, B = amount invested, and R = sales rate

$P = B \cdot R$

$P = \$20,000 \times 0.085$ *Load Fund*

$P = \$1,700$

b. The net investment is the amount invested minus the sales fee or
$\$20,000 - \$1,700 = \$18,300$

c. The commission percent is found using formula 2–3 with

$P = \$1,700, B = \$18,300, R = ?$

$R = \dfrac{P}{B}$

Commissions earned

$R = \dfrac{\$1,700}{\$18,300}$

$R = 0.0929$

$R = 9.3\%$

Thus, the mutual fund will invest $18,300 after paying a fee of $1,700 to the salesperson at a commission rate of 9.3%.   ■

As indicated in example 2, the *net investment* in a load fund differs from the *amount invested*. Suppose in example 2, Johnna desired her net investment to be $20,000. The amount invested is calculated using the formula

(13–7)   Amount invested $= \dfrac{\text{Net investment}}{1 - \text{Sales fee (in decimal form)}}$

In example 2, the calculation is:

$$\text{Amount invested} = \frac{\$20,000}{1 - 0.085}$$

$$= \frac{\$20,000}{0.915}$$

$$= \$21,858 \quad \text{(Rounded)}$$

Figure 13.5
Sample newspaper account of mutual fund prices

Util f	12.60	12.60—0.03	**Fidelity Selects**			Gatwyln	15.51 NL +0.02
ValAd †16.71	16.71—0.01		SIAir r 13.00	13.40—0.06		**Gen Elec Inv**	
WWin	8.90	8.90 +0.02	SIAGI r 12.36	12.74—0.09		ElfDiv u12.83	NL—0.01
WldW †15.01	15.01 +0.09		SIAut ru18.83	19.41—0.04		ElfGl u13.47	NL +0.03
SearT p11.81	11.81 +0.02		SIBio r 28.45	29.33—0.55		Elfnln 11.56	NL +0.01
Delaware Group			SIBrd r 16.09	16.59—0.04		ElfnTx 11.48	NL +0.02
Dectrl u17.10	18.69—0.02		SIBrk r 11.84	12.21—0.08		ElfnTr 33.30	NL—0.05
Dectll pu13.84	14.53—0.04		SIChe r 32.79	33.80—0.05		S&S Lg 11.71	NL +0.02
Delaw 18.26	19.58		SICmp r18.52	19.09 +0.09		S&S 38.25	NL—0.04
Delcp p21.97	23.07 +0.02		SICsh r 13.99	14.42 +0.02		GenSec 12.97	13.66
Deichll 6.78	7.12		SIDef r 14.32	14.76—0.04		**Gintel Group**	
Deichl 6.78	7.27		SelDevC r13.71	14.13		CaAp p 15.05	NL +0.04
Gvt Inc p8.86	9.50 +0.01		SIEUt r 12.81	13.21—0.04		Erisa p 32.71	NL +0.15
Invl 9.98	9.98		*SIElec r12.10*	*12.47 +0.02*		Gintel 77.57	NL +0.43
Inv II p 9.98	NL		SIEng r 14.81	15.27		**Goldman Sachs**	
Txlns 11.04	11.59		SIEnS r 9.73	10.03 +0.11		AdjGv 10.02	10.02
TxFU 11.78	12.37		SIEnv r 11.33	11.68—0.02		CapGr u14.49	15.33—0.02
TxFPa 8.13	8.54		SIFnS ru43.26	44.60 +0.07		SelEq 15.20	16.08
Trend 12.18	12.79—0.02		SIFd r 29.38	30.29—0.10		Glnc 14.23	14.67 +0.02
Value 16.35	17.17—0.01		SIHlth r 70.72	72.91—0.84		ST Gov 10.05	10.05
Dimensional Fds			SIInd ru17.15	17.68 +0.02		**Gradison Funds**	
Cont 13.61	NL +0.02		SIIndT r13.83	14.26—0.07		EstGr p18.45	NL—0.01
Govt 105.29	NL—0.13		SIIns r 18.33	18.90 +0.13		Gvln p 13.10	13.37—0.03
GlBd 100.79	NL—0.10		SILesr r32.14	33.13—0.06		OpGr p 16.55	NL—0.02
IntGv 108.42	NL—0.02		SIMAD r 19.70	20.31—0.12		Grnspg 13.51	NL +0.01
12.63	NL—0.02		SIPap r 15.15	15.62—0.06		GwWsh p 12.70	13.37
Japan 19.74	NL +0.47		SIMetl r10.31	10.63—0.11		**Guardian Funds**	
Fixd u103.29	NL		SIReg ru16.77	17.29—0.02		Bond 12.35	NL—0.02
US Sml 7.22	NL		SIRetl r 22.55	23.25—0.03		ParkA 23.28	24.38—0.03

Information on mutual fund costs are reported daily in the financial section of many newspapers. Figure 13.5 shows a sample of such a financial report. The meaning of the underlined entry is as follows:

Fidelity Selects   The fund's family name. Often, a group of mutual funds will be operated by a single management company or brokerage house.

SIElec   The name of fund, usually abbreviated.

r   Indicates the fund has a redemption fee or that a contingent deferred sales charge may apply. Other letters (symbols) that indicate fees are p and †. Fees are discussed later in this section.

12.10   The net asset value. This is the price per share you would receive if you sold a share, less any deferred sales charges.

12.47   The Offer Price. This is the purchase price per share, or the NAV + load. If NL (no load) appears in this column, the purchase price is the same as the NAV. If the NAV and the offer price are the same, it means the fund has no load, but it does have a contingent deferred sales charge.

+.02   The change in the NAV over the most recent one-day trading period.

The number of shares in a mutual fund that a given amount will purchase is given by the formula

(13–8)   No. of shares = $\dfrac{\text{Net Investment}}{\text{NAV}}$

EXAMPLE 3   Julio invested $2,000 in a mutual fund with front-end load of 5% and an NAV of $12.44. Find to three decimal places the number of shares that he purchased.

Solution: The sales fee is $2,000 × 0.05 = $100. The net investment is $2,000 − $100 = $1,900. Using formula 13–8,

Front End Value

$$\text{No. of shares} = \frac{\text{Net Investment}}{\text{NAV}}$$
$$= \frac{\$1,900}{\$12.44}$$
$$= 152.733$$

   In contrast to load funds, *no-load funds* are purchased directly from the fund, thus there is no sales fee charge and the amount invested is the net investment.

EXAMPLE 4   Lu Ann invested $14,000 in a no-load mutual fund with an NAV of $8.85. Find to three decimal places the number of shares that she purchased.

Solution: Using formula 13–8,

$$\text{No. of shares} = \frac{\text{Net Investment}}{\text{NAV}}$$ — *How much shares worth*
$$= \frac{\$14,000}{\$8.85}$$
$$= 1,581.921$$

   The amount of money received in the sale of shares is also affected by any back-end load, as shown in the next example.

EXAMPLE 5   Mickey and Minnie each owned 100 shares in mutual funds, and after two years both had a NAV of $9.50. Mickey's fund had a back-end load of 6% if the shares were sold in the first year, declining by 1% for each additional year the shares were held. Minnie's fund had no back-end load. If they both sold their shares, what amount would **a.** Mickey receive, **b.** Minnie receive?

Solution: In each case the total value of the shares is $9.50 × 100 = $950.

a. Since Mickey owned the shares for two years, the back-end load is 5% of the total value or $950 × 0.05 = $47.50.

Thus, the amount Mickey receives is $950 − $47.50 = $902.50.

b. Minnie's fund has no back-end load, thus she receives the total value of the shares or $950.

D. Annual Expenses

In addition to loads, the costs of investing and administering a mutual fund are passed on to the share owner in the form of an annual assessment. In most funds, these assessments are lumped together and expressed at a percent of the fund's net assets, called the expense ratio. The average expense ratio is about 1% per year. A breakdown of these expenses can be found in the fund's prospectus under the title "Summary of Fund Expenses" or similar terminology.

The prudent investor will examine expense ratios carefully. While they may seem insignificant, they mount up because they are deducted from the fund's assets each year. For example, over a ten-year period a no-load fund with a 2% expense ratio will cost an investor more than an 8% load fund with a 1% expense ratio.

E. Distribution of Income

Mutual funds that own corporate stocks earn money in the form of dividends or capital gains (see section 13.1). If their portfolios also contain bonds, the funds receive interest (see section 13.4). After expenses are deducted, shareholders share in any profits. In fact, to be exempt from corporate income taxes, most mutual funds must: (1) distribute at least 90% of its taxable income to shareholders, (2) distribute 97% of its income from dividends and interest and 98% of its net capital gains with respect to the year in which they are received. Since this exempts the fund from income taxes, the shareholders must report the distributions on their own tax returns. In lieu of accepting the money, a shareholder may opt to reinvest the profits back into the fund.

EXERCISES FOR SECTION 13.6

In problems 1–10, calculate the net asset value for the given mutual fund.

Fund	Assets	Liabilities/ Expenses	No. Shares
1. ABM Mutual	$116,400,000	$1,097,000	10,000,000
2. CHN Funds	187,510,000	1,856,000	15,280,000
3. Concord Group	226,144,000	3,618,000	21,455,000
4. Providence	245,930,000	2,951,000	12,441,000
5. RCN	178,700,000	1,536,000	18,309,000
6. Sun Investors	112,755,000	1,083,000	10,960,000
7. TBK Select	288,994,000	4,335,000	17,047,000
8. Transcontinental	172,232,000	2,239,000	23,544,000
9. Washington	125,650,000	1,382,000	5,946,000
10. Zeus	126,944,000	1,777,000	9,088,000

*For the given load fund in problems 11–20, find: **a.** the amount of the fee, **b.** the net investment, **c.** the percent earned by the salesperson on the net investment, and **d.** how much would have to be invested for the net investment to equal the amount in the first column.*

Amount Invested	Load		Amount Invested	Load
11. $1,500	8.5%		**16.** $9,500	4.4%
12. $3,000	8%		**17.** $10,500	3.8%
13. $5,000	7.9%		**18.** $15,000	6.2%
14. $6,000	5%		**19.** $18,250	2.2%
15. $8,000	5.7%		**20.** $20,000	6.7%

In problems 21–30, find to three decimal places the number of shares purchased. (All loads are front-end.)

Amount Invested	NAV	Load		Amount Invested	NAV	Load
21. $4,000	$11.29	None		**26.** $18,000	10.20	8%
22. $6,500	10.45	None		**27.** $26,000	12.25	6.8%
23. $2,000	15.90	None		**28.** $88,000	14.37	5.5%
24. $8,600	13.09	None		**29.** $105,000	9.41	3.6%
25. $13,500	18.99	8.5%		**30.** $522,000	11.64	2.4%

Solve.

31. After two years of ownership, Sandra sold 100 shares of a mutual fund with an NAV of $8.80. The fund carries a back-end load of 6% if the shares are sold in the first year, declining 1% per year for each year thereafter. Find the amount that Sandra received.

32. Harold sold 400 shares of a mutual fund with an NAV of $27.81. He purchased the shares five years ago at a price of $19.40 per share. The fund carries a back-end load of 6% if the shares are sold in the first year, declining 1% per year for each year thereafter. How much profit did Harold make on the 400 shares?

33. Virginia sold 200 shares of the Orion Fund with an NAV of $11.17 and used the money to purchase shares in the Jackson Gold fund with an NAV of $10.73. Orion is a no-load fund but Jackson Gold has a front-end load of 8%. How many shares of Jackson Gold did Virginia receive?

34. Roy Eustace invested $4,000 in the Newberger Fund with an offer price of $7.22. When the NAV reached $8.10, he sold all of the shares. How much money did he receive?

35. Lily Massari sold 500 shares of MGS with an NAV of $14.22 and invested the money in the Regency Group with an NAV of $16.27. She sold the Regency shares when the NAV reached $16.90. If both funds were no-load, how much money did she receive?

36. The Primus Pension Fund purchased 125,000 shares of Englehart Metals that had an NAV of $10.85. Two years later, Primus sold the shares when the NAV dropped to $10.60. The fund carried a back-end load of 1%, when the shares were sold. How much did Primus lose on this fund?

Glossary

Bearer bond   A bond that is issued payable to the bearer. Transfer of ownership is effected by the simple act of delivery.

Bond   A written agreement to repay a specified amount of money on a certain date and to pay a specified annual rate of interest during the term of the bond.

Capital gain   The selling price of stock minus the purchase price, provided that the selling price is higher.

Common stock   Partial ownership of a company without guaranteed dividends; represented by transferable certificates.

Current yield   An indicator for evaluating bonds; the percent found by dividing the annual interest by the current market price.

Debenture   A bond that is backed only by the general credit of the company.

Discount   When a bond is sold at a price less than its face value.

Dividend   See *stock dividend*.

Earnings per share   An indicator for evaluating common stock; found by dividing the earnings that are available for common stockholders by the number of outstanding shares of common stock.

Mortgage bond   A bond that pledges the physical property of the company as security.

Mutual fund   A professionally managed investment company that pools the money of many people and invests it in stocks, bonds, and other securities.

Net asset value   The purchase price of a share found by subtracting liabilities and expenses from assets and dividing the result by the number of shares.

Nominal yield   The annual interest rate stated on a bond.

Odd lot   A number of shares of stock that is not a round lot.

Odd-lot differential   An extra commission of $12\frac{1}{2}$¢ per share charged on the purchase or sale of odd-lot orders of stock.

Par value   The face amount of a bond, or the amount printed on a stock certificate. When a corporation first issues stock, it is the usual selling price of one share.

Preferred stock   Stock with a guaranteed dividend per share that is paid before any dividends are paid to common stockholders.

Premium   When a bond is sold at a price greater than its face value.

Price-earnings ratio   An indicator for evaluating common stock; the current market price of a share of stock divided by the earnings per share.

Registered bond   A bond that is issued to a specifically named owner. Registered bonds must be reissued by a transfer office when acquired by new owners.

Round lot   Usually, 100 shares of stock or a multiple thereof; for low-volume stocks, a round lot may be any multiple of 10 shares.

Securities and Exchange Commission (SEC)   A federal regulatory agency created in 1934 to help protect investors.

Share   The unit of issue of stock.

Stock certificate   An engraved or lithographed document that serves as evidence of stock ownership.

Stock dividend   A portion of the profits of a company distributed to stockholders on a per share basis.

Yield   An indicator for evaluating common stock; the percent found by dividing the annual dividend by the current market price.

Yield to maturity   An indicator for evaluating bonds; the percent found by dividing the total annual gain by the average investment.

|||||||||||||||||||||||||||||||||||||||||||||||||||||||||||||||||| Review Test ||||||||||||||||||||||||||||||||||||||||||||||||||||||||||

1. An individual bought 50 shares of a stock at $23\frac{1}{8}$ and later sold them at $30\frac{1}{4}$. The difference in money that the individual received is called _____ .

2. In the event of liquidation, owners of _____ stock have a claim to assets prior to owners of _____ stock.

3. The most frequently used indicator of the relationship between stock prices and earnings is the _____ .

4. A _____ is an example of a secured bond, while a _____ is an example of an unsecured bond.

5. Two reasons for the market price of a bond to differ from the face value are _____ and _____ .

6. One hundred shares of a stock or a multiple thereof is called a _____ .

7. A bond offering the ultimate safety in principal and income to an investor would be rated _____ by an investor service.

8. Mastercraft Industries is distributing 80% of its net profits of $640,000 to its stockholders. If there are 800,000 outstanding shares of common stock, what is the dividend per share?

9. The board of directors of the Amron Company voted $420,000.00 in dividends for the first quarter. The company has issued 80,000 shares of preferred stock that pays a quarterly dividend of $1.20 per share, and there are 720,000 shares of common stock outstanding. Determine the dividend per share of common stock.

10. Gail Barrett purchased 200 shares of stock at $14\frac{3}{8}$ and later sold them at $33\frac{5}{8}$. What was her capital gain?

11. Phil Krueger purchased 60 shares of stock at $27\frac{1}{8}$. If the broker's commission was 2.4% of the trading price, what was the total cost of the stock, including the broker's commission and the odd-lot differential?

12. Last year, Millfield Industries had a net profit of $6,400,000, from which preferred stock dividends were $840,000. If there are 2,400,000 outstanding shares of common stock, what were the earnings per share of common stock?

13. A stock currently sells for $42\frac{1}{2}$ and pays an annual dividend of $2.20. Find the yield. (Round to the nearest tenth of a percent.)

14. Find the current yield on ACC $9\frac{1}{4}$ s02 bonds, each with face value of $1,000 and quoted at 89. (Round to the nearest tenth of a percent.)

15. On October 1, Arnold Snell sold six KMrt $8\frac{1}{2}$ s98 bonds, each with face value of $1,000 and quoted at $84\frac{1}{4}$. If interest is paid on January 1 and July 1, find the net amount Arnold received from the sale of the bonds.

16. Connie and Phil invested $32,000 in a mutual fund with an 8% sales fee. Find: **a.** the amount of the fee, **b.** the net investment, **c.** the percent earned by the salesperson, and **d.** the number of shares purchased if the NAV was $14.10, to three decimal places.

14

Topics in Accounting

Section 14.1   *Financial Statements*

A. Introduction

A requisite of efficient business operation is accurate data. The collection, summarization, and communication of accurate information are essential to sound planning. The kinds of information needed by management and analysts are records

Figure 14.1
Income statement—
Meyer Company

Meyer Company Income Statement for the Year Ended December 31, 19__	
Revenue	
Sales	$ 960,000
Gain from Sale of Land	46,000
Interest and Other	72,000
	$1,078,000
Expenses	
Cost of Merchandise Sold	$ 450,000
Operating Expenses	320,000
Interest Expenses	96,000
Federal and State Taxes	120,000
	$ 986,000
Net Income	$ 92,000

of past activities, data concerning current operating efficiency, and projections for future activities. These three items summarize the role of accounting in business. Accounting techniques are the most widely used means of describing and communicating business operations. This chapter examines some of the basic accounting procedures central to all businesses.

B. The Income Statement

Periodically, a company must appraise its progress. Managers and owners need to check the financial health of the enterprise and note its economic activity. Two documents summarize this information: the income statement and the balance sheet.

The **income statement** is a report on the company income for a period of time, generally a month or a year. The income statement describes the general manner in which the income of the business is earned. There are two basic forms of the statement, the single-step and the multiple-step. The single-step income statement is illustrated in figure 14.1. The basic format of this statement is the fundamental business equation

(14–1)   Revenue − Expenses = Income

where revenue is sales and gains, expenses are costs incurred to generate income, and income is net earnings. The single-step income statement has been adopted by many companies because of its simplicity and readability. The multiple-step income statement is illustrated in figure 14.2. The basic format of this statement is the equation

Figure 14.2
Income statement—
Craft Industries

Craft Industries Income Statement For the Year Ended November 30, 19__		
Sales		$9,250,000
Less Cost of Goods Sold		5,475,000
Gross Margin		$3,775,000
Less Operating Expenses		
Salaries and Commissions	$ 800,000	
Advertising	1,250,000	
Depreciation	225,000	
Income Taxes	650,000	
Other Expenses	230,000	$3,155,000
Income		$ 620,000

(14–2)   Gross margin − Expenses = Income

where gross margin is the difference between net sales and the cost of goods sold. Companies who favor the multiple-step income statement compare the gross margin with that of previous years and with national industry averages to evaluate operating results.

Income statements are used in an analysis of company operations. To management, the income statement is a report on the success or failure of the firm's activities; to owners, it is a measure of the efficiency of management.

C. The Balance Sheet

The **balance sheet** presents the financial condition of a firm at a given moment of time. It is developed from past activities of the company and involves the classification and valuation of the firm's resources.

The balance sheet is a representation of the basic accounting equation

(14–3)   Assets = Liabilities + Owners' equity

Defined in a broad sense, the term **assets** refers to the dollar value of everything the company owns, the term **liabilities** means the dollar value of everything the company owes, and the difference between the two is **owners' equity.*** The term **equities** is used for the sum of liabilities plus owners' equity and represents the claims upon the assets if the business is dissolved.

Traditionally, assets are reported on the left-hand side of the balance sheet and equities on the right-hand side (account form). Alternatively, assets may be at the top of the report and equities at the bottom (report form). In either event, since assets and equities are just two dimensions of the same investment, it follows that the two sides balance—hence, the name balance sheet.

*Assets can also be thought of as the location of investment, and liabilities can be thought of as the source of the funds.

Figure 14.3
Balance sheet—
Vargas Company

THE VARGAS COMPANY

Balance Sheet

December 31, 19___

Assets		Equities	
Current Assets		Current Liabilities	
Cash	$ 4,500	Due to Bank	$ 3,000
Accounts Receivable	6,000	Notes Payable	4,500
Merchandise Inventory	4,700	Total Current Liabilities	$ 7,500
Prepayments	1,300		
Total Current Assets	$16,500	Long-Term Liabilities	
		Mortgage	$20,000
Plant and Equipment		Total Liabilities	$27,500
Equipment	$ 5,000		
Building	22,000	Owners' Equity	
Land	3,000	M. Vargas, Owner	$19,000
Total	$30,000		
Total Assets	$46,500	Total Equities	$46,500

The two forms of balance sheets are illustrated in figures 14.3 and 14.4. On a balance sheet, the general headings of assets and liabilities are subdivided according to short-term and long-term categories. Current assets and current liabilities are short-term transactions; noncurrent assets and long-term liabilities are long-term transactions. Traditionally, short-term categories consist of items that could be converted to cash or disposed of within a period of one year.

D. Vertical and Horizontal Analysis

As public statements, the income statement and the balance sheet describe the economic activities of a company. Properly analyzed, these two statements disclose a company's earning capability and its financial strength. In the short run, a company must have sufficient funds for current needs. In the long run, a company must have sufficient earning and borrowing capacity to provide for continued growth and productivity.

The measure of a company's financial health requires an assessment that is both qualitative and quantitative. Qualitative evaluation is subjective and requires good intuition coupled with sound judgment. Quantitative analysis uses the mathematics of percents and ratios. Thus, financial analysis is both an art and a science.

Figure 14.4
Balance sheet—
Brown Corporation

The Brown Corporation
Statement of Financial Condition
At December 31, 19__

Assets

Current Assets	
Cash	$ 16,288,000
Marketable Securities (at Cost)	60,883,000
Receivables	90,061,000
Inventory	109,758,000
	$276,990,000

Fixed Assets	
Investments in Foreign Branches	$ 50,310,000
Property, Plant, and Equipment	$130,964,000
	$181,274,000

Total Assets	$458,264,000

Liabilities and Stockholders' Equity

Current Liabilities	
Payables and Accruals	$ 38,285,000
Accrued Taxes	26,270,000
Current Installments on Long-Term Debt	1,229,000
Dividends Payable	2,882,000
Customers' Deposits	2,005,000
Customers' Service Prepayments	22,917,000
	93,588,000

Long-Term Debt	123,187,000
Total Liabilities	$216,775,000

Stockholders' Equity	
Common Stock, 8,607,000 shares, $5 par value	$154,187,000
Earnings Retained for Use in the Business	87,302,000
Total Stockholders' Equity	$241,489,000
Total Liabilities and Stockholders' Equity	$458,264,000

The two basic forms of quantitative analysis are vertical analysis and horizontal analysis. **Vertical analysis** expresses in percent form component parts in relation to a whole. The computations in vertical analysis are an application of the basic percentage equation solved for R.

$$R = \frac{P}{B}$$

On an income statement, the base B typically is the value of net sales. This relates all other entries in the statement to sales, as percents.

Figure 14.5
Income statement—
Turner Company

The Turner Company		
Income Statement		
For the Year Ended December 31, 19__		

	Amount	Percent
Net Sales	$375,000	100.0
Less:		
Cost of Sales	$335,000	89.3
Depreciation	6,000	1.6
Maintenance and Repairs	4,200	1.1
Taxes (Other than Federal Income)	6,500	1.7
Total Cost and Operating Expenses	$351,700	93.8
Operating Income	23,300	6.3
Interest Expense	2,500	0.7
Federal Income Taxes	9,900	2.6
Net Income	$ 10,900	2.9

The example of vertical analysis in figure 14.5 answers the question, "Where did the sales dollar go?" In this instance, 89.3% of each dollar (89.3¢) went for cost of goods, 1.6% for depreciation (1.6¢), and so on.

The second type of financial analysis, **horizontal analysis,** compares dollar amounts for different periods shown on the same line of a comparative statement.* Figure 14.6 illustrates horizontal analysis. The earlier year is the base for computing percent increase or decrease.

Horizontal analysis is applicable to income statements as well as to balance sheets. The primary advantage of horizontal analysis is in disclosing trends.

---

*A comparative statement is one that provides financial data for more than one reporting period.

Figure 14.6
Comparative balance
sheet—Troy
Manufacturing
Co., Inc.

Troy Manufacturing Co., Inc.

Comparative Balance Sheet

As of December 31, 1989, 1990

	1990	1989	Increase or (Decrease) Amount	Increase or (Decrease) Percent
Current Assets				
Cash	$ 250,000	$ 249,000	$ 1,000	0.4
Short-Term Investments	382,000	400,000	18,000	(4.5)
Accounts Receivable	237,000	175,000	62,000	35.4
Inventories	300,000	330,000	30,000	(9.1)
Unexpired Insurance	40,000	30,000	10,000	33.3
Total Current Assets	$1,209,000	$1,184,000	$25,000	2.1
Land, Buildings, and Equipment				
Land	$ 135,000	$ 130,000	$ 5,000	3.8
Buildings (Net)	370,000	340,000	30,000	8.8
Machinery and Equipment (Net)	180,000	186,000	6,000	(3.2)
Total	$ 685,000	$ 656,000	$29,000	4.4
Total Assets	$1,894,000	$1,840,000	$54,000	2.9
Liabilities				
Accounts Payable	$ 64,000	$ 70,000	$ 6,000	(8.6)
Bank Loans	100,000	85,000	15,000	17.6
Wages Payable	40,000	30,000	10,000	33.3
Federal Income Tax Payable	215,000	195,000	20,000	10.3
Bonds Payable	300,000	300,000	-0-	-0-
Total Liabilities	$ 719,000	$ 680,000	$39,000	5.7
Owners' Equity				
Common Stock	$ 850,000	$ 832,000	$18,000	2.2
Retained Earnings	325,000	328,000	3,000	0.9
Total Owners' Equity	$1,175,000	$1,160,000	$15,000	1.3
Total Liabilities and Owners' Equity	$1,894,000	$1,840,000	$54,000	2.9

EXERCISES FOR SECTION 14.1

1. Fill in the missing entries in the following income
   statement if the sales for the Topkin Company were
   $870,000 and the operating expenses were $122,000.

	The Topkin Company Income Statement for the Year Ended December 31, 19__	
Revenue		
Sales		_____
Rental Income		$ 73,500
Interest		17,400
	Total	_____
Expenses		
Cost of Merchandise Sold		$642,500
Operating Expenses		_____
Interest Expenses		7,200
Federal and State Taxes		97,000
	Total	_____
Net Income		_____

2. Fill in the missing entries in the following balance
   sheet for the Clinton Corporation if the current
   assets in cash are $10,200, assets in land are $7,300,
   and the long-term mortgage liability is $42,700.

	The Clinton Corporation Balance Sheet December 31, 19__		
Assets		**Equities**	
Current Assets		**Current Liabilities**	
Cash	_____	Due to Bank	$111,200
Accounts Receivable	$12,500	Notes Payable	18,800
Merchandise Inventory	72,300	Total Current	
Prepayments	3,200	Liabilities	_____
Total Current Assets	_____	**Long-Term Liabilities**	
Plant and Equipment		Mortgage	_____
Equipment	$58,000	Total Liabilities	_____
Buildings	97,000	**Owners' Equity**	
Land	_____	R. H. Clinton, Owner	_____
Total	_____		
Total Assets	_____	Total Equities	_____

3. Fill in the missing entries in the following income statement.

The Anderson Corporation Income Statement For the Year Ended December 31, 19__		
Sales		$1,500,000
Cost of Goods Sold		_____
Gross Margin		$ 600,000
Expenses		
Salaries		_____
Advertising		140,000
Administrative Expenses		94,000
Other Expenses		61,000
Total Expenses		510,000
Net Income		$ _____

4. Fill in the missing entries in the following balance sheet for the Elkhorn Company if the current accounts receivable are $218,400, fixed assets in plant and equipment are $430,000, and long-term debts total $257,000.

The Elkhorn Company Balance Sheet December 31, 19__	
Assets	
Current Assets	
Cash	$ 47,500
Marketable Securities	82,000
Accounts Receivable	_____
Inventories	249,000
Total Current Assets	_____
Land, Plant, and Equipment	
Land	$ 98,000
Plant and Equipment	_____
Total Fixed Assets	_____
Total Assets	_____
Equities	
Current Liabilities	
Payables	$748,200
Accrued Taxes	37,400
Long-Term Liabilities	
Long-term Debts	_____
Owners' Equity	
P. H. Elkhorn, Owner	$ 82,300
Total Equities	_____

5. Fill in the missing entries and complete the vertical analysis of the following income statement, using net sales as the base for computing percents (to the nearest tenth).

The Hamilton Company Income Statement Year Ended December 31, 19__			
		Amount	Percent
Net Sales		$450,000	_____
Less:			
Cost of Sales	$375,000		_____
Depreciation	9,700		_____
Maintenance	6,300		_____
Total Cost and Operating Expenses		_____	_____
Operating Income		_____	_____
Interest Expense		4,500	_____
Federal Taxes		7,200	_____
Net Income		_____	_____

6. Fill in the missing entries and complete the vertical analysis of the following income statement, using net sales as the base for computing percents (to the nearest tenth).

Gehrig Brothers Income Statement For the Year Ended June 30, 19__		
	Amount	Percent
Net Sales	$850,000	_____
Cost of Goods Sold	372,900	_____
Gross Margin	_____	_____
Expenses		
Selling Expense	155,800	_____
General and Administrative Expense	51,000	_____
Federal Income Tax	44,800	_____
State Income Tax	14,400	_____
Total Expenses	_____	
Income		

7. Complete the vertical analysis of the following
   income statement, using total income for computing
   percents (to the nearest tenth).

Houser Wholesalers Income Statement December 31, 19__	Amount	Percent
Revenue		
Sales	$730,000	_____
Rentals	60,000	_____
Interest	7,000	_____
Total Income	_____	_____
Expenses		
Cost of Merchandise	$540,000	_____
Operating Expenses	92,000	_____
Interest Expenses	6,000	_____
Taxes	46,000	_____
Total Expenses	_____	_____
Net Income	_____	_____

8. Complete the vertical analysis of the following
   balance sheet, using total assets for computing
   percents (to the nearest tenth).

William Mullins, Inc. Balance Sheet December 31, 19__		
Assets		
Current Assets	Amount	Percent
Cash	$105,000	_____
Accounts Receivable	140,000	_____
Inventory	350,000	_____
Total Current Assets	_____	_____
Land, Plant, and Equipment		
Land	$ 75,000	_____
Plant and Equipment	320,000	_____
Total Fixed Assets	_____	_____
Total Assets	_____	_____
Equities		
Current Liabilities		
Payables	$720,000	_____
Accrued Taxes	42,000	_____
Long-Term Liabilities		
Long-Term Debts	$150,000	_____
Owners' Equity		
W. E. Mullins, Owner	$ 78,000	_____
Total Equities	_____	_____

9. Complete the vertical analysis of the following
   balance sheet, using total assets for computing
   percents (to the nearest tenth).

Felicione & Sons Balance Sheet December 31, 19__		
Assets		
Current Assets	**Amount**	**Percent**
Cash	$ 61,000	_____
Accounts Receivable	184,000	_____
Inventory		_____
Total Current Assets	475,000	_____
Land and Equipment	345,000	_____
Total Assets	$_____	_____
Equities		
Current Liabilities		
Accounts Payable	$180,000	_____
Accrued Liabilities	26,000	_____
Long-Term Liabilities		
Bonds Payable, 12%	90,000	_____
Stockholders' Equity		
Common Stock	300,000	_____
Retained Earnings	224,000	_____
Total Equities	$_____	_____

10. Complete the vertical analysis of the following
    income statement (compute percents to the nearest
    tenth).

AAA Insulation Income Statement for Years Ending December 31, 1989 and 1990			Increase or (Decrease)	
	1990	1989	Amount	Percent
Net Sales	$77,000	$60,000	_____	_____
Cost of Goods Sold	34,000	26,500	_____	_____
Gross Margin	43,000	33,500	_____	_____
Operating Expenses				
Selling Expense	13,200	9,600	_____	_____
Administrative Expense	10,500	8,400	_____	_____
Depreciation Expense	2,750	3,000	_____	_____
Total Operating Expenses	26,450	21,000	_____	_____
Net Income	16,550	12,500	_____	_____

11. Complete the horizontal analysis of the following income statement (compute percents to the nearest tenth).

Oswald Enterprises Income Statement for Years Ending December 31, 1989 and 1990				
			Increase or (Decrease)	
	1990	**1989**	**Amount**	**Percent**
Net Sales	$450,000	$370,000	_____	_____
Less:				
Cost of Sales	310,000	240,000	_____	_____
Depreciation	8,000	6,200	_____	_____
Maintenance	5,200	4,800	_____	_____
Total Cost and Operating Expenses	323,200	251,000	_____	_____
Operating Income	126,800	119,000	_____	_____
Interest Expense	14,000	12,000	_____	_____
Federal Taxes	22,000	18,000	_____	_____
Net Income	90,800	89,000	_____	_____

12. Complete the horizontal analysis of the following balance sheet (compute percents to the nearest tenth).

J. W. Wall, Inc. Balance Sheet for Years Ending December 31, 1989 and 1990						
			Increase or (Decrease)		Percent of Total Assets	
	1990	**1989**	**Amount**	**Percent**	**1990**	**1989**
Assets						
Cash	$ 92,000	$ 74,000	_____	_____	___	___
Accounts Receivable	260,000	240,000	_____	_____	___	___
Inventory	374,000	370,000	_____	_____	___	___
Total Current Assets	_____	684,000	_____	_____	___	___
Fixed Assets	420,000	470,000	_____	_____	___	___
Total Assets	_____	_____	_____	_____	___	___
Equities						
Payables	$816,000	$810,000	_____	_____	___	___
Accrued Taxes	57,000	51,000	_____	_____	___	___
Total Current Liabilities	_____	861,000	_____	_____	___	___
Long-Term Liabilities	170,000	190,000	_____	_____	___	___
Total Liabilities	_____	1,051,000	_____	_____	___	___
Owners' Equity	103,000	103,000	_____	_____	___	___
Total Equities	_____	_____	_____	_____	___	___

13. Complete the horizontal analysis of the following balance sheet (compute percents to the nearest tenth).

Brooker Enterprises
Balance Sheet for Years Ending
December 31, 1989 and 1990

	1990	1989	Increase or (Decrease) Amount	Percent	Percent of Total Assets 1990	1989
Assets						
Cash	$ 3,220,000	$ 4,110,000	_____	_____	____	____
Marketable Securities	11,700,000	9,100,000	_____	_____	____	____
Accounts Receivable	8,756,000	8,386,000	_____	_____	____	____
Inventory	16,750,000	14,200,000	_____	_____	____	____
Total Current Assets	_____	_____	_____	_____	____	____
Plant and Equipment	110,000	70,000	_____	_____	____	____
Total Assets	_____	_____	_____	_____	____	____
Equities						
Payables	$15,700,000	$14,100,000	_____	_____	____	____
Accrued Taxes	2,700,000	2,200,000	_____	_____	____	____
Dividends Payable	4,100,000	3,476,000	_____	_____	____	____
Deposits	1,842,000	1,040,000	_____	_____	____	____
Total Current Liabilities	_____	_____	_____	_____	____	____
Long-Term Debt	6,214,000	5,470,000	_____	_____	____	____
Total Liabilities	_____	_____	_____	_____	____	____
Common Stock	$ 9,740,000	$ 8,840,000	_____	_____	____	____
Retained Earnings	240,000	740,000	_____	_____	____	____
Total Stockholders' Equity	_____	_____	_____	_____	____	____
Total Liabilities and Stockholders' Equity	_____	_____	_____	_____	____	____

Section 14.2 *Financial Ratios*

In financial analysis, numerous ratios have been developed to interpret a company's economic activities. A select group of these are examined.

Ratios Measuring Liquidity

1. Current ratio
2. Acid-test ratio

Ratios Measuring Profitability

3. Gross profit margin
4. Operating ratio

Ratios Measuring Long-Term Financial Condition

5. Stockholders' equity ratio
6. Debt-equity ratio

The income statement and balance sheet of Space-Tronics, Inc., figures 14.7 and 14.8, are used to discuss these basic ratios.

Figure 14.7
Income statement—
Space-Tronics, Inc.

Space-Tronics, Inc.

Income Statement

December 31, 19___

Sales	$250,000
Expenses	
Cost of Goods Sold	$150,000
Operating Expenses	75,000
Interest Charges	600
Common Stock Dividend	12,500
Total	$238,100
Net Income	$ 11,900

Figure 14.8
Balance sheet—Space-
Tronics, Inc.

Space-Tronics, Inc. Balance Sheet December 31, 19___			
Current Assets		**Current Liabilities**	
Cash	$ 12,200	Accounts Payable	$ 13,400
Accounts Receivable	21,900	Notes Payable	4,700
Inventory	18,300	Wages Payable	1,400
Prepaid Insurance	1,200	Income Tax Payable	2,400
Total Current Assets	$ 53,600	Total Current Liabilities	$ 21,900
Fixed Assets		**Long-Term Liabilities**	
Plant and Machinery	$ 97,000	Bonds Payable	$ 12,000
Land	12,400	**Stockholders' Equity**	
		Capital Stock	$120,000
		Retained Earnings	9,100
Total Assets	$163,000	Total Liabilities and Stockholders' Equity	$163,000

Liquidity is the ability of a company to convert assets into cash quickly without incurring a significant loss. The current ratio (also called the working capital ratio) offers a rough measure of whether a company can meet its liabilities in the near future as they come due. The **current ratio** is the ratio of current assets to current liabilities.

(14–4)   Current ratio $= \dfrac{\text{Current assets}}{\text{Current liabilities}}$

EXAMPLE 1   Find the current ratio for Space-Tronics, Inc.

Solution: Current ratio $= \dfrac{\$53,600}{\$21,900}$

$= 2.4$

The current ratio is 2.4 to 1.

The current ratio assumes that current assets could be used to pay current liabilities. Most creditors want more than just a 1:1 current ratio, and traditionally, a 2:1 current ratio is considered a minimum.

A variation of the current ratio is the acid-test ratio. The inference is that the real measure, or the "acid test," of liquidity is to eliminate inventories and prepaid expenses from current assets. Prepaid expenses is money already spent, and inventories, it is argued, require both sales and collection before cash can be obtained. Thus, the **acid-test ratio** is the ratio of cash and receivables to current liabilities.

$$\textbf{(14–5)} \quad \text{Acid-test ratio} = \frac{\text{Cash} + \text{Receivables}}{\text{Current liabilities}}$$

EXAMPLE 2   Find the acid-test ratio of Space-Tronics, Inc.

Solution: $\text{Acid-test ratio} = \dfrac{\$12,200 + \$21,900}{\$21,900}$

$$= 1.6$$

The acid-test ratio is 1.6 to 1.

An acid-test ratio of 1:1 is considered acceptable, but a more practical analysis involves comparing a company's acid-test ratio with the acid-test ratio of other companies in the specific trade or industry.

The difference between net sales and the cost of goods sold is called gross margin. Gross margin should be sufficient to cover all operating expenses, interest expense, and profit for the owners. The percent found by dividing gross margin by net sales is called the **gross profit margin,** and it shows the average spread between the cost of goods sold and the selling price.

$$\textbf{(14–6)} \quad \text{Gross profit margin} = \frac{\text{Net sales} - \text{Cost of goods sold}}{\text{Net sales}}$$

EXAMPLE 3   Find the gross profit margin of Space-Tronics, Inc.

Solution: $\text{Gross profit margin} = \dfrac{\$250,000 - \$150,000}{\$250,000}$

$$= 0.40$$
$$= 40\%$$

Diminishing earnings over a period of time may be explained by a corresponding decline in gross profit margin.

The **operating ratio** is the ratio of cost of goods sold plus operating expenses to net sales.

$$(14\text{--}7) \quad \text{Operating ratio} = \frac{\text{Cost of goods sold} + \text{Operating expenses}}{\text{Net sales}}$$

Expressed as a percent, the operating ratio reflects the amount of sales dollars used to defray the cost of goods and administrative expenses. The higher the operating ratio, the less income to meet interest payments, dividends, and other financial obligations.

EXAMPLE 4   Determine the operating ratio of Space-Tronics, Inc.

Solution: Operating ratio $= \dfrac{\$150,000 + \$75,000}{\$250,000}$

$= 0.90$

$= 90\%$

The ratio of owners' equity to total assets is called the **stockholders' equity ratio.**

$$(14\text{--}8) \quad \text{Stockholders' equity ratio} = \frac{\text{Owners' equity}}{\text{Total assets}}$$

Expressed as a percent, this ratio indicates the investment in assets that is financed by the owners or stockholders.

EXAMPLE 5   Find the stockholders' equity ratio of Space-Tronics, Inc.

Solution: Stockholders' equity ratio $= \dfrac{\$120,000 + \$9,100}{\$163,000}$

$= 0.7920245$

$= 79\%$

Creditors regard a high stockholders' equity ratio as favorable, since it indicates a large cushion of security.

Another safety indicator is the debt-equity ratio. The **debt-equity ratio** is the ratio of total debt to total ownership equity.

$$(14\text{--}9) \quad \text{Debt-equity ratio} = \frac{\text{Current liabilities} + \text{Long-term liabilities}}{\text{Owners' equity}}$$

EXAMPLE 6   Determine the debt-equity ratio of Space-Tronics, Inc.

Solution: Debt-equity ratio $= \dfrac{\$21,900 + \$12,000}{\$120,000 + \$9,100}$

$= 0.2625871$

$= 26\%$

A debt-equity ratio of 1:1 (100%) is considered acceptable for established manufacturing firms; for small firms, a 1:4 (25%) ratio may be the acceptable minimum.

EXERCISES FOR SECTION 14.2

Round current ratios and acid-test ratios to the nearest tenth. Round all other ratios to the nearest percent.

1. The Bilford Company lists current assets of $47,400 and current liabilities of $19,700. Find the current ratio.

2. In problem 1, if inventories and prepaid expenses total $24,300 of the company's current assets, find the acid-test ratio.

3. Find the current ratio and the acid-test ratio for the Sanderson Company which reported current liabilities of $21,400 and current assets of $58,800. Inventories and prepaid expenses of the current assets total $29,100.

4. The Concord Company reported net sales of $174,000. Find the gross profit margin if the cost of the goods sold was $92,000.

5. Tamtek reported net sales of $324,000, with operating expenses of $120,000. If the cost of the goods sold was $190,000, find the gross profit margin and the operating ratio.

6. The net sales of Taylor Enterprises was $520,000, with operating expenses of $260,000. The cost of goods sold was $245,000. Find the gross profit margin and the operating ratio.

7. The owners' equity of the Lewis Company is $91,000, and last year's total assets were $130,000. Find the stockholders' equity ratio.

8. Lerch Enterprises reported current liabilities of $34,000, long-term liabilities of $11,400, and total assets of $210,000. If the owners' equity in the company is $142,000, find the stockholders' equity ratio and the debt-equity ratio.

9. The owners' equity of the Thresher Company is $109,000, and last year's total assets were $183,000. The current liabilities are $31,500, and long-term liabilities are $9,700. Find the stockholders' equity ratio and the debt-equity ratio.

10. The common stock outstanding in the Scott Corporation totals $120,000. Last year, the company retained $14,000 in earnings and reported total assets of $273,000. The current liabilities were $42,300, and the long-term liabilities were $13,200. Find the stockholders' equity ratio and the debt-equity ratio.

For problems 11–15, refer to the following balance sheet and income statement of the Brewster Company.

**The Brewster Company
Balance Sheet
December 31, 19__**

Current Assets		Current Liabilities	
Cash	$18,500	Accounts Payable	$ 15,400
Accounts Receivable	34,000	Notes Payable	5,200
Inventory	28,000	Wages Payable	2,100
Prepaid Insurance	1,750	Income Tax Payable	2,450
Total Current Assets	_____	Total Current Liabilities	_____
Plant, Equipment, and Land		**Long-Term Liabilities**	
Plant and Equipment	$82,500	Bonds Payable	$ 18,400
Land	_____	**Stockholders' Equity**	
Total Assets	_____	Capital Stock	$136,000
		Retained Earnings	_____
		Total Liabilities and Stockholders' Equity	$184,450

**The Brewster Company
Income Statement
December 31, 19__**

Sales	$324,000
Expenses	
Cost of Goods Sold	$182,000
Operating Expenses	92,400
Interest Charges	_____
Common Stock Dividend	8,200
Total Expenses	$285,000
Net Income	_____

11. Fill in the missing entries in the balance sheet and the income statement for the Brewster Company.

12. Find the current ratio for the Brewster Company. What is the acid-test ratio?

13. Compute the gross profit margin and the operating ratio for the Brewster Company.

14. Find the stockholders' equity ratio for the Brewster Company.

15. What is the debt-equity ratio for the Brewster Company?

Section 14.3   *Cash Budgets*

Most people plan expenditures for food, clothing, and other needs on the basis of expected income. Along with these short-term plans, many individuals and families use income estimates to plan for long-term activities, such as college expenses, the purchase of a house, or travel upon retirement. This process of planning for the financial needs of the future is called budgeting. A budget, whether formal or informal, is a plan for utilization of anticipated resources.

The budget of a business serves much the same function as an individual or family budget. Like a personal or family budget, a business budget plans the expenditure of anticipated funds for immediate and long-term goals.

One budget common to both large and small businesses is called the cash budget. The **cash budget** is a detailed plan showing how cash resources will be acquired and used over a specified time period. For many companies, this time period is monthly for the first three months of the budget period, then quarterly for the remainder of the year. A typical cash budget is composed of four major sections:

1. *The receipts section* This section consists of the sum of the opening cash balance and estimated cash receipts for the budget period. For many firms, the major source of cash receipts is sales.
2. *The disbursements section* This section consists of all estimated cash payments for the budget period. Examples are payments for labor and materials, taxes, equipment purchases, and advertising.
3. *The cash excess or cash deficiency section* The entries in this section represent the difference between the totals of the receipts section and the disbursements section. If receipts are greater than disbursements, there is an excess of cash. If receipts are less than disbursements, there is a cash deficiency.
4. *The financing section* This section gives an account of any borrowing or loan repayments projected to take place during the budget period.

The following is an example of a cash budget.

The McQuade Company Cash Budget	
	January
Cash Balance, Beginning	$ 9,000
Receipts	
Cash Sales	14,000
Accounts Receivable Collections	<u>12,000</u>
Total Available Cash	35,000
Disbursements	
Materials	10,000
Labor	9,500
Selling and Administrative Expenses	9,300
Income Taxes	<u>7,200</u>
Total Disbursements	36,000
Excess (Deficiency) of Cash	(1,000)
Financing	
Borrowed Funds Needed	2,000
Repayment of Borrowed Funds	—
Interest (at 10% Per Annum)	—
Total Financing	2,000
Cash Balance, End of Month	1,000

While the cash budget is useful to all companies, it is especially helpful to small firms because management can exercise more control in matching income with disbursements, in negotiating loans with the most favorable interest rates and terms, and in planning investments when there is an excess of cash. Some of the effects of management decisions on the cash budget are illustrated in the next examples.

EXAMPLE 1   For the month of February, the McQuade Company anticipates a decrease in cash sales and accounts receivable collections of 5%, an increase in material costs of 3%, and no payment for income taxes. Assuming there are no other charges in the disbursement section, prepare a cash budget for January and February if the company requires a minimum cash balance of $1,000.

Solution:

<table>
<tr><td colspan="4" align="center">**The McQuade Company**
Cash Budget</td></tr>
<tr><td></td><td>**January**</td><td>**February**</td><td></td></tr>
<tr><td>**Cash Balance, Beginning**</td><td>$9,000</td><td>$1,000</td><td></td></tr>
<tr><td>**Receipts**</td><td></td><td></td><td></td></tr>
<tr><td> Cash Sales</td><td>14,000</td><td>13,300</td><td>(14,000 × 0.95)</td></tr>
<tr><td> Accounts Receivable Collections</td><td>12,000</td><td>11,400</td><td>(12,000 × 0.95)</td></tr>
<tr><td>   Total Available Cash</td><td>35,000</td><td>25,700</td><td></td></tr>
<tr><td>**Disbursements**</td><td></td><td></td><td></td></tr>
<tr><td> Materials</td><td>10,000</td><td>10,300</td><td>(10,000 × 1.03)</td></tr>
<tr><td> Labor</td><td>9,500</td><td>9,500</td><td></td></tr>
<tr><td> Selling and Administrative Expenses</td><td>9,300</td><td>9,300</td><td></td></tr>
<tr><td> Income Taxes</td><td>7,200</td><td>—</td><td></td></tr>
<tr><td>   Total Disbursements</td><td>36,000</td><td>29,100</td><td></td></tr>
<tr><td>Excess (Deficiency) of Cash</td><td>(1,000)</td><td>(3,400)</td><td></td></tr>
<tr><td>**Financing**</td><td></td><td></td><td></td></tr>
<tr><td> Borrowed Funds Needed</td><td>2,000</td><td>4,400</td><td></td></tr>
<tr><td> Repayment of Borrowed Funds</td><td>—</td><td>—</td><td></td></tr>
<tr><td> Interest (at 10% Per Annum)</td><td>—</td><td>—</td><td></td></tr>
<tr><td>   Total Financing</td><td>2,000</td><td>4,400</td><td></td></tr>
<tr><td>**Cash Balance, End of Month**</td><td>1,000</td><td>1,000</td><td></td></tr>
</table>

EXAMPLE 2   With spring approaching, March sales of the McQuade Company are expected to double those of February, and accounts receivable collections are expected to increase by 20%. The cost of materials is estimated at $14,100, anticipated labor costs are $10,000, and selling and administrative expenses are expected to be $9,600. There are no other changes in disbursements. If the January loan plus $35 in interest is repaid at the end of the month, complete the cash budget for the first three months of the year.

Solution:

The McQuade Company Cash Budget			
	January	**February**	**March**
Cash Balance, Beginning	$9,000	$1,000	$1,000
Receipts			
Cash Sales	14,000	13,300	26,600
Accounts Receivable Collections	12,000	11,400	13,680
Total Available Cash	35,000	25,700	41,280
Disbursements			
Materials	10,000	10,300	14,100
Labor	9,500	9,500	10,000
Selling and Administrative Expenses	9,300	9,300	9,600
Income Taxes	7,200	—	—
Total Disbursements	36,000	29,100	33,700
Excess (Deficiency) of Cash	(1,000)	(3,400)	7,580
Financing			
Borrowed Funds Needed	2,000	4,400	—
Repayment of Borrowed Funds	—	—	(2,000)
Interest (at 10% Per Annum)	—	—	(35)
Total Financing	2,000	4,400	(2,035)
Cash Balance, End of Month	1,000	1,000	5,545

EXERCISES FOR SECTION 14.3

Solve.

1. On December 31 of the current year, McGee and Sons expect to have a cash balance of $3,600. For January, they have made the following estimates: raw materials purchased, $24,000; cash sales, $22,000; direct labor costs, $24,000; supervision costs, $2,960; utilities, $6,000; insurance and taxes, $1,700; accounts receivable collections, $38,000. If company policy requires a minimum cash balance of $2,000, prepare a cash budget for January.

2. Using the data in problem 1, prepare a cash budget if disbursements include the purchase of a new machine for $5,000.

3. Repeat problem 1, changing the following data: cash sales, $20,000; accounts receivable collections, $35,000; utility costs, $5,500. All other entries remain the same.

4. Repeat problem 1, using the following data: cash sales, $18,000; labor costs, $28,000; new equipment purchase, $9,700. All other entries remain the same.

5. The Osbourne Company expects cash sales for January to be $28,000 and accounts receivable collections to be $80,400. The company estimates the following expenses: accounts payable, $70,000; taxes, $3,700; advertising, $2,000; merchandise purchases, $24,000; payroll, $12,000; rent, $2,800; insurance, $12,600; other expenses, $1,350. If the balance from the previous month was $20,000 and if the company maintains a minimum monthly cash balance of $15,000, prepare the cash budget for January.

6. Make the following changes in the data for problem 5 and prepare the budget: beginning cash balance, $25,000; insurance, $9,800; rent, $2,500; advertising, $1,500. All other entries remain the same.

7. Repeat problem 5, incorporating the following changes: accounts receivable collections $75,600; accounts payable, $55,000; no insurance premium; machine purchase, $6,600. All other entries remain the same.

8. Repeat problem 5, using the following data: receipts include a state tax refund for $7,000; merchandise purchases, $27,550; other expenses, $1,500; payroll, $15,000. All other entries remain the same.

9. Complete the following cash budget if the corporation maintains a minimum cash balance of $2,500.

Peterson Corporation Cash Budget	
	2nd Quarter
Cash Balance, Beginning	$ 6,600
Receipts	
Cash Sales	16,000
Accounts Receivable Collections	30,000
Total Available Cash	—
Disbursements	
Materials Purchased	19,000
Payroll	23,900
Rent	2,100
Other Expenses	2,400
Equipment Purchase	9,000
Total Disbursements	—
Excess (Deficiency) of Cash	—
Financing	
Borrowed Funds Needed	—
Repayment of Borrowed Funds	0
Interest (at 8% Per Annum)	0
Total Financing	—
Cash Balance, End of Month	—

10. Note: this problem requires information from the solution to problem 9. In the third quarter, when the Peterson Corporation prepares for the Christmas season, the corporation estimates that, compared to the second quarter, cash sales will increase 10%, accounts receivable collections will decrease 5%, cost of materials purchased will double, payroll costs will be $40,000, other expenses will decrease 40%, and there will be no equipment purchases. If there are no other changes in disbursements, if no borrowed funds are repaid, and if there are no interest payments, complete the cash budget for the third quarter.

11. Note: this problem requires information from the solution to problem 10. For the fourth quarter, the Peterson Corporation estimates that, compared to the second quarter, cash sales will increase by 30%, accounts receivable collections will increase by 90%, cost of materials purchased will decrease by 60%, other expenses will increase by 5%, and the payroll will be $20,000. There are no equipment purchases planned, and no other changes in disbursements are anticipated. If both loans are repaid, along with $350 interest, complete the cash budget for the fourth quarter.

12. Complete the following cash budget if the company maintains a minimum cash balance of $1,000.

C. J. Tibbitts Company Cash Budget	
	January
Cash Balance, Beginning	$ 1,200
Receipts	
Cash Sales	14,000
Collection of Receivables	—
Collection of Notes Receivables	0
Total Available Cash	$27,200
Disbursements	
Manufacturing Expenses	19,000
Selling and Administrative Expenses	8,900
Equipment Purchase	0
Total Disbursements	—
Excess (Deficiency) of Cash	—
Financing	
Borrowed Funds Needed	—
Repayment of Borrowed Funds	0
Interest (at 9% Per Annum)	—
Total Financing	—
Cash Balance, End of Month	—

13. Note: this problem requires information from the solution to problem 12. For February, the Tibbitts Company expects cash sales, accounts receivable collections, and manufacturing expenses to increase $1,000 each. No repayment of borrowed money or interest is planned for the month. If selling and administrative expenses are estimated to be $11,100

and there are no other changes in the cash budget from the previous month, prepare the cash budget for February.

14. Note: this problem requires information from the solution to problem 13. For March, cash sales and the collection of receivables for the Tibbitts Company are expected to be $4,000 greater than the January estimates, and the collection of a $4,000 note is anticipated. The purchase of a new machine for $1,200 and manufacturing expenses of $20,600 are expected to result in total disbursements of $30,800. The company plans to repay the January and February loans and will budget $85 for the interest. Prepare the cash budget for March.

15. Complete the following cash budget if the organization maintains a minimum cash balance of $10,000.

Meyers Pharmacies Cash Budget	
	March
Cash Balance, Beginning	$ 16,500
Receipts	
Cash Sales	—
Accounts Receivable Collections	81,000
Total Available Cash	$147,500
Disbursements	
Merchandise Purchases	90,000
Payroll	25,500
Utilities	550
Advertising	16,000
Taxes	0
Other Expenses	2,400
Total Disbursements	—
Excess (Deficiency) of Cash	—
Financing	
Borrowed Funds Needed	—
Repayment of Borrowed Funds	0
Interest (at 12% Per Annum)	—
Total Financing	—
Cash Balance, End of Month	—

16. Note: this problem requires information from the solution to problem 15. In April, the company anticipates a drop in cash sales of 10% and a decrease in merchandise purchases of 15%. Utilities will decrease $50 and the estimated federal income tax payment is $26,450. If all remaining entries are the same, prepare the April cash budget of Meyers Pharmacies.

17. Note: this problem requires information from the solution to problem 16. In May, the company anticipates total available cash of $158,250, of which $84,500 will be accounts receivable collections. Merchandise purchases are anticipated to be $84,000, utilities are expected to double because of air conditioning, and payroll and advertising expenses are expected to decline by 10% from the April estimates. If the loan from April is repaid plus $124 interest, prepare the cash budget for May.

Section 14.4 *Depreciation: MACRS and ACRS*

A. Introduction

Depreciation is a means of partially recovering an investment in an asset. The Internal Revenue Service (IRS) recognizes certain items of property used to operate a business as business expenses and through a tax deduction permits a company to recover a portion of the cost of these items over a specified period of time. Examples of items that may be depreciated are machinery, motor vehicles, buildings, furniture, equipment, and computers.

In general, an asset is depreciable if it meets the following requirements.

1. It is used in the operation of a trade or business or held for the production of income.
2. It has a useful life of more than one year. Useful life is the period that the asset is functional or income producing.
3. It wears out, becomes obsolete, depletes, or loses value from natural causes.

There are several depreciation systems. The system used depends on when the asset was placed in service; that is, when it was operable or ready for use.

B. MACRS

The first system is called the **Modified Accelerated Cost Recovery System (MACRS)** and is used for assets placed in service in 1987 and thereafter. Property that can be depreciated under MACRS is divided into two primary categories: real property and tangible personal property. **Real property** is real estate; that is, anything erected on, attached to, or growing on land. Land by itself is not depreciable. **Tangible personal property** is depreciable property that is not real estate, such as vehicles, machinery, and equipment.

The IRS has assigned each item of depreciable property a **recovery period,** a length of time the property may be depreciated. A description of the recovery periods is shown in table 14.1.

Table 14.1	Recovery Periods
3 year	Tractor units for over the road use, race horses over 2 years old, or any other horse over 12 years old.
5 year	Automobiles, taxis, buses, trucks, computers and peripheral equipment, research equipment and office equipment such as typewriters, calculators, copiers, and so on.
7 year	Office furniture, desks, files, and so on, agricultural machinery, and machinery for manufacturing food, textiles, wood products, paper, rubber, plastic, certain metals, and so on.
10 year	Water transportation vessels, trees or vines bearing fruit or nuts, single purpose agricultural or horticultural structures.
15 year	Roads, shrubbery, and municipal wastewater treatment plants.
20 year	Farm buildings and municipal sewers.
27.5 year	Nonresidential real property such as apartments or rental houses.
31.5 year	Residential real property such as office buildings, stores, and warehouses.

For each year of the recovery period an asset may be depreciated at a percent such as those specified in table 14.2. Note that an asset is depreciated one year more than the recovery period. This is because only a partial depreciation is allowed the first year. The remaining depreciation amount is recovered after the last year of the recovery period.

For a given year, the depreciation amount is calculated using the basic percentage equation $P = B \cdot R$, where P = amount of depreciation, B = cost or purchase price, and R = depreciation percent from tables 14.1 and 14.2.

EXAMPLE 1   A company purchased three computers at a cost of $5,000 each. Find the total amount of depreciation of the computers for the fourth year of the recovery period.

Solution: From table 14.1, computers have a recovery period of five years. From table 14.2, the fourth year depreciation percent is 11.52%. Hence, with P = ?, B = $5,000, and R = 0.1152,

$$P = B \cdot R$$
$$= \$5,000 \times 0.1152$$
$$= \$576$$

For the fourth year of the recovery period, the total amount of depreciation was $576 × 3 = $1,728.

Table 14.2	MACRS Depreciation Percents— Tangible Personal Property and Real Property							
Recovery Period								
	Tangible Personal Property						**Real Property**	
Year	3 Yr	5 Yr	7 Yr	10 Yr	15 Yr	20 Yr	27.5 Yr	31.5 Yr
1	33.33%	20.00%	14.29%	10.00%	5.00%	3.750%	3.485%	3.042%
2	44.45	32.00	24.49	18.00	9.50	7.219	3.636	3.175
3	14.81	19.20	17.49	14.40	8.55	6.677	3.636	3.175
4	7.41	11.52	12.49	11.52	7.70	6.177	3.636	3.175
5		11.52	8.93	9.22	6.93	5.713	3.636	3.175
6		5.76	8.92	7.37	6.23	5.285	3.636	3.175
7			8.93	6.55	5.90	4.888	3.636	3.175
8			4.46	6.55	5.90	4.522	3.636	3.175
9				6.56	5.91	4.462	3.636	3.174
10				6.55	5.90	4.461	3.637	3.175
11				3.28	5.91	4.462	3.636	3.174
12					5.90	4.461	3.637	3.175
13					5.91	4.462	3.636	3.174
14					5.90	4.461	3.637	3.175
15					5.91	4.462	3.636	3.174
16					2.95	4.461	3.637	3.175
17						4.462	3.636	3.174
18						4.461	3.637	3.175
19						4.462	3.636	3.174
20						4.461	3.637	3.175
21						2.231	3.636	3.174
22							3.637	3.175
23							3.636	3.174
24							3.637	3.175
25							3.636	3.174
26							3.637	3.175
27							3.636	3.174
28							1.970	3.175
29								3.174
30								3.175
31								3.174
32								1.720

EXAMPLE 2   The Graham Company purchased 25 desks to furnish a new branch office. If each desk cost $300, find: **a.** the depreciation for each year of the recovery period, and **b.** the total depreciation amount.

Solution: **a.** From table 14.1, desks have a 7 year recovery period. The total amount to be depreciated is $350 \times 12 = $7,500. Using table 14.2,

Year	Cost (B)	Rate (R)	Depreciation (P)
1	$7,500	0.1429	$1,071.75
2	7,500	0.2449	1,836.75
3	7,500	0.1749	1,311.75
4	7,500	0.1249	936.75
5	7,500	0.0893	669.75
6	7,500	0.0892	669.00
7	7,500	0.0893	669.75
8	7,500	0.0446	334.50
			$7,500.00

b. The total cost of $7,500 is depreciated if the asset is held for the entire recovery period. ∎

EXAMPLE 3   A building purchased for $550,000 had a recovery period of 31.5 years. Find: **a.** the amount of depreciation for the tenth year, and **b.** the total depreciation amount.

Solution: **a.** Using table 14.2,

$$P = B \cdot R$$
$$= \$550,000 \times 0.03175$$
$$= \$17,462.50$$

b. Note from table 14.2 there are 12 years in the table for which the depreciation rate is 3.174% and 18 years for which the depreciation rate is 3.175%. Thus,

$ 16,731   Depreciation for year 1   ($550,000 \times 0.03042$)
+ 209,484   Depreciation for 12 of the   ($550,000 \times 0.03174 \times 12$)
            years
+ 314,325   Depreciation for 18 of the   ($550,000 \times 0.03175 \times 18$)
            years
+   9,460   Depreciation for year 32   ($550,000 \times 0.0172$)
$550,000

Again, the total cost of $550,000 is depreciated if the asset is held for the entire recovery period. ∎

Table 14.3	ACRS depreciation on percents

Recovery Period		Type of Property	Depreciation Percent By Year											
Tangible Personal Property	Three Years	Special tools, such as molds, jigs, dies	Year 1	Year 2	Year 3									
			25%	38%	37%									
	Five Years	Equipment; heavy, general purpose trucks; furniture; fixtures; computers	Year 1	Year 2	Years 3-5									
			15%	22%	21%									
	Ten Years	Manufactured homes, certain public utility property, railroad tank cars	Year 1	Year 2	Year 3	Years 4-6	Years 7-10							
			8%	14%	12%	10%	9%							

Real Property	Nineteen Years	Real estate	Year	Month Placed in Service											
				1	2	3	4	5	6	7	8	9	10	11	12
			1st	8.8%	8.1%	7.3%	6.5%	5.8%	5.0%	4.2%	3.5%	2.7%	1.9%	1.1%	0.4%
			2nd	8.4	8.5	8.5	8.6	8.7	8.8	8.8	8.9	9.0	9.0	9.1	9.2
			3rd	7.6	7.7	7.7	7.8	7.9	7.9	8.0	8.1	8.1	8.2	8.3	8.3
			4th	6.9	7.0	7.0	7.1	7.1	7.2	7.3	7.3	7.4	7.4	7.5	7.6
			5th	6.3	6.3	6.4	6.4	6.5	6.5	6.6	6.6	6.7	6.8	6.8	6.9
			6th	5.7	5.7	5.8	5.9	5.9	5.9	6.0	6.0	6.1	6.1	6.2	6.2
			7th	5.2	5.2	5.3	5.3	5.3	5.4	5.4	5.5	5.5	5.6	5.6	5.6
			8th	4.7	4.7	4.8	4.8	4.8	4.9	4.9	5.0	5.0	5.1	5.1	5.1
			9th	4.2	4.3	4.3	4.4	4.4	4.5	4.5	4.5	4.5	4.6	4.6	4.7
			10-19th	4.2	4.2	4.2	4.2	4.2	4.2	4.2	4.2	4.2	4.2	4.2	4.2
			20th	0.2	0.5	0.9	1.2	1.6	1.9	2.3	2.6	3.0	3.3	3.7	4.0

C. ACRS

MACRS is a modification of an earlier depreciation system called the **Accelerated Cost Recovery System (ACRS).** In general, ACRS is used for assets placed in service in the years 1981 through 1986. The primary difference between MACRS and ACRS is that MACRS has more recovery periods and most assets under ACRS were shifted to longer recovery periods under MACRS. Table 14.3 gives the recovery periods and depreciation percents for ACRS.

EXAMPLE 4   A toy company purchased molds for a new line of plastics (3 year recovery period). If the purchase price was $18,000, find the amount of depreciation allowed for each year using ACRS.

Solution: Using table 14.3,

First Year	*Second Year*	*Third Year*
Depreciation amount	*Depreciation amount*	*Depreciation amount*
$P = B \cdot R$	$P = B \cdot R$	$P = B \cdot R$
$= \$18,000 \times 0.25$	$= \$18,000 \times 0.38$	$= \$18,000 \times 0.37$
$= \$4,500$	$= \$6,840$	$= \$6,660$

Note that $\$4,500 + \$6,840 + \$6,660 = \$18,000$. Thus, the entire investment is depreciated over the 3 year period.

EXAMPLE 5   The M & H Construction Company purchased a used mobile home (10 year recovery period) for use as a field office. If the purchase price was $21,600, find the amount of depreciation allowed for the second year.

Solution: From table 14.3, for a 10 year recovery period the second year depreciation percent is 14%. Hence, with $P = ?$, $B = \$21,600$, and $R = 0.14$,

$$P = B \cdot R$$
$$= \$21,600 \times 0.14$$
$$= \$3,024$$

EXAMPLE 6   The Madison Corporation purchased a warehouse (19 year recovery period) for $1,288,000. Find the amount of the first year depreciation if the warehouse was placed in service on April 20.

Solution: From table 14.3, the depreciation percent for the first year is 6.5%, since the warehouse was placed in service in April. Hence, with $P = ?$, $B = \$1,288,000$, and $R = 0.065$,

$$P = B \cdot R$$
$$= \$1,288,000 \times 0.065$$
$$= \$83,720$$

EXERCISES FOR SECTION 14.4

1. Maple Industries spent $34,600 for special tools (5 yr recovery period) to be used in a new branch manufacturing plant. Find the amount of depreciation for the first year using MACRS.

2. Dennison Industries purchased an automobile (5 yr recovery period) for $8,700 to use in the company business. Find the amount of depreciation allowed for the first year of the recovery period using MACRS.

3. The Osborn Company purchased an automobile (5 yr recovery period) for $9,250. The automobile is to be used entirely for company business. Find the amount of depreciation allowed for the first year and the last year of the recovery period using MACRS.

4. Hood and Hoenig bought a $10,200 light duty truck (5 yr recovery period) to be used in their surveying business. The partners depreciated the truck using MACRS method. Find the amount of depreciation allowed for the first year and the fifth year of the recovery period using MACRS.

5. Shoreline Rail Freight acquired five new tank cars (7 yr recovery period) for a total cost of $874,250. If Shoreline uses MACRS, how much depreciation can the company claim for **a.** the first year of the recovery period? **b.** for the sixth year of the recovery period?

6. Mabel Williams has her own consulting business. She purchased a copying machine (5 yr recovery period) for $2,400, but kept it only three years. Find the total amount of depreciation she was allowed under MACRS.

7. Charles Campbell is an independent trucker. He recently bought a used tractor unit (3 yr recovery period) for $9,500 and kept it for 4 years. Find the amount of depreciation allowed for each year using MACRS.

8. The Kalter Realty Company purchased an automobile (5 yr recovery period) for $12,000 to be used in showing real estate to clients but traded the car after three years. The company depreciated the automobile using MACRS. Find the amount of depreciation allowed for each of the 3 years.

9. Derek Fastlane, president of a company, purchased a $4,500 desk (7 yr recovery period) for his personal use in company business. Find the amount of depreciation allowed for each year using MACRS.

10. Woodward Appliance Repair purchased a new welding machine (7 yr recovery period) for $2,185. The machine was depreciated using MACRS. Find the amount of depreciation for each year.

11. In 1982, the accounting firm of Jason, Hancock, & Smith purchased four personal computers (5 yr recovery period) at a cost of $5,300 each and depreciated them using ACRS. Find the amount of depreciation for each year of the recovery period.

12. Suncoast Sprinklers bought ditch-digging equipment (5 year property) for $7,500 and depreciated it using ACRS. Find the amount of depreciation for each year of the recovery period.

13. Use ACRS to find the depreciation for each year of the recovery period on $8,460 worth of furniture (5 yr recovery period) purchased by the Worthington Company.

14. In 1984, Bayside Concrete purchased a heavy-duty truck (5 yr recovery period) for $46,500 and depreciated it using ACRS. Find the amount of depreciation allowed for each year.

15. Entel, Inc. purchased telephone switching equipment (10 yr recovery period) for a central office at a cost of $3,870,000. Find the amount of depreciation allowed for the **a.** first year and **b.** the last year using ACRS.

16. James Jones is a building contractor, and in 1983 he purchased a mobile home (10 yr recovery period) for $18,750 to use as a temporary office at construction sites. Jones depreciated the mobile home using ACRS. Find the amount of depreciation for **a.** the first year and **b.** the last year of the recovery period.

17. A prefabricated housing unit (10 year property) that cost $46,800 was depreciated using ACRS. **a.** Find the depreciation for the first year. **b.** Find the depreciation for the eighth year.

18. A repair shop (19 yr recovery period) was purchased for $420,000 by Overland Trucking Company and placed in service on October 12, 1981. If the company depreciated the shop using ACRS, **a.** what was the amount of the first year depreciation, and **b.** what was the amount of the twelfth year depreciation?

19. Foster Frozen Foods purchased for $845,400 a cold storage building (31.5 yr recovery period) adjacent to the main plant and placed it in service on January 25. Using MACRS, **a.** how much was the first year depreciation, **b.** how much was the fifth year depreciation, and **c.** how much was the fourteenth year depreciation?

20. Using ACRS, find the amount of depreciation for each year of the recovery period for an office building (19 year property) that cost $642,000 and was placed in service in May.

Section 14.5 | *Depreciation: Other Methods*

For federal tax purposes, most businesses elect to use the MACRS depreciation tables (or ACRS, if applicable). However, for federal income taxes, state income tax returns, or for internal accounting other depreciation methods may be optional or appropriate. Among the most widely used are (1) the straight-line method, (2) the declining-balance method, (3) the sum-of-the-years-digits method, and (4) the units-of-production method. For the first three methods, the following information will be used. The Scott Company purchased a forklift for $7,500 (**cost of the asset**). It was estimated that after six years (the **useful life**) the forklift would be worth $1,200 in **trade-in value** (also called the **salvage value**). The salvage value is the minimum value to which the asset may be depreciated.

A. The Straight-line Method

In the straight-line method the depreciation amount is the same for each year of the useful life. The formula for the straight-line method is

$$(14\text{--}10) \quad d = \frac{c - s}{n}$$

where

d = depreciation amount
c = cost of the asset
s = salvage value
n = years of useful life

EXAMPLE 1   For the Scott Company forklift, find: **a.** the depreciation amount for each year using the straight-line method, **b.** prepare a depreciation schedule.

Solution: **a.** $d = \dfrac{\$7,500 - \$1,200}{6}$

$= \$1,050$

The depreciation amount per year is $1,050. Note that this is a constant rate of $16\frac{2}{3}\%$ per year ($\frac{\$1,050}{\$6,300} = 0.166 \ldots$).

b. A depreciation schedule is used to keep track of the depreciation for each asset.

Table 14.4	Depreciation Schedule for the Straight-line Method		
Year	**Annual Depreciation**	**Accumulated Depreciation**	**Book Value***
0	—	—	$7,500
1	$1,050	$1,050	6,450
2	1,050	2,100	5,400
3	1,050	3,150	4,350
4	1,050	4,200	3,300
5	1,050	5,250	2,250
6	1,050	6,300	1,200

*Book value is the current depreciated value of an asset. This is not necessarily the current market value.

In the absence of a depreciation schedule, the accumulated depreciation at the end of any year is the product of the annual depreciation and the number of the year. For example, the accumulated depreciation for the Scott Company forklift after four years is $1,050 \times 4 = $4,200. The book value at the end of any year is the cost minus the accumulated depreciation. For the Scott Company forklift the book value after four years is $7,500 − $4,200 = $3,300.

The advantage of the straight-line method is its simplicity; the depreciation amount for each year is the same. A disadvantage is that is penalizes the later years, when repairs are heaviest.

B. The Declining-Balance Method

This method is a form of **accelerated depreciation,** in which the depreciation amounts are high in the early life of the asset and low in the later years of life. Most machinery follows this pattern; for example, the depreciation of an automobile is greatest in the first year, then less each succeeding year.

In the straight-line method, the *depreciation amount* is the same each year; in the declining-balance method, the *depreciation percent* is the same each year. The percent used most often is twice the straight-line percent; for this reason the declining-balance method is often referred to as the "double declining-balance method" or "200% declining-balance method." To illustrate, the straight-line percent for an asset with a useful life of 5 years is

$$\frac{1}{5} = 0.20 = 20\%$$

For the same period, the double declining-balance percent is

$$20\% \times 2 = 40\%$$

Other common declining-balance percents are 150% and 125% of the straight-line percent.

Once the declining-balance percent is determined, the depreciation amounts are calculated using the formula

(14–11) $d = b \times r$

where d = depreciation amount per year
b = book value of the preceding year
r = declining-balance percent

EXAMPLE 2   Using the double declining-balance (200%) method, prepare a depreciation schedule for the Scott Company forklift.

Solution: With a useful life of 6 years, the straight-line percent was $\frac{1}{6}$, thus double the depreciation percent is

$$\frac{1}{6} \times 2 = \frac{1}{3} = 33\frac{1}{3}\%$$

Since the decimal representation for $33\frac{1}{3}\%$ is infinite repeating, the fraction $\frac{1}{3}$ is used in calculating the depreciation amounts. The formula calculations are shown in parentheses in Table 14.5.

Table 14.5	Depreciation Schedule for the Declining-Balance Method		
Year	**Depreciation**	**Accumulated Depreciation**	**Book Value**
0	—	—	$7,500.00
1	$2,500.00($7,500 × 1/3)	$2,500.00	5,000.00
2	1,666.67($5,000 × 1/3)	4,166.67	3,333.33
3	1,111.11($3,333.33 × 1/3)	5,277.78	2,222.22
4	740.74($2,222.22 × 1/3)	6,018.52	1,481.48
5	281.48($1,481.48 − $1,200)	6,300.00	1,200.00
6	0	6,300.00	1,200.00

Note that in year 5, the depreciation amount calculation $1,481.48 × 1/3 = $493.83 would result in a book value of $1,481.48 − $493.83 = $987.65. Since book value may not be less than salvage value, only $281.48 is allowed in year 5 and $0 in year 6. If an asset has no salvage value, then the book value never reaches zero using this method.

     The high depreciation in the early life of an asset using the declining-balance method is an advantage for income tax purposes. A disadvantage is that the probable maintenance and repair costs will occur late in the life of the asset, when depreciation is low.

C. The Sum-Of-The-Years-Digits Method

Another system of accelerated depreciation is the sum-of-the-years-digits method. The formula for this method is

(14–12) $d = (c - s) \times r$

where d = depreciation amount
                         c = cost of the asset
                         s = salvage value
                         r = depreciation fraction (described below)

The depreciation fraction is a fraction whose denominator is the sum of the digits representing the useful life of the asset, and the numerator is the number of years of useful life remaining at the beginning of the year for which the computation is made.* To illustrate, the Scott Company forklift had a useful life of six years. Hence, the denominator is $1 + 2 + 3 + 4 + 5 + 6 = 21$. The number of years of useful life remaining at the beginning of each depreciation year was 6,5,4,3,2,1. Hence the depreciation fractions are $\frac{6}{21}, \frac{5}{21}, \frac{4}{21}, \frac{3}{21}, \frac{2}{21}$, and $\frac{1}{21}$.

EXAMPLE 3   Prepare a depreciation schedule for the Scott Company forklift using the sum-of-the-years-digits method.

Solution: The depreciation schedule is shown in table 14.6. The formula calculations are shown in parentheses.

Table 14.6   Depreciation Schedule for the Sum-Of-The-Years-Digits Method

Year	Depreciation	Accumulated Depreciation	Book Value
0	—	—	$7,500
1	$1,800($6,300 $\times \frac{6}{21}$)	$1,800	5,700
2	1,500($6,300 $\times \frac{5}{21}$)	3,300	4,200
3	1,200($6,300 $\times \frac{4}{21}$)	4,500	3,000
4	900($6,300 $\times \frac{3}{21}$)	5,400	2,100
5	600($6,300 $\times \frac{2}{21}$)	6,000	1,500
6	300($6,300 $\times \frac{1}{21}$)	6,300	1,200

The sum-of-the-years-digits method of depreciation has the same advantages and disadvantages as the declining-balance method.

The denominator may also be found by using the formula $\frac{n(n + 1)}{2}$ where n = number of years of useful life. This formula is useful when n is a large number.

Calculator entries for the depreciation amounts and book value of table 14.6 are as follows:

Entry	Display	Memory
7500	7500	0
M+	7500	7500
6300	6300	7500
×	6300	7500
6	6	7500
÷	37800	7500
21	21	7500
M−	1800	5700
MR**	5700	5700

D. Comparison of the Three Methods

The three methods can be visually compared by graphing their depreciation schedules on the same graph. (See figures 14.9 and 14.10.)

E. The Units-of-Production Method

In the previous methods, the life of an asset was based on time. In the units-of-production depreciation method, the life of an asset is based on use. Use may be measured in items produced, miles traveled, hours of actual operation, and so on. Calculation of depreciation using this method is in two parts. A per unit depreciation is first calculated, then this is used to calculate an annual depreciation amount.

For example, suppose a stamping machine that cost $120,000 is expected to stamp 2,000,000 parts before being sold at its salvage value of $20,000. The per unit depreciation is

$$\frac{\text{Cost} - \text{Salvage Value}}{\text{Total units produced}} = \frac{\$120,000 - \$20,000}{2,000,000} = \$0.05$$

Thus, if during the first 2 years the actual number of parts stamped was 150,000 and 210,000, then

First Year Depreciation
150,000 × $0.05 = $7,500

Second Year Depreciation
210,000 × $0.05 = $10,500

The units-of-production depreciation method has several shortcomings, among which is the difficulty of estimating the useful life of a machine. Also, there is no depreciation when the machine is not in use, for example when the employees that operate the machine are on strike.

**Now repeat steps 3–9 five times, except instead of the entry 6, use 5,4,3,2, and 1.

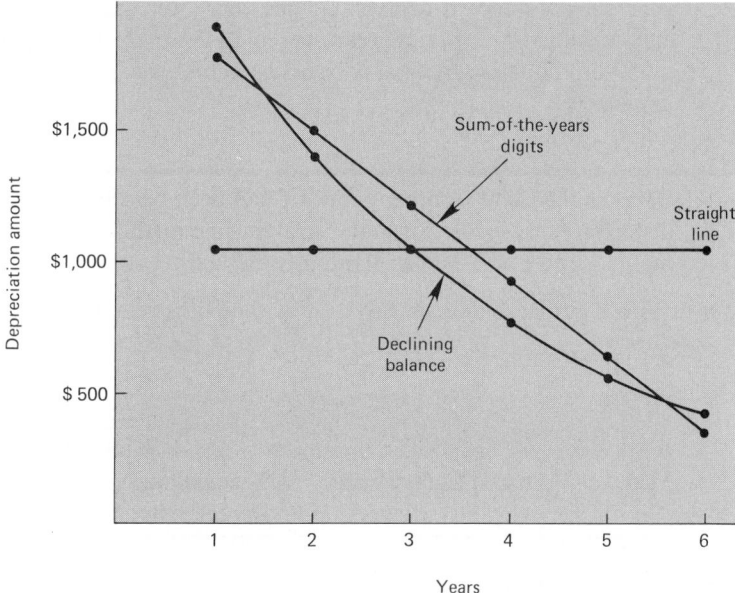

Figure 14.9
Comparison of depreciation amounts resulting from the three depreciation methods

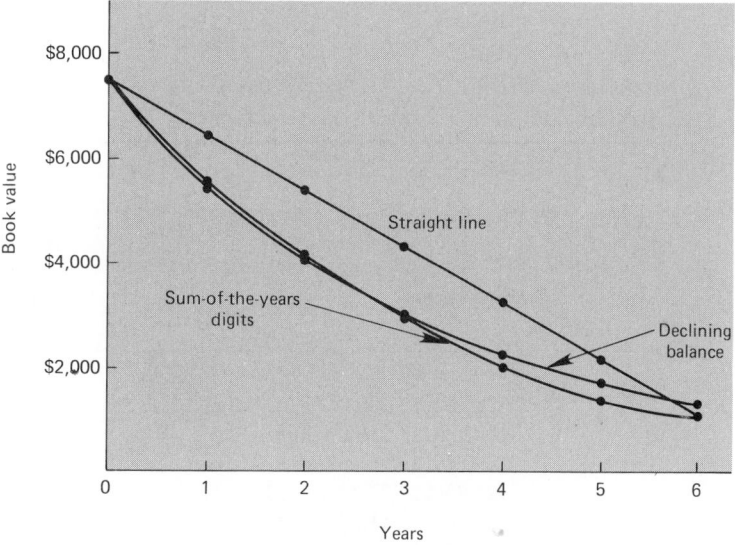

Figure 14.10
Comparison of book values resulting from the three depreciation methods

F. Partial Year Depreciation

The preceding examples assumed that the asset was purchased at the beginning of the year. For assets purchased later in the year, only a partial depreciation is allowed for that year. For example, an asset purchased on February 1 would be allowed only $\frac{11}{12}$ of the first year's depreciation amount. Assets not purchased at the beginning of the month but on or before the 15th of the month may count the full month for depreciation. If only a partial year depreciation is allowed in the first year, the difference is depreciated one year after the end of the useful life. The next example illustrates partial year depreciation for the first three methods. Since the units-of-production method is based on actual use, partial year depreciation is not applicable.

E X A M P L E   4   Suppose the Scott Company forklift had been purchased on July 1. Prepare a depreciation schedule for **a.** the straight-line method, **b.** the declining-balance method, and **c.** the sum-of-the-digits method.

Solution: With a purchase date of July 1, only 6 months remain in the year.

a.

Table 14.7	Depreciation Schedule for the Straight-line Method		
Year	**Annual Depreciation**	**Accumulated Depreciation**	**Book Value**
0	—	—	$7,500
1	$ 525($1,050 ÷ 2)	$ 525	6,975
2	1,050	1,575	5,925
3	1,050	2,625	4,875
4	1,050	3,675	3,825
5	1,050	4,725	2,775
6	1,050	5,775	1,725
7	525	6,300	1,200

b.

Table 14.8	Depreciation Schedule for the Declining-Balance Method		
Year	**Depreciation**	**Accumulated Depreciation**	**Book Value**
0	—	—	$7,500.00
1	$1,250.00($7,500 × 1/3) × 1/2	$1,250.00	6,250.00
2	2,083.33($6,250.00 × 1/3)	3,333.33	4,166.67
3	1,388.89($4,166.67 × 1/3)	4,722.22	2,777.78
4	925.93($2,777.78 × 1/3)	5,648.15	1,851.85
5	617.28($1,851.85 × 1/3)	6,265.43	1,234.57
6	34.57($1,234.57 − $1,200)	6,300.00	1,200.00

c. For year 1, the depreciation allowed is 1/2 the normal annual depreciation for year 1. For year 2, the depreciation allowed equals (1/2 the normal annual depreciation for year 1) + (1/2 the normal annual depreciation for year 2). This pattern continues for the remaining life.

Year	Depreciation	Accumulated Depreciation	Book Value

Table 14.9   Depreciation Schedule for the Sum-Of-The-Years-Digits Method

Year	Depreciation	Accumulated Depreciation	Book Value
0	—	—	$7,500
1	$900 ($6,300 \times \frac{6}{21}) \times \frac{1}{2}$	$ 900	6,600
2	900 (From year 1) $+\ \underline{\ 750}$ ($6,300 \times \frac{5}{21}) \times \frac{1}{2}$ $1,650	2,550	4,950
3	750 (From year 2) $+\ \underline{\ 600}$ ($6,300 \times \frac{4}{21}) \times \frac{1}{2}$ $1,350	3,900	3,600
4	600 (From year 3) $+\ \underline{\ 450}$ ($6,300 \times \frac{3}{21}) \times \frac{1}{2}$ $1,050	4,950	2,550
5	450 (From year 4) $+\ \underline{\ 300}$ ($6,300 \times \frac{2}{21}) \times \frac{1}{2}$ $750	5,700	1,800
6	300 (From year 5) $+\ \underline{\ 150}$ ($6,300 \times \frac{1}{21}) \times \frac{1}{2}$ $450	6,150	1,350
7	150 (From year 6)	6,300	1,200

EXERCISES FOR SECTION 14.5

1. The Madison Manufacturing Company purchased a new conveyor for $10,000. The useful life of the conveyor was 10 years, and its salvage value was $1,000. Find the amount of depreciation per year using the straight-line method.

2. Prepare a depreciation schedule for the conveyor in problem 1 (see table 14.4).

3. Halpen Enterprises purchased some tooling equipment for $23,500. The salvage value of the equipment was $4,000, and its useful life was 8 years. Find the amount of depreciation per year using the straight-line method.

4. Prepare a depreciation schedule for the tooling equipment in problem 3 (see table 14.4).

5. Processing equipment at Central Food Packers had an initial purchase cost of $18,000 and a useful life of 6 years. The equipment was depreciated at twice the straight-line rate using the declining-balance method. Prepare a depreciation schedule for the equipment (see table 14.5).

6. The Carson Company used the declining-balance method at a rate of twice the straight-line rate to depreciate its equipment. If the purchase price of the equipment was $52,000 and the useful life was 8 years, prepare a depreciation schedule for the equipment (see table 14.5).

7. Nelson Meat Packers purchased new meat-cutting equipment for $36,000. The useful life of the equipment was 5 years. Prepare a depreciation schedule for the equipment using a depreciation rate of 1.5 times the straight-line rate and the declining-balance method.

8. The Prescott Company purchased an automobile for $6,000. The salvage value of the car was $1,000, and its useful life was 5 years. Prepare a depreciation schedule for the car using the sum-of-the-years-digits method (see table 14.6).

9. A new platform loader at Holden Industries cost $16,000 and had a useful life of 8 years. If the salvage value of the loader was $2,000, prepare a depreciation schedule for the loader using the sum-of-the-years-digits method (see table 14.6).

10. Use the sum-of-the-years-digits method to prepare a depreciation schedule for a $25,000 piece of machinery at Holden Industries if the machinery had a useful life of 6 years and a salvage value of $5,000.

11. A packing machine cost $10,000, had a salvage value of $4,000, and a useful life of 5 years. Prepare depreciation schedules for the machine using **a.** the straight-line method, **b** the declining-balance method at 1.25 times the straight-line rate, and **c.** the sum-of-the-years-digits method.

12. Repeat problem 11 for a piece of machinery that cost $8,000, had a useful life of 4 years, and a salvage value of $2,000. Use a depreciation rate of 1.5 times the straight-line rate in the declining-balance method.

13. A company car, purchased new for $8,000, had a useful life of 5 years and a salvage value of $600. Use the declining-balance method and the maximum depreciation rate to prepare a depreciation schedule. (Hint: the straight-line rate is $\frac{1}{n}$ where n is the number of years of useful life of the asset.)

14. Lake Scientific Laboratories purchased a new electron microscope for $38,000. It had a useful life of 8 years and a salvage value of $3,800. Use the declining-balance method and the maximum depreciation rate to prepare a depreciation schedule. (Hint: the straight-line rate is $\frac{1}{n}$ where n is the number of years of useful life of the asset.)

15. A crane purchased by the Decker Construction Company cost $15,000 and had a useful life of 8 years. Its salvage value was $5,000. Use the straight-line method to prepare a depreciation schedule for the crane.

16. Use the declining-balance method with a depreciation rate of 1.5 times the straight-line rate to prepare a depreciation schedule for the crane in problem 15.

17. Use the sum-of-the-years-digits method to prepare a depreciation schedule for the crane in problem 15.

18. The Jennings Company purchased new central air-conditioning equipment for $8,000. The useful life was 6 years, and the salvage value was $550. Use the declining-balance method and the maximum depreciation rate to prepare a depreciation schedule.

19. All-Occasion Florists purchased a delivery van for $11,000. The estimated useful life was 70,000 miles with a salvage value of $1,900. Using the units-of-production method, find the depreciation in a year the truck was driven **a.** 18,000 miles, **b.** 22,000 miles.

20. Admiral Motors purchased a robot welding machine for $1,220,000. After its estimated life of 75,000 hours, the salvage value was $140,000. Using the units-of-production method, find the depreciation in a year the machine operated for **a.** 7,100 hours, and **b.** 8,000 hours.

21. The Schmidt Corporation bought a machine for manufacturing carriage bolts with a purchase price of $16,250 and a salvage value of $950 after manufacturing 900,000 boxes of bolts over its lifetime. **a.** Using the units-of-production method, find the annual depreciation if 120,000 boxes were manufactured in the first year and 95,000 boxes were manufactured in the second year. **b.** Find the book value at the end of the second year.

22. A machine with an estimated useful life of 3,500,000 units cost $410,000 with a salvage value of $32,000. The first year depreciation was $46,000. The second year production was 400,000 units. Find the book value for the second year.

23. An asset that was purchased for $8,200 on July 1 had a salvage value of $700 five years later. Prepare a depreciation schedule for **a.** the straight-line method, **b.** the declining-balance method, and **c.** the sum-of-the-digits method.

24. A packaging machine was purchased on July 1 for $16,500. Six years later the machine had a salvage value of $1,200. Prepare a depreciation schedule for **a.** the straight-line method, **b.** the declining-balance method, and **c.** the sum-of-the-digits method.

Section 14.6 *Distribution of Overhead and Profits and Losses*

A. Distribution of Overhead

Overhead was previously defined as operating expenses such as rent, utilities, maintenance, and so on. Since overhead adds to the cost of doing business, it must be kept to a minimum. One way of controlling overhead is to allocate a portion of the total overhead to each department or subunit of the company. If this distribution is done equitably, then management can measure the efficiency of each department or subunit by comparing the amount of money it brings in with its share of the overhead. Two widely used methods of distribution are (1) according to floor space and (2) according to net sales.

EXAMPLE 1   The Banning Corporation distributed its total overhead of $24,000 according to the square feet occupied by each department. Determine the distribution if the floor space of each department is as follows:

Department	Floor Space	Ratio to Total Space
Offices	1,500	$\dfrac{1,500}{30,000} = \dfrac{1}{20}$
Accounting	2,500	$\dfrac{2,500}{30,000} = \dfrac{1}{12}$
Production	14,000	$\dfrac{14,000}{30,000} = \dfrac{7}{15}$
Warehouse	12,000	$\dfrac{12,000}{30,000} = \dfrac{2}{5}$
	30,000	

Solution: The distribution is an application of the basic percentage equation $P = B \cdot R$ with P = allocation method, B = $24,000, and R = ratio of department space to total space.

Office allocation $= \$24,000 \times \dfrac{1}{20} = \$1,200$

Accounting allocation $= \$24,000 \times \dfrac{1}{12} = \$2,000$

Production allocation $= \$24,000 \times \dfrac{7}{15} = \$11,200$

Warehouse allocation $= \$24,000 \times \dfrac{2}{5} = \$9,600$

As a check, the sum of the departmental allocations should equal the total overhead expense: $1,200 + $2,000 + $11,200 + $9,600 = $24,000. ∎

For an alternative calculation, note that each product contains the fraction $\frac{24,000}{30,000}$ = 0.8. For instance, $24,000 \times \frac{1,500}{30,000} = \frac{24,000}{30,000} \times 1,500 = \$0.80 \times 1,500 = \$1,200$. Thus, the floor space could be multiplied by $0.80 to obtain the allocation. If a calculator is available,

Entry	Display	Memory
.8	0.8	0
M+	0.8	0.8
$\times$	0.8	0.8
1500	1500	0.8
=	1200	0.8
MR	0.8	0.8
$\times$	0.8	0.8
2500	2500	0.8
=	2000	0.8
MR	0.8	0.8
$\times$	14000	0.8
=	11200	0.8
MR	0.8	0.8
$\times$	0.8	0.8
12000	12000	0.8
=	9600	0.8

A second method of distributing overhead is according to net sales.

EXAMPLE 2 The Lombard Company had monthly net sales in its departments as follows:

Department	Net Sales	Ratio to Total Sales
Appliances	$1,000	$\frac{1,000}{12,000} = \frac{1}{12}$
Automotive	2,800	$\frac{2,800}{12,000} = \frac{7}{30}$
Ladies' wear	6,200	$\frac{6,200}{12,000} = \frac{31}{60}$
Menswear	1,200	$\frac{1,200}{12,000} = \frac{1}{10}$
Toys	800	$\frac{800}{12,000} = \frac{1}{15}$
	$12,000	

If the month's overhead of $2,400 was distributed according to net sales, what was the allocation to each department?

Solution: $P = ?$, $B = \$2,400$, and $R =$ ratio to total net sales

Appliance allocation	$= \$2,400 \times \dfrac{1}{12}$	$= \$200$
Automotive allocation	$= \$2,400 \times \dfrac{7}{30}$	$= \$560$
Ladies' wear	$= \$2,400 \times \dfrac{31}{60}$	$= \$1,240$
Menswear	$= \$2,400 \times \dfrac{1}{10}$	$= \$240$
Toys	$= \$2,400 \times \dfrac{1}{15}$	$= \$160$

Check: $\$200 + \$560 + \$1,240 + \$240 + \$160 = \$2,480$ ■

B. Distribution of Partnership Profits and Losses

A partnership is formed when two or more individuals join in a business as co-owners. As co-owners, the partners share in both the profits of the business as well as any losses. When establishing a partnership, it is advisable to prepare a written partnership agreement that specifies the responsibilities of each partner and how any profits or losses are to be distributed. One method of distributing profits or losses is according to the amount of money invested in the business, as shown in the next example.

EXAMPLE 3   Collins, Mills, and Tozer formed a business partnership. To start the business, Collins contributed $15,000, Mills contributed $9,000, and Tozer contributed $6,000. During the first year of operation, the business lost $1,280. How much did each partner share in the loss?

Solution: Each partner's share of the loss is the ratio of his or her investment to the total investment.

Partner	Initial Investment	Ratio to Total Investment
Collins	$15,000	$\dfrac{15,000}{30,000} = \dfrac{1}{2} = 0.50$
Mills	9,000	$\dfrac{9,000}{30,000} = \dfrac{3}{10} = 0.30$
Tozer	6,000	$\dfrac{6,000}{30,000} = \dfrac{1}{5} = 0.20$
	$30,000	

The allocation of the loss is an application of $P = B \cdot R$ with $P =$ allocation amount, $B = \$1,280$, and $R =$ ratio to total investment.

Collins	$\$1,280 \times 0.50 = \$640$
Mills	$\$1,280 \times 0.30 = \$384$
Tozer	$\$1,280 \times 0.20 = \$256$

As a check, the sum of the allocations should equal the total loss:
$\$640 + \$384 + \$256 = \$1,280$. ■

Another method of distributing profits or losses considers the time invested in the operation of the business.

E X A M P L E 4   Jones, Barclay, Riddle, and Symanski formed a business partnership. It was agreed that, as manager of the business, Jones would receive 55% of the profits, with the other partners sharing the remaining profits equally. How much did each partner receive in a year when the total profit was $264,000?

Solution: If Jones receives 55%, the other partners receive 45% ÷ 3 = 15%.

Jones $264,000 × 0.55 = $145,200
Barclay $264,000 × 0.15 = $39,600
Riddle $264,000 × 0.15 = $39,600
Symanski $264,000 × 0.15 = $39,600

Check: $145,200 + $39,600 + $39,600 + $39,600 = $264,000   ∎

A third way of distributing profits or losses is according to a fixed ratio.

E X A M P L E 5   Smith, Johnson, and Welch agreed to distribute the profits of their partnership according to a ratio of 3:4:5, respectively. Find the distribution if the profit was $360,000.

Solution: The agreed ratio means that the profit was split into 3 + 4 + 5 = 12 shares.

$$\$360,000 \times \frac{3}{12} = \$90,000 \qquad \text{Smith's share}$$

$$\$360,000 \times \frac{4}{12} = \$120,000 \qquad \text{Johnson's share}$$

$$\$360,000 \times \frac{5}{12} = \$150,000 \qquad \text{Welch's share}$$

Check: $90,000 + $120,000 + $150,000 = $360,000   ∎

If a partner receives a salary from the business, the salary is deducted from profits before distribution.

E X A M P L E 6   Crawford and Freeman are business partners. As a silent partner, Crawford has no part in the business other than his investment. However, Freeman runs the business, and it was agreed that she would receive an annual salary of $50,000, with the remaining profits to be split evenly. In a year when the business has a $145,000 profit, how much was paid to each partner?

Solution: After deducting Freeman's salary, the profit to be split is
$145,000 − $50,000 = $95,000. Crawford is paid $95,000 × $\frac{1}{2}$ = $47,500.
Freeman is paid $47,500 (profit distribution) + $50,000 (salary) = $97,500.   ■

Still another variation in the distribution of profits is for one or more partners to receive a specified percent of their investment prior to distribution of any remaining profits.

EXAMPLE 7   When Acton, Eads, and Nichols formed a partnership, they contributed $20,000, $25,000, and $10,000, respectively to start the business. The partnership agreement specified that annually the partners would receive 9% of their investment, that Nichols would receive a salary of $38,000, and that any remaining profits would be shared equally. Find the distribution on profits of **a.** $50,000 and **b.** $26,000.

Solution: The amount paid before distribution of any remaining profits is

$$
\begin{array}{ll}
\$1,800 & (\$20,000 \times 0.09) \\
+\ \ 2,250 & (\$25,000 \times 0.09) \\
+\ \ \ \ 900 & (\$10,000 \times 0.09) \\
+\ 38,000 & \text{Salary} \\
\hline
\$42,950 & \text{Total}
\end{array}
$$

a. $50,000 − $42,950 = $7,050
$7,050 ÷ 3 = $2,350

The amount received by each partner is

Partner	Return on Investment	Salary	Share of Profits	Total Received
Acton	$1,800		+$2,350	$ 4,150
Eads	2,250		+ 2,350	4,600
Nichols	900	+$38,000	+ 2,350	41,250

b. $42,950 − $26,000 = $16,950 loss
$16,950 ÷ 3 = $5,650

The amount received by each partner is

Partner	Return on Investment	Salary	Share of Loss	Total Received or Lost
Acton	$1,800		−$5,650	−$ 3,850
Eads	2,250		− 5,650	− 3,400
Nichols	900	+$38,000	− 5,650	33,250

■

EXERCISES FOR SECTION 14.6

1. The Stratford Corporation distributed its overhead expense of $62,000 according to the floor space occupied by each department. Determine the distribution of overhead if the floor space (in square feet) of each department is as follows:

Department	Floor Space	Ratio to Total Floor Space
Offices	1,000	$\dfrac{1,000}{40,000} = \dfrac{1}{40}$
Accounting	3,000	$\dfrac{3,000}{40,000} = \dfrac{3}{40}$
Production	16,000	$\dfrac{16,000}{40,000} = \dfrac{2}{5}$
Warehouse	20,000	$\dfrac{20,000}{40,000} = \dfrac{1}{2}$
Total	40,000	

2. The floor space (in square feet) of the Nelson Company is distributed as follows:

Department	Floor Space	Ratio to Total Floor Space
Offices	1,400	$\dfrac{1,400}{8,000} = \dfrac{7}{40}$
Accounting	1,300	$\dfrac{1,300}{8,000} = \dfrac{13}{80}$
Showroom	2,200	$\dfrac{2,200}{8,000} = \dfrac{11}{40}$
Maintenance	900	$\dfrac{900}{8,000} = \dfrac{9}{80}$
Warehouse	2,200	$\dfrac{2,200}{8,000} = \dfrac{11}{40}$
Total	8,000	

Determine the distribution of the company's overhead of $28,000 if the overhead is distributed according to the floor space occupied by each department.

3. For the month of June, the departmental net sales at the Parker Company were as follows:

Department	Net Sales	Ratio to Total Sales
Clothing	$ 4,900	$\dfrac{4,900}{16,000} = \dfrac{49}{160}$
Hardware	2,500	$\dfrac{2,500}{16,000} = \dfrac{5}{32}$
Appliances	3,200	$\dfrac{3,200}{16,000} = \dfrac{1}{5}$
Toys	1,300	$\dfrac{1,300}{16,000} = \dfrac{13}{160}$
Home furnishings	4,100	$\dfrac{4,100}{16,000} = \dfrac{41}{160}$
Total	$16,000	

The total overhead for the month of June was $2,760. If the overhead is distributed according to net sales, find the allocation to each department.

4. The total overhead at Braxton Industries for the month of February was $4,850. The net sales for the month totaled $50,000 and were distributed among the departments as follows:

Department	Net Sales	Ratio to Total Sales
Garden supplies	$ 6,250	$\dfrac{6,250}{50,000} = \dfrac{1}{8}$
Glassware	8,450	$\dfrac{8,450}{50,000} = \dfrac{169}{1000}$
Hardware	12,100	$\dfrac{12,100}{50,000} = \dfrac{121}{500}$
Carpets	16,200	$\dfrac{16,200}{50,000} = \dfrac{81}{250}$
Lightings	7,000	$\dfrac{7,000}{50,000} = \dfrac{7}{50}$
Total	$50,000	

If the month's overhead was distributed according to net sales, what was the allocation to each department?

5. The W.T. Southerd Company reported total overhead of $3,250 for the month of November. The net sales for November were $40,000 and were distributed as follows:

Department	Net Sales
Office supplies	$11,200
Furnishings	7,700
Floor coverings	5,200
Office machines	15,900
Total	$40,000

Find the overhead allocation to each department if the distribution is made according to net sales.

6. The floor space (in square feet) of Frederick's is distributed as follows:

Department	Floor Space
Offices	1,200
Accounting	1,600
Home furnishings	3,200
Hardware	2,100
Paints	1,800
Draperies	2,700
Carpets	2,400
Total	15,000

Determine the distribution of the company's overhead of $44,500 if the overhead is distributed according to the floor space occupied by each department.

7. Elco Enterprises reported total overhead of $5,620 for the month of June. The net sales for June were $65,000 and were distributed as follows: office equipment, $17,500; business forms, $3,500; furnishings, $23,200; art supplies, $4,700; and chemicals, $16,100. The month's overhead was distributed according to net sales. Prepare a table showing the ratio of the net sales of each department to total net sales and the allocation of overhead to each department.

8. The floor space (in square feet) at Prindles is distributed as follows: accounting, 1,400; offices, 900; men's clothing, 2,600; women's clothing, 3,600; children's wear, 1,800; and shoes, 1,000. Prepare a table showing the ratio of the floor space of each department to total floor space and the allocation of the company's overhead of $54,200 to each department if the overhead is distributed according to floor space.

9. Jackson, Peters, and Adams formed a business partnership. To start the business, Jackson contributed $15,000, Peters contributed $40,000, and Adams contributed $25,000. During the first year, the business lost $8,700. Based on the amount of money each partner invested in the business, how much did each partner share in the loss?

10. During the first year of operation, a new business formed by three partners earned a profit of $14,250. To form the business, partner A had invested $36,000, partner B had invested $30,000, and partner C had invested $54,000. Based on the amount that each partner initially invested in the business, determine the amount of profit that each partner received.

11. John Barrett formed a new business with three other partners. It was agreed that Barrett would receive 64% of the profits, since he would manage the business, and the other three partners would share the remaining profits equally. How much did Barrett and each of the other three partners receive in a year when the total profit earned by the business was $76,640?

12. Sheila Bishop and Ann Tucker started an investment counseling service. They formed a partnership with two other people, and it was agreed that Bishop and Tucker would each receive 32% of the profits and that the other two partners would equally share the remainder. Find the distribution of profits for a year when the total profit was $87,500.

13. Criswell, Davis, and Meyer agreed to distribute the profits of their partnership according to a ratio of 2:5:7, respectively. How much was each partner's profit for a year when the total profit was $185,000?

14. A business owned by four partners earned a total profit of $234,420 last year. Find the distribution of profits if the partners have agreed to distribute all profits and losses according to the ratio 3:5:6:10.

15. Foster, Thomas, Harvey, and Daniels distribute all profits and losses from their partnership according to the ratio 7:7:4:2, respectively. Determine each partner's loss for a year when the losses of the business totaled $14,350.

16. Alice Swenson, Joan Hefferman, and Jean Banks formed a partnership. Swenson and Hefferman run the business and receive annual salaries of $27,500 and $22,000, respectively. Banks is a silent partner and receives no salary, but the three partners divide all remaining profits (after salaries) equally. In a year when total profits were $101,190 (before salaries), how much did each partner receive?

17. A business owned by four partners earned a total profit of $316,740 (before salaries) during its third year of operation. Two of the partners run the business, earning annual salaries of $31,500 and $29,500. Remaining profits (after salaries) are divided equally among the four partners. How much was paid to each partner during the third year of operation?

18. Harper, Taylor, Simmons, and Marshall formed a partnership. They agreed that Harper and Taylor would receive salaries of $35,000 and $24,000, respectively, and that remaining profits (after salaries) would be distributed among the four partners according to the ratio 3:3:5:6, respectively. Find the amount paid to each partner for a year when total profits were $186,200 (before salaries).

19. The partnership agreement of Kessler and Schneider specifies that annually each partner will receive 8% on their investments in the business of $50,400 and $75,600, respectively, and that any remaining profits would be shared according to the ratio of their investments. Find the distribution on profits of **a.** $12,000, and **b.** $9,000.

20. To start a business, Buck, Hansley, and Reid contributed $20,000, $22,000, and $15,000, respectively. The partnership agreement specifies that Buck will manage the business and that annually each partner will receive 8.5% of their investment, that Buck will receive a salary of $25,000, and that any remaining profits will be shared equally. Find the distribution on profits of **a.** $33,490, and **b.** $28,885.

Glossary

Accelerated cost recovery system (ACRS)   A method of depreciating assets placed in service after 1980 and before 1987.

Accelerated depreciation   A depreciation method where depreciation amounts are high in the early life of an asset and low in the later life of an asset.

Acid-test ratio   A measure of a firm's ability to meet current liabilities; found by dividing cash plus receivables by current liabilities.

Assets   Possessions owned by a business; money owed to a business.

Balance sheet   A financial statement indicating the financial condition of a business at a given time.

Book value   The current depreciated value of an asset.

Cash budget   A detailed plan showing how cash resources will be acquired and used over a specified time period.

Cost of an asset   The original purchase price of an asset.

Current ratio   A measure of the ability of a firm to meet its debts promptly; found by dividing current assets by current liabilities.

Debt-equity ratio   A measure of the security of a company; found by dividing current liabilities plus long-term liabilities by owners' equity.

Declining-balance method   A depreciation method wherein an asset is depreciated at a constant rate using the formula $d = b \times r$, where d is the depreciation amount per year, b is the book value of the preceding year, and r is the depreciation rate.

Depreciation   A tax deduction that permits a business to partially recover its investment in an asset.

Depreciation schedule   A table showing the depreciation, accumulated depreciation, and book value per year.

Equities   The claims upon the assets if a business is dissolved; liabilities plus owners' equity.

Gross profit margin   A measure of the average spread between the cost of goods sold and the selling price; found by dividing the difference between net sales and the cost of goods sold by net sales.

Horizontal analysis   For entries on a balance sheet or an income statement, the comparison of dollar amounts for different periods of time.

Income statement   A report on a company's income for a period of time, generally a month or a year.

Liabilities   The dollar value of everything a company owes.

Liquidity   The ability of a company to convert assets into cash quickly without incurring a significant loss.

Modified accelerated cost recovery system (MACRS)   A method of depreciating assets placed in service in 1987 and thereafter.

Operating ratio   A measure of the amount of sales dollars used to defray the cost of goods and administrative expenses; found by dividing the cost of goods sold plus operating expenses by net sales.

Overhead   The operating expenses of a business, such as rent, utilities, salaries, supplies, advertising, and maintenance.

Owners' equity   The owners' share of a firm's assets; the difference between total assets and total liabilities.

Partnership   When two or more individuals join in a business venture as co-owners.

Real property   For depreciation purposes, anything erected on, attached to, or growing on land.

Recovery period   A length of time established by the Internal Revenue Service during which property may be depreciated.

Salvage value   For assets placed in service prior to 1981, the value of an asset at the end of its useful life.

Stockholders' equity ratio   A measure of the investment in assets financed by the owners or stockholders; found by dividing the owners' equity by total assets.

Straight-line method   A depreciation method wherein an asset is depreciated a constant amount each year. The constant amount is determined by the formula $\frac{c-s}{n}$ where c is the cost of the asset, s is the salvage value, and n is the number of years the asset is depreciated.

Sum-of-the-years-digits method   A depreciation method wherein an asset is depreciated at a decreasing rate. The formula for each year's depreciation is $(c-s) \times r$, where c is the cost of the asset, s is the salvage value, and r is a fraction whose denominator is the sum of the digits representing the useful life of the asset and the numerator is the number of years of useful life remaining at the beginning of the year.

Tangible personal property   Depreciable property that is not real estate, such as vehicles, machinery, and equipment.

Trade-in value   See *salvage value.*

Units-of-production method   A depreciation method wherein an asset is depreciated at a constant rate. The constant rate is determined by the formula $\frac{c-s}{\ell}$, where c is the cost of the asset, s is the salvage value, and ℓ is the useful life of the asset. The useful life of the asset may be in units other than time such as items produced, miles traveled, etc. The annual depreciation is the product of the annual usage and the constant rate.

Useful life   For depreciation purposes, the period an asset is expected to be functional.

Vertical analysis   Expressed as a percent, the ratio of entries on an income statement or a balance sheet to a particular entry, usually net sales or total assets.

Review Test

1. Complete the missing items in the following balance sheet.

<table>
<tr><td colspan="4">The Aztec Corporation
Balance Sheet

December 31, 19___</td></tr>
<tr><td>Assets</td><td></td><td>Equities</td><td></td></tr>
<tr><td>Current Assets</td><td></td><td>Current Liabilities</td><td></td></tr>
<tr><td>Cash</td><td>$ 10,500</td><td>Due to Bank</td><td>$ 50,000</td></tr>
<tr><td>Accounts Receivable</td><td>_____</td><td>Notes Payable</td><td>12,000</td></tr>
<tr><td>Merchandise Inventory</td><td>20,500</td><td>Total Current Liabilities</td><td>_____</td></tr>
<tr><td>Total Current Assets</td><td>67,000</td><td></td><td></td></tr>
<tr><td>Equipment, Buildings,
and Land</td><td></td><td>Long-Term Liabilities</td><td></td></tr>
<tr><td>Equipment</td><td>$159,000</td><td>Mortgage</td><td>$200,000</td></tr>
<tr><td>Buildings</td><td>240,000</td><td>Total Liabilities</td><td>_____</td></tr>
<tr><td>Land</td><td>100,000</td><td>Owners' Equity</td><td></td></tr>
<tr><td>Total Fixed Assets</td><td>_____</td><td>A. J. Davis, Owner</td><td>$304,000</td></tr>
<tr><td>Total Assets</td><td>_____</td><td>Total Equities</td><td>_____</td></tr>
</table>

2. Find the acid-test ratio of the Aztec Corporation in problem 1.

3. Find the stockholders' equity ratio of the Aztec Corporation in problem 1.

4. Find the debt-equity ratio of the Aztec Corporation in problem 1.

5. The Aztec Corporation purchased a light duty truck for $9,200 and used the ACRS method of depreciation. The depreciation rates for property with a 3 year recovery period are 25%, 38%, and 37%. Find the amount of depreciation for each year of the recovery period, if the maximum depreciation is $3,200 (year 1) and $4,800 (years 2 and 3).

6. A piece of equipment (5 year recovery period) that cost $142,550 was depreciated using MACRS. Find the depreciation for each year if the depreciation percents were 20%, 32%, 19.2%, 11.52%, and 5.76%.

7. The Aztec Corporation purchased a piece of tooling equipment for $12,000. After 5 years, the salvage value was $900. During the 5 years, the company depreciated the equipment using the maximum rate under the declining-balance method. What rate of depreciation did the company use?

8. The stockroom of the Aztec Corporation occupies 5,000 square feet of the total floorspace of 160,000 square feet. How much of the company's overhead of $68,000 should be allocated to the stockroom if overhead is allocated according to floor space?

9. A finishing machine at the Aztec Corporation is valued at $15,000, with a useful life of 6 years. If the salvage value is $2,400, find the book value after three years using the sum-of-the-years-digits method of depreciation.

10. Lombardi and Berra are business partners. The partnership agreement calls for Lombardi to receive a monthly salary of $1,200, with the remaining profits to be distributed as follows: 45% to Lombardi, 55% to Berra. Find the distribution in a year when profits are $44,000.

11. On December 31, the Nichols Company had a cash balance of $12,500. For January, the company made the following estimates: materials purchased, $121,000; cash sales, $400,900; labor costs, $104,500; selling and administrative expenses, $102,300; utilities, $66,000; insurance and taxes, $79,200; accounts receivable collections, $42,600. If the company requires a minimum cash balance of $10,000, prepare a cash budget for January.

15

Insurance

Section 15.1 *Life Insurance*

A. Introduction

The primary purpose of life insurance is to offset financial need resulting from the death of a person. While that person is usually a close relative, it may be a business. For example, consider a drug company with a chemist who is developing a miracle drug expected to be highly profitable to the company. A life insurance policy on the chemist could help offset the financial loss the company might incur if the company's marketing of the drug is delayed because of the unexpected death of the chemist. For a second example, suppose that one of two partners in a partnership dies. The heirs are entitled to the partner's share of the business. A life insurance policy in the amount of the partner's share of the business provides the surviving partner with funds to buy out the other partner's share.

Regardless of the reason for the life insurance policy, upon the death of the insured, the insurance company promises to pay a specified amount of money (the **face value** of the policy) to a person or persons (the **beneficiaries**) named by the policyholder.

There are two categories of life insurance: term insurance and cash-value insurance. Term insurance is pure protection, while cash-value insurance combines protection with a savings account.

B. Term Insurance

Term insurance is protection for a limited period. The period may be as short as an airplane flight or may extend to age 70, but the most common periods are one, five, or ten years. Term insurance is like rent; it provides protection but develops no equity. The advantage of term insurance is that it provides the maximum protection at the lowest cost.

Term insurance may be renewable, convertible, or both. Renewable term insurance means the policy can be renewed for a limited time period, but at a higher cost. Convertibility means the policy can be converted to a form of cash-value insurance regardless of the physical condition of the insured at the time of conversion.

C. Cash-value Insurance

All individual life insurance policies are constructed on a framework of increasing cost with increasing age; that is, the premium per $1,000 increases each year. To counter the unpopularity of an annual price increase, the level premium was developed. A level premium is the same for each installment, higher than the actual cost of the protection in the lower ages but considerably less than the cost of the protection at the upper ages. The excess premium at the lower ages is invested at compound interest, and the accumulated amount is used to offset the higher protection cost at the upper ages. This accumulated amount is called the **cash value,** and represents a savings account with a compound interest rate guaranteed by the insurance company. However, this rate is usually quite conservative, and critics argue that greater savings could be realized if a person purchased term insurance and invested the difference between the premium for cash-value insurance and the premium for term insurance in an account with a higher return than that guaranteed by the insurance company. While possible, this approach assumes that the individual has the discipline to invest the difference, which is not always the case. For some people, the built-in investment feature of cash-value insurance may be the better choice.

There are three basic forms of cash-value insurance: ordinary life, limited pay life, and endowments.

Ordinary Life Insurance

Also known as whole or straight life insurance, **ordinary life insurance** is the basic policy of most life insurance companies and the least expensive of the cash-value plans. A level premium is paid as long as the insured lives, or until one of the non-forfeiture options is exercised (see section 15.3).

Two recent variations of ordinary life insurance are universal life insurance and variable life insurance. In a *universal life insurance* policy, the premium may be increased or decreased (within limits) by the policyholder. Decreasing (increasing) the premium in turn decreases (increases) the growth of the cash value. In a similar fashion, the death benefit may also be adjusted up or down. This flexibility can be important to a young policyholder with limited funds who needs maximum insurance protection for the family, and also to the older policyholder who needs less protection but can use cash value to supplement retirement benefits. Unlike traditional ordinary life insurance, the excess premium in a universal life policy is invested in securities, thus the cash value is subject to fluctuations in interest rates.

Variable life insurance is similar to universal life insurance, except that policyholders are allowed to specify that premiums be placed in one or more of a variety of separate investment funds, such as stock funds, fixed investment funds, bond funds, and so on.

Limited Payment Life Insurance

Limited payment life insurance policies have the same features as ordinary life insurance except the premium payments are limited to a specific number of years. The idea is to pay for a lifetime of coverage during the peak income-earning years. Thus, limited payment policies are sold with payment periods of 10, 15, 20, 25, or 30 years, or to a specified age such as 65 or 70. Upon completion of the payments, the insurance remains in force (unless the policyholder exercises one of the settlement options described in section 15.3), thus providing lifetime protection. The shorter payment period requires a higher premium than a comparable ordinary life policy, but this higher premium also generates a higher cash value, thus providing a larger fund for use if needed.

Endowment Insurance

Like term insurance and the other forms of cash-value insurance, **endowment insurance** pays the face amount of the policy upon death of the insured. Unlike these other policies, endowment insurance also pays the face amount if the insured is alive as of a specified date, called the maturity date. Typical endowment periods are 10, 15, or 20 years, or to a specific age such as 60 or 65. Because of the "can't miss" feature of this insurance, it is the most expensive of the cash-value forms (see section 15.2). Since insurance protection ceases if the insured lives to the maturity date, endowment insurance is not lifetime insurance.

Endowment insurance emphasizes the investment feature of cash-value insurance. A traditional use of endowment policies is to provide educational funds for children. Essentially, endowment insurance is a savings plan with insurance to protect the savings plan against premature death.

D. Life Insurance Premiums

For many years insurance companies have kept records of groups of people, recording the number living and dying at each age. These statistics are used to construct a **mortality table** such as that shown in table 15.1.

Insurance companies use mortality tables to determine the premium for a life insurance policy. To see how this is done, suppose that 100,000 males, all age 30, each purchased a $1,000 term insurance policy. According to table 15.1, 173 of this group will die before reaching age 31. This means the insurance company will have to pay out a total of $1,000 × 173 = $173,000 in claims. Thus, the premium per insured member is $173,000 ÷ 100,000 = $1.73.

Table 15.1 Commissioners 1980 Standard Ordinary Table

	Males		Females			Males		Females	
Age	Deaths per 1,000	Expectation of Life (Years)	Deaths per 1,000	Expectation of Life (Years)	Age	Deaths per 1,000	Expectation of Life (Years)	Deaths per 1,000	Expectation of Life (Years)
0	4.18	70.83	2.89	75.83	28	1.70	45.09	1.26	49.52
1	1.07	70.13	.87	75.04	29	1.71	44.16	1.30	48.59
2	.99	69.20	.81	74.11	30	1.73	43.24	1.35	47.65
3	.98	68.27	.79	73.17	31	1.78	42.31	1.40	46.71
4	.95	67.34	.77	72.23	32	1.83	41.38	1.45	45.78
5	.90	66.40	.76	71.28	33	1.91	40.46	1.50	44.84
6	.86	65.46	.73	70.34	34	2.00	39.54	1.58	43.91
7	.80	64.52	.72	69.39	35	2.11	38.61	1.65	42.98
8	.76	63.57	.70	68.44	36	2.24	37.69	1.76	42.05
9	.74	62.62	.69	67.48	37	2.40	36.78	1.89	41.12
10	.73	61.66	.68	66.53	38	2.58	35.87	2.04	40.20
11	.77	60.71	.69	65.58	39	2.79	34.96	2.22	39.28
12	.85	59.75	.72	64.62	40	3.02	34.05	2.42	38.36
13	.99	58.80	.75	63.67	41	3.29	33.16	2.64	37.46
14	1.15	57.86	.80	62.71	42	3.56	32.26	2.87	36.55
15	1.33	56.93	.85	61.76	43	3.87	31.38	3.09	35.66
16	1.51	56.00	.90	60.82	44	4.19	30.50	3.32	34.77
17	1.67	55.09	.95	59.87	45	4.55	29.62	3.56	33.88
18	1.78	54.18	.98	58.93	46	4.92	28.76	3.80	33.00
19	1.86	53.27	1.02	57.98	47	5.32	27.90	4.05	32.12
20	1.90	52.37	1.05	57.04	48	5.74	27.04	4.33	31.25
21	1.91	51.47	1.07	56.10	49	6.21	26.20	4.63	30.39
22	1.89	50.57	1.09	55.16	50	6.71	25.36	4.96	29.53
23	1.86	49.66	1.11	54.22	51	7.30	24.52	5.31	28.67
24	1.82	48.75	1.14	53.28	52	7.96	23.70	5.70	27.82
25	1.77	47.84	1.16	52.34	53	8.71	22.89	6.15	26.98
26	1.73	46.93	1.19	51.40	54	9.56	22.08	6.61	26.14
27	1.71	46.01	1.22	50.46	55	10.47	21.29	7.09	25.31

| .Table 15.1 | | Commissioners 1980 Standard Ordinary Table   *Continued* | | | | | | | |

	Males		Females			Males		Females	
Age	Deaths per 1,000	Expectation of Life (Years)	Deaths per 1,000	Expectation of Life (Years)	Age	Deaths per 1,000	Expectation of Life (Years)	Deaths per 1,000	Expectation of Life (Years)
56	11.46	20.51	7.57	24.49	78	83.90	6.97	53.45	8.55
57	12.49	19.74	8.03	23.67	79	91.05	6.57	59.35	8.01
58	13.59	18.99	8.47	22.86	80	98.84	6.18	65.99	7.48
59	14.77	18.24	8.94	22.05	81	107.48	5.80	73.60	6.98
60	16.08	17.51	9.47	21.25	82	117.25	5.44	82.40	6.49
61	17.54	16.79	10.13	20.44	83	128.26	5.09	92.53	6.03
62	19.19	16.08	10.96	19.65	84	140.25	4.77	103.81	5.59
63	21.06	15.38	12.02	18.86	85	152.95	4.46	116.10	5.18
64	23.14	14.70	13.25	18.08	86	166.09	4.18	129.29	4.80
65	25.42	14.04	14.59	17.32	87	179.55	3.91	143.32	4.43
66	27.85	13.39	16.00	16.57	88	193.27	3.66	158.18	4.09
67	30.44	12.76	17.43	15.83	89	207.29	3.41	173.94	3.77
68	33.19	12.14	18.84	15.10	90	221.77	3.18	190.75	3.45
69	36.17	11.54	20.36	14.38	91	236.98	2.94	208.87	3.15
70	39.51	10.96	22.11	13.67	92	253.45	2.70	228.81	2.85
71	43.30	10.39	24.23	12.97	93	272.11	2.44	251.51	2.55
72	47.65	9.84	26.87	12.28	94	295.90	2.17	279.31	2.24
73	52.64	9.30	30.11	11.60	95	329.96	1.87	317.32	1.91
74	58.19	8.79	33.93	10.95	96	384.55	1.54	375.74	1.56
75	64.19	8.31	38.24	10.32	97	480.20	1.20	474.97	1.21
76	70.53	7.84	42.97	9.71	98	657.98	.84	655.85	.84
77	77.12	7.40	48.04	9.12	99	1000.00	.50	1000.00	.50

Actually, the premium charged will be less than $1.73. Since insurance premiums are paid in advance, the company could invest the money for one year. The present value of $173,000 at a conservative rate of 5% compounded annually is

$$\$173,000 \times 0.95238095 = \$164,761.89 \qquad \text{(Appendix D)}$$

or $164,761.89 ÷ 100,000 = $1.65 per insured member.

The figure $1.65 is called the **net premium.** The premium actually paid is called the **gross premium** which includes the net premium plus a portion of the company's overhead expenses and contingency reserves.

With a net premium of $1.65 per member, the insurance company records the following:

$$
\begin{array}{rl}
\$165,000 & \text{Premium collected (\$1.65} \times \text{100,000)} \\
+\underline{8,250} & \text{Interest on invested premium (\$165,000} \times \text{0.05)} \\
\$173,250 & \\
-\underline{173,000} & \text{Claims paid (\$1,000} \times \text{173)} \\
\$250 & \text{Surplus (due to rounding of premium calculation)}
\end{array}
$$

It is not necessary to insure 100,000 people to determine the premium per individual. Instead, table 15.1 is used in the following way. At age 30 there are 1.73 deaths per 1,000. This is equivalent to $\frac{1.73}{1000}$ or 0.00173. Multiplying this decimal number by the face value yields

$$\$1,000 \times 0.00173 = \$1.73$$

Multiplying this by the present value of 5% and rounding,

$$\$1.73 \times 0.95238095 = \$1.65$$

EXAMPLE 1   Find the net premium for a one-year term policy of $50,000 sold to a male age 40 if the assumed rate of interest is 5%.

Solution: From table 15.1, the death rate is 3.02 per 1,000, or 0.00302. Thus,

$$\$50,000 \times 0.00302 \times 0.95238095 = \$143.81$$

| | | |
| Face value | Death rate | Present value for one year at 5% |

EXAMPLE 2   Joan Jacobs (age 25) purchased a one-year term policy for $150,000 from the Presidential Insurance Company. Find the net premium if the assumed rate of interest is 5.5%.

Solution: From table 15.1, the death rate is 1.16 per 1,000, or 0.00116.

$$\$150,000 \times 0.00116 \times 0.94786730 = \$164.93$$

EXERCISES FOR SECTION 15.1

In problems 1–10, find the net premium for a one-year term policy with the given face amount and the given interest rate issued to a male of the given age.

1. $150,000; 5%; age 40

2. $80,000; 4%; age 24

3. $120,000; 5%; age 42

4. $70,000; $3\frac{1}{2}$%; age 36

5. $130,000; $4\frac{1}{2}$%; age 52

6. $140,000; 5%; age 49

7. $84,500; $4\frac{1}{2}$%; age 27

8. $47,500; $5\frac{1}{2}$%; age 56

9. $185,000; $4\frac{1}{2}$%; age 37

10. $69,500; $3\frac{1}{2}$%; age 28

In problems 11–16, one-year term policies of the given face amount are issued to females. Find the net premium for the given interest rate.

11. $57,500; 4%; age 24

12. $73,000; 3%; age 42

13. $125,000; 5%; age 34

14. $88,000; $4\frac{1}{2}$%; age 46

15. $120,000; $5\frac{1}{2}$%; age 52

16. $45,000; 4%; age 39

Solve.

17. Eloise Clark, age 22, purchased a one-year term policy for $25,000. If the interest rate is 4% per annum, what was the net premium for the policy?

18. Find the net premium for a one-year term policy of $80,000 sold to a female, age 37 if the assumed rate of interest is 5% per annum.

19. Bob Forester has been assigned to do extensive traveling for his company during the coming year. He decides to purchase a $50,000 one-year term policy. If the interest rate is 5% per annum and if Bob is 34 years old, what is the net premium for the policy?

20. Mary Johnson, age 46, purchased a $30,000 one-year term policy. At an interest rate of $4\frac{1}{2}$% per annum, find the net premium for the policy.

Section 15.2 *Level Premiums*

Premium calculations in the previous section were for a one-year term policy. The premiums grow larger each year, especially in the later years. The solid part of the graph in figure 15.1 is the net premium per $1,000 of a renewable one-year term policy issued to a male at age 30 and assuming an interest rate of 3% per year. Since premiums are based on a mortality table, all insurance plans would have a similar graph.

An annual price increase would make insurance difficult to sell in the early years, and perhaps unaffordable in the later years. To overcome this difficulty, insurance companies developed the level premium. A level premium is the same for each payment. The dashed line in figure 15.1 is the level premium for the same one-year term policy. Note that the level premium is greater than the renewable premium at the early ages but less at the later ages. The insurance company invests the excess premium from the early years and uses the proceeds to offset the difference in premium at the higher ages (see figure 15.2).

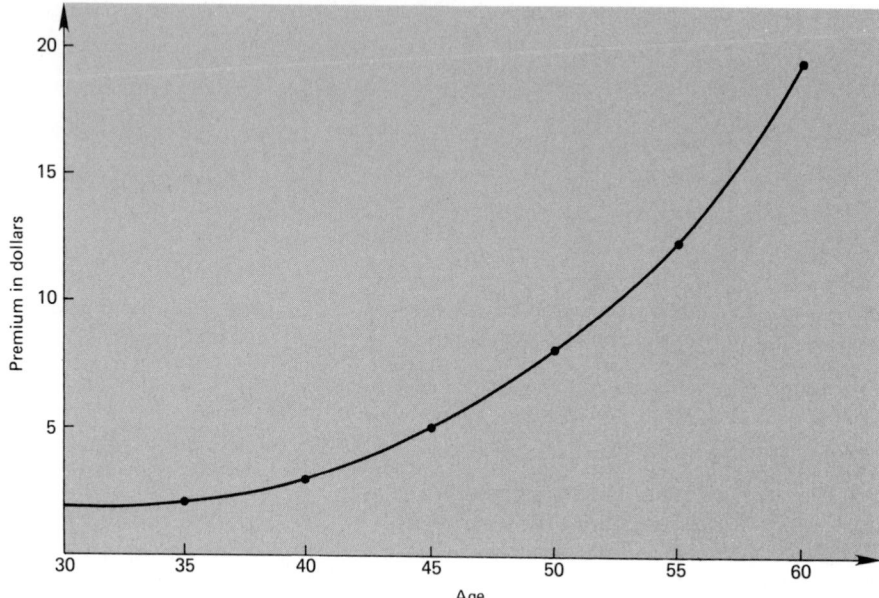

Figure 15.1
Line graph comparison of
a yearly renewable term
premium and a level
premium

Figure 15.2
Investment of premiums

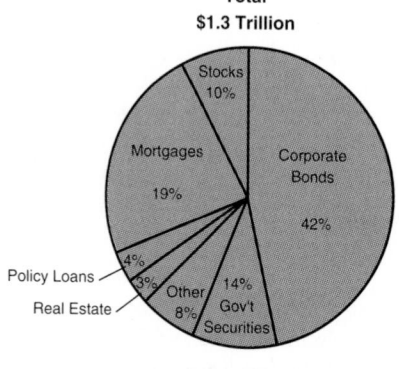

Total
$1.3 Trillion

Investment of Premiums

The excess premium is also used to generate the cash value in cash-value policies.
Table 15.2 illustrates the annual gross premium for four types of policies at selected
ages.

Table 15.2	Annual Level Premium Rates per $1,000 Face Value			
Age	**Renewable Term**	**Ordinary Life**	**Twenty-Payment Life**	**Twenty-Year Endowment**
25	$ 9.97	$12.95	$21.50	$43.13
30	11.79	15.31	24.34	43.55
35	14.17	18.40	27.78	44.24
40	17.22	22.36	31.75	45.32
45	21.13	27.44	36.77	46.89
50	25.87	33.60	42.34	49.12
55	31.90	41.44	48.90	52.94
60	40.74	52.31	58.06	59.26

EXAMPLE 1 Using table 15.2, what is the annual premium for an ordinary life policy of $45,000 issued to a fifty-year old man?

Solution: $33.60 × 45 = $1,512

Table 15.2 is a rate table for males. Since females have a longer life expectancy than males, a separate rate table is needed for females, or an adjustment must be made to table 15.2. One approach is to use table 15.2, but base the premium on an age less than the female's actual age. For example, a female age 25 might have her premiums calculated as though she were age 22. This is illustrated in the next example.

EXAMPLE 2 At age 30, Vicky Williams purchased a 20-payment life policy from Megapolis Life Insurance Company, which uses a five-year setback in calculating rates. If the face value was $80,000 and Megapolis uses the rates of table 15.2, what was Vicky's annual premium?

Solution: A five-year setback means that the premium for age $30 - 5 = 25$ will be used. Thus, $21.50 × 80 = $1,720

The level premiums discussed thus far are annual premiums. However payment periods may also be semiannual, quarterly, or monthly. These rates are percentages of the annual rate and may be approximated by table 15.3.

Table 15.3	Premium Percents for Different Payment Periods

Payment Period	Percent of Annual Premium
Semiannual	52
Quarterly	26
Monthly	9

EXAMPLE 3 At age 40, John Higgins purchased a 20-year endowment policy with a face value of $125,000. If the rates were based on tables 15.2 and 15.3, what was John's monthly premium?

Solution: $45.32 × 125 × 0.09 = $509.85 ■

Although insurance companies are conservative in their estimates of death rates and interest earnings, premiums are based on probabilities, and actual claims could exceed income. One method of guarding against this eventuality is to charge a premium greater than the company expects to need under normal circumstances. The company later refunds a portion of this surplus in the form of dividends. Policies with dividend provisions are called **participating** and are usually marketed by mutual insurance companies.* Generally, dividends begin from one to three years after purchase and increase in size each year. Over a period of time, dividends can substantially reduce the actual insurance cost.

A life insurance policy without the dividend feature is said to be **nonparticipating.** Here the risk of excess claims is borne by the owners of the company, normally the stockholders. As a rule, nonparticipating premiums are considerably less than corresponding participating policies, but there are no provisions for dividends.

EXERCISES FOR SECTION 15.2

In problems 1–10, use table 15.2 to find the annual premium for the given policy if the insured is a male of the given age.

1. $190,000 10-year renewable term; age 40

2. $110,000 20-year endowment; age 30

3. $80,000 20-payment life; age 35

4. $150,000 ordinary life; age 55

5. $225,000 20-payment life; age 25

6. $280,000 10-year renewable term; age 60

7. $95,000 ordinary life; age 45

8. $60,000 20-year endowment; age 60

9. $175,000 ordinary life; age 35

10. $350,000 10-year renewable term; age 40

*A mutual life insurance company is owned by the policyholders who share in the company's surplus earnings in the form of dividends. Nonparticipating policies are usually sold by a stock life insurance company, which is a corporation owned by the stockholders. Surplus earnings of a stock company are distributed to the stockholders as dividends.

In problems 11–16, find the annual premium for the given policy if the insured is a female and the company uses a five-year age reduction.

11. $225,000 20-payment life; age 40

12. $90,000 ordinary life; age 30

13. $175,000 10-year renewable term; age 55

14. $360,000 20-year endowment; age 45

15. $185,000 20-payment life; age 35

16. $85,000 10-year renewable term; age 50

In problems 17–22, use tables 15.2 and 15.3 to find the net premium for the given periodic payment on the given policy if the insured is a male.

17. $65,000 ordinary life; age 35; monthly payment

18. $125,000 10-year renewable term; age 50; quarterly payment

19. $150,000 20-year endowment; age 40; semiannual payment

20. $175,000 20-payment life; age 25; monthly payment

21. $50,000 10-year renewable term; age 60; semiannual payment

22. $200,000 ordinary life; age 45; quarterly payment

In problems 23–28, use tables 15.2 and 15.3 to find the net premium for the given periodic payment on the given policy if the insured is a female. (Use a five-year age reduction.)

23. $185,000 20-year endowment; age 40; monthly payment

24. $165,000 20-payment life; age 35; quarterly payment

25. $200,000 10-year renewable term; age 45; semiannual payment

26. $225,000 20-payment life; age 35; monthly payment

27. $175,000 ordinary life; age 30; quarterly payment

28. $330,000 20-year endowment; age 35; semiannual payment

Solve.

29. Mary Johnson, age 35, purchased a 20-payment life policy of $280,000. The company uses a five-year age reduction for females. How much is the semiannual premium?

30. Preston French bought a $50,000 ordinary life policy upon the birth of his first child. If he was 25 years old at the time, what was his quarterly premium?

31. Victoria Peters decides to buy a 20-year endowment of $165,000. She is 45 years old, and the company uses a five-year age reduction for females. How much is her monthly premium?

32. When Elvin Harrison was married, he purchased a $100,000 10-year renewable term policy. If he was 30 years old at the time, how much was his quarterly premium?

Section 15.3   *Nonforfeiture Values and Settlement Options*

A. Nonforfeiture Values

If premiums are not paid or the policy is canceled, a cash-value policy contains three nonforfeiture values.

1. *Cash value.* The policyholder may receive the cash value of the policy in cash. This terminates the contract. Normally, cash values begin to accrue after one or two years.

2. *Reduced paid-up insurance.* Under this option, the cash value is used to purchase a new policy that requires no further premiums. The face value of the new policy will be less than the original policy. If the original policy was a life policy, the new policy will be a life policy. If the original policy was an endowment, the protection continues to the maturity date, at which time the policyholder receives the reduced face value as a cash settlement.

3. *Extended term insurance.* With this option, the protection of the original policy is continued for a limited time by using the cash value to purchase a paid-up policy. The term depends on the attained age of the insured and the amount of the cash value. This option automatically goes into effect if the policyholder does not elect an option within a specified number of days after failure to pay a premium.

Table 15.4 illustrates minimum paid-up nonforfeiture values per $1,000 face value for a policy issued at age 35.

Table 15.4	Nonforfeiture Value per $1,000 Face Value											
	Ordinary Life				**Twenty-Payment Life**				**Twenty-Year Endowment**				
End of Year	Cash Value	Extended Term Years Days		Reduced Paid-Up	Cash Value	Extended Term Years Days		Reduced Paid-Up	Cash Value	Extended Term Years Days		Pure Endow- ment	Reduced Paid-Up
3	$ 17.00	4	38	$ 37.97	$ 45.93	9	190	$ 102.57	$ 84.12	14	313	—	$ 125.76
5	51.31	9	47	109.84	103.95	15	125	222.53	172.42	15	—	$119.14	246.02
10	140.96	14	91	272.40	259.55	21	291	501.56	412.23	10	—	462.39	523.45
15	235.14	15	183	412.25	431.88	24	352	757.17	684.38	5	—	755.79	772.52
20	331.58	15	72	530.91	624.55	Fully paid up			1000.00 at maturity				
25	427.84	14	60	630.46	—	—	—	—	—	—	—	—	—
30	520.74	12	310	712.57	—	—	—	—	—	—	—	—	—

EXAMPLE 1 Twenty-five years after purchase, Herb Goldberg (age 60) elected to surrender his $40,000 ordinary life policy. To what is Herb entitled under the nonforfeiture options of his policy? (Refer to table 15.4.)

Solution: a. *Cash-value option.* The per $1,000 cash value at the end of 25 years is $427.84. Hence, Herb could elect to receive $427.84 × 40 = $17,113.60 in cash.

b. *Reduced paid-up insurance option.* Herb could elect to receive a paid-up policy with a face value of $630.46 × 40 = $25,218.40.

c. *Extended term insurance option.* Herb could elect to continue his $40,000 coverage for a period of 14 years and 60 days beyond the surrender date.

B. Settlement Options
Upon the death of the insured, the settlement options of the policy allow the policyholder to designate the way the death benefits are to be distributed. Typically, the options fall into the following four categories.

1. *Cash.* The beneficiary may receive the benefits in cash as a lump-sum payment.
2. *Interest option.* The benefits remain with the company, but interest on the benefits is paid to the beneficiary, with provision for later lump-sum payment or gradual withdrawal.
3. *Installment option.* The payments are in the form of an annuity according to one of two plans:
   a. *Fixed period.* A specific length of time is selected, then the insurance company calculates the amount of equal payments that can be made, with the longer the time, the smaller the payments.
   b. *Fixed amount.* A specific payment amount is selected, then the insurance company calculates the number of equal payments that can be made, with the larger the amount, the fewer the number of payments.
4. *Life income annuity.* The annuity is for the lifetime of the beneficiary. Several plans are available and may include a period certain where a guaranteed number of payments will be made to the beneficiary or to a second beneficiary if the primary beneficiary dies before all payments are made.

A table of settlement values such as table 15.5 often appear in the policy.

Table 15.5		Monthly Payment per $1,000					
Fixed Period		**Life Income**			**Life Income with Payments Certain**		
				Life	*Number of Installments*		
Years	*Payment*	*Male*	*Female*	*Income*	*100*	*120*	*240*
1	$84.32	20	25	$2.95	$2.93	$2.92	$2.96
2	42.71	25	30	3.09	3.07	3.06	2.99
3	28.94	30	35	3.26	3.23	3.22	3.15
4	21.91	35	40	3.49	3.46	3.45	3.35
5	17.75	40	45	3.77	3.73	3.72	3.59
6	14.98	45	50	4.12	4.04	4.02	3.85
7	13.00	50	55	4.58	4.50	4.47	4.19
8	11.52	55	60	5.16	5.02	4.97	4.52
9	10.37	60	65	5.90	5.68	5.50	4.86
10	9.45	65	70	6.88	6.40	6.23	5.13

E X A M P L E   2   Nell Butterfield (age 50) is the beneficiary of a $90,000 ordinary life policy. She elects the life income option with 100 payments certain. Find the monthly payment using table 15.5.

Solution: For a female age 50, the payment per $1,000 is $4.04. Hence,

$4.04 × 90 = $363.60

C. Business Uses of Life Insurance

While the primary use of life insurance is to protect the dependents of the insured against financial loss, businesses also need protection against the loss of a valuable worker. At the beginning of this chapter an example was given of a chemist who was developing a drug anticipated to be highly successful and profitable to the company. The unexpected loss of this individual may curtail production, affect credit, reduce dividends, or damage the company in other ways. To offset the estimated financial loss, the company may purchase a life insurance policy for this key employee. The company is the beneficiary of the policy and pays the premiums. This form of insurance is called "key man insurance" and is designed to provide cash for the company during the readjustment period following the death of a key employee.

A second use of life insurance in business is for business continuation. For example, in a partnership form of business organization, the general rule of law calls for the dissolution and liquidation upon death of a general partner, with the surviving partners responsible for paying the estate of the deceased his or her share of the business. Because forced liquidation is costly, many partnerships enter into an agreement that binds the surviving partners to purchase at a predetermined price the interest of the first partner to die. One method of purchase is with a life insurance policy. Each partner is insured for his or her share, the policy being owned by the other partners. In the event of death, the proceeds of the policy are used to purchase the deceased partner's share of the business. All parties benefit by this arrangement, and it eliminates the need for liquidation.

EXERCISES FOR SECTION 15.3

In problems 1–11, use table 15.4 to find the cash value received when the given policy is surrendered after the given number of years.

1. $60,000 ordinary life; 15 years

2. $40,000 20-year endowment; 10 years

3. $50,000 20-payment life; five years

4. $55,000 20-year endowment; five years

5. $45,000 ordinary life; 30 years

6. $65,000 20-payment life; 15 years

7. A $75,000 ordinary life policy is surrendered after 15 years for reduced paid-up insurance. What is the face amount and the term of the new policy?

8. If an $80,000 20-year endowment policy is surrendered after five years for extended term insurance, what is the length of the term of the new policy? What is the face amount of the new term insurance policy?

9. Russ Overmeyer surrendered his $50,000 20-payment life policy after 10 years for reduced paid-up insurance. Find the face amount and the term of the new policy.

10. Find the length of the term when a $35,000 ordinary life policy is surrendered for extended term insurance after 25 years. What is the face amount of the new term insurance policy?

11. A 20-year endowment policy is surrendered after three years for reduced paid-up insurance. If the face amount of the endowment policy was $65,000, what is the face amount and the term of the new policy?

In problems 12–20, use table 15.5 to find the amount of the monthly payment to the beneficiary of a policy with the given proceeds when the given settlement option is selected.

12. Proceeds: $30,000; payee: male, age 40; settlement option: life income

13. Proceeds: $65,000; payee: female, age 60; settlement option: fixed period payments for five years

14. Proceeds: $85,000; payee: male, age 20; settlement option: life income, payments certain, 120 installments

15. Proceeds: $50,000; payee: female, age 45; settlement option: life income

16. Proceeds: $40,000; payee: female, age 35; settlement option: life income, payments certain, 240 installments

17. Proceeds: $80,000; payee: male, age 55; settlement option: life income, payments certain, 100 installments

18. Proceeds: $75,000; payee: male, age 40; settlement option: life income

19. Proceeds: $100,000; payee: male, age 25; settlement option: fixed period payments for 10 years

20. Proceeds: $45,000; payee: female, age 50; settlement option: fixed period payments for six years

21. Pasco Phillips, age 35, is the beneficiary of a $125,000 ordinary life policy, payable as life income. Find the monthly payments that he will receive.

22. Jean Tatum is to receive the proceeds of $40,000 from her father's life insurance in fixed period payments for eight years. If Jean is 45 when her father dies, what are her monthly payments?

23. Find the monthly payments to the beneficiary (male, age 50) of a life insurance policy with proceeds of $130,000 if the proceeds are payable as life income with payments certain in 120 installments.

Section 15.4 *Group Insurance*

A. Introduction

Group insurance provides insurance protection to the employees of a company. Under a group plan, a master contract issued to the company may provide both life insurance and health insurance to participating employees. Many plans also provide coverage for dependents of employees.

Compared with individual insurance, a group insurance plan contains a number of unique features. Among these are

1. Medical examinations usually are not required for employees actively at work.
2. Benefits are automatically determined by wage bracket, position, or some other employee classification.
3. The cost is shared by the employer. This lowers the total cost to the employee and encourages participation in the plan.
4. The cost of the insurance is based on the claims of the insured company rather than claims paid by the insurance company for all plans.

Group insurance policies provide a variety of coverages, including

1. Term life insurance. The basic plan is renewable term insurance with the same features as individual policies.

2. Accidental death and dismemberment insurance. This coverage pays for death or the loss of a limb as a result of an accident. The amount of coverage is usually the same as that for term life insurance.
3. Long term disability. The coverage is designed to pay a portion of income lost as a result of a prolonged absence from work due to illness or an accident. After a stated time period, the insured receives a periodic payment for a term specified in the policy. For example, a policy may call for an employee to receive two-thirds of his or her pay beginning on the 91st day of absence from work.
4. Major medical expense. Designed to cover most expenses of an illness, this coverage pays a percent (usually 80%) of all covered expenses in excess of a deductible (a portion of the expenses paid by the insured). Coverages typically include hospital room and board charges for a semi-private room, anesthetic charges, surgeon's and physician's fees, radiological and laboratory charges, and charges for medical supplies.

B. Group Insurance Premiums

Net premiums for group term life insurance are found by multiplying the rate per $1,000 at each age by the number of thousands insured at that age, adding the results, and dividing by the total amount of insurance to obtain an average rate per $1,000. This rate is charged every employee, regardless of age. The premium is the product of the rate and the number of thousands of insurance. Premiums are paid monthly.

EXAMPLE 1   Rainbow Industries has the following group life insurance coverage for its employees.

Officers	$40,000
Supervisors	$25,000
All other employees	$12,000

What is the monthly premium for an individual in each classification if the total premium is $656 and the total insurance is $800,000?

Solution: The rate per $1,000 is $\dfrac{\$656}{800} = \$0.82$. Thus,

Officers	$0.82 \times 40 = \$32.80$
Supervisors	$0.82 \times 25 = \$20.50$
All other employees	$0.82 \times 12 = \$\ 9.84$

■

The premiums for other group insurance benefits vary according to the amount of coverage and the characteristics of the group. The premium paid by an employee depends on (1) any contribution of the employer and (2) whether or not dependents are also covered.

EXAMPLE 2   Harry Wurts works for a company that provides the following group insurance coverage for its employees: term life insurance, $5,000; accidental death and dismemberment insurance (AD&D), $5,000; long term disability, and major medical insurance. The monthly premiums are as follows: term life insurance, $0.52 per $1,000; accidental death and dismemberment insurance, $0.12 per $1,000; long term disability, $0.61 per $100 of monthly pay; major medical insurance, $150 (employee), $370 (dependents). If Harry earns $3,000 per month and his company contributes 75% of the employee (only) premium, how much is Harry's monthly premium?

Solution:

Coverage	Employee Premium	Dependent Premium
Term life ($0.52 × 5)	$ 2.60	
AD&D ($0.12 × 5)	0.60	
Long term disability $\left(\$0.61 \times \dfrac{\$3,000}{\$100}\right)$	18.30	
Major medical	150.00	$370.00
	$171.50	

Harry pays 25% of the employee premium plus the dependent premium, or $42.88 + $370.00 = $412.88.

EXERCISES FOR SECTION 15.4

1. A company provides $10,000 worth of group term life insurance for each of its employees. Find the monthly premium for each employee if the total monthly premium is $315 and the total insurance is $300,000.

2. If $15,000 worth of group term life insurance is provided to each employee of a company, and if the total monthly premium is $292 and the total insurance is $400,000, what is the monthly premium for each employee?

3. Find the monthly group life insurance premium for each employee of a company that provides all employees with $10,000 worth of group term life insurance if the total monthly premium is $385 and the total insurance is $500,000.

4. The executives of Rockford Enterprises are eligible for $25,000 worth of group term life insurance. All other employees are eligible for $10,000 worth of insurance. Find the monthly premium for each executive and for each of the other employees if the total premium is $195 and the total insurance is $250,000.

5. The Minton Company has the following group life insurance coverage for its employees.

Executives	$20,000
Supervisors	$15,000
Other employees	$10,000

What is the monthly premium for an individual in each classification if the total premium is $528 and the total insurance is $800,000?

6. Find the monthly premium for an employee in each classification at the Buford Corporation if the total premium is $996, the total insurance is $1,200,000, and the company provides the following group life coverages.

Officers	$40,000
Supervisors	$20,000
Other employees	$15,000

7. Michelle Brainard works for a company that pays 100% of the monthly employee group insurance premium. Michelle is insured for group life insurance ($5,000), accidental death and dismemberment ($5,000), and major medical. If the monthly premiums are $0.78 per $1,000 for the life insurance, $0.09 per $1,000 for the accidental death and dismemberment, and $163.30 for the major medical, what amount does the company contribute for Michelle's insurance during a year?

8. Henry Morris insures himself and his family under a company group insurance plan with the following coverages: $10,000 each of life insurance and accidental death and dismemberment (AD&D), and major medical. The respective monthly premiums are: $0.86 per $1,000, $0.12 per $1,000, $166.00 (emp.), $355.94 (dep.). If the company pays 50% of the employee premium, how much does Henry pay each month for the insurance?

9. Barbara Drew and her family are insured under a group policy for the following coverages: $8,000 each of life insurance and AD&D, long term disability, and major medical. The monthly premiums are $0.93 per $1,000 for the life insurance, $0.11 per $1,000 for the AD&D, $0.59 per $100 of monthly salary for the long term disability. Major medical premiums are $161.40 per employee and $380.70 for dependents. If Barbara earns $2,180 per month, what does the insurance company bill each month for Barbara's coverage?

10. Jack Simpson insures himself and his family under the following group insurance plan: $15,000 each of life insurance and AD&D, long term disability, and major medical. The monthly premiums are respectively $0.76 per $1,000, $0.08 per $1,000, $0.49 per $100 of monthly salary, and $141.40 (emp.), $366.22 (dep.). If Jack's monthly salary is $3,100, what does the insurance company bill each month for Jack's coverage?

11. A company group insurance plan contains the following coverages: $6,000 each of life insurance and AD&D, long term disability, and major medical. The monthly premiums are respectively $0.85 per $1,000, $0.09 per $1,000, $0.62 per $100 of monthly pay, and $162.40 (emp.), $332.90 (dep.). The plan calls for each employee to pay all of the dependent premium and 25% of the employee premium. What is the total monthly cost for an employee with dependent coverage who makes $1,600 per month?

12. A group insurance plan at the Helms Corporation contains the following coverages (the monthly premiums are in parentheses): $6,500 life insurance ($0.70 per $1,000), AD&D ($0.10 per $1,000), long term disability ($0.60 per $100 of monthly pay), and major medical ($152.16 emp., $355.40 dep.). Tadashi Iwamoto has both employee and dependent coverage and earns $26,640 per year. If each employee pays the dependent premium and 30% of the employee premium, what amount is deducted from Tadashi's monthly paycheck for group insurance?

Section 15.5 *Fire Insurance*

A. Coinsurance

Both individuals and businesses need to protect their property from loss. Insurance of this type is called property and liability insurance. This section reviews one of the basic coverages of property and liability insurance—fire insurance.

Fire insurance covers the insured for direct losses due to fire or lightning, and also for damage to property while the insured is moving it to safety. Most fire insurance policies conform to a standard fire contract that specifies who is insured; where, when, what property is covered, and what is not covered; the amount of coverage; the premium; and the conditions under which coverage is suspended.

Three factors affect the actual amount paid by the insurance company in the event of a loss: (1) the face value of the policy, (2) the actual damage to the property, and (3) coinsurance. While the face value would be paid in a life insurance claim, most fires seldom cause total destruction, so in a fire insurance claim the company pays for the actual damage if it is less than the face amount. Coinsurance becomes a factor when a business tries to save money by insuring the property for less than it is worth. **Coinsurance** means that the insurance company and the insured share the risk. The most common ratio is 80%–20%. Thus, for property worth $100,000, if the insured carries a policy for $80,000, then in the event of a total loss, the insurance company would pay $80,000, while the insured would absorb $20,000 of the loss.

Summarizing, in a fire insurance policy with a coinsurance clause, the insurer's liability (the amount paid by the insurance company) is the *least* of the following amounts:

1. The face value of the policy
2. The actual loss
3. The amount determined by $\dfrac{\text{Face amount}}{\text{Property value} \times \text{Coinsurance \%}} \times \text{Loss}$

E X A M P L E 1

Property worth $400,000 was insured for $240,000. If the fire insurance policy contained an 80% coinsurance clause and a fire caused $120,000 damage, what was the insurer's liability?

Solution:
1. The face value was $240,000.
2. The actual loss was $120,000.
3. $\dfrac{\$240,000}{\$400,000 \times 0.80} \times \$120,000 = \dfrac{\$240,000}{\$320,000} \times \$120,000 = \$90,000$

The insurer's liability is the least amount, or $90,000.

Had the insured carried the full amount of insurance required by the coinsurance clause ($400,000 × 0.80 = $320,000), the company would have paid the full amount of the loss since

$\dfrac{\$320,000}{\$400,000 \times 0.80} \times \$120,000 = \$120,000$

E X A M P L E 2

Property worth $200,000 was insured for $150,000. If the fire insurance policy contained an 80% coinsurance clause, what was the insurer's liability on a fire that caused $170,000 damage?

Solution:
1. The face value was $150,000.
2. The actual loss was $170,000.
3. $\dfrac{\$150,000}{\$200,000 \times 0.80} \times \$170,000 = \dfrac{\$150,000}{\$160,000} \times \$170,000 = \$159,375$

The insurer's liability is the least amount, or $150,000.

Fire insurance on property may be spread over several companies. This can occur when additional insurance is purchased over a period of time, when new additions are built, or when the value of the property is too great for a single company to accept the risk. The next example illustrates payment of a claim by multiple carriers.

EXAMPLE 3   A building worth $400,000 had fire damage of $150,000. The fire insurance policy of $300,000 contained an 80% coinsurance clause and was divided among Company A ($150,000), Company B ($90,000), and Company C ($60,000). Find the amount paid by each company in the settlement of the claim.

Solution: 1. The face value was $300,000.
2. The actual loss was $150,000.
3. $\dfrac{\$300,000}{\$400,000 \times 0.80} \times \$150,000 = \$140,625$

The least of these amounts was $140,625, which was split among the three companies according to the ratio of the amount of coverage to the total face value. Thus,

Paid by	Amount	
A	$ 70,312.50	$\left(\$140,625 \times \dfrac{\$150,000}{\$300,000}\right)$
B	42,187.50	$\left(\$140,625 \times \dfrac{\$90,000}{\$300,000}\right)$
C	28,125.00	$\left(\$140,625 \times \dfrac{\$60,000}{\$300,000}\right)$
Total	$140,625.00	

B. Fire Insurance Premiums

A number of factors affect the premium charged for fire insurance. Among these are:

1. Construction (brick, wood, etc.)
2. Occupancy (flammability of contents)
3. Protection facilities (availability of fire-fighting equipment, water supply, etc.)
4. Exposure (congestion of area, hazardous property nearby, etc.)
5. Geographic location (losses vary by state)

Fire insurance premiums are quoted as a rate per $100 of insurance coverage, and the calculation is an application of the basic percentage formula $P = B \cdot R$ where P = premium, B = face value of the policy in hundreds of dollars, and R = rate per $100. Premium calculations are rounded to the nearest dollar in the last step.

Table 15.6 lists fire insurance rates for four building construction categories in five areas.

Table 15.6   Annual Rates for Each $100 of Insurance

Building Category

| | A | | B | | C | | D | |
Area	Building	Contents	Building	Contents	Building	Contents	Building	Contents
1	$0.25	$0.26	$0.33	$0.35	$0.37	$0.40	$0.42	$0.46
2	0.27	0.31	0.37	0.40	0.41	0.45	0.46	0.52
3	0.31	0.35	0.42	0.46	0.48	0.52	0.53	0.59
4	0.37	0.44	0.54	0.57	0.58	0.62	0.66	0.70
5	0.45	0.52	0.61	0.68	0.70	0.78	0.84	0.98

EXAMPLE 4   For a building located in area 1 and of construction category B, use table 15.6 to find the total fire insurance premium for a policy insuring the building for $200,000 and its contents for $85,000.

Solution: Building: $P = ?$, $B = \$200,000/\$100 = 2,000$, $R = \$0.33$
$$P = B \cdot R$$
$$= 2,000 \times \$0.33$$
$$= \$660$$
Contents: $P = ?$, $B = \$85,000/\$100 = 850$, $R = \$0.35$
$$P = B \cdot R$$
$$= 850 \times \$0.35$$
$$= \$297.50$$

$660 + $297.50 = $957.50. Rounded to the nearest dollar, the total premium is $958. ∎

EXAMPLE 5   Drs. Avery, Caldwell, and Berstein live in area 4. Their category C office building is insured for $315,000 and its contents for $64,000. Find the total fire insurance premium paid by the doctors.

Solution: Building: $P = ?$, $B = \$315,000/\$100 = 3,150$, $R = \$0.58$
$$P = B \cdot R$$
$$= 3,150 \times \$0.58$$
$$= \$1,827$$

Contents: $P = ?$, $B = \$64,000/\$100 = 640$, $R = \$0.62$
$$P = B \cdot R$$
$$= 640 \times \$0.62$$
$$= \$396.80$$

$1,827 + $396.80 = $2,223.80. Rounded to the nearest dollar, the total premium is $2,224. ∎

While premiums are quoted for one year, policies may be in force for less than one year because of temporary protection need, cancellation by the insured, or cancellation by the insurance company. In this event, the premium charged is a percentage of the annual premium, according to a short-term rate table. Table 15.7 is an abbreviated version of such a table.

Table 15.7	Short-Term Rate Table		
Time in Force	**% of Annual Rate**	**Time in Force**	**% of Annual Rate**
5 days	7	5 months	60
10 days	10	6 months	70
15 days	13	7 months	75
20 days	16	8 months	80
25 days	18	9 months	85
1 month	20	10 months	90
2 months	30	11 months	95
3 months	40	12 months	100
4 months	50		

The premium is less if the insurance company cancels the policy. For the examples and problems in this text, a figure of 10% less than the premium calculated from table 15.7 is used.

EXAMPLE 6   The need for additional space caused Alan Lebeda to sell his property and move his electronics store to a new location. He cancelled a fire insurance policy (coverage: building, $178,000; contents, $90,000; area 1; category B) five months after paying the annual premium. What refund did Alan receive?

Solution: Building: $P = ?$, $B = \$178,000/\$100 = 1,780$, $R = \$0.33$

$$P = B \cdot R$$
$$= 1,780 \times \$0.33$$
$$= \$587.40$$

Contents: $P = ?$, $B = \$90,000/\$100 = 900$, $R = \$0.35$

$$P = B \cdot R$$
$$= 900 \times \$0.35$$
$$= \$315$$

$\$587.40 + \$315 = \$902.40$. Rounded to the nearest dollar, the total annual premium was $902. From table 15.7, the premium is 60% of the total annual premium. Alan received the difference. That is,

$\begin{array}{ll} \$902.00 & \text{Total annual premium} \\ - \underline{541.20} & \text{Short-term premium} \\ \$360.80 & \text{Refund to Alan} \end{array}$

EXAMPLE 7   After a fire of suspicious origin, the Heartford Insurance Company cancelled a seven-month-old policy with an annual premium of $680. What refund did the policyholder receive?

Solution: From table 15.7,

$$P = B \cdot R$$
$$= \$680 \times 0.75$$
$$= \$510$$

Since the insurance company cancelled the policy, the premium is 10% less than $510; that is 90% of $510. Thus,

$\quad$ $680 $\quad$ Annual premium
$-$ $\underline{459}$ $\quad$ Short-term premium ($510 $\times$ 0.90)
$\quad$ $221 $\quad$ Refund

EXERCISES FOR SECTION 15.5

In problems 1–8, find the insurer's liability for a fire that causes the given amount of damage.

1. Property value: $200,000; amount of insurance: $150,000; coinsurance clause: 80%; fire causes $64,000 damage

2. Property value: $320,000; amount of insurance: $224,000; coinsurance clause: 80%; fire causes $190,000 damage

3. Property value: $650,000; amount of insurance: $500,000; coinsurance clause: 80%; fire causes $390,000 damage

4. Property value: $400,000; amount of insurance: $200,000; coinsurance clause: 80%; fire causes $300,000 damage

5. Property value: $580,000; amount of insurance: $400,000; coinsurance clause: 80%; fire causes $478,500 damage

6. Property value: $260,000; amount of insurance: $200,000; coinsurance clause: 80%; fire causes $220,000 damage

7. Property value: $675,000; amount of insurance: $500,000 carried by A ($300,000) and B ($200,000); coinsurance clause: 80%; fire causes $175,500 damage

8. Property value: $625,000; amount of insurance: $400,000 carried by A ($200,000), B ($100,000), and C ($100,000); coinsurance clause: 80%; fire causes $300,000 damage

Solve.

9. Use table 15.6 to find the annual premium for a fire insurance policy that will insure a category D building located in area 3 for $250,000 and the contents for $120,000.

10. Sam Donaldson opened a sporting goods store and purchased $110,000 worth of fire insurance for the building and $65,000 for the contents. If the building is rated category A and is located in area 2, how much was the annual premium for the policy?

11. When Jennifer Smith opened her clothing store, she insured the building for $130,000 and the contents for $80,000. What was her annual insurance premium if the building is located in area 2 and is rated category C?

In problems 12–18, use tables 15.6 and 15.7 to find the premium for a fire insurance policy for the given coverage when the policy is in force for the given period of time.

12. Coverage: building, $230,000; contents, $165,000; category B; area 5; time in force: four months; policy cancelled by insured.

13. Coverage: building, $115,000; contents, $40,000; category C; area 3; time in force: 10 months; policy cancelled by insurance company.

14. Coverage: building, $320,000; contents, $100,000; category D; area 1; time in force: two months; policy cancelled by insurance company.

15. Coverage: building, $180,000; contents, $30,000; category A; area 2; time in force: 20 days; policy cancelled by insured.

16. Coverage: building, $80,000; contents, $20,000; category D; area 5; time in force: seven months; policy cancelled by insurance company.

17. Coverage: building, $145,000; contents, $60,000; category B; area 3; time in force: five days; policy cancelled by insured.

18. Coverage: building, $220,000; contents, $50,000; category C; area 1; time in force: eight months; policy cancelled by insurance company.

19. John Dirkson insured his building for $120,000 and the contents for $70,000, but after six months he went out of business and cancelled his policy. If the building was rated category B and located in area 4, how much did John pay for his insurance coverage for the six months that he was in business?

20. Find the premium for a fire insurance policy to insure a category A building for $130,000 and the contents for $90,000 if the building is located in area 2, the policy is in force for eight months, and the policy is cancelled by the insured.

21. Laura Nesbitt insured her building (category B, area 5) for $110,000 and the contents for $50,000. Eleven months later, the company cancelled her policy because she failed to correct fire hazards in her business. How much did Laura have to pay for the 11 months of coverage?

Section 15.6 *Automobile Insurance*

A. Standard Coverages

In the United States, the automobile has evolved from an expensive luxury to an expensive necessity. Transportation experts predict that the automobile will continue to be the primary means of public transportation for the remainder of the century. At the same time, increased costs and spiraling energy prices have pushed the cost of driving toward 50¢ per mile.

One factor in the increased expense of ówning and operating an automobile has been the spectacular increase in automobile accident costs. For example, in one decade, the average bodily injury claim increased 107%, from $1,604 to $3,316, and the average property damage claim rose 109%, from $294 to an estimated $615.

The likelihood of being involved in an accident is also increasing. According to statistics published by the New York State Insurance Department, during the first year, there is a 1 in 4 chance that the typical driver will be involved in at least one motor vehicle accident. During five years, the chances are better than 3 out of 4. During twenty years, the chances are 99 out of 100.

Faced with the mounting cost of accidents and the probability of involvement, most drivers protect themselves with **automobile insurance.** Indeed, in most states it is compulsory that a driver carry some form of automobile insurance.

Automobile insurance policies are tailored to individual needs. Hence, insurance companies offer a variety of coverages and protection amounts. Among the standard coverages are

1. **Bodily injury liability** This coverage applies when the policyholder's car causes injury or death to persons in other cars or to passengers in his or her car. When claims are brought against the policyholder, the insurance company provides legal defense and pays for bodily injury damages up to the limit of the policy should the policyholder be found legally liable. Bodily injury liability is compulsory in many states, with minimum coverage of 5/10, meaning that the insurance company will pay up to $5,000 for the injuries sustained by one person and up to $10,000 for all injuries resulting from one accident. Many policyholders elect to carry coverage amounts much higher than the minimum.

2. **Property damage liability** This coverage applies when the policyholder's car damages property belonging to others. Usually, the property is another automobile, but it can be other items, such as buildings, lampposts, fire hydrants, and trees. When claims are brought against the policyholder, the insurance company provides legal defense and pays property damage up to the limit of the policy should the policyholder be found legally liable. The minimum coverage is usually $5,000, which means that the insurance company will pay up to this amount for each accident. Many drivers carry more than the minimum amount.

3. **Medical expenses** Under this coverage, the insurance company pays medical, surgical, X-ray, dental, and funeral expenses up to the limit of the policy. The coverage applies to the policyholder and his or her immediate family, whether in their own car, another car, or struck by a car while walking. It also applies to passengers in the policyholder's automobile. Payment is made regardless of who is at fault.

4. **Comprehensive damage** This coverage pays for any damage to the policyholder's car caused by falling objects, fire, theft, missiles, explosion, riot or civil commotion, or collision with a bird or animal. The coverage does not include damage resulting from collision with another automobile or object. Comprehensive insurance can be purchased with a deductible. For example, with a $50 deductible, the policyholder pays for the first $50 of loss per accident, while the insurance company pays any remainder. The higher the deductible, the lower the premium for the insurance.

5. **Collision damage** This coverage applies when the policyholder's car is damaged from collision with a vehicle or an object or as the result of turning over. Damages are paid by the insurance company regardless of who is at fault. Most collision insurance is sold with a $50 or $100 deductible.

6. **Uninsured motorist protection** This coverage reimburses the policyholder for injuries caused by an uninsured motorist or a hit-and-run driver. Coverage is normally limited to bodily injury claims, but some policies may include property damage. Protection is extended to the policyholder, relatives or passengers in the insured automobile, and any other person who would have legal right to collect for bodily injuries suffered through the negligence of an uninsured driver. In some states, uninsured motorist coverage is compulsory.

B. Premiums

Insurance premiums are a function of risk. In automobile insurance, the primary factors affecting risk are

1. *Territory in which the vehicle is operated* The probability of an accident is greater in cities than in rural areas.
2. *Usage and miles driven* The more miles driven, the greater the probability of an accident. Also, vehicles used for business are more likely to be involved in an accident than those driven for personal use.
3. *Make, model, and age of the vehicle* The newer and more expensive the automobile, the greater the cost of repair or replacement.
4. *Age, sex, and marital status of the driver* Statistics indicate that unmarried males under age 25 have more accidents than any other age group.

Factors 1 through 3 are used to establish base rates for the standard insurance coverages, as shown in tables 15.8 through 15.11. The total base rate is then multiplied by the age, sex, and marital status factor contained in table 15.11 to obtain the net semiannual premium.

Table 15.8	Liability and Medical Expense Premiums			
Bodily Injury *Coverage*	*Territory 1*	*Territory 2*	*Territory 3*	*Territory 4*
10/20	$43	$57	$ 72	$ 81
15/30	46	60	77	86
25/50	51	65	86	91
50/100	63	78	98	104
100/200	72	86	104	112
200/300	83	98	117	122
Property Damage				
$ 5,000	$42	$46	$49	$55
10,000	44	48	52	57
25,000	47	51	56	62
50,000	49	53	60	68
100,000	52	56	64	73
Medical Expense				
$1,000	$ 4	$ 7	$10	$18
2,500	8	13	21	26
5,000	10	18	26	33

Table 15.9 — Comprehensive and Collision Premiums

Model Class	Age	Territory 1 Comprehen. Full Cov	Comprehen. $50 Ded.	Collision $50 Ded.	Collision $100 Ded.	Territory 2 Comprehen. Full Cov	Comprehen. $50 Ded.	Collision $50 Ded.	Collision $100 Ded.	Territory 3 Comprehen. Full Cov	Comprehen. $50 Ded.	Collision $50 Ded.	Collision $100 Ded.	Territory 4 Comprehen. Full Cov	Comprehen. $50 Ded.	Collision $50 Ded.	Collision $100 Ded.
A–C	1	$14	$8	$84	$70	$17	$11	$87	$73	$21	$15	$90	$76	$27	$21	$95	$80
	2–3	13	7	71	60	15	10	74	63	20	14	77	66	25	14	88	70
	4–5	11	6	59	49	14	8	62	52	18	13	64	55	24	18	76	57
	6	8	4	49	39	11	7	52	42	15	11	55	45	21	17	66	48
D	1	18	10	94	78	21	13	97	81	25	17	99	84	31	22	104	88
	2–3	15	8	80	66	18	11	83	69	22	15	85	71	28	21	90	76
	4–5	14	7	66	55	17	10	69	57	21	14	71	60	27	20	76	63
	6	10	6	52	43	13	8	55	46	17	13	57	49	22	18	62	52
E	1	21	13	102	85	24	15	105	88	28	20	108	91	34	25	112	94
	2–3	18	10	88	73	21	13	91	76	25	17	94	78	31	22	77	81
	4–5	17	8	71	60	20	11	74	63	24	15	77	66	29	21	91	70
	6	13	7	57	48	15	10	60	50	20	14	63	53	25	20	77	56
F	1	29	17	122	101	32	20	125	104	36	24	127	106	42	29	132	111
	2–3	25	15	104	87	28	18	106	90	32	22	109	92	38	28	115	95
	4–5	22	13	85	71	25	15	88	74	29	20	91	77	35	25	97	81
	6	17	10	67	56	20	13	70	59	24	17	73	62	29	22	78	64
G	1	36	21	140	118	39	24	143	120	43	28	146	125	49	34	150	127
	2–3	31	17	119	99	34	20	122	102	38	24	125	105	46	29	129	109
	4–5	28	15	98	83	31	18	101	85	35	22	104	90	45	28	108	92
	6	20	11	77	64	22	14	80	67	27	18	83	70	36	24	87	74

Table 15.10 — Uninsured Motorist Premiums

Limits	Premium	Limits	Premium
$10,000	$8	$100,000	$29
15,000	14	200,000	32
25,000	17	300,000	35
50,000	22		

Table 15.11	Rating Factors					
	Age	**Driver Training**	**Pleasure**	**Work (Less Than 15 Miles)**	**Work (15 Miles or More)**	**Business Use**
No youthful operator	Female 30–64	—	1.00	1.25	1.45	1.45
	Male or female 65 or over		1.00	1.25	1.45	1.45
	All others	—	1.10	1.35	1.55	1.55
Unmarried female	18–20	Yes	1.30	1.55	1.55	1.55
		No	1.35	1.60	1.60	1.60
	21–24	—	1.10	1.35	1.55	1.55
	25–29	—	1.10	1.35	1.55	1.55
Married male	18–20	Yes	1.65	1.90	1.90	1.90
		No	1.75	2.00	2.00	2.00
	21–24	—	1.15	1.50	1.55	1.55
	25–29	—	1.10	1.35	1.55	1.55
Unmarried male—not owner, not principal operator	18–20	Yes	2.00	2.25	2.25	2.25
		No	2.30	2.55	2.55	2.55
	21–24	—	1.60	1.85	1.85	1.85
	25–29	—	1.10	1.35	1.55	1.55
Unmarried male—owner or principal operator	18–20	Yes	2.65	2.90	2.90	2.90
		No	2.95	3.20	3.20	3.20
	21–24	—	2.10	2.35	2.35	2.35
	25–29	—	1.75	2.00	2.00	2.00

EXAMPLE 1   Find the semiannual premium of an automobile policy for the following driver and coverages.

Driver	*Coverages*
Male, age 30	Bodily injury liability: 25/50
Territory 3	Property damage liability: 25
Car: D class, two years old	Comprehensive: $50 deductible
Miles to and from work: 22	Collision: $50 deductible

Solution:

Base premiums
Bodily injury liability	$ 86.00	(Table 15.8)
Property damage liability	56.00	(Table 15.8)
Comprehensive	15.00	(Table 15.9)
Collision	85.00	(Table 15.9)
Total	$242.00	
Rating factor	× 1.55	(Table 15.11)
Semiannual premium	$375.10	

EXAMPLE 2   Upon graduation from college at age 22, Helen Adkins decided to open a florist shop. Since she would have to use her four-year-old, class F station wagon for delivery, she changed her automobile insurance to insure it as a business vehicle. Helen is unmarried and lives in a territory 2 area. She purchased the following coverage: bodily injury and property damage liability, 50/100/50; medical expense, $5,000; comprehensive and collision, $50 deductible each; and uninsured motorist, $10,000. Find Helen's semiannual premium.

Solution: Base premiums

Bodily injury liability (50/100)	$ 78.00
Property damage liability (50)	53.00
Medical expense ($5,000)	18.00
Comprehensive ($50 deductible, class F)	15.00
Collision ($50 deductible, class F)	88.00
Uninsured motorist ($10,000)	8.00
Total	$260.00
Rating factor	× 1.55
Semiannual premium	$403.00

EXAMPLE 3   Jeff Bachman, age 25 and married, uses his car for business as a customer service representative and is reimbursed for mileage by his company. Jeff lives in a territory 1 area and drives a new class A car that he insures for bodily injury liability, 100/200; property damage liability, 100; comprehensive, full coverage; and collision, $50 deductible. Calculate Jeff's semiannual premium.

Solution: Base premiums

Bodily injury liability (100/200)	$ 72.00
Property damage liability (100)	52.00
Comprehensive (full coverage)	14.00
Collision ($50 deductible)	84.00
Total	$222.00
Rating factor	× 1.55
Semiannual premium	$344.10

E X A M P L E   4   While driving to work on a foggy highway, Janice's car rear-ended a slower moving car, causing $3,800 damage to her car and $1,100 to the other car. The other driver suffered whiplash and other injuries and was awarded $15,000 in a resultant lawsuit. Janice's medical expenses were $750. Janice carried the following automobile insurance: bodily injury and property damage liability, 25/50/10; comprehensive and collision, each with a $50 deductible. **a.** How much did Janice's insurance company pay in settlement of the claim? **b.** How much did Janice pay beyond her insurance coverage?

Solution:

	(a) *Paid by* *Insurance*	*(b)* *Paid by* *Janice*
Collision Damage		
Policyholder car	$ 3,750	$ 50
Other vehicle	1,100	
Bodily injury liability	15,000	
Medical expense		750
Total	$19,850	$800

■

EXERCISES FOR SECTION 15.6

In problems 1–10, find the semiannual premium of an automobile policy for the given driver and indicated coverages.

1. *Driver*
    Male, age 37
    Territory 2
    Car: F class, five years old
    Miles to and from work: 10

    Coverages
    Bodily injury liability: 15/30
    Property damage liability: 10
    Medical expense: $2,500
    Collision: $50 deductible

2. *Driver*
    Female, age 42
    Territory 4
    Car: C class, three years old
    Miles to and from work: 18

    Coverages
    Bodily injury liability: 100/200
    Property damage liability: 100
    Comprehensive: full
    Collision: $100 deductible

3. *Driver*
    Male, age 22, married
    Territory 3
    Car: A class, new
    Miles to and from work: 35

    Coverages
    Bodily injury liability: 10/20
    Property damage liability: 5
    Medical expense: $1,000
    Uninsured motorist: $15,000
    Comprehensive: $50 deductible
    Collision: $50 deductible

4. *Driver*
    Male, age 23, unmarried, owner
    Territory 4
    Car: G class, five years old
    Miles to and from work: 8

    Coverages
    Bodily injury liability: 25/50
    Property damage liability: 25
    Medical expense: $5,000
    Comprehensive: $50 deductible
    Collision: $100 deductible

5. *Driver*
    Female, age 24, unmarried
    Territory 1
    Car: E class, six years old
    Business use

    Coverages
    Bodily injury liability: 15/30
    Property damage liability: 10
    Medical expense: $2,500
    Collision: $100 deductible
    Uninsured motorist: $25,000

6. *Driver*
   Female, age 26, married
   Territory 4
   Car: B class, two years old
   Business use

   Coverages
   Bodily injury liability: 10/20
   Property damage liability: 5
   Collision: $100 deductible
   Comprehensive: $50 deductible
   Uninsured motorist: $15,000

7. *Driver*
   Male, age 18, unmarried, not owner, not principal operator, no driver training
   Territory 2
   Car: G class, three years old
   Pleasure use

   Coverages
   Bodily injury liability: 25/50
   Property damage liability: 10
   Medical expense: $1,000
   Collision: $50 deductible
   Comprehensive: full
   Uninsured motorist: $25,000

8. *Driver*
   Male, age 67
   Territory 1
   Car: F class, new
   Pleasure use

   Coverages
   Bodily injury liability: 200/300
   Property damage liability: 100
   Medical expense: $5,000
   Collision: $50 deductible
   Comprehensive: full
   Uninsured motorist: $300,000

9. *Driver*
   Male, age 20, unmarried, owner, completed driver training
   Territory 3
   Car: C class, six years old
   Miles to and from work: 5

   Coverages
   Bodily injury liability: 15/30
   Property damage liability: 10
   Medical expense: $5,000
   Collision: $100 deductible
   Uninsured motorist: $15,000

10. *Driver*
    Female, age 19, unmarried, completed driver training
    Territory 2
    Car: B class, two years old
    Miles to and from work: 22

    Coverages
    Bodily injury liability: 50/100
    Property damage liability: 50
    Medical expense: $2,500
    Comprehensive: $50 deductible
    Collision: $100 deductible
    Uninsured motorist: $50,000

Solve.

11. Greg Foster sells real estate and uses his own car for business purposes. He lives in a territory 3 area and drives a class F car that is one year old. Greg is married, 28 years old, and has the following insurance coverage: bodily injury and property damage liability, 25/50/10; medical expense, $2,500; comprehensive, full coverage; collision, $50 deductible; and uninsured motorist, $50,000. How much is Greg's semiannual premium?

12. Barbara DeVane is a sales representative for a pharmaceutical company. She uses her own car to call on wholesalers and is reimbursed by the company according to her business mileage. She lives in a territory 4 area and drives a three-year-old, class B car that she insures for the following coverage:

bodily injury and property damage liability, 100/200/50; comprehensive, $50 deductible; collision, $100 deductible; and uninsured motorist, $25,000. If Barbara is married and 32 years old, how much is her semiannual premium?

13. Bob Simmons works as a used book salesman to earn enough money so that he can return to college. Bob is 20 years old, unmarried, owns his own car, and took a driver training course in high school. He uses his car in his sales job and lives in a territory 1 area. Find the amount of the semiannual insurance premium on his two-year-old, class D car for 15/30 bodily injury liability coverage, $50 deductible collision coverage, $5,000 medical expense coverage, and $25,000 uninsured motorist coverage.

14. Tony Mendoza purchased a new class B sports car that he drives only for pleasure, since he also owns a pickup truck that he drives to his construction business. Tony is not married, lives in a territory 2 area, and is 29 years old. He insured his new sports car for the following coverage: bodily injury liability, 50/100; property damage liability, $10,000; medical expense, $2,500; comprehensive, full coverage; collision, $50 deductible; and uninsured motorist, $100,000. How much is Tony's semiannual premium?

15. In example 4, when Janice's policy came up for renewal, Janice lived in territory 1, was a 19-year-old unmarried female without driver training who drove her two-year-old, class D car 20 miles to work. As a result of the accident, the insurance company calculated her normal semiannual premium, then doubled the amount. What was her new premium?

16. Charlene Smith swerved to avoid hitting a child who darted into the street, lost control when the car jumped the curb, and crashed into a brick wall, causing $350 damage to the wall and $780 damage to her car. The cuts and bruises Charlene sustained resulted in a medical bill of $83. Charlene carried the following automobile insurance: bodily injury and property damage liability, 50/100/50; comprehensive and collision, each with a $100 deductible. **a.** How much did Charlene's insurance company pay in settling the claim? **b.** How much out-of-pocket expense did Charlene incur?

17. Hal Stoopid ran a red light and hit another automobile broadside, causing $3,475 damage to the other automobile and $4,200 damage to his own car. A friend in Hal's car and the driver of the other car were seriously injured. When an investigation revealed that Hal's blood alcohol content was above the legal limit, the driver of the other car and his friend's parents sued and were awarded $100,000 and $80,000 respectively. Hal carried the following automobile insurance: bodily injury and property damage liability, 15/30/10; comprehensive and collision, each with a $100 deductible. **a.** Find the amount Hal's insurance company paid in settlement of the claim. **b.** Hal's parents negotiated a loan to pay the difference between the total claim and the amount paid by Hal's insurance company. What was the amount of the loan?

18. Larry Leadfoot failed to negotiate a turn and crashed into a tree causing $5,600 damage to his car. Neither Larry nor his girlfriend were wearing seat belts, and they suffered serious injuries resulting in medical expenses of $6,000 and $11,500 respectively. A suit by the girlfriend's father resulted in an award of $25,000. Larry had the following automobile insurance: bodily injury and property damage liability, 10/20/10; comprehensive and collision, each with a $50 deductible; medical expense, $2,500. In settling the claim, **a.** How much did the insurance company pay, and **b.** how much did Larry have to pay beyond his insurance coverage?

19. Daisy unsuccessfully tried to pass a truck on a two-lane highway and crashed her small foreign car head-on into a full-size sedan. Daisy's car was totaled and damage to the sedan was $6,975. The only survivor of the accident was the driver of the sedan who was hospitalized and incurred medical bills totaling $6,500. Daisy's insurance had recently been canceled, while the other driver carried the following coverage: bodily injury and property damage liability, 100/200/100; comprehensive and collision, full; uninsured motorist, $50,000. Find the amount paid to the surviving driver in settlement of the claim.

Glossary

Automobile insurance   Insurance protection for injuries to persons or damages to property caused by a motor vehicle.

Beneficiary   The person named to receive the proceeds or benefits of an insurance policy.

Bodily injury liability   In automobile insurance, coverage when the policyholder's car causes injury or death to persons in other cars or to passengers in the policyholder's car.

Cash value   A fund that accumulates within a life insurance policy (except for term insurance) that may be borrowed against or paid in cash to the policyholder if the policy is canceled.

Coinsurance   The sharing of a risk by the insurance company and the insured; a feature found in major medical group insurance and in fire insurance.

Collision damage   In automobile insurance, coverage when the policyholder's car is damaged from collision with a vehicle or object.

Comprehensive damage   In automobile insurance, coverage for damage to the policyholder's car by fire, theft, explosion, falling objects, and so on.

Conditions   A description of what an individual must do to receive an insurance policy.

Declaration   In an insurance policy, descriptive material indicating who is covered, what is covered, the amount of coverage, and the premium.

Endowment insurance   Insurance that pays the beneficiary upon death of the insured or pays the insured if the insured is alive on the maturity date of the policy.

Exclusions   A description of what the insuring agreement does not cover in an insurance policy.

Face value   A specified amount of money to be paid to the beneficiary upon the death of the insured or, in the case of endowment insurance, to the insured if the insured is alive on the maturity date.

Gross premium   The premium paid by the policyholder. It includes the cost of the insurance plus the cost of the insurance company's overhead.

Group insurance   Insurance for the employees of a company under a master plan issued to the company. Both life insurance and nonoccupational health coverage are commonly offered under group plans.

Hazard   A condition that may create a peril or increase its probability of occurrence.

Insurance   A contract whereby a party undertakes to guarantee another party against loss by an accidental event.

Insurance policy   The contract wherein the terms and conditions of the insurance are stated.

Insured   The person or organization named in an insurance policy to receive the insurance coverage provided by the policy.

Insurer   Also called *underwriter*. The organization that sells an insurance policy.

Insuring agreement   A description of the perils that are covered by an insurance policy.

Level premium   A premium that is the same for each payment.

Limited payment life insurance   A life insurance plan in which the premiums are limited to a specified number of years.

Medical expenses   In automobile insurance, coverage for medical, surgical, X-ray, dental, and funeral expenses for the policyholder, family of the policyholder, or passengers in the policyholder's car.

Mortality table   A table indicating the probability of death at each age; used by insurance companies as a basis for life insurance rates.

Net premium   A life insurance premium based only on a mortality table, without taking into consideration the expenses of the company.

Nonforfeiture values   Options by which the policyholder may utilize the cash value in the event premium payments are discontinued. These options include cash, reduced paid-up insurance, or extended term insurance.

Nonparticipating policy   An insurance policy with rates lower than the participating rate but with no provision for dividends.

Ordinary life insurance   A life insurance policy characterized by the payment of premiums as long as the insured lives.

Participating policy   An insurance policy offered by a mutual insurance company or a stock insurance company in which an overcharge is made on the premium with the idea of returning a dividend to the policyholder.

Peril   An event that causes a loss, such as fire, accident, illness, and so on.

Policyholder   The owner of an insurance policy.

Premium   The cost of an insurance policy.

Property damage liability   In automobile insurance, coverage when the policyholder's car damages property belonging to others.

Settlement options   Options by which the policyholder (or in some cases the beneficiary) can designate the manner in which the proceeds are to be distributed. Options include cash, interest payments, installments of principal and interest, or a life income annuity.

Term life insurance   Insurance that provides protection for a limited period of time and develops no nonforfeiture values.

Uninsured motorist protection   In automobile insurance, reimbursement to the policyholder for damage caused by an uninsured motorist or a hit-and-run driver.

1. A condition that may create a peril or increase its probability of occurrence is called a _____ .

2. In a typical insurance policy, the _____ sets forth exactly what perils are covered.

3. Life insurance characterized by the payment of premiums as long as the insured lives is called _____ .

4. Life insurance policies marketed by mutual insurance companies that have a dividend provision are called _____ .

5. A nonforfeiture option whereby the cash value is used to purchase life insurance protection without further premiums is called _____ .

6. Automobile insurance that applies when the policyholder's car damages property belonging to others is called _____ .

7. The two categories of life insurance are _____ and _____ .

8. Find the premium for a one-year term policy of $25,000 sold to a 38-year-old male if the assumed interest rate is 4% per annum.

9. Using tables 15.2 and 15.3, find the monthly premium for a 50-year-old female who purchases a 20-payment life policy with a face value of $60,000, if the insurance company uses a five-year setback.

10. Vern Strasberg elected to surrender his Twenty-Pay life insurance policy ten years after purchase for the cash value. How much did he receive if the face value of the policy was $180,000?

11. Juanita Lopez (age 60) was the beneficiary of a $125,000 life insurance policy. If she elected the life income with 120 payments certain option, find the amount of her monthly payment.

12. Property worth $200,000 is insured for $150,000. If the fire insurance policy contains an 80% coinsurance clause and a fire causes $100,000 damage, what is the liability of the insurance company?

13. A married, 25-year-old male who lives in territory 1 insures his new class A car for the following coverage: comprehensive, full coverage; collision, $50 deductible; bodily injury liability, 50/100; property damage liability, $25,000; medical expense, $5,000. If the car is driven 20 miles to work, what is the semiannual premium?

Section 16.1 *Data Organization and Graphs*

A. Introduction

The word *statistics* has more than one meaning. In its most common usage, statistics refers to a collection of numerical data. Statistics may also refer to the analysis and interpretation of such data. In the singular, the word statistic may denote a particular item of data or a measure calculated from data.

Each of these connotations has an application in business. A characterization of the contemporary business enterprise is the accumulation of numerous reports, graphs, and other forms of numerical data from both internal and external sources. The proper utilization of this data is crucial to successful business practices. In this chapter, several of the basic methods used to summarize and categorize numerical data are introduced.

B. Data Organization

1. Arrays

Before statistical analysis can take place, the data to be analyzed must be arranged in a usable form. One such arrangement, called an **array,** involves ordering data from high to low or from low to high. For example, the number of sales at register 9 of the R. D. Davis Company for a two-week period is recorded in table 16.1.

Table 16.1	Sales at Register 9					
Week	**Monday**	**Tuesday**	**Wednesday**	**Thursday**	**Friday**	**Saturday**
1	10	12	15	9	22	32
2	7	15	16	17	20	29

An array of the data in table 16.1 would be

$$7, 9, 10, 12, 15, 15, 16, 17, 20, 22, 29, 32$$

An array serves to detail the overall pattern, but its usefulness is limited to sets with a small number of values. The ordering of data with a large number of values is tedious unless data-processing equipment is available.

2. Frequency Distributions

A second method of summarizing or describing a set of data involves arranging the values in a frequency distribution. In a **frequency distribution,** the values are grouped into **classes;** then a tally is made of the number or frequency of the values in each class. This tally is called the **class frequency.**

Table 16.2 shows a frequency distribution of the data in table 16.1.

Table 16.2	Frequency Distribution of Table 16.1 Data	
Class	**Tally**	**Frequency**
5–9	//	2
10–14	//	2
15–19	////	4
20–24	//	2
25–29	/	1
30–34	/	1

Frequency distributions are described as **numerical** when the data are grouped according to numerical size (such as in table 16.2) and as **categorical** when sorted according to a qualitative description.* The number of classes in a frequency distribution is arbitrary but should range from 6 to 15. It is also desirable to make class intervals of equal length whenever possible.†

Another method of presenting data is the **relative frequency distribution,** in which relative class frequencies are found by dividing class frequencies by the total number in the sample. Table 16.3 is a relative frequency distribution of the data in table 16.1.

Table 16.3	Relative Frequency Distribution of Table 16.1 Data		
Class	**Frequency**	**Relative Frequency**	**Percent**
5–9	2	0.1667	16.67
10–14	2	0.1667	16.67
15–19	4	0.3333	33.33
20–24	2	0.1667	16.67
25–29	1	0.0833	8.33
30–34	1	0.0833	8.33
	12	1.0000	

A **cumulative frequency distribution** is one in which the entry for each line in the table is the class frequency plus the sum of the frequencies of all preceding lines. A cumulative frequency distribution of the data in table 16.1 is shown in table 16.4.

Table 16.4	Cumulative Frequency Distribution of Table 16.1 Data
Class	**Cumulative Frequency**
Less than 10	2
Less than 15	4
Less than 20	8
Less than 25	10
Less than 30	11
Less than 35	12

C. Graphs

In business, graphs are often used to transmit statistical information. Graphs can be more useful than charts or aggregates of figures in presenting data, and graphs are particularly useful in spotting trends. Graphs frequently used in business are line graphs, bar graphs, pictograms, and circle graphs.

*One example of a categorical distribution would be arranging the data according to categories of sales, such as records, tapes, phonographs, televisions, and so on.

†The length of a class interval is the difference between successive lower class limits. For example, the length of the class interval 5–9 is 10 − 5 = 5.

Figure 16.1
Line graph of data for
week one in table 16.1

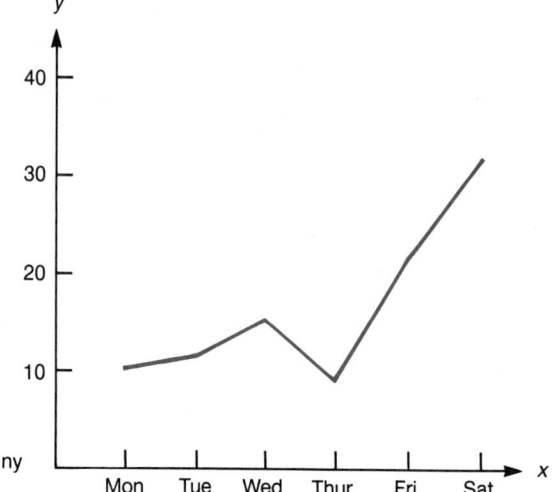

Figure 16.2
Bar graph of table 16.2

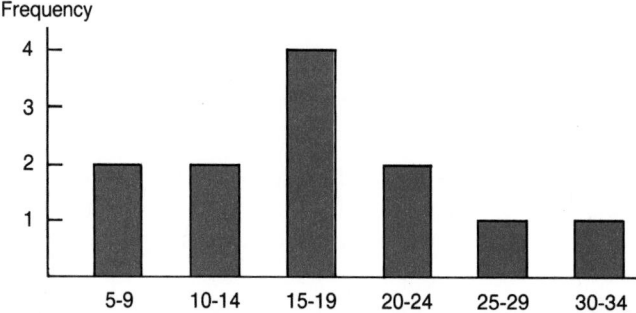

Line graphs are the most widely used kind of graph. Figure 16.1 is a line graph of the data for week one in table 16.1, where the horizontal (x) axis represents time and the vertical (y) axis represents frequency. The dots indicate the frequency for the given day and the graph is formed by connecting the dots with line segments.

A second type of graph is the bar graph. **Bar graphs** are similar to line graphs in that they are also drawn in reference to an x- and y-axis, but instead of points, bar graphs use bars projecting from an axis. Figure 16.2 is a bar graph of the data in table 16.2. Note that the height of the bars in the figure corresponds to points on a line graph.

Circle graphs, also known as pie charts, use a circle as a base for the graph. Figure 16.3 is a circle graph of table 16.3.

To construct a circle graph, each item of data must be converted to degrees. For example, in table 16.3 class 15–19 had a frequency of 4, or 33.33% of the total. Since

$$360° \times 0.3333 = 120°$$

this class is represented by that part of the circle with a central angle of 120 degrees.

Figure 16.3
Circle graph of table 16.3

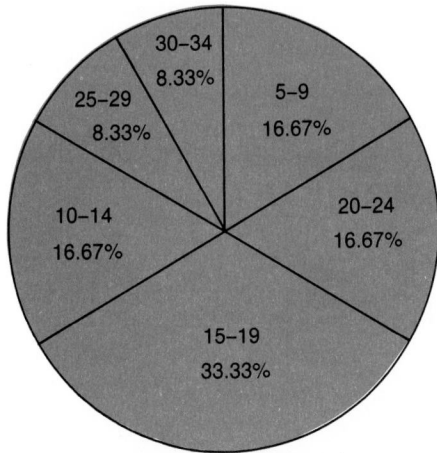

Figure 16.4
Pictogram of the
Whitman Company
employment

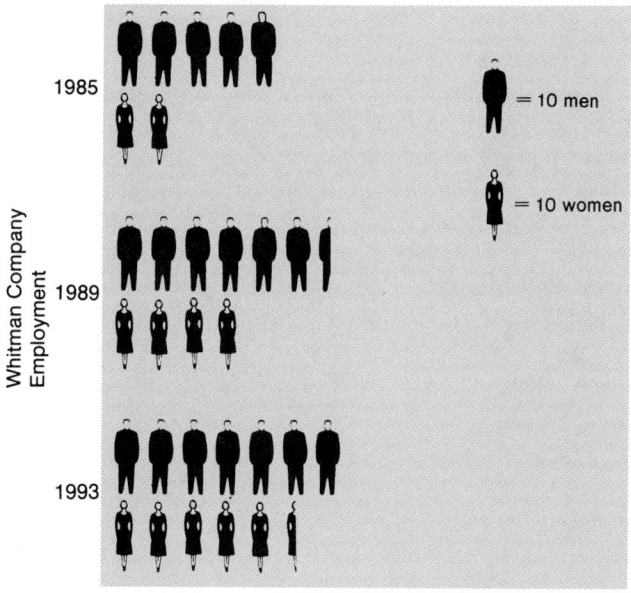

A **pictogram** is a modified form of a bar graph in which pictures are used to represent quantity. Figure 16.4 is a pictogram of the employment record of the Whitman Company taken from the following data.

Total Employment

Year	Men	Women
1985	50	20
1989	65	40
1993	70	55

Pictograms are almost always displayed horizontally; thus, years are scaled on the vertical axis.

D. Graph Distortions

Care must be exercised in the construction of a graph, since it is possible to present a graph that is accurate, yet misleading. To see this, let us see how a graph of the earnings per share of the Armstrong Company (figure 16.5) was reshaped by **a.** the board of directors of the company and **b.** a dissident stockholder seeking control of the company.

Figure 16.5
Earnings per share of the
Armstrong Company

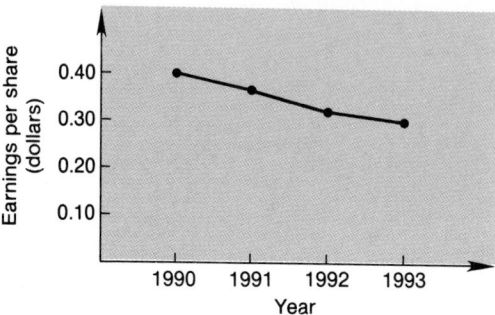

The board of directors naturally wants to minimize the declining earnings of the company. Therefore, in their annual report to stockholders, they present figure 16.6(a) as a graph of the company earnings. By stretching the scale of the *x*-axis and shortening that of the *y*-axis, the decline in earnings appears minimal.

On the other hand, in an open letter to stockholders, Mr. Dissident Stockholder charges the company with mismanagement and calls for an immediate change in the company leadership. He supports his charge with the graph of the company's earnings record shown in figure 16.6(b).

Figure 16.6
Distortions of the earnings
per share of the
Armstrong Company

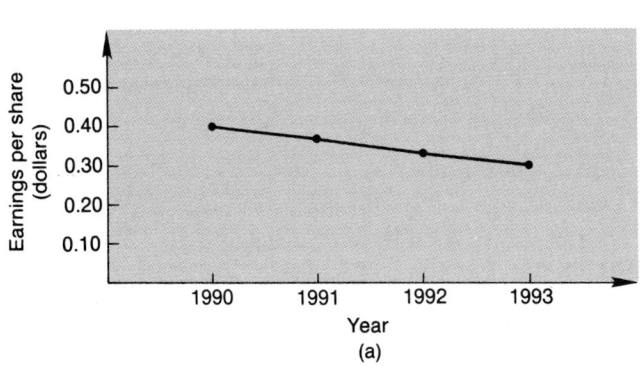

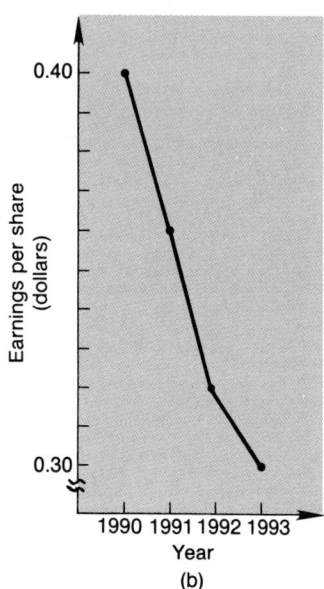

By stretching the scale on the *y*-axis, shortening the scale of the *x*-axis, and eliminating most of the vertical portion of the graph, Mr. D. S. has presented an earnings record that appears calamitous. In both cases, the graphs were accurately drawn but created opposite impressions.

The preceding is an example of how graphs can be manipulated to create an impression. Such manipulations may be accidental, but all too often they are deliberate attempts to deceive. In pointing out these distortions, our purpose is to help you avoid unintentional errors in graph construction and to encourage a critical examination of all published graphs.

Bar graphs are susceptible to the same distortions as line graphs. For example, in a report to the home office on reduction of energy consumption, a branch manager submitted the graph shown in figure 16.7(a).

Figure 16.7
Kilowatt hours consumed
by Oregon branch

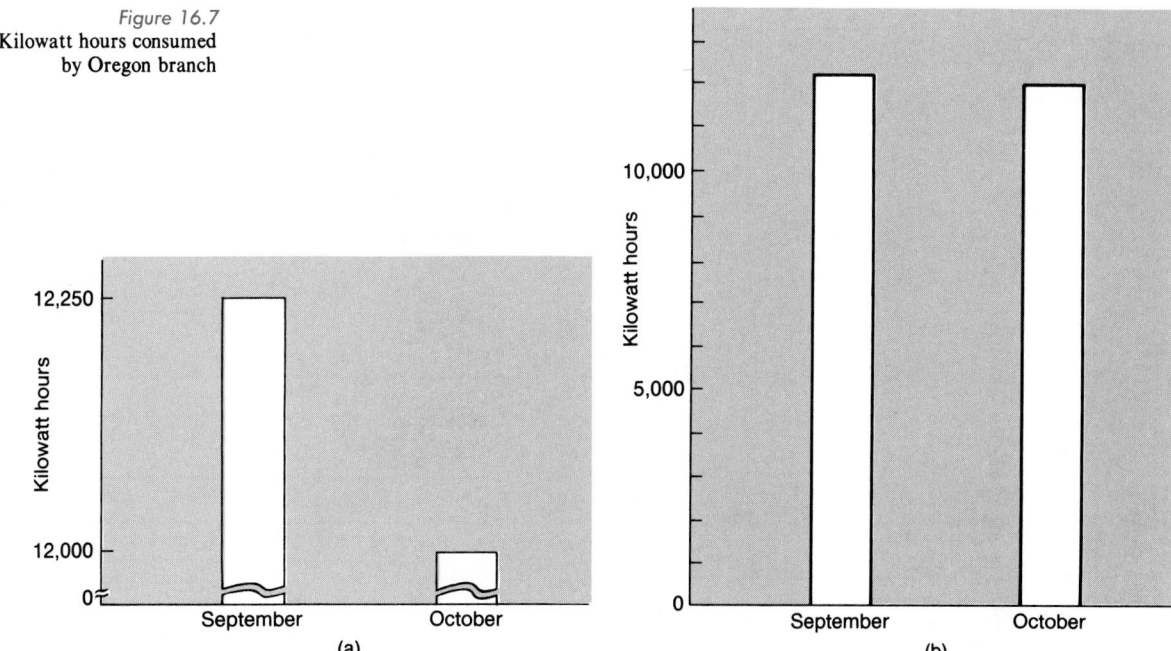

At first glance, the decrease seems impressive; however, the actual reduction is only about 2%. In this instance, a false impression was created by using a detailed scale, then omitting most of the vertical portion of the graph. The correct relationship is shown in figure 16.7(b).

Figure 16.8(a) shows a distortion of a pictogram. In this case, a twofold increase in company assets has been depicted by a figure whose radius is twice that of the 1992 figure. Although the radius is only twice as large, the *area* of the 1993 figure is four *times* that of the 1992 figure!

The correct method of graphing the increase is shown in figure 16.8(b).

Figure 16.8
Assets of a company

1992

1993

1992

1993

(a)

(b)

EXERCISES FOR SECTION 16.1

Use the following data to solve problems 1–12.

A	5	21	14	33	19	27	9	15
B	7	13	24	15	32	37	41	11
C	43	12	8	26	31	23	39	18
D	9	18	27	25	29	19	8	23

1. Arrange the data in line A in an array.

2. Arrange the data in line D in an array.

3. Arrange the data in lines A and C in an array.

4. Arrange the data in lines B and D in an array.

5. Arrange the data in lines B and C in an array.

6. Complete the following table using the data in lines A and C.

Class	Frequency
0–9	
10–19	
20–29	
30–39	
40–49	

7. Complete the following table using the data in lines B and D.

Class	Frequency
0–9	
10–19	
20–29	
30–39	
40–49	

8. Complete the following table using the data in lines B and C.

Class	Frequency
0–9	
10–19	
20–29	
30–39	
40–49	

9. Complete the following table using the data in lines A and D.

Class	Frequency	Relative Frequency	Percent
0–9			
10–19			
20–29			
30–39			
40–49			

10. Complete the following table using the data in lines A and B.

Class	Frequency	Relative Frequency	Percent
0–9			
10–19			
20–29			
30–39			
40–49			

11. Complete the following table using the data in lines A and D.

Class	Frequency	Cumulative Frequency
0–9		
10–19		
20–29		
30–39		
40–49		

12. Complete the following table using the data in lines B and D.

Class	Frequency	Cumulative Frequency
0–9		
10–19		
20–29		
30–39		
40–49		

Solve.

13. The number of sales reported by each of ten salespersons at a used car outlet last week are given in the following table.

Salesperson	Number of Sales	Salesperson	Number of Sales
J. H.	15	R. S.	16
A. B.	7	B. A.	12
D. T.	11	C. D.	9
P. Z.	4	E. T.	8
D. D.	13	E. S.	5

Construct a frequency distribution of this data using class intervals of five.

14. The following numbers represent the number of years that the ten employees at the Simpson Company have yet to work before being eligible for retirement: 5, 11, 14, 2, 21, 8, 14, 9, 18, 12. Construct a frequency distribution of this data using class intervals of four.

15. Construct a relative frequency distribution of the data in problem 13.

16. Construct a relative frequency distribution of the data in problem 14.

17. The biweekly net earnings of 12 employees at the Concord Company are $390, $420, $405, $470, $510, $475, $460, $492, $505, $435, $425, and $395. Construct a cumulative frequency distribution of this data using class intervals of $20 and starting with $380.

18. The following numbers represent the final exam scores of students in a biology class.

62	59	91	80	87	56
72	68	78	87	76	75
42	98	72	75	70	55
52	83	72	71	99	89
69	73	74	59	63	91

Construct a cumulative frequency distribution of this data using class intervals of 10 and starting with 40.

19. The Golden State Corporation reported profits of $1.25 per share in 1990, $1.75 in 1991, $2.00 in 1992, and $1.50 in 1993. Construct a line graph of the company's profits for the four years.

20. The annual maintenance costs of the Omega Manufacturing Company for a five-year period are as follows: 1989, $50,000; 1990, $70,000; 1991, $85,000; 1992, $90,000; 1993, $95,000. Prepare a line graph to illustrate this data.

21. Superior Products manufactures blade housings for lawn mowers. The following table gives the production cost per unit based on the number of units produced per month.

Number of units produced	600	800	1,000	1,200
Production cost per unit	$8.00	$7.00	$6.50	$6.25

Construct a line graph for this data. Use the graph to estimate the production cost per unit if 700 units are produced per month.

22. The following table gives the gross sales and production costs of the Braxton Company for the first six months of the fiscal year:

	Jan.	Feb.	March	April	May	June
Gross sales	$27,000	$31,000	$26,000	$27,500	$33,000	$33,500
Production costs	$18,000	$20,000	$17,000	$17,500	$21,500	$22,000

On the same set of axes, draw a line graph of the gross sales and a line graph of the production costs.

23. Culver Enterprises presented the following bar graph to summarize the number of male and female employees in its work force at the beginning of each of the years shown. How many female employees were at Culver at the beginning of 1985? What was the total work force at the beginning of 1975? How many male employees were there at the beginning of 1990?

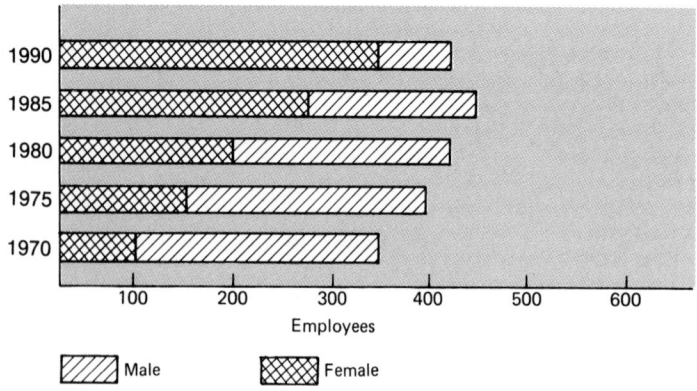

24. Construct a vertical bar graph that shows the number of units produced each month at the Concord Manufacturing Company: January, 4,500; February, 4,800; March, 5,200; April, 5,800; May, 4,200; June, 3,800.

25. Using the data given in the following table, construct a horizontal bar graph of the sales of the five branch stores of the Friendly Wholesale Farm Supply Company.

Branch	Sales
Riverview	$230,000
Eastport	320,000
Gulf	280,000
Brooksville	360,000
Sumter	220,000

26. The employment records of the Bradston Company yield the following data on the number of male and female employees at the company at the beginning of the years indicated.

Year	Male	Female
1965	800	50
1970	850	250
1975	900	400
1980	1,150	700
1985	1,250	950
1990	1,300	1,150

On the same set of axes, construct side-by-side vertical bar graphs showing the number of male employees and the number of female employees for each of the six years.

27. The first-quarter sales of Adamson's Men's Store were distributed as follows: suits, 32%; sport coats, 25%; slacks, 18%; shirts, 16%; shoes, 6%; miscellaneous, 3%. Construct a circle graph of the first-quarter sales.

28. The Eagle Manufacturing Company reported the following use of the company's sales dollar: production, 40¢; operating expenses, 25¢; research, 15¢; taxes, 15¢; miscellaneous, 5¢. Construct a circle graph that represents the use of the sales dollar.

29. The sales last year at Sander's Sporting Goods Store were distributed as follows: sports equipment, 64%; clothing, 28%; books, 6%; miscellaneous, 2%. Prepare a circle graph of the store's sales.

30. John and Pat Weber prepared the following monthly budget for their family: food, $320; housing, $230; clothing, $160; savings, $100; recreation and miscellaneous, $120. Find the percent of each expenditure and construct a circle graph of the budget.

31. Huffman Industries manufactures farm equipment. The company produced 40,000 tractors in 1991, 45,000 in 1992, and 55,000 in 1993. Let the symbol

represent 10,000 tractors, and prepare a pictogram showing the company's production for the three years.

32. Employment records at the Hammond Company reveal that the company employed 20 women and 40 men in 1980, 40 women and 45 men in 1985, and 55 women and 50 men in 1990. Prepare a pictogram for

this data. Use the symbol to represent 10 men

and the symbol to represent 10 women.

33. The net income of the Kenyon Company for the years 1989–1993 is as follows: 1989, $60,000; 1990, $70,000; 1991, $90,000; 1992, $80,000; 1993, $110,000. Construct a pictogram that shows the net income for each year. Use the symbol to

represent $20,000.

34. Sterling Auto Sales sold 2,500 cars in 1975, 3,750 cars in 1980, 4,000 cars in 1985, and 3,500 cars in 1990. Using the symbol to represent 500 cars, construct a pictogram of the company's sales for the four years.

35. Kelsey Industries reported profits of $0.60 per share
in 1990, $0.70 per share in 1991, $0.50 per share in
1992, and $0.40 per share in 1993. Which of the
following line graphs most accurately represents this
data? What is wrong with the other two graphs?

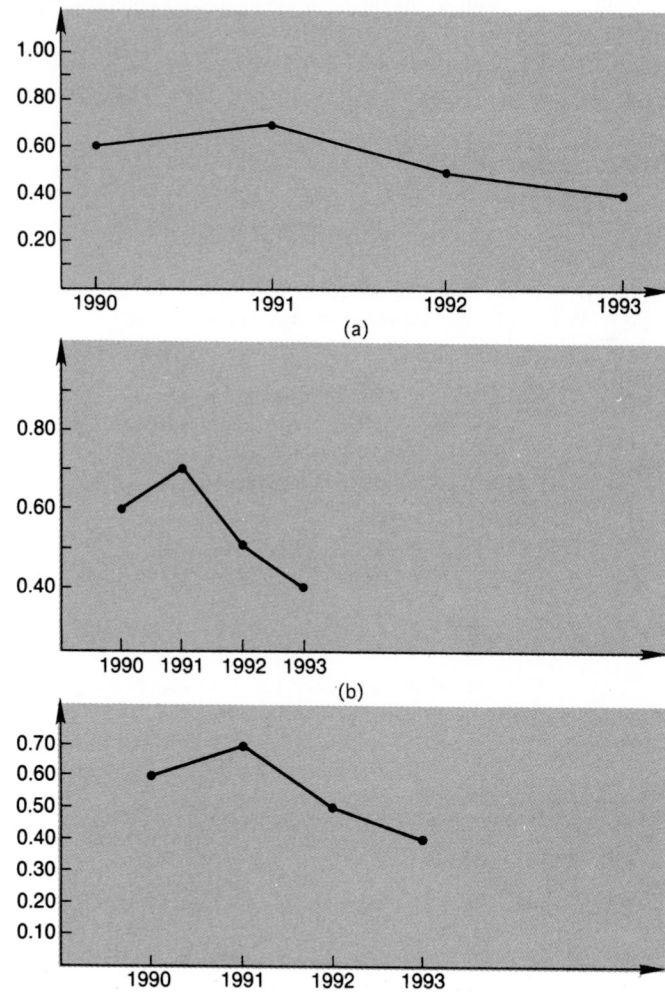

(a)

(b)

(c)

36. Robertson's Electrical Supply recorded sales of
$19,000 in January, $21,500 in February, $17,000 in
March, and $15,000 in April. Which of the following
bar graphs most accurately represents this
information? What is wrong with the other two
graphs?

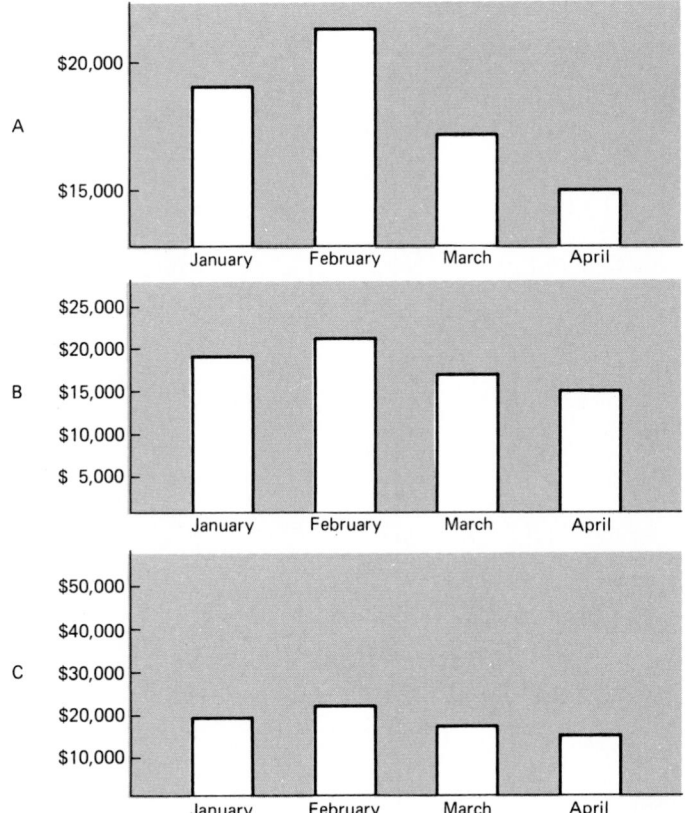

37. Americana Builders constructed 1,000 new homes in
1988 and 4,000 new homes in 1993. If the symbol

represents 1,000 homes, which of the
following pictograms most accurately reflects the
construction record at Americana?

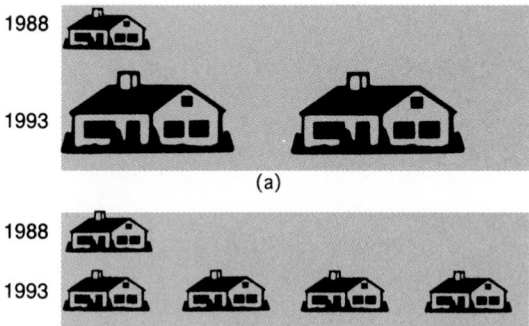

38. Employment records at the Bradshaw Company show that in 1983 15% of the employees were members of minority groups; in 1984, the figure rose to 20%; and in 1993, to 30%. Which of the following line graphs most accurately represents this data? What is wrong with the other two graphs?

39. The sales record at the Clayton Candy Company for the first quarter of this year is as follows: January, $12,000; February, $16,000; March, $8,000; and April, $10,000. Which of the following bar graphs most accurately represents this information? What is wrong with the other two graphs?

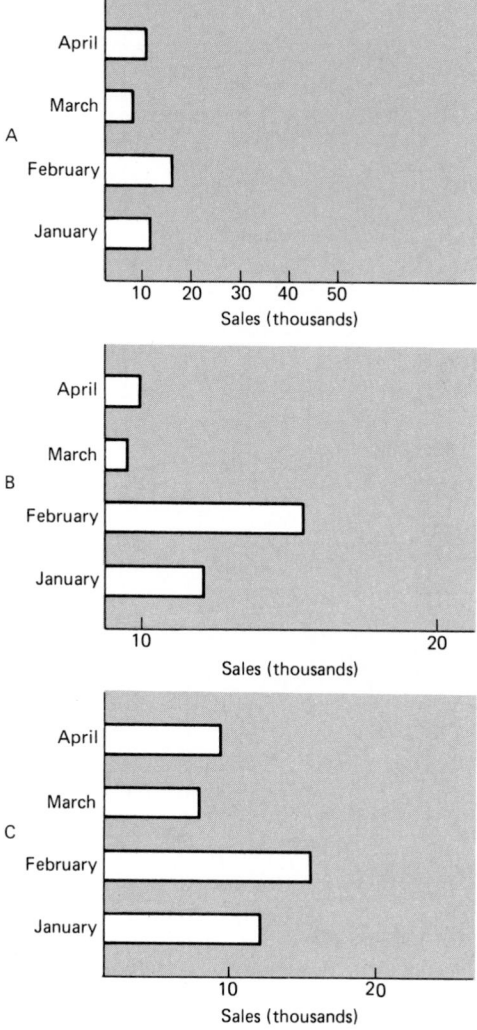

40. Braxton Builders reported net income of $20,000 in 1992 and $40,000 in 1993. If the symbol represents $10,000, which of the following pictograms most accurately represents the net income of the company for the two years?

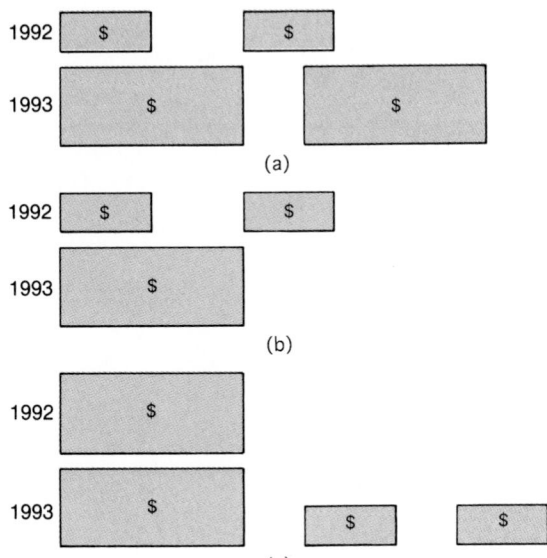

Section 16.2 *Measures of Location*

A. Sigma Notation

Statisticians use a number of techniques to describe quantitative data. Numerical and graphical displays were covered in section 16.1. The sections that follow cover arithmetic methods. Before describing these arithmetic techniques, it is necessary to introduce a mathematical notation used in these measures.

The Greek letter **sigma** (Σ) is a notation used for "sum" or "add." For example, if the values in a distribution are x_1, x_2, x_3, x_4, and x_5, the sum of these values can be denoted by $\sum\limits_{i=1}^{5} x_i$. That is,

$$(16\text{--}1) \quad \sum_{i=1}^{5} x_i = x_1 + x_2 + x_3 + x_4 + x_5$$

The notation Σx_i means sum (add) all of the x_i's. The notation below and above the sigma symbol indicates the range of the x_i's, in this case from one to five. The notation $\sum\limits_{i=1}^{7} y_i$ means the sum of y_1 through y_7; that is,

$$(16\text{-}2) \quad \sum_{i=1}^{7} y_i = y_1 + y_2 + y_3 + y_4 + y_5 + y_6 + y_7$$

EXAMPLE 1   Find: $\sum\limits_{i=1}^{4} x_i$ if $x_1 = 2, x_2 = 4, x_3 = 9, x_4 = 16$

Solution: $\sum\limits_{i=1}^{4} x_i$

$$= x_1 + x_2 + x_3 + x_4$$
$$= 2 + 4 + 9 + 16$$
$$= 31$$

EXAMPLE 2   Find: $\sum\limits_{i=1}^{3} (x_i + y_i)$ if $x_1 = 4, x_2 = 9, x_3 = 14, y_1 = 8, y_2 = 22, y_3 = 7$

Solution: $\sum\limits_{i=1}^{3} (x_i + y_i) = (x_1 + y_1) + (x_2 + y_2) + (x_3 + y_3)$

$$= (4 + 8) + (9 + 22) + (14 + 7)$$
$$= 12 + 31 + 21$$
$$= 64$$

Measures of location (or measures of central tendency) are numbers indicative of the "center" or "average" of a set of data. The measures of location discussed in this section are (1) the arithmetic mean, (2) the median, and (3) the mode. There are advantages and disadvantages to each measure; hence, more than one may be utilized for a given set of data.

B. The Arithmetic Mean

The arithmetic mean is the most popular measure of location and is that value usually associated with the word "average." Average weight, batting average, and average sales are examples of the arithmetic mean. The **arithmetic mean** or **mean** is the sum of the values of a set of data divided by the total number of values. That is, for a set containing n values, the arithmetic mean (denoted by $\bar{x}$) is given by the formula

$$(16\text{-}3) \quad \bar{x} = \frac{\sum\limits_{i=1}^{n} x_i}{n}$$

EXAMPLE 3   Find the mean of the data in the following array.

7, 9, 10, 12, 15, 15, 16, 17, 20, 22, 29, 32

Solution: $x_1 = 7, x_2 = 9, x_3 = 10, \ldots, x_{12} = 32$; hence,

$$\bar{x} = \frac{\sum\limits_{i=1}^{12} x_i}{12}$$
$$= \frac{204}{12}$$
$$= 17 \qquad \blacksquare$$

EXAMPLE 4   Sixteen pieceworkers of the Hudgins Company produced the following number of pieces in one day's work: 22, 24, 20, 22, 26, 26, 23, 30, 28, 22, 20, 24, 28, 27, 26, 24. What was the mean number of pieces produced by the 16 workers?

Solution: $$\bar{x} = \frac{\sum\limits_{i=1}^{16} x_i}{16}$$
$$= \frac{392}{16}$$
$$= 24.5 \qquad \blacksquare$$

As a measure of central tendency, the mean has several advantages. The mean always exists, it is unique in the sense that a set of data has only one mean, and it takes into account each item of the data. A disadvantage of the mean is that it is affected by extreme values; that is, an unusually high or low value shifts the mean toward this value. The mean of the data 2, 3, 4, 5, 6 is $\frac{20}{5} = 4$, but the mean of the data 2, 3, 4, 5, 16 is $\frac{30}{5} = 6$. The mean of the second set of data was shifted toward the extreme value.

C. The Median

In an array of n values, the **median** is (1) the middle value of the array if n is odd and (2) the mean of the two middle values if n is even.

EXAMPLE 5   Find the median of **a.** 2, 4, 6, 8, 10, and **b.** 2, 4, 6, 8, 10, 12.

Solution: **a.** $n = 5$; thus, the median is the middle value 6

b. $n = 6$; thus, the median is the mean of the two middle values; that is,

$$\frac{6 + 8}{2} = 7$$

EXAMPLE 6   Find the median of the data in the following array.

7, 9, 10, 12, 15, 15, 16, 17, 20, 22, 29, 32

Solution: $n = 12$; hence, the median is the mean of the sixth and seventh values.

$$\frac{15 + 16}{2} = \frac{31}{2} = 15.5$$

EXAMPLE 7   During an eleven-day period, the closing stock prices of the Hanson Corporation were

$21\frac{1}{4}$, $21\frac{3}{8}$, $21\frac{1}{4}$, $21\frac{1}{2}$, $21\frac{5}{8}$, $21\frac{1}{2}$, $21\frac{3}{4}$, 22, $22\frac{1}{4}$, $21\frac{7}{8}$, $21\frac{5}{8}$

What was the median closing price of the stock during this period?

Solution: First, arrange the prices in an array

$21\frac{1}{4}$, $21\frac{1}{4}$, $21\frac{3}{8}$, $21\frac{1}{2}$, $21\frac{1}{2}$, $21\frac{5}{8}$, $21\frac{5}{8}$, $21\frac{3}{4}$, $21\frac{7}{8}$, 22, $22\frac{1}{4}$

The sixth or middle value is $21\frac{5}{8}$. This is the median closing price of the stock.

Like the mean, the median is unique and always exists, The median requires a minimum of calculation; unlike the mean, it is not affected by extreme values. On the other hand, to find the median, the values must be arranged in an array, a tedious task for large values of n. A more significant disadvantage is that in statistical problems of estimation and tests of hypotheses, the median is less useful than the mean.

D. The Mode

A third measure of location is the mode. The **mode** is that value, class, or category that has the highest frequency.

E X A M P L E 8   Find the mode of the data in the following array.

7, 9, 10, 12, 15, 15, 16, 17, 20, 22, 29, 32

Solution: The value with the highest frequency is 15, which occurs twice.   ◪

The chief advantage of the mode is that it requires no calculation. On the other hand, the mode may not exist (for example, the set of data 4, 5, 6, 7 has no mode), or if it does exist, it may not be unique. The array 2, 4, 4, 6, 6, 8 has two modes—4 and 6—and is said to be **bimodal.**

The principal value of the mode lies with categorical data. Suppose a poll indicated the following preferences for package size.

Size A = 157

Size B = 84

Size C = 120

Size D = 95

The frequency of 157 clearly indicates that size A is the mode.

EXERCISES FOR SECTION 16.2

1. Compute $\sum\limits_{i=1}^{3} x_i$, when $x_1 = 4$, $x_2 = 3$, and $x_3 = 7$.

2. If $y_1 = 10$, $y_2 = 9$, $y_3 = 4$, and $y_4 = 6$, find $\sum\limits_{i=1}^{4} y_i$.

3. Find $\sum\limits_{i=1}^{3} (y_i - 2)$, when $y_1 = 6$, $y_2 = 8$, and $y_3 = 12$.

4. Find $\sum\limits_{i=1}^{4} (2x_i)$, when $x_1 = 3$, $x_2 = 1$, $x_3 = 5$, and $x_4 = 8$.

5. If $x_1 = 6$, $x_2 = 10$, $x_3 = 8$, and $x_4 = 4$, what is the value of $\sum\limits_{i=1}^{4} (3x_i - 1)$?

6. If $x_1 = 10$, $x_2 = 12$, $x_3 = 20$, $y_1 = 4$, $y_2 = 6$, and $y_3 = 11$, find $\sum\limits_{i=1}^{3} (x_i + y_i)$.

7. In problem 6, find $\sum\limits_{i=1}^{3} (x_i \cdot y_i)$.

8. In problem 6, find $\sum\limits_{i=1}^{3} (4x_i - y_i)$.

9. Find $\sum\limits_{i=1}^{4} (2x_i + 4) + \sum\limits_{i=1}^{3} (4y_i - 1)$, when $x_1 = 2$, $x_2 = 7$, $x_3 = 11$, $x_4 = 6$, $y_1 = 2$, $y_2 = 4$, and $y_3 = 8$.

10. Find $\sum\limits_{i=1}^{3} (6x_i - 1) - \sum\limits_{i=1}^{4} (3y_i + 2)$, when $x_1 = 2$, $x_2 = 3$, $x_3 = 1$, $y_1 = 1$, $y_2 = 1$, $y_3 = 3$, and $y_4 = 2$.

Use the following data to solve problems 11–22.

```
A    7   11    5   19    6   12   12   21   14   12   14
B   18    4    7    2   16   23   15   15    9   14
C    6   11   15   14   13    7   13   24   18   17   16
D   15    9   12   18    7   10   14   15   11   13
```

11. Find the mean of the data in line A.

12. Find the mean of the data in line B.

13. Find the mean of the data in line C.

14. What is the median of line A?

15. What is the median of line B?

16. What is the median of line C?

17. Find the mode of line A.

18. Find the mode of line B.

19. Find the mode of line C.

20. Find the mean, median, and mode of line D.

21. Find the mean, median, and mode of lines A and B.

22. Find the mean, median, and mode of lines C and D.

Solve.

23. A sales representative for the Burns Corporation reported the following daily sales for the past week: Monday, $7,200; Tuesday, $9,200; Wednesday, $10,400; Thursday, $12,100; and Friday, $8,400. Find her mean daily sales for the week.

24. Twelve pieceworkers at Parker Industries produced the following number of pieces in one day's work: 42, 51, 46, 44, 38, 40, 49, 53, 46, 47, 44, 48. What was the mean number of pieces produced by the workers?

25. The prices of nine stocks on the New York Stock Exchange are $14, $47, $60, $22, $12, $38, $67, $54, and $58. Find the median price of the stock.

26. The six employees of the Central Variety Store earn weekly salaries of $260, $265, $280, $240, $244, and $310. Find the median salary.

27. Earl Bowers decided to purchase a new television set and priced the set in seven different stores. The prices he found were $465, $420, $455, $435, $455, $440, and $470. Find: **a.** the mean price and **b.** the mode of the prices.

28. The annual salaries of the employees at the Dunfield Company are given in the following table. Find: **a.** the mean annual salary, **b.** the median of the salaries, and **c.** the mode of the annual salaries.

Annual Salary	Frequency
$24,200	2
25,500	4
25,800	8
25,900	3
26,400	1
27,200	3

Section 16.3 *Frequency Distributions and Measures of Location*

When a set of data contains a large number of values, measures of location are more efficiently calculated using a frequency distribution.

A. The Arithmetic Mean

The mean of a distribution with k classes is found by using the formula

$$(16\text{-}4) \quad \bar{x} = \frac{\sum\limits_{i=1}^{k} f_i x_i}{\sum\limits_{i=1}^{k} f_i}$$

where f_i = class frequency and x_i = midpoint of class interval.*

EXAMPLE 1   Find the mean of the data in table 16.2.

Solution: There are six classes; hence, $k = 6$.

Class	Frequency (f_i)	Class Midpoint (x_i)	$f_i x_i$
5–9	2	7	14
10–14	2	12	24
15–19	4	17	68
20–24	2	22	44
25–29	1	27	27
30–34	1	32	32
	12		209

$$\bar{x} = \frac{\sum\limits_{i=1}^{6} f_i x_i}{\sum\limits_{i=1}^{6} f_i}$$

$$= \frac{209}{12}$$

$$= 17.416$$

$$= 17.42$$

The difference between 17.42 and the actual mean of 17 results from using the midpoint of the class intervals in place of the actual values. If the sample contains a large number of values, this error is quite small.

The class midpoint is the mean of the boundaries of the class interval.

EXAMPLE 2 Gasoline sales at a Sure Oil station were recorded as follows:

Amount	Number of Sales
Less than $10.00	16
$10.00–$19.99	26
20.00–29.99	52
30.00–39.99	12
40.00–49.99	4

Find the mean sale at the station.

Solution:

Class	Frequency (f_i)	Class Midpoint (x_i)	$f_i x_i$
$ 0.00–$ 9.99	16	$ 4.995	$ 79.92
10.00–19.99	26	14.995	389.87
20.00–29.99	52	24.995	1,299.74
30.00–39.99	12	34.995	419.94
40.00–49.99	4	44.995	179.98
	110		$2,369.45

$$\bar{x} = \frac{\sum\limits_{i=1}^{5} f_i x_i}{\sum\limits_{i=1}^{5} f_i}$$

$$= \frac{\$2,369.45}{110}$$

$$= \$21.54$$

B. The Median

In a set of data that contains n values, the median is a number that is at least as large as $\frac{n}{2}$ of the values and no larger than $\frac{n}{2}$ of the values. For the frequency distribution shown in table 16.2, $\frac{n}{2} = \frac{12}{2} = 6$, which means that the median must occur in the class 15–19. Assuming that the values are equally distributed in that interval, the following formula can be used to find the median.

$$\textbf{(16–5)} \quad m = b + \frac{cd}{f_m}$$

where m = median, b = lower boundary of the class containing the median, c = length of the class interval, f_m = frequency of the class containing the median, and d = the difference between $\frac{n}{2}$ and the cumulative frequency up to b.

EXAMPLE 3   Using formula 16–5, find the median of the data in table 16.2.

Solution: $\dfrac{n}{2} = 6, b = 15, c = 5, f_m = 4, d = 6 - 4 = 2$

$$m = b + \frac{cd}{f_m}$$

$$= 15 + \frac{10}{4}$$

$$= 15 + 2.5$$

$$= 17.5$$

■

The discrepancy between 17.5 and the median of 15.5 calculated in example 6 of section 16.2 results from assuming that the values in the class are uniformly distributed over the interval.* For data with a large number of values, uniform distribution is more likely to occur, and the calculated value approximates the median with little error.

EXAMPLE 4   The following table records the reliability of an electronic component.

Hours	Frequency
700–799	86
800–899	82
900–999	64
1,000–1,099	32
1,100–1,199	10

What is the median number of hours the component may be expected to perform?

Solution: $\dfrac{n}{2} = \dfrac{274}{2} = 137$; hence the median class is 800–899.

$b = 800, c = 100, f_m = 82, d = 137 - 86 = 51$

$$m = b + \frac{cd}{f_m}$$

$$= 800 + \frac{100 \times 51}{82}$$

$$= 800 + 62.20$$

$$= 862.20 \text{ hours}$$

■

In class 15–19, the values were distributed as follows: 15—2; 16—2; 17—1; 18—0; 19—0.

C. The Mode

The mode of a frequency distribution cannot be identified; hence, it is customary to report only the modal class. The **modal class** of a frequency distribution is the class with the highest frequency.

EXAMPLE 5   Find the modal class of the data in table 16.2.

Solution: The class with the greatest frequency is the class 15–19; hence, it is the modal class.   ■

If a single value of the mode is necessary, the midpoint of the modal class may be used. In this event, the mode of the data in table 16.2 is

$$\frac{15 + 19}{2} = 17$$

EXAMPLE 6   A survey indicated the following number of flavors of ice cream carried by area supermarkets and drugstores.

Number of Flavors	Frequency
1–5	2
6–10	11
11–15	9
16–20	1

Find: **a.** the modal class and **b.** a single modal value.

Solution: **a.** The modal class is 6–10.

b. The modal value is $\dfrac{6 + 10}{2} = 8$.   ■

EXERCISES FOR SECTION 16.3

In problems 1–5, fill in the missing entries in the given frequency distribution and use the formula

$$\bar{x} = \left(\sum_{i=1}^{k} f_i x_i \right) \div \left(\sum_{i=1}^{k} f_i \right) \text{ to find the mean of the data in the distribution.}$$

1.

Class	Frequency (f_i)	Class Midpoint (x_i)	$f_i x_i$
5–9	1	_____	_____
10–14	3	_____	_____
15–19	4	_____	_____
20–24	4	_____	_____
25–29	2	_____	_____

2.

Class	Frequency (f_i)	Class Midpoint (x_i)	f_ix_i
0–4	2	_____	_____
5–9	6	_____	_____
10–14	8	_____	_____
15–19	8	_____	_____
20–24	10	_____	_____
25–29	7	_____	_____
30–34	6	_____	_____
35–39	3	_____	_____

3.

Class	Frequency (f_i)	Class Midpoint (x_i)	f_ix_i
0–9	2	_____	_____
10–19	3	_____	_____
20–29	2	_____	_____
30–39	4	_____	_____
40–49	1	_____	_____

4.

Class	Frequency (f_i)	Class Midpoint (x_i)	f_ix_i
0–8	1	_____	_____
9–17	2	_____	_____
18–26	3	_____	_____
27–35	2	_____	_____
36–44	4	_____	_____
45–53	1	_____	_____
54–62	1	_____	_____

5.

Class	Frequency (f_i)	Class Midpoint (x_i)	f_ix_i
0–10	2	_____	_____
11–21	4	_____	_____
22–32	6	_____	_____
33–43	5	_____	_____
44–54	7	_____	_____
55–65	3	_____	_____
66–76	1	_____	_____

Solve.

6. Use the formula $m = b + \frac{cd}{f_m}$ to find the median of the data given in problem 1.

7. Repeat problem 6 for the data given in problem 2.

8. Repeat problem 6 for the data given in problem 3.

9. Repeat problem 6 for the data given in problem 4.

10. Find the modal class of the frequency distribution in problem 1. What is the modal value?

11. Find the modal class and the modal value for the frequency distribution in problem 2.

12. Find the modal class and the modal value for the frequency distribution in problem 5.

13. A survey of the number of brands of cereal carried by area supermarkets yielded the following data.

Number of Brands	Frequency
1–5	4
6–10	11
11–15	14
16–20	3

Find: **a.** the mean, **b.** the median, and **c.** the modal class.

14. The Eltec Company manufactures light bulbs. The number of hours of useful life of one of the company's products is indicated by the following data.

Hours	Frequency
160–179	12
180–199	102
200–219	120
220–239	110
240–259	60
260–279	4

Find: **a.** the mean, **b.** the median, and **c.** the modal class.

15. Sales at a local convenience store were recorded as follows:

Amount	Number of Sales
Less than $2.00	42
$ 2.00–$3.99	126
4.00–5.99	130
6.00–7.99	72
8.00–9.99	84
10.00–11.99	20

Find: **a.** the mean, **b.** the median, and **c.** the modal class.

16. A survey of the employees at a manufacturing plant yielded the following frequency distribution of the weekly amount spent for food.

Amount Spent	Frequency
$ 50–$59	38
60–69	62
70–79	74
80–89	46
90–99	23
100–109	18
110–119	5

Find: **a.** the mean, **b.** the median, and **c.** the modal class.

Section 16.4 *Measures of Variation and the Normal Distribution*

Equally important to measures of location that describe the "center" of a set of data are **measures of variation** that describe the amount of scatter or variation among the values.

A. The Range

One measure of variation is the **range,** the difference between the largest and smallest data values. The range is not always reliable in describing the dispersion of data values. To illustrate, consider the following data arrays.

$$A \quad 1, 10, 11, 13, 14, 23$$
$$B \quad 1, 2, 3, 21, 22, 23$$

Each set has the same mean, median, and range (12, 12, and 22, respectively), but most of the values of A are grouped around the mean, while the values of B are near the end values. The most important statistical measure used to describe data variation is the standard deviation.

B. The Standard Deviation

The **standard deviation** is defined by the formula*

$$(16\text{-}6) \quad s = \sqrt{\frac{\displaystyle\sum_{i=1}^{n} (x_i - \bar{x})^2}{n - 1}}$$

---

*$\sqrt{}$ *denotes the square root. The square root of a nonnegative number* a *is that nonnegative number* b *such that* b × b = a. *For example,* $\sqrt{36} = 6$ *because* 6 × 6 = 36.

but is more easily calculated by the formula

$$(16\text{--}7) \quad s = \sqrt{\dfrac{n \cdot \sum\limits_{i=1}^{n} x_i^2 - \left(\sum\limits_{i=1}^{n} x_i\right)^2}{n(n-1)}}$$

where s = standard deviation, n = total number of values, and x_i = data values.

The standard deviation describes the amount of scatter in a set of data in that the larger the value of s the greater the amount of scatter.

EXAMPLE 1   Using table 16.5 to find the necessary square roots, find the standard deviation of each of the data arrays A and B on page 454.

Solution: Using formula 16–7,

	A		B
x_i	x_i^2	x_i	x_i^2
1	1	1	1
10	100	2	4
11	121	3	9
13	169	21	441
14	196	22	484
23	529	23	529

$$\sum_{i=1}^{6} x_i = 72 \qquad \sum_{i=1}^{6} x_i = 1{,}116 \qquad \sum_{i=1}^{6} x_i = 72 \qquad \sum_{i=1}^{6} x_i = 1{,}468$$

$$s = \sqrt{\dfrac{6(1{,}116) - 72^2}{6(5)}} \qquad\qquad s = \sqrt{\dfrac{6(1{,}468) - 72^2}{6(5)}}$$

$$s = \sqrt{50.4} \qquad\qquad\qquad\qquad s = \sqrt{120.8}$$

$$s = 7.07 \qquad\qquad\qquad\qquad\quad s = 11.00$$

The larger standard deviation of B indicates a wider dispersion of data values than for A. ■

For a frequency distribution with k classes, a formula for the standard deviation s is

$$(16\text{--}8) \quad s = \sqrt{\dfrac{\sum\limits_{i=1}^{k} (x_i - \bar{x})^2 \cdot f_i}{n-1}}$$

where the variables have the same meaning as in formula 16–4.

Table 16.5		Square Roots					
n	$\sqrt{n}$	n	$\sqrt{n}$	n	$\sqrt{n}$	n	$\sqrt{n}$
1	1.00	51	7.14	101	10.05	151	12.29
2	1.41	52	7.21	102	10.10	152	12.33
3	1.73	53	7.28	103	10.15	153	12.37
4	2.00	54	7.35	104	10.20	154	12.41
5	2.24	55	7.42	105	10.25	155	12.45
6	2.45	56	7.48	106	10.30	156	12.49
7	2.65	57	7.55	107	10.34	157	12.53
8	2.83	58	7.62	108	10.39	158	12.57
9	3.00	59	7.68	109	10.44	159	12.61
10	3.16	60	7.75	110	10.49	160	12.65
11	3.32	61	7.81	111	10.54	161	12.69
12	3.46	62	7.87	112	10.58	162	12.73
13	3.61	63	7.94	113	10.63	163	12.77
14	3.74	64	8.00	114	10.68	164	12.81
15	3.87	65	8.06	115	10.72	165	12.85
16	4.00	66	8.12	116	10.77	166	12.88
17	4.12	67	8.19	117	10.82	167	12.92
18	4.24	68	8.25	118	10.86	168	12.96
19	4.36	69	8.31	119	10.91	169	13.00
20	4.47	70	8.37	120	10.95	170	13.04
21	4.58	71	8.43	121	11.00	171	13.08
22	4.69	72	8.49	122	11.05	172	13.11
23	4.80	73	8.54	123	11.09	173	13.15
24	4.90	74	8.60	124	11.14	174	13.19
25	5.00	75	8.66	125	11.18	175	13.23
26	5.10	76	8.72	126	11.22	176	13.27
27	5.20	77	8.77	127	11.27	177	13.30
28	5.29	78	8.83	128	11.31	178	13.34
29	5.39	79	8.89	129	11.36	179	13.38
30	5.48	80	8.94	130	11.40	180	13.42
31	5.57	81	9.00	131	11.45	181	13.45
32	5.66	82	9.06	132	11.49	182	13.49
33	5.74	83	9.11	133	11.53	183	13.53
34	5.83	84	9.17	134	11.58	184	13.56
35	5.92	85	9.22	135	11.62	185	13.60
36	6.00	86	9.27	136	11.66	186	13.64
37	6.08	87	9.33	137	11.70	187	13.67
38	6.16	88	9.38	138	11.75	188	13.71
39	6.24	89	9.43	139	11.79	189	13.75
40	6.32	90	9.49	140	11.83	190	13.78
41	6.40	91	9.54	141	11.87	191	13.82

Table 16.5		Square Roots		Continued			
n	$\sqrt{n}$	n	$\sqrt{n}$	n	$\sqrt{n}$	n	$\sqrt{n}$
42	6.48	92	9.59	142	11.92	192	13.86
43	6.56	93	9.64	143	11.96	193	13.89
44	6.63	94	9.70	144	12.00	194	13.93
45	6.71	95	9.75	145	12.04	195	13.96
46	6.78	96	9.80	146	12.08	196	14.00
47	6.86	97	9.85	147	12.12	197	14.04
48	6.93	98	9.90	148	12.17	198	14.07
49	7.00	99	9.95	149	12.21	199	14.11
50	7.07	100	10.00	150	12.25	200	14.14

Measures of central tendency and measures of variation are used to make large collections of data more understandable. With a measure of central tendency, the statistician seeks to produce one number that is representative of all values, while with a measure of variation, one number is sought that describes the "spread" of the values.

C. The Normal Distribution

For many sets of data, if the sample is large, the graph of the frequency distribution tends to resemble the bell-shaped curve shown in figure 16.9. This graph is called a **normal curve,** and distributions of data that are approximated by a normal curve are called **normal distributions.***

Normal distributions are common and occur in a variety of circumstances. For example, I.Q. scores, the heights of adult males or females, baseball batting averages, the size of peas, and the density of the stars are all normally distributed. That is, if a frequency distribution is obtained for a large number of measurements of one of these variables, the corresponding graph tends to look like a normal curve.

The normal curve has several interesting properties. The mean, median, and mode are identical and occur at the point where the curve reaches its maximum height. In addition, approximately 68% of all values differ from the mean by less than one standard deviation, approximately 95% of the data differ from the mean by less than two standard deviations, and approximately 99% of the data differ from the mean by less than three standard deviations. See figure 16.9.

*The data values in a distribution are either discrete or continuous. A count always yields discrete data, while measurements will usually yield continuous data. The normal curve is the graph of a distribution of continuous data, but the graphs of distributions of discrete data may resemble the normal curve.

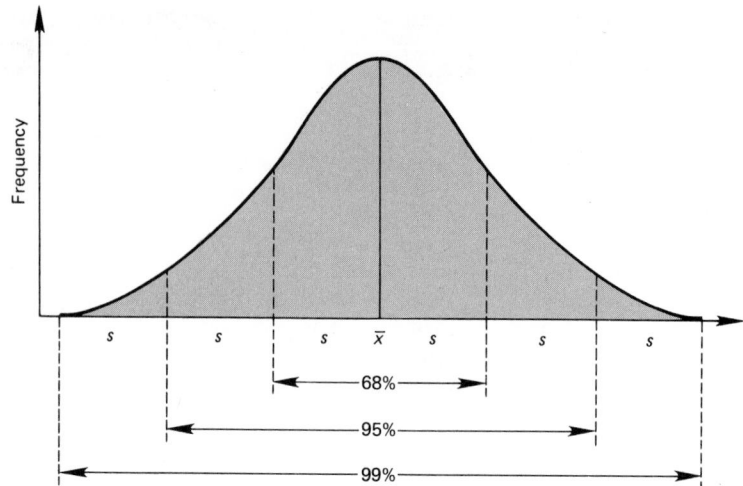

Figure 16.9
A normal curve

EXAMPLE 2   A time study made on 250 workers indicated that the mean time for performing a certain task was 36 minutes with a standard deviation of 8 minutes. Assuming that the times were normally distributed, approximately how many workers completed the task in 28 to 44 minutes?

Solution: The time frame of 28 to 44 minutes is one standard deviation to the left and to the right of the mean. Hence, approximately $250 \times 0.68 = 170$ workers completed the task in 28 to 44 minutes.   ◼

EXERCISES FOR SECTION 16.4

In problems 1–5, use formula 16–7 and table 16.5 to compute the standard deviation of the given data.

1. 11, 4, 23, 16, 4, 15

2. 6, 2, 12, 8, 4, 8

3. 5, 11, 15, 14, 13, 6, 12, 11

4. 10, 15, 11, 20, 25, 14, 16, 21

5. 4, 6, 2, 8, 5, 12, 9, 7, 8, 6, 10, 8

Solve.

6. The weekly salaries of the employees at the Curtis Company are given in the following table.

Weekly Salary	Frequency
$220	3
230	9
250	6
260	2

Compute the standard deviation for this data.

7. The number of sales reported by each of eight salespeople at a furniture store last week were 12, 8, 10, 11, 15, 6, 10, and 8. Compute the standard deviation for this data.

8. The number of years of service of the 10 employees of the Quality Clothing Store are 23, 5, 10, 16, 4, 8, 14, 8, 17, and 8. Compute the standard deviation for this data. What percent of the employees have served a number of years that is within one standard deviation of the mean?

9. A class of 40 students was given an examination. The scores were normally distributed. If the mean score on the exam was 75 and the standard deviation was 10, approximately how many students scored between 65 and 85 on the exam? How many scored between 55 and 95?

10. An analysis of the weekly salaries paid to the assembly-line workers at a manufacturing plant revealed a mean weekly salary of $273 with a standard deviation of $18. If the plant employs 72 assembly-line workers and if their salaries are normally distributed, approximately how many workers earn between $255 and $291 per week? How many earn between $237 and $309 per week?

11. Sunshine Breakfast Cereal is sold in boxes marked with a net weight of 12 ounces. The true net weight is normally distributed, with a mean of 12 ounces and a standard deviation of 0.1 ounce. If a grocer receives a shipment of 200 boxes of the cereal, how many boxes will have an actual net weight between 12.2 and 12.3 ounces? How many will have a net weight between 11.8 and 11.9 ounces?

12. Suppose the waist size of adult men is normally distributed, with a mean of 35 inches and a standard deviation of 1 inch. A clothing manufacturer is introducing a new line of dress slacks for men, and 5,000 pairs of the slacks will be test-marketed. How many of the 5,000 pairs manufactured should be between a size 33 waist and a size 37 waist?

Section 16.5   *Index Numbers*

An **index number** is a statistical measure designed to show changes with respect to some characteristic, such as time, geographic location, income, profession, and so on. Although mainly used in business and economics, index numbers also have applications in such fields as psychology, sociology, public health, and government.

A. The Price Relative

One of the simplest of the index numbers is the **price relative,** the ratio of a given year's price to a base year's price multiplied by 100.

(16–9)   Price relative $= \dfrac{p_n}{p_o} \cdot 100$

where

$p_n =$ new price or the given year price

$p_o =$ old price or the base year price

E X A M P L E   1   The average residential electric bill for 1,000 kilowatt hours in 1975 was $18.31; in 1985, it was $48.76. Compute the price relative (to the nearest whole number) using 1975 as the base year.

Solution: Using formula 16–9, with $p_n = \$48.76$ and $p_o = \$18.31$,

$$\text{Price relative} = \frac{p_n}{p_o} \cdot 100$$

$$= \frac{\$48.76}{\$18.31} \cdot 100$$

$$= 266$$

■

The price relative in example 1 compares 1985 electricity prices with 1975 electricity prices in the following sense: for every $100 spent on electricity in 1975, it took $266 in 1985 to purchase the same number of kilowatt hours.

B. The Simple Aggregate Index

The price relative compares prices of a single item; other indexes seek to compare prices of a related group of items. For example, the **simple aggregate index** is found by dividing the sum of the prices for a given year by the sum of the prices for the base year and then multiplying the result by 100.

(16–10) Simple aggregate index $= \dfrac{\sum p_n}{\sum p_o} \cdot 100$

where

$$\sum p_n = \text{sum of the given year prices}$$

and

$$\sum p_o = \text{sum of the base year prices.}$$

E X A M P L E 2

For selected meats, the price per pound in 1986 and 1992 was as follows.

	1986 Price	**1992 Price**
Sirloin steak	$3.05	$3.99
Pork chops	2.25	3.29
Chicken	0.72	0.99
Bacon	1.89	1.99
Frankfurters	1.75	2.69

Compute the simple aggregate index (to the nearest whole number) using the year 1986 as the base year.

Solution: Using formula 16–10, with $\sum p_n$ = sum of the 1992 prices and $\sum p_o$ = sum of the 1986 prices,

$$
\begin{aligned}
\text{Simple aggregate index} &= \frac{\sum p_n}{\sum p_o} \cdot 100 \\
&= \frac{\$3.99 + \$3.29 + \$0.99 + \$1.99 + \$2.69}{\$3.05 + \$2.25 + \$0.72 + \$1.89 + \$1.75} \cdot 100 \\
&= \frac{\$12.95}{\$9.66} \cdot 100 \\
&= 134
\end{aligned}
$$

If the prices in example 2 are representative of all meats, then the index number 134 indicates that the combined 1992 meat prices are 134% of those of 1986, or that it would take $134 in 1992 to buy the same quantity of meat that $100 would purchase in 1986.

A major weakness of the simple aggregate index is that prices are not related to quantities. For instance, in example 2, sirloin steak and frankfurters were treated equally, although sales of frankfurters undoubtedly far exceeded sales of sirloin steaks.

C. The Laspeyres Index

An index designed to consider both quantity and price is the **Laspeyres index,** named after the statistician who first suggested its use. The formula is

$$(16\text{--}11) \quad I = \frac{\sum p_n q_o}{\sum p_o q_o} \cdot 100$$

where $\sum p_n q_o$ = sum of the products of the *given* year prices and the corresponding base year quantities

and $\sum p_o q_o$ = sum of the products of the *base* year prices and the corresponding base year quantities

EXAMPLE 3

Softwood prices (per 1,000 board feet) and production (in billions of board feet) are shown in the following table.

| | Price | | Production |
	1985	*1990*	*1985*
Douglas fir	$165.90	$432.20	7.33
Southern pine	57.00	155.40	6.97
Ponderosa pine	71.20	206.10	3.54

Using 1985 as the base year, compute (to the nearest whole number) the Laspeyres index.

Solution:

$$I = \frac{\sum p_n q_o}{\sum p_o q_o} \cdot 100$$

$$= \frac{\$432.20(7.33) + \$155.40(6.97) + \$206.10(3.54)}{\$165.90(7.33) + \$57.00(6.97) + \$71.20(3.54)} \cdot 100$$

$$= \frac{\$4,980.76}{\$1,865.39} \cdot 100$$

$$= 267$$

■

The Laspeyres index is an example of a *weighted index* in which the prices are adjusted by the corresponding amount produced. Many of the indexes used today are weighted indexes, particularly those published by the federal government.

D. The Consumer Price Index

Perhaps the most widely known of the weighted indexes is the **Consumer Price Index (CPI).** Calculated monthly by the U.S. Department of Labor, the CPI is a measure of the average change in the prices paid by urban consumers for a fixed market basket of consumption goods and services. The CPI compares what the market basket of goods and services costs this month with what the same market basket cost a month, a year, or several years ago.

The CPI market basket is developed from detailed expenditure information provided by sampling families and individuals on what they actually buy. All expenditure items have been classified into about 250 categories, arranged into seven major groups as shown in table 16.6.

Table 16.6	Consumer Price Index (1982–84 = 100)						
	All Items	**Food**	**Apparel**	**Transportation**	**Shelter**	**Medical Care**	**Entertainment**
Sept.	137.0	136.3	129.9	124.3	146.9	180.1	140.2
Oct.	137.1	136.2	129.4	124.0	147.3	181.1	140.5
Nov.	137.5	137.0	130.7	124.6	147.7	182.0	140.4
Dec.	137.8	137.4	129.9	125.0	148.4	183.4	139.9

For the Consumer Price Index, 1982–84 is the base period. Thus, in September, it costs $136.30 for the same amount of food that $100.00 would buy in the period 1982–84. The Consumer Price Index is an important index in that many government and private cost-of-living increases are linked to the CPI, such as social security payments and cost-of-living increases in collective bargaining contracts.

Other government indexes of importance to businesses include the following:

Gross Domestic Product (GDP) Issued quarterly by the U.S. Department of Commerce, this index measures all the goods and services produced by workers and capital in the United States. It excludes profits on the overseas operations of U.S. companies and includes the earnings of foreign companies in the U.S. The GDP has replaced the Gross National Product as the primary index of the nation's total output of goods and services.

Composite Index of Leading Indicators Prepared monthly by the U.S. Department of Commerce, this index is a composite of 12 other indexes that are weighted to show their importance to the overall economy. This index is designed to foreshadow economic trends in the months ahead. Strong gains in the index are considered signs of healthy economic growth, while several consecutive months of decline are regarded as signaling the onset of a recession.

U.S. Export and Import Merchandise Trade Prepared by the U.S. Bureau of the Census from customs data, this index measures the nation's trade performance in imports and exports.

EXERCISES FOR SECTION 16.5

1. The average monthly residential heating cost in a midwestern city was $24.70 in 1980 and $72.90 in 1990. Compute the price relative, using 1980 as the base year. (Round to the nearest whole number.)

2. The annual company cost of employee benefits at the Preston Company was $984.82 per employee in 1983 and $1,420.36 in 1988. Using 1983 as the base year, find the price relative for employee benefits. (Round to the nearest whole number.)

3. The cost of fuel at Rosen Industries rose from $1.08 per gallon in 1985 to $1.38 per gallon in 1992. To the nearest whole number, find the price relative using 1985 as the base year.

4. Use table 16.6 to determine how much an individual spent in November for medical care that cost $100 in 1982–84. How much did groceries costing $20 in 1982–84 cost in October?

5. Use table 16.6 to determine how much it cost in September to purchase clothing that cost $100 in 1982–84. How much did housing worth $78,500 in 1982–84 cost in November?

6. Use table 16.6 to find the percent increase in the cost of medical care from September to December. What is the percent increase in transportation costs from September to December? (Round to the nearest tenth of a percent.)

7. Production costs (per unit produced) at Carter Enterprises are shown in the following table.

| | Cost | |
	1988	1993
Labor	$400.20	$ 615.10
Materials	931.16	1,540.20
Maintenance	54.08	82.80

Using 1988 as the base year, compute (to the nearest whole number) the simple aggregate index of the production costs.

8. The retail prices of the air-conditioning units produced at Brentwood Refrigeration are shown in the following table.

| | Retail Prices | | Number of Units Produced (Hundreds) |
	1985	1990	1985
Model 12	$302.10	$ 532.18	87.3
Model 12-D	570.90	908.42	101.4
Model 12-XL	924.14	1,514.86	62.3

Compute (to the nearest whole number) the simple aggregate index of the retail prices, using 1985 as the base year.

9. The production costs per unit of the computers produced at Elway Electronics are shown in the following table.

| | Production Costs | | Number of Units Produced (Hundreds) |
	1987	1993	1987
Model E-400	$ 348.20	$ 520.10	76.4
Model E-800	764.80	914.40	112.8
Model E-1200	1,480.10	1,920.30	48.2

Find the simple aggregate index (to the nearest whole number) of the production costs, using 1987 as the base year.

10. Using the 1987 production figures as weights for retail prices, compute (to the nearest whole number) the Laspeyres index for the data given in problem 8.

11. Compute (to the nearest whole number) the Laspeyres index for the data given in problem 9. Use the 1987 production figures as weights for production costs.

Glossary

Arithmetic mean   Also called the *mean*. The sum of the values of a set of data divided by the number of pieces of data.

Array   An arrangement of numerical data in order from low to high or from high to low.

Bar graph   A graph that compares several related pieces of data using horizontal or vertical bars.

Bimodal   A set of data for which two pieces of data occur most frequently, thereby resulting in two modes.

Categorical frequency distribution   A frequency distribution of data sorted according to a qualitative description.

Circle graph   A graph used to illustrate the distribution of goods or money by using portions of a circle.

Classes   The groups into which data are placed in a frequency distribution.

Class frequency   The number of pieces of data in a class of a frequency distribution.

Composite Index of Leading Indicators   An index issued monthly by the U.S. Department of Commerce that is a composite of 12 other indexes and is designed to foreshadow economic trends in the months ahead.

Consumer Price Index (CPI)   An index issued monthly by the U.S. Labor Department that measures retail price changes for specific items of food, clothing, shelter, fuels, and services.

Cumulative frequency distribution   A frequency distribution in which the entry for each line of the table is the class frequency plus the sum of the preceding class frequencies.

Frequency distribution   A tabulation of data obtained by grouping the data into classes and tallying the number or frequency of pieces of data in each class.

Graph   A representation of statistical or numerical data by visual means.

Gross Domestic Product (GDP)   An index issued quarterly by the U.S. Department of Commerce that measures all the goods and services produced by workers and capital in the United States.

Index number   A statistical measure designed to show changes with respect to some characteristic, usually time.

Laspeyres index   The ratio of the sum of the products of the given year prices and the corresponding base year quantities to the sum of the products of the base year prices and the corresponding base year quantities, multiplied by 100.

Line graph   A graph that uses a broken line to illustrate how one quantity changes with respect to another.

Mean   See *arithmetic mean*.

Measures of central tendency   See *measures of location*.

Measures of location   Numbers used to indicate the "center" or "average" of a collection of data. The mean, median, and mode are measures of location.

Measures of variation   Measures that describe the amount of "scatter" or variation in a collection of data.

Median   For an array of n pieces of data, the middle value if n is odd and the mean of the two middle values if n is even.

Modal class   In a frequency distribution, the class with the highest frequency.

Mode   The piece of data that occurs most frequently in a set of data.

Normal curve   The graph of a normal distribution.

Normal distribution   A frequency distribution for which the graph is a bell-shaped curve and approximately 68% of the data differ from the mean by less than one standard deviation, 95% of the data differ from the mean by less than two standard deviations, and 99% of the data differ from the mean by less than three standard deviations.

Numerical frequency distribution   A frequency distribution of data grouped according to numerical size.

Pictogram   A modified form of a bar graph in which pictures are used to represent quantity.

Price relative   The ratio of a given year's price to a base year's price, multiplied by 100.

Range   The difference between the largest and smallest data values.

Relative frequency distribution   A frequency distribution in which relative class frequencies are indicated for each class. Each relative class frequency is the class frequency divided by the total number of pieces of data.

Sigma (Σ)   A notation used to indicate a sum.

Simple aggregate index   The ratio of the sum of the prices for a given year to the sum of the prices for a base year, multiplied by 100.

Standard deviation   A number used to indicate the amount of scatter or variation among the values in a set of data.

U.S. Export and Import Merchandise Trade   An index prepared by the U.S. Bureau of the Census that measures the nation's trade performance in imports and exports.

Review Test

Use the following data for problems 1–4.

12	8	0	3	3	10
10	16	7	14	8	4
2	8	13	8	11	7

1. Arrange the data in an array and find the median.

2. Find the mean of the data.

3. Find the mode of the data.

4. Complete the following cumulative frequency distribution of the data.

Class	Cumulative Frequency
0–3	
4–7	
8–11	
12–15	
16–19	

For problems 5–7, use the information given in the following frequency distribution.

Class	Frequency
0–4	2
5–9	5
10–14	12
15–19	10
20–24	8
25–29	3

5. Find the mean of the data in the distribution.

6. Find the median of the data in the distribution.

7. Find the modal class of the data.

Solve.

8. Compute the standard deviation of the data in the following array: 1, 2, 3, 5, 9. Use table 16.5 to find the necessary square root.

9. Two students each took five exams in an English class. One student scored higher than the other on all but one exam, yet their mean scores for the five exams were the same. Give an example of such exam scores.

10. The breaking strength of a new synthetic fiber is normally distributed, with a mean of 150 pounds and a standard deviation of 3 pounds. If 500 samples of the fiber are tested, approximately how many of the samples will have a breaking strength of between 144 and 156 pounds?

11. The cost of solvent at Burgess Products rose from $0.46 per gallon in 1988 to $0.74 per gallon in 1992. To the nearest whole number, find the price relative using 1988 as the base year.

12. Production costs (per unit produced) at Elpen Enterprises are shown in the following table.

| | Cost | |
	1988	1992
Labor	$204.14	$ 480.20
Materials	612.80	1,042.80
Maintenance	72.14	104.46

Using 1988 as the base year, compute (to the nearest whole number) the simple aggregate index of the production costs.

13. Prices and quantities sold of three brands of shock absorbers are shown in the following table.

| | Prices | | Quantities | |
	1988	1992	1988	1992
A	$ 3	$ 6	240	212
B	5	10	165	104
C	11	15	110	98

Compute (to the nearest whole number) the Laspeyres index, using 1988 as the base year.

14. The profits per share of Elco stock were $0.80 in 1989, $0.40 in 1990, $0.20 in 1991, $1.00 in 1992, and $1.20 in 1993. Construct a line graph to illustrate this data.

15. Glenridge Poultry Products reported the following sales for the years 1989–1993.

Year	Chickens	Turkeys
1989	$180,000	$ 70,000
1990	210,000	100,000
1991	250,000	120,000
1992	260,000	150,000
1993	280,000	180,000

On the same set of axes, construct side-by-side horizontal bar graphs of chicken sales and turkey sales for each of the five years.

16. Allied Parcel Service delivered 80,000 parcels in 1990, 100,000 parcels in 1991, 140,000 parcels in 1992, and 160,000 parcels in 1993.

Using the symbol to represent 40,000 parcels, construct a pictogram showing the number of parcels delivered in each of the four years.

17. Prentice Pharmaceuticals reported that in 1993, 50¢ of each sales dollar was used for research, 25¢ was used for operating expenses, 15¢ was used for taxes, and 10¢ was used for miscellaneous expenses. Construct a circle graph that represents the use of the company's sales dollar in 1993.

17

The Metric System

Section 17.1 *Metric Units of Length and Area*

A. Introduction

The system of weights and measures used in the United States has its heritage in the English system of weights and measures, which in turn can be traced to ancient Roman and Egyptian customs. These ancient standards were imprecise and largely based on anatomical dimensions. For example, in Egypt, a basic unit of length was the cubit, the distance from the elbow to the tip of the middle finger. The Egyptians divided the cubit into seven palms and each palm into four digits, a word also meaning finger. Thus, every person carried his or her own measuring system, but because these lengths vary among individuals, everyone had a different "ruler."

In the latter part of the eighteenth century, a commission of French scientists developed a system that has become the international standard of weights and measures. Called the metric system, it has been adopted by almost every civilized country except the United States (see figures 17.1 and 17.2).*

American scientists already express scientific measurements in metric units, but the general public continues to use the system of feet, miles, pounds, gallons, and so on. Plans to convert the entire country to the metric system currently are being discussed.

Figure 17.1
Islands in a metric world

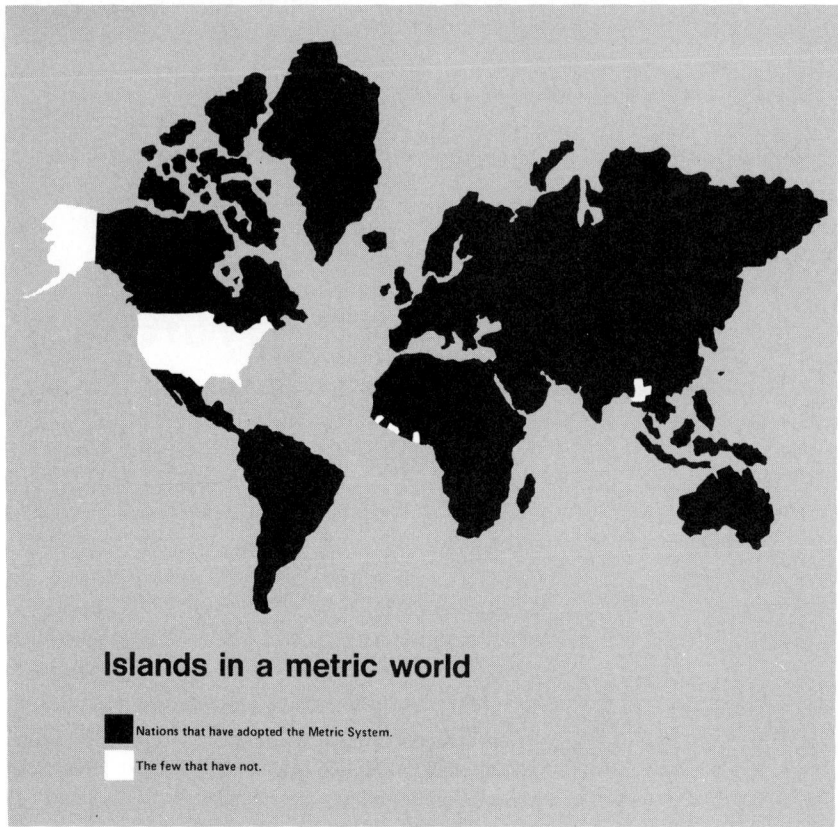

Islands in a metric world

Nations that have adopted the Metric System.

The few that have not.

The metric system has two distinct advantages over other forms of measurement: It has a fixed, invariable base, and its numerical system is decimal based.

The basic unit of measurement is the **meter,** which was defined to be $\frac{1}{10,000,000}$ of the distance from the equator to either the North or South Pole.* As a result, the meter is approximately 39.37 inches or approximately 1.093 yards. This unit of length is also used to establish units of area, capacity, and weight, as will be seen in the sections that follow.

Decimal multiples and fractions of the basic unit are designated by Greek and Latin prefixes. The value and meaning of these designations are shown in table 17.1.

*A more recent definition of the meter is 1,650,763.73 wavelengths of the orange-red light of krypton 86.

Figure 17.2
Australian stamps used to promote metric conversion

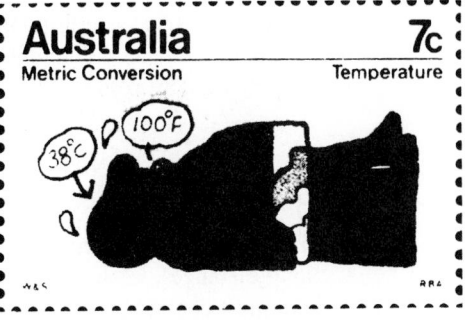

Table 17.1	Prefixes Used in the Metric System	
Prefix (Abbreviation)	**Meaning**	**Numerical Value**
Giga (G)	One billion	1,000,000,000
Mega (M)	One million	1,000,000
Kilo (k)	One thousand	1,000
Hecto (h)	One hundred	100
Deka (dk)	Ten	10
Deci (d)	One tenth	$\frac{1}{10} = 0.1$
Centi (c)	One hundredth	$\frac{1}{100} = 0.01$
Milli (m)	One thousandth	$\frac{1}{1,000} = 0.001$
Micro (u)	One millionth	$\frac{1}{1,000,000} = 0.000001$
Nano (n)	One billionth	$\frac{1}{1,000,000,000} = 0.000000001$

Thus, a dekameter is 10 meters, a kilometer is 1,000 meters, a centimeter is $\frac{1}{100}$ of a meter, and a millimeter is $\frac{1}{1000}$ of a meter. The decimal base makes calculations with the metric system much simpler than with the U.S. system. For example, any denomination can be changed to a higher one by moving the decimal point to the left, and changed to a lower one by moving the decimal point to the right. Thus,

$$1.725 \text{ dekameters} = 17.25 \text{ meters} = 172.5 \text{ decimeters}$$

B. Units of Length

The meter is the basic unit of the metric system. The **kilometer** is used to measure long distances, while for small lengths the **centimeter** and the **millimeter** are the most common forms. Multiples and submultiples of the meter are shown in table 17.2

Table 17.2	Multiples and Submultiples of the Meter		
1 kilometer (km)	= 1,000 meters	1 meter	= 0.001 kilometer
1 hectometer (hm)	= 100 meters	1 meter	= 0.01 hectometer
1 dekameter (dkm)	= 10 meters	1 meter	= 0.1 dekameter
1 meter (m)	= Basic unit of length	1 meter	= Basic unit of length
1 decimeter (dm)	= 0.1 meter	1 meter	= 10 decimeters
1 centimeter (cm)	= 0.01 meter	1 meter	= 100 centimeters
1 millimeter (mm)	= 0.001 meter	1 meter	= 1,000 millimeters

Because the metric system is decimal based, each metric prefix corresponds to a decimal position as indicated in figure 17.3.

Figure 17.3
The metric system

kilo (k)	hecto (h)	deka (dk)	unit	deci (d)	centi (c)	milli (m)
1,000	100	10	1	0.1	0.01	0.001

As a result, converting from one metric measure of length to another is just a matter of relocating the decimal point. To relocate the decimal point, the following steps can be used.

1. Arrange the metric measures according to their decimal position as described in figure 17.3.
2. Count the number of positions from the given measure to the desired measure.
3. Move the decimal point of the given measure the same number of spaces and in the same direction as step 2, adding zeros as necessary.

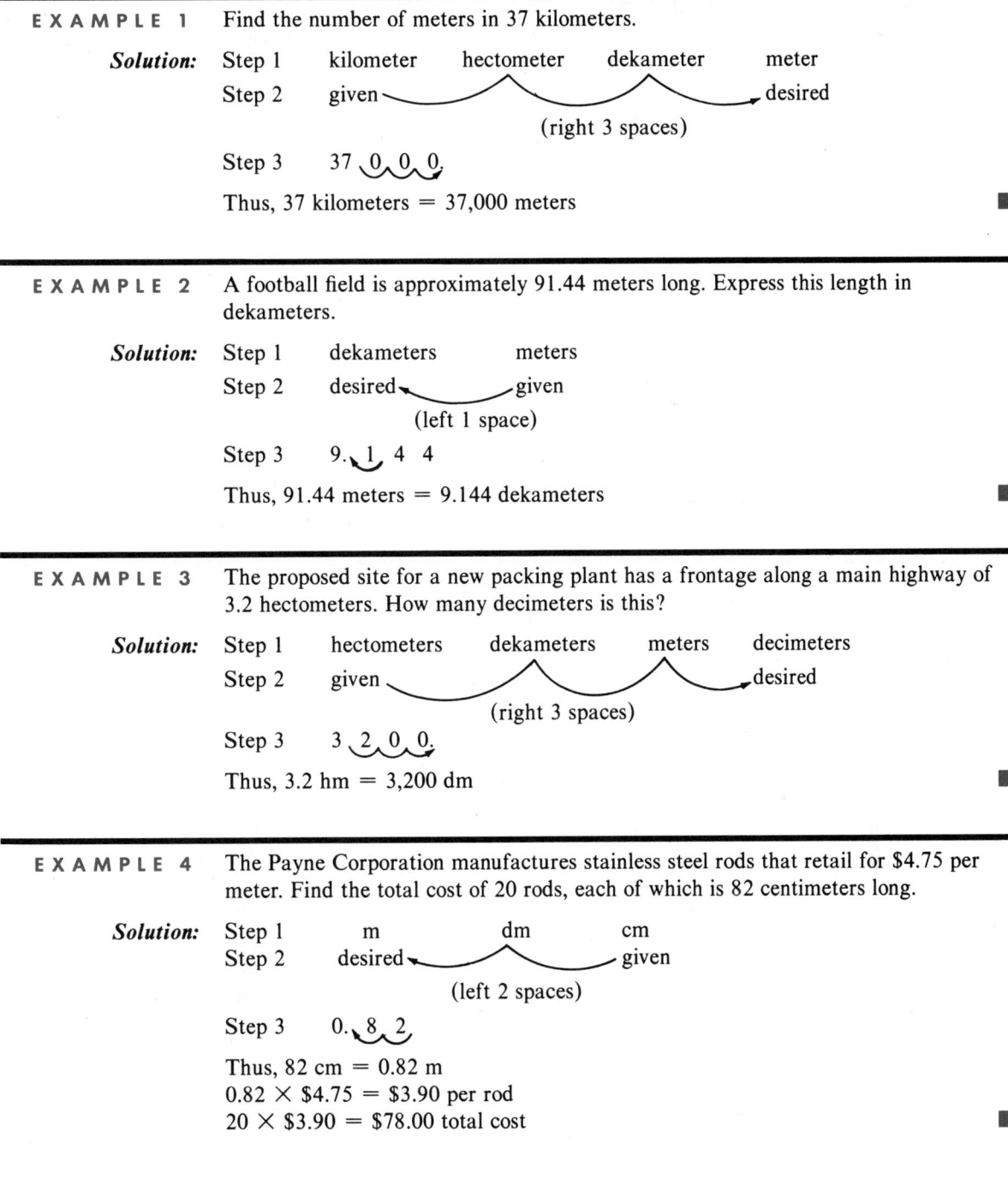

E X A M P L E 1   Find the number of meters in 37 kilometers.

Solution: Step 1   kilometer   hectometer   dekameter   meter
Step 2   given   desired
(right 3 spaces)
Step 3   37 0 0 0
Thus, 37 kilometers = 37,000 meters

E X A M P L E 2   A football field is approximately 91.44 meters long. Express this length in dekameters.

Solution: Step 1   dekameters   meters
Step 2   desired   given
(left 1 space)
Step 3   9. 1 4 4
Thus, 91.44 meters = 9.144 dekameters

E X A M P L E 3   The proposed site for a new packing plant has a frontage along a main highway of 3.2 hectometers. How many decimeters is this?

Solution: Step 1   hectometers   dekameters   meters   decimeters
Step 2   given   desired
(right 3 spaces)
Step 3   3 2 0 0
Thus, 3.2 hm = 3,200 dm

E X A M P L E 4   The Payne Corporation manufactures stainless steel rods that retail for $4.75 per meter. Find the total cost of 20 rods, each of which is 82 centimeters long.

Solution: Step 1   m   dm   cm
Step 2   desired   given
(left 2 spaces)
Step 3   0. 8 2
Thus, 82 cm = 0.82 m
0.82 × $4.75 = $3.90 per rod
20 × $3.90 = $78.00 total cost

C. Units of Area

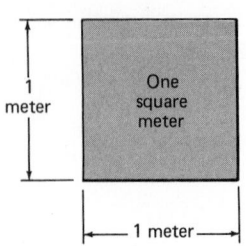

1 meter | One square meter

|— 1 meter —|

Figure 17.4
A square meter, the basic unit of area in the metric system

The basic unit of area in the metric system is the **square meter,** which is the area of a square with sides 1 meter in length (see figure 17.4).

For most land measurements, the **are** (100 square meters), the **hectare** (100 ares), and the square kilometer are used. For small areas, the square meter and the square centimeter are common. Abbreviations for these units are

Square meter	m^2
Are	a
Hectare	ha
Square kilometer	km^2
Square centimeter	cm^2

EXAMPLE 5   Feed-Tex purchased 21.4 hectares of farmland. If the cost was $80 per are, find the total cost of the land.

Solution: 1 ha = 100 a
21.4 ha = 21.4 × 100 a = 2,140 a
2,140 × $80 = $171,200   ∎

EXAMPLE 6   An executive desk is 180 centimeters long and 75 centimeters wide. What is the area of the desk in square meters?

Solution: 1 cm = 0.01 m
180 cm = 180 × 0.01 m = 1.8 m
75 cm = 75 × 0.01 m = 0.75 m
Area = 1.8 m × 0.75 m = 1.35 m^2 ∎

EXERCISES FOR SECTION 17.1

In problems 1–14, convert the given length or area to the metric units specified.

1. **a.** 28 kilometers to meters
   b. 72 meters to dekameters

2. **a.** 109 hectometers to meters
   b. 62 meters to decimeters

3. **a.** 721 dekameters to meters
   b. 7.05 meters to centimeters

4. **a.** 14.78 kilometers to meters
   b. 0.781 meters to millimeters

5. **a.** 157 dekameters to decimeters
   b. 32,214 millimeters to centimeters

6. **a.** 47,100 millimeters to centimeters
   b. 2.17 hectometers to centimeters

7. **a.** 0.0024 square meters to square centimeters
   b. 14 square kilometers to ares

8. **a.** 11,400 square centimeters to square meters
   b. 2,500 ares to hectares

9. 621 dm = _____ dkm = _____ hm

10. 87.2 km = _____ dm = _____ cm

11. 32,240 mm = _____ dkm = _____ dm

12. 0.723 km = _____ hm = _____ dm

13. 0.19 km² = _____ m² = _____ a

14. 481.7 a = _____ ha = _____ km²

Solve.

15. A proposed new office building for the downtown business district is to be 74.2 meters high. Express this height in **a.** dekameters and **b.** hectometers.

16. Jake Scott ordered a new sign for his hardware store. The sign was rectangular in shape, 2.61 meters long, and 0.48 meters high. Express the dimensions of the sign in **a.** decimeters and **b.** centimeters.

17. A new pencil is about 2 decimeters long. The width of the pencil is about 7 millimeters, and the thickness of its lead is about 2 millimeters. Express these measurements in **a.** centimeters and **b.** meters.

18. The scale on a map is 1 centimeter = 80 kilometers. If the distance between two cities on the map is 5.5 centimeters, how long will it take to drive from one city to another at an average speed of 88 kilometers per hour?

19. An art supply store is selling picture-framing material for $5.40 per meter. Find the total cost of six pieces of the material, each of which is 75 centimeters long.

20. Century Developers recently purchased 1.3 square kilometers of property for $92 per are. What was the total purchase price for the property?

21. Joan Barrett is installing new glass shelves in one of the display cases in her shop. Each shelf is 275 centimeters long and 48 centimeters wide, and four shelves will be required. If the glass costs $125.50 per square meter, how much will all four shelves cost?

Section 17.2 *Metric Units of Capacity and Weight*

A. Units of Capacity

The basic unit of capacity in the metric system is the liter. A **liter** is slightly larger than a quart and is the capacity of a cubic container measuring 10 centimeters on each side (see figure 17.5).

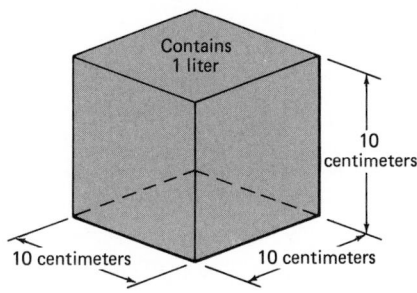

Figure 17.5
A liter, the basic unit of capacity in the metric system

Multiples and submultiples of the liter are shown in table 17.3.

Table 17.3	Multiples and Submultiples of the Liter	
1 kiloliter (kl)	= 1,000 liters	1 liter = 0.001 kiloliter
1 hectoliter (hl)	= 100 liters	1 liter = 0.01 hectoliter
1 dekaliter (dkl)	= 10 liters	1 liter = 0.1 dekaliter
1 liter (l)	= Basic unit of capacity	1 liter = Basic unit of capacity
1 deciliter (dl)	= 0.1 liter	1 liter = 10 deciliters
1 centiliter (cl)	= 0.01 liter	1 liter = 100 centiliters
1 milliliter (ml)	= 0.001 liter	1 liter = 1,000 milliliters

The techniques for converting from one metric unit of capacity to another are similar to the conversion procedures for metric units of length.

EXAMPLE 1 Find the number of liters in 468 centiliters.

Solution: Step 1   liter   deciliter   centiliter

Step 2   desired ⟵‿‿‿‿‿‿‿‿‿‿ given

(left 2 spaces)

Step 3   4. 6 8

Hence, 468 centiliters = 4.68 liters

EXAMPLE 2 A storage tank has a capacity of 550 kiloliters. How many dekaliters will the tank hold?

Solution: Step 1   kl   hl   dkl

Step 2   given ‿‿‿‿‿‿‿‿‿‿ desired

(right 2 spaces)

Step 3   550 0 0

Thus, 550 kl = 55,000 dkl

EXAMPLE 3 A synthetic polymer is sold in 100 milliliter bottles. How many liters are there in a case of 24 bottles?

Solution: The case contains a total of 24 × 100 = 2,400 ml

Step 1   liter   dl   cl   ml

Step 2   desired ⟵‿‿‿‿‿‿‿‿‿‿ given

(left 3 spaces)

Step 3   2. 4 0 0

Thus, there are 2.4 liters in a case of 24 bottles.

B. Units of Weight

The unit of weight in the metric system is the gram. A **gram** is the weight of 1 cubic centimeter of distilled water at its greater density, which is at 39.2° F (4° C) at sea level. Because a gram weighs only 0.353 ounces, the **kilogram** (1,000 grams) is the standard for most small weights. For heavy items, the **metric ton** (1,000 kilograms) is used. Multiples and submultiples of the gram are shown in table 17.4.

Table 17.4	Multiples and Submultiples of the Gram		
1 kilogram (kg)	= 1,000 grams	1 gram = 0.001 kilogram	
1 hectogram (hg)	= 100 grams	1 gram = 0.01 hectogram	
1 dekagram (dkg)	= 10 grams	1 gram = 0.1 dekagram	
1 gram (g)	= Basic unit of weight	1 gram = Basic unit of weight	
1 decigram (dg)	= 0.1 gram	1 gram = 10 decigrams	
1 centigram (cg)	= 0.01 gram	1 gram = 100 centigrams	
1 milligram (mg)	= 0.001 gram	1 gram = 1,000 milligrams	

The techniques for converting from one metric unit of weight to another are similar to the conversion procedures for length and capacity.

E X A M P L E   4   Find the number of kilograms in 1,686 grams.

Solution:

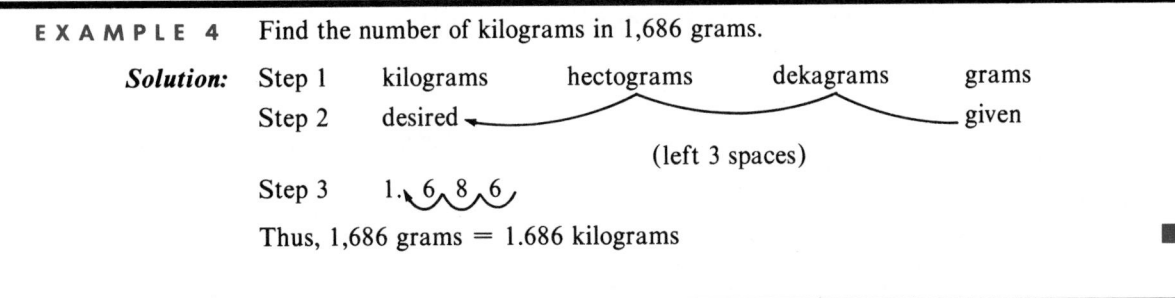

Thus, 1,686 grams = 1.686 kilograms

E X A M P L E   5   Find the number of milligrams in 0.042 hectograms.

Solution:

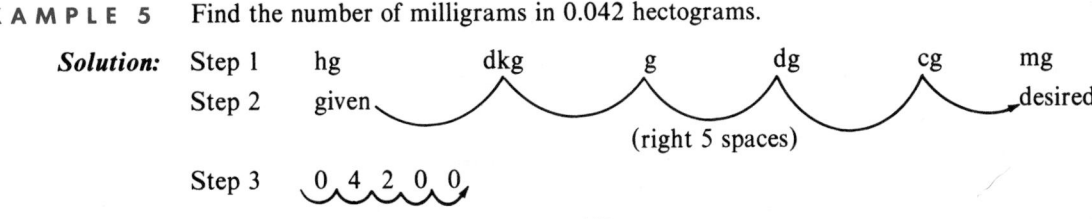

Thus, 0.042 hectograms = 4,200 milligrams

EXAMPLE 6   A tobacco company advertises a low tar brand of cigarette containing an average of 10 milligrams of tar per cigarette. How many decigrams of tar are contained in a carton (200 cigarettes) of this brand?

Solution: At an average of 10 mg per cigarette, a carton contains $200 \times 10 = 2{,}000$ milligrams of tar.

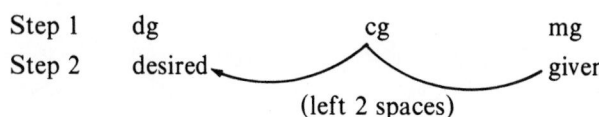

Step 1   dg   cg   mg

Step 2   desired   given

(left 2 spaces)

Step 3   20. 0 0

Thus, a carton contains 20 decigrams of tar.

EXAMPLE 7   A diesel locomotive weighs 150 metric tons. What is its weight in kilograms?

Solution: A metric ton (t) is 1,000 kilograms, Hence,

1 t = 1,000 kg
150 t = 150 × 1,000 = 150,000 kilograms

EXERCISES FOR SECTION 17.2

In problems 1–14, convert the given capacity or weight to the metric units specified.

1. **a.** 47 hectoliters to liters
   b. 27,420 liters to kiloliters

2. **a.** 52 kiloliters to liters
   b. 37 liters to deciliters

3. **a.** 2,710 milliliters to liters
   b. 5.21 liters to centiliters

4. **a.** 251.8 deciliters to liters
   b. 420.8 liters to dekaliters

5. **a.** 67 dekagrams to grams
   b. 38,240 grams to hectograms

6. **a.** 3.14 kilograms to grams
   b. 87 grams to centigrams

7. **a.** 78.3 hectograms to grams
   b. 41.23 grams to decigrams

8. **a.** 18.7 metric tons to kilograms
   b. 9.83 grams to milligrams

9. 420 dl = _____ dkl = _____ ml

10. 27.84 kl = _____ dkl = _____ dl

11. 270,000 ml = _____ hl = _____ cl

12. 2.16 kg = _____ hg = _____ dg

13. 714,000 mg = _____ dg = _____ dkg

14. 0.00214 t = _____ kg = _____ hg

Solve.

15. Beth Walters is planning a party for 15 people. She estimates that each person will drink 600 milliliters of soft drink. How many 1-liter bottles of soft drink should she purchase for the party?

16. A liquid baby formula is sold in 450-milliliter jars, and 48 jars are packed in a case. How many deciliters of formula does a case contain?

17. Betty Patterson takes 25 milliliters of medicine each day. When she filled the prescription, the bottle contained 5.25 deciliters. For how many days will the bottle of medicine last?

18. A 6-hectoliter aquarium is being filled at the rate of 0.5 dekaliters per minute. How long will it take to fill the aquarium?

19. A storage tank for fuel oil is leaking at the rate of 300 centiliters per hour. If the tank contains 0.6 kiloliters of oil, how long will it take for all the oil to leak out?

20. Jake Anderson purchased a new car that gets 14 kilometers per liter. How far can Jake go on **a.** 4 dekaliters of gasoline and **b.** 520 centiliters of gasoline?

21. The Patterson's new baby girl weighed 3.4 kilograms at birth. What was the baby's weight in **a.** dekagrams and **b.** decigrams?

22. The Nut House sells mixed nuts for $6.10 per kilogram. Find the cost of **a.** 8 hectograms and **b.** 400 dekagrams.

23. If a 4.5 kilogram bag of dog food is priced at $3.78, how much does it cost per day to feed a dog 250 grams of the dog food daily?

24. A foreign country purchased 1,200,000 metric tons of fertilizer for $240,000,000. Find the price of the fertilizer per kilogram.

25. The Mid-County Power Company uses 588 metric tons of coal each week at its main generating plant. The plant operates seven days a week, 24 hours a day. How many kilograms of coal per hour does the plant use?

26. A breakfast cereal is packaged in two sizes of boxes. The 250-gram box sells for $1.05, and the 350-gram box sells for $1.54. Find the unit price per gram of the cereal for each of the two sizes of boxes. Which size box is the better buy?

Section 17.3 *Metric Units versus English Units*

Until such time as the United States converts entirely to the metric system, it will be necessary to maintain a conversion table (see table 17.5) showing the relationship between the metric and English units.

Table 17.5   Metric-English Conversion Factors

Metric to English	English to Metric
Length	
Meter (m) = 1.093 yards = 3.281 feet = 39.370 inches	Yard = 0.9144 meter Foot = 0.3048 meter Inch = 0.0254 meter
Kilometer (km) = 0.621 mile	Mile = 1.609 kilometers
Area	
Square meter (m²) = 1.196 square yards = 10.764 square feet	Square yard = 0.836 square meter Square foot = 0.092 square meter
Square centimeter (cm²) = 0.155 square inch	Square inch = 6.45 square centimeters
Square kilometer (km²) = 0.386 square mile	Square mile = 2.590 square kilometers
Hectare (ha) = 2.471 acres	Acre = 0.405 hectare

Table 17.5	Metric-English Conversion Factors *Continued*
Metric to English	**English to Metric**

Capacity

Liter (l)	= 1.056 U.S. Liquid quarts	U.S. Liquid quart	= 0.946 liter
	= 0.908 dry quart	Dry quart	= 1.111 liters
	= 0.264 U.S. gallon	U.S. gallon	= 3.785 liters
Hectoliter (hl)	= 2.837 U.S. bushels	U.S. bushel	= 0.352 hectoliter

Weight

Gram (g)	= 15.432 grains	Grain	= 0.0648 gram
	= 0.0352 avoirdupois ounce	Avoirdupois ounce	= 28.35 grams
Kilogram (kg)	= 2.2046 pounds avoirdupois	Pound	= 0.4536 kilogram
Metric ton (t)	= 2,204.62 pounds avoirdupois	Short ton	= 0.9072 metric ton
	= 1.1023 short tons		

EXAMPLE 1   Karl's Auto Parts specializes in foreign car parts. A voltage regulator 10.1 centimeters in length is to be mailed to a customer. How long a box (in inches) is required if $\frac{1}{2}$ inch of packing is used on each end?

Solution:

$$1 \text{ cm} = .01 \text{ m} = 0.3937 \text{ inches} \quad \text{(Table 17.5)}$$
$$10.1 \text{ cm} = 10.1 \times 0.3937 \text{ inches}$$
$$= 3.98 \text{ inches}$$
$$\text{Packing} = \underline{1.00} \text{ inch}$$
$$\text{Total length} = 4.98 \text{ inches}$$

Karl will no doubt use a 5-inch box to mail the part.   ■

EXAMPLE 2   The Sikes Company purchased 150 hectares of land in Spain for construction of a branch factory. If the total price was $70,000, what was the cost per acre?

Solution:

$$1 \text{ ha} = 2.471 \text{ acres}$$
$$150 \text{ ha} = 150 \times 2.471 \text{ acres}$$
$$= 370.65 \text{ acres}$$
$$\frac{\$70,000}{370.65} = \$188.86 \text{ per acre}$$

■

EXAMPLE 3   The Moroni Import Company received a shipment of 50 hectoliters of olive oil. What was the shipment in gallons?

Solution:
$$1 \text{ hl} = 100 \text{ liters}$$
$$50 \text{ hl} = 50 \times 100 \text{ liters}$$
$$= 5,000 \text{ liters}$$
$$1 \text{ liter} = 0.264 \text{ gallons} \quad \text{(Table 17.5)}$$
$$5,000 \text{ liters} = 5,000 \times 0.264 \text{ gallons}$$
$$= 1,320 \text{ gallons}$$

EXAMPLE 4   A poor grain harvest forced the Russian government to purchase 3,000,000 metric tons of wheat on the open market. What is the U.S. equivalent in tons?

Solution:
$$1 \text{ t} = 1.1023 \text{ tons} \quad \text{(Table 17.5)}$$
$$3,000,000 \text{ t} = 3,000,000 \times 1.1023 \text{ tons}$$
$$= 3,306,900 \text{ tons}$$

A part of the planned conversion to the metric system is a change in temperature measurement. The present system in the United States of measuring temperature by degrees Fahrenheit will be replaced by the degrees Celsius measurement system.

The difference between the two systems involves the freezing and boiling points of water. In the Fahrenheit system, water freezes at 32° and boils at 212°, a difference of 180°. In the Celsius system, water freezes at 0° and boils at 100°. Thus, while the degree Celsius is not defined in terms of the meter, as are the other metric units, it is decimal based.

To convert between degrees Fahrenheit (°F) and degrees Celsius (°C), the following formulas are used.

(17–1) $C = \frac{5}{9}(F - 32)$ To convert from Fahrenheit to Celsius

(17–2) $F = \frac{9}{5}C + 32$ To convert from Celsius to Fahrenheit

Metric Recipe

Queen cakes

100 g butter or margarine
100 g castor sugar
150 g self-raising flour
pinch of salt
2 eggs
25 mℓ milk
100 g currants

Cream the fat and sugar together until light and fluffy.
Sieve or mix the flour and salt.
Add the eggs, one at a time, to the creamed mixture with a spoonful of flour, stir then beat.
Beat in the milk with a little more flour.
Stir in the currants with the remaining flour.
Divide the mixture evenly between about 20 baking cases, smooth level.
Bake for 15–20 minutes at 190° C (375° F) gas mark 5.

Metric recipe leaflets are on sale from UKFEHE, 36 Ravenscroft Avenue, London NW11 8AU.

Recipe supplied by the United Kingdom Home Economics Federation.

EXAMPLE 5   The normal body temperature of a human being is 98.6°F. Express this temperature in degrees Celsius.

Solution: Using formula 17–1,

$$C = \tfrac{5}{9}(F - 32)$$
$$= \tfrac{5}{9}(98.6 - 32)$$
$$= \tfrac{5}{9}(66.6)$$
$$= 37° \text{ C} \qquad ■$$

EXAMPLE 6   Superheated steam used to drive steam turbines can reach 1,050° F. To the nearest tenth of a degree, what is this temperature in degrees Celsius?

Solution: Using formula 17–1,

$$C = \tfrac{5}{9}(F - 32)$$
$$= \tfrac{5}{9}(1,050 - 32)$$
$$= \tfrac{5}{9}(1,018)$$
$$= 565.6° \text{ C} \qquad ■$$

EXAMPLE 7   During the summer, a European city recorded a high temperature of 28° C. To the nearest tenth of a degree, what is this temperature in degrees Fahrenheit?

Solution: Using formula 17–2,

$$F = \tfrac{9}{5}C + 32$$
$$= \tfrac{9}{5}(28) + 32$$
$$= 82.4° \ F$$

■

EXAMPLE 8   As a protection against spoilage during shipping, some meat products were packed in dry ice, which has a temperature of −78.5° C. To the nearest tenth of a degree, what is the temperature of dry ice in degrees Fahrenheit?

Solution: Using formula 17–2,

$$F = \tfrac{9}{5}C + 32$$
$$= \tfrac{9}{5}(-78.5) + 32$$
$$= -109.3° \ F$$

■

EXERCISES FOR SECTION 17.3

In problems 1–28, fill in the blanks. Round your answers to the second decimal place.

1. 10 meters = _____ feet

2. 1,500 meters = _____ miles

3. 45 millimeters = _____ inches

4. 60 kilometers = _____ miles

5. 4,500 meters = _____ yards

6. 48 inches = _____ centimeters

7. 100 yards = _____ meters

8. 12 miles = _____ kilometers

9. 6 feet = _____ meters

10. 350 feet = _____ dekameters

11. 12 square meters = _____ square yards

12. 66 square centimeters = _____ square inches

13. 4 square kilometers = _____ square miles

14. 7 square meters = _____ square feet

15. 44 hectares = _____ acres

16. 12 square yards = _____ square meters

17. 144 square inches = _____ square centimeters

18. $4\tfrac{1}{2}$ square miles = _____ square kilometers

19. 30 square feet = _____ square meters

20. 75 acres = _____ hectares

21. 6 liters = _____ liquid quarts

22. $2\tfrac{1}{2}$ liters = _____ pints

23. 16 liters = _____ gallons

24. 110 hectoliters = _____ bushels

25. 36 gallons = _____ liters

26. 14 liquid quarts = _____ liters

27. 62 bushels = _____ hectoliters

28. 24 liquid quarts = _____ liters

In problems 29–40, round answers to the nearest tenth of a degree.

29. 68° F = _____° C

30. 140° F = _____° C

31. −49° F = _____° C

32. −22° F = _____° C

33. 20° F = _____° C

34. 6° F = _____° C

35. 35° C = _____° F

36. 70° C = _____° F

37. −10° C = _____° F

38. −25° C = _____° F

39. 8° C = _____° F

40. 138° C = _____° F

In problems 41–49, round answers to the second decimal place.

41. The Ferris Company sold 200 gallons of molasses to a European firm for $4.40 per gallon. What was the price per liter?

42. Visitors to a country in the Middle East are advised that the speed limit is 90 kilometers per hour. What is the speed limit in miles per hour?

43. A British plant consumes 12 metric tons of coal every eight hours. How many pounds of coal per hour is this?

44. The Wheeling Tool and Die Company received an order for some brass fittings from a foreign firm. One of the specifications called for a hole of 32 millimeters in diameter. What is the size of the hole in inches?

45. A buyer for the Romulus Corporation can buy an item at $0.26 per pound or $0.55 per kilogram. Which is the best price?

46. The Monroe Packing Company sold a total of 120 metric tons of citrus products to a Japanese import company in one year. Find the number of pounds of citrus products sold.

47. The engine of a foreign car is rated at 1,500 cubic centimeters. How many cubic inches is this? (Note: 1 cubic inch = 16.387 cubic centimeters.)

48. A recipe for a cake called for an oven setting of 175° C. What is this temperature in degrees Fahrenheit?

49. As part of a special military training program, a group of technicians was subjected to temperatures as high as 392° F. How many degrees Celsius is this?

Glossary

Are   100 square meters.

Centimeter $\frac{1}{100}$ meter.

Gram   The weight of 1 cubic centimeter of distilled water at its greatest density.

Hectare   100 ares.

Kilogram   1,000 grams.

Kilometer   1,000 meters.

Liter   The capacity of a cubic container measuring 10 centimeters on each side.

Meter   The basic unit of measurement in the metric system. It was originally defined as $\frac{1}{10,000,000}$ of the distance from the equator to a pole. The current definition of a meter is 1,650,763.73 wavelengths of the orange-red light of krypton 86.

Metric ton   1,000 kilograms.

Millimeter $\frac{1}{1,000}$ meter.

Square meter   The basic unit of area in the metric system. The area of a square with sides 1 meter in length.

||||||||||||||||||||||||||||||||||| Review Test |||||||||||||||||||||||||||||||||||||

In problems 1–10, convert the given measure to the metric units specified.

1. 36 meters to hectometers

2. 16 kiloliters to liters

3. 6.73 grams to decigrams

4. 223 deciliters to dekaliters

5. 7.12 hectometers to centimeters

6. 16 square kilometers to ares

7. 267,490 kilograms to metric tons

8. 720,000 ml = _____ hl = _____ cl

9. 48.72 kl = _____ dkl = _____ dl

10. 4,102 dg = _____ dkg = _____ cg

Solve.

11. A can of refrigeration oil is priced at $4 per liter. What is the cost of 250 milliliters?

12. John Good purchased a 2.25-kilogram bag of fertilizer. If a plant requires three applications of fertilizer during the growing season at 150 grams per application, how many plants can John fertilize for the entire growing season?

13. Cold water for the air-conditioning system of a manufacturing plant is maintained at 50° F. What is this temperature in degrees Celsius?

14. A lens has a focal length of 250 millimeters. Express this length in inches. (Note: 1 meter = 39.37 inches.)

Appendixes

Appendix A   Special purpose calculators

Along with the general purpose calculator described in Section 1.5, financial and scientific calculators are now marketed at increasingly affordable prices. These special purpose calculators have functions that can simplify solutions to exercises in this text. Some keys common to both financial calculators and scientific calculators are as follows:

Keys	*Purpose*
2nd or Shift	To access a second function typically printed above a key.
( )	To postpone a calculation until more numbers can be entered.
y^x	Raises the number y to the power x.
e^x	Raises the number e to the power x.
+/−	Changes the sign of the number in the display.

The following are solutions to examples in the text using a financial calculator with the above keys and special keys for compound interest, annuities, sinking funds, and amortization. Because calculator logic varies among manufacturers, the reader should check the owner's manual to ensure the keys and logic on his or her calculator match those used here. The solutions assume the use of the 2nd or shift key to access the needed function. Answers are rounded to two decimal places.

Use of parentheses in lieu of memory keys

Section 7.4   **Example 3**

Find $\dfrac{\$2{,}000}{1 + (0.12 \times 2/3)}$

Entry	Display
2000	2000
÷	2000
(	2000
1	1
+	1
(	1
.12	0.12
×	0.12
2	2
÷	0.24
3	3
=	1851.85

Section 9.2   **Example 1**

Find $\$670 \left(1 - (0.12 \times \dfrac{5}{12}) \right)$

Entry	Display
670	670
×	670
(	670
1	1
−	1
(	1
.12	0.12
×	0.12
5	5
÷	0.60
12	12
=	636.50

Section 14.2   **Example 6**

Find $\dfrac{\$21,900 + \$12,000}{\$120,000 + \$9,100}$

Entry	Display
(	0
21900	21900
+	21900
12000	12000
)	33900
÷	33900
(	33900
120000	120000
+	120000
9100	9100
=	0.26

Use of the e^x key

Section 8.3   **Example 4**

Find $\$1,200e^{(0.10)(0.5)}$

Entry	Display
1200	1200
×	1200
(	1200
.1	0.1
×	0.1
.5	0.5
)	0.05
e^x	1.05127
=	1261.53

Use of the y^x key

Section 8.1   **Example 1**

Find $\$4,000(1.0275)^{20}$

Entry	Display
4000	4000
×	4000
(	4000
1.0275	1.0275
y^x	1.0275
20	20
=	6881.7137

Section 8.2   **Example 2**

Find $15,000(1.02)^{-20}$

Entry	Display
15000	15000
×	15000
(	15000
1.02	1.02
y^x	1.02
20	20
+/−	−20
=	10094.57

If your financial calculator has the keys

| N | | I/YR | | PV | | PMT | | P/YR | | FV |

you may be able to solve compound interest, present value, annuity, sinking fund, and amortization problems as follows.

Section 8.1   **Example 1**

Find $4,000(1.0275)^{20}$

Entry	Display
20	20
N	20
11	11
I/YR	11
4000	4000
+/−	−4000
PV	−4000
4	4
P/YR	4
FV	6881.71

Section 8.2   **Example 2**

Find $15,000(1.02)^{-20}$

Entry	Display
20	20
N	20
8	8
I/YR	8
4	4
P/YR	4
15000	15000
+/−	−15000
FV	−15000
PV	10094.57

Section 11.2   **Example 1**

Find $1,000 \cdot s_{\overline{10}|0.045}$

Entry	Display
10	10
N	10
9	9
I/YR	9
0	0
PV	0
2	2
P/YR	2
1000	1000
+/−	−1000
PMT	−1000
FV	12288.21

Section 12.1   **Example 1**

Find $240,000 $\times \dfrac{1}{s_{\overline{12}0.02}}$

Entry	Display
12	12
N	12
8	8
I/YR	8
0	0
PV	0
4	4
P/YR	4
240000	240000
+/−	−240000
FV	−240000
PMT	17894.30

If your calculator has the keys

| $\Sigma +$ | $\overline{x}$ | s_x |

you may be able to find the mean and standard deviation of an array as shown next.

Section 16.4

Find the mean and standard deviation of data array A.

Entry	Display
1	1
$\Sigma +$	1
10	10
$\Sigma +$	2
11	11
$\Sigma +$	3
13	13
$\Sigma +$	4
14	14
$\Sigma +$	5
23	23
$\Sigma +$	6
$\overline{x}$	12
s_x	7.10

Appendix B   The number of each day of the year

Day of Month	Jan.	Feb.	Mar.	April	May	June	July	Aug.	Sept.	Oct.	Nov.	Dec.	Day of Month
1	1	32	60	91	121	152	182	213	244	274	305	335	1
2	2	33	61	92	122	153	183	214	245	275	306	336	2
3	3	34	62	93	123	154	184	215	246	276	307	337	3
4	4	35	63	94	124	155	185	216	247	277	308	338	4
5	5	36	64	95	125	156	186	217	248	278	309	339	5
6	6	37	65	96	126	157	187	218	249	279	310	340	6
7	7	38	66	97	127	158	188	219	250	280	311	341	7
8	8	39	67	98	128	159	189	220	251	281	312	342	8
9	9	40	68	99	129	160	190	221	252	282	313	343	9
10	10	41	69	100	130	161	191	222	253	283	314	344	10
11	11	42	70	101	131	162	192	223	254	284	315	345	11
12	12	43	71	102	132	163	193	224	255	285	316	346	12
13	13	44	72	103	133	164	194	225	256	286	317	347	13
14	14	45	73	104	134	165	195	226	257	287	318	348	14
15	15	46	74	105	135	166	196	227	258	288	319	349	15
16	16	47	75	106	136	167	197	228	259	289	320	350	16
17	17	48	76	107	137	168	198	229	260	290	321	351	17
18	18	49	77	108	138	169	199	230	261	291	322	352	18
19	19	50	78	109	139	170	200	231	262	292	323	353	19
20	20	51	79	110	140	171	201	232	263	293	324	354	20
21	21	52	80	111	141	172	202	233	264	294	325	355	21
22	22	53	81	112	142	173	203	234	265	295	326	356	22
23	23	54	82	113	143	174	204	235	266	296	327	357	23
24	24	55	83	114	144	175	205	236	267	297	328	358	24
25	25	56	84	115	145	176	206	237	268	298	329	359	25
26	26	57	85	116	146	177	207	238	269	299	330	360	26
27	27	58	86	117	147	178	208	239	270	300	331	361	27
28	28	59	87	118	148	179	209	240	271	301	332	362	28
29	29		88	119	149	180	210	241	272	302	333	363	29
30	30		89	120	150	181	211	242	273	303	334	364	30
31	31		90		151		212	243		304		365	31

Note. In leap years, after February 28, add 1 to the tabulated number.

Appendixes C–H

Compound amount, present value, amount of annuity, present value of annuity, sinking fund, and amortization

Rate ¼%	C Compound Amount	D Present Value	E Amount of Annuity	F Present Value of Annuity	G Sinking Fund	H Amortization	
n	$(1 + i)^n$	$(1 + i)^{-n}$	$S_{\overline{n}|i}$	$A_{\overline{n}|i}$	$1/S_{\overline{n}|i}$	$1/A_{\overline{n}|i}$	n
1	1.00250000	0.99750623	1.00000000	0.99750623	1.00000000	1.00250000	1
2	1.00500625	0.99501869	2.00250000	1.99252492	0.49937578	0.50187578	2
3	1.00751877	0.99253734	3.00750625	2.98506227	0.33250139	0.33500139	3
4	1.01003756	0.99006219	4.01502502	3.97512446	0.24906445	0.25156445	4
5	1.01256266	0.98759321	5.02506258	4.96271766	0.19900250	0.20150250	5
6	1.01509406	0.98513038	6.03762523	5.94784804	0.16562803	0.16812803	6
7	1.01763180	0.98267370	7.05271930	6.93052174	0.14178928	0.14428928	7
8	1.02017588	0.98022314	8.07035110	7.91074487	0.12391035	0.12641035	8
9	1.02272632	0.97777869	9.09052697	8.88852357	0.11000462	0.11250462	9
10	1.02528313	0.97534034	10.11325329	9.86386391	0.09888015	0.10138015	10
11	1.02784634	0.97290807	11.13853642	10.83677198	0.08977840	0.09227840	11
12	1.03041596	0.97048187	12.16638277	11.80725384	0.08219370	0.08469370	12
13	1.03299200	0.96806171	13.19679872	12.77531555	0.07577595	0.07827595	13
14	1.03557448	0.96564759	14.22979072	13.74096314	0.07027510	0.07277510	14
15	1.03816341	0.96323949	15.26536520	14.70420264	0.06550777	0.06800777	15
16	1.04075882	0.96083740	16.30352861	15.66504004	0.06133642	0.06383642	16
17	1.04336072	0.95844130	17.34428743	16.62348133	0.05765587	0.06015587	17
18	1.04596912	0.95605117	18.38764815	17.57953250	0.05438433	0.05688433	18
19	1.04858404	0.95366700	19.43361727	18.53319950	0.05145722	0.05395722	19
20	1.05120550	0.95128878	20.48220131	19.48448828	0.04882288	0.05132288	20
21	1.05383352	0.94891649	21.53340682	20.43340477	0.04643947	0.04893947	21
22	1.05646810	0.94655011	22.58724033	21.37995488	0.04427278	0.04677278	22
23	1.05910927	0.94418964	23.64370843	22.32414452	0.04229455	0.04479455	23
24	1.06175704	0.94183505	24.70281770	23.26597957	0.04048121	0.04298121	24
25	1.06441144	0.93948634	25.76457475	24.20546591	0.03881298	0.04131298	25
26	1.06707247	0.93714348	26.82898619	25.14260939	0.03727312	0.03977312	26
27	1.06974015	0.93480646	27.89605865	26.07741585	0.03584736	0.03834736	27
28	1.07241450	0.93247527	28.96579880	27.00989112	0.03452347	0.03702347	28
29	1.07509553	0.93014990	30.03821330	27.94004102	0.03329093	0.03579093	29
30	1.07778327	0.92783032	31.11330883	28.86787134	0.03214059	0.03464059	30
31	1.08047773	0.92551653	32.19109210	29.79338787	0.03106449	0.03356449	31
32	1.08317892	0.92320851	33.27156983	30.71659638	0.03005569	0.03255569	32
33	1.08588687	0.92090624	34.35474876	31.63750262	0.02910806	0.03160806	33
34	1.08860159	0.91860972	35.44063563	32.55611234	0.02821620	0.03071620	34
35	1.09132309	0.91631892	36.52923722	33.47243126	0.02737533	0.02987533	35
36	1.09405140	0.91403384	37.62056031	34.38646510	0.02658121	0.02908121	36
37	1.09678653	0.91175445	38.71461171	35.29821955	0.02583004	0.02833004	37
38	1.09952850	0.90948075	39.81139824	36.20770030	0.02511843	0.02761843	38
39	1.10227732	0.90721272	40.91092673	37.11491302	0.02444335	0.02694335	39
40	1.10503301	0.90495034	42.01320405	38.01986336	0.02380204	0.02630204	40
41	1.10779559	0.90269361	43.11823706	38.92255697	0.02319204	0.02569204	41
42	1.11056508	0.90044250	44.22603265	39.82299947	0.02261112	0.02511112	42
43	1.11334149	0.89819701	45.33659774	40.72119648	0.02205724	0.02455724	43
44	1.11612485	0.89595712	46.44993923	41.61715359	0.02152885	0.02402855	44
45	1.11891516	0.89372281	47.56606408	42.51087640	0.02102339	0.02352339	45
46	1.12171245	0.89149407	48.68497924	43.40237047	0.02054022	0.02304022	46
47	1.12451673	0.88927090	49.80669169	44.29164137	0.02007762	0.02257762	47
48	1.12732802	0.88705326	50.93120842	45.17869463	0.01963433	0.02213433	48
49	1.13014634	0.88484116	52.05853644	46.06353580	0.01920915	0.02170915	49
50	1.13297171	0.88263457	53.18868278	46.94617037	0.01880099	0.02130099	50
80	1.22109795	0.81893512	88.43918139	72.42595169	0.01130721	0.01380721	80
100	1.28362489	0.77904379	113.44995550	88.38248346	0.00881446	0.01131446	100
120	1.34935355	0.74109562	139.74141888	103.56175308	0.00715607	0.00965607	120
240	1.82075500	0.54922271	328.30199813	180.31091441	0.00304598	0.00554598	240
360	2.45684221	0.40702655	582.73688460	237.18938150	0.00171604	0.00421604	360

Rate ⅓%	C Compound Amount	D Present Value	E Amount of Annuity	F Present Value of Annuity	G Sinking Fund	H Amortization	
n	$(1 + i)^n$	$(1 + i)^{-n}$	$S_{\overline{n}|i}$	$A_{\overline{n}|i}$	$1/S_{\overline{n}|i}$	$1/A_{\overline{n}|i}$	n
1	1.00333333	0.99667774	1.00000000	0.99667774	1.00000000	1.00333333	1
2	1.00667778	0.99336652	2.00333333	1.99004426	0.49916805	0.50250139	2
3	1.01003337	0.99006630	3.01001111	2.98011056	0.33222469	0.33555802	3
4	1.01340015	0.98677704	4.02004448	3.96688760	0.24875347	0.25208680	4
5	1.01677815	0.98349871	5.03344463	4.95038631	0.19867110	0.20200444	5
6	1.02016741	0.98023127	6.05022278	5.93061759	0.16528317	0.16861650	6
7	1.02356797	0.97697469	7.07039019	6.90759228	0.14143491	0.14476824	7
8	1.02697986	0.97372893	8.09395816	7.88132121	0.12354895	0.12688228	8
9	1.03040313	0.97049395	9.12093802	8.85181516	0.10963785	0.11297118	9
10	1.03383780	0.96726972	10.15134114	9.81908487	0.09850915	0.10184248	10
11	1.03728393	0.96405620	11.18517895	10.78314107	0.08940402	0.09273736	11
12	1.04074154	0.96085335	12.22246288	11.74399442	0.08181657	0.08514990	12
13	1.04421068	0.95766115	13.26320442	12.70165557	0.07539656	0.07872989	13
14	1.04769138	0.95447955	14.30741510	13.65135512	0.06989383	0.07322716	14
15	1.05118369	0.95130852	15.35510648	14.60744364	0.06512491	0.06845825	15
16	1.05468763	0.94814803	16.40629017	15.55559167	0.06095223	0.06428557	16
17	1.05820326	0.94499803	17.46097781	16.50058970	0.05727056	0.06060389	17
18	1.06173060	0.94185851	18.51918107	17.44244821	0.05399807	0.05733140	18
19	1.06526971	0.93872941	19.58091167	18.38117762	0.05107015	0.05440348	19
20	1.06882060	0.93561071	20.64618137	19.31678832	0.04843511	0.05176844	20
21	1.07238334	0.93250236	21.71500198	20.24929069	0.04605111	0.04938445	21
22	1.07595795	0.92940435	22.78738532	21.17869504	0.04388393	0.04721726	22
23	1.07954448	0.92631663	23.86334327	22.10501167	0.04190528	0.04523861	23
24	1.08314296	0.92323916	24.94288775	23.02825083	0.04009159	0.04342492	24
25	1.08675344	0.92017192	26.02603071	23.94842275	0.03842307	0.04175640	25
26	1.09037595	0.91711487	27.11278414	24.86553763	0.03688297	0.04021630	26
27	1.09401053	0.91406798	28.20316009	25.77960561	0.03545702	0.03879035	27
28	1.09765724	0.91103121	29.29717062	26.69063682	0.03413299	0.03746632	28
29	1.10131609	0.90800453	30.39482786	27.59864135	0.03290033	0.03623367	29
30	1.10498715	0.90498790	31.49614395	28.50362925	0.03174992	0.03508325	30
31	1.10867044	0.90198130	32.60113110	29.40561055	0.03067378	0.03400712	31
32	1.11236601	0.89898468	33.70980154	30.30459523	0.02966496	0.03299830	32
33	1.11607389	0.89599802	34.82216754	31.20059325	0.02871734	0.03205067	33
34	1.11979414	0.89302128	35.93824143	32.09361454	0.02782551	0.03115885	34
35	1.12352679	0.89005444	37.05803557	32.98366898	0.02698470	0.03031803	35
36	1.12727187	0.88709745	38.18156236	33.87076642	0.02619065	0.02952399	36
37	1.13102945	0.88415028	39.30883423	34.75491670	0.02543957	0.02877291	37
38	1.13479955	0.88121290	40.43986368	35.63612960	0.02472808	0.02806141	38
39	1.13858221	0.87828528	41.57466322	36.51441488	0.02405311	0.02738644	39
40	1.14237748	0.87536739	42.71324543	37.38978228	0.02341194	0.02674527	40
41	1.14618541	0.87245920	43.85562292	38.26224147	0.02280209	0.02613543	41
42	1.15000603	0.86956066	45.00180833	39.13180213	0.02222133	0.02555466	42
43	1.15383938	0.86667175	46.15181436	39.99847389	0.02166762	0.02500095	43
44	1.15768551	0.86379245	47.30565374	40.86226633	0.02113912	0.02447246	44
45	1.16154446	0.86092270	48.46333925	41.72318903	0.02063415	0.02396749	45
46	1.16541628	0.85806249	49.62488371	42.58125153	0.02015118	0.02348451	46
47	1.16930100	0.85521179	50.79029999	43.43646332	0.01968880	0.02302213	47
48	1.17319867	0.85237055	51.95960099	44.28883387	0.01924572	0.02257905	48
49	1.17710933	0.84953876	53.13279966	45.13837263	0.01882077	0.02215410	49
50	1.18103303	0.84671637	54.30990899	45.98508900	0.01841285	0.02174618	50
80	1.30502632	0.76626807	91.50789532	70.11957849	0.01092802	0.01426135	80
100	1.39483902	0.71692861	118.45170537	84.92141663	0.00844226	0.01177559	100
120	1.49083268	0.67076608	147.24980472	98.77017486	0.00679118	0.01012451	120
240	2.22258209	0.44992714	366.77462607	165.02185825	0.00272647	0.00605980	240
360	3.31349801	0.30179587	694.04940433	209.46124046	0.00144082	0.00477415	360

Rate ½%	C Compound Amount	D Present Value	E Amount of Annuity	F Present Value of Annuity	G Sinking Fund	H Amortization	
n	$(1 + i)^n$	$(1 + i)^{-n}$	$S_{\overline{n}|i}$	$A_{\overline{n}|i}$	$1 / S_{\overline{n}|i}$	$1 / A_{\overline{n}|i}$	n
1	1.00500000	0.99502488	1.00000000	0.99502488	1.00000000	1.00500000	1
2	1.01002500	0.99007450	2.00500000	1.98509938	0.49875312	0.50375312	2
3	1.01507513	0.98514876	3.01502500	2.97024814	0.33167221	0.33667221	3
4	1.02015050	0.98024752	4.03010013	3.95049566	0.24813279	0.25313279	4
5	1.02525125	0.97537067	5.05025063	4.92586633	0.19800997	0.20300997	5
6	1.03037751	0.97051808	6.07550188	5.89638441	0.16459546	0.16959546	6
7	1.03552940	0.96568963	7.10587939	6.86207404	0.14072854	0.14572854	7
8	1.04070704	0.96088520	8.14140879	7.82295924	0.12282886	0.12782886	8
9	1.04591058	0.95610468	9.18211583	8.77906392	0.10890736	0.11390736	9
10	1.05114013	0.95134794	10.22802641	9.73041186	0.09777057	0.10277057	10
11	1.05639583	0.94661487	11.27916654	10.67702673	0.08865903	0.09365903	11
12	1.06167781	0.94190534	12.33556237	11.61893207	0.08106643	0.08606643	12
13	1.06698620	0.93721924	13.39724018	12.55615131	0.07464224	0.07964224	13
14	1.07232113	0.93255646	14.46422639	13.48870777	0.06913609	0.07413609	14
15	1.07768274	0.92791688	15.53654752	14.41662465	0.06436436	0.06936436	15
16	1.08307115	0.92330037	16.61423026	15.33992502	0.06018937	0.06518937	16
17	1.08848651	0.91870684	17.69730141	16.25863186	0.05650579	0.06150579	17
18	1.09392894	0.91413616	18.78578791	17.17276802	0.05323173	0.05823173	18
19	1.09939858	0.90958822	19.87971685	18.08235624	0.05030253	0.05530253	19
20	1.10489558	0.90506290	20.97911544	18.98741915	0.04766645	0.05266645	20
21	1.11042006	0.90056010	22.08401101	19.88797925	0.04528163	0.05028163	21
22	1.11597216	0.89607971	23.19443107	20.78405896	0.04311380	0.04811380	22
23	1.12155202	0.89162160	24.31040322	21.67568055	0.04113465	0.04613465	23
24	1.12715978	0.88718567	25.43195524	22.56286622	0.03932061	0.04432061	24
25	1.13279558	0.88277181	26.55911502	23.44563803	0.03765186	0.04265186	25
26	1.13845955	0.87837991	27.69191059	24.32401794	0.03611163	0.04111163	26
27	1.14415185	0.87400986	28.83037015	25.19802780	0.03468565	0.03968565	27
28	1.14987261	0.86966155	29.97452200	26.06768936	0.03336167	0.03836167	28
29	1.15562197	0.86533488	31.12439461	26.93302423	0.03212914	0.03712914	29
30	1.16140008	0.86102973	32.28001658	27.79405397	0.03097892	0.03597892	30
31	1.16720708	0.85674600	33.44141666	28.65079997	0.02990304	0.03490304	31
32	1.17304312	0.85248358	34.60862375	29.50328355	0.02889453	0.03389453	32
33	1.17890833	0.84824237	35.78166686	30.35152592	0.02794727	0.03294727	33
34	1.18480288	0.84402226	36.96057520	31.19554818	0.02705586	0.03205586	34
35	1.19072689	0.83982314	38.14537807	32.03537132	0.02621550	0.03121550	35
36	1.19668052	0.83564492	39.33610496	32.87101624	0.02542194	0.03042194	36
37	1.20266393	0.83148748	40.53278549	33.70250372	0.02467139	0.02967139	37
38	1.20867725	0.82735073	41.73544942	34.52985445	0.02396045	0.02896045	38
39	1.21472063	0.82323455	42.94412666	35.35308900	0.02328607	0.02828607	39
40	1.22079424	0.81913886	44.15884730	36.17222786	0.02264552	0.02764552	40
41	1.22689821	0.81506354	45.37964153	36.98729141	0.02203631	0.02703631	41
42	1.23303270	0.81100850	46.60653974	37.79829991	0.02145622	0.02645622	42
43	1.23919786	0.80697363	47.83957244	38.60527354	0.02090320	0.02590320	43
44	1.24539385	0.80295884	49.07877030	39.40823238	0.02037541	0.02537541	44
45	1.25162082	0.79896402	50.32416415	40.20719640	0.01987117	0.02487117	45
46	1.25787892	0.79498907	51.57578497	41.00218547	0.01938894	0.02438894	46
47	1.26416832	0.79103390	52.83366390	41.79321937	0.01892733	0.02392733	47
48	1.27048916	0.78709841	54.09783222	42.58031778	0.01848503	0.02348503	48
49	1.27684161	0.78318250	55.36832138	43.36350028	0.01806087	0.02306087	49
50	1.28322581	0.77928607	56.64516299	44.14278635	0.01765376	0.02265376	50
80	1.49033857	0.67098847	98.06771357	65.80230538	0.01019704	0.01519704	80
100	1.64666849	0.60728678	129.33369842	78.54264477	0.00773194	0.01273194	100
120	1.81939673	0.54963273	163.87934681	90.07345333	0.00610205	0.01110205	120
240	3.31020448	0.30209614	462.04089516	139.58077168	0.00216431	0.00716431	240
360	6.02257521	0.16604193	1004.51504245	166.79161439	0.00099551	0.00599551	360

Rate ¾%	C Compound Amount	D Present Value	E Amount of Annuity	F Present Value of Annuity	G Sinking Fund	H Amortization	
n	$(1 + i)^n$	$(1 + i)^{-n}$	$S_{\overline{n}|i}$	$A_{\overline{n}|i}$	$1/S_{\overline{n}|i}$	$1/A_{\overline{n}|i}$	n
1	1.00750000	0.99255583	1.00000000	0.99255583	1.00000000	1.00750000	1
2	1.01505625	0.98516708	2.00750000	1.97772291	0.49813200	0.50563200	2
3	1.02266917	0.97783333	3.02255625	2.95555624	0.33084579	0.33834579	3
4	1.03033919	0.97055417	4.04522542	3.92611041	0.24720501	0.25470501	4
5	1.03806673	0.96332920	5.07556461	4.88943961	0.19702242	0.20452242	5
6	1.04585224	0.95615802	6.11363135	5.84559763	0.16356891	0.17106891	6
7	1.05369613	0.94904022	7.15948358	6.79463785	0.13967488	0.14717488	7
8	1.06159885	0.94197540	8.21317971	7.73661325	0.12175552	0.12925552	8
9	1.06956084	0.93496318	9.27477856	8.67157642	0.10781929	0.11531929	9
10	1.07758255	0.92800315	10.34433940	9.59957958	0.09667123	0.10417123	10
11	1.08566441	0.92109494	11.42192194	10.52067452	0.08755094	0.09505094	11
12	1.09380690	0.91423815	12.50758636	11.43491267	0.07995148	0.08745148	12
13	1.10201045	0.90743241	13.60139325	12.34234508	0.07352188	0.08102188	13
14	1.11027553	0.90067733	14.70340370	13.24302242	0.06801146	0.07551146	14
15	1.11860259	0.89397254	15.81367923	14.13699495	0.06323639	0.07073639	15
16	1.12699211	0.88731766	16.93228183	15.02431261	0.05905879	0.06655879	16
17	1.13544455	0.88071231	18.05927394	15.90502492	0.05537321	0.06287321	17
18	1.14396039	0.87415614	19.19471849	16.77918107	0.05209766	0.05959766	18
19	1.15254009	0.86764878	20.33867888	17.64682984	0.04916740	0.05666740	19
20	1.16118414	0.86118985	21.49121897	18.50801969	0.04653063	0.05403063	20
21	1.16989302	0.85477901	22.65240312	19.36279870	0.04414543	0.05164543	21
22	1.17866722	0.84841589	23.82229614	20.21121459	0.04197748	0.04947748	22
23	1.18750723	0.84210014	25.00096336	21.05331473	0.03999846	0.04749846	23
24	1.19641353	0.83583140	26.18847059	21.88914614	0.03818474	0.04568474	24
25	1.20538663	0.82960933	27.38488412	22.71875547	0.03651650	0.04401650	25
26	1.21442703	0.82343358	28.59027075	23.54218905	0.03497693	0.04247693	26
27	1.22353523	0.81730380	29.80469778	24.35949286	0.03355176	0.04105176	27
28	1.23271175	0.81121966	31.02823301	25.17071251	0.03222871	0.03972871	28
29	1.24195709	0.80518080	32.26094476	25.97589331	0.03099723	0.03849723	29
30	1.25127176	0.79918690	33.50290184	26.77508021	0.02984816	0.03734816	30
31	1.26065630	0.79323762	34.75417361	27.56831783	0.02877352	0.03627352	31
32	1.27011122	0.78733262	36.01482991	28.35565045	0.02776634	0.03526634	32
33	1.27963706	0.78147158	37.28494113	29.13712203	0.02682048	0.03432048	33
34	1.28923434	0.77565418	38.56457819	29.91277621	0.02593053	0.03343053	34
35	1.29890359	0.76988008	39.85381253	30.68265629	0.02509170	0.03259170	35
36	1.30864537	0.76414896	41.15271612	31.44680525	0.02429973	0.03179973	36
37	1.31846021	0.75846051	42.46136149	32.20526576	0.02355082	0.03105082	37
38	1.32834866	0.75281440	43.77982170	32.95808016	0.02284157	0.03034157	38
39	1.33831128	0.74721032	45.10817037	33.70529048	0.02216893	0.02966893	39
40	1.34834861	0.74164796	46.44648164	34.44693844	0.02153016	0.02903016	40
41	1.35846123	0.73612701	47.79483026	35.18306545	0.02092276	0.02842276	41
42	1.36864969	0.73064716	49.15329148	35.91371260	0.02034452	0.02784452	42
43	1.37891456	0.72520809	50.52194117	36.63892070	0.01979338	0.02729338	43
44	1.38925642	0.71980952	51.90085573	37.35873022	0.01926751	0.02676751	44
45	1.39967584	0.71445114	53.29011215	38.07318136	0.01876521	0.02626521	45
46	1.41017341	0.70913264	54.68978799	38.78231401	0.01828495	0.02578495	46
47	1.42074971	0.70385374	56.09996140	39.48616775	0.01782532	0.02532532	47
48	1.43140533	0.69861414	57.52071111	40.18478189	0.01738504	0.02488504	48
49	1.44214087	0.69341353	58.95211644	40.87819542	0.01696292	0.02446292	49
50	1.45295693	0.68825165	60.39425732	41.56644707	0.01655787	0.02405787	50
80	1.81804398	0.55004170	109.07253072	59.99444012	0.00916821	0.01666821	80
100	2.11108384	0.47369033	148.14451201	70.17462272	0.00675017	0.01425017	100
120	2.45135708	0.40793730	193.51427708	78.94169267	0.00516758	0.01266758	120
240	6.00915152	0.16641284	667.88686993	111.14495403	0.00149726	0.00899726	240
360	14.73057612	0.06788601	1830.74348307	124.28186568	0.00054623	0.00804623	360

Rate 1%	C Compound Amount	D Present Value	E Amount of Annuity	F Present Value of Annuity	G Sinking Fund	H Amortization	
n	$(1 + i)^n$	$(1 + i)^{-n}$	$S_{\overline{n}|i}$	$A_{\overline{n}|i}$	$1/S_{\overline{n}|i}$	$1/A_{\overline{n}|i}$	n
1	1.01000000	0.99009901	1.00000000	0.99009901	1.00000000	1.01000000	1
2	1.02010000	0.98029605	2.01000000	1.97039506	0.49751244	0.50751244	2
3	1.03030100	0.97059015	3.03010000	2.94098521	0.33002211	0.34002211	3
4	1.04060401	0.96098034	4.06040100	3.90196555	0.24628109	0.25628109	4
5	1.05101005	0.95146569	5.10100501	4.85343124	0.19603980	0.20603980	5
6	1.06152015	0.94204524	6.15201506	5.79547647	0.16254837	0.17254837	6
7	1.07213535	0.93271805	7.21353521	6.72819453	0.13862828	0.14862828	7
8	1.08285671	0.92348322	8.28567056	7.65167775	0.12069029	0.13069029	8
9	1.09368527	0.91433982	9.36852727	8.56601758	0.10674036	0.11674036	9
10	1.10462213	0.90528695	10.46221254	9.47130453	0.09558208	0.10558208	10
11	1.11566835	0.89632372	11.56683467	10.36762825	0.08645408	0.09645408	11
12	1.12682503	0.88744923	12.68250301	11.25507747	0.07884879	0.08884879	12
13	1.13809328	0.87866260	13.80932804	12.13374007	0.07241482	0.08241482	13
14	1.14947421	0.86996297	14.94742132	13.00370304	0.06690117	0.07690117	14
15	1.16096896	0.86134947	16.09689554	13.86505252	0.06212378	0.07212378	15
16	1.17257864	0.85282126	17.25786449	14.71787378	0.05794460	0.06794460	16
17	1.18430443	0.84437749	18.43044314	15.56225127	0.05425806	0.06425806	17
18	1.19614748	0.83601731	19.61474757	16.39826858	0.05098205	0.06098205	18
19	1.20810895	0.82773992	20.81089504	17.22600850	0.04805175	0.05805175	19
20	1.22019004	0.81954447	22.01900399	18.04555297	0.04541531	0.05541531	20
21	1.23239194	0.81143017	23.23919403	18.85698313	0.04303075	0.05303075	21
22	1.24471586	0.80339621	24.47158598	19.66037934	0.04086372	0.05086372	22
23	1.25716302	0.79544179	25.71630183	20.45582113	0.03888584	0.04888584	23
24	1.26973465	0.78756613	26.97346485	21.24338726	0.03707347	0.04707347	24
25	1.28243200	0.77976844	28.24319950	22.02315570	0.03540675	0.04540675	25
26	1.29525631	0.77204796	29.52563150	22.79520366	0.03386888	0.04386888	26
27	1.30820888	0.76440392	30.82088781	23.55960759	0.03244553	0.04244553	27
28	1.32129097	0.75683557	32.12909669	24.31644316	0.03112444	0.04112444	28
29	1.33450388	0.74934215	33.45038766	25.06578530	0.02989502	0.03989502	29
30	1.34784892	0.74192292	34.78489153	25.80770822	0.02874811	0.03874811	30
31	1.36132740	0.73457715	36.13274045	26.54228537	0.02767573	0.03767573	31
32	1.37494068	0.72730411	37.49406785	27.26958947	0.02667089	0.03667089	32
33	1.38869009	0.72010307	38.86900853	27.98969255	0.02572744	0.03572744	33
34	1.40257699	0.71297334	40.25769862	28.70266589	0.02483997	0.03483997	34
35	1.41660276	0.70591420	41.66027560	29.40858009	0.02400368	0.03400368	35
36	1.43076878	0.69892495	43.07687836	30.10750504	0.02321431	0.03321431	36
37	1.44507647	0.69200490	44.50764714	30.79950994	0.02246805	0.03246805	37
38	1.45952724	0.68515337	45.95272361	31.48466330	0.02176150	0.03176150	38
39	1.47412251	0.67836967	47.41225085	32.16303298	0.02109160	0.03109160	39
40	1.48886373	0.67165314	48.88637336	32.83468611	0.02045560	0.03045560	40
41	1.50375237	0.66500311	50.37523709	33.49968922	0.01985102	0.02985102	41
42	1.51878989	0.65841892	51.87898946	34.15810814	0.01927563	0.02927563	42
43	1.53397779	0.65189992	53.39777936	34.81000806	0.01872737	0.02872737	43
44	1.54931757	0.64544546	54.93175715	35.45545352	0.01820441	0.02820441	44
45	1.56481075	0.63905492	56.48107472	36.09450844	0.01770505	0.02770505	45
46	1.58045885	0.63272764	58.04588547	36.72723608	0.01722775	0.02722775	46
47	1.59626344	0.62646301	59.62634432	37.35369909	0.01677111	0.02677111	47
48	1.61222608	0.62026041	61.22260777	37.97395949	0.01633384	0.02633384	48
49	1.62834834	0.61411921	62.83483385	38.58807871	0.01591474	0.02591474	49
50	1.64463182	0.60803882	64.46318218	39.19611753	0.01551273	0.02551273	50
80	2.21671522	0.45111794	121.67152172	54.88820611	0.00821885	0.01821885	80
100	2.70481383	0.36971121	170.48138294	63.02887877	0.00586574	0.01586574	100
120	3.30038689	0.30299478	230.03886946	69.70052203	0.00434709	0.01434709	120
240	10.89255365	0.09180584	989.25536539	90.81941635	0.00101086	0.01101086	240
360	35.94964133	0.02781669	3494.96413277	97.21833108	0.00028613	0.01028613	360

Rate 1¼%	C Compound Amount	D Present Value	E Amount of Annuity	F Present Value of Annuity	G Sinking Fund	H Amortization	
n	$(1 + i)^n$	$(1 + i)^{-n}$	$S_{\overline{n}\|i}$	$A_{\overline{n}\|i}$	$1/S_{\overline{n}\|i}$	$1/A_{\overline{n}\|i}$	n
1	1.01250000	0.98765432	1.00000000	0.98765432	1.00000000	1.01250000	1
2	1.02515625	0.97546106	2.01250000	1.96311538	0.49689441	0.50939441	2
3	1.03797070	0.96341833	3.03765625	2.92653371	0.32920117	0.34170117	3
4	1.05094534	0.95152428	4.07562695	3.87805798	0.24536102	0.25786102	4
5	1.06408215	0.93977706	5.12657229	4.81783504	0.19506211	0.20756211	5
6	1.07738318	0.92817488	6.19065444	5.74600992	0.16153381	0.17403381	6
7	1.09085047	0.91671593	7.26803762	6.66272585	0.13758872	0.15008872	7
8	1.10448610	0.90539845	8.35888809	7.56812429	0.11963314	0.13213314	8
9	1.11829218	0.89422069	9.46337420	8.46234498	0.10567055	0.11817055	9
10	1.13227083	0.88318093	10.58166637	9.34552591	0.09450307	0.10700307	10
11	1.14642422	0.87227746	11.71393720	10.21780337	0.08536839	0.09786839	11
12	1.16075452	0.86150860	12.86036142	11.07931197	0.07775831	0.09025831	12
13	1.17526395	0.85087269	14.02111594	11.93018466	0.07132100	0.08382100	13
14	1.18995475	0.84036809	15.19637988	12.77055275	0.06580515	0.07830515	14
15	1.20482918	0.82999318	16.38633463	13.60054592	0.06102646	0.07352646	15
16	1.21988955	0.81974635	17.59116382	14.42029227	0.05684672	0.06934672	16
17	1.23513817	0.80962602	18.81105336	15.22991829	0.05316023	0.06566023	17
18	1.25057739	0.79963064	20.04619153	16.02954893	0.04988479	0.06238479	18
19	1.26620961	0.78975866	21.29676893	16.81930759	0.04695548	0.05945548	19
20	1.28203723	0.78000855	22.56297854	17.59931613	0.04432039	0.05682039	20
21	1.29806270	0.77037881	23.84501577	18.36969495	0.04193749	0.05443749	21
22	1.31428848	0.76086796	25.14307847	19.13056291	0.03977238	0.05227238	22
23	1.33071709	0.75147453	26.45736695	19.88203744	0.03779666	0.05029666	23
24	1.34735105	0.74219707	27.78808403	20.62423451	0.03598665	0.04848665	24
25	1.36419294	0.73303414	29.13543508	21.35726865	0.03432247	0.04682247	25
26	1.38124535	0.72398434	30.49962802	22.08125299	0.03278729	0.04528729	26
27	1.39851092	0.71504626	31.88087337	22.79629925	0.03136677	0.04386677	27
28	1.41599230	0.70621853	33.27938429	23.50251778	0.03004863	0.04254863	28
29	1.43369221	0.69749978	34.69537659	24.20001756	0.02882228	0.04132228	29
30	1.45161336	0.68888867	36.12906880	24.88890623	0.02767854	0.04017854	30
31	1.46975853	0.68038387	37.58068216	25.56929010	0.02660942	0.03910942	31
32	1.48813051	0.67198407	39.05044069	26.24127418	0.02560791	0.03810791	32
33	1.50673214	0.66368797	40.53857120	26.90496215	0.02466786	0.03716786	33
34	1.52556629	0.65549429	42.04530334	27.56045644	0.02378387	0.03628387	34
35	1.54463587	0.64740177	43.57086963	28.20785822	0.02295111	0.03545111	35
36	1.56394382	0.63940916	45.11550550	28.84726737	0.02216533	0.03466533	36
37	1.58349312	0.63151522	46.67944932	29.47878259	0.02142270	0.03392270	37
38	1.60328678	0.62371873	48.26294243	30.10250133	0.02071983	0.03321983	38
39	1.62332787	0.61601850	49.86622921	30.71851983	0.02005365	0.03255365	39
40	1.64361946	0.60841334	51.48955708	31.32693316	0.01942141	0.03192141	40
41	1.66416471	0.60090206	53.13317654	31.92783522	0.01882063	0.03132063	41
42	1.68496671	0.59348352	54.79734125	32.52131874	0.01824906	0.03074906	42
43	1.70602885	0.58615656	56.48230801	33.10747530	0.01770466	0.03020466	43
44	1.72735421	0.57892006	58.18833687	33.68639536	0.01718557	0.02968557	44
45	1.74894614	0.57177290	59.91569108	34.25816825	0.01669012	0.02919012	45
46	1.77080797	0.56471397	61.66463721	34.82288222	0.01621675	0.02871675	46
47	1.79294306	0.55774219	63.43544518	35.38062442	0.01576406	0.02826406	47
48	1.81535485	0.55085649	65.22838824	35.93148091	0.01533075	0.02783075	48
49	1.83804679	0.54405579	67.04374310	36.47553670	0.01491563	0.02741563	49
50	1.86102237	0.53733905	68.88178989	37.01287575	0.01451763	0.02701763	50
80	2.70148494	0.37016679	136.11879526	50.38665706	0.00734652	0.01984652	80
100	3.46340427	0.28873326	197.07234200	56.90133936	0.00507428	0.01757428	100
120	4.44021323	0.22521441	275.21705832	61.98284725	0.00363350	0.01613350	120
240	19.71549352	0.05072153	1497.23948148	75.94227758	0.00066790	0.01316790	240
360	87.54099514	0.01142322	6923.27961085	79.08614244	0.00014444	0.01264444	360

Rate 1½%	C Compound Amount	D Present Value	E Amount of Annuity	F Present Value of Annuity	G Sinking Fund	H Amortization	
n	$(1 + i)^n$	$(1 + i)^{-n}$	$S_{\overline{n}|i}$	$A_{\overline{n}|i}$	$1/S_{\overline{n}|i}$	$1/A_{\overline{n}|i}$	n
1	1.01500000	0.98522167	1.00000000	0.98522167	1.00000000	1.01500000	1
2	1.03022500	0.97066175	2.01500000	1.95588342	0.49627792	0.51127792	2
3	1.04567837	0.95631699	3.04522500	2.91220042	0.32838296	0.34338296	3
4	1.06136355	0.94218423	4.09090338	3.85438465	0.24444479	0.25944479	4
5	1.07728400	0.92826033	5.15226693	4.78264497	0.19408932	0.20908932	5
6	1.09344326	0.91454219	6.22955093	5.69718717	0.16052521	0.17552521	6
7	1.10984491	0.90102679	7.32299419	6.59821396	0.13655616	0.15155616	7
8	1.12649259	0.88771112	8.43283911	7.48592508	0.11858402	0.13358402	8
9	1.14338998	0.87459224	9.55933169	8.36051732	0.10460982	0.11960982	9
10	1.16054083	0.86166723	10.70272167	9.22218455	0.09343418	0.10843418	10
11	1.17794894	0.84893323	11.86326249	10.07111779	0.08429384	0.09929384	11
12	1.19561817	0.83638742	13.04121143	10.90750521	0.07667999	0.09167999	12
13	1.21355244	0.82402702	14.23682960	11.73153222	0.07024036	0.08524036	13
14	1.23175573	0.81184928	15.45038205	12.54338150	0.06472332	0.07972332	14
15	1.25023207	0.79985150	16.68213778	13.34323301	0.05994436	0.07494436	15
16	1.26898555	0.78803104	17.93236984	14.13126405	0.05576508	0.07076508	16
17	1.28802033	0.77638526	19.20135539	14.90764931	0.05207966	0.06707966	17
18	1.30734064	0.76491159	20.48937572	15.67256089	0.04880578	0.06380578	18
19	1.32695075	0.75360747	21.79671636	16.42616837	0.04587847	0.06087847	19
20	1.34685501	0.74247042	23.12366710	17.16863879	0.04324574	0.05824574	20
21	1.36705783	0.73149795	24.47052211	17.90013673	0.04086550	0.05586550	21
22	1.38756370	0.72068763	25.83757994	18.62082437	0.03870332	0.05370332	22
23	1.40837715	0.71003708	27.22514364	19.33086145	0.03673075	0.05173075	23
24	1.42950281	0.69954392	28.63352080	20.03040537	0.03492410	0.04992410	24
25	1.45094535	0.68920583	30.06302361	20.71961120	0.03326345	0.04826345	25
26	1.47270953	0.67902052	31.51396896	21.39863172	0.03173196	0.04673196	26
27	1.49480018	0.66898574	32.98667850	22.06761746	0.03031527	0.04531527	27
28	1.51722218	0.65909925	34.48147867	22.72671671	0.02900108	0.04400108	28
29	1.53998051	0.64935887	35.99870085	23.37607558	0.02777878	0.04277878	29
30	1.56308022	0.63976243	37.53868137	24.01583801	0.02663919	0.04163919	30
31	1.58652642	0.63030781	39.10176159	24.64614582	0.02557430	0.04057430	31
32	1.61032432	0.62099292	40.68828801	25.26713874	0.02457710	0.03957710	32
33	1.63447918	0.61181568	42.29861233	25.87895442	0.02364144	0.03864144	33
34	1.65899637	0.60277407	43.93309152	26.48172849	0.02276189	0.03776189	34
35	1.68388132	0.59386608	45.59208789	27.07559458	0.02193363	0.03693363	35
36	1.70913954	0.58508974	47.27596921	27.66068431	0.02115240	0.03615240	36
37	1.73477663	0.57644309	48.98510874	28.23712740	0.02041437	0.03541437	37
38	1.76079828	0.56792423	50.71988538	28.80505163	0.01971613	0.03471613	38
39	1.78721025	0.55953126	52.48068366	29.36458288	0.01905463	0.03405463	39
40	1.81401841	0.55126232	54.26789391	29.91584520	0.01842710	0.03342710	40
41	1.84122868	0.54311559	56.08191232	30.45896079	0.01783106	0.03283106	41
42	1.86884712	0.53508925	57.92314100	30.99405004	0.01726426	0.03226426	42
43	1.89687982	0.52718153	59.79198812	31.52123157	0.01672465	0.03172465	43
44	1.92533302	0.51939067	61.68886794	32.04062223	0.01621038	0.03121038	44
45	1.95421301	0.51171494	63.61420096	32.55233718	0.01571976	0.03071976	45
46	1.98352621	0.50415265	65.56841398	33.05648983	0.01525125	0.03025125	46
47	2.01327910	0.49670212	67.55194018	33.55319195	0.01480342	0.02980342	47
48	2.04347829	0.48936170	69.56521929	34.04255365	0.01437500	0.02937500	48
49	2.07413046	0.48212975	71.60869758	34.52468339	0.01396478	0.02896478	49
50	2.10524242	0.47500468	73.68282804	34.99968807	0.01357168	0.02857168	50
80	3.29066279	0.30389015	152.71085247	46.40732349	0.00654832	0.02154832	80
100	4.43204565	0.22562944	228.80304330	51.62470367	0.00437057	0.01937057	100
120	5.96932287	0.16752319	331.28819149	55.49845411	0.00301852	0.01801852	120
240	35.63281555	0.02806402	2308.85437027	64.79573209	0.00043312	0.01543312	240
360	212.70378089	0.00470137	14113.58539279	66.35324174	0.00007085	0.01507085	360

Rate 1¾%	C Compound Amount	D Present Value	E Amount of Annuity	F Present Value of Annuity	G Sinking Fund	H Amortization	
n	$(1 + i)^n$	$(1 + i)^{-n}$	$S_{\overline{n}|i}$	$A_{\overline{n}|i}$	$1/S_{\overline{n}|i}$	$1/A_{\overline{n}|i}$	n
1	1.01750000	0.98280098	1.00000000	0.98280098	1.00000000	1.01750000	1
2	1.03530625	0.96589777	2.01750000	1.94869875	0.49566295	0.51316295	2
3	1.05342411	0.94928528	3.05280625	2.89798403	0.32756746	0.34506746	3
4	1.07185903	0.93295851	4.10623036	3.83094254	0.24353237	0.26103237	4
5	1.09061656	0.91691254	5.17808939	4.74785508	0.19312142	0.21062142	5
6	1.10970235	0.90114254	6.26870596	5.64899762	0.15952256	0.17702256	6
7	1.12912215	0.88564378	7.37840831	6.53464139	0.13553059	0.15303059	7
8	1.14888178	0.87041157	8.50753045	7.40505297	0.11754292	0.13504292	8
9	1.16898721	0.85544135	9.65641224	8.26049432	0.10355813	0.12105813	9
10	1.18944449	0.84072860	10.82539945	9.10122291	0.09237534	0.10987534	10
11	1.21025977	0.82626889	12.01484394	9.92749181	0.08323038	0.10073038	11
12	1.23143931	0.81205788	13.22510371	10.73954969	0.07561377	0.09311377	12
13	1.25298950	0.79809128	14.45654303	11.53764097	0.06917283	0.08667283	13
14	1.27491682	0.78436490	15.70953253	12.32200587	0.06365562	0.08115562	14
15	1.29722786	0.77087459	16.98444935	13.09288046	0.05887739	0.07637739	15
16	1.31992935	0.75761631	18.28167721	13.85049677	0.05469958	0.07219958	16
17	1.34302811	0.74458605	19.60160656	14.59508282	0.05101623	0.06851623	17
18	1.36653111	0.73177990	20.94463468	15.32686272	0.04774492	0.06524492	18
19	1.39044540	0.71919401	22.31116578	16.04605673	0.04482061	0.06232061	19
20	1.41477820	0.70682458	23.70161119	16.75288130	0.04219122	0.05969122	20
21	1.43953681	0.69466789	25.11638938	17.44754919	0.03981464	0.05731464	21
22	1.46472871	0.68272028	26.55592620	18.13026948	0.03765638	0.05515638	22
23	1.49036146	0.67097817	28.02065490	18.80124764	0.03568796	0.05318796	23
24	1.51644279	0.65943800	29.51101637	19.46068565	0.03388565	0.05138565	24
25	1.54298054	0.64809632	31.02745915	20.10878196	0.03222952	0.04972952	25
26	1.56998269	0.63694970	32.57043969	20.74573166	0.03070269	0.04820269	26
27	1.59745739	0.62599479	34.14042238	21.37172644	0.02929079	0.04679079	27
28	1.62541290	0.61522829	35.73787977	21.98695474	0.02798151	0.04548151	28
29	1.65385762	0.60464697	37.36329267	22.59160171	0.02676424	0.04426424	29
30	1.68280013	0.59424764	39.01715029	23.18584934	0.02562975	0.04312975	30
31	1.71224913	0.58402716	40.69995042	23.76987650	0.02457005	0.04207005	31
32	1.74221349	0.57398247	42.41219955	24.34385897	0.02357812	0.04107812	32
33	1.77270223	0.56411053	44.15441305	24.90796951	0.02264779	0.04014779	33
34	1.80372452	0.55440839	45.92711527	25.46237789	0.02177363	0.03927363	34
35	1.83528970	0.54487311	47.73083979	26.00725100	0.02095082	0.03845082	35
36	1.86740727	0.53550183	49.56612949	26.54275283	0.02017507	0.03767507	36
37	1.90008689	0.52629172	51.43353675	27.06904455	0.01944257	0.03694257	37
38	1.93333841	0.51724002	53.33362365	27.58628457	0.01874990	0.03624990	38
39	1.96717184	0.50834400	55.26696206	28.09462857	0.01809399	0.03559399	39
40	2.00159734	0.49960098	57.23413390	28.59422955	0.01747209	0.03497209	40
41	2.03662530	0.49100834	59.23573124	29.08523789	0.01688170	0.03438170	41
42	2.07226624	0.48256348	61.27235654	29.56780136	0.01632057	0.03382057	42
43	2.10853090	0.47426386	63.34462278	30.04206522	0.01578666	0.03328666	43
44	2.14543019	0.46610699	65.45315367	30.50817221	0.01527810	0.03277810	44
45	2.18297522	0.45809040	67.59858386	30.96626261	0.01479321	0.03229321	45
46	2.22117728	0.45021170	69.78155908	31.41647431	0.01433043	0.03183043	46
47	2.26004789	0.44246850	72.00273637	31.85894281	0.01388836	0.03138836	47
48	2.29959872	0.43485848	74.26278425	32.29380129	0.01346569	0.03096569	48
49	2.33984170	0.42737934	76.56238298	32.72118063	0.01306124	0.03056124	49
50	2.38078893	0.42002883	78.90222468	33.14120946	0.01267391	0.03017391	50
80	4.00639192	0.24960114	171.79382424	42.87993474	0.00582093	0.02332093	80
100	5.66815594	0.17642422	266.75176789	47.06147304	0.00374880	0.02124880	100
120	8.01918343	0.12470098	401.09619608	50.01708709	0.00249317	0.01999317	120
240	64.30730291	0.01555033	3617.56016603	56.25426666	0.00027643	0.01777643	240
360	515.69205797	0.00193914	29410.97474135	57.03204904	0.00003400	0.01753400	360

Rate 2%	C Compound Amount	D Present Value	E Amount of Annuity	F Present Value of Annuity	G Sinking Fund	H Amortization	
n	$(1 + i)^n$	$(1 + i)^{-n}$	$S_{\overline{n}|i}$	$A_{\overline{n}|i}$	$1/S_{\overline{n}|i}$	$1/A_{\overline{n}|i}$	n
1	1.02000000	0.98039216	1.00000000	0.98039216	1.00000000	1.02000000	1
2	1.04040000	0.96116878	2.02000000	1.94156094	0.49504950	0.51504950	2
3	1.06120800	0.94232233	3.06040000	2.88388327	0.32675467	0.34675467	3
4	1.08243216	0.92384543	4.12160800	3.80772870	0.24262375	0.26262375	4
5	1.10408080	0.90573081	5.20404016	4.71345951	0.19215839	0.21215839	5
6	1.12616242	0.88797138	6.30812096	5.60143089	0.15852581	0.17852581	6
7	1.14868567	0.87056018	7.43428338	6.47199107	0.13451196	0.15451196	7
8	1.17165938	0.85349037	8.58296905	7.32548144	0.11650980	0.13650980	8
9	1.19509257	0.83675527	9.75462843	8.16223671	0.10251544	0.12251544	9
10	1.21899442	0.82034830	10.94972100	8.98258501	0.09132653	0.11132653	10
11	1.24337431	0.80426304	12.16871542	9.78684805	0.08217794	0.10217794	11
12	1.26824179	0.78849318	13.41208973	10.57534122	0.07455960	0.09455960	12
13	1.29360663	0.77303253	14.68033152	11.34837375	0.06811835	0.08811835	13
14	1.31947876	0.75787502	15.97393815	12.10624877	0.06260197	0.08260197	14
15	1.34586834	0.74301473	17.29341692	12.84926350	0.05782547	0.07782547	15
16	1.37278571	0.72844581	18.63928525	13.57770931	0.05365013	0.07365013	16
17	1.40024142	0.71416256	20.01207096	14.29187188	0.04996984	0.06996984	17
18	1.42824625	0.70015937	21.41231238	14.99203125	0.04670210	0.06670210	18
19	1.45681117	0.68643076	22.84055863	15.67846201	0.04378177	0.06378177	19
20	1.48594740	0.67297133	24.29736980	16.35143334	0.04115672	0.06115672	20
21	1.51566634	0.65977582	25.78331719	17.01120916	0.03878477	0.05878477	21
22	1.54597967	0.64683904	27.29898354	17.65804820	0.03663140	0.05663140	22
23	1.57689926	0.63415592	28.84496321	18.29220412	0.03466810	0.05466810	23
24	1.60843725	0.62172149	30.42186247	18.91392560	0.03287110	0.05287110	24
25	1.64060599	0.60953087	32.03029972	19.52345647	0.03122044	0.05122044	25
26	1.67341811	0.59757928	33.67090572	20.12103576	0.02969923	0.04969923	26
27	1.70688648	0.58586204	35.34432383	20.70689780	0.02829309	0.04829309	27
28	1.74102421	0.57437455	37.05121031	21.28127236	0.02698967	0.04698967	28
29	1.77584469	0.56311231	38.79223451	21.84438466	0.02577836	0.04577836	29
30	1.81136158	0.55207089	40.56807921	22.39645555	0.02464992	0.04464992	30
31	1.84758882	0.54124597	42.37944079	22.93770152	0.02359635	0.04359635	31
32	1.88454059	0.53063330	44.22702961	23.46833482	0.02261061	0.04261061	32
33	1.92223140	0.52022873	46.11157020	23.98856355	0.02168653	0.04168653	33
34	1.96067603	0.51002817	48.03380160	24.49859172	0.02081867	0.04081867	34
35	1.99988955	0.50002761	49.99447763	24.99861933	0.02000221	0.04000221	35
36	2.03988734	0.49022315	51.99436719	25.48884248	0.01923285	0.03923285	36
37	2.08068509	0.48061093	54.03425453	25.96945341	0.01850678	0.03850678	37
38	2.12229879	0.47118719	56.11493962	26.44064060	0.01782057	0.03782057	38
39	2.16474477	0.46194822	58.23723841	26.90258883	0.01717114	0.03717114	39
40	2.20803966	0.45289042	60.40198318	27.35547924	0.01655575	0.03655575	40
41	2.25220046	0.44401021	62.61002284	27.79948945	0.01597188	0.03597188	41
42	2.29724447	0.43530413	64.86222330	28.23479358	0.01541729	0.03541729	42
43	2.34318936	0.42676875	67.15946777	28.66156233	0.01488993	0.03488993	43
44	2.39005314	0.41840074	69.50265712	29.07996307	0.01438794	0.03438794	44
45	2.43785421	0.41019680	71.89271027	29.49015987	0.01390962	0.03390962	45
46	2.48661129	0.40215373	74.33056447	29.89231360	0.01345342	0.03345342	46
47	2.53634352	0.39426836	76.81717576	30.28658196	0.01301792	0.03301792	47
48	2.58707039	0.38653761	79.35351927	30.67311957	0.01260184	0.03260184	48
49	2.63881179	0.37895844	81.94058966	31.05207801	0.01220396	0.03220396	49
50	2.69158803	0.37152788	84.57940145	31.42360589	0.01182321	0.03182321	50
80	4.87543916	0.20510973	193.77195780	39.74451359	0.00516071	0.02516071	80
100	7.24464612	0.13803297	312.23230591	43.09835164	0.00320274	0.02320274	100
120	10.76516303	0.09289223	488.25815171	45.35538850	0.00204810	0.02204810	120
240	115.88873515	0.00862897	5744.43675765	49.56855168	0.00017408	0.02017408	240
360	1247.56112775	0.00080156	62328.05638744	49.95992180	0.00001604	0.02001604	360

Rate 2¼%	C Compound Amount	D Present Value	E Amount of Annuity	F Present Value of Annuity	G Sinking Fund	H Amortization	
n	$(1 + i)^n$	$(1 + i)^{-n}$	$S_{\overline{n}|i}$	$A_{\overline{n}|i}$	$1/S_{\overline{n}|i}$	$1/A_{\overline{n}|i}$	n
1	1.02250000	0.97799511	1.00000000	0.97799511	1.00000000	1.02250000	1
2	1.04550625	0.95647444	2.02250000	1.93446955	0.49443758	0.51693758	2
3	1.06903014	0.93542732	3.06800625	2.86989687	0.32594458	0.34844458	3
4	1.09308332	0.91484335	4.13703639	3.78474021	0.24171893	0.26421893	4
5	1.11767769	0.89471232	5.23011971	4.67945253	0.19120021	0.21370021	5
6	1.14282544	0.87502427	6.34779740	5.55447680	0.15753496	0.18003496	6
7	1.16853901	0.85576946	7.49062284	6.41024626	0.13350025	0.15600025	7
8	1.19483114	0.83693835	8.65916186	7.24718461	0.11548462	0.13798462	8
9	1.22171484	0.81852161	9.85399300	8.06570622	0.10148170	0.12398170	9
10	1.24920343	0.80051013	11.07570784	8.86621635	0.09028768	0.11278768	10
11	1.27731050	0.78289499	12.32491127	9.64911134	0.08113649	0.10363649	11
12	1.30604999	0.76566748	13.60222177	10.41477882	0.07351740	0.09601740	12
13	1.33543611	0.74881905	14.90827176	11.16359787	0.06707686	0.08957686	13
14	1.36548343	0.73234137	16.24370788	11.89593924	0.06156230	0.08406230	14
15	1.39620680	0.71622628	17.60919130	12.61216551	0.05678852	0.07928852	15
16	1.42762146	0.70046580	19.00539811	13.31263131	0.05261663	0.07511663	16
17	1.45974294	0.68505212	20.43301957	13.99768343	0.04894039	0.07144039	17
18	1.49258716	0.66997763	21.89276251	14.66766106	0.04567720	0.06817720	18
19	1.52617037	0.65523484	23.38534966	15.32289590	0.04276182	0.06526182	19
20	1.56050920	0.64081647	24.91152003	15.96371237	0.04014207	0.06264207	20
21	1.59562066	0.62671538	26.47202923	16.59042775	0.03777572	0.06027572	21
22	1.63152212	0.61292457	28.06764989	17.20335232	0.03562821	0.05812821	22
23	1.66823137	0.59943724	29.69917201	17.80278955	0.03367097	0.05617097	23
24	1.70576658	0.58624668	31.36740338	18.38903624	0.03188023	0.05438023	24
25	1.74414632	0.57334639	33.07316996	18.96238263	0.03023599	0.05273599	25
26	1.78338962	0.56072997	34.81731628	19.52311260	0.02872134	0.05122134	26
27	1.82351588	0.54839117	36.60070590	20.07150376	0.02732188	0.04982188	27
28	1.86454499	0.53632388	38.42422178	20.60782764	0.02602525	0.04852525	28
29	1.90649725	0.52452213	40.28876677	21.13234977	0.02482081	0.04732081	29
30	1.94939344	0.51298008	42.19526402	21.64532985	0.02369934	0.04619934	30
31	1.99325479	0.50169201	44.14465746	22.14702186	0.02265280	0.04515280	31
32	2.03810303	0.49065233	46.13791226	22.63767419	0.02167415	0.04417415	32
33	2.08396034	0.47985558	48.17601528	23.11752977	0.02075722	0.04325722	33
34	2.13084945	0.46929641	50.25997563	23.58682618	0.01989655	0.04239655	34
35	2.17879356	0.45896960	52.39082508	24.04579577	0.01908731	0.04158731	35
36	2.22781642	0.44887002	54.56961864	24.49466579	0.01832522	0.04082522	36
37	2.27794229	0.43899268	56.79743506	24.93365848	0.01760643	0.04010643	37
38	2.32919599	0.42933270	59.07537735	25.36299118	0.01692753	0.03942753	38
39	2.38160290	0.41988528	61.40457334	25.78287646	0.01628543	0.03878543	39
40	2.43518897	0.41064575	63.78617624	26.19352221	0.01567738	0.03817738	40
41	2.48998072	0.40160954	66.22136521	26.59513174	0.01510087	0.03760087	41
42	2.54600528	0.39277216	68.71134592	26.98790390	0.01455364	0.03705364	42
43	2.60329040	0.38412925	71.25735121	27.37203316	0.01403364	0.03653364	43
44	2.66186444	0.37567653	73.86064161	27.74770969	0.01353901	0.03603901	44
45	2.72175639	0.36740981	76.52250605	28.11511950	0.01306805	0.03556805	45
46	2.78299590	0.35932500	79.24426243	28.47444450	0.01261921	0.03511921	46
47	2.84561331	0.35141809	82.02725834	28.82586259	0.01219107	0.03469107	47
48	2.90963961	0.34368518	84.87287165	29.16954777	0.01178233	0.03428233	48
49	2.97510650	0.33612242	87.78251126	29.50567019	0.01139179	0.03389179	49
50	3.04204640	0.32872608	90.75761776	29.83439627	0.01101836	0.03351836	50
80	5.93014530	0.16862993	219.11756877	36.94978079	0.00456376	0.02706376	80
100	9.25404630	0.10806084	366.84650213	39.64174052	0.00272594	0.02522594	100
120	14.44102439	0.06924717	597.37886184	41.36679266	0.00167398	0.02417398	120
240	208.54318547	0.00479517	9224.14157653	44.23132578	0.00010841	0.02260841	240

Rate 2½%	C Compound Amount	D Present Value	E Amount of Annuity	F Present Value of Annuity	G Sinking Fund	H Amortization	
n	$(1 + i)^n$	$(1 + i)^{-n}$	$S_{\overline{n}|i}$	$A_{\overline{n}|i}$	$1/S_{\overline{n}|i}$	$1/A_{\overline{n}|i}$	n
1	1.02500000	0.97560976	1.00000000	0.97560976	1.00000000	1.02500000	1
2	1.05062500	0.95181440	2.02500000	1.92742415	0.49382716	0.51882716	2
3	1.07689062	0.92859941	3.07562500	2.85602356	0.32513717	0.35013717	3
4	1.10381289	0.90595064	4.15251563	3.76197421	0.24081788	0.26581788	4
5	1.13140821	0.88385429	5.25632852	4.64582850	0.19024686	0.21524686	5
6	1.15969342	0.86229687	6.38773673	5.50812536	0.15654997	0.18154997	6
7	1.18868575	0.84126524	7.54743015	6.34939060	0.13249543	0.15749543	7
8	1.21840290	0.82074657	8.73611590	7.17013717	0.11446735	0.13946735	8
9	1.24886297	0.80072836	9.95451880	7.97036553	0.10045689	0.12545689	9
10	1.28008454	0.78119840	11.20338177	8.75206393	0.08925876	0.11425876	10
11	1.31208666	0.76214478	12.48346631	9.51420871	0.08010596	0.10510596	11
12	1.34488882	0.74355589	13.79555297	10.25776460	0.07248713	0.09748713	12
13	1.37851104	0.72542038	15.14044179	10.98318497	0.06604827	0.09104827	13
14	1.41297382	0.70772720	16.51895284	11.69091217	0.06053652	0.08553652	14
15	1.44829817	0.69046556	17.93192666	12.38137773	0.05576646	0.08076646	15
16	1.48450562	0.67362493	19.38022483	13.05500266	0.05159899	0.07659899	16
17	1.52161826	0.65719506	20.86473045	13.71219772	0.04792777	0.07292777	17
18	1.55965872	0.64116591	22.38634871	14.35336363	0.04467008	0.06967008	18
19	1.59865019	0.62552772	23.94600743	14.97889134	0.04176062	0.06676062	19
20	1.63861644	0.61027094	25.54465761	15.58916229	0.03914713	0.06414713	20
21	1.67958185	0.59538629	27.18327405	16.18454857	0.03678733	0.06178733	21
22	1.72157140	0.58086467	28.86285590	16.76541324	0.03464661	0.05964661	22
23	1.76461068	0.56669724	30.58442730	17.33211048	0.03269638	0.05769638	23
24	1.80872595	0.55287535	32.34903798	17.88498583	0.03091282	0.05591282	24
25	1.85394410	0.53939059	34.15776393	18.42437642	0.02927592	0.05427592	25
26	1.90029270	0.52623472	36.01170803	18.95061114	0.02776875	0.05276875	26
27	1.94780002	0.51339973	37.91200073	19.46401087	0.02637687	0.05137687	27
28	1.99649502	0.50087778	39.85980075	19.96488866	0.02508793	0.05008793	28
29	2.04640739	0.48866125	41.85629577	20.45354991	0.02389127	0.04889127	29
30	2.09756758	0.47674269	43.90270316	20.93029259	0.02277764	0.04777764	30
31	2.15000677	0.46511481	46.00027074	21.39540741	0.02173900	0.04673900	31
32	2.20375694	0.45377055	48.15027751	21.84917796	0.02076831	0.04576831	32
33	2.25885086	0.44270298	50.35403445	22.29188094	0.01985938	0.04485938	33
34	2.31532213	0.43190534	52.61288531	22.72378628	0.01900675	0.04400675	34
35	2.37320519	0.42137107	54.92820744	23.14515734	0.01820558	0.04320558	35
36	2.43253532	0.41109372	57.30141263	23.55625107	0.01745158	0.04245158	36
37	2.49334870	0.40106705	59.73394794	23.95731812	0.01674090	0.04174090	37
38	2.55568242	0.39128492	62.22729664	24.34860304	0.01607012	0.04107012	38
39	2.61957448	0.38174139	64.78297906	24.73034443	0.01543615	0.04043615	39
40	2.68506384	0.37243062	67.40255354	25.10277505	0.01483623	0.03983623	40
41	2.75219043	0.36334695	70.08761737	25.46612200	0.01426786	0.03926786	41
42	2.82099520	0.35448483	72.83980781	25.82060683	0.01372876	0.03872876	42
43	2.89152008	0.34583886	75.66080300	26.16644569	0.01321688	0.03821688	43
44	2.96380808	0.33740376	78.55232308	26.50384945	0.01273037	0.03773037	44
45	3.03790328	0.32917440	81.51613116	26.83302386	0.01226751	0.03726751	45
46	3.11385086	0.32114576	84.55403443	27.15416962	0.01182676	0.03682676	46
47	3.19169713	0.31331294	87.66788530	27.46748255	0.01140669	0.03640669	47
48	3.27148956	0.30567116	90.85958243	27.77315371	0.01100599	0.03600599	48
49	3.35327680	0.29821576	94.13107199	28.07136947	0.01062348	0.03562348	49
50	3.43710872	0.29094221	97.48434879	28.36231168	0.01025806	0.03525806	50
80	7.20956782	0.13870457	248.38271265	34.45181722	0.00402605	0.02902605	80
100	11.81371635	0.08464737	432.54865404	36.61410526	0.00231188	0.02731188	100
120	19.35814983	0.05165783	734.32599335	37.93368683	0.00136179	0.02636179	120
240	374.73796499	0.00266853	14949.51859948	39.89325875	0.00006689	0.02506689	240

Rate 2¾%	C Compound Amount	D Present Value	E Amount of Annuity	F Present Value of Annuity	G Sinking Fund	H Amortization	
n	$(1 + i)^n$	$(1 + i)^{-n}$	$S_{\overline{n}|i}$	$A_{\overline{n}|i}$	$1/S_{\overline{n}|i}$	$1/A_{\overline{n}|i}$	n
1	1.02750000	0.97323601	1.00000000	0.97323601	1.00000000	1.02750000	1
2	1.05575625	0.94718833	2.02750000	1.92042434	0.49321825	0.52071825	2
3	1.08478955	0.92183779	3.08325625	2.84226213	0.32433243	0.35183243	3
4	1.11462126	0.89716573	4.16804580	3.73942787	0.23992059	0.26742059	4
5	1.14527334	0.87315400	5.28266706	4.61258186	0.18929832	0.21679832	5
6	1.17676836	0.84978491	6.42794040	5.46236678	0.15557083	0.18307083	6
7	1.20912949	0.82704128	7.60470876	6.28940806	0.13149747	0.15899747	7
8	1.24238055	0.80490635	8.81383825	7.09431441	0.11345795	0.14095795	8
9	1.27654602	0.78336385	10.05621880	7.87767826	0.09944095	0.12694095	9
10	1.31165103	0.76239791	11.33276482	8.64007616	0.08823972	0.11573972	10
11	1.34772144	0.74199310	12.64441585	9.38206926	0.07908629	0.10658629	11
12	1.38478378	0.72213440	13.99213729	10.10420366	0.07146871	0.09896871	12
13	1.42286533	0.70280720	15.37692107	10.80701086	0.06503252	0.09253252	13
14	1.46199413	0.68399728	16.79978639	11.49100814	0.05952457	0.08702457	14
15	1.50219896	0.66569078	18.26178052	12.15669892	0.05475917	0.08225917	15
16	1.54350944	0.64787424	19.76397948	12.80457315	0.05059710	0.07809710	16
17	1.58595595	0.63053454	21.30748892	13.43510769	0.04693186	0.07443186	17
18	1.62956973	0.61365892	22.89344487	14.04876661	0.04368063	0.07118063	18
19	1.67438290	0.59723496	24.52301460	14.64600157	0.04077802	0.06827802	19
20	1.72042843	0.58125057	26.19739750	15.22725213	0.03817173	0.06567173	20
21	1.76774021	0.56569398	27.91782593	15.79294612	0.03581941	0.06331941	21
22	1.81635307	0.55055375	29.68556615	16.34349987	0.03368640	0.06118640	22
23	1.86630278	0.53581874	31.50191921	16.87931861	0.03174410	0.05924410	23
24	1.91762610	0.52147809	33.36822199	17.40079670	0.02996863	0.05746863	24
25	1.97036082	0.50752126	35.28584810	17.90831795	0.02833997	0.05583997	25
26	2.02454575	0.49393796	37.25620892	18.40225592	0.02684116	0.05434116	26
27	2.08022075	0.48071821	39.28075467	18.88297413	0.02545776	0.05295776	27
28	2.13742682	0.46785227	41.36097542	19.35082640	0.02417738	0.05167738	28
29	2.19620606	0.45533068	43.49840224	19.80615708	0.02298935	0.05048935	29
30	2.25660173	0.44314421	45.69460831	20.24930130	0.02188442	0.04938442	30
31	2.31865828	0.43128391	47.95121003	20.68058520	0.02085453	0.04835453	31
32	2.38242138	0.41974103	50.26986831	21.10032623	0.01989263	0.04739263	32
33	2.44793797	0.40850708	52.65228969	21.50883332	0.01899253	0.04649253	33
34	2.51525626	0.39757380	55.10022765	21.90640712	0.01814875	0.04564875	34
35	2.58442581	0.38693314	57.61548391	22.29334026	0.01735645	0.04485645	35
36	2.65549752	0.37657727	60.19990972	22.66991753	0.01661132	0.04411132	36
37	2.72852370	0.36649856	62.85540724	23.03641609	0.01590953	0.04340953	37
38	2.80355810	0.35668959	65.58393094	23.39310568	0.01524764	0.04274764	38
39	2.88065595	0.34714316	68.38748904	23.74024884	0.01462256	0.04212256	39
40	2.95987399	0.33785222	71.26814499	24.07810106	0.01403151	0.04153151	40
41	3.04127052	0.32880995	74.22801898	24.40691101	0.01347200	0.04097200	41
42	3.12490546	0.32000968	77.26928950	24.72692069	0.01294175	0.04044175	42
43	3.21084036	0.31144495	80.39419496	25.03836563	0.01243871	0.03993871	43
44	3.29913847	0.30310944	83.60503532	25.34147507	0.01196100	0.03946100	44
45	3.38986478	0.29499702	86.90417379	25.63647209	0.01150693	0.03900693	45
46	3.48308606	0.28710172	90.29403857	25.92357381	0.01107493	0.03857493	46
47	3.57887093	0.27941773	93.77712463	26.20299154	0.01066358	0.03816358	47
48	3.67728988	0.27193940	97.35599556	26.47493094	0.01027158	0.03777158	48
49	3.77841535	0.26466122	101.03328544	26.73959215	0.00989773	0.03739773	49
50	3.88232177	0.25757783	104.81170079	26.99716998	0.00954092	0.03704092	50
80	8.76085402	0.11414412	282.21287345	32.21294098	0.00354342	0.03104342	80
100	15.07242234	0.06634634	511.72444867	33.95104232	0.00195418	0.02945418	100
120	25.93102392	0.03856385	906.58268797	34.96131471	0.00110304	0.02860304	120
240	672.41800150	0.00148717	24415.20005439	36.30955745	0.00004096	0.02754096	240

Rate 3%	C Compound Amount	D Present Value	E Amount of Annuity	F Present Value of Annuity	G Sinking Fund	H Amortization	
n	$(1 + i)^n$	$(1 + i)^{-n}$	$S_{\overline{n}|i}$	$A_{\overline{n}|i}$	$1/S_{\overline{n}|i}$	$1/A_{\overline{n}|i}$	n
1	1.03000000	0.97087379	1.00000000	0.97087379	1.00000000	1.03000000	1
2	1.06090000	0.94259591	2.03000000	1.91346970	0.49261084	0.52261084	2
3	1.09272700	0.91514166	3.09090000	2.82861135	0.32353036	0.35353036	3
4	1.12550881	0.88848705	4.18362700	3.71709840	0.23902705	0.26902705	4
5	1.15927407	0.86260878	5.30913581	4.57970719	0.18835457	0.21835457	5
6	1.19405230	0.83748426	6.46840988	5.41719144	0.15459750	0.18459750	6
7	1.22987387	0.81309151	7.66246218	6.23028296	0.13050635	0.16050635	7
8	1.26677008	0.78940923	8.89233605	7.01969219	0.11245639	0.14245639	8
9	1.30477318	0.76641673	10.15910613	7.78610892	0.09843386	0.12843386	9
10	1.34391638	0.74409391	11.46387931	8.53020284	0.08723051	0.11723051	10
11	1.38423387	0.72242128	12.80779569	9.25262411	0.07807745	0.10807745	11
12	1.42576089	0.70137988	14.19202956	9.95400399	0.07046209	0.10046209	12
13	1.46853371	0.68095134	15.61779045	10.63495533	0.06402954	0.09402954	13
14	1.51258972	0.66111781	17.08632416	11.29607314	0.05852634	0.08852634	14
15	1.55796742	0.64186195	18.59891389	11.93793509	0.05376658	0.08376658	15
16	1.60470644	0.62316694	20.15688130	12.56110203	0.04961085	0.07961085	16
17	1.65284763	0.60501645	21.76158774	13.16611847	0.04595253	0.07595253	17
18	1.70243306	0.58739461	23.41443537	13.75351308	0.04270870	0.07270870	18
19	1.75350605	0.57028603	25.11686844	14.32379911	0.03981388	0.06981388	19
20	1.80611123	0.55367575	26.87037449	14.87747486	0.03721571	0.06721571	20
21	1.86029457	0.53754928	28.67648572	15.41502414	0.03487178	0.06487178	21
22	1.91610341	0.52189250	30.53678030	15.93691664	0.03274739	0.06274739	22
23	1.97358651	0.50669175	32.45288370	16.44360839	0.03081390	0.06081390	23
24	2.03279411	0.49193374	34.42647022	16.93554212	0.02904742	0.05904742	24
25	2.09377793	0.47760557	36.45926432	17.41314769	0.02742787	0.05742787	25
26	2.15659127	0.46369473	38.55304225	17.87684242	0.02593829	0.05593829	26
27	2.22128901	0.45018906	40.70963352	18.32703147	0.02456421	0.05456421	27
28	2.28792768	0.43707675	42.93092252	18.76410823	0.02329323	0.05329323	28
29	2.35656551	0.42434636	45.21885020	19.18845459	0.02211467	0.05211467	29
30	2.42726247	0.41198676	47.57541571	19.60044135	0.02101926	0.05101926	30
31	2.50008035	0.39998715	50.00267818	20.00042849	0.01999893	0.04999893	31
32	2.57508276	0.38833703	52.50275852	20.38876553	0.01904662	0.04904662	32
33	2.65233524	0.37702625	55.07784128	20.76579178	0.01815612	0.04815612	33
34	2.73190530	0.36604490	57.73017652	21.13183668	0.01732196	0.04732196	34
35	2.81386245	0.35538340	60.46208181	21.48722007	0.01653929	0.04653929	35
36	2.89827833	0.34503243	63.27594427	21.83225250	0.01580379	0.04580379	36
37	2.98522668	0.33498294	66.17422259	22.16723544	0.01511162	0.04511162	37
38	3.07478348	0.32522615	69.15944927	22.49246159	0.01445934	0.04445934	38
39	3.16702698	0.31575355	72.23423275	22.80821513	0.01384385	0.04384385	39
40	3.26203779	0.30655684	75.40125973	23.11477197	0.01326238	0.04326238	40
41	3.35989893	0.29762800	78.66329753	23.41239997	0.01271241	0.04271241	41
42	3.46069589	0.28895922	82.02319645	23.70135920	0.01219167	0.04219167	42
43	3.56451677	0.28054294	85.48389234	23.98190213	0.01169811	0.04169811	43
44	3.67145227	0.27237178	89.04840911	24.25427392	0.01122985	0.04122985	44
45	3.78159584	0.26443862	92.71986139	24.51871254	0.01078518	0.04078518	45
46	3.89504372	0.25673653	96.50145723	24.77544907	0.01036254	0.04036254	46
47	4.01189503	0.24925876	100.39650095	25.02470783	0.00996051	0.03996051	47
48	4.13225188	0.24199880	104.40839598	25.26670664	0.00957777	0.03957777	48
49	4.25621944	0.23495029	108.54064785	25.50165693	0.00921314	0.03921314	49
50	4.38390602	0.22810708	112.79686729	25.72976401	0.00886549	0.03886549	50
80	10.64089056	0.09397710	321.36301855	30.20076345	0.00311175	0.03311175	80
100	19.21863198	0.05203284	607.28773270	31.59890534	0.00164667	0.03164667	100
120	34.71098714	0.02880932	1123.69957119	32.37302261	0.00088992	0.03088992	120
240	1204.85262793	0.00082998	40128.42093093	33.30566743	0.00002492	0.03002492	240

Rate 3¼%	C Compound Amount	D Present Value	E Amount of Annuity	F Present Value of Annuity	G Sinking Fund	H Amortization	
n	$(1 + i)^n$	$(1 + i)^{-n}$	$S_{\overline{n}|i}$	$A_{\overline{n}|i}$	$1/S_{\overline{n}|i}$	$1/A_{\overline{n}|i}$	n
1	1.03250000	0.96852300	1.00000000	0.96852300	1.00000000	1.03250000	1
2	1.06605625	0.93803681	2.03250000	1.90655981	0.49200492	0.52450492	2
3	1.10070308	0.90851022	3.09855625	2.81507003	0.32273095	0.35523095	3
4	1.13647593	0.87991305	4.19925933	3.69498308	0.23813723	0.27063723	4
5	1.17341140	0.85221603	5.33573526	4.54719911	0.18741560	0.21991560	5
6	1.21154727	0.82539083	6.50914665	5.37258994	0.15362997	0.18612997	6
7	1.25092255	0.79941000	7.72069392	6.17199994	0.12952204	0.16202204	7
8	1.29157754	0.77424698	8.97161647	6.94624692	0.11146263	0.14396263	8
9	1.33355381	0.74987601	10.26319401	7.69612292	0.09743555	0.12993555	9
10	1.37689430	0.72627216	11.59674781	8.42239508	0.08623107	0.11873107	10
11	1.42164337	0.70341129	12.97364212	9.12580637	0.07707936	0.10957936	11
12	1.46784678	0.68127002	14.39528548	9.80707639	0.06946719	0.10196719	12
13	1.51555180	0.65982568	15.86313226	10.46690207	0.06303925	0.09553925	13
14	1.56480723	0.63905635	17.37868406	11.10595842	0.05754176	0.09004176	14
15	1.61566347	0.61894078	18.94349129	11.72489920	0.05278858	0.08528858	15
16	1.66817253	0.59945838	20.55915476	12.32435758	0.04864013	0.08114013	16
17	1.72238814	0.58058923	22.22732729	12.90494681	0.04498966	0.07748966	17
18	1.77836575	0.56231402	23.94971543	13.46726083	0.04175415	0.07425415	18
19	1.83616264	0.54461407	25.72808118	14.01187490	0.03886804	0.07136804	19
20	1.89583792	0.52747125	27.56424382	14.53934615	0.03627888	0.06877888	20
21	1.95745266	0.51086804	29.46008174	15.05021419	0.03394424	0.06644424	21
22	2.02106987	0.49478745	31.41753440	15.54500163	0.03182936	0.06432936	22
23	2.08675464	0.47921302	33.43860426	16.02421466	0.02990555	0.06240555	23
24	2.15457416	0.46412884	35.52535890	16.48834349	0.02814891	0.06064891	24
25	2.22459782	0.44951945	37.67993307	16.93786295	0.02653933	0.05903933	25
26	2.29689725	0.43536993	39.90453089	17.37323288	0.02505981	0.05755981	26
27	2.37154641	0.42166579	42.20142815	17.79489867	0.02369588	0.05619588	27
28	2.44862167	0.40839302	44.57297456	18.20329169	0.02243512	0.05493512	28
29	2.52820188	0.39553803	47.02159623	18.59882973	0.02126682	0.05376682	29
30	2.61036844	0.38308768	49.54979811	18.98191741	0.02018172	0.05268172	30
31	2.69520541	0.37102923	52.16016655	19.35294664	0.01917172	0.05167172	31
32	2.78279959	0.35935035	54.85537196	19.71229699	0.01822976	0.05072976	32
33	2.87324058	0.34803908	57.63817155	20.06033607	0.01734961	0.04984961	33
34	2.96662089	0.33708385	60.51141213	20.39741992	0.01652581	0.04902581	34
35	3.06303607	0.32647346	63.47803302	20.72389339	0.01575348	0.04825348	35
36	3.16258475	0.31619706	66.54106909	21.04009045	0.01502831	0.04752831	36
37	3.26536875	0.30624413	69.70365384	21.34633457	0.01434645	0.04684645	37
38	3.37149323	0.29660448	72.96902259	21.64293905	0.01370445	0.04620445	38
39	3.48106676	0.28726826	76.34051582	21.93020732	0.01309920	0.04559920	39
40	3.59420143	0.27822592	79.82158259	22.20843324	0.01252794	0.04502794	40
41	3.71101298	0.26946820	83.41578402	22.47790144	0.01198814	0.04448814	41
42	3.83162090	0.26098615	87.12679700	22.73888759	0.01147753	0.04397753	42
43	3.95614858	0.25277109	90.95841791	22.99165869	0.01099403	0.04349403	43
44	4.08472341	0.24481462	94.91456649	23.23647330	0.01053579	0.04303579	44
45	4.21747692	0.23710859	98.99928990	23.47358189	0.01010108	0.04260108	45
46	4.35454492	0.22964512	103.21676682	23.70322701	0.00968835	0.04218835	46
47	4.49606763	0.22241658	107.57131174	23.92564360	0.00929616	0.04179616	47
48	4.64218983	0.21541558	112.06737937	24.14105917	0.00892320	0.04142320	48
49	4.79306100	0.20863494	116.70956920	24.34969412	0.00856828	0.04106828	49
50	4.94883548	0.20206774	121.50263020	24.55176185	0.00823027	0.04073027	50
80	12.91828395	0.07740966	366.71642920	28.38739500	0.00272690	0.03522690	80
100	24.49097262	0.04083137	722.79915765	29.51288088	0.00138351	0.03388351	100
120	46.43091470	0.02153737	1397.87429832	30.10654232	0.00071537	0.03321537	120
240	2155.82983946	0.00046386	66302.45659888	30.75495820	0.00001508	0.03251508	240

Rate 3½%	C Compound Amount	D Present Value	E Amount of Annuity	F Present Value of Annuity	G Sinking Fund	H Amortization	
n	$(1 + i)^n$	$(1 + i)^{-n}$	$S_{\overline{n}\rceil i}$	$A_{\overline{n}\rceil i}$	$1/S_{\overline{n}\rceil i}$	$1/A_{\overline{n}\rceil i}$	n
1	1.03500000	0.96618357	1.00000000	0.96618357	1.00000000	1.03500000	1
2	1.07122500	0.93351070	2.03500000	1.89969428	0.49140049	0.52640049	2
3	1.10871788	0.90194271	3.10622500	2.80163698	0.32193418	0.35693418	3
4	1.14752300	0.87144223	4.21494287	3.67307921	0.23725114	0.27225114	4
5	1.18768631	0.84197317	5.36246588	4.51505238	0.18648137	0.22148137	5
6	1.22925533	0.81350064	6.55015218	5.32855302	0.15266821	0.18766821	6
7	1.27227926	0.78599096	7.77940751	6.11454398	0.12854449	0.16354449	7
8	1.31680904	0.75941156	9.05168677	6.87395554	0.11047665	0.14547665	8
9	1.36289735	0.73373097	10.36849581	7.60768651	0.09644601	0.13144601	9
10	1.41059876	0.70891881	11.73139316	8.31660532	0.08524137	0.12024137	10
11	1.45996972	0.68494571	13.14199192	9.00155104	0.07609197	0.11109197	11
12	1.51106866	0.66178330	14.60196164	9.66333433	0.06848395	0.10348395	12
13	1.56395606	0.63940415	16.11303030	10.30273849	0.06206157	0.09706157	13
14	1.61869452	0.61778179	17.67698636	10.92052028	0.05657073	0.09157073	14
15	1.67534883	0.59689062	19.29568088	11.51741090	0.05182507	0.08682507	15
16	1.73398604	0.57670591	20.97102971	12.09411681	0.04768483	0.08268483	16
17	1.79467555	0.55720378	22.70501575	12.65132059	0.04404313	0.07904313	17
18	1.85748920	0.53836114	24.49969130	13.18968173	0.04081684	0.07581684	18
19	1.92250132	0.52015569	26.35718050	13.70983742	0.03794033	0.07294033	19
20	1.98978886	0.50256588	28.27968181	14.21240330	0.03536108	0.07036108	20
21	2.05943147	0.48557090	30.26947068	14.69797420	0.03303659	0.06803659	21
22	2.13151158	0.46915063	32.32890215	15.16712484	0.03093207	0.06593207	22
23	2.20611448	0.45328563	34.46041373	15.62041047	0.02901880	0.06401880	23
24	2.28332849	0.43795713	36.66652821	16.05836760	0.02727283	0.06227283	24
25	2.36324498	0.42314699	38.94985669	16.48151459	0.02567404	0.06067404	25
26	2.44595856	0.40883767	41.31310168	16.89035226	0.02420540	0.05920540	26
27	2.53156711	0.39501224	43.75906024	17.28536451	0.02285241	0.05785241	27
28	2.62017196	0.38165434	46.29062734	17.66701885	0.02160265	0.05660265	28
29	2.71187798	0.36874815	48.91079930	18.03576700	0.02044538	0.05544538	29
30	2.80679370	0.35627841	51.62267728	18.39204541	0.01937133	0.05437133	30
31	2.90503148	0.34423035	54.42947098	18.73627576	0.01837240	0.05337240	31
32	3.00670759	0.33258971	57.33450247	19.06886547	0.01744150	0.05244150	32
33	3.11194235	0.32134271	60.34121005	19.39020818	0.01657242	0.05157242	33
34	3.22086033	0.31047605	63.45315240	19.70068423	0.01575966	0.05075966	34
35	3.33359045	0.29997686	66.67401274	20.00066110	0.01499835	0.04999835	35
36	3.45026611	0.28983272	70.00760318	20.29049381	0.01428416	0.04928416	36
37	3.57102543	0.28003161	73.45786930	20.57052542	0.01361325	0.04861325	37
38	3.69601132	0.27056194	77.02889472	20.84108736	0.01298214	0.04798214	38
39	3.82537171	0.26141250	80.72490604	21.10249987	0.01238775	0.04738775	39
40	3.95925972	0.25257247	84.55027775	21.35507234	0.01182728	0.04682728	40
41	4.09783381	0.24403137	88.50953747	21.59910371	0.01129822	0.04629822	41
42	4.24125799	0.23577910	92.60737128	21.83488281	0.01079828	0.04579828	42
43	4.38970202	0.22780590	96.84862928	22.06268870	0.01032539	0.04532539	43
44	4.54334160	0.22010231	101.23833130	22.28279102	0.00987768	0.04487768	44
45	4.70235855	0.21265924	105.78167290	22.49545026	0.00945343	0.04445343	45
46	4.86694110	0.20546787	110.48403145	22.70091813	0.00905108	0.04405108	46
47	5.03728404	0.19851968	115.35097255	22.89943780	0.00866919	0.04366919	47
48	5.21358898	0.19180645	120.38825659	23.09124425	0.00830646	0.04330646	48
49	5.39606459	0.18532024	125.60184557	23.27656450	0.00796167	0.04296167	49
50	5.58492686	0.17905337	130.99791016	23.45561787	0.00763371	0.04263371	50
80	15.67573754	0.06379285	419.30678685	26.74877567	0.00238489	0.03738489	80
100	31.19140798	0.03206011	862.61165666	27.65542540	0.00115927	0.03615927	100
120	62.06431624	0.01611232	1744.69474973	28.11107663	0.00057317	0.03557317	120

Rate 3¾%	C Compound Amount	D Present Value	E Amount of Annuity	F Present Value of Annuity	G Sinking Fund	H Amortization	
n	$(1 + i)^n$	$(1 + i)^{-n}$	$S_{\overline{n}|i}$	$A_{\overline{n}|i}$	$1/S_{\overline{n}|i}$	$1/A_{\overline{n}|i}$	n
1	1.03750000	0.96385542	1.00000000	0.96385542	1.00000000	1.03750000	1
2	1.07640625	0.92901727	2.03750000	1.89287270	0.49079755	0.52829755	2
3	1.11677148	0.89543834	3.11390625	2.78831103	0.32114005	0.35864005	3
4	1.15865042	0.86307310	4.23067773	3.65138413	0.23636875	0.27386875	4
5	1.20209981	0.83187768	5.38932815	4.48326181	0.18555189	0.22305189	5
6	1.24717855	0.80180981	6.59142796	5.28507162	0.15171219	0.18921219	6
7	1.29394774	0.77282874	7.83860650	6.05790036	0.12757370	0.16507370	7
8	1.34247078	0.74489517	9.13255425	6.80279553	0.10949839	0.14699839	8
9	1.39281344	0.71797125	10.47502503	7.52076677	0.09546517	0.13296517	9
10	1.44504394	0.69202048	11.86783847	8.21278725	0.08426134	0.12176134	10
11	1.49923309	0.66700769	13.31288241	8.87979494	0.07511521	0.11261521	11
12	1.55545433	0.64289898	14.81211550	9.52269392	0.06751230	0.10501230	12
13	1.61378387	0.61966167	16.36756983	10.14235558	0.06109642	0.09859642	13
14	1.67430076	0.59726426	17.98135370	10.73961984	0.05561317	0.09311317	14
15	1.73708704	0.57567639	19.65565447	11.31529623	0.05087595	0.08837595	15
16	1.80222781	0.55486881	21.39274151	11.87016504	0.04674483	0.08424483	16
17	1.86981135	0.53481331	23.19496932	12.40497835	0.04311280	0.08061280	17
18	1.93992927	0.51548271	25.06478067	12.92046106	0.03989662	0.07739662	18
19	2.01267662	0.49685080	27.00470994	13.41731187	0.03703058	0.07453058	19
20	2.08815200	0.47889234	29.01738656	13.89620421	0.03446210	0.07196210	20
21	2.16645770	0.46158298	31.10553856	14.35778719	0.03214862	0.06964862	21
22	2.24769986	0.44489926	33.27199626	14.80268645	0.03005531	0.06755531	22
23	2.33198860	0.42881856	35.51969612	15.23150501	0.02815339	0.06565339	23
24	2.41943818	0.41331910	37.85168472	15.64482411	0.02641890	0.06391890	24
25	2.51016711	0.39837985	40.27112290	16.04320396	0.02483169	0.06233169	25
26	2.60429838	0.38398058	42.78129001	16.42718454	0.02337470	0.06087470	26
27	2.70195956	0.37010176	45.38558838	16.79728630	0.02203343	0.05953343	27
28	2.80328305	0.35672459	48.08754794	17.15401089	0.02079540	0.05829540	28
29	2.90840616	0.34383093	50.89083099	17.49784183	0.01964991	0.05714991	29
30	3.01747139	0.33140331	53.79923715	17.82924513	0.01858762	0.05608762	30
31	3.13062657	0.31942487	56.81670855	18.14867001	0.01760046	0.05510046	31
32	3.24802507	0.30787940	59.94733512	18.45654941	0.01668131	0.05418131	32
33	3.36982601	0.29675123	63.19536019	18.75330063	0.01582395	0.05332395	33
34	3.49619448	0.28602528	66.56518619	19.03932591	0.01502287	0.05252287	34
35	3.62730178	0.27568702	70.06138067	19.31501293	0.01427320	0.05177320	35
36	3.76332559	0.26572242	73.68868245	19.58073535	0.01357060	0.05107060	36
37	3.90445030	0.25611800	77.45200804	19.83685335	0.01291122	0.05041122	37
38	4.05086719	0.24686072	81.35645834	20.08371407	0.01229159	0.04979159	38
39	4.20277471	0.23793805	85.40732553	20.32165212	0.01170860	0.04920860	39
40	4.36037876	0.22933788	89.61010024	20.55098999	0.01115946	0.04865946	40
41	4.52389296	0.22104855	93.97047900	20.77203855	0.01064164	0.04814164	41
42	4.69353895	0.21305885	98.49437196	20.98509739	0.01015286	0.04765286	42
43	4.86954666	0.20535793	103.18791091	21.19045532	0.00969106	0.04719106	43
44	5.05215466	0.19793535	108.05745757	21.38839067	0.00925434	0.04675434	44
45	5.24161046	0.19078106	113.10961223	21.57917173	0.00884098	0.04634098	45
46	5.43817085	0.18388536	118.35122269	21.76305709	0.00844943	0.04594943	46
47	5.64210226	0.17723890	123.78939354	21.94029599	0.00807824	0.04557824	47
48	5.85368109	0.17083268	129.43149579	22.11112866	0.00772609	0.04522609	48
49	6.07319413	0.16465800	135.28517689	22.27578666	0.00739179	0.04489179	49
50	6.30093891	0.15870651	141.35837102	22.43449317	0.00707422	0.04457422	50
80	19.01290292	0.05259586	480.34407791	25.26411037	0.00208184	0.03958184	80
100	39.70183119	0.02518776	1032.04883168	25.99499320	0.00096895	0.03846895	100
120	82.90345805	0.01206222	2184.09221454	26.34500739	0.00045786	0.03795786	120

Rate 4%	C Compound Amount	D Present Value	E Amount of Annuity	F Present Value of Annuity	G Sinking Fund	H Amortization	
n	$(1 + i)^n$	$(1 + i)^{-n}$	$S_{\overline{n}|i}$	$A_{\overline{n}|i}$	$1/S_{\overline{n}|i}$	$1/A_{\overline{n}|i}$	n
1	1.04000000	0.96153846	1.00000000	0.96153846	1.00000000	1.04000000	1
2	1.08160000	0.92455621	2.04000000	1.88609467	0.49019608	0.53019608	2
3	1.12486400	0.88899636	3.12160000	2.77509103	0.32034854	0.36034854	3
4	1.16985856	0.85480419	4.24646400	3.62989522	0.23549005	0.27549005	4
5	1.21665290	0.82192711	5.41632256	4.45182233	0.18462711	0.22462711	5
6	1.26531902	0.79031453	6.63297546	5.24213686	0.15076190	0.19076190	6
7	1.31593178	0.75991781	7.89829448	6.00205467	0.12660961	0.16660961	7
8	1.36856905	0.73069021	9.21422626	6.73274487	0.10852783	0.14852783	8
9	1.42331181	0.70258674	10.58279531	7.43533161	0.09449299	0.13449299	9
10	1.48024428	0.67556417	12.00610712	8.11089578	0.08329094	0.12329094	10
11	1.53945406	0.64958093	13.48635141	8.76047671	0.07414904	0.11414904	11
12	1.60103222	0.62459705	15.02580546	9.38507376	0.06655217	0.10655217	12
13	1.66507351	0.60057409	16.62683768	9.98564785	0.06014373	0.10014373	13
14	1.73167645	0.57747508	18.29191119	10.56312293	0.05466897	0.09466897	14
15	1.80094351	0.55526450	20.02358764	11.11838743	0.04994110	0.08994110	15
16	1.87298125	0.53390818	21.82453114	11.65229561	0.04582000	0.08582000	16
17	1.94790050	0.51337325	23.69751239	12.16566885	0.04219852	0.08219852	17
18	2.02581652	0.49362812	25.64541288	12.65929697	0.03899333	0.07899333	18
19	2.10684918	0.47464242	27.67122940	13.13393940	0.03613862	0.07613862	19
20	2.19112314	0.45638695	29.77807858	13.59032634	0.03358175	0.07358175	20
21	2.27876807	0.43883360	31.96920172	14.02915995	0.03128011	0.07128011	21
22	2.36991879	0.42195539	34.24796979	14.45111533	0.02919881	0.06919881	22
23	2.46471554	0.40572633	36.61788858	14.85684167	0.02730906	0.06730906	23
24	2.56330416	0.39012147	39.08260412	15.24696314	0.02558683	0.06558683	24
25	2.66583633	0.37511680	41.64590829	15.62207994	0.02401196	0.06401196	25
26	2.77246978	0.36068923	44.31174462	15.98276918	0.02256738	0.06256738	26
27	2.88336858	0.34681657	47.08421440	16.32958575	0.02123854	0.06123854	27
28	2.99870332	0.33347747	49.96758298	16.66306322	0.02001298	0.06001298	28
29	3.11865145	0.32065141	52.96628630	16.98371463	0.01887993	0.05887993	29
30	3.24339751	0.30831867	56.08493775	17.29203330	0.01783010	0.05783010	30
31	3.37313341	0.29646026	59.32833526	17.58849356	0.01685535	0.05685535	31
32	3.50805875	0.28505794	62.70146867	17.87355150	0.01594859	0.05594859	32
33	3.64838110	0.27409417	66.20952742	18.14764567	0.01510357	0.05510357	33
34	3.79431634	0.26355209	69.85790851	18.41119776	0.01431477	0.05431477	34
35	3.94608899	0.25341547	73.65222486	18.66461323	0.01357732	0.05357732	35
36	4.10393255	0.24366872	77.59831385	18.90828195	0.01288688	0.05288688	36
37	4.26808986	0.23429685	81.70224640	19.14257880	0.01223957	0.05223957	37
38	4.43881345	0.22528543	85.97033626	19.36786423	0.01163192	0.05163192	38
39	4.61636599	0.21662061	90.40914971	19.58448484	0.01106083	0.05106083	39
40	4.80102063	0.20828904	95.02551570	19.79277388	0.01052349	0.05052349	40
41	4.99306145	0.20027793	99.82653633	19.99305181	0.01001738	0.05001738	41
42	5.19278391	0.19257493	104.81959778	20.18562674	0.00954020	0.04954020	42
43	5.40049527	0.18516820	110.01238169	20.37079494	0.00908989	0.04908989	43
44	5.61651508	0.17804635	115.41287696	20.54884129	0.00866454	0.04866454	44
45	5.84117568	0.17119841	121.02939204	20.72003970	0.00826246	0.04826246	45
46	6.07482271	0.16461386	126.87056772	20.88465356	0.00788205	0.04788205	46
47	6.31781562	0.15828256	132.94539043	21.04293612	0.00752189	0.04752189	47
48	6.57052824	0.15219476	139.26320604	21.19513088	0.00718065	0.04718065	48
49	6.83334937	0.14634112	145.83373429	21.34147200	0.00685712	0.04685712	49
50	7.10668335	0.14071262	152.66708366	21.48218462	0.00655020	0.04655020	50
80	23.04979907	0.04338433	551.24497675	23.91539185	0.00181408	0.04181408	80
100	50.50494818	0.01980004	1237.62370461	24.50499900	0.00080800	0.04080800	100
120	110.66256080	0.00903648	2741.56402011	24.77408800	0.00036476	0.04036476	120

Rate 4½%	C Compound Amount	D Present Value	E Amount of Annuity	F Present Value of Annuity	G Sinking Fund	H Amortization	
n	$(1 + i)^n$	$(1 + i)^{-n}$	$S_{\overline{n}|i}$	$A_{\overline{n}|i}$	$1/S_{\overline{n}|i}$	$1/A_{\overline{n}|i}$	n
1	1.04500000	0.95693780	1.00000000	0.95693780	1.00000000	1.04500000	1
2	1.09202500	0.91572995	2.04500000	1.87266775	0.48899756	0.53399756	2
3	1.14116612	0.87629660	3.13702500	2.74896435	0.31877336	0.36377336	3
4	1.19251860	0.83856134	4.27819112	3.58752570	0.23374365	0.27874365	4
5	1.24618194	0.80245105	5.47070973	4.38997674	0.18279164	0.22779164	5
6	1.30226012	0.76789574	6.71689166	5.15787248	0.14887839	0.19387839	6
7	1.36086183	0.73482846	8.01915179	5.89270094	0.12470147	0.16970147	7
8	1.42210061	0.70318513	9.38001362	6.59588607	0.10660965	0.15160965	8
9	1.48609514	0.67290443	10.80211423	7.26879050	0.09257447	0.13757447	9
10	1.55296942	0.64392768	12.28820937	7.91271818	0.08137882	0.12637882	10
11	1.62285305	0.61619874	13.84117879	8.52891692	0.07224818	0.11724818	11
12	1.69588143	0.58966386	15.46403184	9.11858078	0.06466619	0.10966619	12
13	1.77219610	0.56427164	17.15991327	9.68285242	0.05827535	0.10327535	13
14	1.85191492	0.53997286	18.93210937	10.22282528	0.05282032	0.09782032	14
15	1.93528244	0.51672044	20.78405429	10.73954573	0.04811381	0.09311381	15
16	2.02237015	0.49446932	22.71933673	11.23401505	0.04401537	0.08901537	16
17	2.11337681	0.47317639	24.74170689	11.70719143	0.04041758	0.08541758	17
18	2.20847877	0.45280037	26.85508370	12.15999180	0.03723690	0.08223690	18
19	2.30786031	0.43330179	29.06356246	12.59329359	0.03440734	0.07940734	19
20	2.41171402	0.41464286	31.37142277	13.00793645	0.03187614	0.07687614	20
21	2.52024116	0.39678743	33.78313680	13.40472388	0.02960057	0.07460057	21
22	2.63365201	0.37970089	36.30337795	13.78442476	0.02754565	0.07254565	22
23	2.75216635	0.36335013	38.93702996	14.14777489	0.02568249	0.07068249	23
24	2.87601383	0.34770347	41.68919631	14.49547837	0.02398703	0.06898703	24
25	3.00543446	0.33273060	44.56521015	14.82820896	0.02243903	0.06743903	25
26	3.14067901	0.31840248	47.57064460	15.14661145	0.02102137	0.06602137	26
27	3.28200956	0.30469137	50.71132361	15.45130282	0.01971946	0.06471946	27
28	3.42969999	0.29157069	53.99333317	15.74287351	0.01852081	0.06352081	28
29	3.58403649	0.27901502	57.42303316	16.02188853	0.01741461	0.06241461	29
30	3.74531813	0.26700002	61.00706966	16.28888854	0.01639154	0.06139154	30
31	3.91385745	0.25550241	64.75238779	16.54439095	0.01544345	0.06044345	31
32	4.08998104	0.24449991	68.66624524	16.78889086	0.01456320	0.05956320	32
33	4.27403018	0.23397121	72.75622628	17.02286207	0.01374453	0.05874453	33
34	4.46636154	0.22389589	77.03025646	17.24675796	0.01298191	0.05798191	34
35	4.66734781	0.21425444	81.49661800	17.46101240	0.01227045	0.05727045	35
36	4.87737846	0.20502817	86.16396581	17.66604058	0.01160578	0.05660578	36
37	5.09686049	0.19619921	91.04134427	17.86223979	0.01098402	0.05598402	37
38	5.32621921	0.18775044	96.13820476	18.04999023	0.01040169	0.05540169	38
39	5.56589908	0.17966549	101.46442398	18.22965572	0.00985567	0.05485567	39
40	5.81636454	0.17192870	107.03032306	18.40158442	0.00934315	0.05434315	40
41	6.07810094	0.16452507	112.84668760	18.56610949	0.00886158	0.05386158	41
42	6.35161548	0.15744026	118.92478854	18.72354975	0.00840868	0.05340868	42
43	6.63743818	0.15066054	125.27640402	18.87421029	0.00798235	0.05298235	43
44	6.93612290	0.14417276	131.91384220	19.01838305	0.00758071	0.05258071	44
45	7.24824843	0.13796437	138.84996510	19.15634742	0.00720202	0.05220202	45
46	7.57441961	0.13202332	146.09821353	19.28837074	0.00684471	0.05184471	46
47	7.91526849	0.12633810	153.67263314	19.41470884	0.00650734	0.05150734	47
48	8.27145557	0.12089771	161.58790163	19.53560654	0.00618858	0.05118858	48
49	8.64367107	0.11569158	169.85935720	19.65129813	0.00588722	0.05088722	49
50	9.03263627	0.11070965	178.50302828	19.76200778	0.00560215	0.05060215	50
80	33.83009643	0.02955948	729.55769854	21.56534493	0.00137069	0.04637069	80
100	81.58851803	0.01225663	1790.85595627	21.94985274	0.00055839	0.04555839	100
120	196.76817320	0.00508212	4350.40384897	22.10928616	0.00022986	0.04522986	120

Rate 5%	C Compound Amount	D Present Value	E Amount of Annuity	F Present Value of Annuity	G Sinking Fund	H Amortization	
n	$(1 + i)^n$	$(1 + i)^{-n}$	$S_{\overline{n}|i}$	$A_{\overline{n}|i}$	$1/S_{\overline{n}|i}$	$1/A_{\overline{n}|i}$	n
1	1.05000000	0.95238095	1.00000000	0.95238095	1.00000000	1.05000000	1
2	1.10250000	0.90702948	2.05000000	1.85941043	0.48780488	0.53780488	2
3	1.15762500	0.86383760	3.15250000	2.72324803	0.31720856	0.36720856	3
4	1.21550625	0.82270247	4.31012500	3.54595050	0.23201183	0.28201183	4
5	1.27628156	0.78352617	5.52563125	4.32947667	0.18097480	0.23097480	5
6	1.34009564	0.74621540	6.80191281	5.07569207	0.14701747	0.19701747	6
7	1.40710042	0.71068133	8.14200845	5.78637340	0.12281982	0.17281982	7
8	1.47745544	0.67683936	9.54910888	6.46321276	0.10472181	0.15472181	8
9	1.55132822	0.64460892	11.02656432	7.10782168	0.09069008	0.14069008	9
10	1.62889463	0.61391325	12.57789254	7.72173493	0.07950457	0.12950457	10
11	1.71033936	0.58467929	14.20678716	8.30641422	0.07038889	0.12038889	11
12	1.79585633	0.55683742	15.91712652	8.86325164	0.06282541	0.11282541	12
13	1.88564914	0.53032135	17.71298285	9.39357299	0.05645577	0.10645577	13
14	1.97993160	0.50506795	19.59863199	9.89864094	0.05102397	0.10102397	14
15	2.07892818	0.48101710	21.57856359	10.37965804	0.04634229	0.09634229	15
16	2.18287459	0.45811152	23.65749177	10.83776956	0.04226991	0.09226991	16
17	2.29201832	0.43629669	25.84036636	11.27406625	0.03869914	0.08869914	17
18	2.40661923	0.41552065	28.13238467	11.68958690	0.03554622	0.08554622	18
19	2.52695020	0.39573396	30.53900391	12.08532086	0.03274501	0.08274501	19
20	2.65329771	0.37688948	33.06595410	12.46221034	0.03024259	0.08024259	20
21	2.78596259	0.35894236	35.71925181	12.82115271	0.02799611	0.07799611	21
22	2.92526072	0.34184987	38.50521440	13.16300258	0.02597051	0.07597051	22
23	3.07152376	0.32557131	41.43047512	13.48857388	0.02413682	0.07413682	23
24	3.22509994	0.31006791	44.50199887	13.79864179	0.02247090	0.07247090	24
25	3.38635494	0.29530277	47.72709882	14.09394457	0.02095246	0.07095246	25
26	3.55567269	0.28124073	51.11345376	14.37518530	0.01956432	0.06956432	26
27	3.73345632	0.26784832	54.66912645	14.64303362	0.01829186	0.06829186	27
28	3.92012914	0.25509364	58.40258277	14.89812726	0.01712253	0.06712253	28
29	4.11613560	0.24294632	62.32271191	15.14107358	0.01604551	0.06604551	29
30	4.32194238	0.23137745	66.43884750	15.37245103	0.01505144	0.06505144	30
31	4.53803949	0.22035947	70.76078988	15.59281050	0.01413212	0.06413212	31
32	4.76494147	0.20986617	75.29882937	15.80267667	0.01328040	0.06328040	32
33	5.00318854	0.19987254	80.06377084	16.00254921	0.01249004	0.06249004	33
34	5.25334797	0.19035480	85.06695938	16.19290401	0.01175545	0.06175545	34
35	5.51601537	0.18129029	90.32030735	16.37419429	0.01107171	0.06107171	35
36	5.79181614	0.17265741	95.83632272	16.54685171	0.01043446	0.06043446	36
37	6.08140694	0.16443563	101.62813886	16.71128734	0.00983979	0.05983979	37
38	6.38547729	0.15660536	107.70954580	16.86789271	0.00928423	0.05928423	38
39	6.70475115	0.14914797	114.09502309	17.01704067	0.00876462	0.05876462	39
40	7.03998871	0.14204568	120.79977424	17.15908635	0.00827816	0.05827816	40
41	7.39198815	0.13528160	127.83976295	17.29436796	0.00782229	0.05782229	41
42	7.76158756	0.12883962	135.23175110	17.42320758	0.00739471	0.05739471	42
43	8.14966693	0.12270440	142.99333866	17.54591198	0.00699333	0.05699333	43
44	8.55715028	0.11686133	151.14300559	17.66277331	0.00661625	0.05661625	44
45	8.98500779	0.11129651	159.70015587	17.77406982	0.00626173	0.05626173	45
46	9.43425818	0.10599668	168.68516366	17.88006650	0.00592820	0.05592820	46
47	9.90597109	0.10094921	178.11942185	17.98101571	0.00561421	0.05561421	47
48	10.40126965	0.09614211	188.02539294	18.07715782	0.00531843	0.05531843	48
49	10.92133313	0.09156391	198.42666259	18.16872173	0.00503965	0.05503965	49
50	11.46739979	0.08720373	209.34799572	18.25592546	0.00477674	0.05477674	50
80	49.56144107	0.02017698	971.22882134	19.59646048	0.00102962	0.05102962	80
100	131.50125785	0.00760449	2610.02515693	19.84791020	0.00038314	0.05038314	100
120	348.91198567	0.00286605	6958.23971334	19.94267895	0.00014371	0.05014371	120

Rate 5½%	C Compound Amount	D Present Value	E Amount of Annuity	F Present Value of Annuity	G Sinking Fund	H Amortization	
n	$(1 + i)^n$	$(1 + i)^{-n}$	$S_{\overline{n}|i}$	$A_{\overline{n}|i}$	$1/S_{\overline{n}|i}$	$1/A_{\overline{n}|i}$	n
1	1.05500000	0.94786730	1.00000000	0.94786730	1.00000000	1.05500000	1
2	1.11302500	0.89845242	2.05500000	1.84631971	0.48661800	0.54161800	2
3	1.17424137	0.85161366	3.16802500	2.69793338	0.31565407	0.37065407	3
4	1.23882465	0.80721674	4.34226638	3.50515012	0.23029449	0.28529449	4
5	1.30696001	0.76513435	5.58109103	4.27028448	0.17917644	0.23417644	5
6	1.37884281	0.72524583	6.88805103	4.99553031	0.14517895	0.20017895	6
7	1.45467916	0.68743681	8.26689384	5.68296712	0.12096442	0.17596442	7
8	1.53468651	0.65159887	9.72157300	6.33456599	0.10286401	0.15786401	8
9	1.61909427	0.61762926	11.25625951	6.95219525	0.08883946	0.14383946	9
10	1.70814446	0.58543058	12.87535379	7.53762583	0.07766777	0.13266777	10
11	1.80209240	0.55491050	14.58349825	8.09253633	0.06857065	0.12357065	11
12	1.90120749	0.52598152	16.38559065	8.61851785	0.06102923	0.11602923	12
13	2.00577390	0.49856068	18.28679814	9.11707853	0.05468426	0.10968426	13
14	2.11609146	0.47256937	20.29257203	9.58964790	0.04927912	0.10427912	14
15	2.23247649	0.44793305	22.40866350	10.03758094	0.04462560	0.09962560	15
16	2.35526270	0.42458109	24.64113999	10.46216203	0.04058254	0.09558254	16
17	2.48480215	0.40244653	26.99640269	10.86460856	0.03704197	0.09204197	17
18	2.62146627	0.38146590	29.48120483	11.24607447	0.03391992	0.08891992	18
19	2.76564691	0.36157906	32.10267110	11.60765352	0.03115006	0.08615006	19
20	2.91775749	0.34272896	34.86831801	11.95038248	0.02867933	0.08367933	20
21	3.07823415	0.32486158	37.78607550	12.27524406	0.02646478	0.08146478	21
22	3.24753703	0.30792567	40.86430965	12.58316973	0.02447123	0.07947123	22
23	3.42615157	0.29187267	44.11184669	12.87504239	0.02266965	0.07766965	23
24	3.61458990	0.27665656	47.53799825	13.15169895	0.02103580	0.07603580	24
25	3.81339235	0.26223370	51.15258816	13.41393266	0.01954935	0.07454935	25
26	4.02312893	0.24856275	54.96598051	13.66249541	0.01819307	0.07319307	26
27	4.24440102	0.23560450	58.98910943	13.89809991	0.01695228	0.07195228	27
28	4.47784307	0.22332181	63.23351045	14.12142172	0.01581440	0.07081440	28
29	4.72412444	0.21167944	67.71135353	14.33310116	0.01476857	0.06976857	29
30	4.98395129	0.20064402	72.43547797	14.53374517	0.01380539	0.06880539	30
31	5.25806861	0.19018390	77.41942926	14.72392907	0.01291665	0.06791665	31
32	5.54726238	0.18026910	82.67749787	14.90419817	0.01209519	0.06709519	32
33	5.85236181	0.17087119	88.22476025	15.07506936	0.01133469	0.06633469	33
34	6.17424171	0.16196321	94.07712207	15.23703257	0.01062958	0.06562958	34
35	6.51382501	0.15351963	100.25136378	15.39055220	0.00997493	0.06497493	35
36	6.87208538	0.14551624	106.76518879	15.53606843	0.00936635	0.06436635	36
37	7.25005008	0.13793008	113.63727417	15.67399851	0.00879993	0.06379993	37
38	7.64880283	0.13073941	120.88732425	15.80473793	0.00827217	0.06327217	38
39	8.06948690	0.12392362	128.53612708	15.92866154	0.00777991	0.06277991	39
40	8.51330877	0.11746314	136.60561407	16.04612469	0.00732034	0.06232034	40
41	8.98154076	0.11133947	145.11892285	16.15746416	0.00689090	0.06189090	41
42	9.47552550	0.10553504	154.10046360	16.26299920	0.00648927	0.06148927	42
43	9.99667940	0.10003322	163.57598910	16.36303242	0.00611337	0.06111337	43
44	10.54649677	0.09481822	173.57266850	16.45785063	0.00576128	0.06076128	44
45	11.12655409	0.08987509	184.11916527	16.54772572	0.00543127	0.06043127	45
46	11.73851456	0.08518965	195.24571936	16.63291537	0.00512175	0.06012175	46
47	12.38413287	0.08074849	206.98423392	16.71366386	0.00483129	0.05983129	47
48	13.06526017	0.07653885	219.36836679	16.79020271	0.00455854	0.05955854	48
49	13.78384948	0.07254867	232.43362696	16.86275139	0.00430230	0.05930230	49
50	14.54196120	0.06876652	246.21747645	16.93151790	0.00406145	0.05906145	50
80	72.47642628	0.01379759	1299.57138693	17.93095291	0.00076948	0.05576948	80
100	211.46863567	0.00472883	3826.70246680	18.09583939	0.00026132	0.05526132	100
120	617.01419577	0.00162071	11200.25810482	18.15235076	0.00008928	0.05508928	120

Rate 6%	C Compound Amount	D Present Value	E Amount of Annuity	F Present Value of Annuity	G Sinking Fund	H Amortization	
n	$(1 + i)^n$	$(1 + i)^{-n}$	$S_{\overline{n}|i}$	$A_{\overline{n}|i}$	$1/S_{\overline{n}|i}$	$1/A_{\overline{n}|i}$	n
1	1.06000000	0.94339623	1.00000000	0.94339623	1.00000000	1.06000000	1
2	1.12360000	0.88999644	2.06000000	1.83339267	0.48543689	0.54543689	2
3	1.19101600	0.83961928	3.18360000	2.67301195	0.31410981	0.37410981	3
4	1.26247696	0.79209366	4.37461600	3.46510561	0.22859149	0.28859149	4
5	1.33822558	0.74725817	5.63709296	4.21236379	0.17739640	0.23739640	5
6	1.41851911	0.70496054	6.97531854	4.91732433	0.14336263	0.20336263	6
7	1.50363026	0.66505711	8.39383765	5.58238144	0.11913502	0.17913502	7
8	1.59384807	0.62741237	9.89746791	6.20979381	0.10103594	0.16103594	8
9	1.68947896	0.59189846	11.49131598	6.80169227	0.08702224	0.14702224	9
10	1.79084770	0.55839478	13.18079494	7.36008705	0.07586796	0.13586796	10
11	1.89829856	0.52678753	14.97164264	7.88687458	0.06679294	0.12679294	11
12	2.01219647	0.49696936	16.86994120	8.38384394	0.05927703	0.11927703	12
13	2.13292826	0.46883902	18.88213767	8.85268296	0.05296011	0.11296011	13
14	2.26090396	0.44230096	21.01506593	9.29498393	0.04758491	0.10758491	14
15	2.39655819	0.41726506	23.27596988	9.71224899	0.04296276	0.10296276	15
16	2.54035168	0.39364628	25.67252808	10.10589527	0.03895214	0.09895214	16
17	2.69277279	0.37136442	28.21287976	10.47725969	0.03544480	0.09544480	17
18	2.85433915	0.35034379	30.90565255	10.82760348	0.03235654	0.09235654	18
19	3.02559950	0.33051301	33.75999170	11.15811649	0.02962086	0.08962086	19
20	3.20713547	0.31180473	36.78559120	11.46992122	0.02718456	0.08718456	20
21	3.39956360	0.29415540	39.99272668	11.76407662	0.02500455	0.08500455	21
22	3.60353742	0.27750510	43.39229028	12.04158172	0.02304557	0.08304557	22
23	3.81974966	0.26179726	46.99582769	12.30337898	0.02127848	0.08127848	23
24	4.04893464	0.24697855	50.81557735	12.55035753	0.01967900	0.07967900	24
25	4.29187072	0.23299863	54.86451200	12.78335616	0.01822672	0.07822672	25
26	4.54938296	0.21981003	59.15638272	13.00316619	0.01690435	0.07690435	26
27	4.82234564	0.20736795	63.70576568	13.21053414	0.01569717	0.07569717	27
28	5.11168670	0.19563014	68.52811162	13.40616428	0.01459255	0.07459255	28
29	5.41838790	0.18455674	73.63979832	13.59072102	0.01357961	0.07357961	29
30	5.74349117	0.17411013	79.05818622	13.76483115	0.01264891	0.07264891	30
31	6.08810064	0.16425484	84.80167739	13.92908599	0.01179222	0.07179222	31
32	6.45338668	0.15495740	90.88977803	14.08404339	0.01100234	0.07100234	32
33	6.84058988	0.14618622	97.34316471	14.23022961	0.01027293	0.07027293	33
34	7.25102528	0.13791153	104.18375460	14.36814114	0.00959843	0.06959843	34
35	7.68608679	0.13010522	111.43477987	14.49824636	0.00897386	0.06897386	35
36	8.14725200	0.12274077	119.12086666	14.62098713	0.00839483	0.06839483	36
37	8.63608712	0.11579318	127.26811866	14.73678031	0.00785743	0.06785743	37
38	9.15425235	0.10923885	135.90420578	14.84601916	0.00735812	0.06735812	38
39	9.70350749	0.10305552	145.05845813	14.94907468	0.00689377	0.06689377	39
40	10.28571794	0.09722219	154.76196562	15.04629687	0.00646154	0.06646154	40
41	10.90286101	0.09171905	165.04768356	15.13801592	0.00605886	0.06605886	41
42	11.55703267	0.08652740	175.95054457	15.22454332	0.00568342	0.06568342	42
43	12.25045463	0.08162962	187.50757724	15.30617294	0.00533312	0.06533312	43
44	12.98548191	0.07700908	199.75803188	15.38318202	0.00500606	0.06500606	44
45	13.76461083	0.07265007	212.74351379	15.45583209	0.00470050	0.06470050	45
46	14.59048748	0.06853781	226.50812462	15.52436990	0.00441485	0.06441485	46
47	15.46591673	0.06465831	241.09861210	15.58902821	0.00414768	0.06414768	47
48	16.39387173	0.06099840	256.56452882	15.65002661	0.00389765	0.06389765	48
49	17.37750403	0.05754566	272.95840055	15.70757227	0.00366356	0.06366356	49
50	18.42015427	0.05428836	290.33590458	15.76186064	0.00344429	0.06344429	50
80	105.79599348	0.00945215	1746.59989137	16.50913077	0.00057254	0.06057254	80
100	339.30208351	0.00294723	5638.36805857	16.61754623	0.00017736	0.06017736	100
120	1088.18774784	0.00091896	18119.79579725	16.65135068	0.00005519	0.06005519	120

Rate 6½%	C Compound Amount	D Present Value	E Amount of Annuity	F Present Value of Annuity	G Sinking Fund	H Amortization	
n	$(1 + i)^n$	$(1 + i)^{-n}$	$S_{\overline{n}|i}$	$A_{\overline{n}|i}$	$1/S_{\overline{n}|i}$	$1/A_{\overline{n}|i}$	n
1	1.06500000	0.93896714	1.00000000	0.93896714	1.00000000	1.06500000	1
2	1.13422500	0.88165928	2.06500000	1.82062642	0.48426150	0.54926150	2
3	1.20794963	0.82784909	3.19922500	2.64847551	0.31257570	0.37757570	3
4	1.28646635	0.77732309	4.40717463	3.42579860	0.22690274	0.29190274	4
5	1.37008666	0.72988084	5.69364098	4.15567944	0.17563454	0.24063454	5
6	1.45914230	0.68533412	7.06372764	4.84101356	0.14156831	0.20656831	6
7	1.55398655	0.64350621	8.52286994	5.48451977	0.11733137	0.18233137	7
8	1.65499567	0.60423119	10.07685648	6.08875096	0.09923730	0.16423730	8
9	1.76257039	0.56735323	11.73185215	6.65610419	0.08523803	0.15023803	9
10	1.87713747	0.53272604	13.49442254	7.18883022	0.07410469	0.13910469	10
11	1.99915140	0.50021224	15.37156001	7.68904246	0.06505521	0.13005521	11
12	2.12909624	0.46968285	17.37071141	8.15872532	0.05756817	0.12256817	12
13	2.26748750	0.44101676	19.49980765	8.59974208	0.05128256	0.11628256	13
14	2.41487418	0.41410025	21.76729515	9.01384233	0.04594048	0.11094048	14
15	2.57184101	0.38882652	24.18216933	9.40266885	0.04135278	0.10635278	15
16	2.73901067	0.36509533	26.75401034	9.76776418	0.03737757	0.10237757	16
17	2.91704637	0.34281251	29.49302101	10.11057670	0.03390633	0.09890633	17
18	3.10665438	0.32188969	32.41006738	10.43246638	0.03085461	0.09585461	18
19	3.30858691	0.30224384	35.51672176	10.73471022	0.02815575	0.09315575	19
20	3.52364506	0.28379703	38.82530867	11.01850725	0.02575640	0.09075640	20
21	3.75268199	0.26647608	42.34895373	11.28498333	0.02361333	0.08861333	21
22	3.99660632	0.25021228	46.10163573	11.53519562	0.02169120	0.08669120	22
23	4.25638573	0.23494111	50.09824205	11.77013673	0.01996078	0.08496078	23
24	4.53305081	0.22060198	54.35462778	11.99073871	0.01839770	0.08339770	24
25	4.82769911	0.20713801	58.88767859	12.19787673	0.01698148	0.08198148	25
26	5.14149955	0.19449579	63.71537769	12.39237251	0.01569480	0.08069480	26
27	5.47569702	0.18262515	68.85687725	12.57499766	0.01452288	0.07952288	27
28	5.83161733	0.17147902	74.33257427	12.74647668	0.01345305	0.07845305	28
29	6.21067245	0.16101316	80.16419159	12.90748984	0.01247440	0.07747440	29
30	6.61436616	0.15118607	86.37486405	13.05867591	0.01157744	0.07657744	30
31	7.04429996	0.14195875	92.98923021	13.20063465	0.01075393	0.07575393	31
32	7.50217946	0.13329460	100.03353017	13.33392925	0.00999665	0.07499665	32
33	7.98982113	0.12515925	107.53570963	13.45908850	0.00929924	0.07429924	33
34	8.50915950	0.11752042	115.52553076	13.57660892	0.00865610	0.07365610	34
35	9.06225487	0.11034781	124.03469026	13.68695673	0.00806226	0.07306226	35
36	9.65130143	0.10361297	133.09694513	13.79056970	0.00751332	0.07251332	36
37	10.27863603	0.09728917	142.74824656	13.88785887	0.00700534	0.07200534	37
38	10.94674737	0.09135134	153.02688259	13.97921021	0.00653480	0.07153480	38
39	11.65828595	0.08577590	163.97362996	14.06498611	0.00609854	0.07109854	39
40	12.41607453	0.08054075	175.63191590	14.14552687	0.00569373	0.07069373	40
41	13.22311938	0.07562512	188.04799044	14.22115199	0.00531779	0.07031779	41
42	14.08262214	0.07100950	201.27110981	14.29216149	0.00496842	0.06996842	42
43	14.99799258	0.06667559	215.35373195	14.35883708	0.00464352	0.06964352	43
44	15.97286209	0.06260619	230.35172453	14.42144327	0.00434119	0.06934119	44
45	17.01109813	0.05878515	246.32458662	14.48022842	0.00405968	0.06905968	45
46	18.11681951	0.05519733	263.33568475	14.53542575	0.00379743	0.06879743	46
47	19.29441278	0.05182848	281.45250426	14.58725422	0.00355300	0.06855300	47
48	20.54854961	0.04866524	300.74691704	14.63591946	0.00332505	0.06832505	48
49	21.88420533	0.04569506	321.29546665	14.68161451	0.00311240	0.06811240	49
50	23.30667868	0.04290616	343.17967198	14.72452067	0.00291393	0.06791393	50
80	154.15890683	0.00648681	2356.29087423	15.28481826	0.00042440	0.06542440	80
100	543.20127103	0.00184094	8341.55801588	15.35629326	0.00011988	0.06511988	100
120	1914.04847717	0.00052245	29431.51503337	15.37657765	0.00003398	0.06503398	120

Rate 7%	C Compound Amount	D Present Value	E Amount of Annuity	F Present Value of Annuity	G Sinking Fund	H Amortization	
n	$(1 + i)^n$	$(1 + i)^{-n}$	$S_{\overline{n}|i}$	$A_{\overline{n}|i}$	$1/S_{\overline{n}|i}$	$1/A_{\overline{n}|i}$	n
1	1.07000000	0.93457944	1.00000000	0.93457944	1.00000000	1.07000000	1
2	1.14490000	0.87343873	2.07000000	1.80801817	0.48309179	0.55309179	2
3	1.22504300	0.81629788	3.21490000	2.62431604	0.31105167	0.38105167	3
4	1.31079601	0.76289521	4.43994300	3.38721126	0.22522812	0.29522812	4
5	1.40255173	0.71298618	5.75073901	4.10019744	0.17389069	0.24389069	5
6	1.50073035	0.66634222	7.15329074	4.76653966	0.13979580	0.20979580	6
7	1.60578148	0.62274974	8.65402109	5.38928940	0.11555322	0.18555322	7
8	1.71818618	0.58200910	10.25980257	5.97129851	0.09746776	0.16746776	8
9	1.83845921	0.54393374	11.97798875	6.51523225	0.08348647	0.15348647	9
10	1.96715136	0.50834929	13.81644796	7.02358154	0.07237750	0.14237750	10
11	2.10485195	0.47509280	15.78359932	7.49867434	0.06335690	0.13335690	11
12	2.25219159	0.44401196	17.88845127	7.94268630	0.05590199	0.12590199	12
13	2.40984500	0.41496445	20.14064286	8.35765074	0.04965085	0.11965085	13
14	2.57853415	0.38781724	22.55048786	8.74546799	0.04434494	0.11434494	14
15	2.75903154	0.36244602	25.12902201	9.10791401	0.03979462	0.10979462	15
16	2.95216375	0.33873460	27.88805355	9.44664860	0.03585765	0.10585765	16
17	3.15881521	0.31657439	30.84021730	9.76322299	0.03242519	0.10242519	17
18	3.37993228	0.29586392	33.99903251	10.05908691	0.02941260	0.09941260	18
19	3.61652754	0.27650833	37.37896479	10.33559524	0.02675301	0.09675301	19
20	3.86968446	0.25841900	40.99549232	10.59401425	0.02439293	0.09439293	20
21	4.14056237	0.24151309	44.86517678	10.83552733	0.02228900	0.09228900	21
22	4.43040174	0.22571317	49.00573916	11.06124050	0.02040577	0.09040577	22
23	4.74052986	0.21094688	53.43614090	11.27218738	0.01871393	0.08871393	23
24	5.07236695	0.19714662	58.17667076	11.46933400	0.01718902	0.08718902	24
25	5.42743264	0.18424918	63.24903772	11.65358318	0.01581052	0.08581052	25
26	5.80735292	0.17219549	68.67647036	11.82577867	0.01456103	0.08456103	26
27	6.21386763	0.16093037	74.48382328	11.98670904	0.01342573	0.08342573	27
28	6.64883836	0.15040221	80.69769091	12.13711125	0.01239193	0.08239193	28
29	7.11425705	0.14056282	87.34652927	12.27767407	0.01144865	0.08144865	29
30	7.61225504	0.13136712	94.46078632	12.40904118	0.01058640	0.08058640	30
31	8.14511290	0.12277301	102.07304137	12.53181419	0.00979691	0.07979691	31
32	8.71527080	0.11474113	110.21815426	12.64655532	0.00907292	0.07907292	32
33	9.32533975	0.10723470	118.93342506	12.75379002	0.00840807	0.07840807	33
34	9.97811354	0.10021934	128.25876481	12.85400936	0.00779674	0.07779674	34
35	10.67658148	0.09366294	138.23687835	12.94767230	0.00723396	0.07723396	35
36	11.42394219	0.08753546	148.91345984	13.03520776	0.00671531	0.07671531	36
37	12.22361814	0.08180884	160.33740202	13.11701660	0.00623685	0.07623685	37
38	13.07927141	0.07645686	172.56102017	13.19347345	0.00579505	0.07579505	38
39	13.99482041	0.07145501	185.64029158	13.26492846	0.00538676	0.07538676	39
40	14.97445784	0.06678038	199.63511199	13.33170884	0.00500914	0.07500914	40
41	16.02266989	0.06241157	214.60956983	13.39412041	0.00465962	0.07465962	41
42	17.14425678	0.05832857	230.63223972	13.45244898	0.00433591	0.07433591	42
43	18.34435475	0.05451268	247.77649650	13.50696167	0.00403590	0.07403590	43
44	19.62845959	0.05094643	266.12085125	13.55790810	0.00375769	0.07375769	44
45	21.00245176	0.04761349	285.74931084	13.60552159	0.00349957	0.07349957	45
46	22.47262338	0.04449859	306.75176260	13.65002018	0.00325996	0.07325996	46
47	24.04570702	0.04158747	329.22438598	13.69160764	0.00303744	0.07303744	47
48	25.72890651	0.03886679	353.27009300	13.73047443	0.00283070	0.07283070	48
49	27.52992997	0.03632410	378.99899951	13.76679853	0.00263853	0.07263853	49
50	29.45702506	0.03394776	406.52892947	13.80074629	0.00245985	0.07245985	50
80	224.23438758	0.00445962	3189.06267969	14.22200544	0.00031357	0.07031357	80
100	867.71632557	0.00115245	12381.66179381	14.26925071	0.00008076	0.07008076	100
120	3357.78838289	0.00029782	47954.11975557	14.28145978	0.00002085	0.07002085	120

Rate 7½%	C Compound Amount	D Present Value	E Amount of Annuity	F Present Value of Annuity	G Sinking Fund	H Amortization	
n	$(1 + i)^n$	$(1 + i)^{-n}$	$S_{\overline{n}|i}$	$A_{\overline{n}|i}$	$1/S_{\overline{n}|i}$	$1/A_{\overline{n}|i}$	n
1	1.07500000	0.93023256	1.00000000	0.93023256	1.00000000	1.07500000	1
2	1.15562500	0.86533261	2.07500000	1.79556517	0.48192771	0.55692771	2
3	1.24229688	0.80496057	3.23062500	2.60052574	0.30953763	0.38453763	3
4	1.33546914	0.74880053	4.47292188	3.34932627	0.22356751	0.29856751	4
5	1.43562933	0.69655863	5.80839102	4.04588490	0.17216472	0.24716472	5
6	1.54330153	0.64796152	7.24402034	4.69384642	0.13804489	0.21304489	6
7	1.65904914	0.60275490	8.78732187	5.29660132	0.11380032	0.18880032	7
8	1.78347783	0.56070223	10.44637101	5.85730355	0.09572702	0.17072702	8
9	1.91723866	0.52158347	12.22984883	6.37888703	0.08176716	0.15676716	9
10	2.06103156	0.48519393	14.14708750	6.86408096	0.07068593	0.14568593	10
11	2.21560893	0.45134319	16.20811906	7.31542415	0.06169747	0.13669747	11
12	2.38177960	0.41985413	18.42372799	7.73527827	0.05427783	0.12927783	12
13	2.56041307	0.39056198	20.80550759	8.12584026	0.04806420	0.12306420	13
14	2.75244405	0.36331347	23.36592066	8.48915373	0.04279737	0.11779737	14
15	2.95887735	0.33796602	26.11836470	8.82711975	0.03828724	0.11328724	15
16	3.18079315	0.31438699	29.07724206	9.14150674	0.03439116	0.10939116	16
17	3.41935264	0.29245302	32.25803521	9.43395976	0.03100003	0.10600003	17
18	3.67580409	0.27204932	35.67738785	9.70600908	0.02802896	0.10302896	18
19	3.95148940	0.25306913	39.35319194	9.95907821	0.02541090	0.10041090	19
20	4.24785110	0.23541315	43.30468134	10.19449136	0.02309219	0.09809219	20
21	4.56643993	0.21898897	47.55253244	10.41348033	0.02102937	0.09602937	21
22	4.90892293	0.20371067	52.11897237	10.61719101	0.01918687	0.09418687	22
23	5.27709215	0.18949830	57.02789530	10.80668931	0.01753528	0.09253528	23
24	5.67287406	0.17627749	62.30498744	10.98296680	0.01605008	0.09105008	24
25	6.09833961	0.16397906	67.97786150	11.14694586	0.01471067	0.08971067	25
26	6.55571508	0.15253866	74.07620112	11.29948452	0.01349961	0.08849961	26
27	7.04739371	0.14189643	80.63191620	11.44138095	0.01240204	0.08740204	27
28	7.57594824	0.13199668	87.67930991	11.57337763	0.01140520	0.08640520	28
29	8.14414436	0.12278761	95.25525816	11.69616524	0.01049811	0.08549811	29
30	8.75495519	0.11422103	103.39940252	11.81038627	0.00967124	0.08467124	30
31	9.41157683	0.10625212	112.15435771	11.91663839	0.00891628	0.08391628	31
32	10.11744509	0.09883918	121.56593454	12.01547757	0.00822599	0.08322599	32
33	10.87625347	0.09194343	131.68337963	12.10742099	0.00759397	0.08259397	33
34	11.69197248	0.08552877	142.55963310	12.19294976	0.00701461	0.08201461	34
35	12.56887042	0.07956164	154.25160558	12.27251141	0.00648291	0.08148291	35
36	13.51153570	0.07401083	166.82047600	12.34652224	0.00599447	0.08099447	36
37	14.52490088	0.06884729	180.33201170	12.41536952	0.00554533	0.08054533	37
38	15.61426844	0.06404399	194.85691258	12.47941351	0.00513197	0.08013197	38
39	16.78533858	0.05957580	210.47118102	12.53898931	0.00475124	0.07975124	39
40	18.04423897	0.05541935	227.25651960	12.59440866	0.00440031	0.07940031	40
41	19.39755689	0.05155288	245.30075857	12.64596155	0.00407663	0.07907663	41
42	20.85237366	0.04795617	264.69831546	12.69391772	0.00377789	0.07877789	42
43	22.41630168	0.04461039	285.55068912	12.73852811	0.00350201	0.07850201	43
44	24.09752431	0.04149804	307.96699080	12.78002615	0.00324710	0.07824710	44
45	25.90483863	0.03860283	332.06451511	12.81862898	0.00301146	0.07801146	45
46	27.84770153	0.03590961	357.96935375	12.85453858	0.00279354	0.07779354	46
47	29.93627915	0.03340428	385.81705528	12.88794287	0.00259190	0.07759190	47
48	32.18150008	0.03107375	415.75333442	12.91901662	0.00240527	0.07740527	48
49	34.59511259	0.02890582	447.93483451	12.94792244	0.00223247	0.07723247	49
50	37.18974603	0.02688913	482.52994709	12.97481157	0.00207241	0.07707241	50
80	325.59456000	0.00307130	4327.92746666	13.29238261	0.00023106	0.07523106	80
100	1383.07720993	0.00072303	18427.69613233	13.32369299	0.00005427	0.07505427	100
120	5875.10604790	0.00017021	78321.41397195	13.33106387	0.00001277	0.07501277	120

Rate 8%	C Compound Amount	D Present Value	E Amount of Annuity	F Present Value of Annuity	G Sinking Fund	H Amortization	
n	$(1+i)^n$	$(1+i)^{-n}$	$S_{\overline{n}|i}$	$A_{\overline{n}|i}$	$1/S_{\overline{n}|i}$	$1/A_{\overline{n}|i}$	n
1	1.08000000	0.92592593	1.00000000	0.92592593	1.00000000	1.08000000	1
2	1.16640000	0.85733882	2.08000000	1.78326475	0.48076923	0.56076923	2
3	1.25971200	0.79383224	3.24640000	2.57709699	0.30803351	0.38803351	3
4	1.36048896	0.73502985	4.50611200	3.31212684	0.22192080	0.30192080	4
5	1.46932808	0.68058320	5.86660096	3.99271004	0.17045645	0.25045645	5
6	1.58687432	0.63016963	7.33592904	4.62287966	0.13631539	0.21631539	6
7	1.71382427	0.58349040	8.92280336	5.20637006	0.11207240	0.19207240	7
8	1.85093021	0.54026888	10.63662763	5.74663894	0.09401476	0.17401476	8
9	1.99900463	0.50024897	12.48755784	6.24688791	0.08007971	0.16007971	9
10	2.15892500	0.46319349	14.48656247	6.71008140	0.06902949	0.14902949	10
11	2.33163900	0.42888286	16.64548746	7.13896426	0.06007634	0.14007634	11
12	2.51817012	0.39711376	18.97712646	7.53607802	0.05269502	0.13269502	12
13	2.71962373	0.36769792	21.49529658	7.90377594	0.04652181	0.12652181	13
14	2.93719362	0.34046104	24.21492030	8.24423698	0.04129685	0.12129685	14
15	3.17216911	0.31524170	27.15211393	8.55947869	0.03682954	0.11682954	15
16	3.42594264	0.29189047	30.32428304	8.85136916	0.03297687	0.11297687	16
17	3.70001805	0.27026895	33.75022569	9.12163811	0.02962943	0.10962943	17
18	3.99601950	0.25024903	37.45024374	9.37188714	0.02670210	0.10670210	18
19	4.31570106	0.23171206	41.44626324	9.60359920	0.02412763	0.10412763	19
20	4.66095714	0.21454821	45.76196430	9.81814741	0.02185221	0.10185221	20
21	5.03383372	0.19865575	50.42292144	10.01680316	0.01983225	0.09983225	21
22	5.43654041	0.18394051	55.45675516	10.20074366	0.01803207	0.09803207	22
23	5.87146365	0.17031528	60.89329557	10.37105895	0.01642217	0.09642217	23
24	6.34118074	0.15769934	66.76475922	10.52875828	0.01497796	0.09497796	24
25	6.84847520	0.14601790	73.10593995	10.67477619	0.01367878	0.09367878	25
26	7.39635321	0.13520176	79.95441515	10.80997795	0.01250713	0.09250713	26
27	7.98806147	0.12518682	87.35076836	10.93516477	0.01144810	0.09144810	27
28	8.62710639	0.11591372	95.33882983	11.05107849	0.01048891	0.09048891	28
29	9.31727490	0.10732752	103.96593622	11.15840601	0.00961854	0.08961854	29
30	10.06265689	0.09937733	113.28321111	11.25778334	0.00882743	0.08882743	30
31	10.86766944	0.09201605	123.34586800	11.34979939	0.00810728	0.08810728	31
32	11.73708300	0.08520005	134.21353744	11.43499944	0.00745081	0.08745081	32
33	12.67604964	0.07888893	145.95062044	11.51388837	0.00685163	0.08685163	33
34	13.69013361	0.07304531	158.62667007	11.58693367	0.00630411	0.08630411	34
35	14.78534429	0.06763454	172.31680368	11.65456822	0.00580326	0.08580326	35
36	15.96817184	0.06262458	187.10214797	11.71719279	0.00534467	0.08534467	36
37	17.24562558	0.05798572	203.07031981	11.77517851	0.00492440	0.08492440	37
38	18.62527563	0.05369048	220.31594540	11.82886899	0.00453894	0.08453894	38
39	20.11529768	0.04971341	238.94122103	11.87858240	0.00418513	0.08418513	39
40	21.72452150	0.04603093	259.05651871	11.92461333	0.00386016	0.08386016	40
41	23.46248322	0.04262123	280.78104021	11.96723457	0.00356149	0.08356149	41
42	25.33948187	0.03946411	304.24352342	12.00669867	0.00328684	0.08328684	42
43	27.36664042	0.03654084	329.58300530	12.04323951	0.00303414	0.08303414	43
44	29.55597166	0.03383411	356.94964572	12.07707362	0.00280152	0.08280152	44
45	31.92044939	0.03132788	386.50561738	12.10840150	0.00258728	0.08258728	45
46	34.47408534	0.02900730	418.42606677	12.13740880	0.00238991	0.08238991	46
47	37.23201217	0.02685861	452.90015211	12.16426741	0.00220799	0.08220799	47
48	40.21057314	0.02486908	490.13216428	12.18913649	0.00204027	0.08204027	48
49	43.42741899	0.02302693	530.34273742	12.21216341	0.00188557	0.08188557	49
50	46.90161251	0.02132123	573.77015642	12.23348464	0.00174286	0.08174286	50
80	471.95483426	0.00211885	5886.93542831	12.47351441	0.00016987	0.08016987	80
100	2199.76125634	0.00045459	27484.51570427	12.49431757	0.00003638	0.08003638	100

Rate 8½%	C Compound Amount	D Present Value	E Amount of Annuity	F Present Value of Annuity	G Sinking Fund	H Amortization	
n	$(1 + i)^n$	$(1 + i)^{-n}$	$S_{\overline{n}|i}$	$A_{\overline{n}|i}$	$1/S_{\overline{n}|i}$	$1/A_{\overline{n}|i}$	n
1	1.08500000	0.92165899	1.00000000	0.92165899	1.00000000	1.08500000	1
2	1.17722500	0.84945529	2.08500000	1.77111427	0.47961631	0.56461631	2
3	1.27728913	0.78290810	3.26222500	2.55402237	0.30653925	0.39153925	3
4	1.38585870	0.72157428	4.53951413	3.27559666	0.22028789	0.30528789	4
5	1.50365669	0.66504542	5.92537283	3.94064208	0.16876575	0.25376575	5
6	1.63146751	0.61294509	7.42902952	4.55358717	0.13460708	0.21960708	6
7	1.77014225	0.56492635	9.06049702	5.11851352	0.11036922	0.19536922	7
8	1.92060434	0.52066945	10.83063927	5.63918297	0.09233065	0.17733065	8
9	2.08385571	0.47987968	12.75124361	6.11906264	0.07842372	0.16342372	9
10	2.26098344	0.44228542	14.83509932	6.56134806	0.06740771	0.15240771	10
11	2.45316703	0.40763633	17.09608276	6.96898439	0.05849293	0.14349293	11
12	2.66168623	0.37570168	19.54924979	7.34468607	0.05115286	0.13615286	12
13	2.88792956	0.34626883	22.21093603	7.69095490	0.04502287	0.13002287	13
14	3.13340357	0.31914178	25.09886559	8.01009668	0.03984244	0.12484244	14
15	3.39974288	0.29413989	28.23226916	8.30423658	0.03542046	0.12042046	15
16	3.68872102	0.27109667	31.63201204	8.57533325	0.03161354	0.11661354	16
17	4.00226231	0.24985869	35.32073306	8.82519194	0.02831198	0.11331198	17
18	4.34245461	0.23028450	39.32299538	9.05547644	0.02543041	0.11043041	18
19	4.71156325	0.21224378	43.66544998	9.26772022	0.02290140	0.10790140	19
20	5.11204612	0.19561639	48.37701323	9.46333661	0.02067097	0.10567097	20
21	5.54657005	0.18029160	53.48905936	9.64362821	0.01869541	0.10369541	21
22	6.01802850	0.16616738	59.03562940	9.80979559	0.01693892	0.10193892	22
23	6.52956092	0.15314965	65.05365790	9.96294524	0.01537193	0.10037193	23
24	7.08457360	0.14115176	71.58321882	10.10409700	0.01396975	0.09896975	24
25	7.68676236	0.13009378	78.66779242	10.23419078	0.01271168	0.09771168	25
26	8.34013716	0.11990210	86.35455478	10.35409288	0.01158017	0.09658017	26
27	9.04904881	0.11050885	94.69469193	10.46460174	0.01056025	0.09556025	27
28	9.81821796	0.10185148	103.74374075	10.56645321	0.00963914	0.09463914	28
29	10.65276649	0.09387233	113.56195871	10.66032554	0.00880577	0.09380577	29
30	11.55825164	0.08651828	124.21472520	10.74684382	0.00805058	0.09305058	30
31	12.54070303	0.07974035	135.77297684	10.82658416	0.00736524	0.09236524	31
32	13.60666279	0.07349341	148.31367987	10.90007757	0.00674247	0.09174247	32
33	14.76322913	0.06773586	161.92034266	10.96781343	0.00617588	0.09117588	33
34	16.01810340	0.06242906	176.68357179	11.03024279	0.00565984	0.09065984	34
35	17.37964241	0.05753858	192.70167539	11.08778137	0.00518937	0.09018937	35
36	18.85691201	0.05303095	210.08131780	11.14081233	0.00476006	0.08976006	36
37	20.45974953	0.04887645	228.93822981	11.18968878	0.00436799	0.08936799	37
38	22.19882824	0.04504742	249.39797935	11.23473620	0.00400966	0.08900966	38
39	24.08572865	0.04151836	271.59680759	11.27625457	0.00368193	0.08868193	39
40	26.13301558	0.03826577	295.68253624	11.31452034	0.00338201	0.08838201	40
41	28.35432190	0.03526799	321.81555182	11.34978833	0.00310737	0.08810737	41
42	30.76443927	0.03250506	350.16987372	11.38229339	0.00285576	0.08785576	42
43	33.37941660	0.02995858	380.93431299	11.41225197	0.00262512	0.08762512	43
44	36.21666702	0.02761160	414.31372959	11.43986357	0.00241363	0.08741363	44
45	39.29508371	0.02544848	450.53039661	11.46531205	0.00221961	0.08721961	45
46	42.63516583	0.02345482	489.82548032	11.48876686	0.00204154	0.08704154	46
47	46.25915492	0.02161734	532.46064615	11.51038420	0.00187807	0.08687807	47
48	50.19118309	0.01992382	578.71980107	11.53030802	0.00172795	0.08672795	48
49	54.45743365	0.01836297	628.91098416	11.54867099	0.00159005	0.08659005	49
50	59.08631551	0.01692439	683.36841782	11.56559538	0.00146334	0.08646334	50
80	682.93450332	0.00146427	8022.75886259	11.74747919	0.00012465	0.08512465	80
100	3491.19268107	0.00028644	41061.09036551	11.76133606	0.00002435	0.08502435	100

Rate 9%	C Compound Amount	D Present Value	E Amount of Annuity	F Present Value of Annuity	G Sinking Fund	H Amortization	
n	$(1 + i)^n$	$(1 + i)^{-n}$	$S_{\overline{n}|i}$	$A_{\overline{n}|i}$	$1/S_{\overline{n}|i}$	$1/A_{\overline{n}|i}$	n
1	1.09000000	0.91743119	1.00000000	0.91743119	1.00000000	1.09000000	1
2	1.18810000	0.84167999	2.09000000	1.75911119	0.47846890	0.56846890	2
3	1.29502900	0.77218348	3.27810000	2.53129467	0.30505476	0.39505476	3
4	1.41158161	0.70842521	4.57312900	3.23971988	0.21866866	0.30866866	4
5	1.53862395	0.64993139	5.98471061	3.88965126	0.16709246	0.25709246	5
6	1.67710011	0.59626733	7.52333456	4.48591859	0.13291978	0.22291978	6
7	1.82803912	0.54703424	9.20043468	5.03295284	0.10869052	0.19869052	7
8	1.99256264	0.50186628	11.02847380	5.53481911	0.09067438	0.18067438	8
9	2.17189328	0.46042778	13.02103644	5.99524689	0.07679880	0.16679880	9
10	2.36736367	0.42241081	15.19292972	6.41765770	0.06582009	0.15582009	10
11	2.58042641	0.38753285	17.56029339	6.80519055	0.05694666	0.14694666	11
12	2.81266478	0.35553473	20.14071980	7.16072528	0.04965066	0.13965066	12
13	3.06580461	0.32617865	22.95338458	7.48690392	0.04356656	0.13356656	13
14	3.34172703	0.29924647	26.01918919	7.78615039	0.03843317	0.12843317	14
15	3.64248246	0.27453804	29.36091622	8.06068843	0.03405888	0.12405888	15
16	3.97030588	0.25186976	33.00339868	8.31255819	0.03029991	0.12029991	16
17	4.32763341	0.23107318	36.97370456	8.54363137	0.02704625	0.11704625	17
18	4.71712042	0.21199374	41.30133797	8.75562511	0.02421229	0.11421229	18
19	5.14166125	0.19448967	46.01845839	8.95011478	0.02173041	0.11173041	19
20	5.60441077	0.17843089	51.16011964	9.12854567	0.01954648	0.10954648	20
21	6.10880774	0.16369806	56.76453041	9.29224373	0.01761663	0.10761663	21
22	6.65860043	0.15018171	62.87333815	9.44242544	0.01590499	0.10590499	22
23	7.25787447	0.13778139	69.53193858	9.58020683	0.01438188	0.10438188	23
24	7.91108317	0.12640494	76.78981305	9.70661177	0.01302256	0.10302256	24
25	8.62308066	0.11596784	84.70089623	9.82257960	0.01180625	0.10180625	25
26	9.39915792	0.10639251	93.32397689	9.92897211	0.01071536	0.10071536	26
27	10.24508213	0.09760781	102.72313481	10.02657992	0.00973491	0.09973491	27
28	11.16713952	0.08954845	112.96821694	10.11612837	0.00885205	0.09885205	28
29	12.17218208	0.08215454	124.13535646	10.19828291	0.00805572	0.09805572	29
30	13.26767847	0.07537114	136.30753855	10.27365404	0.00733635	0.09733635	30
31	14.46176953	0.06914783	149.57521702	10.34280187	0.00668560	0.09668560	31
32	15.76332879	0.06343838	164.03698655	10.40624025	0.00609619	0.09609619	32
33	17.18202838	0.05820035	179.80031534	10.46444000	0.00556173	0.09556173	33
34	18.72841093	0.05339481	196.98234372	10.51783541	0.00507660	0.09507660	34
35	20.41396792	0.04898607	215.71075465	10.56682148	0.00463584	0.09463584	35
36	22.25122503	0.04494135	236.12472257	10.61176282	0.00423505	0.09423505	36
37	24.25383528	0.04123059	258.37594760	10.65299342	0.00387033	0.09387033	37
38	26.43668046	0.03782623	282.62978288	10.69081965	0.00353820	0.09353820	38
39	28.81598170	0.03470296	309.06646334	10.72552261	0.00323555	0.09323555	39
40	31.40942005	0.03183758	337.88244504	10.75736020	0.00295961	0.09295961	40
41	34.23626786	0.02920879	369.29186510	10.78656899	0.00270789	0.09270789	41
42	37.31753197	0.02679706	403.52813296	10.81336604	0.00247814	0.09247814	42
43	40.67610984	0.02458446	440.84566492	10.83795050	0.00226837	0.09226837	43
44	44.33695973	0.02255455	481.52177477	10.86050504	0.00207675	0.09207675	44
45	48.32728610	0.02069224	525.85873450	10.88119729	0.00190165	0.09190165	45
46	52.67674185	0.01898371	574.18602060	10.90018100	0.00174160	0.09174160	46
47	57.41764862	0.01741625	626.86276245	10.91759725	0.00159525	0.09159525	47
48	62.58523700	0.01597821	684.28041107	10.93357546	0.00146139	0.09146139	48
49	68.21790833	0.01465891	746.86564807	10.94823436	0.00133893	0.09133893	49
50	74.35752008	0.01344854	815.08355640	10.96168290	0.00122687	0.09122687	50
80	986.55166813	0.00101363	10950.57409031	11.09984854	0.00009132	0.09009132	80
100	5529.04079183	0.00018086	61422.67546473	11.10910152	0.00001628	0.09001628	100

Rate 9½%	C Compound Amount	D Present Value	E Amount of Annuity	F Present Value of Annuity	G Sinking Fund	H Amortization	
n	$(1 + i)^n$	$(1 + i)^{-n}$	$S_{\overline{n}|i}$	$A_{\overline{n}|i}$	$1/S_{\overline{n}|i}$	$1/A_{\overline{n}|i}$	n
1	1.09500000	0.91324201	1.00000000	0.91324201	1.00000000	1.09500000	1
2	1.19902500	0.83401097	2.09500000	1.74725298	0.47732697	0.57232697	2
3	1.31293237	0.76165385	3.29402500	2.50890683	0.30357997	0.39857997	3
4	1.43766095	0.69557429	4.60695737	3.20448112	0.21706300	0.31206300	4
5	1.57423874	0.63522767	6.04461833	3.83970879	0.16543642	0.26043642	5
6	1.72379142	0.58011659	7.61885707	4.41982538	0.13125328	0.22625328	6
7	1.88755161	0.52978684	9.34264849	4.94961222	0.10703603	0.20203603	7
8	2.06686901	0.48382360	11.23020009	5.43343581	0.08904561	0.18404561	8
9	2.26322156	0.44184803	13.29706910	5.87528385	0.07520454	0.17020454	9
10	2.47822761	0.40351419	15.56029067	6.27879803	0.06426615	0.15926615	10
11	2.71365924	0.36850611	18.03851828	6.64730414	0.05543693	0.15043693	11
12	2.97145686	0.33653526	20.75217752	6.98383940	0.04818771	0.14318771	12
13	3.25374527	0.30733813	23.72363438	7.29117753	0.04215206	0.13715206	13
14	3.56285107	0.28067410	26.97737965	7.57185163	0.03706809	0.13206809	14
15	3.90132192	0.25632337	30.54023072	7.82817500	0.03274370	0.12774370	15
16	4.27194750	0.23408527	34.44155263	8.06226028	0.02903470	0.12403470	16
17	4.67778251	0.21371651	38.71350013	8.27603678	0.02583078	0.12083078	17
18	5.12217185	0.19522969	43.39128265	8.47126647	0.02304610	0.11804610	18
19	5.60877818	0.17829195	48.51345450	8.64955842	0.02061284	0.11561284	19
20	6.14161210	0.16282370	54.12223267	8.81238212	0.01847670	0.11347670	20
21	6.72506525	0.14869744	60.26384478	8.96107956	0.01659370	0.11159370	21
22	7.36394645	0.13579675	66.98891003	9.09687631	0.01492784	0.10992784	22
23	8.06352137	0.12401530	74.35285649	9.22089161	0.01344938	0.10844938	23
24	8.82955590	0.11325598	82.41637785	9.33414759	0.01213351	0.10713351	24
25	9.66836371	0.10343012	91.24593375	9.43757770	0.01095939	0.10595939	25
26	10.58685826	0.09445673	100.91429745	9.53203443	0.00990940	0.10490940	26
27	11.59260979	0.08626185	111.50115571	9.61829629	0.00896852	0.10396852	27
28	12.69390772	0.07877795	123.09376551	9.69707423	0.00812389	0.10312389	28
29	13.89982896	0.07194333	135.78767323	9.76901756	0.00736444	0.10236444	29
30	15.22031271	0.06570167	149.68750218	9.83471924	0.00668058	0.10168058	30
31	16.66624241	0.06000153	164.90781489	9.89472076	0.00606399	0.10106399	31
32	18.24953544	0.05479592	181.57405731	9.94951668	0.00550739	0.10050739	32
33	19.98324193	0.05004193	199.82359275	9.99955861	0.00500441	0.10000441	33
34	21.88164924	0.04570039	219.80683406	10.04525901	0.00454945	0.09954945	34
35	23.96040591	0.04173552	241.68848330	10.08699453	0.00413756	0.09913756	35
36	26.23664448	0.03811463	265.64888921	10.12510916	0.00376437	0.09876437	36
37	28.72912570	0.03480788	291.88553369	10.15991704	0.00342600	0.09842600	37
38	31.45839264	0.03178802	320.61465939	10.19170506	0.00311901	0.09811901	38
39	34.44693994	0.02903015	352.07305203	10.22073521	0.00284032	0.09784032	39
40	37.71939924	0.02651156	386.51999197	10.24724677	0.00258719	0.09758719	40
41	41.30274216	0.02421147	424.23939121	10.27145824	0.00235716	0.09735716	41
42	45.22650267	0.02211093	465.54213337	10.29356917	0.00214803	0.09714803	42
43	49.52302042	0.02019263	510.76863604	10.31376180	0.00195783	0.09695783	43
44	54.22770736	0.01844076	560.29165647	10.33220255	0.00178478	0.09678478	44
45	59.37933956	0.01684087	614.51936383	10.34904343	0.00162729	0.09662729	45
46	65.02037682	0.01537979	673.89870340	10.36442322	0.00148390	0.09648390	46
47	71.19731262	0.01404547	738.91908022	10.37846870	0.00135333	0.09635333	47
48	77.96105732	0.01282692	810.11639284	10.39129561	0.00123439	0.09623439	48
49	85.36735777	0.01171408	888.07745016	10.40300969	0.00112603	0.09612603	49
50	93.47725675	0.01069779	973.44480793	10.41370748	0.00102728	0.09602728	50
80	1422.75307883	0.00070286	14965.82188238	10.51891724	0.00006682	0.09506682	80
100	8737.99753007	0.00011444	91968.39505341	10.52511113	0.00001087	0.09501087	100

Rate 10%	C Compound Amount	D Present Value	E Amount of Annuity	F Present Value of Annuity	G Sinking Fund	H Amortization	
n	$(1 + i)^n$	$(1 + i)^{-n}$	$S_{\overline{n}|i}$	$A_{\overline{n}|i}$	$1/S_{\overline{n}|i}$	$1/A_{\overline{n}|i}$	n
1	1.10000000	0.90909091	1.00000000	0.90909091	1.00000000	1.10000000	1
2	1.21000000	0.82644628	2.10000000	1.73553719	0.47619048	0.57619048	2
3	1.33100000	0.75131480	3.31000000	2.48685199	0.30211480	0.40211480	3
4	1.46410000	0.68301346	4.64100000	3.16986545	0.21547080	0.31547080	4
5	1.61051000	0.62092132	6.10510000	3.79078677	0.16379748	0.26379748	5
6	1.77156100	0.56447393	7.71561000	4.35526070	0.12960738	0.22960738	6
7	1.94871710	0.51315812	9.48717100	4.86841882	0.10540550	0.20540550	7
8	2.14358881	0.46650738	11.43588810	5.33492620	0.08744402	0.18744402	8
9	2.35794769	0.42409762	13.57947691	5.75902382	0.07364054	0.17364054	9
10	2.59374246	0.38554329	15.93742460	6.14456711	0.06274539	0.16274539	10
11	2.85311671	0.35049390	18.53116706	6.49506101	0.05396314	0.15396314	11
12	3.13842838	0.31863082	21.38428377	6.81369182	0.04676332	0.14676332	12
13	3.45227121	0.28966438	24.52271214	7.10335620	0.04077852	0.14077852	13
14	3.79749834	0.26333125	27.97498336	7.36668746	0.03574622	0.13574622	14
15	4.17724817	0.23939205	31.77248169	7.60607951	0.03147378	0.13147378	15
16	4.59497299	0.21762914	35.94972986	7.82370864	0.02781662	0.12781662	16
17	5.05447028	0.19784467	40.54470285	8.02155331	0.02466413	0.12466413	17
18	5.55991731	0.17985879	45.59917313	8.20141210	0.02193022	0.12193022	18
19	6.11590904	0.16350799	51.15909045	8.36492009	0.01954687	0.11954687	19
20	6.72749995	0.14864363	57.27499949	8.51356372	0.01745962	0.11745962	20
21	7.40024994	0.13513057	64.00249944	8.64869429	0.01562439	0.11562439	21
22	8.14027494	0.12284597	71.40274939	8.77154026	0.01400506	0.11400506	22
23	8.95430243	0.11167816	79.54302433	8.88321842	0.01257181	0.11257181	23
24	9.84973268	0.10152560	88.49732676	8.98474402	0.01129978	0.11129978	24
25	10.83470594	0.09229600	98.34705943	9.07704002	0.01016807	0.11016807	25
26	11.91817654	0.08390545	109.18176538	9.16094547	0.00915904	0.10915904	26
27	13.10999419	0.07627768	121.09994191	9.23722316	0.00825764	0.10825764	27
28	14.42099361	0.06934335	134.20993611	9.30656651	0.00745101	0.10745101	28
29	15.86309297	0.06303941	148.63092972	9.36960591	0.00672807	0.10672807	29
30	17.44940227	0.05730855	164.49402269	9.42691447	0.00607925	0.10607925	30
31	19.19434250	0.05209868	181.94342496	9.47901315	0.00549621	0.10549621	31
32	21.11377675	0.04736244	201.13776745	9.52637559	0.00497172	0.10497172	32
33	23.22515442	0.04305676	222.25154420	9.56943236	0.00449941	0.10449941	33
34	25.54766986	0.03914251	245.47669862	9.60857487	0.00407371	0.10407371	34
35	28.10243685	0.03558410	271.02436848	9.64415897	0.00368971	0.10368971	35
36	30.91268053	0.03234918	299.12680533	9.67650816	0.00334306	0.10334306	36
37	34.00394859	0.02940835	330.03948586	9.70591651	0.00302994	0.10302994	37
38	37.40434344	0.02673486	364.04343445	9.73265137	0.00274692	0.10274692	38
39	41.14477779	0.02430442	401.44777789	9.75695579	0.00249098	0.10249098	39
40	45.25925557	0.02209493	442.59255568	9.77905072	0.00225941	0.10225941	40
41	49.78518112	0.02008630	487.85181125	9.79913702	0.00204980	0.10204980	41
42	54.76369924	0.01826027	537.63699237	9.81739729	0.00185999	0.10185999	42
43	60.24006916	0.01660025	592.40069161	9.83399753	0.00168805	0.10168805	43
44	66.26407608	0.01509113	652.64076077	9.84908867	0.00153224	0.10153224	44
45	72.89048369	0.01371921	718.90483685	9.86280788	0.00139100	0.10139100	45
46	80.17953205	0.01247201	791.79532054	9.87527989	0.00126295	0.10126295	46
47	88.19748526	0.01133819	871.97485259	9.88661808	0.00114682	0.10114682	47
48	97.01723378	0.01030745	960.17233785	9.89692553	0.00104148	0.10104148	48
49	106.71895716	0.00937041	1057.18957163	9.90629594	0.00094590	0.10094590	49
50	117.39085288	0.00851855	1163.90852880	9.91481449	0.00085917	0.10085917	50
80	2048.40021459	0.00048819	20474.00214585	9.99511814	0.00004884	0.10004884	80

Rate 11%	C Compound Amount	D Present Value	E Amount of Annuity	F Present Value of Annuity	G Sinking Fund	H Amortization	
n	$(1 + i)^n$	$(1 + i)^{-n}$	$S_{\overline{n}|i}$	$A_{\overline{n}|i}$	$1/S_{\overline{n}|i}$	$1/A_{\overline{n}|i}$	n
1	1.11000000	0.90090090	1.00000000	0.90090090	1.00000000	1.11000000	1
2	1.23210000	0.81162243	2.11000000	1.71252333	0.47393365	0.58393365	2
3	1.36763100	0.73119138	3.34210000	2.44371472	0.29921307	0.40921307	3
4	1.51807041	0.65873097	4.70973100	3.10244569	0.21232635	0.32232635	4
5	1.68505816	0.59345133	6.22780141	3.69589702	0.16057031	0.27057031	5
6	1.87041455	0.53464084	7.91285957	4.23053785	0.12637656	0.23637656	6
7	2.07616015	0.48165841	9.78327412	4.71219626	0.10221527	0.21221527	7
8	2.30453777	0.43392650	11.85943427	5.14612276	0.08432105	0.19432105	8
9	2.55803692	0.39092477	14.16397204	5.53704753	0.07060166	0.18060166	9
10	2.83942099	0.35218448	16.72200896	5.88923201	0.05980143	0.16980143	10
11	3.15175729	0.31728331	19.56142995	6.20651533	0.05112101	0.16112101	11
12	3.49845060	0.28584082	22.71318724	6.49235615	0.04402729	0.15402729	12
13	3.88328016	0.25751426	26.21163784	6.74987040	0.03815099	0.14815099	13
14	4.31044098	0.23199482	30.09491800	6.98186523	0.03322820	0.14322820	14
15	4.78458949	0.20900435	34.40535898	7.19086958	0.02906524	0.13906524	15
16	5.31089433	0.18829220	39.18994847	7.37916178	0.02551675	0.13551675	16
17	5.89509271	0.16963262	44.50084281	7.54879440	0.02247148	0.13247148	17
18	6.54355291	0.15282218	50.39593551	7.70161657	0.01984287	0.12984287	18
19	7.26334373	0.13767764	56.93948842	7.83929421	0.01756250	0.12756250	19
20	8.06231154	0.12403391	64.20283215	7.96332812	0.01557564	0.12557564	20
21	8.94916581	0.11174226	72.26514368	8.07507038	0.01383793	0.12383793	21
22	9.93357404	0.10066870	81.21430949	8.17573908	0.01231310	0.12231310	22
23	11.02626719	0.09069252	91.14788353	8.26643160	0.01097118	0.12097118	23
24	12.23915658	0.08170498	102.17415072	8.34813658	0.00978721	0.11978721	24
25	13.58546380	0.07360809	114.41330730	8.42174466	0.00874024	0.11874024	25
26	15.07986482	0.06631359	127.99877110	8.48805826	0.00781258	0.11781258	26
27	16.73864995	0.05974197	143.07863592	8.54780023	0.00698916	0.11698916	27
28	18.57990145	0.05382160	159.81728587	8.60162183	0.00625715	0.11625715	28
29	20.62369061	0.04848793	178.39718732	8.65010976	0.00560547	0.11560547	29
30	22.89229657	0.04368282	199.02087793	8.69379257	0.00502460	0.11502460	30
31	25.41044919	0.03935389	221.91317450	8.73314646	0.00450627	0.11450627	31
32	28.20559861	0.03545395	247.32362369	8.76860042	0.00404329	0.11404329	32
33	31.30821445	0.03194050	275.52922230	8.80054092	0.00362938	0.11362938	33
34	34.75211804	0.02877522	306.83743675	8.82931614	0.00325905	0.11325905	34
35	38.57485103	0.02592363	341.58955480	8.85523977	0.00292749	0.11292749	35
36	42.81808464	0.02335462	380.16440582	8.87859438	0.00263044	0.11263044	36
37	47.52807395	0.02104020	422.98249046	8.89963458	0.00236416	0.11236416	37
38	52.75616209	0.01895513	470.51056441	8.91858971	0.00212535	0.11212535	38
39	58.55933991	0.01707670	523.26672650	8.93566641	0.00191107	0.11191107	39
40	65.00086731	0.01538441	581.82606641	8.95105082	0.00171873	0.11171873	40
41	72.15096271	0.01385983	646.82693372	8.96491065	0.00154601	0.11154601	41
42	80.08756861	0.01248633	718.97789643	8.97739698	0.00139086	0.11139086	42
43	88.89720115	0.01124895	799.06546504	8.98864593	0.00125146	0.11125146	43
44	98.67589328	0.01013419	887.96266619	8.99878011	0.00112617	0.11112617	44
45	109.53024154	0.00912990	986.63855947	9.00791001	0.00101354	0.11101354	45
46	121.57856811	0.00822513	1096.16880101	9.01613515	0.00091227	0.11091227	46
47	134.95221060	0.00741003	1217.74736912	9.02354518	0.00082119	0.11082119	47
48	149.79695377	0.00667570	1352.69957973	9.03022088	0.00073926	0.11073926	48
49	166.27461868	0.00601415	1502.49653350	9.03623503	0.00066556	0.11066556	49
50	184.56482674	0.00541815	1668.77115218	9.04165318	0.00059924	0.11059924	50
80	4225.11275048	0.00023668	38401.02500437	9.08875745	0.00002604	0.11002604	80

Rate 12%	C Compound Amount	D Present Value	E Amount of Annuity	F Present Value of Annuity	G Sinking Fund	H Amortization	
n	$(1 + i)^n$	$(1 + i)^{-n}$	$S_{\overline{n}|i}$	$A_{\overline{n}|i}$	$1/S_{\overline{n}|i}$	$1/A_{\overline{n}|i}$	n
1	1.12000000	0.89285714	1.00000000	0.89285714	1.00000000	1.12000000	1
2	1.25440000	0.79719388	2.12000000	1.69005102	0.47169811	0.59169811	2
3	1.40492800	0.71178025	3.37440000	2.40183127	0.29634898	0.41634898	3
4	1.57351936	0.63551808	4.77932800	3.03734935	0.20923444	0.32923444	4
5	1.76234168	0.56742686	6.35284736	3.60477620	0.15740973	0.27740973	5
6	1.97382269	0.50663112	8.11518904	4.11140732	0.12322572	0.24322572	6
7	2.21068141	0.45234922	10.08901173	4.56375654	0.09911774	0.21911774	7
8	2.47596318	0.40388323	12.29969314	4.96763977	0.08130284	0.20130284	8
9	2.77307876	0.36061002	14.77565631	5.32824979	0.06767889	0.18767889	9
10	3.10584821	0.32197324	17.54873507	5.65022303	0.05698416	0.17698416	10
11	3.47854999	0.28747610	20.65458328	5.93769913	0.04841540	0.16841540	11
12	3.89597599	0.25667509	24.13313327	6.19437423	0.04143681	0.16143681	12
13	4.36349311	0.22917419	28.02910926	6.42354842	0.03567720	0.15567720	13
14	4.88711229	0.20461981	32.39260238	6.62816823	0.03087125	0.15087125	14
15	5.47356576	0.18269626	37.27971466	6.81086449	0.02682424	0.14682424	15
16	6.13039365	0.16312166	42.75328042	6.97398615	0.02339002	0.14339002	16
17	6.86604089	0.14564434	48.88367407	7.11963049	0.02045673	0.14045673	17
18	7.68996580	0.13003959	55.74971496	7.24967008	0.01793731	0.13793731	18
19	8.61276169	0.11610678	63.43968075	7.36577686	0.01576300	0.13576300	19
20	9.64629309	0.10366677	72.05244244	7.46944362	0.01387878	0.13387878	20
21	10.80384826	0.09255961	81.69873554	7.56200324	0.01224009	0.13224009	21
22	12.10031006	0.08264251	92.50258380	7.64464575	0.01081051	0.13081051	22
23	13.55234726	0.07378796	104.60289386	7.71843370	0.00955996	0.12955996	23
24	15.17862893	0.06588210	118.15524112	7.78431581	0.00846344	0.12846344	24
25	17.00006441	0.05882331	133.33387006	7.84313911	0.00749997	0.12749997	25
26	19.04007214	0.05252081	150.33393446	7.89565992	0.00665186	0.12665186	26
27	21.32488079	0.04689358	169.37400660	7.94255350	0.00590409	0.12590409	27
28	23.88386649	0.04186927	190.69888739	7.98442277	0.00524387	0.12524387	28
29	26.74993047	0.03738327	214.58275388	8.02180604	0.00466021	0.12466021	29
30	29.95992212	0.03337792	241.33268434	8.05518397	0.00414366	0.12414366	30
31	33.55511278	0.02980172	271.29260646	8.08498569	0.00368606	0.12368606	31
32	37.58172631	0.02660868	304.84771924	8.11159436	0.00328033	0.12328033	32
33	42.09153347	0.02375775	342.42944555	8.13535211	0.00292031	0.12292031	33
34	47.14251748	0.02121227	384.52097901	8.15656438	0.00260064	0.12260064	34
35	52.79961958	0.01893953	431.66349649	8.17550391	0.00231662	0.12231662	35
36	59.13557393	0.01691029	484.46311607	8.19241421	0.00206414	0.12206414	36
37	66.23184280	0.01509848	543.59869000	8.20751269	0.00183959	0.12183959	37
38	74.17966394	0.01348078	609.83053280	8.22099347	0.00163980	0.12163980	38
39	83.08122361	0.01203641	684.01019674	8.23302988	0.00146197	0.12146197	39
40	93.05097044	0.01074680	767.09142034	8.24377668	0.00130363	0.12130363	40
41	104.21708689	0.00959536	860.14239079	8.25337204	0.00116260	0.12116260	41
42	116.72313732	0.00856728	964.35947768	8.26193932	0.00103696	0.12103696	42
43	130.72991380	0.00764936	1081.08261500	8.26958868	0.00092500	0.12092500	43
44	146.41750346	0.00682978	1211.81252880	8.27641846	0.00082521	0.12082521	44
45	163.98760387	0.00609802	1358.23003226	8.28251648	0.00073625	0.12073625	45
46	183.66611634	0.00544466	1522.21763613	8.28796115	0.00065694	0.12065694	46
47	205.70605030	0.00486131	1705.88375247	8.29282245	0.00058621	0.12058621	47
48	230.39077633	0.00434045	1911.58980276	8.29716290	0.00052312	0.12052312	48
49	258.03766949	0.00387540	2141.98057909	8.30103831	0.00046686	0.12046686	49
50	289.00218983	0.00346018	2400.01824858	8.30449849	0.00041666	0.12041666	50
80	8658.48310008	0.00011549	72145.69250066	8.33237089	0.00001386	0.12001386	80

Rate 13%	C Compound Amount	D Present Value	E Amount of Annuity	F Present Value of Annuity	G Sinking Fund	H Amortization	
n	$(1 + i)^n$	$(1 + i)^{-n}$	$S_{\overline{n}|i}$	$A_{\overline{n}|i}$	$1/S_{\overline{n}|i}$	$1/A_{\overline{n}|i}$	n
1	1.13000000	0.88495575	1.00000000	0.88495575	1.00000000	1.13000000	1
2	1.27690000	0.78314668	2.13000000	1.66810244	0.46948357	0.59948357	2
3	1.44289700	0.69305016	3.40690000	2.36115260	0.29352197	0.42352197	3
4	1.63047361	0.61331873	4.84979700	2.97447133	0.20619420	0.33619420	4
5	1.84243518	0.54275994	6.48027061	3.51723126	0.15431454	0.28431454	5
6	2.08195175	0.48031853	8.32270579	3.99754979	0.12015323	0.25015323	6
7	2.35260548	0.42506064	10.40465754	4.42261043	0.09611080	0.22611080	7
8	2.65844419	0.37615986	12.75726302	4.79877029	0.07838672	0.20838672	8
9	3.00404194	0.33288483	15.41570722	5.13165513	0.06486890	0.19486890	9
10	3.39456739	0.29458835	18.41974915	5.42624348	0.05428956	0.18428956	10
11	3.83586115	0.26069765	21.81431654	5.68694113	0.04584145	0.17584145	11
12	4.33452310	0.23070589	25.65017769	5.91764702	0.03898608	0.16898608	12
13	4.89801110	0.20416450	29.98470079	6.12181152	0.03335034	0.16335034	13
14	5.53475255	0.18067655	34.88271190	6.30248807	0.02866750	0.15866750	14
15	6.25427038	0.15989075	40.41746444	6.46237882	0.02474178	0.15474178	15
16	7.06732553	0.14149624	46.67173482	6.60387506	0.02142624	0.15142624	16
17	7.98607785	0.12521791	53.73906035	6.72909298	0.01860844	0.14860844	17
18	9.02426797	0.11081231	61.72513819	6.83990529	0.01620085	0.14620085	18
19	10.19742280	0.09806399	70.74940616	6.93796928	0.01413439	0.14413439	19
20	11.52308776	0.08678229	80.94682896	7.02475158	0.01235379	0.14235379	20
21	13.02108917	0.07679849	92.46991672	7.10155007	0.01081433	0.14081433	21
22	14.71383077	0.06796327	105.49100590	7.16951334	0.00947948	0.13947948	22
23	16.62662877	0.06014448	120.20483667	7.22965782	0.00831913	0.13831913	23
24	18.78809051	0.05322521	136.83146543	7.28288303	0.00730826	0.13730826	24
25	21.23054227	0.04710195	155.61955594	7.32998498	0.00642593	0.13642593	25
26	23.99051277	0.04168314	176.85009821	7.37166812	0.00565451	0.13565451	26
27	27.10927943	0.03688774	200.84061098	7.40855586	0.00497907	0.13497907	27
28	30.63348575	0.03264402	227.94989040	7.44119988	0.00438693	0.13438693	28
29	34.61583890	0.02888851	258.58337616	7.47008839	0.00386722	0.13386722	29
30	39.11589796	0.02556505	293.19921506	7.49565344	0.00341065	0.13341065	30
31	44.20096469	0.02262394	332.31511301	7.51827738	0.00300919	0.13300919	31
32	49.94709010	0.02002119	376.51607771	7.53829857	0.00265593	0.13265593	32
33	56.44021181	0.01771786	426.46316781	7.55601643	0.00234487	0.13234487	33
34	63.77743935	0.01567953	482.90337962	7.57169596	0.00207081	0.13207081	34
35	72.06850647	0.01387569	546.68081897	7.58557164	0.00182922	0.13182922	35
36	81.43741231	0.01227937	618.74932544	7.59785101	0.00161616	0.13161616	36
37	92.02427591	0.01086670	700.18673775	7.60871771	0.00142819	0.13142819	37
38	103.98743178	0.00961655	792.21101365	7.61833426	0.00126229	0.13126229	38
39	117.50579791	0.00851022	896.19844543	7.62684447	0.00111582	0.13111582	39
40	132.78155163	0.00753117	1013.70424333	7.63437564	0.00098648	0.13098648	40
41	150.04315335	0.00666475	1146.48579497	7.64104039	0.00087223	0.13087223	41
42	169.54876328	0.00589801	1296.52894831	7.64693840	0.00077129	0.13077129	42
43	191.59010251	0.00521948	1466.07771159	7.65215787	0.00068209	0.13068209	43
44	216.49681583	0.00461901	1657.66781410	7.65677688	0.00060326	0.13060326	44
45	244.64140189	0.00408762	1874.16462994	7.66086450	0.00053357	0.13053357	45
46	276.44478414	0.00361736	2118.80603183	7.66448185	0.00047196	0.13047196	46
47	312.38260608	0.00320120	2395.25081596	7.66768306	0.00041749	0.13041749	47
48	352.99234487	0.00283292	2707.63342204	7.67051598	0.00036933	0.13036933	48
49	398.88134970	0.00250701	3060.62576691	7.67302299	0.00032673	0.13032673	49
50	450.73592516	0.00221859	3459.50711660	7.67524158	0.00028906	0.13028906	50

Rate 14%	C Compound Amount	D Present Value	E Amount of Annuity	F Present Value of Annuity	G Sinking Fund	H Amortization	
n	$(1 + i)^n$	$(1 + i)^{-n}$	$S_{\overline{n}|i}$	$A_{\overline{n}|i}$	$1/S_{\overline{n}|i}$	$1/A_{\overline{n}|i}$	n
1	1.14000000	0.87719298	1.00000000	0.87719298	1.00000000	1.14000000	1
2	1.29960000	0.76946753	2.14000000	1.64666051	0.46728972	0.60728972	2
3	1.48154400	0.67497152	3.43960000	2.32163203	0.29073148	0.43073148	3
4	1.68896016	0.59208028	4.92114400	2.91371230	0.20320478	0.34320478	4
5	1.92541458	0.51936866	6.61010416	3.43308097	0.15128355	0.29128355	5
6	2.19497262	0.45558655	8.53551874	3.88866752	0.11715750	0.25715750	6
7	2.50226879	0.39963732	10.73049137	4.28830484	0.09319238	0.23319238	7
8	2.85258642	0.35055905	13.23276016	4.63886389	0.07557002	0.21557002	8
9	3.25194852	0.30750794	16.08534658	4.94637184	0.06216838	0.20216838	9
10	3.70722131	0.26974381	19.33729510	5.21611565	0.05171354	0.19171354	10
11	4.22623230	0.23661738	23.04451641	5.45273302	0.04339427	0.18339427	11
12	4.81790482	0.20755910	27.27074871	5.66029213	0.03666933	0.17666933	12
13	5.49241149	0.18206939	32.08865353	5.84236151	0.03116366	0.17116366	13
14	6.26134910	0.15970999	37.58106503	6.00207150	0.02660914	0.16660914	14
15	7.13793798	0.14009648	43.84241413	6.14216799	0.02280896	0.16280896	15
16	8.13724930	0.12289165	50.98035211	6.26505964	0.01961540	0.15961540	16
17	9.27646420	0.10779969	59.11760141	6.37285933	0.01691544	0.15691544	17
18	10.57516918	0.09456113	68.39406560	6.46742046	0.01462115	0.15462115	18
19	12.05569287	0.08294836	78.96923479	6.55036883	0.01266316	0.15266316	19
20	13.74348987	0.07276172	91.02492766	6.62313055	0.01098600	0.15098600	20
21	15.66757845	0.06382607	104.76841753	6.68695662	0.00954486	0.14954486	21
22	17.86103944	0.05598778	120.43599598	6.74294441	0.00830317	0.14830317	22
23	20.36158496	0.04911209	138.29703542	6.79205650	0.00723081	0.14723081	23
24	23.21220685	0.04308078	158.65862038	6.83513728	0.00630284	0.14630284	24
25	26.46191581	0.03779016	181.87082723	6.87292744	0.00549841	0.14549841	25
26	30.16658403	0.03314926	208.33274304	6.90607670	0.00480001	0.14480001	26
27	34.38990579	0.02907830	238.49932707	6.93515500	0.00419288	0.14419288	27
28	39.20449260	0.02550728	272.88923286	6.96066228	0.00366449	0.14366449	28
29	44.69312156	0.02237481	312.09372546	6.98303709	0.00320417	0.14320417	29
30	50.95015858	0.01962702	356.78684702	7.00266411	0.00280279	0.14280279	30
31	58.08318078	0.01721669	407.73700561	7.01988080	0.00245256	0.14245256	31
32	66.21482609	0.01510236	465.82018639	7.03498316	0.00214675	0.14214675	32
33	75.48490175	0.01324768	532.03501249	7.04823084	0.00187958	0.14187958	33
34	86.05278799	0.01162077	607.51991423	7.05985161	0.00164604	0.14164604	34
35	98.10017831	0.01019366	693.57270223	7.07004528	0.00144181	0.14144181	35
36	111.83420328	0.00894181	791.67288054	7.07898708	0.00126315	0.14126315	36
37	127.49099173	0.00784369	903.50708382	7.08683078	0.00110680	0.14110680	37
38	145.33973058	0.00688043	1030.99807555	7.09371121	0.00096993	0.14096993	38
39	165.68729286	0.00603547	1176.33780613	7.09974667	0.00085010	0.14085010	39
40	188.88351386	0.00529427	1342.02509898	7.10504094	0.00074514	0.14074514	40
41	215.32720580	0.00464410	1530.90861284	7.10968504	0.00065321	0.14065321	41
42	245.47301461	0.00407377	1746.23581864	7.11375880	0.00057266	0.14057266	42
43	279.83923665	0.00357348	1991.70883325	7.11733228	0.00050208	0.14050208	43
44	319.01672979	0.00313463	2271.54806990	7.12046692	0.00044023	0.14044023	44
45	363.67907196	0.00274968	2590.56479969	7.12321659	0.00038602	0.14038602	45
46	414.59414203	0.00241200	2954.24387165	7.12562859	0.00033850	0.14033850	46
47	472.63732191	0.00211579	3368.83801368	7.12774438	0.00029684	0.14029684	47
48	538.80654698	0.00185595	3841.47533559	7.12960033	0.00026032	0.14026032	48
49	614.23946356	0.00162803	4380.28188258	7.13122836	0.00022830	0.14022830	49
50	700.23298846	0.00142810	4994.52134614	7.13265646	0.00020022	0.14020022	50

Rate 15%	C Compound Amount	D Present Value	E Amount of Annuity	F Present Value of Annuity	G Sinking Fund	H Amortization	
n	$(1 + i)^n$	$(1 + i)^{-n}$	$S_{\overline{n}|i}$	$A_{\overline{n}|i}$	$1/S_{\overline{n}|i}$	$1/A_{\overline{n}|i}$	n
1	1.15000000	0.86956522	1.00000000	0.86956522	1.00000000	1.15000000	1
2	1.32250000	0.75614367	2.15000000	1.62570888	0.46511628	0.61511628	2
3	1.52087500	0.65751623	3.47250000	2.28322512	0.28797696	0.43797696	3
4	1.74900625	0.57175325	4.99337500	2.85497836	0.20026535	0.35026535	4
5	2.01135719	0.49717674	6.74238125	3.35215510	0.14831555	0.29831555	5
6	2.31306077	0.43232760	8.75373844	3.78448269	0.11423691	0.26423691	6
7	2.66001988	0.37593704	11.06679920	4.16041973	0.09036036	0.24036036	7
8	3.05902286	0.32690177	13.72681908	4.48732151	0.07285009	0.22285009	8
9	3.51787629	0.28426241	16.78584195	4.77158392	0.05957402	0.20957402	9
10	4.04555774	0.24718471	20.30371824	5.01876863	0.04925206	0.19925206	10
11	4.65239140	0.21494322	24.34927597	5.23371185	0.04106898	0.19106898	11
12	5.35025011	0.18690715	29.00166737	5.42061900	0.03448078	0.18448078	12
13	6.15278762	0.16252796	34.35191748	5.58314696	0.02911046	0.17911046	13
14	7.07570576	0.14132866	40.50470510	5.72447561	0.02468849	0.17468849	14
15	8.13706163	0.12289449	47.58041086	5.84737010	0.02101705	0.17101705	15
16	9.35762087	0.10686477	55.71747249	5.95423487	0.01794769	0.16794769	16
17	10.76126400	0.09292589	65.07509336	6.04716076	0.01536686	0.16536686	17
18	12.37545361	0.08080512	75.83635737	6.12796587	0.01318629	0.16318629	18
19	14.23177165	0.07026532	88.21181097	6.19823119	0.01133635	0.16133635	19
20	16.36653739	0.06110028	102.44358262	6.25933147	0.00976147	0.15976147	20
21	18.82151800	0.05313068	118.81012001	6.31246215	0.00841679	0.15841679	21
22	21.64474570	0.04620059	137.63163801	6.35866274	0.00726577	0.15726577	22
23	24.89145756	0.04017443	159.27638372	6.39883717	0.00627839	0.15627839	23
24	28.62517619	0.03493428	184.16784127	6.43377145	0.00542983	0.15542983	24
25	32.91895262	0.03037764	212.79301747	6.46414909	0.00469940	0.15469940	25
26	37.85679551	0.02641534	245.71197009	6.49056442	0.00406981	0.15406981	26
27	43.53531484	0.02296986	283.56876560	6.51353428	0.00352648	0.15352648	27
28	50.06561207	0.01997379	327.10408044	6.53350807	0.00305713	0.15305713	28
29	57.57545388	0.01736851	377.16969250	6.55087658	0.00265133	0.15265133	29
30	66.21177196	0.01510305	434.74514638	6.56597964	0.00230020	0.15230020	30
31	76.14353775	0.01313309	500.95691834	6.57911273	0.00199618	0.15199618	31
32	87.56506841	0.01142008	577.10045609	6.59053281	0.00173280	0.15173280	32
33	100.69982867	0.00993050	664.66552450	6.60046331	0.00150452	0.15150452	33
34	115.80480298	0.00863522	765.36535317	6.60909853	0.00130657	0.15130657	34
35	133.17552342	0.00750889	881.17015615	6.61660742	0.00113485	0.15113485	35
36	153.15185194	0.00652947	1014.34567957	6.62313689	0.00098586	0.15098586	36
37	176.12462973	0.00567780	1167.49753151	6.62881468	0.00085653	0.15085653	37
38	202.54332419	0.00493722	1343.62216123	6.63375190	0.00074426	0.15074426	38
39	232.92482281	0.00429323	1546.16548542	6.63804513	0.00064676	0.15064676	39
40	267.86354623	0.00373324	1779.09030823	6.64177837	0.00056209	0.15056209	40
41	308.04307817	0.00324630	2046.95385447	6.64502467	0.00048853	0.15048853	41
42	354.24953990	0.00282287	2354.99693264	6.64784754	0.00042463	0.15042463	42
43	407.38697088	0.00245467	2709.24647253	6.65030221	0.00036911	0.15036911	43
44	468.49501651	0.00213449	3116.63344341	6.65243670	0.00032086	0.15032086	44
45	538.76926899	0.00185608	3585.12845992	6.65429279	0.00027893	0.15027893	45
46	619.58465934	0.00161398	4123.89772891	6.65590677	0.00024249	0.15024249	46
47	712.52235824	0.00140346	4743.48238825	6.65731024	0.00021082	0.15021082	47
48	819.40071197	0.00122040	5456.00474648	6.65853064	0.00018328	0.15018328	48
49	942.31081877	0.00106122	6275.40545846	6.65959186	0.00015935	0.15015935	49
50	1083.65744158	0.00092280	7217.71627723	6.66051466	0.00013855	0.15013855	50

Rate 16%	C Compound Amount	D Present Value	E Amount of Annuity	F Present Value of Annuity	G Sinking Fund	H Amortization	
n	$(1 + i)^n$	$(1 + i)^{-n}$	$S_{\overline{n}|i}$	$A_{\overline{n}|i}$	$1/S_{\overline{n}|i}$	$1/A_{\overline{n}|i}$	n
1	1.16000000	0.86206897	1.00000000	0.86206897	1.00000000	1.16000000	1
2	1.34560000	0.74316290	2.16000000	1.60523187	0.46296296	0.62296296	2
3	1.56089600	0.64065767	3.50560000	2.24588954	0.28525787	0.44525787	3
4	1.81063936	0.55229110	5.06649600	2.79818064	0.19737507	0.35737507	4
5	2.10034166	0.47611302	6.87713536	3.27429365	0.14540938	0.30540938	5
6	2.43639632	0.41044225	8.97747702	3.68473591	0.11138987	0.27138987	6
7	2.82621973	0.35382953	11.41387334	4.03856544	0.08761268	0.24761268	7
8	3.27841489	0.30502546	14.24009307	4.34359090	0.07022426	0.23022426	8
9	3.80296127	0.26295298	17.51850797	4.60654388	0.05708249	0.21708249	9
10	4.41143508	0.22668360	21.32146924	4.83322748	0.04690108	0.20690108	10
11	5.11726469	0.19541690	25.73290432	5.02864438	0.03886075	0.19886075	11
12	5.93602704	0.16846284	30.85016901	5.19710722	0.03241473	0.19241473	12
13	6.88579137	0.14522659	36.78619605	5.34233381	0.02718411	0.18718411	13
14	7.98751799	0.12519534	43.67198742	5.46752915	0.02289797	0.18289797	14
15	9.26552087	0.10792701	51.65950541	5.57545616	0.01935752	0.17935752	15
16	10.74800420	0.09304053	60.92502627	5.66849669	0.01641362	0.17641362	16
17	12.46768488	0.08020735	71.67303048	5.74870404	0.01395225	0.17395225	17
18	14.46251446	0.06914427	84.14071536	5.81784831	0.01188485	0.17188485	18
19	16.77651677	0.05960713	98.60322981	5.87745544	0.01014166	0.17014166	19
20	19.46075945	0.05138546	115.37974658	5.92884090	0.00866703	0.16866703	20
21	22.57448097	0.04429781	134.84050604	5.97313871	0.00741617	0.16741617	21
22	26.18639792	0.03818776	157.41498700	6.01132647	0.00635264	0.16635264	22
23	30.37622159	0.03292049	183.60138492	6.04424696	0.00544658	0.16544658	23
24	35.23641704	0.02837973	213.97760651	6.07262669	0.00467339	0.16467339	24
25	40.87424377	0.02446528	249.21402355	6.09709197	0.00401262	0.16401262	25
26	47.41412277	0.02109076	290.08826732	6.11818273	0.00344723	0.16344723	26
27	55.00038241	0.01818169	337.50239009	6.13636443	0.00296294	0.16296294	27
28	63.80044360	0.01567387	392.50277250	6.15203830	0.00254775	0.16254775	28
29	74.00851458	0.01351196	456.30321610	6.16555026	0.00219153	0.16219153	29
30	85.84987691	0.01164824	530.31173068	6.17719850	0.00188568	0.16188568	30
31	99.58585721	0.01004159	616.16160759	6.18724008	0.00162295	0.16162295	31
32	115.51959437	0.00865654	715.74746480	6.19589662	0.00139714	0.16139714	32
33	134.00272947	0.00746253	831.26705917	6.20335916	0.00120298	0.16120298	33
34	155.44316618	0.00643322	965.26978864	6.20979238	0.00103598	0.16103598	34
35	180.31407277	0.00554588	1120.71295482	6.21533826	0.00089229	0.16089229	35
36	209.16432441	0.00478093	1301.02702759	6.22011919	0.00076862	0.16076862	36
37	242.63061632	0.00412149	1510.19135201	6.22424068	0.00066217	0.16066217	37
38	281.45151493	0.00355301	1752.82196833	6.22779369	0.00057051	0.16057051	38
39	326.48375732	0.00306294	2034.27348326	6.23085663	0.00049158	0.16049158	39
40	378.72115849	0.00264047	2360.75724058	6.23349709	0.00042359	0.16042359	40
41	439.31654385	0.00227626	2739.47839907	6.23577336	0.00036503	0.16036503	41
42	509.60719087	0.00196230	3178.79494293	6.23773565	0.00031458	0.16031458	42
43	591.14434141	0.00169163	3688.40213380	6.23942729	0.00027112	0.16027112	43
44	685.72743603	0.00145831	4279.54647520	6.24088559	0.00023367	0.16023367	44
45	795.44382580	0.00125716	4965.27391123	6.24214275	0.00020140	0.16020140	45
46	922.71483793	0.00108376	5760.71773703	6.24322651	0.00017359	0.16017359	46
47	1070.34921199	0.00093427	6683.43257496	6.24416078	0.00014962	0.16014962	47
48	1241.60508591	0.00080541	7753.78178695	6.24496619	0.00012897	0.16012897	48
49	1440.26189966	0.00069432	8995.38687286	6.24566051	0.00011117	0.16011117	49
50	1670.70380360	0.00059855	10435.64877252	6.24625906	0.00009583	0.16009583	50

Rate 17%	C Compound Amount	D Present Value	E Amount of Annuity	F Present Value of Annuity	G Sinking Fund	H Amortization	
n	$(1 + i)^n$	$(1 + i)^{-n}$	$S_{\overline{n}|i}$	$A_{\overline{n}|i}$	$1/S_{\overline{n}|i}$	$1/A_{\overline{n}|i}$	n
1	1.17000000	0.85470085	1.00000000	0.85470085	1.00000000	1.17000000	1
2	1.36890000	0.73051355	2.17000000	1.58521441	0.46082949	0.63082949	2
3	1.60161300	0.62437056	3.53890000	2.20958496	0.28257368	0.45257368	3
4	1.87388721	0.53365005	5.14051300	2.74323501	0.19453311	0.36453311	4
5	2.19244804	0.45611115	7.01440021	3.19934616	0.14256386	0.31256386	5
6	2.56516420	0.38983859	9.20684825	3.58918475	0.10861480	0.27861480	6
7	3.00124212	0.33319538	11.77201245	3.92238013	0.08494724	0.25494724	7
8	3.51145328	0.28478237	14.77325456	4.20716251	0.06768989	0.23768989	8
9	4.10840033	0.24340374	18.28470784	4.45056624	0.05469051	0.22469051	9
10	4.80682839	0.20803738	22.39310817	4.65860363	0.04465660	0.21465660	10
11	5.62398922	0.17780973	27.19993656	4.83641336	0.03676479	0.20676479	11
12	6.58006738	0.15197413	32.82392578	4.98838748	0.03046558	0.20046558	12
13	7.69867884	0.12989242	39.40399316	5.11827990	0.02537814	0.19537814	13
14	9.00745424	0.11101916	47.10267200	5.22929906	0.02123022	0.19123022	14
15	10.53872146	0.09488817	56.11012623	5.32418723	0.01782209	0.18782209	15
16	12.33030411	0.08110100	66.64884769	5.40528823	0.01500401	0.18500401	16
17	14.42645581	0.06931709	78.97915180	5.47460533	0.01266157	0.18266157	17
18	16.87895329	0.05924538	93.40560761	5.53385071	0.01070600	0.18070600	18
19	19.74837535	0.05063708	110.28456090	5.58448778	0.00906745	0.17906745	19
20	23.10559916	0.04327955	130.03293626	5.62776734	0.00769036	0.17769036	20
21	27.03355102	0.03699107	153.13853542	5.66475841	0.00653004	0.17653004	21
22	31.62925470	0.03161630	180.17208644	5.69637471	0.00555025	0.17555025	22
23	37.00622799	0.02702248	211.80134114	5.72339719	0.00472141	0.17472141	23
24	43.29728675	0.02309614	248.80756913	5.74649332	0.00401917	0.17401917	24
25	50.65782550	0.01974029	292.10485588	5.76623361	0.00342343	0.17342343	25
26	59.26965584	0.01687204	342.76268138	5.78310565	0.00291747	0.17291747	26
27	69.34549733	0.01442055	402.03233722	5.79752619	0.00248736	0.17248736	27
28	81.13423187	0.01232525	471.37783454	5.80985145	0.00212144	0.17212144	28
29	94.92705129	0.01053440	552.51206642	5.82038585	0.00180992	0.17180992	29
30	111.06465001	0.00900376	647.43911771	5.82938962	0.00154455	0.17154455	30
31	129.94564051	0.00769553	758.50376772	5.83708514	0.00131839	0.17131839	31
32	152.03639940	0.00657737	888.44940823	5.84366252	0.00112556	0.17112556	32
33	177.88258730	0.00562169	1040.48580763	5.84928420	0.00096109	0.17096109	33
34	208.12262714	0.00480486	1218.36839493	5.85408906	0.00082077	0.17082077	34
35	243.50347375	0.00410672	1426.49102206	5.85819578	0.00070102	0.17070102	35
36	284.89906429	0.00351002	1669.99449581	5.86170579	0.00059880	0.17059880	36
37	333.33190522	0.00300001	1954.89356010	5.86470581	0.00051154	0.17051154	37
38	389.99832910	0.00256411	2288.22546532	5.86726992	0.00043702	0.17043702	38
39	456.29804505	0.00219155	2678.22379443	5.86946147	0.00037338	0.17037338	39
40	533.86871271	0.00187312	3134.52183948	5.87133459	0.00031903	0.17031903	40
41	624.62639387	0.00160096	3668.39055219	5.87293555	0.00027260	0.17027260	41
42	730.81288083	0.00136834	4293.01694606	5.87430389	0.00023294	0.17023294	42
43	855.05107057	0.00116952	5023.82982689	5.87547341	0.00019905	0.17019905	43
44	1000.40975257	0.00099959	5878.88089746	5.87647300	0.00017010	0.17017010	44
45	1170.47941051	0.00085435	6879.29065003	5.87732735	0.00014536	0.17014536	45
46	1369.46091029	0.00073021	8049.77006054	5.87805756	0.00012423	0.17012423	46
47	1602.26926504	0.00062411	9419.23097083	5.87868168	0.00010617	0.17010617	47
48	1874.65504010	0.00053343	11021.50023587	5.87921511	0.00009073	0.17009073	48
49	2193.34639691	0.00045592	12896.15527597	5.87967103	0.00007754	0.17007754	49
50	2566.21528439	0.00038968	15089.50167288	5.88006071	0.00006627	0.17006627	50

Rate 18%	C Compound Amount	D Present Value	E Amount of Annuity	F Present Value of Annuity	G Sinking Fund	H Amortization	
n	$(1 + i)^n$	$(1 + i)^{-n}$	$S_{\overline{n}|i}$	$A_{\overline{n}|i}$	$1/S_{\overline{n}|i}$	$1/A_{\overline{n}|i}$	n
1	1.18000000	0.84745763	1.00000000	0.84745763	1.00000000	1.18000000	1
2	1.39240000	0.71818443	2.18000000	1.56564206	0.45871560	0.63871560	2
3	1.64303200	0.60863087	3.57240000	2.17427293	0.27992386	0.45992386	3
4	1.93877776	0.51578888	5.21543200	2.69006180	0.19173867	0.37173867	4
5	2.28775776	0.43710922	7.15420976	3.12717102	0.13977784	0.31977784	5
6	2.69955415	0.37043154	9.44196752	3.49760256	0.10591013	0.28591013	6
7	3.18547390	0.31392503	12.14152167	3.81152759	0.08236200	0.26236200	7
8	3.75885920	0.26603816	15.32699557	4.07756576	0.06524436	0.24524436	8
9	4.43545386	0.22545607	19.08585477	4.30302183	0.05239482	0.23239482	9
10	5.23383555	0.19106447	23.52130863	4.49408629	0.04251464	0.22251464	10
11	6.17592595	0.16191904	28.75514419	4.65600533	0.03477639	0.21477639	11
12	7.28759263	0.13721953	34.93107014	4.79322486	0.02862781	0.20862781	12
13	8.59935930	0.11628773	42.21866276	4.90951259	0.02368621	0.20368621	13
14	10.14724397	0.09854893	50.81802206	5.00806152	0.01967806	0.19967806	14
15	11.97374789	0.08351604	60.96526603	5.09157756	0.01640278	0.19640278	15
16	14.12902251	0.07077630	72.93901392	5.16235386	0.01371008	0.19371008	16
17	16.67224656	0.05997992	87.06803642	5.22233378	0.01148527	0.19148527	17
18	19.67325094	0.05083044	103.74028298	5.27316422	0.00963946	0.18963946	18
19	23.21443611	0.04307664	123.41353392	5.31624087	0.00810284	0.18810284	19
20	27.39303460	0.03650563	146.62797002	5.35274650	0.00681998	0.18681998	20
21	32.32378083	0.03093698	174.02100463	5.38368347	0.00574643	0.18574643	21
22	38.14206138	0.02621778	206.34478546	5.40990125	0.00484626	0.18484626	22
23	45.00763243	0.02221845	244.48684684	5.43211970	0.00409020	0.18409020	23
24	53.10900627	0.01882920	289.49447928	5.45094890	0.00345430	0.18345430	24
25	62.66862740	0.01595695	342.60348554	5.46690585	0.00291883	0.18291883	25
26	73.94898033	0.01352284	405.27211294	5.48042868	0.00246748	0.18246748	26
27	87.25979679	0.01146003	479.22109327	5.49188872	0.00208672	0.18208672	27
28	102.96656021	0.00971189	566.48089006	5.50160061	0.00176528	0.18176528	28
29	121.50054105	0.00823042	669.44745027	5.50983102	0.00149377	0.18149377	29
30	143.37063844	0.00697493	790.94799132	5.51680595	0.00126431	0.18126431	30
31	169.17735336	0.00591096	934.31862976	5.52271691	0.00107030	0.18107030	31
32	199.62927696	0.00500929	1103.49598312	5.52772619	0.00090621	0.18090621	32
33	235.56254681	0.00424516	1303.12526008	5.53197135	0.00076739	0.18076739	33
34	277.96380524	0.00359759	1538.68780689	5.53556894	0.00064990	0.18064990	34
35	327.99729018	0.00304881	1816.65161213	5.53861775	0.00055046	0.18055046	35
36	387.03680242	0.00258373	2144.64890232	5.54120148	0.00046628	0.18046628	36
37	456.70342685	0.00218960	2531.68570473	5.54339108	0.00039499	0.18039499	37
38	538.91004369	0.00185560	2988.38913158	5.54524668	0.00033463	0.18033463	38
39	635.91385155	0.00157254	3527.29917527	5.54681922	0.00028350	0.18028350	39
40	750.37834483	0.00133266	4163.21302682	5.54815188	0.00024020	0.18024020	40
41	885.44644690	0.00112937	4913.59137165	5.54928126	0.00020352	0.18020352	41
42	1044.82680734	0.00095710	5799.03781854	5.55023835	0.00017244	0.18017244	42
43	1232.89563266	0.00081110	6843.86462588	5.55104945	0.00014612	0.18014612	43
44	1454.81684654	0.00068737	8076.76025854	5.55173682	0.00012381	0.18012381	44
45	1716.68387891	0.00058252	9531.57710507	5.55231934	0.00010491	0.18010491	45
46	2025.68697712	0.00049366	11248.26098399	5.55281300	0.00008890	0.18008890	46
47	2390.31063300	0.00041836	13273.94796110	5.55323136	0.00007534	0.18007534	47
48	2820.56654694	0.00035454	15664.25859410	5.55358590	0.00006384	0.18006384	48
49	3328.26852539	0.00030046	18484.82514104	5.55388635	0.00005410	0.18005410	49
50	3927.35685996	0.00025462	21813.09366643	5.55414098	0.00004584	0.18004584	50

Rate 19%	C Compound Amount	D Present Value	E Amount of Annuity	F Present Value of Annuity	G Sinking Fund	H Amortization	
n	$(1 + i)^n$	$(1 + i)^{-n}$	$S_{\overline{n}|i}$	$A_{\overline{n}|i}$	$1/S_{\overline{n}|i}$	$1/A_{\overline{n}|i}$	n
1	1.19000000	0.84033613	1.00000000	0.84033613	1.00000000	1.19000000	1
2	1.41610000	0.70616482	2.19000000	1.54650095	0.45662100	0.64662100	2
3	1.68515900	0.59341581	3.60610000	2.13991677	0.27730789	0.46730789	3
4	2.00533921	0.49866875	5.29125900	2.63858552	0.18899094	0.37899094	4
5	2.38635366	0.41904937	7.29659821	3.05763489	0.13705017	0.32705017	5
6	2.83976086	0.35214233	9.68295187	3.40977722	0.10327429	0.29327429	6
7	3.37931542	0.29591792	12.52271273	3.70569514	0.07985490	0.26985490	7
8	4.02138535	0.24867052	15.90202814	3.95436567	0.06288506	0.25288506	8
9	4.78544856	0.20896683	19.92341349	4.16333249	0.05019220	0.24019220	9
10	5.69468379	0.17560238	24.70886205	4.33893487	0.04047131	0.23047131	10
11	6.77667371	0.14756502	30.40354584	4.48649989	0.03289090	0.22289090	11
12	8.06424172	0.12400422	37.18021955	4.61050411	0.02689602	0.21689602	12
13	9.59644764	0.10420523	45.24446127	4.71470933	0.02210215	0.21210215	13
14	11.41977269	0.08756742	54.84090891	4.80227675	0.01823456	0.20823456	14
15	13.58952950	0.07358606	66.26068160	4.87586282	0.01509191	0.20509191	15
16	16.17154011	0.06183703	79.85021111	4.93769985	0.01252345	0.20252345	16
17	19.24413273	0.05196389	96.02175122	4.98966374	0.01041431	0.20041431	17
18	22.90051795	0.04366713	115.26588395	5.03333087	0.00867559	0.19867559	18
19	27.25161636	0.03669507	138.16640190	5.07002594	0.00723765	0.19723765	19
20	32.42942347	0.03083619	165.41801826	5.10086214	0.00604529	0.19604529	20
21	38.59101393	0.02591277	197.84744173	5.12677490	0.00505440	0.19505440	21
22	45.92330658	0.02177544	236.43845566	5.14855034	0.00422943	0.19422943	22
23	54.64873482	0.01829869	282.36176223	5.16684902	0.00354156	0.19354156	23
24	65.03199444	0.01537705	337.01049706	5.18222607	0.00296727	0.19296727	24
25	77.38807338	0.01292189	402.04249150	5.19514796	0.00248730	0.19248730	25
26	92.09180733	0.01085873	479.43056488	5.20600669	0.00208581	0.19208581	26
27	109.58925072	0.00912498	571.52237221	5.21513167	0.00174971	0.19174971	27
28	130.41120836	0.00766805	681.11162293	5.22279972	0.00146819	0.19146819	28
29	155.18933794	0.00644374	811.52283129	5.22924347	0.00123225	0.19123225	29
30	184.67531215	0.00541491	966.71216923	5.23465837	0.00103443	0.19103443	30
31	219.76362146	0.00455034	1151.38748139	5.23920872	0.00086852	0.19086852	31
32	261.51870954	0.00382382	1371.15110285	5.24303254	0.00072931	0.19072931	32
33	311.20726435	0.00321329	1632.66981239	5.24624583	0.00061249	0.19061249	33
34	370.33664458	0.00270025	1943.87707675	5.24894607	0.00051444	0.19051444	34
35	440.70060705	0.00226911	2314.21372133	5.25121519	0.00043211	0.19043211	35
36	524.43372239	0.00190682	2754.91432838	5.25312201	0.00036299	0.19036299	36
37	624.07612965	0.00160237	3279.34805077	5.25472438	0.00030494	0.19030494	37
38	742.65059428	0.00134653	3903.42418042	5.25607090	0.00025619	0.19025619	38
39	883.75420719	0.00113154	4646.07477470	5.25720244	0.00021524	0.19021524	39
40	1051.66750656	0.00095087	5529.82898189	5.25815331	0.00018084	0.19018084	40
41	1251.48433281	0.00079905	6581.49648845	5.25895236	0.00015194	0.19015194	41
42	1489.26635604	0.00067147	7832.98082126	5.25962383	0.00012767	0.19012767	42
43	1772.22696369	0.00056426	9322.24717730	5.26018810	0.00010727	0.19010727	43
44	2108.95008679	0.00047417	11094.47414099	5.26066227	0.00009013	0.19009013	44
45	2509.65060328	0.00039846	13203.42422777	5.26106073	0.00007574	0.19007574	45
46	2986.48421790	0.00033484	15713.07483105	5.26139557	0.00006364	0.19006364	46
47	3553.91621930	0.00028138	18699.55904895	5.26167695	0.00005348	0.19005348	47
48	4229.16030097	0.00023645	22253.47526825	5.26191340	0.00004494	0.19004494	48
49	5032.70075815	0.00019870	26482.63556922	5.26211210	0.00003776	0.19003776	49
50	5988.91390220	0.00016698	31515.33632737	5.26227908	0.00003173	0.19003173	50

Rate 20%	C Compound Amount	D Present Value	E Amount of Annuity	F Present Value of Annuity	G Sinking Fund	H Amortization	
n	$(1 + i)^n$	$(1 + i)^{-n}$	$S_{\overline{n}|i}$	$A_{\overline{n}|i}$	$1/S_{\overline{n}|i}$	$1/A_{\overline{n}|i}$	n
1	1.20000000	0.83333333	1.00000000	0.83333333	1.00000000	1.20000000	1
2	1.44000000	0.69444444	2.20000000	1.52777778	0.45454545	0.65454545	2
3	1.72800000	0.57870370	3.64000000	2.10648148	0.27472527	0.47472527	3
4	2.07360000	0.48225309	5.36800000	2.58873457	0.18628912	0.38628912	4
5	2.48832000	0.40187757	7.44160000	2.99061214	0.13437970	0.33437970	5
6	2.98598400	0.33489798	9.92992000	3.32551012	0.10070575	0.30070575	6
7	3.58318080	0.27908165	12.91590400	3.60459176	0.07742393	0.27742393	7
8	4.29981696	0.23256804	16.49908480	3.83715980	0.06060942	0.26060942	8
9	5.15978035	0.19380670	20.79890176	4.03096650	0.04807946	0.24807946	9
10	6.19173642	0.16150558	25.95868211	4.19247209	0.03852276	0.23852276	10
11	7.43008371	0.13458799	32.15041853	4.32706007	0.03110379	0.23110379	11
12	8.91610045	0.11215665	39.58050224	4.43921673	0.02526496	0.22526496	12
13	10.69932054	0.09346388	48.49660269	4.53268061	0.02062000	0.22062000	13
14	12.83918465	0.07788657	59.19592323	4.61056717	0.01689306	0.21689306	14
15	15.40702157	0.06490547	72.03510787	4.67547264	0.01388212	0.21388212	15
16	18.48842589	0.05408789	87.44212945	4.72956054	0.01143614	0.21143614	16
17	22.18611107	0.04507324	105.93055534	4.77463378	0.00944015	0.20944015	17
18	26.62333328	0.03756104	128.11666640	4.81219482	0.00780539	0.20780539	18
19	31.94799994	0.03130086	154.73999969	4.84349568	0.00646245	0.20646245	19
20	38.33759992	0.02608405	186.68799962	4.86957973	0.00535653	0.20535653	20
21	46.00511991	0.02173671	225.02559955	4.89131644	0.00444394	0.20444394	21
22	55.20614389	0.01811393	271.03071946	4.90943037	0.00368962	0.20368962	22
23	66.24737267	0.01509494	326.23686335	4.92452531	0.00306526	0.20306526	23
24	79.49684720	0.01257912	392.48423602	4.93710442	0.00254787	0.20254787	24
25	95.39621664	0.01048260	471.98108322	4.94758702	0.00211873	0.20211873	25
26	114.47545997	0.00873550	567.37729986	4.95632252	0.00176250	0.20176250	26
27	137.37055197	0.00727958	681.85275984	4.96360210	0.00146659	0.20146659	27
28	164.84466236	0.00606632	819.22331180	4.96966841	0.00122067	0.20122067	28
29	197.81359483	0.00505526	984.06797417	4.97472368	0.00101619	0.20101619	29
30	237.37631380	0.00421272	1181.88156900	4.97893640	0.00084611	0.20084611	30
31	284.85157656	0.00351060	1419.25788280	4.98244700	0.00070459	0.20070459	31
32	341.82189187	0.00292550	1704.10945936	4.98537250	0.00058682	0.20058682	32
33	410.18627025	0.00243792	2045.93135123	4.98781042	0.00048877	0.20048877	33
34	492.22352430	0.00203160	2456.11762148	4.98984201	0.00040715	0.20040715	34
35	590.66822915	0.00169300	2948.34114577	4.99153501	0.00033917	0.20033917	35
36	708.80187499	0.00141083	3539.00937493	4.99294584	0.00028256	0.20028256	36
37	850.56224998	0.00117569	4247.81124991	4.99412154	0.00023542	0.20023542	37
38	1020.67469998	0.00097974	5098.37349989	4.99510128	0.00019614	0.20019614	38
39	1224.80963997	0.00081645	6119.04819987	4.99591773	0.00016342	0.20016342	39
40	1469.77156797	0.00068038	7343.85783985	4.99659811	0.00013617	0.20013617	40
41	1763.72588156	0.00056698	8813.62940781	4.99716509	0.00011346	0.20011346	41
42	2116.47105788	0.00047248	10577.35528938	4.99763758	0.00009454	0.20009454	42
43	2539.76526945	0.00039374	12693.82634725	4.99803131	0.00007878	0.20007878	43
44	3047.71832334	0.00032811	15233.59161670	4.99835943	0.00006564	0.20006564	44
45	3657.26198801	0.00027343	18281.30994004	4.99863286	0.00005470	0.20005470	45
46	4388.71438561	0.00022786	21938.57192805	4.99886071	0.00004558	0.20004558	46
47	5266.45726273	0.00018988	26327.28631366	4.99905060	0.00003798	0.20003798	47
48	6319.74871528	0.00015823	31593.74357640	4.99920883	0.00003165	0.20003165	48
49	7583.69845834	0.00013186	37913.49229168	4.99934069	0.00002638	0.20002638	49
50	9100.43815000	0.00010988	45497.19075001	4.99945058	0.00002198	0.20002198	50

Appendix I   Compound daily interest factors for a 365-day year

Day	6.00%	6.25%	6.50%	6.75%	7.00%	7.25%	7.50%	7.75%
1	1.00016438	1.00017123	1.00017808	1.00018493	1.00019178	1.00019863	1.00020548	1.00021233
2	1.00032879	1.00034250	1.00035620	1.00036990	1.00038360	1.00039730	1.00041100	1.00042470
3	1.00049323	1.00051379	1.00053434	1.00055490	1.00057545	1.00059601	1.00061657	1.00063712
4	1.00065770	1.00068511	1.00071252	1.00073993	1.00076734	1.00079476	1.00082217	1.00084959
5	1.00082219	1.00085646	1.00089073	1.00092500	1.00095927	1.00099355	1.00102782	1.00106209
6	1.00098671	1.00102784	1.00106897	1.00111010	1.00115124	1.00119237	1.00123351	1.00127465
7	1.00115125	1.00119925	1.00124724	1.00129524	1.00134324	1.00139124	1.00143924	1.00148725
8	1.00131583	1.00137068	1.00142555	1.00148041	1.00153528	1.00159015	1.00164502	1.00169989
9	1.00148043	1.00154215	1.00160388	1.00166562	1.00172735	1.00178909	1.00185084	1.00191258
10	1.00164505	1.00171365	1.00178225	1.00185085	1.00191946	1.00198808	1.00205670	1.00212532
11	1.00180971	1.00188518	1.00196065	1.00203613	1.00211161	1.00218710	1.00226260	1.00233810
12	1.00197439	1.00205673	1.00213908	1.00222144	1.00230380	1.00238617	1.00246854	1.00255092
13	1.00213910	1.00222832	1.00231754	1.00240678	1.00249602	1.00258527	1.00267453	1.00276379
14	1.00230383	1.00239993	1.00249604	1.00259216	1.00268828	1.00278441	1.00288056	1.00297671
15	1.00246859	1.00257157	1.00267457	1.00277757	1.00288058	1.00298360	1.00308663	1.00318967
16	1.00263338	1.00274325	1.00285312	1.00296301	1.00307291	1.00318282	1.00329274	1.00340268
17	1.00279820	1.00291495	1.00303171	1.00314849	1.00326528	1.00338208	1.00349890	1.00361573
18	1.00296304	1.00308668	1.00321034	1.00333400	1.00345769	1.00358139	1.00370510	1.00382882
19	1.00312791	1.00325844	1.00338899	1.00351955	1.00365013	1.00378073	1.00391134	1.00404196
20	1.00329281	1.00343023	1.00356768	1.00370514	1.00384261	1.00398011	1.00411762	1.00425515
21	1.00345774	1.00360205	1.00374639	1.00389075	1.00403513	1.00417953	1.00432395	1.00446838
22	1.00362269	1.00377390	1.00392514	1.00407640	1.00422769	1.00437899	1.00453031	1.00468166
23	1.00378767	1.00394578	1.00410392	1.00426209	1.00442028	1.00457849	1.00473672	1.00489498
24	1.00395267	1.00411769	1.00428274	1.00444781	1.00461291	1.00477803	1.00494318	1.00510835
25	1.00411771	1.00428963	1.00446158	1.00463356	1.00480557	1.00497761	1.00514967	1.00532177
26	1.00428277	1.00446160	1.00464046	1.00481935	1.00499827	1.00517723	1.00535621	1.00553522
27	1.00444785	1.00463359	1.00481937	1.00500517	1.00519101	1.00537688	1.00556279	1.00574873
28	1.00461297	1.00480562	1.00499831	1.00519103	1.00538379	1.00557658	1.00576941	1.00596228
29	1.00477811	1.00497768	1.00517728	1.00537692	1.00557660	1.00577632	1.00597608	1.00617587
30	1.00494328	1.00514976	1.00535628	1.00556285	1.00576945	1.00597610	1.00618279	1.00638951
31	1.00510848	1.00532188	1.00553532	1.00574881	1.00596234	1.00617592	1.00638953	1.00660320
32	1.00527370	1.00549402	1.00571439	1.00593480	1.00615526	1.00637577	1.00659633	1.00681693
33	1.00543895	1.00566619	1.00589349	1.00612083	1.00634823	1.00657567	1.00680316	1.00703071
34	1.00560423	1.00583840	1.00607262	1.00630689	1.00654122	1.00677561	1.00701004	1.00724453
35	1.00576953	1.00601063	1.00625178	1.00649299	1.00673426	1.00697558	1.00721696	1.00745839
36	1.00593486	1.00618289	1.00643098	1.00667913	1.00692733	1.00717560	1.00742392	1.00767231
37	1.00610022	1.00635518	1.00661021	1.00686529	1.00712044	1.00737565	1.00763093	1.00788626
38	1.00626561	1.00652750	1.00678947	1.00705149	1.00731359	1.00757575	1.00783797	1.00810027
39	1.00643102	1.00669985	1.00696876	1.00723773	1.00750677	1.00777588	1.00804506	1.00831432
40	1.00659646	1.00687223	1.00714808	1.00742400	1.00769999	1.00797606	1.00825220	1.00852841
41	1.00676193	1.00704464	1.00732743	1.00761030	1.00789325	1.00817627	1.00845937	1.00874255
42	1.00692743	1.00721708	1.00750682	1.00779664	1.00808654	1.00837653	1.00866659	1.00895673
43	1.00709295	1.00738955	1.00768624	1.00798302	1.00827987	1.00857682	1.00887385	1.00917097
44	1.00725850	1.00756205	1.00786569	1.00816942	1.00847324	1.00877715	1.00908115	1.00938524
45	1.00742407	1.00773458	1.00804517	1.00835587	1.00866665	1.00897753	1.00928850	1.00959956
46	1.00758968	1.00790714	1.00822469	1.00854234	1.00886009	1.00917794	1.00949589	1.00981393
47	1.00775531	1.00807972	1.00840424	1.00872885	1.00905357	1.00937839	1.00970332	1.01002834
48	1.00792097	1.00825234	1.00858382	1.00891540	1.00924709	1.00957889	1.00991079	1.01024280
49	1.00808665	1.00842498	1.00876343	1.00910198	1.00944064	1.00977942	1.01011831	1.01045730
50	1.00825237	1.00859766	1.00894307	1.00928859	1.00963423	1.00997999	1.01032586	1.01067185

Day	6.00%	6.25%	6.50%	6.75%	7.00%	7.25%	7.50%	7.75%
51	1.00841811	1.00877037	1.00912274	1.00947524	1.00982786	1.01018060	1.01053347	1.01088645
52	1.00858387	1.00894310	1.00930245	1.00966193	1.01002153	1.01038126	1.01074111	1.01110109
53	1.00874967	1.00911586	1.00948219	1.00984865	1.01021523	1.01058195	1.01094880	1.01131577
54	1.00891549	1.00928866	1.00966196	1.01003540	1.01040897	1.01078268	1.01115653	1.01153051
55	1.00908134	1.00946148	1.00984176	1.01022219	1.01060275	1.01098345	1.01136430	1.01174528
56	1.00924722	1.00963433	1.01002160	1.01040901	1.01079656	1.01118426	1.01157211	1.01196011
57	1.00941312	1.00980722	1.01020146	1.01059586	1.01099041	1.01138512	1.01177997	1.01217497
58	1.00957905	1.00998013	1.01038136	1.01078275	1.01118430	1.01158601	1.01198787	1.01238989
59	1.00974501	1.01015307	1.01056129	1.01096968	1.01137823	1.01178694	1.01219581	1.01260485
60	1.00991099	1.01032604	1.01074126	1.01115664	1.01157219	1.01198791	1.01240380	1.01281985
61	1.01007701	1.01049904	1.01092125	1.01134364	1.01176619	1.01218892	1.01261183	1.01303490
62	1.01024305	1.01067207	1.01110128	1.01153066	1.01196023	1.01238997	1.01281990	1.01325000
63	1.01040911	1.01084513	1.01128134	1.01171773	1.01215430	1.01259106	1.01302801	1.01346514
64	1.01057521	1.01101822	1.01146143	1.01190483	1.01234842	1.01279220	1.01323617	1.01368033
65	1.01074133	1.01119134	1.01164155	1.01209196	1.01254256	1.01299337	1.01344437	1.01389556
66	1.01090748	1.01136449	1.01182171	1.01227913	1.01273675	1.01319458	1.01365261	1.01411084
67	1.01107366	1.01153767	1.01200190	1.01246633	1.01293097	1.01339583	1.01386089	1.01432617
68	1.01123986	1.01171088	1.01218212	1.01265357	1.01312523	1.01359712	1.01406922	1.01454154
69	1.01140609	1.01188412	1.01236237	1.01284084	1.01331953	1.01379845	1.01427759	1.01475695
70	1.01157235	1.01205739	1.01254265	1.01302814	1.01351387	1.01399982	1.01448600	1.01497242
71	1.01173864	1.01223068	1.01272297	1.01321549	1.01370824	1.01420123	1.01469446	1.01518792
72	1.01190495	1.01240401	1.01290331	1.01340286	1.01390265	1.01440268	1.01490296	1.01540348
73	1.01207129	1.01257737	1.01308369	1.01359027	1.01409710	1.01460417	1.01511150	1.01561908
74	1.01223766	1.01275075	1.01326411	1.01377772	1.01429158	1.01480570	1.01532008	1.01583472
75	1.01240405	1.01292417	1.01344455	1.01396520	1.01448610	1.01500728	1.01552871	1.01605041
76	1.01257048	1.01309762	1.01362503	1.01415271	1.01468066	1.01520889	1.01573738	1.01626615
77	1.01273693	1.01327109	1.01380554	1.01434026	1.01487526	1.01541054	1.01594610	1.01648193
78	1.01290340	1.01344460	1.01398608	1.01452784	1.01506989	1.01561223	1.01615485	1.01669776
79	1.01306991	1.01361813	1.01416665	1.01471546	1.01526456	1.01581396	1.01636365	1.01691363
80	1.01323644	1.01379170	1.01434725	1.01490311	1.01545927	1.01601573	1.01657249	1.01712955
81	1.01340300	1.01396529	1.01452789	1.01509080	1.01565402	1.01621754	1.01678138	1.01734552
82	1.01356959	1.01413892	1.01470856	1.01527852	1.01584880	1.01641939	1.01699030	1.01756153
83	1.01373620	1.01431257	1.01488926	1.01546628	1.01604362	1.01662129	1.01719928	1.01777759
84	1.01390284	1.01448625	1.01507000	1.01565407	1.01623848	1.01682322	1.01740829	1.01799369
85	1.01406951	1.01465997	1.01525076	1.01584190	1.01643337	1.01702519	1.01761735	1.01820984
86	1.01423621	1.01483371	1.01543156	1.01602976	1.01662831	1.01722720	1.01782644	1.01842604
87	1.01440293	1.01500748	1.01561239	1.01621765	1.01682328	1.01742925	1.01803559	1.01864228
88	1.01456968	1.01518129	1.01579325	1.01640559	1.01701828	1.01763134	1.01824477	1.01885857
89	1.01473646	1.01535512	1.01597415	1.01659355	1.01721333	1.01783348	1.01845400	1.01907490
90	1.01490327	1.01552898	1.01615507	1.01678155	1.01740841	1.01803565	1.01866327	1.01929128
91	1.01507010	1.01570287	1.01633603	1.01696959	1.01760353	1.01823786	1.01887259	1.01950770
92	1.01523696	1.01587679	1.01651703	1.01715766	1.01779869	1.01844011	1.01908194	1.01972417
93	1.01540385	1.01605075	1.01669805	1.01734576	1.01799388	1.01864241	1.01929134	1.01994069
94	1.01557077	1.01622473	1.01687910	1.01753390	1.01818911	1.01884474	1.01950079	1.02015725
95	1.01573771	1.01639874	1.01706019	1.01772207	1.01838438	1.01904711	1.01971027	1.02037386
96	1.01590468	1.01657278	1.01724131	1.01791028	1.01857969	1.01924953	1.01991980	1.02059052
97	1.01607168	1.01674685	1.01742247	1.01809853	1.01877503	1.01945198	1.02012938	1.02080722
98	1.01623870	1.01692095	1.01760365	1.01828680	1.01897041	1.01965447	1.02033899	1.02102396
99	1.01640576	1.01709508	1.01778487	1.01847512	1.01916583	1.01985701	1.02054865	1.02124076
100	1.01657284	1.01726924	1.01796612	1.01866347	1.01936129	1.02005958	1.02075835	1.02145760

Day	6.00%	6.25%	6.50%	6.75%	7.00%	7.25%	7.50%	7.75%
101	1.01673994	1.01744343	1.01814740	1.01885185	1.01955678	1.02026220	1.02096810	1.02167448
102	1.01690708	1.01761765	1.01832871	1.01904027	1.01975231	1.02046485	1.02117789	1.02189141
103	1.01707424	1.01779190	1.01851006	1.01922872	1.01994788	1.02066755	1.02138772	1.02210839
104	1.01724143	1.01796618	1.01869144	1.01941721	1.02014349	1.02087028	1.02159759	1.02232541
105	1.01740865	1.01814049	1.01887285	1.01960573	1.02033913	1.02107306	1.02180751	1.02254248
106	1.01757589	1.01831483	1.01905429	1.01979429	1.02053481	1.02127587	1.02201747	1.02275959
107	1.01774317	1.01848920	1.01923577	1.01998288	1.02073053	1.02147873	1.02222747	1.02297676
108	1.01791047	1.01866359	1.01941727	1.02017151	1.02092629	1.02168163	1.02243752	1.02319396
109	1.01807780	1.01883802	1.01959881	1.02036017	1.02112208	1.02188456	1.02264761	1.02341122
110	1.01824515	1.01901248	1.01978039	1.02054886	1.02131792	1.02208754	1.02285774	1.02362852
111	1.01841253	1.01918697	1.01996199	1.02073760	1.02151378	1.02229056	1.02306792	1.02384586
112	1.01857994	1.01936149	1.02014363	1.02092636	1.02170969	1.02249362	1.02327814	1.02406325
113	1.01874738	1.01953604	1.02032530	1.02111516	1.02190564	1.02269671	1.02348840	1.02428069
114	1.01891485	1.01971062	1.02050700	1.02130400	1.02210162	1.02289985	1.02369871	1.02449818
115	1.01908234	1.01988522	1.02068873	1.02149287	1.02229764	1.02310303	1.02390905	1.02471571
116	1.01924986	1.02005986	1.02087050	1.02168178	1.02249369	1.02330625	1.02411945	1.02493328
117	1.01941741	1.02023453	1.02105230	1.02187072	1.02268979	1.02350951	1.02432988	1.02515091
118	1.01958498	1.02040923	1.02123413	1.02205969	1.02288592	1.02371281	1.02454036	1.02536858
119	1.01975259	1.02058395	1.02141599	1.02224871	1.02308209	1.02391615	1.02475088	1.02558629
120	1.01992022	1.02075871	1.02159789	1.02243775	1.02327830	1.02411953	1.02496145	1.02580405
121	1.02008788	1.02093350	1.02177982	1.02262683	1.02347454	1.02432295	1.02517206	1.02602186
122	1.02025556	1.02110832	1.02196178	1.02281595	1.02367083	1.02452641	1.02538271	1.02623971
123	1.02042327	1.02128316	1.02214377	1.02300510	1.02386715	1.02472991	1.02559340	1.02645761
124	1.02059102	1.02145804	1.02232580	1.02319429	1.02406351	1.02493346	1.02580414	1.02667556
125	1.02075878	1.02163295	1.02250786	1.02338351	1.02425990	1.02513704	1.02601492	1.02689355
126	1.02092658	1.02180789	1.02268995	1.02357276	1.02445633	1.02534066	1.02622575	1.02711159
127	1.02109440	1.02198285	1.02287207	1.02376205	1.02465281	1.02554433	1.02643662	1.02732968
128	1.02126225	1.02215785	1.02305422	1.02395138	1.02484931	1.02574803	1.02664753	1.02754781
129	1.02143013	1.02233288	1.02323641	1.02414074	1.02504586	1.02595177	1.02685848	1.02776599
130	1.02159804	1.02250793	1.02341863	1.02433014	1.02524244	1.02615556	1.02706948	1.02798421
131	1.02176597	1.02268302	1.02360088	1.02451957	1.02543907	1.02635939	1.02728052	1.02820248
132	1.02193393	1.02285814	1.02378317	1.02470903	1.02563573	1.02656325	1.02749161	1.02842080
133	1.02210192	1.02303328	1.02396549	1.02489853	1.02583242	1.02676716	1.02770274	1.02863916
134	1.02226994	1.02320846	1.02414784	1.02508807	1.02602916	1.02697110	1.02791391	1.02885757
135	1.02243798	1.02338367	1.02433022	1.02527764	1.02622593	1.02717509	1.02812512	1.02907603
136	1.02260606	1.02355891	1.02451263	1.02546725	1.02642274	1.02737912	1.02833638	1.02929453
137	1.02277416	1.02373417	1.02469508	1.02565689	1.02661959	1.02758319	1.02854768	1.02951308
138	1.02294228	1.02390947	1.02487756	1.02584656	1.02681648	1.02778730	1.02875903	1.02973167
139	1.02311044	1.02408480	1.02506007	1.02603628	1.02701340	1.02799145	1.02897042	1.02995032
140	1.02327862	1.02426015	1.02524262	1.02622602	1.02721036	1.02819564	1.02918185	1.03016900
141	1.02344683	1.02443554	1.02542520	1.02641580	1.02740736	1.02839987	1.02939333	1.03038774
142	1.02361507	1.02461096	1.02560781	1.02660562	1.02760440	1.02860414	1.02960485	1.03060652
143	1.02378333	1.02478640	1.02579045	1.02679547	1.02780147	1.02880845	1.02981641	1.03082535
144	1.02395163	1.02496188	1.02597312	1.02698536	1.02799858	1.02901280	1.03002801	1.03104422
145	1.02411995	1.02513739	1.02615583	1.02717528	1.02819573	1.02921720	1.03023966	1.03126314
146	1.02428830	1.02531293	1.02633857	1.02736524	1.02839292	1.02942163	1.03045136	1.03148211
147	1.02445667	1.02548849	1.02652134	1.02755523	1.02859015	1.02962610	1.03066309	1.03170112
148	1.02462508	1.02566409	1.02670415	1.02774526	1.02878741	1.02983062	1.03087487	1.03192018
149	1.02479351	1.02583972	1.02688699	1.02793532	1.02898471	1.03003517	1.03108670	1.03213929
150	1.02496197	1.02601538	1.02706986	1.02812542	1.02918205	1.03023977	1.03129856	1.03235844

Day	6.00%	6.25%	6.50%	6.75%	7.00%	7.25%	7.50%	7.75%
151	1.02513045	1.02619106	1.02725276	1.02831555	1.02937943	1.03044441	1.03151048	1.03257764
152	1.02529897	1.02636678	1.02743570	1.02850572	1.02957685	1.03064908	1.03172243	1.03279689
153	1.02546751	1.02654253	1.02761866	1.02869592	1.02977430	1.03085380	1.03193443	1.03301618
154	1.02563608	1.02671831	1.02780166	1.02888616	1.02997179	1.03105856	1.03214647	1.03323552
155	1.02580468	1.02689411	1.02798470	1.02907643	1.03016932	1.03126336	1.03235855	1.03345490
156	1.02597330	1.02706995	1.02816776	1.02926674	1.03036689	1.03146820	1.03257068	1.03367434
157	1.02614196	1.02724582	1.02835086	1.02945709	1.03056449	1.03167308	1.03278285	1.03389381
158	1.02631064	1.02742172	1.02853399	1.02964746	1.03076213	1.03187800	1.03299507	1.03411334
159	1.02647935	1.02759765	1.02871716	1.02983788	1.03095981	1.03208296	1.03320733	1.03433291
160	1.02664808	1.02777361	1.02890035	1.03002833	1.03115753	1.03228797	1.03341963	1.03455253
161	1.02681685	1.02794959	1.02908358	1.03021881	1.03135529	1.03249301	1.03363198	1.03477220
162	1.02698564	1.02812561	1.02926684	1.03040933	1.03155308	1.03269809	1.03384437	1.03499191
163	1.02715446	1.02830166	1.02945014	1.03059989	1.03175091	1.03290322	1.03405680	1.03521167
164	1.02732331	1.02847774	1.02963346	1.03079048	1.03194878	1.03310838	1.03426928	1.03543147
165	1.02749218	1.02865385	1.02981682	1.03098110	1.03214669	1.03331359	1.03448180	1.03565132
166	1.02766108	1.02882999	1.03000022	1.03117176	1.03234464	1.03351884	1.03469437	1.03587122
167	1.02783001	1.02900616	1.03018364	1.03136246	1.03254262	1.03372413	1.03490697	1.03609117
168	1.02799897	1.02918236	1.03036710	1.03155319	1.03274064	1.03392945	1.03511963	1.03631116
169	1.02816796	1.02935859	1.03055059	1.03174396	1.03293870	1.03413482	1.03533232	1.03653120
170	1.02833697	1.02953485	1.03073411	1.03193476	1.03313680	1.03434023	1.03554506	1.03675128
171	1.02850601	1.02971114	1.03091767	1.03212560	1.03333494	1.03454569	1.03575784	1.03697141
172	1.02867508	1.02988746	1.03110125	1.03231647	1.03353311	1.03475118	1.03597067	1.03719159
173	1.02884418	1.03006381	1.03128487	1.03250738	1.03373132	1.03495671	1.03618354	1.03741182
174	1.02901331	1.03024019	1.03146853	1.03269832	1.03392957	1.03516228	1.03639646	1.03763209
175	1.02918246	1.03041660	1.03165221	1.03288930	1.03412786	1.03536790	1.03660941	1.03785241
176	1.02935164	1.03059304	1.03183593	1.03308031	1.03432619	1.03557355	1.03682242	1.03807278
177	1.02952085	1.03076951	1.03201968	1.03327136	1.03452455	1.03577925	1.03703546	1.03829319
178	1.02969009	1.03094602	1.03220347	1.03346245	1.03472295	1.03598499	1.03724855	1.03851365
179	1.02985935	1.03112255	1.03238729	1.03365357	1.03492139	1.03619076	1.03746168	1.03873416
180	1.03002864	1.03129911	1.03257114	1.03384472	1.03511987	1.03639658	1.03767486	1.03895471
181	1.03019796	1.03147570	1.03275502	1.03403591	1.03531839	1.03660244	1.03788808	1.03917531
182	1.03036731	1.03165232	1.03293893	1.03422714	1.03551694	1.03680834	1.03810135	1.03939596
183	1.03053668	1.03182898	1.03312288	1.03441840	1.03571553	1.03701429	1.03831466	1.03961665
184	1.03070609	1.03200566	1.03330686	1.03460970	1.03591416	1.03722027	1.03852801	1.03983739
185	1.03087552	1.03218237	1.03349088	1.03480103	1.03611283	1.03742629	1.03874140	1.04005818
186	1.03104498	1.03235912	1.03367492	1.03499240	1.03631154	1.03763235	1.03895484	1.04027901
187	1.03121446	1.03253589	1.03385900	1.03518380	1.03651028	1.03783846	1.03916833	1.04049989
188	1.03138398	1.03271269	1.03404311	1.03537524	1.03670907	1.03804461	1.03938186	1.04072082
189	1.03155352	1.03288953	1.03422726	1.03556671	1.03690789	1.03825079	1.03959543	1.04094180
190	1.03172309	1.03306639	1.03441144	1.03575822	1.03710675	1.03845702	1.03980904	1.04116282
191	1.03189269	1.03324329	1.03459565	1.03594976	1.03730564	1.03866329	1.04002270	1.04138389
192	1.03206232	1.03342021	1.03477989	1.03614134	1.03750458	1.03886960	1.04023641	1.04160500
193	1.03223197	1.03359717	1.03496416	1.03633296	1.03770355	1.03907595	1.04045015	1.04182616
194	1.03240165	1.03377416	1.03514847	1.03652461	1.03790256	1.03928234	1.04066394	1.04204737
195	1.03257136	1.03395117	1.03533281	1.03671629	1.03810161	1.03948877	1.04087778	1.04226863
196	1.03274110	1.03412822	1.03551719	1.03690802	1.03830070	1.03969525	1.04109166	1.04248993
197	1.03291087	1.03430529	1.03570160	1.03709977	1.03849983	1.03990176	1.04130558	1.04271128
198	1.03308066	1.03448240	1.03588604	1.03729157	1.03869899	1.04010832	1.04151955	1.04293268
199	1.03325048	1.03465954	1.03607051	1.03748339	1.03889819	1.04031492	1.04173356	1.04315413
200	1.03342033	1.03483671	1.03625501	1.03767526	1.03909744	1.04052155	1.04194761	1.04337562

Day	6.00%	6.25%	6.50%	6.75%	7.00%	7.25%	7.50%	7.75%
201	1.03359021	1.03501390	1.03643955	1.03786716	1.03929671	1.04072823	1.04216171	1.04359716
202	1.03376011	1.03519113	1.03662412	1.03805909	1.03949603	1.04093495	1.04237586	1.04381874
203	1.03393005	1.03536839	1.03680873	1.03825106	1.03969539	1.04114171	1.04259004	1.04404038
204	1.03410001	1.03554568	1.03699337	1.03844306	1.03989478	1.04134852	1.04280427	1.04426206
205	1.03427000	1.03572300	1.03717804	1.03863511	1.04009421	1.04155536	1.04301855	1.04448378
206	1.03444001	1.03590035	1.03736274	1.03882718	1.04029368	1.04176224	1.04323287	1.04470556
207	1.03461006	1.03607773	1.03754747	1.03901929	1.04049319	1.04196917	1.04344723	1.04492738
208	1.03478013	1.03625514	1.03773224	1.03921144	1.04069274	1.04217614	1.04366164	1.04514925
209	1.03495023	1.03643258	1.03791705	1.03940362	1.04089232	1.04238314	1.04387609	1.04537116
210	1.03512036	1.03661005	1.03810188	1.03959584	1.04109195	1.04259019	1.04409058	1.04559312
211	1.03529052	1.03678755	1.03828675	1.03978810	1.04129161	1.04279728	1.04430512	1.04581513
212	1.03546070	1.03696509	1.03847165	1.03998039	1.04149131	1.04300441	1.04451971	1.04603719
213	1.03563091	1.03714265	1.03865658	1.04017271	1.04169105	1.04321158	1.04473433	1.04625929
214	1.03580116	1.03732024	1.03884155	1.04036507	1.04189082	1.04341880	1.04494900	1.04648144
215	1.03597142	1.03749787	1.03902655	1.04055747	1.04209064	1.04362605	1.04516372	1.04670364
216	1.03614172	1.03767552	1.03921158	1.04074990	1.04229049	1.04383335	1.04537848	1.04692589
217	1.03631205	1.03785320	1.03939664	1.04094237	1.04249038	1.04404068	1.04559328	1.04714818
218	1.03648240	1.03803092	1.03958174	1.04113487	1.04269031	1.04424806	1.04580813	1.04737052
219	1.03665278	1.03820866	1.03976687	1.04132741	1.04289028	1.04445548	1.04602302	1.04759291
220	1.03682319	1.03838644	1.03995204	1.04151998	1.04309028	1.04466294	1.04623796	1.04781534
221	1.03699362	1.03856424	1.04013723	1.04171259	1.04329033	1.04487044	1.04645294	1.04803782
222	1.03716409	1.03874208	1.04032246	1.04190524	1.04349041	1.04507799	1.04666796	1.04826035
223	1.03733458	1.03891995	1.04050773	1.04209792	1.04369053	1.04528557	1.04688303	1.04848293
224	1.03750510	1.03909785	1.04069302	1.04229064	1.04389069	1.04549320	1.04709815	1.04870555
225	1.03767565	1.03927577	1.04087835	1.04248339	1.04409089	1.04570086	1.04731330	1.04892822
226	1.03784623	1.03945373	1.04106371	1.04267618	1.04429113	1.04590857	1.04752850	1.04915094
227	1.03801683	1.03963172	1.04124911	1.04286900	1.04449140	1.04611632	1.04774375	1.04937370
228	1.03818747	1.03980974	1.04143454	1.04306186	1.04469172	1.04632411	1.04795904	1.04959651
229	1.03835813	1.03998779	1.04162000	1.04325476	1.04489207	1.04653194	1.04817437	1.04981937
230	1.03852882	1.04016587	1.04180549	1.04344769	1.04509246	1.04673981	1.04838975	1.05004228
231	1.03869953	1.04034398	1.04199102	1.04364065	1.04529289	1.04694773	1.04860517	1.05026523
232	1.03887028	1.04052212	1.04217658	1.04383365	1.04549335	1.04715568	1.04882064	1.05048824
233	1.03904105	1.04070029	1.04236217	1.04402669	1.04569386	1.04736368	1.04903615	1.05071129
234	1.03921185	1.04087849	1.04254780	1.04421977	1.04589440	1.04757172	1.04925171	1.05093438
235	1.03938268	1.04105673	1.04273346	1.04441287	1.04609499	1.04777980	1.04946731	1.05115752
236	1.03955354	1.04123499	1.04291915	1.04460602	1.04629561	1.04798792	1.04968295	1.05138072
237	1.03972442	1.04141328	1.04310487	1.04479920	1.04649627	1.04819608	1.04989864	1.05160395
238	1.03989534	1.04159161	1.04329063	1.04499242	1.04669697	1.04840428	1.05011437	1.05182724
239	1.04006628	1.04176996	1.04347642	1.04518567	1.04689770	1.04861253	1.05033015	1.05205057
240	1.04023725	1.04194835	1.04366225	1.04537896	1.04709848	1.04882081	1.05054597	1.05227395
241	1.04040825	1.04212676	1.04384811	1.04557228	1.04729929	1.04902914	1.05076184	1.05249738
242	1.04057927	1.04230521	1.04403400	1.04576564	1.04750014	1.04923751	1.05097775	1.05272086
243	1.04075033	1.04248369	1.04421992	1.04595903	1.04770103	1.04944592	1.05119370	1.05294438
244	1.04092141	1.04266219	1.04440588	1.04615246	1.04790196	1.04965437	1.05140970	1.05316795
245	1.04109252	1.04284073	1.04459187	1.04634593	1.04810293	1.04986286	1.05162574	1.05339157
246	1.04126366	1.04301930	1.04477789	1.04653943	1.04830393	1.05007140	1.05184183	1.05361523
247	1.04143483	1.04319790	1.04496395	1.04673297	1.04850498	1.05027997	1.05205796	1.05383895
248	1.04160602	1.04337653	1.04515004	1.04692655	1.04870606	1.05048859	1.05227414	1.05406271
249	1.04177724	1.04355519	1.04533616	1.04712015	1.04890718	1.05069725	1.05249036	1.05428651
250	1.04194849	1.04373388	1.04552231	1.04731380	1.04910834	1.05090595	1.05270662	1.05451037

Day	6.00%	6.25%	6.50%	6.75%	7.00%	7.25%	7.50%	7.75%
251	1.04211977	1.04391260	1.04570850	1.04750748	1.04930954	1.05111469	1.05292293	1.05473427
252	1.04229108	1.04409135	1.04589473	1.04770120	1.04951078	1.05132347	1.05313929	1.05495822
253	1.04246242	1.04427014	1.04608098	1.04789495	1.04971206	1.05153230	1.05335569	1.05518222
254	1.04263378	1.04444895	1.04626727	1.04808874	1.04991337	1.05174117	1.05357213	1.05540627
255	1.04280517	1.04462779	1.04645359	1.04828257	1.05011472	1.05195007	1.05378862	1.05563036
256	1.04297659	1.04480667	1.04663995	1.04847643	1.05031612	1.05215902	1.05400515	1.05585450
257	1.04314804	1.04498557	1.04682633	1.04867032	1.05051755	1.05236801	1.05422172	1.05607869
258	1.04331952	1.04516451	1.04701275	1.04886425	1.05071902	1.05257704	1.05443835	1.05630292
259	1.04349102	1.04534348	1.04719921	1.04905822	1.05092052	1.05278612	1.05465501	1.05652721
260	1.04366255	1.04552247	1.04738570	1.04925223	1.05112207	1.05299523	1.05487172	1.05675154
261	1.04383411	1.04570150	1.04757222	1.04944627	1.05132366	1.05320439	1.05508847	1.05697592
262	1.04400570	1.04588056	1.04775877	1.04964034	1.05152528	1.05341359	1.05530527	1.05720034
263	1.04417732	1.04605965	1.04794536	1.04983445	1.05172694	1.05362283	1.05552212	1.05742482
264	1.04434897	1.04623877	1.04813198	1.05002860	1.05192864	1.05383211	1.05573901	1.05764934
265	1.04452064	1.04641792	1.04831863	1.05022278	1.05213038	1.05404143	1.05595594	1.05787391
266	1.04469234	1.04659710	1.04850532	1.05041700	1.05233216	1.05425080	1.05617292	1.05809853
267	1.04486407	1.04677631	1.04869204	1.05061126	1.05253398	1.05446020	1.05638994	1.05832319
268	1.04503583	1.04695556	1.04887879	1.05080555	1.05273583	1.05466965	1.05660700	1.05854790
269	1.04520762	1.04713483	1.04906558	1.05099988	1.05293773	1.05487914	1.05682411	1.05877266
270	1.04537943	1.04731413	1.04925240	1.05119424	1.05313966	1.05508867	1.05704127	1.05899747
271	1.04555128	1.04749347	1.04943925	1.05138864	1.05334163	1.05529824	1.05725847	1.05922233
272	1.04572315	1.04767283	1.04962614	1.05158307	1.05354364	1.05550786	1.05747572	1.05944723
273	1.04589505	1.04785223	1.04981306	1.05177754	1.05374569	1.05571751	1.05769301	1.05967218
274	1.04606698	1.04803166	1.05000001	1.05197205	1.05394778	1.05592721	1.05791034	1.05989718
275	1.04623893	1.04821111	1.05018700	1.05216659	1.05414991	1.05613695	1.05812772	1.06012223
276	1.04641092	1.04839060	1.05037402	1.05236117	1.05435207	1.05634673	1.05834514	1.06034732
277	1.04658293	1.04857012	1.05056107	1.05255579	1.05455428	1.05655655	1.05856261	1.06057246
278	1.04675497	1.04874967	1.05074816	1.05275044	1.05475652	1.05676641	1.05878012	1.06079765
279	1.04692704	1.04892925	1.05093528	1.05294512	1.05495880	1.05697632	1.05899768	1.06102289
280	1.04709914	1.04910886	1.05112243	1.05313985	1.05516113	1.05718627	1.05921528	1.06124818
281	1.04727126	1.04928850	1.05130962	1.05333461	1.05536348	1.05739626	1.05943293	1.06147351
282	1.04744342	1.04946818	1.05149683	1.05352940	1.05556588	1.05760629	1.05965062	1.06169889
283	1.04761560	1.04964788	1.05168409	1.05372423	1.05576832	1.05781636	1.05986836	1.06192432
284	1.04778781	1.04982761	1.05187137	1.05391910	1.05597080	1.05802647	1.06008614	1.06214980
285	1.04796005	1.05000738	1.05205869	1.05411400	1.05617331	1.05823663	1.06030396	1.06237532
286	1.04813232	1.05018717	1.05224605	1.05430894	1.05637587	1.05844683	1.06052184	1.06260090
287	1.04830461	1.05036700	1.05243343	1.05450392	1.05657846	1.05865707	1.06073975	1.06282652
288	1.04847694	1.05054686	1.05262085	1.05469893	1.05678109	1.05886735	1.06095771	1.06305219
289	1.04864929	1.05072675	1.05280831	1.05489397	1.05698376	1.05907767	1.06117572	1.06327790
290	1.04882167	1.05090667	1.05299579	1.05508906	1.05718647	1.05928804	1.06139377	1.06350367
291	1.04899408	1.05108661	1.05318331	1.05528418	1.05738922	1.05949844	1.06161186	1.06372948
292	1.04916652	1.05126660	1.05337086	1.05547933	1.05759200	1.05970889	1.06183000	1.06395534
293	1.04933898	1.05144661	1.05355845	1.05567452	1.05779483	1.05991938	1.06204818	1.06418125
294	1.04951148	1.05162665	1.05374607	1.05586975	1.05799769	1.06012991	1.06226641	1.06440720
295	1.04968400	1.05180672	1.05393372	1.05606501	1.05820060	1.06034049	1.06248469	1.06463321
296	1.04985655	1.05198683	1.05412141	1.05626031	1.05840354	1.06055110	1.06270301	1.06485926
297	1.05002913	1.05216696	1.05430913	1.05645565	1.05860652	1.06076176	1.06292137	1.06508536
298	1.05020174	1.05234713	1.05449689	1.05665102	1.05880954	1.06097246	1.06313978	1.06531151
299	1.05037437	1.05252732	1.05468467	1.05684643	1.05901260	1.06118320	1.06335823	1.06553771
300	1.05054704	1.05270755	1.05487249	1.05704187	1.05921570	1.06139398	1.06357673	1.06576395

Day	6.00%	6.25%	6.50%	6.75%	7.00%	7.25%	7.50%	7.75%
301	1.05071973	1.05288781	1.05506035	1.05723735	1.05941884	1.06160481	1.06379527	1.06599024
302	1.05089245	1.05306810	1.05524823	1.05743287	1.05962201	1.06181567	1.06401386	1.06621658
303	1.05106520	1.05324842	1.05543616	1.05762842	1.05982523	1.06202658	1.06423249	1.06644297
304	1.05123798	1.05342877	1.05562411	1.05782401	1.06002848	1.06223753	1.06445117	1.06666941
305	1.05141078	1.05360915	1.05581210	1.05801964	1.06023178	1.06244853	1.06466989	1.06689589
306	1.05158362	1.05378956	1.05600012	1.05821530	1.06043511	1.06265956	1.06488866	1.06712242
307	1.05175648	1.05397001	1.05618817	1.05841099	1.06063848	1.06287064	1.06510747	1.06734901
308	1.05192937	1.05415048	1.05637626	1.05860673	1.06084189	1.06308175	1.06532633	1.06757563
309	1.05210229	1.05433098	1.05656438	1.05880250	1.06104534	1.06329291	1.06554524	1.06780231
310	1.05227524	1.05451152	1.05675254	1.05899830	1.06124883	1.06350412	1.06576418	1.06802904
311	1.05244822	1.05469209	1.05694073	1.05919415	1.06145235	1.06371536	1.06598318	1.06825581
312	1.05262122	1.05487269	1.05712895	1.05939002	1.06165592	1.06392665	1.06620221	1.06848263
313	1.05279426	1.05505331	1.05731721	1.05958594	1.06185953	1.06413797	1.06642130	1.06870950
314	1.05296732	1.05523397	1.05750550	1.05978189	1.06206317	1.06434934	1.06664042	1.06893642
315	1.05314041	1.05541467	1.05769382	1.05997788	1.06226685	1.06456076	1.06685960	1.06916338
316	1.05331353	1.05559539	1.05788217	1.06017390	1.06247058	1.06477221	1.06707881	1.06939040
317	1.05348667	1.05577614	1.05807056	1.06036996	1.06267434	1.06498371	1.06729808	1.06961746
318	1.05365985	1.05595692	1.05825899	1.06056606	1.06287814	1.06519524	1.06751738	1.06984457
319	1.05383305	1.05613774	1.05844745	1.06076219	1.06308198	1.06540682	1.06773674	1.07007173
320	1.05400629	1.05631858	1.05863594	1.06095836	1.06328586	1.06561845	1.06795614	1.07029894
321	1.05417955	1.05649946	1.05882446	1.06115456	1.06348977	1.06583011	1.06817558	1.07052619
322	1.05435284	1.05668037	1.05901302	1.06135080	1.06369373	1.06604181	1.06839507	1.07075350
323	1.05452616	1.05686131	1.05920161	1.06154708	1.06389773	1.06625356	1.06861460	1.07098085
324	1.05469950	1.05704228	1.05939023	1.06174339	1.06410176	1.06646535	1.06883418	1.07120825
325	1.05487288	1.05722328	1.05957889	1.06193974	1.06430584	1.06667719	1.06905380	1.07143570
326	1.05504628	1.05740431	1.05976758	1.06213613	1.06450995	1.06688906	1.06927347	1.07166319
327	1.05521971	1.05758537	1.05995631	1.06233255	1.06471410	1.06710098	1.06949318	1.07189074
328	1.05539318	1.05776646	1.06014507	1.06252901	1.06491829	1.06731293	1.06971294	1.07211833
329	1.05556666	1.05794759	1.06033386	1.06272550	1.06512252	1.06752493	1.06993275	1.07234597
330	1.05574018	1.05812874	1.06052269	1.06292204	1.06532680	1.06773698	1.07015260	1.07257366
331	1.05591373	1.05830993	1.06071155	1.06311860	1.06553110	1.06794906	1.07037249	1.07280140
332	1.05608730	1.05849115	1.06090044	1.06331521	1.06573545	1.06816119	1.07059243	1.07302919
333	1.05626091	1.05867239	1.06108937	1.06351185	1.06593984	1.06837336	1.07081241	1.07325702
334	1.05643454	1.05885367	1.06127833	1.06370853	1.06614427	1.06858557	1.07103244	1.07348491
335	1.05660820	1.05903498	1.06146733	1.06390524	1.06634873	1.06879782	1.07125252	1.07371284

Day	6.00%	6.25%	6.50%	6.75%	7.00%	7.25%	7.50%	7.75%
336	1.05678189	1.05921633	1.06165636	1.06410199	1.06655324	1.06901012	1.07147264	1.07394082
337	1.05695561	1.05939770	1.06184542	1.06429877	1.06675778	1.06922246	1.07169281	1.07416885
338	1.05712935	1.05957910	1.06203451	1.06449560	1.06696237	1.06943484	1.07191302	1.07439692
339	1.05730313	1.05976054	1.06222364	1.06469246	1.06716699	1.06964726	1.07213327	1.07462505
340	1.05747693	1.05994200	1.06241281	1.06488935	1.06737165	1.06985972	1.07235357	1.07485322
341	1.05765076	1.06012350	1.06260200	1.06508628	1.06757635	1.07007223	1.07257392	1.07508144
342	1.05782462	1.06030503	1.06279123	1.06528325	1.06778109	1.07028478	1.07279431	1.07530972
343	1.05799851	1.06048659	1.06298050	1.06548025	1.06798587	1.07049737	1.07301475	1.07553803
344	1.05817243	1.06066818	1.06316980	1.06567730	1.06819069	1.07071000	1.07323523	1.07576640
345	1.05834638	1.06084980	1.06335913	1.06587437	1.06839555	1.07092268	1.07345576	1.07599482
346	1.05852035	1.06103145	1.06354849	1.06607149	1.06860045	1.07113539	1.07367633	1.07622328
347	1.05869435	1.06121313	1.06373789	1.06626864	1.06880539	1.07134815	1.07389695	1.07645180
348	1.05886839	1.06139485	1.06392732	1.06646582	1.06901036	1.07156095	1.07411761	1.07668036
349	1.05904245	1.06157659	1.06411679	1.06666305	1.06921538	1.07177380	1.07433832	1.07690897
350	1.05921654	1.06175837	1.06430629	1.06686031	1.06942043	1.07198669	1.07455908	1.07713763
351	1.05939065	1.06194018	1.06449582	1.06705760	1.06962553	1.07219961	1.07477988	1.07736633
352	1.05956480	1.06212202	1.06468539	1.06725493	1.06983066	1.07241259	1.07500072	1.07759509
353	1.05973897	1.06230389	1.06487499	1.06745230	1.07003583	1.07262560	1.07522161	1.07782389
354	1.05991318	1.06248579	1.06506463	1.06764971	1.07024105	1.07283865	1.07544255	1.07805275
355	1.06008741	1.06266772	1.06525430	1.06784715	1.07044630	1.07305175	1.07566353	1.07828165
356	1.06026167	1.06284969	1.06544400	1.06804463	1.07065159	1.07326489	1.07588456	1.07851060
357	1.06043596	1.06303168	1.06563374	1.06824214	1.07085692	1.07347808	1.07610563	1.07873960
358	1.06061028	1.06321371	1.06582351	1.06843970	1.07106229	1.07369130	1.07632675	1.07896865
359	1.06078463	1.06339576	1.06601331	1.06863728	1.07126770	1.07390457	1.07654791	1.07919774
360	1.06095900	1.06357785	1.06620315	1.06883491	1.07147315	1.07411788	1.07676912	1.07942689
361	1.06113341	1.06375997	1.06639302	1.06903257	1.07167864	1.07433123	1.07699037	1.07965608
362	1.06130784	1.06394212	1.06658293	1.06923027	1.07188416	1.07454463	1.07721167	1.07988532
363	1.06148230	1.06412430	1.06677287	1.06942800	1.07208973	1.07475806	1.07743302	1.08011461
364	1.06165679	1.06430652	1.06696284	1.06962577	1.07229534	1.07497154	1.07765441	1.08034395
365	1.06183131	1.06448876	1.06715285	1.06982358	1.07250098	1.07518506	1.07787584	1.08057334

Day	8.00%	8.25%	8.50%	8.75%	9.00%	9.25%	9.50%	9.75%
1	1.00021918	1.00022603	1.00023288	1.00023973	1.00024658	1.00025342	1.00026027	1.00026712
2	1.00043840	1.00045211	1.00046581	1.00047951	1.00049321	1.00050691	1.00052062	1.00053432
3	1.00065768	1.00067824	1.00069879	1.00071935	1.00073991	1.00076047	1.00078103	1.00080158
4	1.00087700	1.00090442	1.00093183	1.00095925	1.00098667	1.00101408	1.00104150	1.00106892
5	1.00109637	1.00113065	1.00116493	1.00119920	1.00123348	1.00126777	1.00130205	1.00133633
6	1.00131579	1.00135693	1.00139807	1.00143922	1.00148036	1.00152151	1.00156266	1.00160381
7	1.00153526	1.00158327	1.00163128	1.00167929	1.00172730	1.00177532	1.00182334	1.00187136
8	1.00175477	1.00180965	1.00186453	1.00191942	1.00197431	1.00202920	1.00208409	1.00213899
9	1.00197433	1.00203609	1.00209784	1.00215960	1.00222137	1.00228314	1.00234491	1.00240668
10	1.00219394	1.00226257	1.00233121	1.00239985	1.00246849	1.00253714	1.00260579	1.00267445
11	1.00241360	1.00248911	1.00256463	1.00264015	1.00271568	1.00279121	1.00286674	1.00294228
12	1.00263331	1.00271570	1.00279810	1.00288051	1.00296292	1.00304534	1.00312776	1.00321019
13	1.00285307	1.00294234	1.00303163	1.00312092	1.00321023	1.00329953	1.00338885	1.00347817
14	1.00307287	1.00316904	1.00326521	1.00336140	1.00345759	1.00355380	1.00365001	1.00374623
15	1.00329272	1.00339578	1.00349885	1.00360193	1.00370502	1.00380812	1.00391123	1.00401435
16	1.00351262	1.00362258	1.00373254	1.00384252	1.00395251	1.00406251	1.00417252	1.00428255
17	1.00373257	1.00384942	1.00396629	1.00408317	1.00420006	1.00431696	1.00443388	1.00455081
18	1.00395256	1.00407632	1.00420009	1.00432387	1.00444767	1.00457148	1.00469531	1.00481915
19	1.00417261	1.00430327	1.00443394	1.00456463	1.00469534	1.00482607	1.00495681	1.00508756
20	1.00439270	1.00453027	1.00466785	1.00480546	1.00494308	1.00508071	1.00521837	1.00535604
21	1.00461284	1.00475732	1.00490182	1.00504633	1.00519087	1.00533543	1.00548000	1.00562460
22	1.00483303	1.00498442	1.00513583	1.00528727	1.00543873	1.00559020	1.00574170	1.00589322
23	1.00505327	1.00521158	1.00536991	1.00552826	1.00568664	1.00584504	1.00600347	1.00616192
24	1.00527355	1.00543878	1.00560403	1.00576931	1.00593462	1.00609995	1.00626531	1.00643069
25	1.00549389	1.00566604	1.00583822	1.00601042	1.00618266	1.00635492	1.00652721	1.00669953
26	1.00571427	1.00589335	1.00607245	1.00625159	1.00643076	1.00660996	1.00678919	1.00696845
27	1.00593470	1.00612071	1.00630674	1.00649281	1.00667892	1.00686506	1.00705123	1.00723743
28	1.00615518	1.00634812	1.00654109	1.00673410	1.00692714	1.00712022	1.00731334	1.00750649
29	1.00637571	1.00657558	1.00677549	1.00697544	1.00717542	1.00737545	1.00757551	1.00777561
30	1.00659628	1.00680309	1.00700994	1.00721684	1.00742377	1.00763074	1.00783776	1.00804482
31	1.00681691	1.00703066	1.00724445	1.00745829	1.00767217	1.00788610	1.00810007	1.00831409
32	1.00703758	1.00725827	1.00747902	1.00769981	1.00792064	1.00814152	1.00836245	1.00858343
33	1.00725830	1.00748594	1.00771363	1.00794138	1.00816917	1.00839701	1.00862491	1.00885285
34	1.00747907	1.00771366	1.00794831	1.00818301	1.00841776	1.00865257	1.00888742	1.00912234
35	1.00769988	1.00794143	1.00818304	1.00842469	1.00866641	1.00890818	1.00915001	1.00939190
36	1.00792075	1.00816925	1.00841782	1.00866644	1.00891512	1.00916387	1.00941267	1.00966153
37	1.00814166	1.00839713	1.00865265	1.00890824	1.00916390	1.00941961	1.00967539	1.00993123
38	1.00836263	1.00862505	1.00888755	1.00915011	1.00941273	1.00967542	1.00993818	1.01020101
39	1.00858364	1.00885303	1.00912249	1.00939203	1.00966163	1.00993130	1.01020104	1.01047086
40	1.00880470	1.00908106	1.00935749	1.00963400	1.00991059	1.01018724	1.01046397	1.01074078
41	1.00902581	1.00930914	1.00959255	1.00987604	1.01015960	1.01044325	1.01072697	1.01101077
42	1.00924696	1.00953727	1.00982766	1.01011813	1.01040868	1.01069932	1.01099004	1.01128083
43	1.00946817	1.00976545	1.01006283	1.01036028	1.01065783	1.01095546	1.01125317	1.01155097
44	1.00968942	1.00999369	1.01029805	1.01060249	1.01090703	1.01121166	1.01151637	1.01182118
45	1.00991072	1.01022197	1.01053332	1.01084476	1.01115629	1.01146792	1.01177964	1.01209146
46	1.01013207	1.01045031	1.01076865	1.01108709	1.01140562	1.01172425	1.01204298	1.01236181
47	1.01035347	1.01067870	1.01100403	1.01132947	1.01165501	1.01198065	1.01230639	1.01263224
48	1.01057492	1.01090714	1.01123947	1.01157191	1.01190446	1.01223711	1.01256987	1.01290274
49	1.01079641	1.01113564	1.01147497	1.01181441	1.01215397	1.01249364	1.01283342	1.01317331
50	1.01101796	1.01136418	1.01171052	1.01205697	1.01240354	1.01275023	1.01309703	1.01344395

Day	8.00%	8.25%	8.50%	8.75%	9.00%	9.25%	9.50%	9.75%
51	1.01123955	1.01159278	1.01194612	1.01229959	1.01265317	1.01300688	1.01336071	1.01371466
52	1.01146119	1.01182142	1.01218178	1.01254226	1.01290287	1.01326360	1.01362446	1.01398545
53	1.01168288	1.01205012	1.01241749	1.01278499	1.01315263	1.01352039	1.01388828	1.01425631
54	1.01190462	1.01227887	1.01265326	1.01302779	1.01340245	1.01377724	1.01415217	1.01452724
55	1.01212641	1.01250768	1.01288909	1.01327063	1.01365233	1.01403416	1.01441613	1.01479824
56	1.01234825	1.01273653	1.01312496	1.01351354	1.01390227	1.01429114	1.01468016	1.01506932
57	1.01257013	1.01296544	1.01336090	1.01375651	1.01415227	1.01454818	1.01494425	1.01534047
58	1.01279206	1.01319440	1.01359688	1.01399953	1.01440234	1.01480530	1.01520841	1.01561169
59	1.01301404	1.01342340	1.01383293	1.01424261	1.01465246	1.01506247	1.01547265	1.01588298
60	1.01323608	1.01365247	1.01406903	1.01448575	1.01490265	1.01531971	1.01573695	1.01615435
61	1.01345815	1.01388158	1.01430518	1.01472895	1.01515290	1.01557702	1.01600132	1.01642579
62	1.01368028	1.01411074	1.01454139	1.01497221	1.01540321	1.01583439	1.01626576	1.01669730
63	1.01390246	1.01433996	1.01477765	1.01521552	1.01565358	1.01609183	1.01653026	1.01696888
64	1.01412468	1.01456923	1.01501397	1.01545890	1.01590402	1.01634933	1.01679484	1.01724054
65	1.01434696	1.01479855	1.01525034	1.01570233	1.01615452	1.01660690	1.01705949	1.01751227
66	1.01456928	1.01502792	1.01548677	1.01594582	1.01640508	1.01686454	1.01732420	1.01778407
67	1.01479165	1.01525735	1.01572325	1.01618937	1.01665570	1.01712223	1.01758898	1.01805594
68	1.01501407	1.01548682	1.01595979	1.01643298	1.01690638	1.01738000	1.01785383	1.01832789
69	1.01523654	1.01571635	1.01619638	1.01667664	1.01715712	1.01763783	1.01811876	1.01859991
70	1.01545906	1.01594593	1.01643303	1.01692037	1.01740793	1.01789572	1.01838375	1.01887200
71	1.01568162	1.01617556	1.01666974	1.01716415	1.01765880	1.01815368	1.01864880	1.01914416
72	1.01590424	1.01640525	1.01690650	1.01740799	1.01790973	1.01841171	1.01891393	1.01941640
73	1.01612690	1.01663498	1.01714331	1.01765189	1.01816072	1.01866980	1.01917913	1.01968871
74	1.01634962	1.01686477	1.01738018	1.01789585	1.01841177	1.01892795	1.01944439	1.01996109
75	1.01657238	1.01709461	1.01761710	1.01813986	1.01866289	1.01918617	1.01970973	1.02023355
76	1.01679519	1.01732450	1.01785408	1.01838394	1.01891406	1.01944446	1.01997513	1.02050608
77	1.01701805	1.01755444	1.01809112	1.01862807	1.01916530	1.01970281	1.02024061	1.02077868
78	1.01724096	1.01778444	1.01832821	1.01887226	1.01941660	1.01996123	1.02050615	1.02105135
79	1.01746391	1.01801448	1.01856535	1.01911651	1.01966797	1.02021972	1.02077176	1.02132410
80	1.01768692	1.01824458	1.01880255	1.01936082	1.01991939	1.02047826	1.02103744	1.02159692
81	1.01790997	1.01847473	1.01903981	1.01960519	1.02017088	1.02073688	1.02130319	1.02186981
82	1.01813308	1.01870494	1.01927712	1.01984961	1.02042243	1.02099556	1.02156901	1.02214278
83	1.01835623	1.01893519	1.01951448	1.02009410	1.02067404	1.02125430	1.02183490	1.02241581
84	1.01857943	1.01916550	1.01975190	1.02033864	1.02092571	1.02151311	1.02210085	1.02268892
85	1.01880268	1.01939586	1.01998938	1.02058324	1.02117745	1.02177199	1.02236688	1.02296211
86	1.01902598	1.01962627	1.02022691	1.02082790	1.02142924	1.02203093	1.02263297	1.02323537
87	1.01924933	1.01985673	1.02046450	1.02107262	1.02168110	1.02228994	1.02289914	1.02350870
88	1.01947273	1.02008725	1.02070214	1.02131740	1.02193302	1.02254901	1.02316537	1.02378210
89	1.01969617	1.02031782	1.02093984	1.02156224	1.02218501	1.02280815	1.02343168	1.02405557
90	1.01991967	1.02054844	1.02117759	1.02180713	1.02243705	1.02306736	1.02369805	1.02432912
91	1.02014321	1.02077911	1.02141540	1.02205208	1.02268916	1.02332663	1.02396449	1.02460275
92	1.02036680	1.02100983	1.02165326	1.02229710	1.02294133	1.02358597	1.02423100	1.02487644
93	1.02059045	1.02124061	1.02189118	1.02254217	1.02319356	1.02384537	1.02449758	1.02515021
94	1.02081414	1.02147144	1.02212916	1.02278730	1.02344586	1.02410483	1.02476423	1.02542405
95	1.02103788	1.02170232	1.02236719	1.02303249	1.02369821	1.02436437	1.02503095	1.02569797
96	1.02126167	1.02193325	1.02260527	1.02327773	1.02395063	1.02462397	1.02529774	1.02597195
97	1.02148550	1.02216424	1.02284342	1.02352304	1.02420311	1.02488363	1.02556460	1.02624601
98	1.02170939	1.02239527	1.02308161	1.02376841	1.02445566	1.02514336	1.02583153	1.02652015
99	1.02193333	1.02262636	1.02331986	1.02401383	1.02470826	1.02540316	1.02609852	1.02679436
100	1.02215731	1.02285750	1.02355817	1.02425931	1.02496093	1.02566302	1.02636559	1.02706864

Day	8.00%	8.25%	8.50%	8.75%	9.00%	9.25%	9.50%	9.75%
101	1.02238135	1.02308870	1.02379653	1.02450485	1.02521366	1.02592295	1.02663273	1.02734299
102	1.02260543	1.02331994	1.02403495	1.02475045	1.02546645	1.02618294	1.02689993	1.02761742
103	1.02282956	1.02355124	1.02427343	1.02499611	1.02571931	1.02644300	1.02716721	1.02789192
104	1.02305375	1.02378259	1.02451196	1.02524183	1.02597222	1.02670313	1.02743455	1.02816649
105	1.02327798	1.02401400	1.02475054	1.02548761	1.02622520	1.02696332	1.02770197	1.02844114
106	1.02350226	1.02424545	1.02498918	1.02573345	1.02647825	1.02722358	1.02796945	1.02871586
107	1.02372659	1.02447696	1.02522788	1.02597934	1.02673135	1.02748390	1.02823701	1.02899065
108	1.02395096	1.02470852	1.02546663	1.02622529	1.02698452	1.02774429	1.02850463	1.02926552
109	1.02417539	1.02494013	1.02570544	1.02647131	1.02723774	1.02800475	1.02877232	1.02954046
110	1.02439987	1.02517180	1.02594430	1.02671738	1.02749104	1.02826527	1.02904008	1.02981548
111	1.02462439	1.02540351	1.02618322	1.02696351	1.02774439	1.02852586	1.02930792	1.03009056
112	1.02484897	1.02563528	1.02642219	1.02720970	1.02799781	1.02878651	1.02957582	1.03036572
113	1.02507359	1.02586710	1.02666122	1.02745595	1.02825129	1.02904723	1.02984379	1.03064096
114	1.02529827	1.02609898	1.02690031	1.02770226	1.02850483	1.02930802	1.03011183	1.03091627
115	1.02552299	1.02633090	1.02713945	1.02794862	1.02875843	1.02956887	1.03037994	1.03119165
116	1.02574776	1.02656288	1.02737864	1.02819505	1.02901210	1.02982979	1.03064812	1.03146710
117	1.02597258	1.02679491	1.02761790	1.02844153	1.02926583	1.03009077	1.03091638	1.03174263
118	1.02619745	1.02702700	1.02785721	1.02868808	1.02951962	1.03035182	1.03118470	1.03201824
119	1.02642237	1.02725913	1.02809657	1.02893468	1.02977347	1.03061294	1.03145309	1.03229391
120	1.02664734	1.02749132	1.02833599	1.02918134	1.03002739	1.03087412	1.03172155	1.03256966
121	1.02687236	1.02772356	1.02857546	1.02942807	1.03028137	1.03113537	1.03199008	1.03284549
122	1.02709743	1.02795586	1.02881500	1.02967485	1.03053541	1.03139669	1.03225868	1.03312138
123	1.02732255	1.02818820	1.02905458	1.02992169	1.03078951	1.03165807	1.03252735	1.03339735
124	1.02754771	1.02842060	1.02929423	1.03016859	1.03104368	1.03191952	1.03279609	1.03367340
125	1.02777293	1.02865305	1.02953392	1.03041554	1.03129791	1.03218103	1.03306490	1.03394952
126	1.02799820	1.02888556	1.02977368	1.03066256	1.03155220	1.03244261	1.03333378	1.03422571
127	1.02822351	1.02911811	1.03001349	1.03090964	1.03180656	1.03270426	1.03360273	1.03450197
128	1.02844887	1.02935072	1.03025336	1.03115677	1.03206098	1.03296597	1.03387175	1.03477831
129	1.02867429	1.02958338	1.03049328	1.03140397	1.03231546	1.03322775	1.03414084	1.03505473
130	1.02889975	1.02981610	1.03073326	1.03165122	1.03257000	1.03348959	1.03441000	1.03533121
131	1.02912526	1.03004886	1.03097329	1.03189854	1.03282461	1.03375151	1.03467923	1.03560777
132	1.02935082	1.03028168	1.03121338	1.03214591	1.03307928	1.03401348	1.03494853	1.03588441
133	1.02957644	1.03051456	1.03145352	1.03239334	1.03333401	1.03427553	1.03521790	1.03616112
134	1.02980210	1.03074748	1.03169373	1.03264083	1.03358880	1.03453764	1.03548734	1.03643790
135	1.03002781	1.03098046	1.03193398	1.03288838	1.03384366	1.03479982	1.03575685	1.03671476
136	1.03025357	1.03121349	1.03217430	1.03313599	1.03409858	1.03506206	1.03602643	1.03699169
137	1.03047937	1.03144657	1.03241467	1.03338366	1.03435357	1.03532437	1.03629608	1.03726869
138	1.03070523	1.03167971	1.03265509	1.03363139	1.03460861	1.03558675	1.03656580	1.03754577
139	1.03093114	1.03191289	1.03289557	1.03387918	1.03486372	1.03584919	1.03683559	1.03782292
140	1.03115710	1.03214613	1.03313611	1.03412703	1.03511889	1.03611170	1.03710545	1.03810015
141	1.03138311	1.03237943	1.03337670	1.03437494	1.03537413	1.03637428	1.03737538	1.03837745
142	1.03160916	1.03261277	1.03361735	1.03462290	1.03562942	1.03663692	1.03764539	1.03865483
143	1.03183527	1.03284617	1.03385806	1.03487093	1.03588479	1.03689963	1.03791546	1.03893228
144	1.03206142	1.03307962	1.03409882	1.03511901	1.03614021	1.03716240	1.03818560	1.03920980
145	1.03228763	1.03331313	1.03433964	1.03536716	1.03639570	1.03742525	1.03845581	1.03948740
146	1.03251388	1.03354668	1.03458051	1.03561536	1.03665125	1.03768816	1.03872610	1.03976507
147	1.03274019	1.03378029	1.03482144	1.03586363	1.03690686	1.03795113	1.03899645	1.04004281
148	1.03296654	1.03401396	1.03506243	1.03611195	1.03716253	1.03821417	1.03926687	1.04032063
149	1.03319295	1.03424767	1.03530347	1.03636033	1.03741827	1.03847728	1.03953737	1.04059853
150	1.03341940	1.03448144	1.03554457	1.03660878	1.03767407	1.03874046	1.03980793	1.04087649

Day	8.00%	8.25%	8.50%	8.75%	9.00%	9.25%	9.50%	9.75%
151	1.03364590	1.03471526	1.03578572	1.03685728	1.03792994	1.03900370	1.04007857	1.04115454
152	1.03387245	1.03494914	1.03602693	1.03710584	1.03818587	1.03926701	1.04034927	1.04143265
153	1.03409906	1.03518306	1.03626820	1.03735446	1.03844186	1.03953039	1.04062005	1.04171084
154	1.03432571	1.03541704	1.03650952	1.03760314	1.03869791	1.03979383	1.04089089	1.04198911
155	1.03455241	1.03565108	1.03675090	1.03785188	1.03895403	1.04005734	1.04116181	1.04226745
156	1.03477916	1.03588516	1.03699233	1.03810068	1.03921021	1.04032091	1.04143280	1.04254586
157	1.03500596	1.03611930	1.03723383	1.03834954	1.03946645	1.04058456	1.04170386	1.04282435
158	1.03523281	1.03635349	1.03747537	1.03859846	1.03972276	1.04084827	1.04197498	1.04310291
159	1.03545971	1.03658773	1.03771698	1.03884744	1.03997913	1.04111204	1.04224618	1.04338155
160	1.03568666	1.03682203	1.03795864	1.03909648	1.04023556	1.04137589	1.04251745	1.04366026
161	1.03591366	1.03705638	1.03820035	1.03934558	1.04049206	1.04163980	1.04278879	1.04393905
162	1.03614071	1.03729079	1.03844213	1.03959474	1.04074862	1.04190377	1.04306020	1.04421791
163	1.03636781	1.03752524	1.03868396	1.03984395	1.04100524	1.04216782	1.04333169	1.04449684
164	1.03659496	1.03775975	1.03892584	1.04009323	1.04126193	1.04243193	1.04360324	1.04477585
165	1.03682216	1.03799431	1.03916778	1.04034257	1.04151868	1.04269611	1.04387486	1.04505494
166	1.03704941	1.03822893	1.03940978	1.04059197	1.04177549	1.04296035	1.04414655	1.04533410
167	1.03727671	1.03846360	1.03965183	1.04084142	1.04203237	1.04322466	1.04441832	1.04561333
168	1.03750406	1.03869832	1.03989395	1.04109094	1.04228931	1.04348904	1.04469015	1.04589264
169	1.03773145	1.03893309	1.04013611	1.04134052	1.04254631	1.04375349	1.04496206	1.04617202
170	1.03795890	1.03916792	1.04037834	1.04159015	1.04280338	1.04401800	1.04523403	1.04645148
171	1.03818640	1.03940280	1.04062062	1.04183985	1.04306051	1.04428258	1.04550608	1.04673101
172	1.03841395	1.03963773	1.04086295	1.04208961	1.04331770	1.04454723	1.04577820	1.04701061
173	1.03864155	1.03987272	1.04110534	1.04233942	1.04357495	1.04481194	1.04605039	1.04729029
174	1.03886919	1.04010776	1.04134779	1.04258930	1.04383227	1.04507672	1.04632265	1.04757005
175	1.03909689	1.04034285	1.04159030	1.04283923	1.04408966	1.04534157	1.04659498	1.04784988
176	1.03932464	1.04057800	1.04183286	1.04308923	1.04434710	1.04560649	1.04686738	1.04812978
177	1.03955243	1.04081320	1.04207548	1.04333929	1.04460461	1.04587147	1.04713985	1.04840976
178	1.03978028	1.04104845	1.04231816	1.04358940	1.04486219	1.04613652	1.04741240	1.04868982
179	1.04000818	1.04128375	1.04256089	1.04383958	1.04511983	1.04640164	1.04768501	1.04896995
180	1.04023613	1.04151911	1.04280367	1.04408981	1.04537753	1.04666682	1.04795770	1.04925015
181	1.04046412	1.04175453	1.04304652	1.04434011	1.04563529	1.04693207	1.04823045	1.04953043
182	1.04069217	1.04198999	1.04328942	1.04459046	1.04589312	1.04719739	1.04850328	1.04981079
183	1.04092027	1.04222551	1.04353238	1.04484088	1.04615101	1.04746278	1.04877618	1.05009122
184	1.04114841	1.04246108	1.04377539	1.04509135	1.04640897	1.04772823	1.04904915	1.05037172
185	1.04137661	1.04269670	1.04401846	1.04534189	1.04666698	1.04799375	1.04932219	1.05065230
186	1.04160486	1.04293238	1.04426159	1.04559249	1.04692507	1.04825934	1.04959530	1.05093295
187	1.04183315	1.04316811	1.04450478	1.04584314	1.04718321	1.04852499	1.04986848	1.05121368
188	1.04206150	1.04340390	1.04474802	1.04609386	1.04744142	1.04879071	1.05014173	1.05149448
189	1.04228990	1.04363974	1.04499131	1.04634463	1.04769969	1.04905650	1.05041506	1.05177536
190	1.04251834	1.04387563	1.04523467	1.04659547	1.04795803	1.04932236	1.05068845	1.05205632
191	1.04274684	1.04411157	1.04547808	1.04684636	1.04821643	1.04958828	1.05096192	1.05233734
192	1.04297539	1.04434757	1.04572155	1.04709732	1.04847490	1.04985427	1.05123546	1.05261845
193	1.04320399	1.04458362	1.04596507	1.04734834	1.04873342	1.05012033	1.05150907	1.05289963
194	1.04343263	1.04481973	1.04620865	1.04759941	1.04899202	1.05038646	1.05178275	1.05318088
195	1.04366133	1.04505588	1.04645229	1.04785055	1.04925067	1.05065265	1.05205650	1.05346221
196	1.04389008	1.04529209	1.04669598	1.04810175	1.04950939	1.05091892	1.05233032	1.05374361
197	1.04411888	1.04552836	1.04693973	1.04835301	1.04976817	1.05118524	1.05260422	1.05402509
198	1.04434773	1.04576468	1.04718354	1.04860432	1.05002702	1.05145164	1.05287818	1.05430665
199	1.04457662	1.04600105	1.04742741	1.04885570	1.05028593	1.05171810	1.05315222	1.05458828
200	1.04480557	1.04623747	1.04767133	1.04910714	1.05054491	1.05198464	1.05342633	1.05486998

Day	8.00%	8.25%	8.50%	8.75%	9.00%	9.25%	9.50%	9.75%
201	1.04503457	1.04647395	1.04791531	1.04935864	1.05080395	1.05225123	1.05370051	1.05515176
202	1.04526362	1.04671048	1.04815934	1.04961020	1.05106305	1.05251790	1.05397476	1.05543362
203	1.04549272	1.04694707	1.04840343	1.04986181	1.05132221	1.05278463	1.05424908	1.05571555
204	1.04572187	1.04718371	1.04864758	1.05011349	1.05158144	1.05305144	1.05452347	1.05599756
205	1.04595107	1.04742040	1.04889179	1.05036523	1.05184074	1.05331831	1.05479794	1.05627964
206	1.04618032	1.04765715	1.04913605	1.05061703	1.05210010	1.05358524	1.05507247	1.05656180
207	1.04640962	1.04789395	1.04938037	1.05086889	1.05235952	1.05385225	1.05534708	1.05684403
208	1.04663897	1.04813080	1.04962475	1.05112081	1.05261900	1.05411932	1.05562176	1.05712634
209	1.04686837	1.04836770	1.04986918	1.05137279	1.05287855	1.05438646	1.05589651	1.05740872
210	1.04709782	1.04860466	1.05011367	1.05162484	1.05313817	1.05465367	1.05617133	1.05769118
211	1.04732732	1.04884168	1.05035822	1.05187694	1.05339785	1.05492094	1.05644623	1.05797371
212	1.04755687	1.04907874	1.05060282	1.05212910	1.05365759	1.05518828	1.05672119	1.05825632
213	1.04778647	1.04931586	1.05084748	1.05238132	1.05391739	1.05545569	1.05699623	1.05853901
214	1.04801612	1.04955304	1.05109220	1.05263361	1.05417726	1.05572317	1.05727134	1.05882177
215	1.04824582	1.04979027	1.05133697	1.05288595	1.05443720	1.05599072	1.05754652	1.05910460
216	1.04847558	1.05002755	1.05158181	1.05313835	1.05469720	1.05625833	1.05782177	1.05938751
217	1.04870538	1.05026488	1.05182670	1.05339082	1.05495726	1.05652602	1.05809710	1.05967050
218	1.04893523	1.05050227	1.05207164	1.05364334	1.05521738	1.05679377	1.05837249	1.05995356
219	1.04916514	1.05073971	1.05231664	1.05389593	1.05547758	1.05706158	1.05864796	1.06023670
220	1.04939509	1.05097721	1.05256170	1.05414858	1.05573783	1.05732947	1.05892350	1.06051991
221	1.04962509	1.05121476	1.05280682	1.05440128	1.05599815	1.05759742	1.05919911	1.06080320
222	1.04985515	1.05145236	1.05305200	1.05465405	1.05625853	1.05786544	1.05947479	1.06108657
223	1.05008525	1.05169002	1.05329723	1.05490688	1.05651898	1.05813353	1.05975054	1.06137001
224	1.05031541	1.05192773	1.05354251	1.05515977	1.05677949	1.05840169	1.06002637	1.06165353
225	1.05054562	1.05216550	1.05378786	1.05541272	1.05704007	1.05866991	1.06030226	1.06193712
226	1.05077587	1.05240331	1.05403326	1.05566573	1.05730071	1.05893821	1.06057823	1.06222079
227	1.05100618	1.05264119	1.05427872	1.05591880	1.05756141	1.05920657	1.06085427	1.06250453
228	1.05123654	1.05287911	1.05452424	1.05617193	1.05782218	1.05947500	1.06113039	1.06278835
229	1.05146695	1.05311709	1.05476981	1.05642512	1.05808301	1.05974349	1.06140657	1.06307225
230	1.05169740	1.05335512	1.05501545	1.05667837	1.05834391	1.06001206	1.06168283	1.06335622
231	1.05192791	1.05359321	1.05526113	1.05693169	1.05860487	1.06028069	1.06195916	1.06364027
232	1.05215847	1.05383135	1.05550688	1.05718506	1.05886590	1.06054939	1.06223556	1.06392439
233	1.05238908	1.05406955	1.05575268	1.05743849	1.05912699	1.06081816	1.06251203	1.06420859
234	1.05261974	1.05430780	1.05599854	1.05769199	1.05938814	1.06108700	1.06278857	1.06449286
235	1.05285045	1.05454610	1.05624446	1.05794555	1.05964936	1.06135591	1.06306519	1.06477721
236	1.05308122	1.05478445	1.05649043	1.05819916	1.05991064	1.06162488	1.06334188	1.06506164
237	1.05331203	1.05502286	1.05673647	1.05845284	1.06017199	1.06189392	1.06361864	1.06534614
238	1.05354289	1.05526133	1.05698256	1.05870658	1.06043340	1.06216303	1.06389547	1.06563072
239	1.05377380	1.05549985	1.05722870	1.05896038	1.06069488	1.06243221	1.06417237	1.06591538
240	1.05400477	1.05573842	1.05747491	1.05921424	1.06095642	1.06270146	1.06444935	1.06620011
241	1.05423578	1.05597704	1.05772117	1.05946816	1.06121803	1.06297077	1.06472640	1.06648491
242	1.05446685	1.05621572	1.05796749	1.05972214	1.06147970	1.06324015	1.06500352	1.06676980
243	1.05469797	1.05645446	1.05821386	1.05997619	1.06174143	1.06350961	1.06528071	1.06705476
244	1.05492913	1.05669324	1.05846030	1.06023029	1.06200323	1.06377913	1.06555798	1.06733979
245	1.05516035	1.05693209	1.05870679	1.06048445	1.06226510	1.06404871	1.06583531	1.06762490
246	1.05539162	1.05717098	1.05895334	1.06073868	1.06252702	1.06431837	1.06611272	1.06791009
247	1.05562294	1.05740993	1.05919994	1.06099297	1.06278902	1.06458809	1.06639020	1.06819535
248	1.05585431	1.05764894	1.05944660	1.06124731	1.06305107	1.06485789	1.06666776	1.06848069
249	1.05608573	1.05788799	1.05969332	1.06150172	1.06331320	1.06512775	1.06694538	1.06876611
250	1.05631720	1.05812710	1.05994010	1.06175619	1.06357538	1.06539768	1.06722308	1.06905160

Day	8.00%	8.25%	8.50%	8.75%	9.00%	9.25%	9.50%	9.75%
251	1.05654872	1.05836627	1.06018694	1.06201072	1.06383763	1.06566768	1.06750085	1.06933717
252	1.05678029	1.05860549	1.06043383	1.06226531	1.06409995	1.06593774	1.06777870	1.06962281
253	1.05701191	1.05884476	1.06068078	1.06251997	1.06436233	1.06620788	1.06805661	1.06990854
254	1.05724359	1.05908409	1.06092779	1.06277468	1.06462478	1.06647808	1.06833460	1.07019433
255	1.05747531	1.05932347	1.06117485	1.06302946	1.06488729	1.06674835	1.06861266	1.07048021
256	1.05770709	1.05956291	1.06142198	1.06328429	1.06514986	1.06701869	1.06889079	1.07076616
257	1.05793891	1.05980240	1.06166916	1.06353919	1.06541250	1.06728910	1.06916899	1.07105218
258	1.05817079	1.06004194	1.06191640	1.06379415	1.06567521	1.06755958	1.06944727	1.07133829
259	1.05840272	1.06028154	1.06216369	1.06404917	1.06593798	1.06783012	1.06972562	1.07162447
260	1.05863470	1.06052120	1.06241104	1.06430425	1.06620081	1.06810074	1.07000404	1.07191072
261	1.05886673	1.06076090	1.06265845	1.06455939	1.06646371	1.06837142	1.07028254	1.07219705
262	1.05909881	1.06100066	1.06290592	1.06481459	1.06672667	1.06864217	1.07056110	1.07248346
263	1.05933094	1.06124048	1.06315345	1.06506985	1.06698970	1.06891299	1.07083974	1.07276995
264	1.05956312	1.06148035	1.06340103	1.06532518	1.06725279	1.06918388	1.07111845	1.07305651
265	1.05979535	1.06172027	1.06364867	1.06558057	1.06751595	1.06945484	1.07139724	1.07334315
266	1.06002764	1.06196025	1.06389637	1.06583601	1.06777918	1.06972587	1.07167609	1.07362986
267	1.06025997	1.06220028	1.06414413	1.06609152	1.06804246	1.06999696	1.07195502	1.07391666
268	1.06049236	1.06244037	1.06439194	1.06634709	1.06830582	1.07026813	1.07223403	1.07420352
269	1.06072479	1.06268051	1.06463982	1.06660272	1.06856923	1.07053936	1.07251310	1.07449047
270	1.06095728	1.06292070	1.06488775	1.06685841	1.06883272	1.07081066	1.07279225	1.07477749
271	1.06118982	1.06316095	1.06513573	1.06711417	1.06909626	1.07108203	1.07307147	1.07506459
272	1.06142241	1.06340126	1.06538378	1.06736998	1.06935988	1.07135347	1.07335076	1.07535176
273	1.06165505	1.06364161	1.06563188	1.06762586	1.06962356	1.07162497	1.07363013	1.07563901
274	1.06188774	1.06388203	1.06588004	1.06788180	1.06988730	1.07189655	1.07390956	1.07592634
275	1.06212048	1.06412249	1.06612826	1.06813780	1.07015111	1.07216820	1.07418907	1.07621375
276	1.06235328	1.06436301	1.06637654	1.06839386	1.07041498	1.07243991	1.07446866	1.07650123
277	1.06258612	1.06460359	1.06662487	1.06864998	1.07067892	1.07271169	1.07474831	1.07678879
278	1.06281902	1.06484422	1.06687326	1.06890616	1.07094292	1.07298354	1.07502804	1.07707642
279	1.06305196	1.06508490	1.06712171	1.06916241	1.07120699	1.07325546	1.07530784	1.07736414
280	1.06328496	1.06532564	1.06737022	1.06941871	1.07147112	1.07352745	1.07558772	1.07765192
281	1.06351801	1.06556643	1.06761879	1.06967508	1.07173532	1.07379951	1.07586767	1.07793979
282	1.06375111	1.06580728	1.06786741	1.06993151	1.07199958	1.07407164	1.07614769	1.07822773
283	1.06398426	1.06604818	1.06811609	1.07018800	1.07226391	1.07434384	1.07642778	1.07851575
284	1.06421746	1.06628914	1.06836483	1.07044455	1.07252831	1.07461610	1.07670795	1.07880385
285	1.06445072	1.06653015	1.06861363	1.07070116	1.07279276	1.07488844	1.07698819	1.07909202
286	1.06468402	1.06677121	1.06886248	1.07095784	1.07305729	1.07516084	1.07726850	1.07938027
287	1.06491738	1.06701233	1.06911140	1.07121458	1.07332188	1.07543331	1.07754888	1.07966860
288	1.06515078	1.06725351	1.06936037	1.07147137	1.07358653	1.07570585	1.07782934	1.07995701
289	1.06538424	1.06749474	1.06960940	1.07172823	1.07385125	1.07597846	1.07810987	1.08024549
290	1.06561775	1.06773602	1.06985848	1.07198515	1.07411604	1.07625114	1.07839048	1.08053405
291	1.06585131	1.06797736	1.07010763	1.07224214	1.07438089	1.07652389	1.07867115	1.08082268
292	1.06608492	1.06821875	1.07035683	1.07249918	1.07464580	1.07679671	1.07895190	1.08111139
293	1.06631858	1.06846020	1.07060609	1.07275629	1.07491079	1.07706959	1.07923273	1.08140018
294	1.06655230	1.06870170	1.07085541	1.07301346	1.07517583	1.07734255	1.07951362	1.08168905
295	1.06678606	1.06894325	1.07110479	1.07327068	1.07544094	1.07761558	1.07979459	1.08197800
296	1.06701988	1.06918486	1.07135423	1.07352798	1.07570612	1.07788867	1.08007563	1.08226702
297	1.06725375	1.06942653	1.07160372	1.07378533	1.07597136	1.07816183	1.08035675	1.08255612
298	1.06748766	1.06966825	1.07185327	1.07404274	1.07623667	1.07843507	1.08063794	1.08284529
299	1.06772163	1.06991002	1.07210288	1.07430022	1.07650205	1.07870837	1.08091920	1.08313455
300	1.06795566	1.07015185	1.07235255	1.07455776	1.07676748	1.07898174	1.08120053	1.08342388

Day	8.00%	8.25%	8.50%	8.75%	9.00%	9.25%	9.50%	9.75%
301	1.06818973	1.07039373	1.07260227	1.07481536	1.07703299	1.07925518	1.08148194	1.08371328
302	1.06842385	1.07063567	1.07285206	1.07507302	1.07729856	1.07952869	1.08176342	1.08400277
303	1.06865803	1.07087767	1.07310190	1.07533074	1.07756419	1.07980227	1.08204498	1.08429233
304	1.06889225	1.07111971	1.07335180	1.07558852	1.07782989	1.08007592	1.08232661	1.08458197
305	1.06912653	1.07136182	1.07360176	1.07584637	1.07809566	1.08034964	1.08260831	1.08487169
306	1.06936086	1.07160397	1.07385178	1.07610428	1.07836149	1.08062342	1.08289008	1.08516148
307	1.06959524	1.07184619	1.07410185	1.07636225	1.07862739	1.08089728	1.08317193	1.08545135
308	1.06982967	1.07208845	1.07435199	1.07662028	1.07889335	1.08117121	1.08345385	1.08574130
309	1.07006416	1.07233077	1.07460218	1.07687838	1.07915938	1.08144520	1.08373585	1.08603133
310	1.07029869	1.07257315	1.07485243	1.07713653	1.07942548	1.08171927	1.08401792	1.08632143
311	1.07053328	1.07281558	1.07510273	1.07739475	1.07969163	1.08199340	1.08430006	1.08661162
312	1.07076791	1.07305807	1.07535310	1.07765303	1.07995786	1.08226760	1.08458227	1.08690188
313	1.07100260	1.07330061	1.07560353	1.07791137	1.08022415	1.08254188	1.08486456	1.08719221
314	1.07123734	1.07354320	1.07585401	1.07816977	1.08049051	1.08281622	1.08514692	1.08748263
315	1.07147213	1.07378585	1.07610455	1.07842824	1.08075693	1.08309063	1.08542936	1.08777312
316	1.07170698	1.07402856	1.07635515	1.07868677	1.08102342	1.08336511	1.08571187	1.08806369
317	1.07194187	1.07427132	1.07660581	1.07894536	1.08128997	1.08363967	1.08599445	1.08835434
318	1.07217682	1.07451413	1.07685652	1.07920401	1.08155659	1.08391429	1.08627711	1.08864506
319	1.07241182	1.07475700	1.07710730	1.07946272	1.08182328	1.08418898	1.08655984	1.08893586
320	1.07264687	1.07499993	1.07735813	1.07972150	1.08209003	1.08446374	1.08684264	1.08922674
321	1.07288197	1.07524291	1.07760902	1.07998033	1.08235684	1.08473857	1.08712552	1.08951770
322	1.07311712	1.07548594	1.07785997	1.08023923	1.08262373	1.08501347	1.08740847	1.08980874
323	1.07335232	1.07572903	1.07811098	1.08049819	1.08289067	1.08528844	1.08769149	1.09009985
324	1.07358758	1.07597217	1.07836205	1.08075722	1.08315769	1.08556348	1.08797459	1.09039104
325	1.07382288	1.07621537	1.07861317	1.08101630	1.08342477	1.08583858	1.08825776	1.09068231
326	1.07405824	1.07645863	1.07886436	1.08127545	1.08369191	1.08611376	1.08854101	1.09097366
327	1.07429365	1.07670194	1.07911560	1.08153466	1.08395913	1.08638901	1.08882432	1.09126508
328	1.07452911	1.07694530	1.07936690	1.08179393	1.08422640	1.08666433	1.08910772	1.09155658
329	1.07476463	1.07718872	1.07961826	1.08205327	1.08449375	1.08693972	1.08939118	1.09184816
330	1.07500019	1.07743219	1.07986968	1.08231266	1.08476116	1.08721517	1.08967472	1.09213982
331	1.07523581	1.07767572	1.08012116	1.08257212	1.08502863	1.08749070	1.08995834	1.09243156
332	1.07547148	1.07791931	1.08037269	1.08283164	1.08529617	1.08776630	1.09024202	1.09272337
333	1.07570720	1.07816295	1.08062428	1.08309122	1.08556378	1.08804196	1.09052579	1.09301526
334	1.07594297	1.07840664	1.08087594	1.08335087	1.08583145	1.08831770	1.09080962	1.09330723
335	1.07617879	1.07865039	1.08112765	1.08361058	1.08609919	1.08859351	1.09109353	1.09359928

Day	8.00%	8.25%	8.50%	8.75%	9.00%	9.25%	9.50%	9.75%
336	1.07641467	1.07889419	1.08137942	1.08387035	1.08636700	1.08886938	1.09137751	1.09389141
337	1.07665059	1.07913805	1.08163125	1.08413018	1.08663487	1.08914533	1.09166157	1.09418361
338	1.07688657	1.07938197	1.08188313	1.08439007	1.08690281	1.08942135	1.09194570	1.09447589
339	1.07712260	1.07962594	1.08213508	1.08465003	1.08717081	1.08969743	1.09222991	1.09476825
340	1.07735868	1.07986996	1.08238708	1.08491005	1.08743888	1.08997359	1.09251419	1.09506069
341	1.07759482	1.08011404	1.08263914	1.08517013	1.08770702	1.09024981	1.09279854	1.09535321
342	1.07783100	1.08035818	1.08289127	1.08543027	1.08797522	1.09052611	1.09308297	1.09564580
343	1.07806724	1.08060237	1.08314345	1.08569048	1.08824349	1.09080248	1.09336747	1.09593847
344	1.07830353	1.08084662	1.08339568	1.08595075	1.08851182	1.09107891	1.09365204	1.09623122
345	1.07853987	1.08109092	1.08364798	1.08621108	1.08878022	1.09135542	1.09393669	1.09652405
346	1.07877626	1.08133527	1.08390034	1.08647147	1.08904869	1.09163200	1.09422142	1.09681696
347	1.07901270	1.08157968	1.08415275	1.08673193	1.08931722	1.09190864	1.09450621	1.09710994
348	1.07924920	1.08182415	1.08440523	1.08699244	1.08958582	1.09218536	1.09479108	1.09740301
349	1.07948575	1.08206867	1.08465776	1.08725302	1.08985448	1.09246215	1.09507603	1.09769615
350	1.07972235	1.08231325	1.08491035	1.08751367	1.09012321	1.09273900	1.09536105	1.09798937
351	1.07995900	1.08255788	1.08516300	1.08777437	1.09039201	1.09301593	1.09564614	1.09828267
352	1.08019570	1.08280257	1.08541571	1.08803514	1.09066087	1.09329293	1.09593131	1.09857605
353	1.08043246	1.08304731	1.08566848	1.08829597	1.09092980	1.09356999	1.09621655	1.09886950
354	1.08066926	1.08329211	1.08592131	1.08855686	1.09119880	1.09384713	1.09650187	1.09916303
355	1.08090612	1.08353696	1.08617419	1.08881782	1.09146786	1.09412434	1.09678726	1.09945665
356	1.08114303	1.08378187	1.08642714	1.08907884	1.09173699	1.09440162	1.09707273	1.09975034
357	1.08138000	1.08402684	1.08668014	1.08933992	1.09200619	1.09467897	1.09735827	1.10004411
358	1.08161701	1.08427186	1.08693320	1.08960106	1.09227545	1.09495638	1.09764388	1.10033795
359	1.08185408	1.08451693	1.08718632	1.08986227	1.09254478	1.09523387	1.09792957	1.10063188
360	1.08209120	1.08476206	1.08743950	1.09012354	1.09281417	1.09551143	1.09821533	1.10092588
361	1.08232837	1.08500725	1.08769274	1.09038487	1.09308363	1.09578906	1.09850117	1.10121997
362	1.08256559	1.08525249	1.08794604	1.09064626	1.09335316	1.09606676	1.09878708	1.10151413
363	1.08280286	1.08549779	1.08819940	1.09090772	1.09362276	1.09634453	1.09907306	1.10180837
364	1.08304019	1.08574314	1.08845282	1.09116923	1.09389242	1.09662237	1.09935912	1.10210269
365	1.08327757	1.08598855	1.08870629	1.09143082	1.09416214	1.09690028	1.09964526	1.10239708

Day	10.00%	10.25%	10.50%	10.75%	11.00%	11.25%	11.50%	11.75%
1	1.00027397	1.00028082	1.00028767	1.00029452	1.00030137	1.00030822	1.00031507	1.00032192
2	1.00054802	1.00056172	1.00057543	1.00058913	1.00060283	1.00061653	1.00063024	1.00064394
3	1.00082214	1.00084270	1.00086326	1.00088382	1.00090438	1.00092494	1.00094550	1.00096606
4	1.00109634	1.00112376	1.00115118	1.00117860	1.00120602	1.00123345	1.00126087	1.00128829
5	1.00137061	1.00140490	1.00143918	1.00147347	1.00150776	1.00154205	1.00157634	1.00161063
6	1.00164496	1.00168611	1.00172727	1.00176842	1.00180958	1.00185074	1.00189190	1.00193306
7	1.00191939	1.00196741	1.00201544	1.00206347	1.00211150	1.00215953	1.00220757	1.00225560
8	1.00219388	1.00224878	1.00230369	1.00235859	1.00241350	1.00246841	1.00252333	1.00257825
9	1.00246846	1.00253024	1.00259202	1.00265381	1.00271560	1.00277739	1.00283919	1.00290099
10	1.00274311	1.00281177	1.00288044	1.00294911	1.00301779	1.00308647	1.00315516	1.00322385
11	1.00301783	1.00309338	1.00316894	1.00324450	1.00332007	1.00339564	1.00347122	1.00354680
12	1.00329263	1.00337507	1.00345752	1.00353998	1.00362244	1.00370491	1.00378738	1.00386986
13	1.00356750	1.00365684	1.00374619	1.00383554	1.00392490	1.00401427	1.00410364	1.00419302
14	1.00384245	1.00393869	1.00403494	1.00413119	1.00422745	1.00432372	1.00442000	1.00451629
15	1.00411748	1.00422062	1.00432377	1.00442693	1.00453010	1.00463328	1.00473646	1.00483966
16	1.00439258	1.00450263	1.00461268	1.00472275	1.00483283	1.00494292	1.00505303	1.00516314
17	1.00466776	1.00478471	1.00490168	1.00501866	1.00513566	1.00525267	1.00536969	1.00548672
18	1.00494301	1.00506688	1.00519076	1.00531466	1.00543858	1.00556250	1.00568645	1.00581040
19	1.00521833	1.00534912	1.00547993	1.00561075	1.00574158	1.00587244	1.00600331	1.00613419
20	1.00549374	1.00563145	1.00576918	1.00590692	1.00604468	1.00618247	1.00632027	1.00645808
21	1.00576921	1.00591385	1.00605851	1.00620318	1.00634788	1.00649259	1.00663733	1.00678208
22	1.00604477	1.00619633	1.00634792	1.00649953	1.00665116	1.00680281	1.00695449	1.00710618
23	1.00632040	1.00647890	1.00663742	1.00679596	1.00695453	1.00711313	1.00727175	1.00743039
24	1.00659610	1.00676154	1.00692700	1.00709249	1.00725800	1.00742354	1.00758911	1.00775470
25	1.00687188	1.00704426	1.00721666	1.00738910	1.00756156	1.00773405	1.00790656	1.00807911
26	1.00714774	1.00732706	1.00750641	1.00768579	1.00786521	1.00804465	1.00822412	1.00840363
27	1.00742367	1.00760994	1.00779624	1.00798258	1.00816895	1.00835535	1.00854178	1.00872825
28	1.00769967	1.00789290	1.00808615	1.00827945	1.00847278	1.00866614	1.00885954	1.00905298
29	1.00797576	1.00817593	1.00837615	1.00857641	1.00877670	1.00897703	1.00917740	1.00937781
30	1.00825191	1.00845905	1.00866623	1.00887345	1.00908072	1.00928802	1.00949536	1.00970275
31	1.00852815	1.00874225	1.00895640	1.00917059	1.00938482	1.00959910	1.00981342	1.01002779
32	1.00880446	1.00902553	1.00924664	1.00946781	1.00968902	1.00991028	1.01013158	1.01035294
33	1.00908084	1.00930888	1.00953698	1.00976512	1.00999331	1.01022155	1.01044984	1.01067819
34	1.00935730	1.00959232	1.00982739	1.01006251	1.01029769	1.01053292	1.01076821	1.01100354
35	1.00963384	1.00987583	1.01011789	1.01036000	1.01060216	1.01084439	1.01108667	1.01132900
36	1.00991045	1.01015943	1.01040847	1.01065757	1.01090673	1.01115595	1.01140523	1.01165457
37	1.01018714	1.01044310	1.01069914	1.01095523	1.01121139	1.01146761	1.01172389	1.01198024
38	1.01046390	1.01072686	1.01098988	1.01125298	1.01151614	1.01177936	1.01204265	1.01230601
39	1.01074074	1.01101069	1.01128072	1.01155081	1.01182098	1.01209121	1.01236152	1.01263189
40	1.01101766	1.01129461	1.01157163	1.01184873	1.01212591	1.01240316	1.01268048	1.01295787
41	1.01129465	1.01157860	1.01186263	1.01214674	1.01243093	1.01271520	1.01299954	1.01328396
42	1.01157171	1.01186267	1.01215372	1.01244484	1.01273605	1.01302734	1.01331871	1.01361016
43	1.01184886	1.01214683	1.01244488	1.01274303	1.01304126	1.01333957	1.01363797	1.01393646
44	1.01212608	1.01243106	1.01273614	1.01304130	1.01334656	1.01365190	1.01395734	1.01426286
45	1.01240337	1.01271537	1.01302747	1.01333966	1.01365195	1.01396433	1.01427680	1.01458937
46	1.01268074	1.01299977	1.01331889	1.01363811	1.01395743	1.01427685	1.01459637	1.01491598
47	1.01295819	1.01328424	1.01361039	1.01393665	1.01426301	1.01458947	1.01491604	1.01524270
48	1.01323571	1.01356879	1.01390198	1.01423527	1.01456868	1.01490219	1.01523580	1.01556953
49	1.01351331	1.01385342	1.01419365	1.01453399	1.01487444	1.01521500	1.01555567	1.01589646
50	1.01379098	1.01413814	1.01448540	1.01483279	1.01518029	1.01552791	1.01587564	1.01622349

Day	10.00%	10.25%	10.50%	10.75%	11.00%	11.25%	11.50%	11.75%
51	1.01406873	1.01442293	1.01477724	1.01513168	1.01548624	1.01584091	1.01619571	1.01655063
52	1.01434656	1.01470780	1.01506916	1.01543066	1.01579227	1.01615402	1.01651588	1.01687788
53	1.01462447	1.01499275	1.01536117	1.01572972	1.01609840	1.01646721	1.01683616	1.01720523
54	1.01490244	1.01527778	1.01565326	1.01602887	1.01640462	1.01678051	1.01715653	1.01753269
55	1.01518050	1.01556290	1.01594544	1.01632811	1.01671094	1.01709390	1.01747700	1.01786025
56	1.01545863	1.01584809	1.01623769	1.01662744	1.01701734	1.01740739	1.01779758	1.01818792
57	1.01573684	1.01613336	1.01653004	1.01692686	1.01732384	1.01772097	1.01811825	1.01851569
58	1.01601512	1.01641871	1.01682246	1.01722637	1.01763043	1.01803465	1.01843903	1.01884357
59	1.01629348	1.01670415	1.01711497	1.01752596	1.01793711	1.01834843	1.01875991	1.01917155
60	1.01657192	1.01698966	1.01740757	1.01782564	1.01824389	1.01866230	1.01908089	1.01949964
61	1.01685043	1.01727525	1.01770025	1.01812541	1.01855076	1.01897628	1.01940197	1.01982784
62	1.01712902	1.01756093	1.01799301	1.01842527	1.01885772	1.01929034	1.01972315	1.02015614
63	1.01740769	1.01784668	1.01828586	1.01872522	1.01916477	1.01960451	1.02004443	1.02048454
64	1.01768643	1.01813251	1.01857879	1.01902526	1.01947192	1.01991877	1.02036582	1.02081306
65	1.01796525	1.01841843	1.01887180	1.01932538	1.01977916	1.02023313	1.02068730	1.02114167
66	1.01824414	1.01870442	1.01916490	1.01962559	1.02008649	1.02054758	1.02100889	1.02147040
67	1.01852311	1.01899050	1.01945809	1.01992589	1.02039391	1.02086214	1.02133058	1.02179923
68	1.01880216	1.01927665	1.01975136	1.02022628	1.02070143	1.02117679	1.02165237	1.02212816
69	1.01908128	1.01956289	1.02004471	1.02052676	1.02100903	1.02149153	1.02197426	1.02245720
70	1.01936048	1.01984920	1.02033815	1.02082733	1.02131674	1.02180638	1.02229625	1.02278635
71	1.01963976	1.02013560	1.02063167	1.02112798	1.02162453	1.02212132	1.02261834	1.02311560
72	1.01991912	1.02042207	1.02092528	1.02142872	1.02193242	1.02243635	1.02294054	1.02344496
73	1.02019855	1.02070863	1.02121897	1.02172956	1.02224040	1.02275149	1.02326283	1.02377443
74	1.02047805	1.02099527	1.02151274	1.02203048	1.02254847	1.02306672	1.02358523	1.02410400
75	1.02075763	1.02128199	1.02180660	1.02233148	1.02285663	1.02338205	1.02390773	1.02443368
76	1.02103729	1.02156878	1.02210055	1.02263258	1.02316489	1.02369747	1.02423033	1.02476346
77	1.02131703	1.02185566	1.02239458	1.02293377	1.02347324	1.02401300	1.02455303	1.02509335
78	1.02159684	1.02214262	1.02268869	1.02323504	1.02378169	1.02432862	1.02487584	1.02542335
79	1.02187673	1.02242966	1.02298289	1.02353641	1.02409022	1.02464434	1.02519874	1.02575345
80	1.02215670	1.02271678	1.02327717	1.02383786	1.02439885	1.02496015	1.02552175	1.02608366
81	1.02243674	1.02300398	1.02357154	1.02413940	1.02470758	1.02527606	1.02584486	1.02641397
82	1.02271686	1.02329127	1.02386599	1.02444103	1.02501639	1.02559207	1.02616807	1.02674439
83	1.02299706	1.02357863	1.02416053	1.02474275	1.02532530	1.02590818	1.02649139	1.02707492
84	1.02327733	1.02386607	1.02445515	1.02504456	1.02563430	1.02622438	1.02681480	1.02740555
85	1.02355768	1.02415360	1.02474985	1.02534645	1.02594340	1.02654069	1.02713832	1.02773629
86	1.02383811	1.02444120	1.02504464	1.02564844	1.02625259	1.02685709	1.02746194	1.02806714
87	1.02411861	1.02472889	1.02533952	1.02595051	1.02656187	1.02717358	1.02778566	1.02839809
88	1.02439919	1.02501665	1.02563448	1.02625268	1.02687124	1.02749018	1.02810948	1.02872915
89	1.02467985	1.02530450	1.02592953	1.02655493	1.02718071	1.02780687	1.02843341	1.02906032
90	1.02496058	1.02559243	1.02622466	1.02685727	1.02749027	1.02812366	1.02875743	1.02939159
91	1.02524139	1.02588044	1.02651987	1.02715970	1.02779993	1.02844055	1.02908156	1.02972297
92	1.02552228	1.02616853	1.02681517	1.02746222	1.02810968	1.02875753	1.02940579	1.03005446
93	1.02580325	1.02645670	1.02711056	1.02776483	1.02841952	1.02907461	1.02973013	1.03038605
94	1.02608429	1.02674495	1.02740603	1.02806753	1.02872945	1.02939180	1.03005456	1.03071775
95	1.02636541	1.02703328	1.02770158	1.02837032	1.02903948	1.02970907	1.03037910	1.03104956
96	1.02664660	1.02732169	1.02799722	1.02867319	1.02934960	1.03002645	1.03070374	1.03138147
97	1.02692788	1.02761019	1.02829295	1.02897616	1.02965982	1.03034392	1.03102848	1.03171349
98	1.02720923	1.02789876	1.02858876	1.02927921	1.02997012	1.03066150	1.03135333	1.03204562
99	1.02749065	1.02818742	1.02888465	1.02958236	1.03028053	1.03097917	1.03167827	1.03237785
100	1.02777216	1.02847616	1.02918064	1.02988559	1.03059102	1.03129693	1.03200332	1.03271019

Day	10.00%	10.25%	10.50%	10.75%	11.00%	11.25%	11.50%	11.75%
101	1.02805374	1.02876498	1.02947670	1.03018891	1.03090161	1.03161480	1.03232847	1.03304264
102	1.02833540	1.02905388	1.02977285	1.03049232	1.03121229	1.03193276	1.03265373	1.03337519
103	1.02861713	1.02934286	1.03006909	1.03079582	1.03152307	1.03225082	1.03297908	1.03370785
104	1.02889895	1.02963192	1.03036541	1.03109942	1.03183394	1.03256898	1.03330454	1.03404062
105	1.02918084	1.02992106	1.03066182	1.03140310	1.03214490	1.03288724	1.03363011	1.03437350
106	1.02946281	1.03021029	1.03095831	1.03170686	1.03245596	1.03320560	1.03395577	1.03470648
107	1.02974485	1.03049959	1.03125488	1.03201072	1.03276711	1.03352405	1.03428154	1.03503957
108	1.03002697	1.03078898	1.03155155	1.03231467	1.03307836	1.03384260	1.03460741	1.03537277
109	1.03030917	1.03107845	1.03184829	1.03261871	1.03338970	1.03416125	1.03493338	1.03570608
110	1.03059145	1.03136800	1.03214513	1.03292284	1.03370113	1.03448000	1.03525945	1.03603949
111	1.03087380	1.03165763	1.03244205	1.03322705	1.03401265	1.03479885	1.03558563	1.03637301
112	1.03115623	1.03194734	1.03273905	1.03353136	1.03432427	1.03511779	1.03591191	1.03670663
113	1.03143874	1.03223713	1.03303614	1.03383576	1.03463599	1.03543683	1.03623829	1.03704037
114	1.03172133	1.03252701	1.03333331	1.03414024	1.03494780	1.03575598	1.03656478	1.03737421
115	1.03200399	1.03281696	1.03363057	1.03444482	1.03525970	1.03607522	1.03689137	1.03770816
116	1.03228673	1.03310700	1.03392792	1.03474948	1.03557170	1.03639455	1.03721806	1.03804222
117	1.03256955	1.03339712	1.03422535	1.03505424	1.03588379	1.03671399	1.03754486	1.03837638
118	1.03285244	1.03368732	1.03452287	1.03535908	1.03619597	1.03703353	1.03787175	1.03871065
119	1.03313542	1.03397760	1.03482047	1.03566402	1.03650825	1.03735316	1.03819875	1.03904503
120	1.03341847	1.03426797	1.03511816	1.03596904	1.03682062	1.03767289	1.03852586	1.03937952
121	1.03370160	1.03455841	1.03541593	1.03627416	1.03713309	1.03799272	1.03885306	1.03971411
122	1.03398480	1.03484894	1.03571379	1.03657936	1.03744565	1.03831265	1.03918037	1.04004882
123	1.03426809	1.03513955	1.03601174	1.03688465	1.03775830	1.03863268	1.03950779	1.04038363
124	1.03455145	1.03543024	1.03630977	1.03719004	1.03807105	1.03895281	1.03983530	1.04071854
125	1.03483489	1.03572101	1.03660788	1.03749551	1.03838389	1.03927303	1.04016292	1.04105357
126	1.03511840	1.03601186	1.03690609	1.03780108	1.03869683	1.03959335	1.04049065	1.04138870
127	1.03540200	1.03630280	1.03720437	1.03810673	1.03900986	1.03991378	1.04081847	1.04172395
128	1.03568567	1.03659381	1.03750275	1.03841247	1.03932299	1.04023430	1.04114640	1.04205930
129	1.03596942	1.03688491	1.03780121	1.03871831	1.03963621	1.04055492	1.04147443	1.04239475
130	1.03625325	1.03717609	1.03809975	1.03902423	1.03994953	1.04087564	1.04180257	1.04273032
131	1.03653715	1.03746735	1.03839838	1.03933024	1.04026294	1.04119646	1.04213081	1.04306599
132	1.03682113	1.03775870	1.03869710	1.03963635	1.04057644	1.04151737	1.04245915	1.04340177
133	1.03710519	1.03805012	1.03899591	1.03994254	1.04089004	1.04183839	1.04278760	1.04373766
134	1.03738933	1.03834163	1.03929479	1.04024883	1.04120373	1.04215950	1.04311615	1.04407366
135	1.03767355	1.03863322	1.03959377	1.04055520	1.04151752	1.04248072	1.04344480	1.04440977
136	1.03795784	1.03892489	1.03989283	1.04086167	1.04183140	1.04280203	1.04377356	1.04474598
137	1.03824221	1.03921664	1.04019198	1.04116822	1.04214538	1.04312344	1.04410242	1.04508230
138	1.03852666	1.03950848	1.04049121	1.04147487	1.04245945	1.04344495	1.04443138	1.04541873
139	1.03881119	1.03980039	1.04079053	1.04178160	1.04277361	1.04376656	1.04476045	1.04575527
140	1.03909580	1.04009239	1.04108994	1.04208843	1.04308787	1.04408827	1.04508962	1.04609192
141	1.03938048	1.04038447	1.04138943	1.04239535	1.04340223	1.04441008	1.04541889	1.04642868
142	1.03966524	1.04067664	1.04168901	1.04270235	1.04371668	1.04473198	1.04574827	1.04676554
143	1.03995008	1.04096888	1.04198867	1.04300945	1.04403122	1.04505399	1.04607775	1.04710251
144	1.04023500	1.04126121	1.04228842	1.04331664	1.04434586	1.04537610	1.04640734	1.04743959
145	1.04052000	1.04155362	1.04258826	1.04362392	1.04466060	1.04569830	1.04673703	1.04777678
146	1.04080507	1.04184611	1.04288818	1.04393128	1.04497543	1.04602061	1.04706682	1.04811408
147	1.04109022	1.04213868	1.04318819	1.04423874	1.04529035	1.04634301	1.04739672	1.04845149
148	1.04137545	1.04243134	1.04348828	1.04454629	1.04560537	1.04666551	1.04772672	1.04878900
149	1.04166076	1.04272407	1.04378846	1.04485393	1.04592048	1.04698811	1.04805683	1.04912663
150	1.04194615	1.04301689	1.04408873	1.04516166	1.04623569	1.04731082	1.04838704	1.04946436

Day	10.00%	10.25%	10.50%	10.75%	11.00%	11.25%	11.50%	11.75%
151	1.04223161	1.04330980	1.04438909	1.04546949	1.04655100	1.04763362	1.04871735	1.04980220
152	1.04251716	1.04360278	1.04468953	1.04577740	1.04686640	1.04795652	1.04904777	1.05014015
153	1.04280278	1.04389585	1.04499005	1.04608540	1.04718189	1.04827952	1.04937829	1.05047821
154	1.04308848	1.04418900	1.04529067	1.04639350	1.04749748	1.04860262	1.04970892	1.05081638
155	1.04337425	1.04448223	1.04559137	1.04670168	1.04781316	1.04892582	1.05003965	1.05115465
156	1.04366011	1.04477554	1.04589215	1.04700995	1.04812894	1.04924912	1.05037048	1.05149304
157	1.04394604	1.04506894	1.04619303	1.04731832	1.04844482	1.04957252	1.05070142	1.05183153
158	1.04423206	1.04536241	1.04649399	1.04762678	1.04876079	1.04989601	1.05103246	1.05217014
159	1.04451815	1.04565597	1.04679503	1.04793533	1.04907685	1.05021961	1.05136361	1.05250885
160	1.04480432	1.04594962	1.04709617	1.04824396	1.04939301	1.05054331	1.05169486	1.05284767
161	1.04509057	1.04624334	1.04739739	1.04855269	1.04970927	1.05086711	1.05202622	1.05318660
162	1.04537689	1.04653715	1.04769869	1.04886151	1.05002562	1.05119101	1.05235768	1.05352564
163	1.04566330	1.04683104	1.04800008	1.04917042	1.05034206	1.05151500	1.05268924	1.05386479
164	1.04594978	1.04712502	1.04830156	1.04947943	1.05065860	1.05183910	1.05302091	1.05420405
165	1.04623634	1.04741907	1.04860313	1.04978852	1.05097524	1.05216330	1.05335269	1.05454341
166	1.04652298	1.04771321	1.04890478	1.05009770	1.05129197	1.05248759	1.05368456	1.05488289
167	1.04680970	1.04800743	1.04920652	1.05040698	1.05160880	1.05281199	1.05401655	1.05522247
168	1.04709650	1.04830173	1.04950835	1.05071635	1.05192572	1.05313649	1.05434863	1.05556217
169	1.04738337	1.04859612	1.04981026	1.05102580	1.05224274	1.05346108	1.05468083	1.05590197
170	1.04767033	1.04889059	1.05011226	1.05133535	1.05255986	1.05378578	1.05501312	1.05624189
171	1.04795736	1.04918514	1.05041435	1.05164499	1.05287707	1.05411058	1.05534552	1.05658191
172	1.04824447	1.04947977	1.05071652	1.05195472	1.05319437	1.05443548	1.05567803	1.05692204
173	1.04853166	1.04977449	1.05101879	1.05226455	1.05351177	1.05476047	1.05601064	1.05726228
174	1.04881893	1.05006929	1.05132113	1.05257446	1.05382927	1.05508557	1.05634336	1.05760264
175	1.04910628	1.05036417	1.05162357	1.05288446	1.05414686	1.05541077	1.05667618	1.05794310
176	1.04939370	1.05065914	1.05192609	1.05319456	1.05446455	1.05573607	1.05700910	1.05828367
177	1.04968121	1.05095419	1.05222870	1.05350475	1.05478234	1.05606146	1.05734213	1.05862435
178	1.04996879	1.05124932	1.05253139	1.05381503	1.05510021	1.05638696	1.05767527	1.05896514
179	1.05025646	1.05154453	1.05283418	1.05412540	1.05541819	1.05671256	1.05800851	1.05930604
180	1.05054420	1.05183983	1.05313705	1.05443586	1.05573626	1.05703826	1.05834185	1.05964705
181	1.05083202	1.05213521	1.05344000	1.05474641	1.05605443	1.05736406	1.05867530	1.05998817
182	1.05111992	1.05243067	1.05374305	1.05505706	1.05637269	1.05768996	1.05900886	1.06032940
183	1.05140789	1.05272622	1.05404618	1.05536779	1.05669105	1.05801596	1.05934252	1.06067073
184	1.05169595	1.05302184	1.05434940	1.05567862	1.05700951	1.05834206	1.05967629	1.06101218
185	1.05198409	1.05331756	1.05465271	1.05598954	1.05732806	1.05866826	1.06001016	1.06135374
186	1.05227230	1.05361335	1.05495610	1.05630055	1.05764670	1.05899456	1.06034413	1.06169541
187	1.05256060	1.05390923	1.05525958	1.05661165	1.05796545	1.05932097	1.06067821	1.06203719
188	1.05284897	1.05420519	1.05556315	1.05692284	1.05828428	1.05964747	1.06101240	1.06237908
189	1.05313742	1.05450123	1.05586680	1.05723413	1.05860322	1.05997407	1.06134669	1.06272108
190	1.05342595	1.05479736	1.05617054	1.05754551	1.05892225	1.06030078	1.06168109	1.06306319
191	1.05371456	1.05509357	1.05647437	1.05785698	1.05924138	1.06062758	1.06201559	1.06340540
192	1.05400325	1.05538986	1.05677829	1.05816854	1.05956060	1.06095449	1.06235020	1.06374773
193	1.05429202	1.05568624	1.05708230	1.05848019	1.05987992	1.06128149	1.06268491	1.06409017
194	1.05458087	1.05598270	1.05738639	1.05879193	1.06019934	1.06160860	1.06301973	1.06443272
195	1.05486979	1.05627924	1.05769057	1.05910377	1.06051885	1.06193581	1.06335465	1.06477538
196	1.05515880	1.05657587	1.05799484	1.05941570	1.06083846	1.06226312	1.06368968	1.06511815
197	1.05544788	1.05687258	1.05829919	1.05972772	1.06115816	1.06259053	1.06402482	1.06546103
198	1.05573705	1.05716937	1.05860363	1.06003983	1.06147796	1.06291804	1.06436006	1.06580402
199	1.05602629	1.05746625	1.05890816	1.06035203	1.06179786	1.06324565	1.06469540	1.06614713
200	1.05631561	1.05776321	1.05921278	1.06066433	1.06211785	1.06357336	1.06503086	1.06649034

Day	10.00%	10.25%	10.50%	10.75%	11.00%	11.25%	11.50%	11.75%
201	1.05660501	1.05806025	1.05951748	1.06097671	1.06243794	1.06390118	1.06536641	1.06683366
202	1.05689449	1.05835738	1.05982228	1.06128919	1.06275813	1.06422909	1.06570208	1.06717709
203	1.05718405	1.05865459	1.06012716	1.06160177	1.06307841	1.06455711	1.06603785	1.06752064
204	1.05747369	1.05895188	1.06043213	1.06191443	1.06339879	1.06488522	1.06637372	1.06786429
205	1.05776341	1.05924926	1.06073718	1.06222718	1.06371927	1.06521344	1.06670970	1.06820805
206	1.05805321	1.05954672	1.06104233	1.06254003	1.06403984	1.06554176	1.06704579	1.06855193
207	1.05834309	1.05984426	1.06134756	1.06285297	1.06436051	1.06587018	1.06738198	1.06889591
208	1.05863304	1.06014189	1.06165288	1.06316600	1.06468128	1.06619870	1.06771828	1.06924001
209	1.05892308	1.06043960	1.06195828	1.06347913	1.06500214	1.06652733	1.06805468	1.06958422
210	1.05921320	1.06073740	1.06226378	1.06379234	1.06532310	1.06685605	1.06839119	1.06992854
211	1.05950339	1.06103527	1.06256936	1.06410565	1.06564416	1.06718488	1.06872781	1.07027297
212	1.05979367	1.06133324	1.06287503	1.06441905	1.06596531	1.06751380	1.06906453	1.07061751
213	1.06008402	1.06163128	1.06318079	1.06473255	1.06628656	1.06784283	1.06940136	1.07096216
214	1.06037446	1.06192941	1.06348664	1.06504613	1.06660791	1.06817196	1.06973830	1.07130692
215	1.06066497	1.06222762	1.06379257	1.06535981	1.06692935	1.06850119	1.07007534	1.07165179
216	1.06095556	1.06252592	1.06409859	1.06567358	1.06725089	1.06883052	1.07041248	1.07199678
217	1.06124623	1.06282430	1.06440470	1.06598744	1.06757253	1.06915996	1.07074974	1.07234187
218	1.06153699	1.06312277	1.06471090	1.06630140	1.06789426	1.06948949	1.07108710	1.07268708
219	1.06182782	1.06342131	1.06501719	1.06661545	1.06821609	1.06981913	1.07142456	1.07303239
220	1.06211873	1.06371995	1.06532356	1.06692959	1.06853802	1.07014887	1.07176214	1.07337782
221	1.06240972	1.06401866	1.06563003	1.06724382	1.06886005	1.07047871	1.07209981	1.07372336
222	1.06270079	1.06431746	1.06593658	1.06755815	1.06918217	1.07080865	1.07243760	1.07406901
223	1.06299194	1.06461635	1.06624322	1.06787256	1.06950439	1.07113870	1.07277549	1.07441477
224	1.06328318	1.06491531	1.06654994	1.06818707	1.06982671	1.07146884	1.07311349	1.07476065
225	1.06357449	1.06521436	1.06685676	1.06850168	1.07014912	1.07179909	1.07345159	1.07510663
226	1.06386588	1.06551350	1.06716366	1.06881637	1.07047163	1.07212944	1.07378980	1.07545273
227	1.06415735	1.06581272	1.06747066	1.06913116	1.07079424	1.07245989	1.07412812	1.07579893
228	1.06444890	1.06611202	1.06777774	1.06944604	1.07111694	1.07279044	1.07446654	1.07614525
229	1.06474053	1.06641141	1.06808491	1.06976102	1.07143974	1.07312110	1.07480507	1.07649168
230	1.06503224	1.06671088	1.06839216	1.07007608	1.07176264	1.07345185	1.07514371	1.07683823
231	1.06532403	1.06701044	1.06869951	1.07039124	1.07208564	1.07378271	1.07548246	1.07718488
232	1.06561589	1.06731008	1.06900694	1.07070649	1.07240874	1.07411367	1.07582131	1.07753164
233	1.06590784	1.06760980	1.06931447	1.07102184	1.07273193	1.07444473	1.07616026	1.07787852
234	1.06619987	1.06790961	1.06962208	1.07133728	1.07305522	1.07477590	1.07649933	1.07822551
235	1.06649198	1.06820950	1.06992978	1.07165281	1.07337860	1.07510716	1.07683850	1.07857261
236	1.06678417	1.06850948	1.07023756	1.07196843	1.07370209	1.07543853	1.07717778	1.07891982
237	1.06707644	1.06880954	1.07054544	1.07228415	1.07402567	1.07577000	1.07751716	1.07926714
238	1.06736879	1.06910969	1.07085341	1.07259996	1.07434935	1.07610158	1.07785665	1.07961458
239	1.06766122	1.06940991	1.07116146	1.07291586	1.07467312	1.07643325	1.07819625	1.07996213
240	1.06795373	1.06971023	1.07146960	1.07323186	1.07499700	1.07676503	1.07853596	1.08030979
241	1.06824632	1.07001063	1.07177783	1.07354795	1.07532097	1.07709691	1.07887577	1.08065756
242	1.06853899	1.07031111	1.07208615	1.07386413	1.07564504	1.07742889	1.07921569	1.08100544
243	1.06883174	1.07061168	1.07239456	1.07418040	1.07596921	1.07776098	1.07955572	1.08135343
244	1.06912457	1.07091233	1.07270306	1.07449677	1.07629347	1.07809316	1.07989585	1.08170154
245	1.06941748	1.07121306	1.07301164	1.07481323	1.07661783	1.07842545	1.08023609	1.08204976
246	1.06971048	1.07151388	1.07332032	1.07512979	1.07694229	1.07875784	1.08057644	1.08239809
247	1.07000355	1.07181479	1.07362908	1.07544643	1.07726685	1.07909034	1.08091690	1.08274653
248	1.07029670	1.07211578	1.07393793	1.07576318	1.07759151	1.07942293	1.08125746	1.08309509
249	1.07058993	1.07241685	1.07424687	1.07608001	1.07791626	1.07975563	1.08159813	1.08344376
250	1.07088324	1.07271801	1.07455590	1.07639694	1.07824111	1.08008843	1.08193891	1.08379254

Day	10.00%	10.25%	10.50%	10.75%	11.00%	11.25%	11.50%	11.75%
251	1.07117664	1.07301925	1.07486502	1.07671396	1.07856606	1.08042134	1.08227979	1.08414143
252	1.07147011	1.07332058	1.07517423	1.07703107	1.07889111	1.08075434	1.08262078	1.08449043
253	1.07176366	1.07362199	1.07548353	1.07734828	1.07921625	1.08108745	1.08296188	1.08483955
254	1.07205730	1.07392349	1.07579291	1.07766558	1.07954150	1.08142066	1.08330309	1.08518878
255	1.07235101	1.07422507	1.07610239	1.07798298	1.07986684	1.08175398	1.08364440	1.08553812
256	1.07264480	1.07452673	1.07641195	1.07830046	1.08019228	1.08208740	1.08398583	1.08588758
257	1.07293868	1.07482848	1.07672160	1.07861805	1.08051781	1.08242092	1.08432736	1.08623714
258	1.07323264	1.07513032	1.07703135	1.07893572	1.08084345	1.08275454	1.08466899	1.08658682
259	1.07352667	1.07543224	1.07734118	1.07925349	1.08116918	1.08308826	1.08501074	1.08693661
260	1.07382079	1.07573424	1.07765110	1.07957135	1.08149502	1.08342209	1.08535259	1.08728652
261	1.07411499	1.07603633	1.07796111	1.07988931	1.08182095	1.08375603	1.08569455	1.08763653
262	1.07440926	1.07633851	1.07827121	1.08020736	1.08214697	1.08409006	1.08603662	1.08798666
263	1.07470362	1.07664077	1.07858139	1.08052550	1.08247310	1.08442420	1.08637880	1.08833691
264	1.07499806	1.07694311	1.07889167	1.08084374	1.08279933	1.08475844	1.08672108	1.08868726
265	1.07529258	1.07724554	1.07920204	1.08116207	1.08312565	1.08509278	1.08706347	1.08903773
266	1.07558718	1.07754806	1.07951249	1.08148049	1.08345207	1.08542723	1.08740597	1.08938831
267	1.07588186	1.07785066	1.07982304	1.08179901	1.08377859	1.08576178	1.08774858	1.08973900
268	1.07617663	1.07815334	1.08013367	1.08211762	1.08410521	1.08609643	1.08809129	1.09008981
269	1.07647147	1.07845611	1.08044439	1.08243633	1.08443192	1.08643118	1.08843412	1.09044073
270	1.07676639	1.07875896	1.08075521	1.08275513	1.08475874	1.08676604	1.08877705	1.09079176
271	1.07706140	1.07906190	1.08106611	1.08307402	1.08508565	1.08710101	1.08912009	1.09114291
272	1.07735648	1.07936493	1.08137710	1.08339301	1.08541267	1.08743607	1.08946323	1.09149416
273	1.07765165	1.07966804	1.08168818	1.08371209	1.08573978	1.08777124	1.08980649	1.09184554
274	1.07794690	1.07997123	1.08199935	1.08403127	1.08606699	1.08810651	1.09014985	1.09219702
275	1.07824222	1.08027451	1.08231061	1.08435054	1.08639429	1.08844189	1.09049333	1.09254862
276	1.07853763	1.08057787	1.08262196	1.08466990	1.08672170	1.08877737	1.09083691	1.09290033
277	1.07883312	1.08088132	1.08293340	1.08498936	1.08704920	1.08911295	1.09118059	1.09325215
278	1.07912869	1.08118486	1.08324493	1.08530891	1.08737681	1.08944863	1.09152439	1.09360409
279	1.07942435	1.08148848	1.08355655	1.08562855	1.08770451	1.08978442	1.09186830	1.09395614
280	1.07972008	1.08179219	1.08386826	1.08594829	1.08803231	1.09012031	1.09221231	1.09430830
281	1.08001589	1.08209598	1.08418005	1.08626813	1.08836021	1.09045631	1.09255643	1.09466058
282	1.08031179	1.08239985	1.08449194	1.08658806	1.08868821	1.09079241	1.09290066	1.09501297
283	1.08060776	1.08270381	1.08480392	1.08690808	1.08901631	1.09112861	1.09324500	1.09536548
284	1.08090382	1.08300786	1.08511598	1.08722820	1.08934451	1.09146492	1.09358945	1.09571809
285	1.08119996	1.08331199	1.08542814	1.08754841	1.08967280	1.09180133	1.09393400	1.09607083
286	1.08149618	1.08361621	1.08574039	1.08786871	1.09000120	1.09213784	1.09427867	1.09642367
287	1.08179248	1.08392051	1.08605272	1.08818911	1.09032969	1.09247446	1.09462344	1.09677663
288	1.08208886	1.08422490	1.08636515	1.08850961	1.09065828	1.09281118	1.09496832	1.09712970
289	1.08238532	1.08452938	1.08667767	1.08883019	1.09098697	1.09314801	1.09531331	1.09748289
290	1.08268186	1.08483394	1.08699027	1.08915088	1.09131576	1.09348494	1.09565841	1.09783618
291	1.08297849	1.08513858	1.08730297	1.08947166	1.09164465	1.09382197	1.09600362	1.09818960
292	1.08327520	1.08544331	1.08761575	1.08979253	1.09197364	1.09415911	1.09634893	1.09854312
293	1.08357198	1.08574813	1.08792863	1.09011349	1.09230273	1.09449635	1.09669436	1.09889677
294	1.08386885	1.08605303	1.08824159	1.09043455	1.09263192	1.09483369	1.09703989	1.09925052
295	1.08416580	1.08635802	1.08855465	1.09075571	1.09296120	1.09517114	1.09738553	1.09960439
296	1.08446284	1.08666309	1.08886780	1.09107696	1.09329059	1.09550870	1.09773129	1.09995837
297	1.08475995	1.08696825	1.08918103	1.09139830	1.09362007	1.09584635	1.09807715	1.10031247
298	1.08505714	1.08727349	1.08949436	1.09171974	1.09394966	1.09618411	1.09842312	1.10066668
299	1.08535442	1.08757882	1.08980777	1.09204128	1.09427934	1.09652198	1.09876919	1.10102100
300	1.08565178	1.08788424	1.09012128	1.09236291	1.09460912	1.09685995	1.09911538	1.10137544

Day	10.00%	10.25%	10.50%	10.75%	11.00%	11.25%	11.50%	11.75%
301	1.08594921	1.08818974	1.09043488	1.09268463	1.09493901	1.09719802	1.09946168	1.10172999
302	1.08624674	1.08849533	1.09074856	1.09300645	1.09526899	1.09753620	1.09980808	1.10208466
303	1.08654434	1.08880100	1.09106234	1.09332836	1.09559907	1.09787448	1.10015460	1.10243944
304	1.08684202	1.08910676	1.09137621	1.09365037	1.09592925	1.09821287	1.10050122	1.10279433
305	1.08713979	1.08941261	1.09169017	1.09397247	1.09625953	1.09855136	1.10084796	1.10314934
306	1.08743763	1.08971854	1.09200421	1.09429467	1.09658991	1.09888995	1.10119480	1.10350447
307	1.08773556	1.09002456	1.09231835	1.09461696	1.09692039	1.09922865	1.10154175	1.10385970
308	1.08803357	1.09033066	1.09263258	1.09493935	1.09725097	1.09956745	1.10188881	1.10421506
309	1.08833166	1.09063685	1.09294690	1.09526183	1.09758165	1.09990636	1.10223598	1.10457052
310	1.08862983	1.09094312	1.09326131	1.09558441	1.09791242	1.10024537	1.10258326	1.10492610
311	1.08892809	1.09124948	1.09357581	1.09590708	1.09824330	1.10058449	1.10293065	1.10528180
312	1.08922643	1.09155593	1.09389040	1.09622985	1.09857428	1.10092371	1.10327815	1.10563761
313	1.08952484	1.09186246	1.09420508	1.09655271	1.09890536	1.10126304	1.10362576	1.10599353
314	1.08982334	1.09216908	1.09451985	1.09687566	1.09923653	1.10160247	1.10397348	1.10634957
315	1.09012193	1.09247579	1.09483471	1.09719872	1.09956781	1.10194200	1.10432130	1.10670573
316	1.09042059	1.09278258	1.09514967	1.09752186	1.09989919	1.10228164	1.10466924	1.10706199
317	1.09071933	1.09308945	1.09546471	1.09784511	1.10023066	1.10262139	1.10501729	1.10741838
318	1.09101816	1.09339642	1.09577984	1.09816845	1.10056224	1.10296123	1.10536544	1.10777487
319	1.09131707	1.09370347	1.09609507	1.09849188	1.10089392	1.10330119	1.10571371	1.10813149
320	1.09161606	1.09401060	1.09641038	1.09881541	1.10122569	1.10364125	1.10606208	1.10848821
321	1.09191513	1.09431783	1.09672579	1.09913903	1.10155757	1.10398141	1.10641057	1.10884506
322	1.09221429	1.09462513	1.09704128	1.09946275	1.10188954	1.10432168	1.10675916	1.10920201
323	1.09251353	1.09493253	1.09735687	1.09978656	1.10222162	1.10466205	1.10710787	1.10955908
324	1.09281284	1.09524001	1.09767255	1.10011047	1.10255380	1.10500253	1.10745668	1.10991627
325	1.09311225	1.09554758	1.09798832	1.10043448	1.10288607	1.10534311	1.10780561	1.11027357
326	1.09341173	1.09585523	1.09830418	1.10075858	1.10321845	1.10568380	1.10815464	1.11063099
327	1.09371129	1.09616297	1.09862013	1.10108278	1.10355093	1.10602459	1.10850379	1.11098852
328	1.09401094	1.09647080	1.09893617	1.10140707	1.10388350	1.10636549	1.10885304	1.11134617
329	1.09431067	1.09677871	1.09925230	1.10173145	1.10421618	1.10670649	1.10920241	1.11170393
330	1.09461048	1.09708671	1.09956852	1.10205594	1.10454896	1.10704760	1.10955188	1.11206181
331	1.09491037	1.09739480	1.09988484	1.10238051	1.10488184	1.10738882	1.10990147	1.11241980
332	1.09521035	1.09770297	1.10020124	1.10270519	1.10521481	1.10773013	1.11025116	1.11277791
333	1.09551041	1.09801123	1.10051774	1.10302996	1.10554789	1.10807156	1.11060097	1.11313613
334	1.09581055	1.09831957	1.10083433	1.10335482	1.10588107	1.10841309	1.11095088	1.11349447
335	1.09611077	1.09862801	1.10115101	1.10367978	1.10621435	1.10875472	1.11130091	1.11385292

Day	10.00%	10.25%	10.50%	10.75%	11.00%	11.25%	11.50%	11.75%
336	1.09641107	1.09893652	1.10146778	1.10400484	1.10654773	1.10909646	1.11165104	1.11421149
337	1.09671146	1.09924513	1.10178464	1.10432999	1.10688121	1.10943831	1.11200129	1.11457018
338	1.09701193	1.09955382	1.10210159	1.10465524	1.10721479	1.10978026	1.11235165	1.11492898
339	1.09731248	1.09986260	1.10241863	1.10498058	1.10754847	1.11012231	1.11270211	1.11528789
340	1.09761311	1.10017147	1.10273577	1.10530602	1.10788225	1.11046447	1.11305269	1.11564692
341	1.09791383	1.10048042	1.10305299	1.10563156	1.10821614	1.11080674	1.11340338	1.11600607
342	1.09821463	1.10078946	1.10337031	1.10595719	1.10855012	1.11114911	1.11375418	1.11636533
343	1.09851551	1.10109858	1.10368771	1.10628292	1.10888420	1.11149159	1.11410509	1.11672471
344	1.09881647	1.10140780	1.10400521	1.10660874	1.10921839	1.11183417	1.11445611	1.11708420
345	1.09911752	1.10171710	1.10432280	1.10693466	1.10955267	1.11217686	1.11480724	1.11744381
346	1.09941864	1.10202648	1.10464049	1.10726067	1.10988706	1.11251965	1.11515848	1.11780354
347	1.09971986	1.10233595	1.10495826	1.10758678	1.11022154	1.11286255	1.11550983	1.11816338
348	1.10002115	1.10264551	1.10527612	1.10791299	1.11055613	1.11320556	1.11586129	1.11852334
349	1.10032252	1.10295516	1.10559408	1.10823929	1.11089082	1.11354867	1.11621286	1.11888341
350	1.10062398	1.10326490	1.10591213	1.10856569	1.11122561	1.11389189	1.11656455	1.11924360
351	1.10092552	1.10357472	1.10623027	1.10889219	1.11156050	1.11423521	1.11691634	1.11960390
352	1.10122715	1.10388462	1.10654850	1.10921878	1.11189549	1.11457864	1.11726824	1.11996432
353	1.10152885	1.10419462	1.10686682	1.10954547	1.11223058	1.11492217	1.11762026	1.12032486
354	1.10183064	1.10450470	1.10718523	1.10987225	1.11256577	1.11526581	1.11797239	1.12068551
355	1.10213251	1.10481487	1.10750374	1.11019913	1.11290107	1.11560956	1.11832463	1.12104628
356	1.10243447	1.10512513	1.10782234	1.11052611	1.11323646	1.11595341	1.11867697	1.12140716
357	1.10273650	1.10543547	1.10814102	1.11085318	1.11357196	1.11629737	1.11902943	1.12176817
358	1.10303862	1.10574590	1.10845981	1.11118035	1.11390756	1.11664144	1.11938201	1.12212928
359	1.10334083	1.10605642	1.10877868	1.11150762	1.11424325	1.11698561	1.11973469	1.12249052
360	1.10364311	1.10636702	1.10909764	1.11183498	1.11457905	1.11732988	1.12008748	1.12285187
361	1.10394548	1.10667772	1.10941670	1.11216244	1.11491495	1.11767426	1.12044038	1.12321333
362	1.10424793	1.10698850	1.10973584	1.11248999	1.11525096	1.11801875	1.12079340	1.12357491
363	1.10455046	1.10729936	1.11005508	1.11281764	1.11558706	1.11836335	1.12114653	1.12393661
364	1.10485308	1.10761032	1.11037441	1.11314539	1.11592326	1.11870805	1.12149976	1.12429843
365	1.10515578	1.10792136	1.11069384	1.11347323	1.11625957	1.11905286	1.12185311	1.12466036

Day	12.00%	12.25%	12.50%	12.75%	13.00%	13.25%	13.50%	13.75%
1	1.00032877	1.00033562	1.00034247	1.00034932	1.00035616	1.00036301	1.00036986	1.00037671
2	1.00065764	1.00067135	1.00068505	1.00069875	1.00071246	1.00072616	1.00073986	1.00075357
3	1.00098663	1.00100719	1.00102775	1.00104831	1.00106887	1.00108944	1.00111000	1.00113056
4	1.00131572	1.00134314	1.00137057	1.00139799	1.00142542	1.00145285	1.00148027	1.00150770
5	1.00164492	1.00167921	1.00171350	1.00174780	1.00178209	1.00181639	1.00185068	1.00188498
6	1.00197422	1.00201539	1.00205655	1.00209772	1.00213889	1.00218006	1.00222123	1.00226240
7	1.00230364	1.00235168	1.00239972	1.00244777	1.00249582	1.00254386	1.00259192	1.00263997
8	1.00263317	1.00268809	1.00274301	1.00279794	1.00285287	1.00290780	1.00296274	1.00301768
9	1.00296280	1.00302461	1.00308642	1.00314823	1.00321005	1.00327187	1.00333370	1.00339552
10	1.00329254	1.00336124	1.00342994	1.00349865	1.00356736	1.00363607	1.00370479	1.00377352
11	1.00362239	1.00369798	1.00377358	1.00384918	1.00392479	1.00400041	1.00407603	1.00415165
12	1.00395235	1.00403484	1.00411734	1.00419984	1.00428235	1.00436487	1.00444740	1.00452993
13	1.00428241	1.00437181	1.00446121	1.00455063	1.00464004	1.00472947	1.00481890	1.00490834
14	1.00461259	1.00470889	1.00480521	1.00490153	1.00499786	1.00509420	1.00519055	1.00528691
15	1.00494287	1.00504609	1.00514932	1.00525256	1.00535581	1.00545906	1.00556233	1.00566561
16	1.00527326	1.00538340	1.00549355	1.00560371	1.00571388	1.00582406	1.00593425	1.00604446
17	1.00560377	1.00572082	1.00583790	1.00595498	1.00607208	1.00618919	1.00630631	1.00642345
18	1.00593437	1.00605836	1.00618236	1.00630638	1.00643040	1.00655445	1.00667851	1.00680258
19	1.00626509	1.00639601	1.00652694	1.00665789	1.00678886	1.00691984	1.00705084	1.00718185
20	1.00659592	1.00673377	1.00687164	1.00700953	1.00714744	1.00728537	1.00742331	1.00756127
21	1.00692686	1.00707165	1.00721646	1.00736130	1.00750615	1.00765102	1.00779592	1.00794083
22	1.00725790	1.00740964	1.00756140	1.00771318	1.00786499	1.00801682	1.00816866	1.00832054
23	1.00758905	1.00774774	1.00790646	1.00806519	1.00822395	1.00838274	1.00854155	1.00870038
24	1.00792032	1.00808596	1.00825163	1.00841733	1.00858305	1.00874880	1.00891457	1.00908037
25	1.00825169	1.00842429	1.00859692	1.00876958	1.00894227	1.00911499	1.00928773	1.00946050
26	1.00858317	1.00876273	1.00894233	1.00912196	1.00930162	1.00948131	1.00966103	1.00984078
27	1.00891476	1.00910129	1.00928786	1.00947446	1.00966110	1.00984776	1.01003447	1.01022120
28	1.00924645	1.00943996	1.00963351	1.00982709	1.01002070	1.01021435	1.01040804	1.01060176
29	1.00957826	1.00977875	1.00997927	1.01017983	1.01038043	1.01058107	1.01078175	1.01098247
30	1.00991018	1.01011764	1.01032515	1.01053270	1.01074030	1.01094793	1.01115560	1.01136332
31	1.01024220	1.01045666	1.01067116	1.01088570	1.01110029	1.01131492	1.01152959	1.01174431
32	1.01057434	1.01079578	1.01101728	1.01123882	1.01146040	1.01168204	1.01190372	1.01212545
33	1.01090658	1.01113502	1.01136351	1.01159206	1.01182065	1.01204929	1.01227799	1.01250673
34	1.01123893	1.01147438	1.01170987	1.01194542	1.01218102	1.01241668	1.01265239	1.01288815
35	1.01157139	1.01181384	1.01205635	1.01229891	1.01254153	1.01278420	1.01302693	1.01326972
36	1.01190397	1.01215342	1.01240294	1.01265252	1.01290216	1.01315186	1.01340161	1.01365143
37	1.01223665	1.01249312	1.01274966	1.01300626	1.01326292	1.01351964	1.01377643	1.01403329
38	1.01256944	1.01283293	1.01309649	1.01336011	1.01362381	1.01388757	1.01415139	1.01441528
39	1.01290234	1.01317285	1.01344344	1.01371410	1.01398482	1.01425562	1.01452649	1.01479743
40	1.01323535	1.01351289	1.01379051	1.01406820	1.01434597	1.01462381	1.01490172	1.01517971
41	1.01356846	1.01385304	1.01413770	1.01442243	1.01470724	1.01499213	1.01527710	1.01556214
42	1.01390169	1.01419331	1.01448500	1.01477678	1.01506864	1.01536059	1.01565261	1.01594472
43	1.01423503	1.01453369	1.01483243	1.01513126	1.01543018	1.01572918	1.01602827	1.01632744
44	1.01456848	1.01487418	1.01517998	1.01548586	1.01579184	1.01609790	1.01640406	1.01671030
45	1.01490203	1.01521479	1.01552764	1.01584059	1.01615362	1.01646676	1.01677999	1.01709331
46	1.01523570	1.01555551	1.01587542	1.01619543	1.01651554	1.01683575	1.01715606	1.01747646
47	1.01556948	1.01589635	1.01622333	1.01655041	1.01687759	1.01720488	1.01753226	1.01785976
48	1.01590336	1.01623730	1.01657135	1.01690550	1.01723976	1.01757413	1.01790861	1.01824320
49	1.01623736	1.01657837	1.01691949	1.01726072	1.01760207	1.01794353	1.01828510	1.01862678
50	1.01657146	1.01691955	1.01726775	1.01761607	1.01796450	1.01831306	1.01866172	1.01901051

Day	12.00%	12.25%	12.50%	12.75%	13.00%	13.25%	13.50%	13.75%
51	1.01690568	1.01726084	1.01761613	1.01797154	1.01832707	1.01868272	1.01903849	1.01939438
52	1.01724000	1.01760225	1.01796463	1.01832713	1.01868976	1.01905251	1.01941539	1.01977840
53	1.01757444	1.01794378	1.01831325	1.01868285	1.01905258	1.01942244	1.01979244	1.02016257
54	1.01790898	1.01828541	1.01866198	1.01903869	1.01941553	1.01979251	1.02016962	1.02054687
55	1.01824364	1.01862717	1.01901084	1.01939465	1.01977861	1.02016271	1.02054694	1.02093133
56	1.01857840	1.01896904	1.01935982	1.01975074	1.02014182	1.02053304	1.02092441	1.02131592
57	1.01891328	1.01931102	1.01970891	1.02010696	1.02050516	1.02090351	1.02130201	1.02170067
58	1.01924826	1.01965312	1.02005813	1.02046330	1.02086862	1.02127411	1.02167975	1.02208555
59	1.01958336	1.01999533	1.02040746	1.02081976	1.02123222	1.02164484	1.02205763	1.02247059
60	1.01991856	1.02033766	1.02075692	1.02117635	1.02159595	1.02201572	1.02243565	1.02285576
61	1.02025388	1.02068010	1.02110649	1.02153306	1.02195980	1.02238672	1.02281382	1.02324109
62	1.02058931	1.02102265	1.02145618	1.02188990	1.02232379	1.02275786	1.02319212	1.02362655
63	1.02092484	1.02136533	1.02180600	1.02224686	1.02268790	1.02312914	1.02357056	1.02401217
64	1.02126049	1.02170811	1.02215593	1.02260394	1.02305215	1.02350055	1.02394914	1.02439792
65	1.02159625	1.02205102	1.02250599	1.02296115	1.02341652	1.02387209	1.02432786	1.02478383
66	1.02193211	1.02239403	1.02285616	1.02331849	1.02378103	1.02424377	1.02470672	1.02516988
67	1.02226809	1.02273717	1.02320645	1.02367595	1.02414566	1.02461559	1.02508572	1.02555607
68	1.02260418	1.02308041	1.02355687	1.02403354	1.02451043	1.02498753	1.02546486	1.02594241
69	1.02294038	1.02342378	1.02390740	1.02439125	1.02487532	1.02535962	1.02584414	1.02632889
70	1.02327669	1.02376725	1.02425805	1.02474908	1.02524034	1.02573184	1.02622357	1.02671553
71	1.02361311	1.02411085	1.02460882	1.02510704	1.02560550	1.02610419	1.02660313	1.02710230
72	1.02394964	1.02445455	1.02495972	1.02546513	1.02597078	1.02647668	1.02698283	1.02748922
73	1.02428628	1.02479838	1.02531073	1.02582334	1.02633620	1.02684931	1.02736267	1.02787629
74	1.02462303	1.02514232	1.02566187	1.02618167	1.02670174	1.02722207	1.02774266	1.02826350
75	1.02495989	1.02548637	1.02601312	1.02654013	1.02706742	1.02759496	1.02812278	1.02865086
76	1.02529686	1.02583054	1.02636449	1.02689872	1.02743322	1.02796800	1.02850305	1.02903837
77	1.02563395	1.02617483	1.02671599	1.02725743	1.02779916	1.02834116	1.02888345	1.02942602
78	1.02597114	1.02651923	1.02706760	1.02761627	1.02816522	1.02871446	1.02926400	1.02981382
79	1.02630845	1.02686375	1.02741934	1.02797523	1.02853142	1.02908790	1.02964468	1.03020176
80	1.02664586	1.02720838	1.02777120	1.02833432	1.02889774	1.02946147	1.03002551	1.03058985
81	1.02698339	1.02755313	1.02812317	1.02869353	1.02926420	1.02983518	1.03040648	1.03097809
82	1.02732103	1.02789799	1.02847527	1.02905287	1.02963079	1.03020903	1.03078759	1.03136647
83	1.02765878	1.02824297	1.02882749	1.02941233	1.02999751	1.03058301	1.03116884	1.03175500
84	1.02799664	1.02858806	1.02917982	1.02977192	1.03036435	1.03095712	1.03155023	1.03214367
85	1.02833461	1.02893328	1.02953228	1.03013164	1.03073133	1.03133137	1.03193176	1.03253249
86	1.02867269	1.02927860	1.02988486	1.03049148	1.03109844	1.03170576	1.03231344	1.03292146
87	1.02901089	1.02962405	1.03023756	1.03085144	1.03146568	1.03208029	1.03269525	1.03331058
88	1.02934919	1.02996960	1.03059038	1.03121153	1.03183305	1.03245494	1.03307721	1.03369984
89	1.02968761	1.03031528	1.03094333	1.03157175	1.03220056	1.03282974	1.03345930	1.03408924
90	1.03002614	1.03066107	1.03129639	1.03193210	1.03256819	1.03320467	1.03384154	1.03447880
91	1.03036478	1.03100698	1.03164957	1.03229256	1.03293595	1.03357974	1.03422392	1.03486850
92	1.03070353	1.03135300	1.03200288	1.03265316	1.03330385	1.03395494	1.03460644	1.03525835
93	1.03104239	1.03169914	1.03235630	1.03301388	1.03367187	1.03433028	1.03498910	1.03564834
94	1.03138136	1.03204539	1.03270985	1.03337473	1.03404003	1.03470576	1.03537191	1.03603848
95	1.03172044	1.03239176	1.03306352	1.03373570	1.03440832	1.03508137	1.03575485	1.03642877
96	1.03205964	1.03273825	1.03341731	1.03409680	1.03477674	1.03545712	1.03613794	1.03681921
97	1.03239895	1.03308486	1.03377122	1.03445803	1.03514529	1.03583300	1.03652117	1.03720979
98	1.03273837	1.03343158	1.03412525	1.03481938	1.03551397	1.03620903	1.03690454	1.03760052
99	1.03307790	1.03377841	1.03447940	1.03518086	1.03588278	1.03658518	1.03728805	1.03799140
100	1.03341754	1.03412537	1.03483367	1.03554246	1.03625173	1.03696148	1.03767171	1.03838242

Day	12.00%	12.25%	12.50%	12.75%	13.00%	13.25%	13.50%	13.75%
101	1.03375729	1.03447244	1.03518807	1.03590419	1.03662081	1.03733791	1.03805551	1.03877359
102	1.03409716	1.03481962	1.03554258	1.03626605	1.03699001	1.03771448	1.03843944	1.03916491
103	1.03443713	1.03516692	1.03589722	1.03662803	1.03735935	1.03809118	1.03882352	1.03955638
104	1.03477722	1.03551434	1.03625198	1.03699014	1.03772882	1.03846802	1.03920775	1.03994799
105	1.03511742	1.03586188	1.03660686	1.03735238	1.03809842	1.03884500	1.03959211	1.04033975
106	1.03545774	1.03620953	1.03696187	1.03771474	1.03846816	1.03922212	1.03997662	1.04073166
107	1.03579816	1.03655730	1.03731699	1.03807723	1.03883802	1.03959937	1.04036127	1.04112372
108	1.03613870	1.03690519	1.03767223	1.03843985	1.03920802	1.03997676	1.04074606	1.04151592
109	1.03647935	1.03725319	1.03802760	1.03880259	1.03957815	1.04035428	1.04113099	1.04190827
110	1.03682011	1.03760131	1.03838309	1.03916546	1.03994841	1.04073195	1.04151607	1.04230077
111	1.03716098	1.03794954	1.03873870	1.03952845	1.04031880	1.04110975	1.04190129	1.04269342
112	1.03750196	1.03829790	1.03909443	1.03989158	1.04068933	1.04148768	1.04228665	1.04308622
113	1.03784306	1.03864637	1.03945029	1.04025483	1.04105998	1.04186576	1.04267215	1.04347916
114	1.03818427	1.03899495	1.03980626	1.04061820	1.04143077	1.04224397	1.04305779	1.04387225
115	1.03852559	1.03934366	1.04016236	1.04098171	1.04180169	1.04262232	1.04344358	1.04426549
116	1.03886702	1.03969248	1.04051858	1.04134534	1.04217275	1.04300080	1.04382951	1.04465888
117	1.03920857	1.04004142	1.04087492	1.04170910	1.04254393	1.04337943	1.04421559	1.04505241
118	1.03955023	1.04039047	1.04123139	1.04207298	1.04291525	1.04375819	1.04460181	1.04544610
119	1.03989200	1.04073964	1.04158797	1.04243699	1.04328670	1.04413709	1.04498816	1.04583993
120	1.04023388	1.04108893	1.04194468	1.04280113	1.04365828	1.04451612	1.04537467	1.04623391
121	1.04057587	1.04143834	1.04230151	1.04316540	1.04402999	1.04489530	1.04576131	1.04662804
122	1.04091798	1.04178786	1.04265847	1.04352979	1.04440184	1.04527461	1.04614810	1.04702232
123	1.04126020	1.04213750	1.04301554	1.04389431	1.04477382	1.04565406	1.04653503	1.04741674
124	1.04160253	1.04248726	1.04337274	1.04425896	1.04514593	1.04603364	1.04692211	1.04781132
125	1.04194498	1.04283714	1.04373006	1.04462373	1.04551817	1.04641337	1.04730932	1.04820604
126	1.04228753	1.04318713	1.04408750	1.04498864	1.04589055	1.04679323	1.04769669	1.04860091
127	1.04263020	1.04353724	1.04444506	1.04535367	1.04626306	1.04717323	1.04808419	1.04899594
128	1.04297299	1.04388747	1.04480275	1.04571883	1.04663570	1.04755337	1.04847184	1.04939111
129	1.04331588	1.04423782	1.04516056	1.04608411	1.04700847	1.04793365	1.04885963	1.04978642
130	1.04365889	1.04458828	1.04551849	1.04644952	1.04738138	1.04831406	1.04924756	1.05018189
131	1.04400201	1.04493886	1.04587654	1.04681506	1.04775442	1.04869461	1.04963564	1.05057751
132	1.04434524	1.04528956	1.04623472	1.04718073	1.04812759	1.04907530	1.05002386	1.05097327
133	1.04468859	1.04564037	1.04659302	1.04754653	1.04850090	1.04945613	1.05041223	1.05136919
134	1.04503205	1.04599131	1.04695144	1.04791245	1.04887434	1.04983710	1.05080074	1.05176525
135	1.04537562	1.04634236	1.04730999	1.04827850	1.04924791	1.05021820	1.05118939	1.05216146
136	1.04571931	1.04669353	1.04766866	1.04864468	1.04962161	1.05059945	1.05157818	1.05255783
137	1.04606310	1.04704482	1.04802745	1.04901099	1.04999545	1.05098083	1.05196712	1.05295434
138	1.04640701	1.04739622	1.04838636	1.04937743	1.05036942	1.05136235	1.05235621	1.05335100
139	1.04675104	1.04774775	1.04874540	1.04974399	1.05074353	1.05174401	1.05274544	1.05374781
140	1.04709518	1.04809939	1.04910456	1.05011068	1.05111776	1.05212581	1.05313481	1.05414477
141	1.04743943	1.04845115	1.04946384	1.05047750	1.05149213	1.05250774	1.05352432	1.05454188
142	1.04778379	1.04880302	1.04982324	1.05084445	1.05186664	1.05288982	1.05391398	1.05493914
143	1.04812827	1.04915502	1.05018277	1.05121152	1.05224128	1.05327203	1.05430379	1.05533655
144	1.04847286	1.04950713	1.05054242	1.05157873	1.05261605	1.05365438	1.05469373	1.05573410
145	1.04881756	1.04985937	1.05090220	1.05194606	1.05299095	1.05403687	1.05508383	1.05613181
146	1.04916238	1.05021172	1.05126210	1.05231352	1.05336599	1.05441950	1.05547406	1.05652967
147	1.04950731	1.05056418	1.05162212	1.05268111	1.05374116	1.05480227	1.05586444	1.05692768
148	1.04985235	1.05091677	1.05198226	1.05304883	1.05411647	1.05518518	1.05625497	1.05732584
149	1.05019751	1.05126948	1.05234253	1.05341667	1.05449190	1.05556823	1.05664564	1.05772414
150	1.05054278	1.05162230	1.05270292	1.05378465	1.05486748	1.05595141	1.05703645	1.05812260

Day	12.00%	12.25%	12.50%	12.75%	13.00%	13.25%	13.50%	13.75%
151	1.05088816	1.05197524	1.05306344	1.05415275	1.05524318	1.05633474	1.05742741	1.05852121
152	1.05123366	1.05232830	1.05342407	1.05452098	1.05561902	1.05671820	1.05781851	1.05891997
153	1.05157927	1.05268148	1.05378484	1.05488934	1.05599500	1.05710180	1.05820976	1.05931888
154	1.05192500	1.05303478	1.05414572	1.05525783	1.05637110	1.05748555	1.05860116	1.05971793
155	1.05227083	1.05338819	1.05450673	1.05562645	1.05674735	1.05786943	1.05899269	1.06011714
156	1.05261679	1.05374173	1.05486786	1.05599519	1.05712372	1.05825345	1.05938437	1.06051650
157	1.05296285	1.05409538	1.05522912	1.05636407	1.05750023	1.05863761	1.05977620	1.06091601
158	1.05330903	1.05444915	1.05559050	1.05673307	1.05787688	1.05902191	1.06016817	1.06131567
159	1.05365532	1.05480304	1.05595200	1.05710221	1.05825365	1.05940635	1.06056029	1.06171548
160	1.05400173	1.05515705	1.05631363	1.05747147	1.05863057	1.05979093	1.06095255	1.06211544
161	1.05434825	1.05551118	1.05667538	1.05784086	1.05900761	1.06017565	1.06134496	1.06251556
162	1.05469489	1.05586543	1.05703726	1.05821038	1.05938479	1.06056050	1.06173751	1.06291582
163	1.05504164	1.05621979	1.05739925	1.05858003	1.05976211	1.06094550	1.06213021	1.06331623
164	1.05538850	1.05657428	1.05776138	1.05894980	1.06013956	1.06133064	1.06252305	1.06371680
165	1.05573548	1.05692888	1.05812362	1.05931971	1.06051714	1.06171592	1.06291604	1.06411751
166	1.05608257	1.05728360	1.05848600	1.05968975	1.06089486	1.06210134	1.06330917	1.06451838
167	1.05642977	1.05763845	1.05884849	1.06005991	1.06127271	1.06248689	1.06370245	1.06491939
168	1.05677709	1.05799341	1.05921111	1.06043021	1.06165070	1.06287259	1.06409588	1.06532056
169	1.05712453	1.05834849	1.05957385	1.06080063	1.06202882	1.06325843	1.06448945	1.06572188
170	1.05747207	1.05870369	1.05993672	1.06117119	1.06240708	1.06364440	1.06488316	1.06612335
171	1.05781974	1.05905900	1.06029971	1.06154187	1.06278547	1.06403052	1.06527702	1.06652497
172	1.05816751	1.05941444	1.06066283	1.06191268	1.06316400	1.06441678	1.06567103	1.06692675
173	1.05851540	1.05977000	1.06102607	1.06228362	1.06354266	1.06480318	1.06606518	1.06732867
174	1.05886341	1.06012567	1.06138944	1.06265470	1.06392146	1.06518972	1.06645948	1.06773075
175	1.05921153	1.06048147	1.06175293	1.06302590	1.06430039	1.06557639	1.06685392	1.06813297
176	1.05955976	1.06083738	1.06211654	1.06339723	1.06467945	1.06596321	1.06724851	1.06853535
177	1.05990811	1.06119342	1.06248028	1.06376869	1.06505865	1.06635017	1.06764325	1.06893788
178	1.06025657	1.06154957	1.06284414	1.06414028	1.06543799	1.06673727	1.06803813	1.06934057
179	1.06060515	1.06190585	1.06320813	1.06451200	1.06581746	1.06712451	1.06843316	1.06974340
180	1.06095384	1.06226224	1.06357224	1.06488385	1.06619707	1.06751189	1.06882833	1.07014639
181	1.06130265	1.06261875	1.06393648	1.06525583	1.06657681	1.06789941	1.06922365	1.07054952
182	1.06165157	1.06297538	1.06430084	1.06562794	1.06695668	1.06828708	1.06961912	1.07095281
183	1.06200061	1.06333214	1.06466533	1.06600018	1.06733670	1.06867488	1.07001473	1.07135625
184	1.06234976	1.06368901	1.06502994	1.06637255	1.06771684	1.06906282	1.07041049	1.07175985
185	1.06269902	1.06404600	1.06539467	1.06674505	1.06809713	1.06945091	1.07080639	1.07216359
186	1.06304840	1.06440311	1.06575954	1.06711768	1.06847754	1.06983913	1.07120245	1.07256749
187	1.06339790	1.06476034	1.06612452	1.06749044	1.06885810	1.07022750	1.07159864	1.07297154
188	1.06374751	1.06511769	1.06648963	1.06786333	1.06923879	1.07061601	1.07199499	1.07337574
189	1.06409723	1.06547516	1.06685487	1.06823635	1.06961961	1.07100465	1.07239148	1.07378009
190	1.06444707	1.06583276	1.06722023	1.06860950	1.07000057	1.07139344	1.07278812	1.07418460
191	1.06479703	1.06619047	1.06758572	1.06898278	1.07038167	1.07178237	1.07318490	1.07458926
192	1.06514710	1.06654830	1.06795133	1.06935619	1.07076290	1.07217145	1.07358183	1.07499407
193	1.06549729	1.06690625	1.06831706	1.06972974	1.07114427	1.07256066	1.07397891	1.07539903
194	1.06584759	1.06726432	1.06868293	1.07010341	1.07152577	1.07295001	1.07437614	1.07580415
195	1.06619800	1.06762251	1.06904891	1.07047721	1.07190741	1.07333951	1.07477351	1.07620942
196	1.06654853	1.06798082	1.06941503	1.07085115	1.07228919	1.07372915	1.07517103	1.07661484
197	1.06689918	1.06833925	1.06978126	1.07122521	1.07267110	1.07411892	1.07556869	1.07702041
198	1.06724994	1.06869781	1.07014763	1.07159941	1.07305314	1.07450884	1.07596651	1.07742614
199	1.06760082	1.06905648	1.07051412	1.07197373	1.07343533	1.07489891	1.07636447	1.07783202
200	1.06795181	1.06941527	1.07088073	1.07234819	1.07381765	1.07528911	1.07676258	1.07823805

Day	12.00%	12.25%	12.50%	12.75%	13.00%	13.25%	13.50%	13.75%
201	1.06830292	1.06977419	1.07124747	1.07272278	1.07420010	1.07567945	1.07716083	1.07864424
202	1.06865414	1.07013322	1.07161434	1.07309749	1.07458269	1.07606994	1.07755923	1.07905058
203	1.06900548	1.07049237	1.07198133	1.07347234	1.07496542	1.07646057	1.07795778	1.07945707
204	1.06935693	1.07085165	1.07234845	1.07384732	1.07534829	1.07685134	1.07835648	1.07986371
205	1.06970850	1.07121104	1.07271569	1.07422243	1.07573129	1.07724225	1.07875532	1.08027051
206	1.07006019	1.07157056	1.07308306	1.07459768	1.07611442	1.07763330	1.07915431	1.08067746
207	1.07041199	1.07193020	1.07345055	1.07497305	1.07649770	1.07802450	1.07955345	1.08108457
208	1.07076390	1.07228995	1.07381817	1.07534855	1.07688111	1.07841584	1.07995274	1.08149182
209	1.07111593	1.07264983	1.07418592	1.07572419	1.07726465	1.07880732	1.08035217	1.08189924
210	1.07146808	1.07300983	1.07455379	1.07609996	1.07764834	1.07919894	1.08075176	1.08230680
211	1.07182035	1.07336995	1.07492179	1.07647585	1.07803216	1.07959070	1.08115149	1.08271452
212	1.07217273	1.07373019	1.07528991	1.07685188	1.07841611	1.07998261	1.08155137	1.08312239
213	1.07252522	1.07409055	1.07565816	1.07722804	1.07880021	1.08037466	1.08195139	1.08353042
214	1.07287783	1.07445104	1.07602654	1.07760434	1.07918444	1.08076685	1.08235156	1.08393860
215	1.07323056	1.07481164	1.07639504	1.07798076	1.07956881	1.08115918	1.08275189	1.08434693
216	1.07358340	1.07517236	1.07676367	1.07835731	1.07995331	1.08155166	1.08315236	1.08475542
217	1.07393636	1.07553321	1.07713242	1.07873400	1.08033795	1.08194427	1.08355297	1.08516406
218	1.07428943	1.07589418	1.07750130	1.07911082	1.08072273	1.08233703	1.08395374	1.08557285
219	1.07464263	1.07625526	1.07787031	1.07948777	1.08110764	1.08272994	1.08435465	1.08598180
220	1.07499593	1.07661647	1.07823944	1.07986485	1.08149270	1.08312298	1.08475572	1.08639090
221	1.07534936	1.07697780	1.07860870	1.08024206	1.08187788	1.08351617	1.08515693	1.08680016
222	1.07570290	1.07733925	1.07897809	1.08061941	1.08226321	1.08390950	1.08555829	1.08720957
223	1.07605655	1.07770083	1.07934760	1.08099688	1.08264867	1.08430298	1.08595980	1.08761913
224	1.07641032	1.07806252	1.07971724	1.08137449	1.08303428	1.08469659	1.08636145	1.08802885
225	1.07676421	1.07842434	1.08008701	1.08175223	1.08342001	1.08509035	1.08676326	1.08843873
226	1.07711822	1.07878627	1.08045690	1.08213011	1.08380589	1.08548426	1.08716521	1.08884876
227	1.07747234	1.07914833	1.08082692	1.08250811	1.08419190	1.08587830	1.08756731	1.08925894
228	1.07782658	1.07951051	1.08119707	1.08288625	1.08457805	1.08627249	1.08796956	1.08966928
229	1.07818093	1.07987281	1.08156734	1.08326451	1.08496434	1.08666682	1.08837196	1.09007977
230	1.07853540	1.08023524	1.08193774	1.08364291	1.08535077	1.08706130	1.08877451	1.09049041
231	1.07888999	1.08059778	1.08230827	1.08402145	1.08573733	1.08745592	1.08917721	1.09090122
232	1.07924469	1.08096045	1.08267892	1.08440011	1.08612403	1.08785068	1.08958006	1.09131217
233	1.07959951	1.08132324	1.08304970	1.08477891	1.08651087	1.08824558	1.08998305	1.09172328
234	1.07995445	1.08168615	1.08342061	1.08515784	1.08689785	1.08864063	1.09038620	1.09213455
235	1.08030950	1.08204918	1.08379164	1.08553690	1.08728496	1.08903582	1.09078949	1.09254597
236	1.08066467	1.08241233	1.08416280	1.08591610	1.08767221	1.08943116	1.09119293	1.09295754
237	1.08101996	1.08277561	1.08453409	1.08629542	1.08805960	1.08982663	1.09159652	1.09336927
238	1.08137536	1.08313900	1.08490551	1.08667488	1.08844713	1.09022226	1.09200026	1.09378116
239	1.08173088	1.08350252	1.08527705	1.08705447	1.08883480	1.09061802	1.09240416	1.09419320
240	1.08208652	1.08386616	1.08564872	1.08743420	1.08922260	1.09101393	1.09280820	1.09460540
241	1.08244227	1.08422993	1.08602052	1.08781406	1.08961054	1.09140998	1.09321238	1.09501775
242	1.08279815	1.08459381	1.08639244	1.08819405	1.08999862	1.09180618	1.09361672	1.09543026
243	1.08315413	1.08495782	1.08676450	1.08857417	1.09038684	1.09220252	1.09402121	1.09584292
244	1.08351024	1.08532195	1.08713668	1.08895442	1.09077520	1.09259901	1.09442585	1.09625574
245	1.08386646	1.08568620	1.08750898	1.08933481	1.09116369	1.09299563	1.09483064	1.09666871
246	1.08422280	1.08605058	1.08788142	1.08971533	1.09155233	1.09339241	1.09523557	1.09708184
247	1.08457926	1.08641507	1.08825398	1.09009599	1.09194110	1.09378932	1.09564066	1.09749512
248	1.08493583	1.08677969	1.08862667	1.09047677	1.09233001	1.09418638	1.09604590	1.09790856
249	1.08529252	1.08714443	1.08899949	1.09085769	1.09271906	1.09458359	1.09645129	1.09832216
250	1.08564933	1.08750929	1.08937243	1.09123875	1.09310825	1.09498094	1.09685682	1.09873591

Day	12.00%	12.25%	12.50%	12.75%	13.00%	13.25%	13.50%	13.75%
251	1.08600626	1.08787428	1.08974550	1.09161993	1.09349757	1.09537843	1.09726251	1.09914982
252	1.08636330	1.08823939	1.09011870	1.09200125	1.09388704	1.09577607	1.09766835	1.09956388
253	1.08672046	1.08860462	1.09049203	1.09238270	1.09427664	1.09617385	1.09807433	1.09997810
254	1.08707774	1.08896997	1.09086549	1.09276429	1.09466638	1.09657178	1.09848047	1.10039247
255	1.08743514	1.08933545	1.09123907	1.09314601	1.09505627	1.09696985	1.09888676	1.10080700
256	1.08779265	1.08970105	1.09161279	1.09352786	1.09544629	1.09736806	1.09929319	1.10122169
257	1.08815028	1.09006677	1.09198663	1.09390985	1.09583644	1.09776642	1.09969978	1.10163654
258	1.08850803	1.09043262	1.09236059	1.09429197	1.09622674	1.09816492	1.10010652	1.10205154
259	1.08886589	1.09079858	1.09273469	1.09467422	1.09661718	1.09856357	1.10051341	1.10246669
260	1.08922388	1.09116467	1.09310891	1.09505661	1.09700776	1.09896237	1.10092045	1.10288201
261	1.08958198	1.09153088	1.09348327	1.09543913	1.09739847	1.09936131	1.10132764	1.10329747
262	1.08994020	1.09189722	1.09385775	1.09582178	1.09778932	1.09976039	1.10173498	1.10371310
263	1.09029853	1.09226368	1.09423236	1.09620457	1.09818032	1.10015962	1.10214247	1.10412888
264	1.09065699	1.09263026	1.09460709	1.09658749	1.09857145	1.10055899	1.10255011	1.10454482
265	1.09101556	1.09299697	1.09498196	1.09697054	1.09896272	1.10095851	1.10295790	1.10496092
266	1.09137425	1.09336379	1.09535695	1.09735373	1.09935413	1.10135817	1.10336585	1.10537717
267	1.09173306	1.09373074	1.09573207	1.09773705	1.09974568	1.10175798	1.10377394	1.10579358
268	1.09209198	1.09409782	1.09610732	1.09812051	1.10013738	1.10215793	1.10418219	1.10621014
269	1.09245103	1.09446502	1.09648270	1.09850410	1.10052920	1.10255803	1.10459058	1.10662687
270	1.09281019	1.09483234	1.09685821	1.09888782	1.10092117	1.10295827	1.10499913	1.10704375
271	1.09316947	1.09519978	1.09723385	1.09927168	1.10131328	1.10335866	1.10540783	1.10746078
272	1.09352887	1.09556735	1.09760961	1.09965567	1.10170553	1.10375920	1.10581668	1.10787798
273	1.09388838	1.09593504	1.09798551	1.10003980	1.10209792	1.10415988	1.10622568	1.10829533
274	1.09424802	1.09630285	1.09836153	1.10042406	1.10249045	1.10456070	1.10663483	1.10871284
275	1.09460777	1.09667079	1.09873768	1.10080845	1.10288312	1.10496167	1.10704413	1.10913050
276	1.09496764	1.09703885	1.09911396	1.10119298	1.10327592	1.10536279	1.10745359	1.10954833
277	1.09532763	1.09740703	1.09949037	1.10157765	1.10366887	1.10576405	1.10786319	1.10996631
278	1.09568774	1.09777534	1.09986691	1.10196244	1.10406196	1.10616546	1.10827295	1.11038445
279	1.09604796	1.09814377	1.10024357	1.10234738	1.10445519	1.10656701	1.10868286	1.11080274
280	1.09640831	1.09851233	1.10062037	1.10273244	1.10484855	1.10696871	1.10909292	1.11122119
281	1.09676877	1.09888101	1.10099729	1.10311764	1.10524206	1.10737056	1.10950313	1.11163981
282	1.09712935	1.09924981	1.10137435	1.10350298	1.10563571	1.10777255	1.10991350	1.11205857
283	1.09749005	1.09961873	1.10175153	1.10388845	1.10602950	1.10817468	1.11032401	1.11247750
284	1.09785087	1.09998779	1.10212884	1.10427405	1.10642343	1.10857697	1.11073468	1.11289658
285	1.09821181	1.10035696	1.10250628	1.10465979	1.10681749	1.10897939	1.11114550	1.11331583
286	1.09857286	1.10072626	1.10288386	1.10504567	1.10721170	1.10938197	1.11155647	1.11373523
287	1.09893404	1.10109568	1.10326156	1.10543168	1.10760605	1.10978469	1.11196760	1.11415478
288	1.09929533	1.10146522	1.10363938	1.10581782	1.10800054	1.11018756	1.11237887	1.11457450
289	1.09965675	1.10183489	1.10401734	1.10620410	1.10839517	1.11059057	1.11279030	1.11499437
290	1.10001828	1.10220469	1.10439543	1.10659051	1.10878994	1.11099373	1.11320188	1.11541441
291	1.10037993	1.10257461	1.10477365	1.10697706	1.10918485	1.11139704	1.11361361	1.11583460
292	1.10074169	1.10294465	1.10515200	1.10736375	1.10957991	1.11180049	1.11402550	1.11625494
293	1.10110358	1.10331481	1.10553047	1.10775056	1.10997510	1.11220409	1.11443753	1.11667545
294	1.10146559	1.10368511	1.10590908	1.10813752	1.11037043	1.11260783	1.11484972	1.11709612
295	1.10182771	1.10405552	1.10628781	1.10852461	1.11076591	1.11301172	1.11526206	1.11751694
296	1.10218996	1.10442606	1.10666668	1.10891183	1.11116152	1.11341576	1.11567456	1.11793792
297	1.10255232	1.10479672	1.10704568	1.10929919	1.11155728	1.11381995	1.11608721	1.11835906
298	1.10291481	1.10516751	1.10742480	1.10968669	1.11195318	1.11422428	1.11650001	1.11878036
299	1.10327741	1.10553842	1.10780406	1.11007432	1.11234921	1.11462876	1.11691296	1.11920182
300	1.10364013	1.10590946	1.10818344	1.11046208	1.11274539	1.11503338	1.11732606	1.11962344

Day	12.00%	12.25%	12.50%	12.75%	13.00%	13.25%	13.50%	13.75%
301	1.10400297	1.10628062	1.10856296	1.11084998	1.11314171	1.11543816	1.11773932	1.12004521
302	1.10436593	1.10665191	1.10894260	1.11123802	1.11353818	1.11584308	1.11815273	1.12046715
303	1.10472901	1.10702332	1.10932238	1.11162619	1.11393478	1.11624814	1.11856629	1.12088924
304	1.10509221	1.10739485	1.10970228	1.11201450	1.11433152	1.11665335	1.11898001	1.12131150
305	1.10545553	1.10776651	1.11008232	1.11240294	1.11472841	1.11705872	1.11939388	1.12173391
306	1.10581896	1.10813830	1.11046248	1.11279152	1.11512543	1.11746422	1.11980790	1.12215648
307	1.10618252	1.10851021	1.11084278	1.11318024	1.11552260	1.11786988	1.12022208	1.12257921
308	1.10654620	1.10888224	1.11122320	1.11356909	1.11591991	1.11827568	1.12063641	1.12300210
309	1.10690999	1.10925440	1.11160376	1.11395807	1.11631736	1.11868163	1.12105089	1.12342515
310	1.10727391	1.10962668	1.11198444	1.11434720	1.11671495	1.11908773	1.12146552	1.12384836
311	1.10763794	1.10999909	1.11236526	1.11473645	1.11711269	1.11949397	1.12188031	1.12427172
312	1.10800210	1.11037163	1.11274621	1.11512585	1.11751056	1.11990036	1.12229525	1.12469525
313	1.10836637	1.11074429	1.11312729	1.11551538	1.11790858	1.12030690	1.12271035	1.12511894
314	1.10873077	1.11111707	1.11350849	1.11590505	1.11830674	1.12071359	1.12312560	1.12554278
315	1.10909528	1.11148998	1.11388983	1.11629485	1.11870504	1.12112042	1.12354100	1.12596679
316	1.10945992	1.11186301	1.11427130	1.11668479	1.11910348	1.12152740	1.12395656	1.12639095
317	1.10982467	1.11223617	1.11465290	1.11707486	1.11950207	1.12193453	1.12437227	1.12681528
318	1.11018954	1.11260946	1.11503463	1.11746507	1.11990080	1.12234181	1.12478813	1.12723976
319	1.11055454	1.11298287	1.11541649	1.11785542	1.12029967	1.12274924	1.12520415	1.12766441
320	1.11091965	1.11335640	1.11579848	1.11824590	1.12069868	1.12315681	1.12562032	1.12808921
321	1.11128488	1.11373006	1.11618061	1.11863652	1.12109783	1.12356453	1.12603664	1.12851418
322	1.11165024	1.11410385	1.11656286	1.11902728	1.12149712	1.12397240	1.12645312	1.12893931
323	1.11201571	1.11447776	1.11694524	1.11941817	1.12189656	1.12438042	1.12686976	1.12936459
324	1.11238131	1.11485180	1.11732776	1.11980920	1.12229614	1.12478858	1.12728654	1.12979004
325	1.11274702	1.11522596	1.11771041	1.12020037	1.12269586	1.12519690	1.12770349	1.13021564
326	1.11311286	1.11560025	1.11809318	1.12059167	1.12309573	1.12560536	1.12812058	1.13064141
327	1.11347881	1.11597466	1.11847609	1.12098311	1.12349573	1.12601397	1.12853783	1.13106733
328	1.11384489	1.11634920	1.11885913	1.12137469	1.12389588	1.12642273	1.12895524	1.13149342
329	1.11421108	1.11672387	1.11924230	1.12176640	1.12429617	1.12683163	1.12937280	1.13191967
330	1.11457740	1.11709866	1.11962561	1.12215825	1.12469661	1.12724069	1.12979051	1.13234608
331	1.11494383	1.11747358	1.12000904	1.12255024	1.12509719	1.12764989	1.13020838	1.13277265
332	1.11531039	1.11784862	1.12039260	1.12294236	1.12549791	1.12805925	1.13062640	1.13319938
333	1.11567707	1.11822379	1.12077630	1.12333462	1.12589877	1.12846875	1.13104458	1.13362627
334	1.11604387	1.11859908	1.12116013	1.12372702	1.12629977	1.12887840	1.13146291	1.13405332
335	1.11641078	1.11897450	1.12154409	1.12411955	1.12670092	1.12928819	1.13188139	1.13448053

Day	12.00%	12.25%	12.50%	12.75%	13.00%	13.25%	13.50%	13.75%
336	1.11677782	1.11935005	1.12192818	1.12451223	1.12710221	1.12969814	1.13230003	1.13490790
337	1.11714498	1.11972572	1.12231240	1.12490504	1.12750364	1.13010824	1.13271883	1.13533543
338	1.11751226	1.12010152	1.12269675	1.12529798	1.12790522	1.13051848	1.13313778	1.13576313
339	1.11787967	1.12047744	1.12308124	1.12569107	1.12830694	1.13092888	1.13355689	1.13619099
340	1.11824719	1.12085349	1.12346585	1.12608429	1.12870880	1.13133942	1.13397615	1.13661900
341	1.11861483	1.12122967	1.12385060	1.12647764	1.12911081	1.13175011	1.13439556	1.13704718
342	1.11898259	1.12160597	1.12423548	1.12687114	1.12951296	1.13216095	1.13481513	1.13747552
343	1.11935048	1.12198240	1.12462050	1.12726477	1.12991525	1.13257194	1.13523486	1.13790402
344	1.11971848	1.12235896	1.12500564	1.12765854	1.13031769	1.13298308	1.13565474	1.13833268
345	1.12008661	1.12273564	1.12539092	1.12805245	1.13072027	1.13339437	1.13607478	1.13876151
346	1.12045486	1.12311245	1.12577632	1.12844650	1.13112299	1.13380581	1.13649497	1.13919049
347	1.12082323	1.12348938	1.12616186	1.12884068	1.13152585	1.13421739	1.13691532	1.13961964
348	1.12119172	1.12386645	1.12654753	1.12923500	1.13192886	1.13462913	1.13733582	1.14004895
349	1.12156033	1.12424363	1.12693334	1.12962946	1.13233202	1.13504102	1.13775648	1.14047842
350	1.12192906	1.12462095	1.12731927	1.13002406	1.13273531	1.13545305	1.13817729	1.14090805
351	1.12229791	1.12499839	1.12770534	1.13041879	1.13313875	1.13586524	1.13859826	1.14133785
352	1.12266689	1.12537596	1.12809154	1.13081366	1.13354234	1.13627757	1.13901939	1.14176780
353	1.12303598	1.12575365	1.12847788	1.13120867	1.13394606	1.13669006	1.13944067	1.14219792
354	1.12340520	1.12613147	1.12886434	1.13160382	1.13434993	1.13710269	1.13986211	1.14262820
355	1.12377454	1.12650942	1.12925094	1.13199911	1.13475395	1.13751547	1.14028370	1.14305864
356	1.12414400	1.12688750	1.12963767	1.13239453	1.13515811	1.13792841	1.14070545	1.14348925
357	1.12451358	1.12726570	1.13002453	1.13279010	1.13556241	1.13834149	1.14112735	1.14392001
358	1.12488329	1.12764403	1.13041153	1.13318580	1.13596686	1.13875472	1.14154941	1.14435094
359	1.12525311	1.12802248	1.13079865	1.13358163	1.13637145	1.13916811	1.14197163	1.14478203
360	1.12562306	1.12840107	1.13118591	1.13397761	1.13677618	1.13958164	1.14239400	1.14521329
361	1.12599312	1.12877978	1.13157330	1.13437373	1.13718106	1.13999532	1.14281653	1.14564470
362	1.12636331	1.12915861	1.13196083	1.13476998	1.13758609	1.14040916	1.14323922	1.14607628
363	1.12673362	1.12953758	1.13234849	1.13516637	1.13799125	1.14082314	1.14366206	1.14650802
364	1.12710406	1.12991667	1.13273628	1.13556290	1.13839657	1.14123728	1.14408506	1.14693993
365	1.12747461	1.13029589	1.13312420	1.13595957	1.13880202	1.14165156	1.14450821	1.14737199

Appendix J   Continuous compound interest

x	e^x	x	e^x	x	e^x	x	e^x	x	e^x	x	e^x	x	e^x
0.00	1.0000	0.25	1.2840	0.50	1.6487	0.75	2.1170	1.00	2.7183	1.25	3.4903	1.50	4.4817
0.01	1.0101	0.26	1.2969	0.51	1.6653	0.76	2.1383	1.01	2.7456	1.26	3.5254	1.51	4.5267
0.02	1.0202	0.27	1.3100	0.52	1.6820	0.77	2.1598	1.02	2.7732	1.27	3.5609	1.52	4.5722
0.03	1.0305	0.28	1.3231	0.53	1.6989	0.78	2.1815	1.03	2.8011	1.28	3.5966	1.53	4.6182
0.04	1.0408	0.29	1.3364	0.54	1.7160	0.79	2.2034	1.04	2.8292	1.29	3.6328	1.54	4.6646
0.05	1.0513	0.30	1.3499	0.55	1.7333	0.80	2.2255	1.05	2.8577	1.30	3.6693	1.55	4.7115
0.06	1.0618	0.31	1.3634	0.56	1.7507	0.81	2.2479	1.06	2.8864	1.31	3.7062	1.56	4.7588
0.07	1.0725	0.32	1.3771	0.57	1.7683	0.82	2.2705	1.07	2.9154	1.32	3.7434	1.57	4.8066
0.08	1.0833	0.33	1.3910	0.58	1.7860	0.83	2.2933	1.08	2.9447	1.33	3.7810	1.58	4.8550
0.09	1.0942	0.34	1.4049	0.59	1.8040	0.84	2.3164	1.09	2.9743	1.34	3.8190	1.59	4.9037
0.10	1.1052	0.35	1.4191	0.60	1.8221	0.85	2.3396	1.10	3.0042	1.35	3.8574	1.60	4.9530
0.11	1.1163	0.36	1.4333	0.61	1.8404	0.86	2.3632	1.11	3.0344	1.36	3.8962	1.61	5.0028
0.12	1.1275	0.37	1.4477	0.62	1.8589	0.87	2.3869	1.12	3.0649	1.37	3.9354	1.62	5.0531
0.13	1.1388	0.38	1.4623	0.63	1.8776	0.88	2.4109	1.13	3.0957	1.38	3.9749	1.63	5.1039
0.14	1.1503	0.39	1.4770	0.64	1.8965	0.89	2.4351	1.14	3.1268	1.39	4.0149	1.64	5.1552
0.15	1.1618	0.40	1.4918	0.65	1.9155	0.90	2.4596	1.15	3.1582	1.40	4.0552	1.65	5.2070
0.16	1.1735	0.41	1.5068	0.66	1.9348	0.91	2.4843	1.16	3.1899	1.41	4.0960	1.66	5.2593
0.17	1.1853	0.42	1.5220	0.67	1.9542	0.92	2.5093	1.17	3.2220	1.42	4.1371	1.67	5.3122
0.18	1.1972	0.43	1.5373	0.68	1.9739	0.93	2.5345	1.18	3.2544	1.43	4.1787	1.68	5.3656
0.19	1.2092	0.44	1.5527	0.69	1.9937	0.94	2.5600	1.19	3.2871	1.44	4.2207	1.69	5.4195
0.20	1.2214	0.45	1.5683	0.70	2.0138	0.95	2.5857	1.20	3.3201	1.45	4.2631	1.70	5.4739
0.21	1.2337	0.46	1.5841	0.71	2.0340	0.96	2.6117	1.21	3.3535	1.46	4.3060	1.71	5.5290
0.22	1.2461	0.47	1.6000	0.72	2.0544	0.97	2.6379	1.22	3.3872	1.47	4.3492	1.72	5.5845
0.23	1.2586	0.48	1.6161	0.73	2.0751	0.98	2.6645	1.23	3.4212	1.48	4.3929	1.73	5.6407
0.24	1.2712	0.49	1.6323	0.74	2.0959	0.99	2.6912	1.24	3.4556	1.49	4.4371	1.74	5.6973

x	e^x	x	e^x	x	e^x	x	e^x	x	e^x	x	e^x	x	e^x
1.75	5.7546	2.00	7.3891	2.25	9.4877	2.50	12.182	2.75	15.643	3.00	20.086	4.50	90.017
1.76	5.8124	2.01	7.4633	2.26	9.5831	2.51	12.305	2.76	15.800	3.05	21.115	4.60	99.484
1.77	5.8709	2.02	7.5383	2.27	9.6794	2.52	12.429	2.77	15.959	3.10	22.198	4.70	109.95
1.78	5.9299	2.03	7.6141	2.28	9.7767	2.53	12.554	2.78	16.119	3.15	23.336	4.80	121.51
1.79	5.9895	2.04	7.6906	2.29	9.8749	2.54	12.680	2.79	16.281	3.20	24.533	4.90	134.29
1.80	6.0496	2.05	7.7679	2.30	9.9742	2.55	12.807	2.80	16.445	3.25	25.790	5.00	148.41
1.81	6.1104	2.06	7.8460	2.31	10.074	2.56	12.936	2.81	16.610	3.30	27.113	5.10	164.02
1.82	6.1719	2.07	7.9248	2.32	10.176	2.57	13.066	2.82	16.777	3.35	28.503	5.20	181.27
1.83	6.2339	2.08	8.0045	2.33	10.278	2.58	13.197	2.83	16.945	3.40	29.964	5.30	200.34
1.84	6.2965	2.09	8.0849	2.34	10.381	2.59	13.330	2.84	17.116	3.45	31.500	5.40	221.41
1.85	6.3598	2.10	8.1662	2.35	10.486	2.60	13.464	2.85	17.288	3.50	33.115	5.50	244.69
1.86	6.4237	2.11	8.2482	2.36	10.591	2.61	13.599	2.86	17.462	3.55	34.813	5.60	270.43
1.87	6.4883	2.12	8.3311	2.37	10.697	2.62	13.736	2.87	17.637	3.60	36.598	5.70	298.87
1.88	6.5535	2.13	8.4149	2.38	10.805	2.63	13.874	2.88	17.814	3.65	38.475	5.80	330.30
1.89	6.6194	2.14	8.4994	2.39	10.913	2.64	14.013	2.89	17.993	3.70	40.447	5.90	365.04
1.90	6.6859	2.15	8.5849	2.40	11.023	2.65	14.154	2.90	18.174	3.75	42.521	6.00	403.43
1.91	6.7531	2.16	8.6711	2.41	11.134	2.66	14.296	2.91	18.357	3.80	44.701	6.25	518.01
1.92	6.8210	2.17	8.7583	2.42	11.246	2.67	14.440	2.92	18.541	3.85	46.993	6.50	665.14
1.93	6.8895	2.18	8.8463	2.43	11.359	2.68	14.585	2.93	18.728	3.90	49.402	6.75	854.06
1.94	6.9588	2.19	8.9352	2.44	11.473	2.69	14.732	2.94	18.916	3.95	51.935	7.00	1096.6
1.95	7.0287	2.20	9.0250	2.45	11.588	2.70	14.880	2.95	19.106	4.00	54.598	7.50	1808.0
1.96	7.0993	2.21	9.1157	2.46	11.705	2.71	15.029	2.96	19.298	4.10	60.340	8.00	2981.0
1.97	7.1707	2.22	9.2073	2.47	11.822	2.72	15.180	2.97	19.492	4.20	66.686	8.50	4914.8
1.98	7.2427	2.23	9.2999	2.48	11.941	2.73	15.333	2.98	19.688	4.30	73.700	9.00	8103.1
1.99	7.3155	2.24	9.3933	2.49	12.061	2.74	15.487	2.99	19.886	4.40	81.451	9.50	13360.
												10.00	22026.

Appendix K   Annual percentage rate tables for monthly payment plans

Number of Payments	Annual Percentage Rate													
	10.00%	10.25%	10.50%	10.75%	11.00%	11.25%	11.50%	11.75%	12.00%	12.25%	12.50%	12.75%	13.00%	13.25%
	Finance Charge per $100 of Amount Financed													
1	0.83	0.85	0.88	0.90	0.92	0.94	0.96	0.98	1.00	1.02	1.04	1.06	1.08	1.10
2	1.25	1.28	1.31	1.35	1.38	1.41	1.44	1.47	1.50	1.53	1.57	1.60	1.63	1.66
3	1.67	1.71	1.76	1.80	1.84	1.88	1.92	1.96	2.01	2.05	2.09	2.13	2.17	2.22
4	2.09	2.14	2.20	2.25	2.30	2.35	2.41	2.46	2.51	2.57	2.62	2.67	2.72	2.78
5	2.51	2.58	2.64	2.70	2.77	2.83	2.89	2.96	3.02	3.08	3.15	3.21	3.27	3.34
6	2.94	3.01	3.08	3.16	3.23	3.31	3.38	3.45	3.53	3.60	3.68	3.75	3.83	3.90
7	3.36	3.45	3.53	3.62	3.70	3.78	3.87	3.95	4.04	4.12	4.21	4.29	4.38	4.47
8	3.79	3.88	3.98	4.07	4.17	4.26	4.36	4.46	4.55	4.65	4.74	4.84	4.94	5.03
9	4.21	4.32	4.43	4.53	4.64	4.75	4.85	4.96	5.07	5.17	5.28	5.39	5.49	5.60
10	4.64	4.76	4.88	4.99	5.11	5.23	5.35	5.46	5.58	5.70	5.82	5.94	6.05	6.17
11	5.07	5.20	5.33	5.45	5.58	5.71	5.84	5.97	6.10	6.23	6.36	6.49	6.62	6.75
12	5.50	5.64	5.78	5.92	6.06	6.20	6.34	6.48	6.62	6.76	6.90	7.04	7.18	7.32
13	5.93	6.08	6.23	6.38	6.53	6.68	6.84	6.99	7.14	7.29	7.44	7.59	7.75	7.90
14	6.36	6.52	6.69	6.85	7.01	7.17	7.34	7.50	7.66	7.82	7.99	8.15	8.31	8.48
15	6.80	6.97	7.14	7.32	7.49	7.66	7.84	8.01	8.19	8.36	8.53	8.71	8.88	9.06
16	7.23	7.41	7.60	7.78	7.97	8.15	8.34	8.53	8.71	8.90	9.08	9.27	9.46	9.64
17	7.67	7.86	8.06	8.25	8.45	8.65	8.84	9.04	9.24	9.44	9.63	9.83	10.03	10.23
18	8.10	8.31	8.52	8.73	8.93	9.14	9.35	9.56	9.77	9.98	10.19	10.40	10.61	10.82
19	8.54	8.76	8.98	9.20	9.42	9.64	9.86	10.08	10.30	10.52	10.74	10.96	11.18	11.41
20	8.98	9.21	9.44	9.67	9.90	10.13	10.37	10.60	10.83	11.06	11.30	11.53	11.76	12.00
21	9.42	9.66	9.90	10.15	10.39	10.63	10.88	11.12	11.36	11.61	11.85	12.10	12.34	12.59
22	9.86	10.12	10.37	10.62	10.88	11.13	11.39	11.64	11.90	12.16	12.41	12.67	12.93	13.19
23	10.30	10.57	10.84	11.10	11.37	11.63	11.90	12.17	12.44	12.71	12.97	13.24	13.51	13.78
24	10.75	11.02	11.30	11.58	11.86	12.14	12.42	12.70	12.98	13.26	13.54	13.82	14.10	14.38
25	11.19	11.48	11.77	12.06	12.35	12.64	12.93	13.22	13.52	13.81	14.10	14.40	14.69	14.98
26	11.64	11.94	12.24	12.54	12.85	13.15	13.45	13.75	14.06	14.36	14.67	14.97	15.28	15.59
27	12.09	12.40	12.71	13.03	13.34	13.66	13.97	14.29	14.60	14.92	15.24	15.56	15.87	16.19
28	12.53	12.86	13.18	13.51	13.84	14.16	14.49	14.82	15.15	15.48	15.81	16.14	16.47	16.80
29	12.98	13.32	13.66	14.00	14.33	14.67	15.01	15.35	15.70	16.04	16.38	16.72	17.07	17.41
30	13.43	13.78	14.13	14.48	14.83	15.19	15.54	15.89	16.24	16.60	16.95	17.31	17.66	18.02

Number of Payments	Annual Percentage Rate													
	10.00%	10.25%	10.50%	10.75%	11.00%	11.25%	11.50%	11.75%	12.00%	12.25%	12.50%	12.75%	13.00%	13.25%
	Finance Charge per $100 of Amount Financed													
31	13.89	14.25	14.61	14.97	15.33	15.70	16.06	16.43	16.79	17.16	17.53	17.90	18.27	18.63
32	14.34	14.71	15.09	15.46	15.84	16.21	16.59	16.97	17.35	17.73	18.11	18.49	18.87	19.25
33	14.79	15.18	15.57	15.95	16.34	16.73	17.12	17.51	17.90	18.29	18.69	19.08	19.47	19.87
34	15.25	15.65	16.05	16.44	16.85	17.25	17.65	18.05	18.46	18.86	19.27	19.67	20.08	20.49
35	15.70	16.11	16.53	16.94	17.35	17.77	18.18	18.60	19.01	19.43	19.85	20.27	20.69	21.11
36	16.16	16.58	17.01	17.43	17.86	18.29	18.71	19.14	19.57	20.00	20.43	20.87	21.30	21.73
37	16.62	17.06	17.49	17.93	18.37	18.81	19.25	19.69	20.13	20.58	21.02	21.46	21.91	22.36
38	17.08	17.53	17.98	18.43	18.88	19.33	19.78	20.24	20.69	21.15	21.61	22.07	22.52	22.99
39	17.54	18.00	18.46	18.93	19.39	19.86	20.32	20.79	21.26	21.73	22.20	22.67	23.14	23.61
40	18.00	18.48	18.95	19.43	19.90	20.38	20.86	21.34	21.82	22.30	22.79	23.27	23.76	24.25
41	18.47	18.95	19.44	19.93	20.42	20.91	21.40	21.89	22.39	22.88	23.38	23.88	24.38	24.88
42	18.93	19.43	19.93	20.43	20.93	21.44	21.94	22.45	22.96	23.47	23.98	24.49	25.00	25.51
43	19.40	19.91	20.42	20.94	21.45	21.97	22.49	23.01	23.53	24.05	24.57	25.10	25.62	26.15
44	19.86	20.39	20.91	21.44	21.97	22.50	23.03	23.57	24.10	24.64	25.17	25.71	26.25	26.79
45	20.33	20.87	21.41	21.95	22.49	23.03	23.58	24.12	24.67	25.22	25.77	26.32	26.88	27.43
46	20.80	21.35	21.90	22.46	23.01	23.57	24.13	24.69	25.25	25.81	26.37	26.94	27.51	28.08
47	21.27	21.83	22.40	22.97	23.53	24.10	24.68	25.25	25.82	26.40	26.98	27.56	28.14	28.72
48	21.74	22.32	22.90	23.48	24.06	24.64	25.23	25.81	26.40	26.99	27.58	28.18	28.77	29.37
49	22.21	22.80	23.39	23.99	24.58	25.18	25.78	26.38	26.98	27.59	28.19	28.80	29.41	30.02
50	22.69	23.29	23.89	24.50	25.11	25.72	26.33	26.95	27.56	28.18	28.80	29.42	30.04	30.67
51	23.16	23.78	24.40	25.02	25.64	26.26	26.89	27.52	28.15	28.78	29.41	30.05	30.68	31.32
52	23.64	24.27	24.90	25.53	26.17	26.81	27.45	28.09	28.73	29.38	30.02	30.67	31.32	31.98
53	24.11	24.76	25.40	26.05	26.70	27.35	28.00	28.66	29.32	29.98	30.64	31.30	31.97	32.63
54	24.59	25.25	25.91	26.57	27.23	27.90	28.56	29.23	29.91	30.58	31.25	31.93	32.61	33.29
55	25.07	25.74	26.41	27.09	27.77	28.44	29.13	29.81	30.50	31.18	31.87	32.56	33.26	33.95
56	25.55	26.23	26.92	27.61	28.30	28.99	29.69	30.39	31.09	31.79	32.49	33.20	33.91	34.62
57	26.03	26.73	27.43	28.13	28.84	29.54	30.25	30.97	31.68	32.39	33.11	33.83	34.56	35.28
58	26.51	27.23	27.94	28.66	29.37	30.10	30.82	31.55	32.27	33.00	33.74	34.47	35.21	35.95
59	27.00	27.72	28.45	29.18	29.91	30.65	31.39	32.13	32.87	33.61	34.36	35.11	35.86	36.62
60	27.48	28.22	28.96	29.71	30.45	31.20	31.96	32.71	33.47	34.23	34.99	35.75	36.52	37.29

Number of Payments	Annual Percentage Rate													
	13.50%	13.75%	14.00%	14.25%	14.50%	14.75%	15.00%	15.25%	15.50%	15.75%	16.00%	16.25%	16.50%	16.75%
	Finance Charge per $100 of Amount Financed													
1	1.13	1.15	1.17	1.19	1.21	1.23	1.25	1.27	1.29	1.31	1.33	1.35	1.38	1.40
2	1.69	1.72	1.75	1.78	1.82	1.85	1.88	1.91	1.94	1.97	2.00	2.04	2.07	2.10
3	2.26	2.30	2.34	2.38	2.43	2.47	2.51	2.55	2.59	2.64	2.68	2.72	2.76	2.80
4	2.83	2.88	2.93	2.99	3.04	3.09	3.14	3.20	3.25	3.30	3.36	3.41	3.46	3.51
5	3.40	3.46	3.53	3.59	3.65	3.72	3.78	3.84	3.91	3.97	4.04	4.10	4.16	4.23
6	3.97	4.05	4.12	4.20	4.27	4.35	4.42	4.49	4.57	4.64	4.72	4.79	4.87	4.94
7	4.55	4.64	4.72	4.81	4.89	4.98	5.06	5.15	5.23	5.32	5.40	5.49	5.58	5.66
8	5.13	5.22	5.32	5.42	5.51	5.61	5.71	5.80	5.90	6.00	6.09	6.19	6.29	6.38
9	5.71	5.82	5.92	6.03	6.14	6.25	6.35	6.46	6.57	6.68	6.78	6.89	7.00	7.11
10	6.29	6.41	6.53	6.65	6.77	6.88	7.00	7.12	7.24	7.36	7.48	7.60	7.72	7.84
11	6.88	7.01	7.14	7.27	7.40	7.53	7.66	7.79	7.92	8.05	8.18	8.31	8.44	8.57
12	7.46	7.60	7.74	7.89	8.03	8.17	8.31	8.45	8.59	8.74	8.88	9.02	9.16	9.30
13	8.05	8.20	8.36	8.51	8.66	8.81	8.97	9.12	9.27	9.43	9.58	9.73	9.89	10.04
14	8.64	8.81	8.97	9.13	9.30	9.46	9.63	9.79	9.96	10.12	10.29	10.45	10.62	10.78
15	9.23	9.41	9.59	9.76	9.94	10.11	10.29	10.47	10.64	10.82	11.00	11.17	11.35	11.53
16	9.83	10.02	10.20	10.39	10.58	10.77	10.95	11.14	11.33	11.52	11.71	11.90	12.09	12.28
17	10.43	10.63	10.82	11.02	11.22	11.42	11.62	11.82	12.02	12.22	12.42	12.62	12.83	13.03
18	11.03	11.24	11.45	11.66	11.87	12.08	12.29	12.50	12.72	12.93	13.14	13.35	13.57	13.78
19	11.63	11.85	12.07	12.30	12.52	12.74	12.97	13.19	13.41	13.64	13.86	14.09	14.31	14.54
20	12.23	12.46	12.70	12.93	13.17	13.41	13.64	13.88	14.11	14.35	14.59	14.82	15.06	15.30
21	12.84	13.08	13.33	13.58	13.82	14.07	14.32	14.57	14.82	15.06	15.31	15.56	15.81	16.06
22	13.44	13.70	13.96	14.22	14.48	14.74	15.00	15.26	15.52	15.78	16.04	16.30	16.57	16.83
23	14.05	14.32	14.59	14.87	15.14	15.41	15.68	15.96	16.23	16.50	16.78	17.05	17.32	17.60
24	14.66	14.95	15.23	15.51	15.80	16.08	16.37	16.65	16.94	17.22	17.51	17.80	18.09	18.37
25	15.28	15.57	15.87	16.17	16.46	16.76	17.06	17.35	17.65	17.95	18.25	18.55	18.85	19.15
26	15.89	16.20	16.51	16.82	17.13	17.44	17.75	18.06	18.37	18.68	18.99	19.30	19.62	19.93
27	16.51	16.83	17.15	17.47	17.80	18.12	18.44	18.76	19.09	19.41	19.74	20.06	20.39	20.71
28	17.13	17.46	17.80	18.13	18.47	18.80	19.14	19.47	19.81	20.15	20.48	20.82	21.16	21.50
29	17.75	18.10	18.45	18.79	19.14	19.49	19.83	20.18	20.53	20.88	21.23	21.58	21.94	22.29
30	18.38	18.74	19.10	19.45	19.81	20.17	20.54	20.90	21.26	21.62	21.99	22.35	22.72	23.08

Number of Payments	Annual Percentage Rate													
	13.50%	13.75%	14.00%	14.25%	14.50%	14.75%	15.00%	15.25%	15.50%	15.75%	16.00%	16.25%	16.50%	16.75%
	Finance Charge per $100 of Amount Financed													
31	19.00	19.38	19.75	20.12	20.49	20.87	21.24	21.61	21.99	22.37	22.74	23.12	23.50	23.88
32	19.63	20.02	20.40	20.79	21.17	21.56	21.95	22.33	22.72	23.11	23.50	23.89	24.28	24.68
33	20.26	20.66	21.06	21.46	21.85	22.25	22.65	23.06	23.46	23.86	24.26	24.67	25.07	25.48
34	20.90	21.31	21.72	22.13	22.54	22.95	23.37	23.78	24.19	24.61	25.03	25.44	25.86	26.28
35	21.53	21.95	22.38	22.80	23.23	23.65	24.08	24.51	24.94	25.36	25.79	26.23	26.66	27.09
36	22.17	22.60	23.04	23.48	23.92	24.35	24.80	25.24	25.68	26.12	26.57	27.01	27.46	27.90
37	22.81	23.25	23.70	24.16	24.61	25.06	25.51	25.97	26.42	26.88	27.34	27.80	28.26	28.72
38	23.45	23.91	24.37	24.84	25.30	25.77	26.24	26.70	27.17	27.64	28.11	28.59	29.06	29.53
39	24.09	24.56	25.04	25.52	26.00	26.48	26.96	27.44	27.92	28.41	28.89	29.38	29.87	30.36
40	24.73	25.22	25.71	26.20	26.70	27.19	27.69	28.18	28.68	29.18	29.68	30.18	30.68	31.18
41	25.38	25.88	26.39	26.89	27.40	27.91	28.41	28.92	29.44	29.95	30.46	30.97	31.49	32.01
42	26.03	26.55	27.06	27.58	28.10	28.62	29.15	29.67	30.19	30.72	31.25	31.78	32.31	32.84
43	26.68	27.21	27.74	28.27	28.81	29.34	29.88	30.42	30.96	31.50	32.04	32.58	33.13	33.67
44	27.33	27.88	28.42	28.97	29.52	30.07	30.62	31.17	31.72	32.28	32.83	33.39	33.95	34.51
45	27.99	28.55	29.11	29.67	30.23	30.79	31.36	31.92	32.49	33.06	33.63	34.20	34.77	35.35
46	28.65	29.22	29.79	30.36	30.94	31.52	32.10	32.68	33.26	33.84	34.43	35.01	35.60	36.19
47	29.31	29.89	30.48	31.07	31.66	32.25	32.84	33.44	34.03	34.63	35.23	35.83	36.43	37.04
48	29.97	30.57	31.17	31.77	32.37	32.98	33.59	34.20	34.81	35.42	36.03	36.65	37.27	37.88
49	30.63	31.24	31.86	32.48	33.09	33.71	34.34	34.96	35.59	36.21	36.84	37.47	38.10	38.74
50	31.29	31.92	32.55	33.18	33.82	34.45	35.09	35.73	36.37	37.01	37.65	38.30	38.94	39.59
51	31.96	32.60	33.25	33.89	34.54	35.19	35.84	36.50	37.15	37.81	38.46	39.12	39.79	40.45
52	32.63	33.29	33.95	34.61	35.27	35.93	36.60	37.27	37.94	38.61	39.28	39.96	40.63	41.31
53	33.30	33.97	34.65	35.32	36.00	36.68	37.36	38.04	38.72	39.41	40.10	40.79	41.48	42.17
54	33.98	34.66	35.35	36.04	36.73	37.42	38.12	38.82	39.52	40.22	40.92	41.63	42.33	43.04
55	34.65	35.35	36.05	36.76	37.46	38.17	38.88	39.60	40.31	41.03	41.74	42.47	43.19	43.91
56	35.33	36.04	36.76	37.48	38.20	38.92	39.65	40.38	41.11	41.84	42.57	43.31	44.05	44.79
57	36.01	36.74	37.47	38.20	38.94	39.68	40.42	41.16	41.91	42.65	43.40	44.15	44.91	45.66
58	36.69	37.43	38.18	38.93	39.68	40.43	41.19	41.95	42.71	43.47	44.23	45.00	45.77	46.54
59	37.37	38.13	38.89	39.66	40.42	41.19	41.96	42.74	43.51	44.29	45.07	45.85	46.64	47.42
60	38.06	38.83	39.61	40.39	41.17	41.95	42.74	43.53	44.32	45.11	45.91	46.71	47.51	48.31

Number of Payments	Annual Percentage Rate													
	17.00%	17.25%	17.50%	17.75%	18.00%	18.25%	18.50%	18.75%	19.00%	19.25%	19.50%	19.75%	20.00%	20.25%
	Finance Charge per $100 of Amount Financed													
1	1.42	1.44	1.46	1.48	1.50	1.52	1.54	1.56	1.58	1.60	1.63	1.65	1.67	1.69
2	2.13	2.16	2.19	2.22	2.26	2.29	2.32	2.35	2.38	2.41	2.44	2.48	2.51	2.54
3	2.85	2.89	2.93	2.97	3.01	3.06	3.10	3.14	3.18	3.23	3.27	3.31	3.35	3.39
4	3.57	3.62	3.67	3.73	3.78	3.83	3.88	3.94	3.99	4.04	4.10	4.15	4.20	4.25
5	4.29	4.35	4.42	4.48	4.54	4.61	4.67	4.74	4.80	4.86	4.93	4.99	5.06	5.12
6	5.02	5.09	5.17	5.24	5.32	5.39	5.46	5.54	5.61	5.69	5.76	5.84	5.91	5.99
7	5.75	5.83	5.92	6.00	6.09	6.18	6.26	6.35	6.43	6.52	6.60	6.69	6.78	6.86
8	6.48	6.58	6.67	6.77	6.87	6.96	7.06	7.16	7.26	7.35	7.45	7.55	7.64	7.74
9	7.22	7.32	7.43	7.54	7.65	7.76	7.87	7.97	8.08	8.19	8.30	8.41	8.52	8.63
10	7.96	8.08	8.19	8.31	8.43	8.55	8.67	8.79	8.91	9.03	9.15	9.27	9.39	9.51
11	8.70	8.83	8.96	9.09	9.22	9.35	9.49	9.62	9.75	9.88	10.01	10.14	10.28	10.41
12	9.45	9.59	9.73	9.87	10.02	10.16	10.30	10.44	10.59	10.73	10.87	11.02	11.16	11.31
13	10.20	10.35	10.50	10.66	10.81	10.97	11.12	11.28	11.43	11.59	11.74	11.90	12.05	12.21
14	10.95	11.11	11.28	11.45	11.61	11.78	11.95	12.11	12.28	12.45	12.61	12.78	12.95	13.11
15	11.71	11.88	12.06	12.24	12.42	12.59	12.77	12.95	13.13	13.31	13.49	13.67	13.85	14.03
16	12.46	12.65	12.84	13.03	13.22	13.41	13.60	13.80	13.99	14.18	14.37	14.56	14.75	14.94
17	13.23	13.43	13.63	13.83	14.04	14.24	14.44	14.64	14.85	15.05	15.25	15.46	15.66	15.86
18	13.99	14.21	14.42	14.64	14.85	15.07	15.28	15.49	15.71	15.93	16.14	16.36	16.57	16.79
19	14.76	14.99	15.22	15.44	15.67	15.90	16.12	16.35	16.58	16.81	17.03	17.26	17.49	17.72
20	15.54	15.78	16.01	16.25	16.49	16.73	16.97	17.21	17.45	17.69	17.93	18.17	18.41	18.66
21	16.31	16.56	16.81	17.07	17.32	17.57	17.82	18.07	18.33	18.58	18.83	19.09	19.34	19.60
22	17.09	17.36	17.62	17.88	18.15	18.41	18.68	18.94	19.21	19.47	19.74	20.01	20.27	20.54
23	17.88	18.15	18.43	18.70	18.98	19.26	19.54	19.81	20.09	20.37	20.65	20.93	21.21	21.49
24	18.66	18.95	19.24	19.53	19.82	20.11	20.40	20.69	20.98	21.27	21.56	21.86	22.15	22.44
25	19.45	19.75	20.05	20.36	20.66	20.96	21.27	21.57	21.87	22.18	22.48	22.79	23.10	23.40
26	20.24	20.56	20.87	21.19	21.50	21.82	22.14	22.45	22.77	23.09	23.41	23.73	24.04	24.36
27	21.04	21.37	21.69	22.02	22.35	22.68	23.01	23.34	23.67	24.00	24.33	24.67	25.00	25.33
28	21.84	22.18	22.52	22.86	23.20	23.55	23.89	24.23	24.58	24.92	25.27	25.61	25.96	26.30
29	22.64	22.99	23.35	23.70	24.06	24.41	24.77	25.13	25.49	25.84	26.20	26.56	26.92	27.28
30	23.45	23.81	24.18	24.55	24.92	25.29	25.66	26.03	26.40	26.77	27.14	27.52	27.89	28.26

Number of Payments	Annual Percentage Rate													
	17.00%	17.25%	17.50%	17.75%	18.00%	18.25%	18.50%	18.75%	19.00%	19.25%	19.50%	19.75%	20.00%	20.25%
Finance Charge per $100 of Amount Financed														
31	24.26	24.64	25.02	25.40	25.78	26.16	26.55	26.93	27.32	27.70	28.09	28.47	28.86	29.25
32	25.07	25.46	25.86	26.25	26.65	27.04	27.44	27.84	28.24	28.64	29.04	29.44	29.84	30.24
33	25.88	26.29	26.70	27.11	27.52	27.93	28.34	28.75	29.16	29.57	29.99	30.40	30.82	31.23
34	26.70	27.12	27.54	27.97	28.39	28.81	29.24	29.66	30.09	30.52	30.95	31.37	31.80	32.23
35	27.52	27.96	28.39	28.83	29.27	29.71	30.14	30.58	31.02	31.47	31.91	32.35	32.79	33.24
36	28.35	28.80	29.25	29.70	30.15	30.60	31.05	31.51	31.96	32.42	32.87	33.33	33.79	34.25
37	29.18	29.64	30.10	30.57	31.03	31.50	31.97	32.43	32.90	33.37	33.84	34.32	34.79	35.26
38	30.01	30.49	30.96	31.44	31.92	32.40	32.88	33.37	33.85	34.33	34.82	35.30	35.79	36.28
39	30.85	31.34	31.83	32.32	32.81	33.31	33.80	34.30	34.80	35.30	35.80	36.30	36.80	37.30
40	31.68	32.19	32.69	33.20	33.71	34.22	34.73	35.24	35.75	36.26	36.78	37.29	37.81	38.33
41	32.52	33.04	33.56	34.08	34.61	35.13	35.66	36.18	36.71	37.24	37.77	38.30	38.83	39.36
42	33.37	33.90	34.44	34.97	35.51	36.05	36.59	37.13	37.67	38.21	38.76	39.30	39.85	40.40
43	34.22	34.76	35.31	35.86	36.42	36.97	37.52	38.08	38.63	39.19	39.75	40.31	40.87	41.44
44	35.07	35.63	36.19	36.76	37.33	37.89	38.46	39.03	39.60	40.18	40.75	41.33	41.90	42.48
45	35.92	36.50	37.08	37.66	38.24	38.82	39.41	39.99	40.58	41.17	41.75	42.35	42.94	43.53
46	36.78	37.37	37.96	38.56	39.16	39.75	40.35	40.95	41.55	42.16	42.76	43.37	43.98	44.58
47	37.64	38.25	38.86	39.46	40.08	40.69	41.30	41.92	42.54	43.15	43.77	44.40	45.02	45.64
48	38.50	39.13	39.75	40.37	41.00	41.63	42.26	42.89	43.52	44.15	44.79	45.43	46.07	46.71
49	39.37	40.01	40.65	41.29	41.93	42.57	43.22	43.86	44.51	45.16	45.81	46.46	47.12	47.77
50	40.24	40.89	41.55	42.20	42.86	43.52	44.18	44.84	45.50	46.17	46.83	47.50	48.17	48.84
51	41.11	41.78	42.45	43.12	43.79	44.47	45.14	45.82	46.50	47.18	47.86	48.55	49.23	49.92
52	41.99	42.67	43.36	44.04	44.73	45.42	46.11	46.80	47.50	48.20	48.89	49.59	50.30	51.00
53	42.87	43.57	44.27	44.97	45.67	46.38	47.08	47.79	48.50	49.22	49.93	50.65	51.37	52.09
54	43.75	44.47	45.18	45.90	46.62	47.34	48.06	48.79	49.51	50.24	50.97	51.70	52.44	53.17
55	44.64	45.37	46.10	46.83	47.57	48.30	49.04	49.78	50.52	51.27	52.02	52.76	53.52	54.27
56	45.53	46.27	47.02	47.77	48.52	49.27	50.03	50.78	51.54	52.30	53.06	53.83	54.60	55.37
57	46.42	47.18	47.94	48.71	49.47	50.24	51.01	51.79	52.56	53.34	54.12	54.90	55.68	56.47
58	47.32	48.09	48.87	49.65	50.43	51.22	52.00	52.79	53.58	54.38	55.17	55.97	56.77	57.57
59	48.21	49.01	49.80	50.60	51.39	52.20	53.00	53.80	54.61	55.42	56.23	57.05	57.87	58.68
60	49.12	49.92	50.73	51.55	52.36	53.18	54.00	54.82	55.64	56.47	57.30	58.13	58.96	59.80

Number of Payments	Annual Percentage Rate													
	20.50%	20.75%	21.00%	21.25%	21.50%	21.75%	22.00%	22.25%	22.50%	22.75%	23.00%	23.25%	23.50%	23.75%
	Finance Charge per $100 of Amount Financed													
1	1.71	1.73	1.75	1.77	1.79	1.81	1.83	1.85	1.88	1.90	1.92	1.94	1.96	1.98
2	2.57	2.60	2.63	2.66	2.70	2.73	2.76	2.79	2.82	2.85	2.88	2.92	2.95	2.98
3	3.44	3.48	3.52	3.56	3.60	3.65	3.69	3.73	3.77	3.82	3.86	3.90	3.94	3.98
4	4.31	4.36	4.41	4.47	4.52	4.57	4.62	4.68	4.73	4.78	4.84	4.89	4.94	5.00
5	5.18	5.25	5.31	5.37	5.44	5.50	5.57	5.63	5.69	5.76	5.82	5.89	5.95	6.02
6	6.06	6.14	6.21	6.29	6.36	6.44	6.51	6.59	6.66	6.74	6.81	6.89	6.96	7.04
7	6.95	7.04	7.12	7.21	7.29	7.38	7.47	7.55	7.64	7.73	7.81	7.90	7.99	8.07
8	7.84	7.94	8.03	8.13	8.23	8.33	8.42	8.52	8.62	8.72	8.82	8.91	9.01	9.11
9	8.73	8.84	8.95	9.06	9.17	9.28	9.39	9.50	9.61	9.72	9.83	9.94	10.04	10.15
10	9.63	9.75	9.88	10.00	10.12	10.24	10.36	10.48	10.60	10.72	10.84	10.96	11.08	11.21
11	10.54	10.67	10.80	10.94	11.07	11.20	11.33	11.47	11.60	11.73	11.86	12.00	12.13	12.26
12	11.45	11.59	11.74	11.88	12.02	12.17	12.31	12.46	12.60	12.75	12.89	13.04	13.18	13.33
13	12.36	12.52	12.67	12.83	12.99	13.14	13.30	13.46	13.61	13.77	13.93	14.08	14.24	14.40
14	13.28	13.45	13.62	13.79	13.95	14.12	14.29	14.46	14.63	14.80	14.97	15.13	15.30	15.47
15	14.21	14.39	14.57	14.75	14.93	15.11	15.29	15.47	15.65	15.83	16.01	16.19	16.37	16.56
16	15.14	15.33	15.52	15.71	15.90	16.10	16.29	16.48	16.68	16.87	17.06	17.26	17.45	17.65
17	16.07	16.27	16.48	16.68	16.89	17.09	17.30	17.50	17.71	17.92	18.12	18.33	18.53	18.74
18	17.01	17.22	17.44	17.66	17.88	18.09	18.31	18.53	18.75	18.97	19.19	19.41	19.62	19.84
19	17.95	18.18	18.41	18.64	18.87	19.10	19.33	19.56	19.79	20.02	20.26	20.49	20.72	20.95
20	18.90	19.14	19.38	19.63	19.87	20.11	20.36	20.60	20.84	21.09	21.33	21.58	21.82	22.07
21	19.85	20.11	20.36	20.62	20.87	21.13	21.38	21.64	21.90	22.16	22.41	22.67	22.93	23.19
22	20.81	21.08	21.34	21.61	21.88	22.15	22.42	22.69	22.96	23.23	23.50	23.77	24.04	24.32
23	21.77	22.05	22.33	22.61	22.90	23.18	23.46	23.74	24.03	24.31	24.60	24.88	25.17	25.45
24	22.74	23.03	23.33	23.62	23.92	24.21	24.51	24.80	25.10	25.40	25.70	25.99	26.29	26.59
25	23.71	24.02	24.32	24.63	24.94	25.25	25.56	25.87	26.18	26.49	26.80	27.11	27.43	27.74
26	24.68	25.01	25.33	25.65	25.97	26.29	26.62	26.94	27.26	27.59	27.91	28.24	28.56	28.89
27	25.67	26.00	26.34	26.67	27.01	27.34	27.68	28.02	28.35	28.69	29.03	29.37	29.71	30.05
28	26.65	27.00	27.35	27.70	28.05	28.40	28.75	29.10	29.45	29.80	30.15	30.51	30.86	31.22
29	27.64	28.00	28.37	28.73	29.09	29.46	29.82	30.19	30.55	30.92	31.28	31.65	32.02	32.39
30	28.64	29.01	29.39	29.77	30.14	30.52	30.90	31.28	31.66	32.04	32.42	32.80	33.18	33.57

Number of Payments	Annual Percentage Rate													
	20.50%	20.75%	21.00%	21.25%	21.50%	21.75%	22.00%	22.25%	22.50%	22.75%	23.00%	23.25%	23.50%	23.75%
	Finance Charge per $100 of Amount Financed													
31	29.64	30.03	30.42	30.81	31.20	31.59	31.98	32.38	32.77	33.17	33.56	33.96	34.35	34.75
32	30.64	31.05	31.45	31.85	32.26	32.67	33.07	33.48	33.89	34.30	34.71	35.12	35.53	35.94
33	31.65	32.07	32.49	32.91	33.33	33.75	34.17	34.59	35.01	35.44	35.86	36.29	36.71	37.14
34	32.67	33.10	33.53	33.96	34.40	34.83	35.27	35.71	36.14	36.58	37.02	37.46	37.90	38.34
35	33.68	34.13	34.58	35.03	35.47	35.92	36.37	36.83	37.28	37.73	38.18	38.64	39.09	39.55
36	34.71	35.17	35.63	36.09	36.56	37.02	37.49	37.95	38.42	38.89	39.35	39.82	40.29	40.77
37	35.74	36.21	36.69	37.16	37.64	38.12	38.60	39.08	39.56	40.05	40.53	41.02	41.50	41.99
38	36.77	37.26	37.75	38.24	38.73	39.23	39.72	40.22	40.72	41.21	41.71	42.21	42.71	43.22
39	37.81	38.31	38.82	39.32	39.83	40.34	40.85	41.36	41.87	42.39	42.90	43.42	43.93	44.45
40	38.85	39.37	39.89	40.41	40.93	41.46	41.98	42.51	43.04	43.56	44.09	44.62	45.16	45.69
41	39.89	40.43	40.96	41.50	42.04	42.58	43.12	43.66	44.20	44.75	45.29	45.84	46.39	46.94
42	40.95	41.50	42.05	42.60	43.15	43.71	44.26	44.82	45.38	45.94	46.50	47.06	47.62	48.19
43	42.00	42.57	43.13	43.70	44.27	44.84	45.41	45.98	46.56	47.13	47.71	48.29	48.87	49.45
44	43.06	43.64	44.22	44.81	45.39	45.98	46.56	47.15	47.74	48.33	48.93	49.52	50.11	50.71
45	44.13	44.72	45.32	45.92	46.52	47.12	47.72	48.33	48.93	49.54	50.15	50.76	51.37	51.98
46	45.20	45.81	46.42	47.03	47.65	48.27	48.89	49.51	50.13	50.75	51.38	52.00	52.63	53.26
47	46.27	46.90	47.53	48.16	48.79	49.42	50.06	50.69	51.33	51.97	52.61	53.25	53.89	54.54
48	47.35	47.99	48.64	49.28	49.93	50.58	51.23	51.88	52.54	53.19	53.85	54.51	55.16	55.83
49	48.43	49.09	49.75	50.41	51.08	51.74	52.41	53.08	53.75	54.42	55.09	55.77	56.44	57.12
50	49.52	50.19	50.87	51.55	52.23	52.91	53.59	54.28	54.96	55.65	56.34	57.03	57.73	58.42
51	50.61	51.30	51.99	52.69	53.38	54.08	54.78	55.48	56.19	56.89	57.60	58.30	59.01	59.73
52	51.71	52.41	53.12	53.83	54.55	55.26	55.98	56.69	57.41	58.13	58.86	59.58	60.31	61.04
53	52.81	53.53	54.26	54.98	55.71	56.44	57.18	57.91	58.65	59.38	60.12	60.87	61.61	62.35
54	53.91	54.65	55.39	56.14	56.88	57.63	58.38	59.13	59.88	60.64	61.40	62.16	62.92	63.68
55	55.02	55.78	56.54	57.30	58.06	58.82	59.59	60.36	61.13	61.90	62.67	63.45	64.23	65.01
56	56.14	56.91	57.68	58.46	59.24	60.02	60.80	61.59	62.38	63.17	63.96	64.75	65.54	66.34
57	57.26	58.04	58.84	59.63	60.43	61.22	62.02	62.83	63.63	64.44	65.25	66.06	66.87	67.68
58	58.38	59.18	59.99	60.80	61.62	62.43	63.25	64.07	64.89	65.71	66.54	67.37	68.20	69.03
59	59.51	60.33	61.15	61.98	62.81	63.64	64.48	65.32	66.15	67.00	67.84	68.68	69.53	70.38
60	60.64	61.48	62.32	63.17	64.01	64.86	65.71	66.57	67.42	68.28	69.14	70.01	70.87	71.74

Number of Payments	Annual Percentage Rate													
	24.00%	24.25%	24.50%	24.75%	25.00%	25.25%	25.50%	25.75%	26.00%	26.25%	26.50%	26.75%	27.00%	27.25%
	Finance Charge per $100 of Amount Financed													
1	2.00	2.02	2.04	2.06	2.08	2.10	2.12	2.15	2.17	2.19	2.21	2.23	2.25	2.27
2	3.01	3.04	3.07	3.10	3.14	3.17	3.20	3.23	3.26	3.29	3.32	3.36	3.39	3.42
3	4.03	4.07	4.11	4.15	4.20	4.24	4.28	4.32	4.36	4.41	4.45	4.49	4.53	4.58
4	5.05	5.10	5.16	5.21	5.26	5.32	5.37	5.42	5.47	5.53	5.58	5.63	5.69	5.74
5	6.08	6.14	6.21	6.27	6.34	6.40	6.46	6.53	6.59	6.66	6.72	6.79	6.85	6.91
6	7.12	7.19	7.27	7.34	7.42	7.49	7.57	7.64	7.72	7.79	7.87	7.95	8.02	8.10
7	8.16	8.25	8.33	8.42	8.51	8.59	8.68	8.77	8.85	8.94	9.03	9.11	9.20	9.29
8	9.21	9.31	9.40	9.50	9.60	9.70	9.80	9.90	9.99	10.09	10.19	10.29	10.39	10.49
9	10.26	10.37	10.48	10.59	10.70	10.81	10.92	11.03	11.14	11.25	11.36	11.47	11.58	11.69
10	11.33	11.45	11.57	11.69	11.81	11.93	12.06	12.18	12.30	12.42	12.54	12.67	12.79	12.91
11	12.40	12.53	12.66	12.80	12.93	13.06	13.20	13.33	13.46	13.60	13.73	13.87	14.00	14.13
12	13.47	13.62	13.76	13.91	14.05	14.20	14.34	14.49	14.64	14.78	14.93	15.07	15.22	15.37
13	14.55	14.71	14.87	15.03	15.18	15.34	15.50	15.66	15.82	15.97	16.13	16.29	16.45	16.61
14	15.64	15.81	15.98	16.15	16.32	16.49	16.66	16.83	17.00	17.17	17.35	17.52	17.69	17.86
15	16.74	16.92	17.10	17.28	17.47	17.65	17.83	18.02	18.20	18.38	18.57	18.75	18.93	19.12
16	17.84	18.03	18.23	18.42	18.62	18.81	19.01	19.21	19.40	19.60	19.79	19.99	20.19	20.38
17	18.95	19.16	19.36	19.57	19.78	19.99	20.20	20.40	20.61	20.82	21.03	21.24	21.45	21.66
18	20.06	20.28	20.50	20.72	20.95	21.17	21.39	21.61	21.83	22.05	22.27	22.50	22.72	22.94
19	21.19	21.42	21.65	21.89	22.12	22.35	22.59	22.82	23.06	23.29	23.53	23.76	24.00	24.23
20	22.31	22.56	22.81	23.05	23.30	23.55	23.79	24.04	24.29	24.54	24.79	25.04	25.28	25.53
21	23.45	23.71	23.97	24.23	24.49	24.75	25.01	25.27	25.53	25.79	26.05	26.32	26.58	26.84
22	24.59	24.86	25.13	25.41	25.68	25.96	26.23	26.50	26.78	27.05	27.33	27.61	27.88	28.16
23	25.74	26.02	26.31	26.60	26.88	27.17	27.46	27.75	28.04	28.32	28.61	28.90	29.19	29.48
24	26.89	27.19	27.49	27.79	28.09	28.39	28.69	29.00	29.30	29.60	29.90	30.21	30.51	30.82
25	28.05	28.36	28.68	28.99	29.31	29.62	29.94	30.25	30.57	30.89	31.20	31.52	31.84	32.16
26	29.22	29.55	29.87	30.20	30.53	30.86	31.19	31.52	31.85	32.18	32.51	32.84	33.18	33.51
27	30.39	30.73	31.07	31.42	31.76	32.10	32.45	32.79	33.14	33.48	33.83	34.17	34.52	34.87
28	31.57	31.93	32.28	32.64	33.00	33.35	33.71	34.07	34.43	34.79	35.15	35.51	35.87	36.23
29	32.76	33.13	33.50	33.87	34.24	34.61	34.98	35.36	35.73	36.10	36.48	36.85	37.23	37.61
30	33.95	34.33	34.72	35.10	35.49	35.88	36.26	36.65	37.04	37.43	37.82	38.21	38.60	38.99

Number of Payments	Annual Percentage Rate													
	24.00%	24.25%	24.50%	24.75%	25.00%	25.25%	25.50%	25.75%	26.00%	26.25%	26.50%	26.75%	27.00%	27.25%
	Finance Charge per $100 of Amount Financed													
31	35.15	35.55	35.95	36.35	36.75	37.15	37.55	37.95	38.36	38.76	39.16	39.57	39.97	40.38
32	36.35	36.77	37.18	37.60	38.01	38.43	38.84	39.26	39.68	40.10	40.52	40.94	41.36	41.78
33	37.57	37.99	38.42	38.85	39.28	39.71	40.14	40.58	41.01	41.44	41.88	42.31	42.75	43.19
34	38.78	39.23	39.67	40.11	40.56	41.01	41.45	41.90	42.35	42.80	43.25	43.70	44.15	44.60
35	40.01	40.47	40.92	41.38	41.84	42.31	42.77	43.23	43.69	44.16	44.62	45.09	45.56	46.02
36	41.24	41.71	42.19	42.66	43.14	43.61	44.09	44.57	45.05	45.53	46.01	46.49	46.97	47.45
37	42.48	42.96	43.45	43.94	44.43	44.93	45.42	45.91	46.41	46.90	47.40	47.90	48.39	48.89
38	43.72	44.22	44.73	45.23	45.74	46.25	46.75	47.26	47.77	48.29	48.80	49.31	49.82	50.34
39	44.97	45.49	46.01	46.53	47.05	47.57	48.10	48.62	49.15	49.68	50.20	50.73	51.26	51.79
40	46.22	46.76	47.29	47.83	48.37	48.91	49.45	49.99	50.53	51.07	51.62	52.16	52.71	53.26
41	47.48	48.04	48.59	49.14	49.69	50.25	50.80	51.36	51.92	52.48	53.04	53.60	54.16	54.73
42	48.75	49.32	49.89	50.46	51.03	51.60	52.17	52.74	53.32	53.89	54.47	55.05	55.63	56.21
43	50.03	50.61	51.19	51.78	52.36	52.95	53.54	54.13	54.72	55.31	55.90	56.50	57.09	57.69
44	51.31	51.91	52.51	53.11	53.71	54.31	54.92	55.52	56.13	56.74	57.35	57.96	58.57	59.19
45	52.59	53.21	53.82	54.44	55.06	55.68	56.30	56.92	57.55	58.17	58.80	59.43	60.06	60.69
46	53.89	54.52	55.15	55.78	56.42	57.05	57.69	58.33	58.97	59.61	60.26	60.90	61.55	62.20
47	55.18	55.83	56.48	57.13	57.78	58.44	59.09	59.75	60.40	61.06	61.72	62.39	63.05	63.71
48	56.49	57.15	57.82	58.49	59.15	59.82	60.50	61.17	61.84	62.52	63.20	63.87	64.56	65.24
49	57.80	58.48	59.16	59.85	60.53	61.22	61.91	62.60	63.29	63.98	64.68	65.37	66.07	66.77
50	59.12	59.81	60.51	61.21	61.92	62.62	63.33	64.03	64.74	65.45	66.16	66.88	67.59	68.31
51	60.44	61.15	61.87	62.59	63.31	64.03	64.75	65.48	66.20	66.93	67.66	68.39	69.12	69.86
52	61.77	62.50	63.23	63.97	64.70	65.44	66.18	66.92	67.67	68.41	69.16	69.91	70.66	71.41
53	63.10	63.85	64.60	65.35	66.11	66.86	67.62	68.38	69.14	69.90	70.67	71.43	72.20	72.97
54	64.44	65.21	65.98	66.75	67.52	68.29	69.07	69.84	70.62	71.40	72.18	72.97	73.75	74.54
55	65.79	66.57	67.36	68.14	68.93	69.72	70.52	71.31	72.11	72.91	73.71	74.51	75.31	76.12
56	67.14	67.94	68.74	69.55	70.36	71.16	71.97	72.79	73.60	74.42	75.24	76.06	76.88	77.70
57	68.50	69.32	70.14	70.96	71.78	72.61	73.44	74.27	75.10	75.94	76.77	77.61	78.45	79.29
58	69.86	70.70	71.54	72.38	73.22	74.06	74.91	75.76	76.61	77.46	78.32	79.17	80.03	80.89
59	71.23	72.09	72.94	73.80	74.66	75.52	76.39	77.25	78.12	78.99	79.87	80.74	81.62	82.50
60	72.61	73.48	74.35	75.23	76.11	76.99	77.87	78.76	79.64	80.53	81.42	82.32	83.21	84.11

Number of Payments	Annual Percentage Rate													
	27.50%	27.75%	28.00%	28.25%	28.50%	28.75%	29.00%	29.25%	29.50%	29.75%	30.00%	30.25%	30.50%	30.75%
	Finance Charge per $100 of Amount Financed													
1	2.29	2.31	2.33	2.35	2.37	2.40	2.42	2.44	2.46	2.48	2.50	2.52	2.54	2.56
2	3.45	3.48	3.51	3.54	3.58	3.61	3.64	3.67	3.70	3.73	3.77	3.80	3.83	3.86
3	4.62	4.66	4.70	4.74	4.79	4.83	4.87	4.91	4.96	5.00	5.04	5.08	5.13	5.17
4	5.79	5.85	5.90	5.95	6.01	6.06	6.11	6.17	6.22	6.27	6.33	6.38	6.43	6.49
5	6.98	7.04	7.11	7.17	7.24	7.30	7.37	7.43	7.49	7.56	7.62	7.69	7.75	7.82
6	8.17	8.25	8.32	8.40	8.48	8.55	8.63	8.70	8.78	8.85	8.93	9.01	9.08	9.16
7	9.37	9.46	9.55	9.64	9.72	9.81	9.90	9.98	10.07	10.16	10.25	10.33	10.42	10.51
8	10.58	10.68	10.78	10.88	10.98	11.08	11.18	11.28	11.38	11.47	11.57	11.67	11.77	11.87
9	11.80	11.91	12.03	12.14	12.25	12.36	12.47	12.58	12.69	12.80	12.91	13.02	13.13	13.24
10	13.03	13.15	13.28	13.40	13.52	13.64	13.77	13.89	14.01	14.14	14.26	14.38	14.50	14.63
11	14.27	14.40	14.54	14.67	14.81	14.94	15.08	15.21	15.35	15.48	15.62	15.75	15.89	16.02
12	15.51	15.66	15.81	15.95	16.10	16.25	16.40	16.54	16.69	16.84	16.98	17.13	17.28	17.43
13	16.77	16.93	17.09	17.24	17.40	17.56	17.72	17.88	18.04	18.20	18.36	18.52	18.68	18.84
14	18.03	18.20	18.37	18.54	18.72	18.89	19.06	19.23	19.41	19.58	19.75	19.92	20.10	20.27
15	19.30	19.48	19.67	19.85	20.04	20.22	20.41	20.59	20.78	20.96	21.15	21.34	21.52	21.71
16	20.58	20.78	20.97	21.17	21.37	21.57	21.76	21.96	22.16	22.36	22.56	22.76	22.96	23.16
17	21.87	22.08	22.29	22.50	22.71	22.92	23.13	23.34	23.55	23.77	23.98	24.19	24.40	24.61
18	23.16	23.39	23.61	23.83	24.06	24.28	24.51	24.73	24.96	25.18	25.41	25.63	25.86	26.08
19	24.47	24.71	24.94	25.18	25.42	25.65	25.89	26.13	26.37	26.61	26.85	27.08	27.32	27.56
20	25.78	26.03	26.28	26.53	26.78	27.04	27.29	27.54	27.79	28.04	28.29	28.55	28.80	29.05
21	27.11	27.37	27.63	27.90	28.16	28.43	28.69	28.96	29.22	29.49	29.75	30.02	30.29	30.55
22	28.44	28.71	28.99	29.27	29.55	29.82	30.10	30.38	30.66	30.94	31.22	31.50	31.78	32.07
23	29.77	30.07	30.36	30.65	30.94	31.23	31.53	31.82	32.11	32.41	32.70	33.00	33.29	33.59
24	31.12	31.43	31.73	32.04	32.34	32.65	32.96	33.27	33.57	33.88	34.19	34.50	34.81	35.12
25	32.48	32.80	33.12	33.44	33.76	34.08	34.40	34.72	35.04	35.37	35.69	36.01	36.34	36.66
26	33.84	34.18	34.51	34.84	35.18	35.51	35.85	36.19	36.52	36.86	37.20	37.54	37.88	38.21
27	35.21	35.56	35.91	36.26	36.61	36.96	37.31	37.66	38.01	38.36	38.72	39.07	39.42	39.78
28	36.59	36.96	37.32	37.68	38.05	38.41	38.78	39.15	39.51	39.88	40.25	40.61	40.98	41.35
29	37.98	38.36	38.74	39.12	39.50	39.88	40.26	40.64	41.02	41.40	41.78	42.17	42.55	42.94
30	39.38	39.77	40.17	40.56	40.95	41.35	41.75	42.14	42.54	42.94	43.33	43.73	44.13	44.53

Number of Payments	Annual Percentage Rate													
	27.50%	27.75%	28.00%	28.25%	28.50%	28.75%	29.00%	29.25%	29.50%	29.75%	30.00%	30.25%	30.50%	30.75%
	Finance Charge per $100 of Amount Financed													
31	40.79	41.19	41.60	42.01	42.42	42.83	43.24	43.65	44.07	44.48	44.89	45.30	45.72	46.13
32	42.20	42.62	43.05	43.47	43.90	44.32	44.75	45.17	45.60	46.03	46.46	46.89	47.32	47.75
33	43.62	44.06	44.50	44.94	45.38	45.82	46.26	46.70	47.15	47.59	48.04	48.48	48.93	49.37
34	45.05	45.51	45.96	46.42	46.87	47.33	47.79	48.24	48.70	49.16	49.62	50.08	50.55	51.01
35	46.49	46.96	47.43	47.90	48.37	48.85	49.32	49.79	50.27	50.74	51.22	51.70	52.17	52.65
36	47.94	48.42	48.91	49.40	49.88	50.37	50.86	51.35	51.84	52.33	52.83	53.32	53.81	54.31
37	49.39	49.89	50.40	50.90	51.40	51.91	52.41	52.92	53.42	53.93	54.44	54.95	55.46	55.97
38	50.86	51.37	51.89	52.41	52.93	53.45	53.97	54.49	55.02	55.54	56.07	56.59	57.12	57.65
39	52.33	52.86	53.39	53.93	54.46	55.00	55.54	56.08	56.62	57.16	57.70	58.24	58.79	59.33
40	53.81	54.35	54.90	55.46	56.01	56.56	57.12	57.67	58.23	58.79	59.34	59.90	60.47	61.03
41	55.29	55.86	56.42	56.99	57.56	58.13	58.70	59.28	59.85	60.42	61.00	61.57	62.15	62.73
42	56.79	57.37	57.95	58.54	59.12	59.71	60.30	60.89	61.48	62.07	62.66	63.25	63.85	64.44
43	58.29	58.89	59.49	60.09	60.69	61.30	61.90	62.51	63.11	63.72	64.33	64.94	65.56	66.17
44	59.80	60.42	61.03	61.65	62.27	62.89	63.51	64.14	64.76	65.39	66.01	66.64	67.27	67.90
45	61.32	61.95	62.59	63.22	63.86	64.50	65.13	65.77	66.42	67.06	67.70	68.35	69.00	69.64
46	62.84	63.49	64.15	64.80	65.45	66.11	66.76	67.42	68.08	68.74	69.40	70.07	70.73	71.40
47	64.38	65.05	65.71	66.38	67.06	67.73	68.40	69.08	69.75	70.43	71.11	71.79	72.47	73.16
48	65.92	66.60	67.29	67.98	68.67	69.36	70.05	70.74	71.44	72.13	72.83	73.53	74.23	74.93
49	67.47	68.17	68.87	69.58	70.29	70.99	71.70	72.41	73.13	73.84	74.56	75.27	75.99	76.71
50	69.03	69.75	70.47	71.19	71.91	72.64	73.37	74.10	74.83	75.56	76.29	77.02	77.76	78.50
51	70.59	71.33	72.07	72.81	73.55	74.29	75.04	75.78	76.53	77.28	78.03	78.79	79.54	80.30
52	72.16	72.92	73.67	74.43	75.19	75.95	76.72	77.48	78.25	79.02	79.79	80.56	81.33	82.11
53	73.74	74.52	75.29	76.07	76.85	77.62	78.41	79.19	79.97	80.76	81.55	82.34	83.13	83.92
54	75.33	76.12	76.91	77.71	78.50	79.30	80.10	80.90	81.71	82.51	83.32	84.13	84.94	85.75
55	76.92	77.73	78.55	79.36	80.17	80.99	81.81	82.63	83.45	84.27	85.10	85.93	86.75	87.58
56	78.53	79.35	80.18	81.02	81.85	82.68	83.52	84.36	85.20	86.04	86.89	87.73	88.58	89.43
57	80.14	80.98	81.83	82.68	83.53	84.39	85.24	86.10	86.96	87.82	88.68	89.55	90.41	91.28
58	81.75	82.62	83.48	84.35	85.22	86.10	86.97	87.85	88.72	89.60	90.49	91.37	92.26	93.14
59	83.38	84.26	85.15	86.03	86.92	87.81	88.71	89.60	90.50	91.40	92.30	93.20	94.11	95.01
60	85.01	85.91	86.81	87.72	88.63	89.54	90.45	91.37	92.28	93.20	94.12	95.04	95.97	96.89

Annual Percentage Rate

Number of Payments	31.00%	31.25%	31.50%	31.75%	32.00%	32.25%	32.50%	32.75%	33.00%	33.25%	33.50%	33.75%	34.00%	34.25%
				Finance Charge per $100 of Amount Financed										
1	2.58	2.60	2.63	2.65	2.67	2.69	2.71	2.73	2.75	2.77	2.79	2.81	2.83	2.85
2	3.89	3.92	3.95	3.99	4.02	4.05	4.08	4.11	4.14	4.18	4.21	4.24	4.27	4.30
3	5.21	5.25	5.30	5.34	5.38	5.42	5.46	5.51	5.55	5.59	5.63	5.68	5.72	5.76
4	6.54	6.59	6.65	6.70	6.75	6.81	6.86	6.91	6.97	7.02	7.08	7.13	7.18	7.24
5	7.88	7.95	8.01	8.08	8.14	8.21	8.27	8.33	8.40	8.46	8.53	8.59	8.66	8.72
6	9.23	9.31	9.39	9.46	9.54	9.61	9.69	9.77	9.84	9.92	9.99	10.07	10.15	10.22
7	10.60	10.68	10.77	10.86	10.95	11.03	11.12	11.21	11.30	11.39	11.47	11.56	11.65	11.74
8	11.97	12.07	12.17	12.27	12.37	12.47	12.57	12.67	12.77	12.87	12.97	13.07	13.17	13.27
9	13.36	13.47	13.58	13.69	13.80	13.91	14.02	14.14	14.25	14.36	14.47	14.58	14.69	14.81
10	14.75	14.87	15.00	15.12	15.24	15.37	15.49	15.62	15.74	15.86	15.99	16.11	16.24	16.36
11	16.16	16.29	16.43	16.56	16.70	16.84	16.97	17.11	17.24	17.38	17.52	17.65	17.79	17.93
12	17.58	17.72	17.87	18.02	18.17	18.32	18.47	18.61	18.76	18.91	19.06	19.21	19.36	19.51
13	19.00	19.16	19.33	19.49	19.65	19.81	19.97	20.13	20.29	20.45	20.62	20.78	20.94	21.10
14	20.44	20.62	20.79	20.96	21.14	21.31	21.49	21.66	21.83	22.01	22.18	22.36	22.53	22.71
15	21.89	22.08	22.27	22.45	22.64	22.83	23.01	23.20	23.39	23.58	23.76	23.95	24.14	24.33
16	23.35	23.55	23.75	23.95	24.15	24.35	24.55	24.75	24.96	25.16	25.36	25.56	25.76	25.96
17	24.83	25.04	25.25	25.47	25.68	25.89	26.11	26.32	26.53	26.75	26.96	27.18	27.39	27.61
18	26.31	26.54	26.76	26.99	27.22	27.44	27.67	27.90	28.13	28.35	28.58	28.81	29.04	29.27
19	27.80	28.04	28.28	28.52	28.76	29.00	29.25	29.49	29.73	29.97	30.21	30.45	30.70	30.94
20	29.31	29.56	29.81	30.07	30.32	30.58	30.83	31.09	31.34	31.60	31.86	32.11	32.37	32.63
21	30.82	31.09	31.36	31.62	31.89	32.16	32.43	32.70	32.97	33.24	33.51	33.78	34.05	34.32
22	32.35	32.63	32.91	33.19	33.48	33.76	34.04	34.33	34.61	34.89	35.18	35.46	35.75	36.04
23	33.88	34.18	34.48	34.77	35.07	35.37	35.66	35.96	36.26	36.56	36.86	37.16	37.46	37.76
24	35.43	35.74	36.05	36.36	36.67	36.99	37.30	37.61	37.92	38.24	38.55	38.87	39.18	39.50
25	36.99	37.31	37.64	37.96	38.29	38.62	38.94	39.27	39.60	39.93	40.26	40.59	40.92	41.25
26	38.55	38.89	39.23	39.58	39.92	40.26	40.60	40.94	41.29	41.63	41.97	42.32	42.66	43.01
27	40.13	40.49	40.84	41.20	41.56	41.91	42.27	42.63	42.99	43.34	43.70	44.06	44.42	44.78
28	41.72	42.09	42.46	42.83	43.20	43.58	43.95	44.32	44.70	45.07	45.45	45.82	46.20	46.57
29	43.32	43.71	44.09	44.48	44.87	45.25	45.64	46.03	46.42	46.81	47.20	47.59	47.98	48.37
30	44.93	45.33	45.73	46.13	46.54	46.94	47.34	47.75	48.15	48.56	48.96	49.37	49.78	50.19

Number of Payments	Annual Percentage Rate													
	31.00%	31.25%	31.50%	31.75%	32.00%	32.25%	32.50%	32.75%	33.00%	33.25%	33.50%	33.75%	34.00%	34.25%
	Finance Charge per $100 of Amount Financed													
31	46.55	46.97	47.38	47.80	48.22	48.64	49.06	49.48	49.90	50.32	50.74	51.17	51.59	52.01
32	48.18	48.61	49.05	49.48	49.91	50.35	50.78	51.22	51.66	52.09	52.53	52.97	53.41	53.85
33	49.82	50.27	50.72	51.17	51.62	52.07	52.52	52.97	53.43	53.88	54.33	54.79	55.24	55.70
34	51.47	51.94	52.40	52.87	53.33	53.80	54.27	54.74	55.21	55.68	56.15	56.62	57.09	57.56
35	53.13	53.61	54.09	54.58	55.06	55.54	56.03	56.51	57.00	57.48	57.97	58.46	58.95	59.44
36	54.80	55.30	55.80	56.30	56.80	57.30	57.80	58.30	58.80	59.30	59.81	60.31	60.82	61.33
37	56.49	57.00	57.51	58.03	58.54	59.06	59.58	60.10	60.62	61.14	61.66	62.18	62.70	63.22
38	58.18	58.71	59.24	59.77	60.30	60.84	61.37	61.90	62.44	62.98	63.52	64.06	64.59	65.14
39	59.88	60.42	60.97	61.52	62.07	62.62	63.17	63.72	64.28	64.83	65.39	65.94	66.50	67.06
40	61.59	62.15	62.72	63.28	63.85	64.42	64.99	65.56	66.13	66.70	67.27	67.84	68.42	68.99
41	63.31	63.89	64.47	65.06	65.64	66.22	66.81	67.40	67.99	68.57	69.16	69.76	70.35	70.94
42	65.04	65.64	66.24	66.84	67.44	68.04	68.65	69.25	69.86	70.46	71.07	71.68	72.29	72.90
43	66.78	67.40	68.01	68.63	69.25	69.87	70.49	71.11	71.74	72.36	72.99	73.61	74.24	74.87
44	68.53	69.17	69.80	70.43	71.07	71.71	72.35	72.99	73.63	74.27	74.91	75.56	76.20	76.85
45	70.29	70.94	71.60	72.25	72.90	73.56	74.21	74.87	75.53	76.19	76.85	77.52	78.18	78.84
46	72.06	72.73	73.40	74.07	74.74	75.42	76.09	76.77	77.44	78.12	78.80	79.48	80.17	80.85
47	73.84	74.53	75.22	75.91	76.60	77.29	77.98	78.67	79.37	80.07	80.76	81.46	82.16	82.87
48	75.63	76.34	77.04	77.75	78.46	79.17	79.88	80.59	81.30	82.02	82.74	83.45	84.17	84.89
49	77.43	78.15	78.88	79.60	80.33	81.06	81.79	82.52	83.25	83.98	84.72	85.45	86.19	86.93
50	79.24	79.98	80.72	81.46	82.21	82.96	83.70	84.45	85.20	85.96	86.71	87.47	88.22	88.98
51	81.06	81.81	82.58	83.34	84.10	84.87	85.63	86.40	87.17	87.94	88.71	89.49	90.26	91.04
52	82.88	83.66	84.44	85.22	86.00	86.79	87.57	88.36	89.15	89.94	90.73	91.52	92.32	93.11
53	84.72	85.51	86.31	87.11	87.91	88.72	89.52	90.33	91.13	91.94	92.75	93.57	94.38	95.20
54	86.56	87.38	88.19	89.01	89.83	90.66	91.48	92.30	93.13	93.96	94.79	95.62	96.45	97.29
55	88.42	89.25	90.09	90.92	91.76	92.60	93.45	94.29	95.14	95.99	96.83	97.69	98.54	99.39
56	90.28	91.13	91.99	92.84	93.70	94.56	95.43	96.29	97.15	98.02	98.89	99.76	100.63	101.51
57	92.15	93.02	93.90	94.77	95.65	96.53	97.41	98.30	99.18	100.07	100.96	101.85	102.74	103.63
58	94.03	94.92	95.82	96.71	97.61	98.51	99.41	100.31	101.22	102.12	103.03	103.94	104.85	105.77
59	95.92	96.83	97.75	98.66	99.58	100.50	101.42	102.34	103.26	104.19	105.12	106.05	106.98	107.91
60	97.82	98.75	99.68	100.62	101.56	102.49	103.43	104.38	105.32	106.27	107.21	108.16	109.12	110.07

Annual Percentage Rate

Number of Payments	34.50%	34.75%	35.00%	35.25%	35.50%	35.75%	36.00%	36.25%	36.50%	36.75%	37.00%	37.25%	37.50%	37.75%
	Finance Charge per $100 of Amount Financed													
1	2.87	2.90	2.92	2.94	2.96	2.98	3.00	3.02	3.04	3.06	3.08	3.10	3.12	3.15
2	4.33	4.36	4.40	4.43	4.46	4.49	4.52	4.55	4.59	4.62	4.65	4.68	4.71	4.74
3	5.80	5.85	5.89	5.93	5.97	6.02	6.06	6.10	6.14	6.19	6.23	6.27	6.31	6.36
4	7.29	7.34	7.40	7.45	7.50	7.56	7.61	7.66	7.72	7.77	7.83	7.88	7.93	7.99
5	8.79	8.85	8.92	8.98	9.05	9.11	9.18	9.24	9.31	9.37	9.44	9.50	9.57	9.63
6	10.30	10.38	10.45	10.53	10.61	10.68	10.76	10.83	10.91	10.99	11.06	11.14	11.22	11.29
7	11.83	11.91	12.00	12.09	12.18	12.27	12.35	12.44	12.53	12.62	12.71	12.80	12.88	12.97
8	13.36	13.46	13.56	13.66	13.76	13.86	13.97	14.07	14.17	14.27	14.37	14.47	14.57	14.67
9	14.92	15.03	15.14	15.25	15.37	15.48	15.59	15.70	15.82	15.93	16.04	16.15	16.27	16.38
10	16.48	16.61	16.73	16.86	16.98	17.11	17.23	17.36	17.48	17.60	17.73	17.85	17.98	18.10
11	18.06	18.20	18.34	18.47	18.61	18.75	18.89	19.02	19.16	19.30	19.43	19.57	19.71	19.85
12	19.66	19.81	19.96	20.11	20.25	20.40	20.55	20.70	20.85	21.00	21.15	21.31	21.46	21.61
13	21.26	21.43	21.59	21.75	21.91	22.08	22.24	22.40	22.56	22.73	22.89	23.05	23.22	23.38
14	22.88	23.06	23.23	23.41	23.59	23.76	23.94	24.11	24.29	24.47	24.64	24.82	25.00	25.17
15	24.52	24.71	24.89	25.08	25.27	25.46	25.65	25.84	26.03	26.22	26.41	26.60	26.79	26.98
16	26.16	26.37	26.57	26.77	26.97	27.17	27.38	27.58	27.78	27.99	28.19	28.39	28.60	28.80
17	27.82	28.04	28.25	28.47	28.69	28.90	29.12	29.34	29.55	29.77	29.99	30.20	30.42	30.64
18	29.50	29.73	29.96	30.19	30.42	30.65	30.88	31.11	31.34	31.57	31.80	32.03	32.26	32.49
19	31.18	31.43	31.67	31.91	32.16	32.40	32.65	32.89	33.14	33.38	33.63	33.87	34.12	34.36
20	32.88	33.14	33.40	33.66	33.91	34.17	34.43	34.69	34.95	35.21	35.47	35.73	35.99	36.25
21	34.60	34.87	35.14	35.41	35.68	35.96	36.23	36.50	36.78	37.05	37.33	37.60	37.88	38.15
22	36.32	36.61	36.89	37.18	37.47	37.76	38.04	38.33	38.62	38.91	39.20	39.49	39.78	40.07
23	38.06	38.36	38.66	38.96	39.27	39.57	39.87	40.18	40.48	40.78	41.09	41.39	41.70	42.00
24	39.81	40.13	40.44	40.76	41.08	41.40	41.71	42.03	42.35	42.67	42.99	43.31	43.63	43.95
25	41.58	41.91	42.24	42.57	42.90	43.24	43.57	43.90	44.24	44.57	44.91	45.24	45.58	45.91
26	43.36	43.70	44.05	44.40	44.74	45.09	45.44	45.79	46.14	46.49	46.84	47.19	47.54	47.89
27	45.15	45.51	45.87	46.23	46.60	46.96	47.32	47.69	48.05	48.42	48.78	49.15	49.52	49.89
28	46.95	47.33	47.70	48.08	48.46	48.84	49.22	49.60	49.98	50.36	50.75	51.13	51.51	51.89
29	48.77	49.16	49.55	49.95	50.34	50.74	51.13	51.53	51.93	52.32	52.72	53.12	53.52	53.92
30	50.60	51.00	51.41	51.82	52.23	52.65	53.06	53.47	53.88	54.30	54.71	55.13	55.54	55.96

Number of Payments	Annual Percentage Rate													
	34.50%	34.75%	35.00%	35.25%	35.50%	35.75%	36.00%	36.25%	36.50%	36.75%	37.00%	37.25%	37.50%	37.75%
	Finance Charge per $100 of Amount Financed													
31	52.44	52.86	53.29	53.71	54.14	54.57	55.00	55.43	55.85	56.28	56.72	57.15	57.58	58.01
32	54.29	54.73	55.17	55.62	56.06	56.50	56.95	57.39	57.84	58.29	58.73	59.18	59.63	60.08
33	56.16	56.62	57.07	57.53	57.99	58.45	58.92	59.38	59.84	60.30	60.77	61.23	61.70	62.16
34	58.04	58.51	58.99	59.46	59.94	60.42	60.89	61.37	61.85	62.33	62.81	63.30	63.78	64.26
35	59.93	60.42	60.91	61.40	61.90	62.39	62.89	63.38	63.88	64.38	64.88	65.37	65.87	66.37
36	61.83	62.34	62.85	63.36	63.87	64.38	64.89	65.41	65.92	66.44	66.95	67.47	67.98	68.50
37	63.75	64.27	64.80	65.33	65.85	66.38	66.91	67.44	67.97	68.51	69.04	69.57	70.11	70.64
38	65.68	66.22	66.76	67.31	67.85	68.40	68.95	69.49	70.04	70.59	71.14	71.69	72.25	72.80
39	67.62	68.18	68.74	69.30	69.86	70.43	70.99	71.56	72.12	72.69	73.26	73.83	74.40	74.97
40	69.57	70.15	70.73	71.31	71.89	72.47	73.05	73.63	74.22	74.80	75.39	75.98	76.56	77.15
41	71.53	72.13	72.73	73.32	73.92	74.52	75.12	75.72	76.32	76.93	77.53	78.14	78.74	79.35
42	73.51	74.12	74.74	75.35	75.97	76.59	77.21	77.82	78.44	79.07	79.69	80.31	80.94	81.56
43	75.50	76.13	76.76	77.40	78.03	78.67	79.30	79.94	80.58	81.22	81.86	82.50	83.14	83.79
44	77.50	78.15	78.80	79.45	80.10	80.76	81.41	82.07	82.72	83.38	84.04	84.70	85.36	86.03
45	79.51	80.18	80.85	81.52	82.19	82.86	83.53	84.21	84.88	85.56	86.24	86.92	87.60	88.28
46	81.53	82.22	82.91	83.60	84.28	84.98	85.67	86.36	87.06	87.75	88.45	89.15	89.85	90.55
47	83.57	84.27	84.98	85.69	86.39	87.10	87.81	88.53	89.24	89.95	90.67	91.39	92.11	92.83
48	85.61	86.34	87.06	87.79	88.52	89.24	89.97	90.70	91.44	92.17	92.91	93.64	94.38	95.12
49	87.67	88.41	89.16	89.90	90.65	91.40	92.14	92.89	93.65	94.40	95.15	95.91	96.67	97.42
50	89.74	90.50	91.26	92.03	92.79	93.56	94.33	95.10	95.87	96.64	97.41	98.19	98.96	99.74
51	91.82	92.60	93.38	94.16	94.95	95.74	96.52	97.31	98.10	98.89	99.69	100.48	101.28	102.07
52	93.91	94.71	95.51	96.31	97.12	97.92	98.73	99.54	100.35	101.16	101.97	102.79	103.60	104.42
53	96.01	96.83	97.65	98.47	99.30	100.12	100.95	101.78	102.61	103.44	104.27	105.10	105.94	106.78
54	98.13	98.96	99.80	100.64	101.49	102.33	103.18	104.03	104.88	105.73	106.58	107.43	108.29	109.14
55	100.25	101.11	101.97	102.83	103.69	104.55	105.42	106.29	107.16	108.03	108.90	109.77	110.65	111.53
56	102.38	103.26	104.14	105.02	105.90	106.79	107.67	108.56	109.45	110.34	111.23	112.13	113.02	113.92
57	104.53	105.43	106.32	107.22	108.13	109.03	109.94	110.85	111.75	112.67	113.58	114.49	115.41	116.33
58	106.68	107.60	108.52	109.44	110.36	111.29	112.21	113.14	114.07	115.00	115.93	116.87	117.81	118.74
59	108.85	109.79	110.73	111.67	112.61	113.55	114.50	115.45	116.40	117.35	118.30	119.26	120.22	121.17
60	111.03	111.98	112.94	113.90	114.87	115.83	116.80	117.77	118.74	119.71	120.68	121.66	122.64	123.62

Chapter 1

Student's self-examination for chapter 1

1. 144,691 **2.** 62,621 **3.** 6,876 **4.** 766 **5.** 1,027,004
6. 6,699,615 **7.** 524 **8.** 515 **9.** $\frac{5}{12}$ **10.** $\frac{19}{20}$ **11.** $\frac{3}{14}$ **12.** $2\frac{47}{50}$

13. $3\frac{1}{3}$ **14.** $4\frac{5}{8}$ **15.** $2\frac{11}{12}$ **16.** $2\frac{8}{13}$ **17.** 4,124.97
18. 1,716.55 **19.** 3.2318 **20.** 2.4 **21.** 13.38 **22.** 64,
rem. 5 **23.** 8, rem. 195 **24.** 14,626 **25.** 1,081 **26.** 3,619
27. 37 **28.** 1,687 **29.** \$189 **30.** \$34,793 **31.** \$11,483
32. \$49 **33.** \$238 **34. a.** 27.5, **b.** 27 **35. a.** 4.847,
b. 4.85 **36.** 28 **37.** \$11.70 **38.** $5\frac{3}{8}$ **39.** \$5,057.94
40. 15

Section 1.1

1. 525 **3.** 562 **5.** 1,699 **7.** 1,294 **9.** 11,873
11. 3,596,541 **13.** 326 **15.** 344 **17.** 669 **19.** 4,748
21. 796 **23.** 12,953 **25.** 4,164 **27.** 58,899 **29.** 165,400
31. 409,184 **33.** 2,858,769 **35.** 3,925,050 **37.** 151
39. 15 **41.** 92, rem. 13 **43.** 47, rem. 22 **45.** 8, rem. 111
47. 1,370, rem. 6 **49.** 145, rem. 246 **51.** 1,452, rem. 118

Section 1.2

1. $\frac{22}{5}$ **3.** $\frac{24}{5}$ **5.** $\frac{65}{7}$ **7.** $\frac{17}{8}$ **9.** $\frac{32}{9}$ **11.** $1\frac{5}{9}$ **13.** $2\frac{1}{2}$ **15.** $1\frac{9}{15}$
17. $1\frac{2}{3}$ **19.** $1\frac{2}{9}$ **21.** Equal **23.** Unequal **25.** Equal
27. Equal **29.** Equal **31.** 6 **33.** 21 **35.** 78 **37.** 6
39. 21 **41.** $\frac{1}{2}$ **43.** $\frac{2}{3}$ **45.** $\frac{3}{4}$ **47.** $\frac{59}{62}$ **49.** $\frac{7}{10}$ **51.** $\frac{2}{9}$ **53.** $\frac{1}{9}$
55. $\frac{4}{5}$ **57.** $\frac{2}{5}$ **59.** Sally: $\frac{5}{8}$; Dr. Denton $\frac{3}{8}$ **61. a.** $\frac{16}{41}$,
b. $\frac{22}{41}$ **63. a.** $\frac{39}{55}$; **b.** $\frac{2}{5}$; **c.** $\frac{7}{11}$

Section 1.3

1. $\frac{1}{2}$ **3.** $\frac{3}{5}$ **5.** $\frac{7}{10}$ **7.** $\frac{23}{56}$ **9.** $\frac{19}{36}$ **11.** $\frac{11}{24}$ **13.** $\frac{23}{24}$ **15.** $\frac{2}{3}$ **17.** $\frac{3}{10}$
19. $\frac{11}{70}$ **21.** $\frac{17}{70}$ **23.** $\frac{1}{6}$ **25.** $\frac{1}{3}$ **27.** $\frac{1}{12}$ **29.** $1\frac{1}{4}$ **31.** $\frac{2}{3}$ **33.** $\frac{4}{63}$
35. $\frac{1}{15}$ **37.** $\frac{5}{14}$ **39.** $2\frac{1}{2}$ **41.** $1\frac{11}{17}$ **43.** $\frac{73}{117}$ **45.** $4\frac{1}{3}$ **47.** $5\frac{1}{2}$
49. $21\frac{4}{15}$ **51.** $2\frac{1}{12}$ **53.** $13\frac{1}{15}$ **55.** $85\frac{23}{45}$ **57.** $71\frac{32}{63}$ **59.** $1\frac{21}{26}$
61. $\frac{7}{13}$ **63.** $\frac{31}{40}$ **65.** $\frac{29}{45}$ **67.** $\frac{2}{15}$ **69.** $\frac{1}{5}$ **71.** $\frac{11}{15}$ **73.** \$82.89

Section 1.4

1. 77.9 **3.** 385.5 **5.** 56.56 **7.** 808.180 **9.** 367.820
11. 848.58 **13.** 540.737 **15.** 442.84 **17.** 77.0009
19. 25.78378 **21.** 249.3764 **23.** 4009.806
25. 25.6979456 **27.** 23.1 **29.** 4.47 **31.** 84.53
33. \$1,147.33 **35.** \$38,262.46 **37.** \$216.85 **39.** \$4.24
41. a. 35 **b.** 34.6 **c.** 34.60 **43. a.** 329 **b.** 328.6
c. 328.59 **45. a.** 5,321 **b.** 5,320.9 **c.** 5,320.90
47. a. 107,389 **b.** 107,388.9 **c.** 107,388.87 **49. a.** 12,342
b. 12,341.8 **c.** 12,341.79 **51. a.** 4,000 **b.** 3,800
c. 3,761.57 **53. a.** 6,000 **b.** 5,900 **c.** 5,864.00

55. a. 19,000 **b.** 18,800 **c.** 18,831.08 **57. a.** 138,000
b. 138,500 **c.** 138,489.07 **59. a.** 251,000 **b.** 250,900
c. 250,902.70 **61.** \$74,899.88 **63.** \$1,940.37
65. \$14,847.80 **67.** \$1,305,891.72 **69.** \$9,826.96
71. a. \$59,227.35 **b.** \$81,913.65 **73.** \$24,594.04

Section 1.5

1. 1,717 **3.** 19,050 **5.** 12,660 **7.** 1,541 **9.** 347.55
11. 1,124.11 **13.** 1,031,507.2 **15.** 1,877.29
17. 167985.75 **19.** 17,684.75 **21.** 285.50752
23. 5233.562 **25.** 822.1 **27.** 788.98 **29.** 419.69777
31. 16981.6 **33.** 1370.3981 **35.** 1398.9622
37. 3579.8598 **39.** 3566.525

Chapter 1 Review Test

1. 82,975 **3.** 172,598 **5.** 107,889 **7.** 356 **9.** 568
11. $1\frac{3}{7}$ **13.** $\frac{29}{36}$ **15.** $\frac{3}{4}$ **17.** 1 **19.** 3 **21.** $\frac{1}{7}$ **23.** 415
25. \$184 **27.** \$454 **29.** \$7,608 **31.** 41.40 **33.** 35.298
35. \$67,545.79 **37.** $543\frac{1}{3}$

Chapter 2

Section 2.1

1. a. $B = \dfrac{P}{R}$ **b.** $B = 20,000$ **3. a.** $r = \dfrac{I}{Pt}$

b. 0.0675 **5. a.** $d = \dfrac{D}{At}$ **b.** 0.12

7. a. Current liabilities $= \dfrac{\text{Cash} + \text{Receivables}}{\text{Acid-test ratio}}$

b. \$77,500 **9. a.** $P = \dfrac{A}{1 + rt}$ **b.** \$1,200 **11.** $\frac{3}{8}$; 3 to 8;
3:8 **13.** $\frac{3}{8}$; 3 to 8; 3:8 **15.** $\frac{3}{2}$; 3 to 2; 3:2 **17.** $\frac{9}{50}$; 9 to
50; 9:50 **19.** $\frac{13}{90}$; 13 to 90; 13:90 **21.** $\frac{10}{3}$; 10 to 3; 10:3
23. $\frac{27}{55}$; 27 to 55; 27:55 **25.** $\frac{115}{27}$; 115 to 27; 115:27
27. $\frac{36}{97}$; 36 to 97; 36:97 **29.** $\frac{2}{3}$ **31.** $\frac{2}{5}$ **33.** $\frac{1}{100}$ **35.** $\frac{1}{8}$

37. 4 **39.** 6 **41.** 2 **43.** 80 **45. a.** $n = \dfrac{G}{p}$ **b.** 642

47. a. \$3.30 **b.** \$3.35 **c.** \$3.40 **49. a.** \$8,500
b. \$13,000 **51. a.** \$49 **b.** \$81 **c.** \$97 **53. a.** 2,800
b. 2,000 **c.** 1,000 **55. a.** 38,000 **b.** 28,000 **c.** 23,000
57. $\frac{1}{15}$ **59.** $\frac{5}{7}$ **61. a.** $\frac{3}{1}$ **b.** $\frac{2}{1}$ **63. a.** $\frac{2}{9}$ **b.** $\frac{1}{12}$ **65.** 130
67. 216 **69.** 10 **71.** \$14.70 **73.** 12,600 **75.** 0.125

Section 2.2

1. 0.03 **3.** 0.67 **5.** 0.837 **7.** 0.0892 **9.** 0.8351
11. 0.1325 **13.** 0.002 **15.** 2.12 **17.** 1.834 **19.** 2%
21. 64% **23.** 80% **25.** 6.4% **27.** 60.45% **29.** 0.43%
31. 543% **33.** 835.7% **35.** 813.74% **37.** $\frac{11}{100}$ **39.** $\frac{23}{50}$

41. $\frac{1}{500}$ **43.** $\frac{49}{10,000}$ **45.** $\frac{11}{2,000}$ **47.** $\frac{7}{800}$ **49.** $\frac{3}{500}$ **51.** $\frac{7}{400}$ **53.** $\frac{26}{25}$
55. $\frac{63}{50}$ **57.** $\frac{437}{500}$ **59.** $\frac{291}{200}$ **61.** 25% **63.** 75% **65.** 45%
67. 87.5% **69.** 93.75% **71.** $81\frac{9}{11}$% **73.** $46\frac{2}{3}$% **75.** 225%

Section 2.3
1. 20 **3.** 9 **5.** 380 **7.** 230 **9.** 35% **11.** 15% **13.** 33.15
15. 629.30 **17.** 154.8 **19.** 118 **21.** 336.5 **23.** 615.9
25. 4% **27.** 8% **29.** 113.25 **31.** 0.525 **33.** 229.6
35. 760 **37.** 12% **39.** 2.5% **41.** $106.20 **43.** 27 **45.** 6%
47. 4% **49.** $64.48 **51.** $124,500 **53.** $14.35
55. $1,400.70 **57.** 21.04% **59.** 75% **61.** $5,000
63. $490,500 **65.** 7.5% **67.** 12.4% **69.** 160
71. $1,192.26 **73.** $15,625 **75.** 144 **77.** 3% **79.** 8.75%

Section 2.4
1. 50% increase **3.** 30% increase **5.** 40% increase
7. 15% decrease **9.** 12% decrease **11.** 20% decrease
13. 288 **15.** 150 **17.** $5,267.18 **19.** 81 **21.** 119.04
23. $11,180.09 **25.** 6% increase **27.** 22% increase
29. 12.5% increase **31.** 20% decrease **33.** 11% decrease
35. 5.39% decrease **37.** 1,325 **39.** $169.60 **41.** $90,160
43. $415.80 **45.** $1,608 **47.** $686.65

Chapter 2 Review Test
1. 5 **2. a.** $P = \dfrac{A}{1 + rt}$ **b.** $2,750 **3.** $\frac{29}{61}$ **4.** 12 **5.** 3
6. a. 0.43 **b.** 0.195 **7. a.** 73% **b.** 2.4% **8. a.** 72 **b.** 93.6
9. a. 60% **b.** 275% **10.** $\frac{13}{20}$ **11. a.** 2000% **b.** 20 **12.** 350
13. 40% **14.** 38% **15.** 60% **16.** $\frac{3}{5}$ **17.** 559 **18.** 60
19. $9,720 **20.** $1,672 **21.** 35% **22.** $73.44 **23.** 12.5%
24. 30% **25.** $13.33

Chapter 3
Section 3.1
1. $170.00 **3.** $517.50 **5.** $219.62 **7.** $278.96
9. $438.81 **11.** $617.62 **13.** $107.60 **15.** $109.45
17. $23.43 **19.** $2,093.40 **21.** $399.60 **23.** $604.00
25. $5,032.32 **27.** 35% **29.** 40%

Section 3.2
1. a. 40% **b.** 60% **3. a.** 76% **b.** 24% **5. a.** 67.5%
b. 32.5% **7. a.** 75.44% **b.** 24.56% **9. a.** 40.5% **b.** 59.5%
11. a. 45.6% **b.** 54.4% **13. a.** 57.6% **b.** 42.4%
15. a. 53.2% **b.** 46.8% **17. a.** 76.95% **b.** 23.05%
19. a. $\frac{4}{9}$ = 44.44% **b.** $\frac{5}{9}$ = 55.56% **21. a.** $\frac{11}{36}$ = 30.56%
b. $\frac{25}{36}$ = 69.44% **23. a.** $\frac{275}{432}$ = 63.66% **b.** $\frac{157}{432}$ = 36.34%
25. a. $10.80, $1.62 **b.** $14.58 **27. a.** $9.00, $12.15
b. $68.85 **29. a.** $8.25, $2.48 **b.** $22.27 **31. a.** $48,
$64.80/$18.36 **b.** $348.84 **33. a.** $23.50, $10.58, $10.05
b. $190.87 **35. a.** $212.80, $42.56, $121.30
b. $687.34 **37.** $81.60 **39.** $149.64 **41.** $249.90
43. $292.49 **45.** $70.29 **47.** $101.04 **49.** $171.00
51. $24.36 **53.** $203.49 **55.** $284.28 **57.** $253.78
59. First supplier

Section 3.3
1. $1,344.00 **3.** $667.56 **5.** $4,216.22 **7.** $616.45
9. $719.82

Section 3.4
1. $230.43 **3.** $350.21 **5.** $774.31 **7.** $1,119.36
9. $1,244.75 **11.** $3,206.31 **13.** $2,687.76
15. $3,779.84 **17.** $127.35 **19.** $80.02 **21.** $67.46
23. $216.92 **25.** $254.10 **27. a.** $1,722.25 **b.** $1,739.83
29. $633.73 **31.** Amount column: Extensions: $372,
$216, $144; Chain discount: $175.68; Net: $556.32.
Amount to be remitted: $534.07.

Section 3.5
1. a. May 10 **b.** $502.56 **3. a.** February 18 **b.** $825.81
5. a. October 3 **b.** $1,284.34 **7. a.** February
b. $1,323.03 **9. a.** November 1 **b.** $855.59
11. a. April 1 **b.** $3,784.53 **13. a.** $280.84 **b.** $286.57
15. a. December 10 **b.** $132.84 **17. a.** $918.36
b. $966.70 **19. a.** $549.60 **b.** $572.50 **21.** $741.07
23. a. September 14 **b.** $966.84 **25.** $1,826.24
27. $575.82 **29. a.** April 26 **b.** $731.36 **31. a.** $665.62
b. $679.20 **c.** $679.20 **d.** $658.82
33. February 14 Payment: $362.05
    March 9 Payment: $255.40 **35.** 533.12 **37.** Amount
column: Extension, $960; Chain discount, $266.88; Total,
$700.41. Amount to be remitted, $679.62.

Chapter 3 Review Test
1. List price **2.** Net price is list less any discounts. Billing
price is net price plus any freight charges or
transportation charges **3.** 55% **4.** $15.00 **5.** $15.13
6. $32.67 **7.** $102.37 **8.** 0.456 **9.** $57.67 **10.** 7%
11. $351.07 **12.** $590.38 **13.** October 21 **14. a.** May 28
b. $687.50 **15. a.** November 10 **b.** $294.98 **16. a.** June
18; July 18 **b.** $87.04

Chapter 4
Section 4.1
1. $30 **3.** $218.68 **5.** 52% **7.** 70% **9.** $139.46
11. $243.45 **13.** $1,253.64 **15.** $110.60 **17. a.** $28.13
b. $29.70 **19. a.** $187.05 **b.** $206.40 **21.** $675.02
23. 66.7% **25.** 47% **27.** 95% **29.** $175.46 **31.** $220.77
33. $23.81

Section 4.2
1. $30 **3.** $56.60 **5.** $174.75 **7.** $12.87 **9.** $42.46
11. $94.86 **13.** $67.74 **15.** $8.00 **17.** $140 **19.** $180
21. $155 **23.** $6.68 **25.** $30.16 **27.** 8% **29.** $42
31. a. 67% **b.** 82% **33. a.** 138% **b.** $339.29

Section 4.3
1. 25% **3.** 34.2% **5.** $2,029.30 **7.** $15.90 **9.** $39.98
11. a. $127.99 **b.** $108.79 **13. a.** $483.96 **b.** $454.92
15. $218.88 **17. a.** $536.60 **b.** $375.62 **19.** Profit of $10
21. Profit of $4.39 **23.** $180.00 **25.** Loss of $12.27
27. Loss of $12.72

Section 4.4
1. $0.90 **3.** $0.71 **5.** $1.22 **7.** $20.25 **9.** $150
11. $486
Section 4.5
1. $1,410 **3.** $522.50 **5.** $494 **7.** $2,304.50
9. $1,447.60 **11.** $1,339.50 **13.** $391,080
15. $120,476.80 **17.** $30,798 **19.** $28,270 **21.** $68,803
23. 5.5 **25.** 17.6
Chapter 4 Review Test
1. Overhead **2.** Trade discount **3.** $91.98 **4.** $169
5. $51.95 **6.** 23% **7.** 56.25% **8.** 29% **9.** Profit of
$15.90 **10.** $0.55 **11.** $10.00 **12.** $42.00 **13. a.** $62.40
b. $62.10 **14.** $34,850 **15.** 4.3

Chapter 5
Section 5.1
1. $1,230.77 **3.** $1,769.23 **5.** $2,055.67 **7.** $784.17
9. $481.85 **11.** $1,854.67 **13.** $524.16 **15.** $614.79
17. $640.00 **19.** $644.50 **21.** $43.68 **23.** $391.50
25. $365.40 **27.** $591.81 **29.** $213.60 **31.** $57.96
33. $485.00 **35.** $420.00 **37.** $12.41 **39.** $413.60
41. $412.80
Section 5.2
1. $2,348.50 **3.** $1,759.17 **5.** $2,708.28 **7.** $282.23
9. 2%

11.

Month	Net Sales	Earned Commission	Draw Advance	Draw Deficit Brought Fwd.	Gross Earnings	Draw Deficit Carried Fwd.
Jan.	$15,200	$1,368.00	$207.00	—	$1,575.00	$207.00
Feb.	11,850	1,066.50	508.50	$207.00	1,575.00	715.50
Mar.	20,540	1,848.60	—	715.50	1,575.00	441.90

13.

Month	Net Sales	Earned Commission	Draw Advance	Draw Deficit Brought Fwd.	Gross Earnings	Draw Deficit Carried Fwd.
Aug.	$12,842	$1,797.88	—	$ 70.00	$1,750.00	$ 22.12
	11,540	1,615.60	134.40	22.12	1,750.00	156.52
	18,760	2,626.40	—	156.52	2,469.88	—

15. $1,465.80 **17.** $1,037.50 **19.** $2,303.56 **21.** $370.00
23. $1,235.20 **25.** $522.51

27.

Sam's Style Shoppe							Week ending April 6
Name	Net Sales	Returns	Sales	Quota	Commission	Salary	Gross Earnings
Mazurek, S.	$2,452	$47	$2,405	$800	6.5%	$245	$349.33
Reese, S.	3,187	63	3,124	—	4.0	255	379.96
Taylor, J.	2,740	18	2,722	1,200	7.0	250	356.54
Velasco, R.	3,416	27	3,389	—	5.5	240	426.40
Williams, P.	3,141	36	3,105	1,000	5.75	260	381.04

29. Net proceeds $14,180.43
31. Net proceeds $37,446.20
Section 5.3
1. $418.00   **3.** $655.20   **5.** $872.95   **7.** $290.16
9. $393.90   **11.** $242.52   **13.** $384.56   **15.** $2,064.00
17. $703.10   **19.** $477.40   **21.** $333.75
Section 5.4
1. $34   **3.** $193   **5.** $128   **7.** $49   **9.** $33   **11.** $65
13. a. $147.12   **b.** Will contribute to SSM for entire year.
15. $50.34   **17.** $723.87   **19.** $263.85   **21. a.** $2,751.20
b. $3,504.71
Section 5.5
1. a. $89.72   **b.** $4,665.44   **3. a.** $214.20   **b.** $8,931.20
5. $18,662   **7.** $2,898   **9. a.** $2,697.78   **b.** $1,084.98
Section 5.6
1. $166.79   **3.** $3,704.89   **5.** $1,599.66   **7.** $2,397.15
9. $1,935.29   **11.** Stub no. 87: balance carried forward =
$909.21   **13.** Adjusted balance = $381.84   **15.** Adjusted
balance = $3,188.31   **17.** Adjusted balance = $2,029.13
19. Final check register balance = $536.52; final bank
statement balance = $697.85; adjusted balance =
$191.34
Chapter 5 Review Test
1. $1,033.85   **2.** $2,361   **3.** $513.13   **4.** $1,142.80
5. $211.60   **6.** $606.57   **7.** $6,276.74   **8.** $1,076.40
9. $2,263   **10.** $353.03   **11.** $945.75   **12.** $16,422
13. $324.94   **14.** $498.64

15.

Month	Net Sales	Commission	Draw Advance	Draw Deficit Brought Fwd.	Gross Earnings	Draw Deficit Carried Fwd.
Jan.	$19,422	$1,747.98	$ 52.02	$600.00	$1,800.00	$652.02
Feb.	21,112	1,900.08	0.00	652.02	1,800.00	551.94
Mar.	18,748	1,687.32	112.68	551.94	1,800.00	664.62

Chapter 6
Section 6.1
1. a. $2.40 **b.** $62.40 **3. a.** $5.75 **b.** $120.75
5. a. $7.42 **b.** $131.10 **7. a.** $34.70 **b.** $568.58
9. a. $61.90 **b.** $1,299.85 **11.** $2.15 **13.** $6.18
15. $14.05 **17.** $23.43 **19.** $178.41 **21.** $73.45
23. $201.27 **25.** $2,218.17 **27. a.** $29.25 **b.** $29.25
29. $0.82 **31.** $449.95, $22.50 **33.** $319.00 **35.** $435.50
Section 6.2
1. $2,355 **3.** $4,558.65 **5.** $669.90 **7.** $18,943.60
9. $1,184.09 **11.** $14,158.13 **13.** $258.72
15. $22,762.80 **17.** $132,875 **19.** $20,976
21. a. $7,905.60 **b.** $9,720 **23.** $5,155.20 **25.** $3,026.70
27. Marion **29.** $3,950,000
Section 6.3
1. $24,227 **3.** $47,638 **5.** $50,862 **7.** Standard
deduction **9.** Itemize deductions **11.** Itemize deductions
13. $5,856 **15.** $2,269 **17.** $3,949 **19.** $2,501
21. $7,421 **23.** $3,611 **25.** $7,029 **27.** $8,989
Chapter 6 Review Test
1. Excise **2.** Assessed value **3.** Mill **4.** Adjusted gross
income **5.** Standard deduction **6.** $4.20 **7.** $48.83
8. $5.24 **9.** $83.17 **10.** $33.05 **11.** $32,121.60
12. 3.5% **13.** $180,000 **14.** $30,530 **15.** $62,410
16. $20,050

Chapter 7
Section 7.1
1. $70 **3.** $3,000 **5.** 9% **7.** 4 **9.** $158.33 **11.** 8%
13. $6,400 **15.** $2,119.50 **17.** $120 **19.** $65.63
21. $128.13 **23.** $6,000 **25.** 9.83% **27.** 11.83%
29. $984.38 **31.** No **33.** 11.11%
Section 7.2
1. 154 **3.** 60 **5.** 109 **7.** 252 **9.** 281 **11.** June 5
13. December 27 **15.** May 20 **17.** June 4 **19.** April 22
Section 7.3
1. $190.85 **3.** $58.32 **5.** $70.12 **7.** $92.47 **9.** $161.48
11. $667.54 **13.** $265.30 **15.** $207.57 **17.** $58.00
19. $104.55 **21.** $356.90 **23. a.** $209.59 **b.** $212.50
25. a. $84.08 **b.** $85.25 **27. a.** $49.62 **b.** $50.31
29. a. $85.07 **b.** $86.25 **31. a.** $120.21 **b.** $121.88
33. a. $274.25 **b.** $278.06 **35. a.** $193.06 **b.** $195.74
37. a. $260.77 **b.** $264.40 **39. a.** $189.74 **b.** $192.38
41. 9% **43.** 8% **45.** 9.5% **47.** 6.25% **49.** 9.25% **51.** 60
53. 300 **55.** 150 **57.** $5,333 **59.** $2,500 **61.** $4,455
63. 5,600 **65.** 48.98% **67.** 16.32% **69.** 94.74%
71. a. $485 **b.** $11.77 **73. a.** $766.85 **b.** $5.11

Section 7.4
1. $2,120 **3.** $4,080 **5.** $2,617.50 **7.** $3,451.09
9. $2,315.63 **11.** $1,200 **13.** $1,000 **15.** $2,000
17. $3,600 **19.** $2,905.57 **21.** $2,543.75 **23.** $3,806.25
25. $2,758.62 **27.** $2,350.06 **29.** $20,000 now
31. $1,000 now, $625 in 6 months **33.** 12% **35.** 1.5 years
Chapter 7 Review Test
1. $56 **2.** $70 **3.** $2,200 **4.** $3,200 **5.** 7.75%
6. 11.25% **7.** 14 months **8.** 3 months **9.** $23.75
10. 165 days **11.** $28.60; $29.00 **12.** 8.14% **13.** 55.67%
14. $769.73 **15.** $562.17 **16.** $5,647.06 **17.** $825 later
18. $525 later

Chapter 8
Section 8.1
1. $2,289.80 **3.** $850.85 **5.** $1,311.70 **7.** $1,052.87
9. $332.80 **11.** $13.57 **13.** $358.24 **15.** $2,100.60
17. 4 years **19.** 6 years **21.** 20 months **23.** 10% **25.** 6%
27. 6% **29.** $5,412.16 **31.** $2,155.17 **33.** $187,870.33
35. 6 years **37.** $5.63 **39.** $9\frac{1}{2}$ % compounded annually
41. $1,811.12
Section 8.2
1. $3,168.37 **3.** $2,448.89 **5.** $459.84 **7.** $3,493.07
9. $730.07 **11.** $1,700 **13.** $9,658.92 **15.** Program B
17. First proposal
Section 8.3
1. $615.18 **3.** $964.07 **5.** $2,558.89 **7.** $2,644.08
9. $1,889.56 **11.** $509.96 **13.** $2,827.52 **15.** $612.79
17. $1,010.49 **19.** $1,610.42 **21.** $1,008.71
23. $2,265.51 **25.** $2,281.10 **27.** 10% compounded
semiannually
Section 8.4
1. 11.46% **3.** 9.31% **5.** 8.24% **7.** 9.20% **9.** 6.17%
11. 11% **13.** 7% **15.** 6%
Chapter 8 Review Test
1. a. $2\frac{1}{2}$% **b.** $\frac{3}{4}$% **c.** 3% **d.** $2\frac{1}{4}$% **2.** $1,011.24
3. $3,600.44, $1,000.44 **4.** 7% **5.** $3.89 **6.** $20,937.11
7. $3\frac{3}{4}$ years **8.** $808.13 **9.** $4,000 **10.** 8.24%
11. a. $5,978.09 **b.** $5,954.40 **c.** Program (c)
12. Program B

Chapter 9
Section 9.1
1. $1,500, $3,500 **3.** $204, $2,516 **5.** $132.19, $2,117.81
7. $257.55, $2,617.45 **9.** $737.44, $3,537.56 **11.** $9.50,
$1,890.50 **13.** $12.66, $1,337.34 **15.** $58.97, $1,291.03
17. $975, $6,525 **19.** $592.08, $11,407.92
21. a. $344.50 **b.** $9,655.50 **23.** $510.62

Section 9.2
1. 3 years   **3.** $8\frac{1}{2}$%   **5.** 11%   **7.** $2,700   **9.** $10.40
11. $2,200   **13.** $4,252.50   **15.** $1,067.02   **17.** $6,382.98
19. $8\frac{1}{2}$%   **21.** 8.59%

Section 9.3
1. $3,037.05, $37.05   **3.** $151.90, $528.10   **5.** $2,792.99,
$7.01, $127.57   **7.** $3,639.88, $113.32   **9.** $1,568, $24.78
11. No. Discount rate exceeds calculated rate.

Section 9.4
1. 9.52%   **3.** 13.53%   **5.** 9.99%   **7.** 12.68%   **9.** 6.90%
11. 8.47%   **13.** 6.15%   **15.** 9.30%   **17.** 11.28%
19. Friend   **21.** Other sources

Chapter 9 Review Test
1. $2,632.50   **2.** $1,587   **3.** $3,750   **4.** 9%   **5.** $918.33
6. $1,719.38   **7.** 10.26%   **8.** 11.11%   **9.** $22.61
10. $843.87

Chapter 10
Section 10.1
1. $282.79   **3.** $1,828.25   **5.** $1,970.65   **7.** $571.36
9. $3,150.53   **11.** $3,655.04

Section 10.2
1. $304.32, $20.12   **3.** $224.05, $16.79   **5.** $595.61,
$71.39   **7.** $412.65   **9.** $232.65   **11.** $506.27   **13. a.** May
31   **b.** $216.40, $350.74   **15. a.** February 22   **b.** $359.15,
$201.43   **17. a.** May 26   **b.** $444.15, $357.36
19. $152.96   **21.** $379.31   **23.** $123.34   **25.** $4.23
27. $5.66   **29.** $3.25   **31.** $210.66   **33.** $151.73

Section 10.3
1. a. $117.32   **b.** $999.46   **c.** $49.97   **3. a.** $99.24
b. $1,151.42   **c.** $83.45   **5. a.** $187.28   **b.** $1,799.54
c. $87.47   **7. a.** $492.34   **b.** $3,763.94   **c.** $141.19
9. a. $865.17   **b.** $5,104.62   **c.** $127.40   **11. a.** $436.25
b. $599.40   **c.** $88.15   **13. a.** $375.92   **b.** $438.86
c. $17.68   **15. a.** $952.00   **b.** $1,392.34   **c.** $268.16
17. a. $882.23   **b.** $1,117.10   **c.** $124.15   **19. a.** $2,528.30
b. $3,593.37   **c.** $701.26   **21. a.** $245.62   **b.** $2,408.95
c. $104.39

Section 10.4
1. 15%   **3.** 30%   **5.** 21.6%   **7.** 16.25%   **9.** 14.75%
11. 11.00%   **13.** 14.50%   **15.** 17.00%   **17.** 20.25%
19. 13.25%   **21.** 13.00%   **23.** 16.50%   **25.** 12.25%
27. 14.75%

Section 10.5
1. $21.54   **3.** $0.92   **5.** $6.15   **7.** $23.16   **9.** $12.86
11. $8.72   **13.** $11.24   **15.** $299.69

Chapter 10 Review Test
1. F   **2.** F   **3.** T   **4.** T   **5.** T   **6.** Amount due: $435.96
7. New balance: $235.39   **8.** Finance charge: $4.78
9. a. $101.51   **b.** $741.46   **c.** $37.64   **10. a.** $24.12
b. $377.38

Chapter 11
Section 11.1
1. $2,389.66   **3.** $7,039.92   **5.** $13,965.58   **7.** $22,905.17
9. $398,333.30   **11.** $44,797.60   **13.** $79,061.30
15. $181,425.37   **17.** $185,717.87   **19.** $1,689,328.79
21. $7,623.42, $14,759.63   **23.** $12,190.17, $33,203.48
25. $6,961.50, $14,230.76

Section 11.2
1. $2,401.22   **3.** $21,331.45   **5.** $2,832.26   **7.** $5,412.41
9. $43,466.97   **11.** 30   **13.** 30 years   **15.** 49 months,
$826.56   **17.** 11 quarters, $1,510.71   **19.** $12,894.73,
$894.73

Section 11.3
1. $14,047.16   **3.** $11,080.40   **5.** $3,754.03
7. $60,277.17   **9.** $52,202.39   **11.** 41   **13.** $151,777.40
15. 44   **17.** $5,167.04

Section 11.4
1. $7,115.19   **3.** $8,740.45   **5.** $7,906.56   **7.** $8,190.61
9. $23,180.85   **11.** $8,759.11   **13.** 9 years
15. a. $6,569.83   **b.** $6,701.23   **17.** $5,276.98
19. $529,297.78

Section 11.5
1. $3,229.88   **3.** $9,694.48   **5.** $10,122.40   **7.** $8,558.64
9. $30,181.45   **11. a.** $50,191.61   **b.** $52,952.14
13. $3,644.70   **15.** $621.75   **17.** $38,309.50

Chapter 11 Review Test
1. $5,596.85   **2.** $51,015.87   **3.** Annuity due   **4.** 4 years
5. $15,002.33   **6.** $1,125.69   **7.** 21   **8.** $3,480.96
9. $551,847.82   **10.** $494.67

Chapter 12
Section 12.1
1. $2,880.97
3. $2,869.22
5. $388.80

7.

Period	Accumulated Amount	Earned Interest	Periodic Payment	Accumulated Amount
1	—	—	$2,563.22	$2,563.22
2	$2,563.22	$51.26	2,563.22	5,177.70
3	5,177.70	103.55	2,563.22	7,844.47
4	7,844.47	156.89	2,563.22	10,564.58
5	10,564.58	211.29	2,563.22	13,339.09
6	13,339.09	266.78	2,563.22	16,169.09
7	16,169.09	323.38	2,563.22	19,055.69
8	19,055.69	381.11	2,563.22	22,000.02
Total		$1,494.26		

9.

Period	Accumulated Amount	Earned Interest	Periodic Payment	Accumulated Amount
1	—	—	$1,316.76	$1,316.76
2	$1,316.76	$ 6.58	1,316.76	2,640.10
3	2,640.10	13.20	1,316.76	3,970.06
4	3,970.06	19.85	1,316.76	5,306.67
5	5,306.67	26.53	1,316.76	6,649.96
6	6,649.96	33.25	1,316.76	7,999.97
Total		$99.41		

11.

Period	Accumulated Amount	Earned Interest	Periodic Payment	Accumulated Amount
1	—	—	$6,848.89	$ 6,848.89
2	$ 6,848.89	$ 171.22	6,848.89	13,869.00
3	13,869.00	346.73	6,848.89	21,064.62
4	21,064.62	526.62	6,848.89	28,440.13
5	28,440.13	711.00	6,848.89	36,000.02
Total		$1,755.57		

13.

Period	Accumulated Amount	Earned Interest	Periodic Payment	Accumulated Amount
1	—	—	$2,073.72	$ 2,073.72
2	$ 2,073.72	$ 207.37	2,073.72	4,354.81
3	4,354.81	435.48	2,073.72	6,864.01
4	6,864.01	686.40	2,073.72	9,624.13
5	9,624.13	962.41	2,073.72	12,660.26
6	12,660.26	1,266.03	2,073.72	16,000.01

15.

Period	Accumulated Amount	Earned Interest	Periodic Payment	Accumulated Amount
1	—	—	$6,694.41	$ 6,694.41
2	$ 6,694.41	$ 167.36	6,694.41	13,556.18
3	13,556.18	338.90	6,694.41	20,589.49
4	20,589.49	514.74	6,694.41	27,798.64
5	27,798.64	694.97	6,694.41	35,188.02
6	35,188.02	879.70	6,694.41	42,762.13
7	42,762.13	1,069.05	6,694.41	50,525.59
8	50,525.59	1,263.14	6,694.41	58,483.14
9	58,483.14	1,462.08	6,694.41	66,639.63
10	66,639.73	1,665.99	6,694.41	75,000.03

17. $25,182.82
19. $343.66

Section 12.2

1. $543.47   **3.** $932.45   **5.** $238.50

7.

Period	Amount of Debt	Payment	Interest	Applied to Principal	Remaining Debt
1	$5,250.00	$1,585.08	$420.00	$1,165.08	$4,084.92
2	4,084.92	1,585.08	326.79	1,258.29	2,826.63
3	2,826.63	1,585.08	226.13	1,358.95	1,467.68
4	1,467.68	1,585.08	117.41	1,467.67	0.01

9.

Period	Amount of Debt	Payment	Interest	Applied to Principal	Remaining Debt
1	$3,200.00	$451.07	$88.00	$363.07	$2,836.93
2	2,836.93	451.07	78.02	373.05	2,463.88
3	2,463.88	451.07	67.76	383.31	2.080.57
4	2,080.57	451.07	57.22	393.85	1,686.72
5	1,686.72	451.07	46.38	404.69	1,282.03
6	1,282.03	451.07	35.26	415.81	866.22
7	866.22	451.07	23.82	427.25	438.97
8	438.97	451.07	12.07	439.00	−0.03

11.

Period	Amount of Debt	Payment	Interest	Applied to Principal	Remaining Debt
1	$8,700.00	$760.83	$65.25	$695.58	$8,004.42
2	8,004.42	760.83	60.03	700.80	7,303.62
3	7,303.62	760.83	54.78	706.05	6,597.57
4	6,597.57	760.83	49.48	711.35	5,886.22
5	5,886.22	760.83	44.15	716.68	5,169.54
6	5,169.54	760.83	38.77	722.06	4,447.48
7	4,447.48	760.83	33.36	727.47	3,720.01
8	3,720.01	760.83	27.90	732.93	2,987.08
9	2,987.08	760.83	22.40	738.43	2,248.65
10	2,248.65	760.83	16.86	743.97	1,504.68
11	1,504.68	760.83	11.29	749.54	755.14
12	755.14	760.83	5.66	755.17	−0.03

13.

Period	Amount of Debt	Payment	Interest	Applied to Principal	Remaining Debt
1	$1,500.00	$423.02	$75.00	$348.02	$1,151.98
2	1,151.98	423.02	57.60	365.42	786.56
3	786.56	423.02	39.33	383.69	402.87
4	402.87	423.02	20.14	402.88	−0.01

15.

Period	Amount of Debt	Payment	Interest	Applied to Principal	Remaining Debt
1	$11,000.00	$1,583.59	$357.50	$1,226.09	$9,733.91
2	9,773.91	1,583.59	317.65	1,265.94	8,507.97
3	8,507.97	1,583.59	276.51	1,307.08	7,200.89
4	7,200.89	1,583.59	234.03	1,349.56	5,851.33
5	5,851.33	1,583.59	190.17	1,393.42	4,457.91
6	4,457.91	1,583.59	144.88	1,438.71	3,019.20
7	3,019.20	1,583.59	98.12	1,485.47	1,533.73
8	1,533.73	1,583.59	49.85	1,533.74	−0.01

17. $12,689.06   **19.** $13,404.82   **21.** $627.61
23. a. $4,612.57   **b.** $2,795.38   **c.** $56,464.36   **25.** 9.2%
27. 9.75%

Chapter 12 Review Test
1. $5,565.68   **2. a.** $2,907.69   **b.** $333,692.40
3. $1,002.27   **4.** $1,085.48

5.

Period	Amount of Debt	Payment	Interest	Applied to Principal	Remaining Debt
1	$4,700.00	$925.98	$235.00	$690.98	$4,009.02
2	4,009.02	925.98	200.45	725.53	3,283.49
3	3,283.49	925.98	164.17	761.81	2,521.68
4	2,521.68	925.98	126.08	799.90	1,721.78
5	1,721.78	925.98	86.09	839.89	881.89
6	881.89	925.98	44.09	881.89	0.00

6. $2,404.16 **7. a.** $5,723.95 **b.** $26,062.20
c. $226,062.20 **8.** $3,662.30

Chapter 13
Section 13.1
1. $1.10 **3.** $0.70 **5.** I: $0.52; II: $0.40; III: $0.35; IV: $0.43 **7.** $675.00 **9.** $0.36 **11.** $210 **13.** $0.15
Section 13.2
1. $970.40 **3.** $4,295.41 **5.** $51,823.80 **7.** $1,604.32
9. $2,271.95 **11.** $1,176.37 **13.** $15,247.19
15. $8,630.52 **17.** $531.78 **19.** $1,566.22
21. $547.01 Paid **23.** $604.27 Received
Section 13.3
1. $2.02 **3.** $2.21 **5.** $1.81 **7.** 26 to 1 **9.** 35 to 1
11. 14 to 1 **13.** 2.9% **15.** 3.8% **17.** 2.6% **19.** 6.2%
Section 13.4
1. $8,525 **3.** $7,615 **5.** $8,194.23 **7.** $8,530
9. $2,984.94 **11.** $4,884.56 **13.** $14,982.90
15. $16,658.97 **17.** $457.81
Section 13.5
1. 8.9% **3.** 8.8% **5.** 8.5% **7.** 8.5% **9.** 9.8% **11.** 10.0%
13. 9.2% **15.** 13.5% **17.** NLL
Section 13.6
1. $11.53 **3.** $10.37 **5.** $9.67 **7.** $16.70 **9.** $20.90
11. a. $127.50 **b.** $1,372.50 **c.** 9.3% **d.** $1,639.34
13. a. $395.00 **b.** $4,605.00 **c.** 8.6% **d.** $5,428.88
15. a. $456.00 **b.** $7,544.00 **c.** 6.0% **d.** $8,483.56
17. a. $399.00 **b.** $10,101.00 **c.** 4.0% **d.** $10,914.76
19. a. $401.50 **b.** $17,848.50 **c.** 2.2% **d.** $18,660.53
21. 354.296 **23.** 125.786 **25.** 650.474 **27.** 1,978.122
29. 10,756.64 **31.** $836 **33.** 191.545 **35.** $7,385.32
Chapter 13 Review Test
1. Capital gain **2.** Preferred, common **3.** Price-earnings ratio **4.** Mortgage bond, debenture **5.** Financial risk, interest rates **6.** Round lot **7.** Triple A **8.** $0.64
9. $0.45 **10.** $3,850.00 **11.** $1,674.06 **12.** $2.32
13. 5.2% **14.** 10.4% **15.** $5,122.39 **16. a.** $2,560
b. $29,440 **c.** 8.7% **d.** 2,087.943

Chapter 14
Section 14.1
1. Sales—$870,000; Total Revenue—$960,900; Operating Expenses—$122,000; Total Expenses—$868,700; Net Income—$92,200.
3. Cost of Goods Sold—$900,000; Salaries—$215,000; Net Income—$90,000.
5. Net Sales—100.0%; Cost of Sales—83.3%; Depreciation—2.2%; Maintenance—1.4%; Total Cost and Operating Expenses—$391,000, 86.9%; Operating Income—$59,000, 13.1%; Interest Expense—1.0%; Federal Taxes—1.6%; Net Income—$47,300, 10.5%.
7. Sales—91.6%; Rentals—7.5%; Interest—0.9%; Total Income—$797,000, 100.0%; Cost of Merchandise—67.8%; Operating Expenses—11.5%; Interest Expenses—0.8%; Taxes—5.8%; Total Expenses—$684,000, 85.8%; Net Income—$113,000, 14.2%.
9. Cash—7.4%; Accounts Receivable—22.4%; Inventory—$230,000, 28.0%; Total Current Assets—57.9%; Land and Equipment—42.1%; Total Assets—$820,000, 100.0%; Accounts Payable—22.0%; Accrued Liabilities—3.2%; Bonds Payable—11.0%; Common Stock—36.6%; Retained Earnings—27.3%; Total Equities—$820,000, 100.0%.
11. Net Sales—$80,000, 21.6%; Cost of Sales—$70,000, 29.2%; Depreciation—$1,800, 29.0%; Maintenance—$400, 8.3%; Total Cost and Operating Expenses—$72,200, 28.8%; Operating Income—$7,800, 6.6%; Interest Expense—$2,000, 16.7%; Federal Taxes—$4,000, 22.2%; Net Income—$1,800, 2.0%.
13. 1990: Total Current Assets—$40,426,000; Total Assets—$40,536,000; Total Current Liabilities—$24,342,000; Total Liabilities—$30,556,000; Total Stockholders' Equity—$9,980,000; Total Liabilities and Stockholders' Equity—$40,536,000. 1989: Total Current Assets—$35,796,000; Total Assets—$35,866,000; Total Current Liabilities—$20,816,000; Total Liabilities—$26,286,000; Total Stockholders'

Equity—$9,580,000; Total Liabilities and Stockholders' Equity—$35,866,000.

Increase or Decrease—Amount (*top to bottom*): ($890,000); 2,600,000; 370,000; 2,550,000; 4,630,000; 40,000; 4,670,000; 1,600,000; 500,000; 624,000; 802,000; 3,526,000; 744,000; 4,270,000; 900,000; (500,000); 400,000; 4,670,000.

Increase or Decrease—Percent (*top to bottom*): (21.7); 28.6; 4.4; 18.0; 12.9; 57.1; 13.0; 11.3; 22.7; 18.0; 77.1; 16.9; 13.6; 16.2; 10.2; (67.6); 4.2; 13.0.

Percent of Total Assets—1990 (*top to bottom*): 7.9; 28.9; 21.6; 41.3; 99.7; 0.3; 100.0; 38.7; 6.7; 10.1; 4.5; 60.1; 15.3; 75.4; 24.0; 0.6; 24.6; 100.0.

Percent of Total Assets—1989 (*top to bottom*): 11.5; 25.4; 23.4; 39.6; 99.8; 0.2; 100.0; 39.3; 6.1; 9.7; 2.9; 58.0; 15.3; 73.3; 24.6; 2.1; 26.7; 100.0.

Section 14.2

1. 2.4:1

3. Current ratio = 2.7:1; acid-test ratio = 1.4:1

5. Gross profit margin = 41%; operating ratio = 96%

7. 70%

9. Stockholder's equity ratio = 60%; debt-equity ratio = 38%

11. Total current assets = $82,250; total current liabilities = $25,150; land = $19,700; total assets = $184,450; retained earnings = $4,900; net income = $39,000; interest charges = $2,400

13. Gross profit margin = 44%; operating ratio = 85%

15. 31%

Section 14.3

1. Total Available Cash, $63,600; Total Disbursements, $58,660; Excess of Cash, $4,940; Borrowed Funds Needed, $0; Repayment of Borrowed Funds, $0; Interest, $0; Total Financing, $0; Cash Balance, End of Month, $4,940

3. Total Available Cash, $58,600; Total Disbursements, $58,160; Excess of Cash, $440; Borrowed Funds Needed, $1,560; Repayment of Borrowed Funds, $0; Interest, $0; Total Financing, $1,560; Cash Balance, End of Month, $2,000

5. Total Available Cash, $128,400; Total Disbursements, $128,450; Deficiency of Cash, ($50); Borrowed Funds Needed, $15,050; Repayment of Borrowed Funds, $0; Interest, $0; Total Financing, $15,050; Cash Balance, End of Month, $15,000

7. Total Available Cash, $123,600; Total Disbursements, $107,450; Excess of Cash, $16,150; Borrowed Funds Needed, $0; Repayment of Borrowed Funds, $0; Interest, $0; Total Financing, $0; Cash Balance, End of Month, $16,150

9. Total Available Cash, $52,600; Total Disbursements, $56,400; Deficiency of Cash, ($3,800); Borrowed Funds Needed, $6,300; Repayment of Borrowed Funds, $0; Interest, $0; Total Financing, $6,300; Cash Balance, End of Month, $2,500

11. Beginning Cash Balance: $2,500. Receipts: Cash sales, $20,800; Accounts Receivable Collections, $57,000; Total Available Cash, $80,300. Disbursements: Materials Purchased, $7,600; Payroll, $20,000; Rent, $2,100; Other Expenses, $1,512; Equipment Purchase, $0; Total Disbursements, $31,212. Excess of Cash, $49,088. Financing: Borrowed Funds Needed, $0; Repayment of Borrowed Funds ($41,740); Interest, ($350); Total Financing, ($42,090). Cash Balance, End of Month, $6,998

13. Beginning Cash Balance: $1,000. Receipts: Cash sales, $15,000; Accounts Receivable Collections, $13,000; Collection of Notes Receivable, $0; Total Available Cash, $29,000. Disbursements: Manufacturing Expenses, $20,000; Selling and Administrative Expenses, $11,100; Equipment Purchase, $0; Total Disbursements, $31,100. Deficiency of Cash, ($2,100). Financing: Borrowed Funds Needed, $3,100; Repayment of Borrowed Funds, $0; Interest, $0; Total Financing, $3,100. Cash Balance, End of Month, $1,000

15. Cash Sales, $50,000; Total Disbursements, $134,450; Excess of Cash, $13,050; Borrowed Funds Needed, $0; Repayment of Borrowed Funds, $0; Interest, $0; Total Financing, $0; Cash Balance, End of Month, $13,050

17. Beginning Cash Balance: $10,000. Receipts: Cash sales, $63,750; Accounts Receivable Collections, $84,500; Total Available Cash, $158,250. Disbursements: Merchandise Purchases, $84,000; Payroll, $22,950; Utilities, $1,000; Advertising, $14,400; Taxes, $0; Other Expenses, $2,400; Total Disbursements, $124,750; Excess of Cash, $33,500. Financing: Borrowed Funds Needed, $0; Repayment of Borrowed Funds, ($18,300); Interest, ($124); Total Financing, ($18,424). Cash Balance, End of Month, $15,076

Section 14.4

1. $6,920

3. First year, $1,850; Sixth year, $532.80

5. First year, $124,930.32; Sixth year, $77,983.10

7. First year, $3,166.35; Second year, $4,222.75; Third year, $1,460.95; Fourth year, $703.95

9. First year, $643.05; Second year, $1,102.05; Third year, $787.05; Fourth year, $562.05; Fifth year, $401.85; Sixth year, $401.40; Seventh year, $401.85; Eighth year, $200.70

11. First year, $3,180; Second year, $4,664; Third through fifth years, $4,452

13. First year, $1,269; Second year, $1,861.20; Third through fifth years, $1,776.60

15. First year, $309,600; Tenth year, $348,300

17. First year, $3,744; Eighth year, $4,212

19. First year, $25,717.07; Fifth year, $26,841.45; Fourteenth year, $26,841.45

Section 14.5

1. $900

3. $2,437.50

5.

Year	Depreciation	Accumulated Depreciation	Book Value
0	—	—	$18,000.00
1	$6,000.00 ($18,000 $\times \frac{1}{3}$)	$6,000.00	12,000.00
2	4,000.00 ($12,000 $\times \frac{1}{3}$)	10,000.00	8,000.00
3	2,666.67 ($8,000 $\times \frac{1}{3}$)	12,666.67	5,333.33
4	1,777.78 ($5,333.33 $\times \frac{1}{3}$)	14,444.45	3,555.55
5	1,185.18 ($3,555.55 $\times \frac{1}{3}$)	15,629.63	2,370.37
6	790.12 ($2,370.37 $\times \frac{1}{3}$)	16,419.75	1,580.25

7.

Year	Depreciation	Accumulated Depreciation	Book Value
0	—	—	$36,000.00
1	$10,800.00 ($36,000 $\times$ 0.30)	$10,800.00	25,200.00
2	7,560.00 ($25,200 $\times$ 0.30)	18,360.00	17,640.00
3	5,292.00 ($17,640 $\times$ 0.30)	23,652.00	12,348.00
4	3,704.40 ($12,348 $\times$ 0.30)	27,356.40	8,643.60
5	2,593.08 ($8,643.60 $\times$ 0.30)	29,949.48	6,050.52

9.

Year	Depreciation	Accumulated Depreciation	Book Value
0	—	—	$16,000.00
1	$3,111.11 ($14,000 $\times \frac{8}{36}$)	$3,111.11	12,888.89
2	2,722.22 ($14,000 $\times \frac{7}{36}$)	5,833.33	10,166.67
3	2,333.33 ($14,000 $\times \frac{6}{36}$)	8,166.66	7,833.34
4	1,944.44 ($14,000 $\times \frac{5}{36}$)	10,111.10	5,888.90
5	1,555.56 ($14,000 $\times \frac{4}{36}$)	11,666.66	4,333.34
6	1,166.67 ($14,000 $\times \frac{3}{36}$)	12,833.33	3,166.67
7	777.78 ($14,000 $\times \frac{2}{365}$)	13,611.11	2,388.89
8	388.89 ($14,000 $\times \frac{1}{36}$)	14,000.00	2,000.00

11. a.

Year	Depreciation	Accumulated Depreciation	Book Value
0	—	—	$10,000
1	$1,200	$1,200	8,800
2	1,200	2,400	7,600
3	1,200	3,600	6,400
4	1,200	4,800	5,200
5	1,200	6,000	4,000

b.

Year	Depreciation	Accumulated Depreciation	Book Value
0	—	—	$10,000.00
1	$2,500.00 ($10,000 $\times$ 0.25)	$2,500.00	7,500.00
2	1,875.00 ($7,500 $\times$ 0.25)	4,375.00	5,625.00
3	1,406.25 ($5,625 $\times$ 0.25)	5,781.25	4,218.75
4	218.75	6,000.00	4,000.00
5	—	—	—

c.

Year	Depreciation	Accumulated Depreciation	Book Value
0	—	—	$10,000.00
1	$2,000.00 ($6,000 $\times \frac{5}{15}$)	$2,000.00	8,000.00
2	1,600.00 ($6,000 $\times \frac{4}{15}$)	3,600.00	6,400.00
3	1,200.00 ($6,000 $\times \frac{3}{15}$)	4,800.00	5,200.00
4	800.00 ($6,000 $\times \frac{2}{15}$)	5,600.00	4,400.00
5	400.00 ($6,000 $\times \frac{1}{15}$)	6,000.00	4,000.00

13.

Year	Depreciation	Accumulated Depreciation	Book Value
0	—	—	$8,000.00
1	$3,200.00 ($8,000 $\times$ 0.40)	$3,200.00	4,800.00
2	1,920.00 ($4,800 $\times$ 0.40)	5,120.00	2,880.00
3	1,152.00 ($2,880 $\times$ 0.40)	6,272.00	1,728.00
4	691.20 ($1,728 $\times$ 0.40)	6,963.20	1,036.80
5	414.72 ($1,036.80 $\times$ 0.40)	7,377.92	622.08

15.

Year	Depreciation	Accumulated Depreciation	Book Value
0	—	—	$15,000
1	$1,250	$1,250	13,750
2	1,250	2,500	12,500
3	1,250	3,750	11,250
4	1,250	5,000	10,000
5	1,250	6,250	8,750
6	1,250	7,500	7,500
7	1,250	8,750	6,250
8	1,250	10,000	5,000

17.

Year	Depreciation	Accumulated Depreciation	Book Value
0	—	—	$15,000.00
1	$2,222.22 ($10,000 $\times \frac{8}{36}$)	$ 2,222.22	12,777.78
2	1,944.44 ($10,000 $\times \frac{7}{36}$)	4,166.66	10,833.34
3	1,666.67 ($10,000 $\times \frac{6}{36}$)	5,833.33	9,166.67
4	1,388.89 ($10,000 $\times \frac{5}{36}$)	7,222.22	7,777.78
5	1,111.11 ($10,000 $\times \frac{4}{36}$)	8,333.33	6,666.67
6	833.33 ($10,000 $\times \frac{3}{36}$)	9,166.66	5,833.34
7	555.56 ($10,000 $\times \frac{2}{36}$)	9,722.22	5,277.78
8	277.78 ($10,000 $\times \frac{1}{36}$)	10,000.00	5,000.00

19. a. $2,340   **b.** $2,860
21. a. $2,040, $1,615   **b.** 12,595
23. a.

Year	Depreciation	Accumulated Depreciation	Book Value
0	—	—	$8,200
1	$ 750 ($1,500 $\times \frac{1}{2}$)	$ 750	7,450
2	1,500	2,250	5,950
3	1,500	3,750	4,450
4	1,500	5,250	2,950
5	1,500	6,750	1,450
6	750	7,500	700

b.

Year	Depreciation	Accumulated Depreciation	Book Value
0	—	—	$8,200.00
1	$1,640.00 ($8,200.00 $\times$ 0.40 $\times \frac{1}{2}$)	$1,640.00	6,560.00
2	2,624.00 ($6,560.00 $\times$ 0.40)	4,264.00	3,936.00
3	1,574.40 ($3,936.00 $\times$ 0.40)	5,838.40	2,361.60
4	944.64 ($2,361.60 $\times$ 0.40)	6,783.04	1,416.96
5	566.78 ($1,416.96 $\times$ 0.40)	7,349.82	850.18
6	150.18 ($850.18 − $700.00)	7,500.00	700.00

c.

Year	Depreciation	Accumulated Depreciation	Book Value
0	—	—	$8,200
1	$1,250 ($7,500 $\times \frac{5}{15} \times \frac{1}{2}$)	$1,250	6,950
2	1,250		
	1,000 ($7,500 $\times \frac{4}{15} \times \frac{1}{2}$)	3,500	4,700
	2,250		
3	1,000		
	750 ($7,500 $\times \frac{3}{15} \times \frac{1}{2}$)	5,250	2,950
	1,750		
4	750		
	500 ($7,500 $\times \frac{2}{15} \times \frac{1}{2}$)	6,500	1,700
	1,250		
5	500		
	250 ($7,500 $\times \frac{1}{15} \times \frac{1}{2}$)	7,250	950
	750		
6	250	7,500	700

Section 14.6

1. Offices, $1,550; accounting, $4,650; production, $24,800; warehouse, $31,000

3. Clothing, $845.25; hardware, $431.25; appliances, $552.00; toys, $224.25; home furnishings, $707.25

5. Office supplies, $910.00; furnishings, $625.63; floor coverings, $422.50; office machines, $1,291.88

7. Office equipment, $1,513.08; business forms, $302.62; furnishings, $2,005.91; art supplies, $406.37; chemicals, $1,392.03

9. Jackson, $1,631.25; Peters, $4,350.00; Adams, $2,718.75

11. Barrett, $49,049.60; other partners (each), $9,196.80

13. Criswell, $26,428.57; Davis, $66,071.43; Meyer, $92,500.00

15. Foster, $5,022.50; Thomas, $5,022.50; Harvey, $2,870.00; Daniels, $1,435.00

17. A, $95,435; B, $93,435; C, $63,935; D, $63,935

19. (a) Kessler, $4,800; Schneider, $7,200; (b) Kessler, $3,600; Schneider, $5,400

Chapter 14 Review Test

1. Accounts Receivable = $36,000; Total Fixed Assets = $499,000; Total Assets = $566,000; Total Current Liabilities = $62,000; Total Liabilities = $262,000; Total Equities = $566,000 **2.** 0.8 to 1 **3.** 54% **4.** 86% **5.** 1st year = $2,300; 2nd year = $3,496; 3rd year = $3,404 **6.** 1st year = $28,510; 2nd year = $45,616; 3rd year = $27,369.60; 4th year = $16,421.76; 4th year = $16,421.76; 5th year = $16,421.76; 6th year = $8,210.88 **7.** 40% **8.** f(L($2,125 **9.** $6,000

10. Lombardi = $27,720; Berra = $16,280 **11.** Total available cash, $456,000; Total disbursements, $473,000; Deficiency of cash, ($17,000); Borrowed funds needed, $27,000; Repayment of borrowed funds, $0; Interest, $0; Total financing, $27,000; Cash balance, end of month, $10,000

Chapter 15

Section 15.1

1. $431.43 **3.** $406.86 **5.** $990.24 **7.** $138.27 **9.** $424.88 **11.** $63.03 **13.** $188.10 **15.** $648.34 **17.** $26.20 **19.** $95.24

Section 15.2

1. $3,271.80 **3.** $2,222.40 **5.** $4,837.50 **7.** $2,606.80 **9.** $3,220.00 **11.** $6,250.50 **13.** $4,527.25 **15.** $4,502.90 **17.** $107.64 **19.** $3,534.96 **21.** $1,059.24 **23.** $736.60 **25.** $1,790.88 **27.** $589.23 **29.** $3,543.90 **31.** $673.00

Section 15.3

1. $14,108.40 **3.** $5,197.50 **5.** $23,433.30 **7.** $30,918.75; life **9.** $25,078.00; life **11.** $8,174.40; 17 years **13.** $1,153.75 **15.** $188.50 **17.** $401.60 **19.** $945.00 **21.** $436.25 **23.** $581.10

Section 15.4

1. $10.50 **3.** $7.70 **5.** Executives, $13.20; Supervisors, $9.90; Others, $6.60 **7.** $2,011.80 **9.** $563.28 **11.** $377.39

Section 15.5

1. $60,000 **3.** $375,000 **5.** $400,000 **7. a.** $97,500 **b.** $65,000 **9.** $2,033 **11.** $893 **13.** $615.60 **15.** $92.64 **17.** $61.95 **19.** $732.90 **21.** $864.41

Section 15.6
1. $282.15 **3.** $387.50 **5.** $252.65 **7.** $673.90
9. $620.60 **11.** $533.20 **13.** $443.70 **15.** $585.60
17. Paid by Ins. Co., $37,575; Paid by Policyholder,
$150,100 **19.** $13,475

Chapter 15 Review Test
1. Hazard **2.** Insuring agreement **3.** Ordinary life
insurance **4.** Participating **5.** Reduced paid-up
insurance **6.** Property damage liability **7.** Term
insurance, cash value insurance **8.** $62.02 **9.** $198.56
10. $46,719 **11.** $621.25 **12.** $93,750 **13.** $337.90

Chapter 16

Section 16.1
1. 5, 9, 14, 15, 19, 21, 27, 33 **3.** 5, 8, 9, 12, 14, 15, 18,
19, 21, 23, 26, 27, 31, 33, 39, 43 **5.** 7, 8, 11, 12, 13, 15,
18, 23, 24, 26, 31, 32, 37, 39, 41, 43 **7.** Frequency: 3, 5,
5, 2, 1
9.

Frequency	Relative Frequency	Percent
4	0.2500	25.00
5	0.3125	31.25
6	0.3750	37.50
1	0.0625	6.25
0	0.0000	0.00
16	1.0000	

11.

Frequency	Cumulative Frequency
4	4
5	9
6	15
1	16
0	16

13.

Class	Frequency
0–4	1
5–9	4
10–14	3
15–19	2

15.

Frequency	Relative Frequency	Percent
1	0.1	10
4	0.4	40
3	0.3	30
2	0.2	20
10	1.0	

17.

Class	Frequency	Cumulative Frequency
380–399	2	2
400–419	1	3
420–439	3	6
440–459	0	6
460–479	3	9
480–499	1	10
500–519	2	12

19.

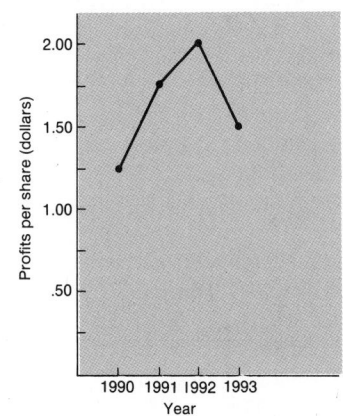

21.

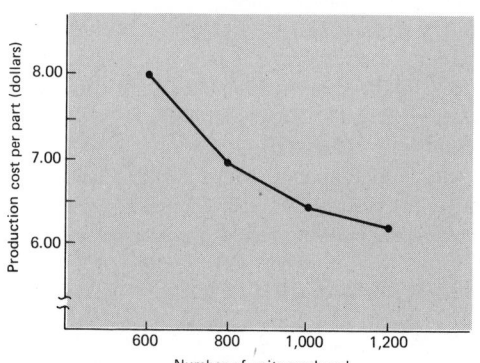

23. a. 280   **b.** 550   **c.** 425

25.

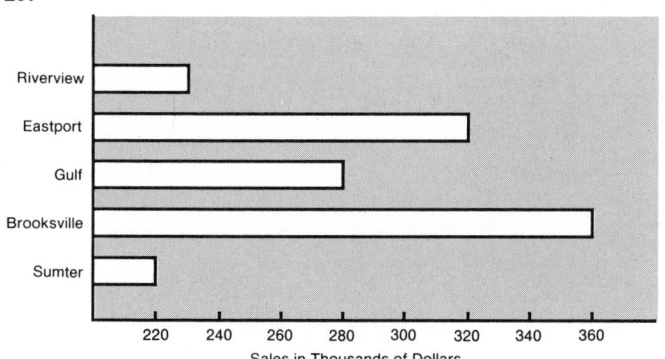

27.

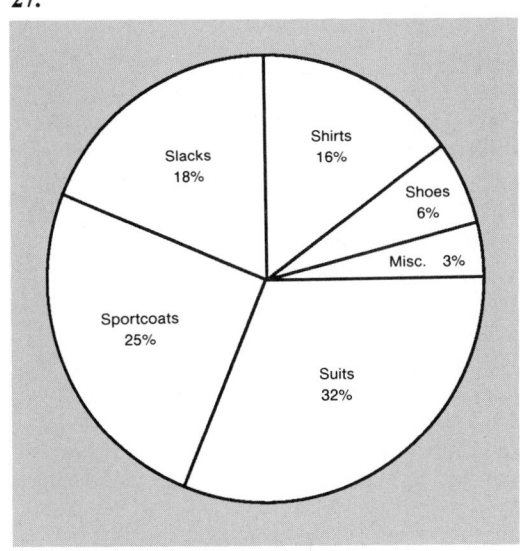

29.

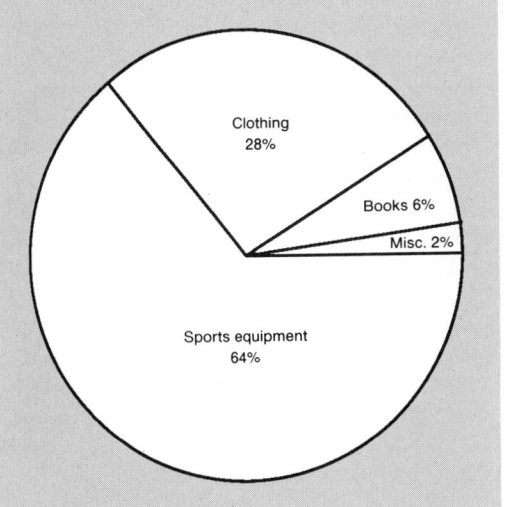

31.

33.

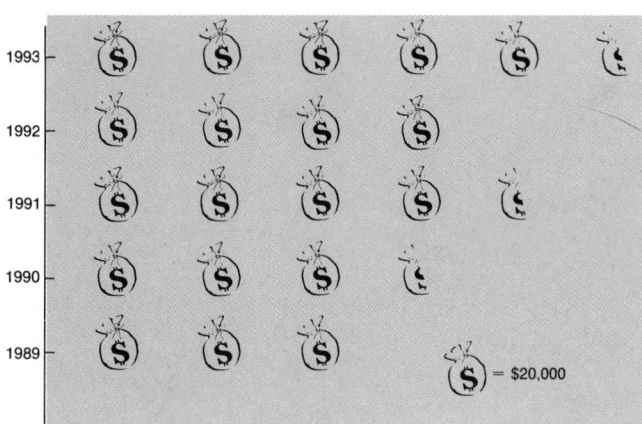

35. Graph C; Graph A—horizontal scale is too spread out; Graph B—vertical scale is too spread out and does not begin at zero
37. Graph B
39. Graph C; Graph A—horizontal scale is too compressed; Graph B—horizontal scale is too spread out and does not begin at zero

Section 16.2
1. 14   **3.** 20   **5.** 80   **7.** 332   **9.** 121   **11.** 12.09   **13.** 14
15. 14.5   **17.** 12   **19.** 13   **21.** Mean = 12.19; median = 12; mode: bimodal, 12, 14   **23.** $9,460   **25.** $47
27. Mean = $448.57; mode = $455

Section 16.3

1.

Class Midpoint (x_i)	$f_i x_i$
7	7
12	36
17	68
22	88
27	54
	253

Mean = $\frac{253}{14}$ = 18.07

3.

Class Midpoint (x_i)	$f_i x_i$
4.5	9
14.5	43.5
24.5	49
34.5	138
44.5	44.5
	284

Mean = $\frac{284}{12}$ = 23.67

5.

Class Midpoint (x_i)	$f_i x_i$
5	10
16	64
27	162
38	190
49	343
60	180
71	71
	1,020

Mean = $\frac{1,020}{28}$ = 36.43

7. 20.5   **9.** 31.5

11. Modal class: 20–24; modal value: 22
13. Mean = 10.5; median = 11.36; modal class: 11–15
15. Mean = $5.37; median = $5.06; modal class: $4.00–$5.99

Section 16.4
1. 7.42   **3.** 3.61   **5.** 2.65   **7.** 2.83   **9. a.** 27 students;
b. 38 students   **11. a.** 4 boxes;   **b.** 27 boxes

Section 16.5
1. 295   **3.** 128   **5. a.** $129.90;   **b.** $115,945   **7.** 162
9. 129   **11.** 128

Chapter 16 Review Test
1. 0, 2, 3, 3, 4, 7, 7, 8, 8, 8, 8, 10, 10, 11, 12, 13, 14, 16;
median = 8   **2.** 8   **3.** 8   **4.** Cumulative Frequency 4, 7, 14, 17, 18   **5.** 15.25   **6.** 15.5   **7.** 10–14   **8.** 3.16
9. a. 100, 100, 100, 100, 0   **b.** 80, 80, 80, 80, 80   **10.** 475
11. 161   **12.** 183   **13.** 172

Chapter 17
Section 17.1
1. a. 28,000 m   **b.** 7.2 dkm   **3. a.** 7,210 m   **b.** 705 cm
5. a. 15,700 dm   **b.** 3,221.4 cm   **7. a.** 24 cm²   **b.** 140,000 ares   **9.** 6.21 dkm, 0.621 hm   **11.** 3.224 dkm, 322.4 dm
13. 190,000 m², 1,900 ares   **15. a.** 7.42 dkm   **b.** 0.742 hm
17. a. 20 cm long, 0.7 cm wide, lead is 0.2 cm thick;
b. 0.2 m long, 0.007 m wide, lead is 0.002 m thick
19. $24.30   **21.** $662.64

Section 17.2
1. a. 4,700 liters   **b.** 27.42 kl   **3. a.** 2.71 liters   **b.** 521 cl
5. a. 670 g   **b.** 382.4 hg   **7. a.** 7,830 g   **b.** 412.3 dg
9. 4.2 dkl, 42,000 ml   **11.** 2.7 hl, 27,000 cl   **13.** 7,140 dg, 71.4 dkg   **15.** Nine bottles   **17.** 21 days   **19.** 200 hours
21. a. 340 dkg   **b.** 34,000 dg   **23.** $0.21   **25.** 3,500 kg per hour

Section 17.3
1. 32.81 ft.   **3.** 1.77 in.   **5.** 4,918.50 yds.   **7.** 91.44 m
9. 1.83 m   **11.** 14.35 sq. yds.   **13.** 1.54 sq. miles
15. 108.72 acres   **17.** 928.80 cm²   **19.** 2.76 m²   **21.** 6.34 quarts   **23.** 4.22 gallons   **25.** 136.26 liters   **27.** 21.82 hl
29. 20° C   **31.** −45° C   **33.** −6.7° C   **35.** 95° F
37. 14° F   **39.** 46.4° F   **41.** $1.16 per liter   **43.** 3,306.93 lb/hr   **45.** $0.26/lb. = $0.57/kg; $0.55 per kg is better
47. 91.54 cubic inches   **49.** 200° C

Chapter 17 Review Test
1. 0.36hm   **2.** 16,000 liters   **3.** 67.3dg   **4.** 2.23dkl
5. 71,200cm   **6.** 160,000 ares   **7.** 267.49 t   **8.** 7.2hl = 72,000cl   **9.** 4.872 dkl = 487,200dl   **10.** 41.02dkg, 41,020cg   **11.** $1   **12.** 5   **13.** 10° C   **14.** 9.84 in

Index

An investment carried a nominal rate of 6% compounded semiannually
What is the effective rate

$$A = [(1 + i)n \quad (1 + \frac{6\%}{2})^2 = (1.03)^2 = 1.0609$$

$$\text{\&} (1.0609 + 100) - 100] = 6.09.$$

Rate = 6.09

Ans 6.09%

$A = 4400$

$P = 4100 + \dfrac{1}{48/0.2}$

$\qquad = 10,000 + 032601.84$

$\qquad\qquad = 326.04$

Page 127

Present

To find P

$$S = P \times S_{\overline{n}|i}$$

$$P = \frac{S}{S_{\overline{n}|i}} = \frac{5000}{.8 \times 0.0225} = \frac{5000}{.865916186}$$

$$= 577.43$$

$$P = S\left(\frac{(1+i)^n - 1}{i}\right)$$

$$= \frac{S}{\frac{(1+i)^n - 1}{i}} \cdot \frac{5000}{}$$

$S = 40,000 \quad n = 20 \quad i = 0.05$

$$P = S \frac{i}{S_{\overline{n}|i}}$$

$$4000 = 0.3024259$$

$$= 12097.036$$

Ans 12097.036

Chapter 11

Annuity Calculations pp. 285, 289, 291, 294

Ordinary Annuity

$$S = P \cdot s_{\overline{n}|i}$$

where S = accumulated amount, P = payment, n = number of payments, i = rate per period.

Present Value of an Ordinary Annuity

$$A = P \cdot a_{\overline{n}|i}$$

where A = present value of an ordinary annuity, P = amount of each future payment, and $a_{\overline{n}|i}$ = present value of a deposit of \$1 at interest rate per period i for n conversion periods.

Annuity Due

$$\overline{S} = P \cdot (s_{\overline{n+1}|i} - 1)$$

where $\overline{S}$ = accumulated amount of annuity due, P = payment or deposit, n = number of payments or deposits, and i = rate per period.

Present Value of an Annuity Due

$$\overline{A} = P(a_{\overline{n-1}|i} + 1)$$

where $\overline{A}$ = present value of an annuity due, P = amount of each future payment, n = number of payments, and i = rate per period.

Chapter 12

Sinking Funds p. 300

$$P = S \times \frac{1}{s_{\overline{n}|i}}$$

Amortization p. 304

$$P = A \times \frac{1}{a_{\overline{n}|i}}$$

Chapter 13

Valuation Indices—Stocks pp. 323–324

Earnings Per Share

$$E/S = \frac{\text{Net profit} - \text{Preferred dividends}}{\text{Outstanding shares}}$$

Price-Earnings Ratio

$$P/E = \frac{\text{Current market price}}{\text{Earnings per share}}$$

$$\text{Yield} = \frac{\text{Annual dividend}}{\text{Current market price}}$$

Valuation Indices—Bonds p. 331

Current Yield

$$\text{Current yield} = \frac{\text{Annual interest}}{\text{Current market price}}$$

Yield to Maturity

Yield to maturity

$$= \frac{\text{Annual interest} + \text{Average capital gain}}{500 + 1/2 \text{ Market price}}$$

Mutual Fund Calculations pp. 334–336

$$\text{NAV} = \frac{\text{Assets} - \text{Liabilities and Expenses}}{\text{No. of shares}}$$

$$\text{Amount invested} = \frac{\text{Net investment}}{1 - \text{Sales fee (in decimal form)}}$$

$$\text{No. of shares} = \frac{\text{Net Investment}}{\text{NAV}}$$

Chapter 14

Financial Ratios pp. 358–360

$$\text{Current ratio} = \frac{\text{Current assets}}{\text{Current liabilities}}$$

$$\text{Gross profit margin} = \frac{\text{Net sales} - \text{Cost of goods sold}}{\text{Net sales}}$$

$$\text{Acid-test ratio} = \frac{\text{Cash} + \text{Receivables}}{\text{Current liabilities}}$$

$$\text{Operating ratio} = \frac{\text{Cost of goods sold} + \text{Operating expenses}}{\text{Net sales}}$$

$$\text{Stockholders' equity ratio} = \frac{\text{Owners' equity}}{\text{Total assets}}$$

$$\text{Debt-equity ratio} = \frac{\text{Current liabilities} + \text{Long-term liabilities}}{\text{Owners' equity}}$$

Depreciation Methods pp. 370, 373, 376–380

MACRS and ACRS

For a given year, the depreciation amount is calculated using the basic percentage equation $P = B \cdot R$, where P = amount of depreciation, B = cost or purchase price, and R = depreciation percent from tables 14.1, 14.2, and 14.3.

The Straight-Line Method

$$d = \frac{c - s}{n}$$

where d = depreciation amount per year, c = cost of asset, s = salvage value, and n = years of useful life.

The Declining-Balance Method

$$d = b \times r$$

where d = depreciation amount per year, b = book value of the preceding year, and r = depreciation rate.

The Sum-of-the-Years-Digits Method

$$d = (c - s) \times r$$

where r is a fraction determined as follows: The denominator is the sum of the digits representing the useful life of the asset, and the numerator is the number of years of useful life remaining at the beginning of the year for which the computation is made.